LOUIS MACNEICE

LOUIS MACNEICE

Jon Stallworthy

faber and faber

LONDON · BOSTON

First published in 1995
by Faber and Faber Limited
3 Queen Square London WC1N 3AU

Photoset in Linotron Sabon by Parker Typesetting Service, Leicester
Printed in England by Mackays of Chatham plc, Chatham, Kent

© Jon Stallworthy, 1995

Jon Stallworthy is hereby identified as author of this work
in accordance with Section 77 of the Copyright, Designs
and Patents Act 1968

A CIP record for this book is available
from the British Library

ISBN 0-571-16019-0

2 4 6 8 10 9 7 5 3

IN MEMORY
OF E. R. DODDS
AN IRISHMAN, A POET, AND A SCHOLAR,
WHO KNEW MORE ABOUT IT ALL
THAN I DO

Contents

List of Illustrations

Abbreviations

AB	Anthony Blunt
AMHM	Antoinette Millicent Hedley MacNeice (née Anderson)
ABD	*Apollo's Blended Dream*
Bod	Bodleian Library, Oxford
CM	Corinna MacNeice
CP	*The Collected Poems of Louis MacNeice*
DM	Daniel MacNeice
EC	Eleanor Clark
EN	Elizabeth Nicholson (née MacNeice)
ERD	Eric Robertson Dodds
FLM	Frederick Louis MacNeice
GBM	Georgina Beatrice MacNeice
GMTBM	Giovanna Marie Thérèse Babette MacNeice (née Ezra)
HRC	Humanities Research Center, University of Texas, Austin, Texas
ICM	*I Crossed the Minch*
JFM	John Frederick MacNeice
JH	John Hilton
JS	Jon Stallworthy
LI	*Letters from Iceland*
LMBBC	*Louis MacNeice in the BBC*
MP	*Modern Poetry*
NYPL/BC	New York Public Library, Berg Collection
Plays	*Selected Plays of Louis MacNeice*
RW	*Roundabout Way*
SAF	*The Strings are False*
SLC	*Selected Literary Criticism of Louis MacNeice*
SP	*Selected Prose of Louis MacNeice*
TWA	*Time Was Away*
TSE	T. S. Eliot

Preface

In 1976, as an editor at the Clarendon Press, it was my good fortune to oversee the publication of Professor E. R. Dodds's autobiography, *Missing Persons*. Acquaintance ripened into friendship when he found me a house close to his own in the Oxfordshire village of Old Marston. Over many midnight glasses of Irish whiskey, we spoke of the famous friends of his 'missing persons' (his own past selves) – Yeats, Eliot, Auden, and MacNeice. The last and the least-known of these was closest to his heart: he had given MacNeice his first job and after a lifetime's friendship had, as his Literary Executor, edited his 'unfinished autobiography', *The Strings are False*, and his *Collected Poems*. He was concerned that MacNeice's reputation still bobbed – as it seemed to him, unfairly – in the wake of Auden's and, concluding that it would take a biography to initiate a revaluation, invited me to write one. I declined, regretfully, unable to imagine myself having time to write a prose book while publishing books by other people.

Dodds died in 1979 and some years later Dan Davin, his successor as MacNeice's Literary Executor, invited me for the second time to write the first biography. Having by then exchanged a publisher's office for a professor's, I accepted and, with Dodds's ghostly presence at my elbow, went back to his editions of the *Collected Poems* and *The Strings are False*.

MacNeice's autobiography, perhaps the most brilliant of his generation, must be his biographer's key document, but it poses problems. *The Strings are False* makes no mention of poems produced on those harp-strings, and it ends in December 1940. The first problem is alleviated by the personal 'casebook' sections of his *Modern Poetry*, which trace the development of the poet up to 1930, and the second is alleviated by Barbara Coulton's book, *Louis MacNeice in the BBC*. Her portrait of the poet as scriptwriter-producer was invaluable in the composition of my portrait of the scriptwriter-producer as poet.

Modern biographers of lyric poets tend to follow literary critics in assuming a close acquaintance with their subject's work. I do not and, because I hoped to achieve a speaking likeness, have allowed MacNeice, in certain important letters and poems, to speak for himself more than is customary. Ideally, readers – especially readers new to the poet – should meet them in full, rather than in paraphrase or fractured and filtered through critical commentary.

While writing this book, I have become increasingly aware of the apprehension with which many twentieth-century writers regard the prospect of a twentieth-century biographer or – to use Henry James's phrase – a 'postmortem exploiter'. James made the biographer of *The Aspern Papers* a deceiving homicide, and William Golding made the biographer of *The Paper Men* a murderer. I was therefore relieved to find a letter of 17 November 1940 in which MacNeice, about to cross the submarine-infested Atlantic, advised Dodds – and someone he would never meet:

In case any super-mug wants to do a life of me I would warn him against accepting, without careful scrutiny, any alleged information from my family (including Elizabeth). The best authorities (though each only from a certain angle) are Graham Shepard, Nancy Coldstream, yourself, Eleanor Clark, &, I suppose Wystan. [How mortuary-egotistical all this sounds.]

Chastened, I have followed his advice – but better a mug than a murderer.

It was MacNeice's family, however, who with Dodds and Davin invited me to undertake his biography, and it could not have been completed but for their assistance at every stage. My principal debts of gratitude are to them – especially to Hedli MacNeice who, sadly, did not live to read it – and to the British Academy for a Research Readership in which to write it.

I wish to thank the staff of the following institutions for their help: BBC Written Archives Centre, Caversham Park; Berg Collection, New York Public Library; Birmingham University Library; Bodleian Library, Oxford; British Film Institute; British Library; Britten-Pears Library, Aldeburgh; Butler Library, Columbia University; Dublin Public Libraries; English Faculty Library, Oxford; Esther Raushenbush Library, Sarah Lawrence College; Geneseo College Library, New York;

Humanities Research Center, University of Texas at Austin; Joseph Regenstein Library, University of Chicago; Kenneth Spencer Research Library, University of Kansas; King's College Library, Cambridge; Library of Congress, Washington; Livingstone Lord Library, Moorhead State University, Minnesota; Marlborough College Library; Milton S. Eisenhower Library, Johns Hopkins University; National Library of Scotland; National Theatre Society Limited, Dublin; Olin Library, Cornell University; Oxford University Press Library; Poetry/Rare Books Collection, University Libraries, State University of New York at Buffalo; Princeton University Library; Queen's University Library, Belfast; Royal Holloway and Bedford New College Library; Rush Rhees Library, University of Rochester; Trinity College Library, Dublin; University of Iowa Library; University of Minnesota (Duluth Campus) Library; Wolfson College Library, Oxford; and Yale University Library.

A biography of this kind is a collaborative venture, and I am indebted to many people for advice or assistance of one form or another: Dr Gerald Abraham, Professor J. C. Adams, Mr Martyn Adkins, Professor William Alfred, Professor Walter Allen, Professor Anthony Andrewes, Mr Kevin Andrews, Mr Alf Armstrong, Ms Dorothy Baker, Dr Caroline Barron, Dr Linna Bentley, Sir Isaiah Berlin, Professor Martin Bernal, Mr Robert J. Bertholf, Sir John Betjeman, Mr Paul Bloomfield, Dr Anthony Blunt, Professor Roger Bowen, Mr Dallas Bower, Dr David Bradshaw, Mr John Malcolm Brinnin, Professor Harold Brooks, Professor Terence Brown, Ms Cécile Chevreau, Ms Margaret Clark, Mr Douglas Cleverdon, Mrs Marg Clouts, Professor Richard Cobb, Ms Beatrix Collingham, Mr Tim Cook, Mr Jack Cope, Ms Barbara Coulton, Sir Ponsonby Moore Crosthwaite, Ms Eileen Cullen, Mr and Mrs Dan Davin, Mr Frank Duncan, Sir William and Lady Empson, Mr Martin Esslin, the Revd A. S. T. Fisher, Dr Jennifer Fitzgerald, Mr Peter Foden, Ms Margaret Gardiner, Dame Helen Gardner, Mrs Ann Gould, Professor John Gouws, Mr Paul Gregorowski, Mr and Mrs Geoffrey Grigson, Professor Adolphe Haberer, Mr Michael Halls, Sir Keith Hancock, Ms Christina Harris, Mr John Harris, Sir Rupert and Lady Hart-Davis, Mr Denys Hawthorne, Professor Seamus Heaney, Dr Roger Highfield, Mrs Christopher Holme, Mr Oliver Holt, Ms Pamela Howe, Ms Wendy Jennings, Professor Dillon Johnston, Mr Neil Johnston, Professor Ronald Johnston, Ms Gwyniver Jones, Mrs Alice Kadel, Mr John

Keohane, Mr Francis King, Professor Tom Kinsella, Mrs Sylvia Krige, Dr Donna Kurtz, Ms Julia Lang, Mr Patrick Leigh Fermor, Mr Hal Lidderdale, Mr Robin Lindsay, Sir Hugh Lloyd-Jones, Professor David Lodge, Dr Edward Lowbury, Mrs Mercy MacCann, Professor N. H. MacKenzie, Dr Robyn Marsack, Dr Francis O. Mattson, Ms Martha McCulloch, Dr Peter McDonald, Dr David Medalie, Mr Charles Monteith, Mr Richard Murphy, Mr P. H. Newby, Mr George Newsom, Mr John Ormond, Professor Kenneth Parker, Professor A. C. Partridge, Dr David Pascoe, Mr Sebastian Peake, Dr John Penney, Mr Bob Pocock, Mrs Caroline Powell, Mr John Press, Dr Judith Priestman, Sir V. S. Pritchett, Mr and Mrs John Rendall, Mr Richard Rickett, Professor Christopher Ricks, Professor Martin Robertson, Mr Fortie Ross, Professor Peter Sacks, Mr Charles M. Saffer Jr., Mr William St Clair, Mr John Sharp, Mrs Ann Shepard, Professor Philip Sherrard, Professor Michael Sidnell, Mr Michael Silver, Mrs Robert Simpson, Professor Reggie Smith, Mr Shepard Smith, Professor Richard Sorabji, Mrs Nancy Spender, Sir Stephen Spender, Ms Anita Sterner, Ms M. P. Stevens, Mrs Sarah and Mr Panico Theodosiou, Mr and Mrs David Thompson, the Rt Revd Jim Thompson, Dr Sally Thompson, Mrs Ann Thwaite, Mr Terence Tiller, Mr and Mrs J. McC. Todd, Ms Kathleen Tynan, Mrs Kathy Villiers-Tuthill, Ms Jackie Wall, Mr John Warrack, Ms Eleanor Clark Warren, Mr J. C. G. Waterhouse, Mr J. F. Waterhouse, Mr Adam Weisman, Mr Sam Wells, Mr David West, Professor R. F. Willetts, Mrs Lindy Wilson, Ms Mary Wimbush, Ms Ruth Winawer, and Mr Wesley Woods.

I am particularly grateful to Ms Sarah Barker for her impeccable word-processing, and to ten friends who read the typescript and improved it with their comments and corrections: Mr Freddie Baveystock, Professor Alan Heuser, Mr John Hilton, Mr Bruce Hunter, Professor Edna Longley, Mr Michael Longley, Ms Corinna MacNeice, Mr Dan MacNeice, Mr Tom Paulin, and Mr Anthony Thwaite.

I am conscious that my infiltration of MacNeice's extended family has involved a reciprocal process; and so, finally, I must thank my wife and children for admitting the poet and his entourage (not to mention the dogs) into our family circle so good-naturedly for so many years.

Wolfson College, Oxford
September 1993

Acknowledgements

The author and publishers are grateful to David Higham Associates on behalf of the Estate of Louis MacNeice for permission to reprint copyright material from Louis MacNeice's published works and from previously unpublished letters and documents. The locations of letters quoted are given in the Select Bibliography on page 492, which also includes a complete list of titles published by Louis MacNeice.

For permission to reprint material from other sources, acknowledgements are due to the following: to Mr A. Alvarez for an extract from a review published in *The New Statesman*, 11 December 1954; to the Kevin Andrews Estate for an extract from 'Time and the Will Lie Sidestepped: Athens, the Interval' in Terence Brown and Alec Reid, eds, *Time was Away: The World of Louis MacNeice* (Dublin, 1974); to John Murray (Publishers) Ltd for lines from 'Greek Orthodox' (from *A Nip in the Air*, 1974) by John Betjeman, and for an extract from *Young Betjeman* (1988) by Bevis Hillier; to the Anthony Blunt Estate for an extract from 'From Bloomsbury to Marxism' (*Studio International*, vol. 186, November 1973); to the Blackstaff Press, Belfast, for an extract from *The Middle of My Journey* (1990) by John Boyd; to Francisco Campbell Custodio and Ad. Donker (Pty) Ltd for an extract from a review by Roy Campbell published in *Poetry Review*, August/September 1949; to Mrs Douglas Cleverdon for an extract from *The Art of Radio in Britain* (unpublished typescript); to David Higham Associates for extracts from *Closing Times* (Oxford, 1975) by Dan Davin; to Faber and Faber Ltd and Mrs Valerie Eliot for quotations from letters by T. S. Eliot; to Patrick Leigh Fermor for extracts from a letter and from 'The Background of Ghika' (*Encounter*, 41, February 1957); to the author for extracts from *A Scatter of Memories* (London, 1988) by Margaret Gardiner; to Alice Kadel and Chatto &

Windus Ltd for an extract from *Mrs Donald* (London, 1983) by Mary Keene; to Sheil Land Associates Ltd for an extract from *John is Easy to Please* by Ved Mehta; to David Higham Associates for an extract from 'Footnote to a Poet's House' (*Independent Magazine*, 5 November 1988) by Muriel Spark; to Mr Anthony Thwaite for an extract from 'Memories of Rothwell House' (*Poetry Review*, vol. 78, no. 2, Summer 1988); and to the BBC for extracts from material held at the BBC Written Archives Centre, Caversham Park.

For permission to reproduce illustrative material, acknowledgements are due to the following: to the BBC for the frontispiece; to Mr Dan MacNeice for the illustrations on pages 7, 13, 24, 27, 40, 63, 84, 149, 162, 173; to Mr Patrick James Doulton, pages 10, 20, 44; to Mr T. McNally, page 23; to the Keeper of Western Manuscripts, Bodleian Library, Oxford, pages 30, 47, 50, 58, 85, 136, 179, 282, 363, 396; to the Hulton-Deutsch Collection, pages 33, 137, 162 (photo by Howard Coster), 230, 235, 288, 289, 333, 359, 370, 371 (photo by Haywood Magee); to the Trustees of the Ulster Museum, Belfast, page 36; to the Preparatory School, Sherborne, page 55; to Marlborough College, pages 78, 79; to Mrs Graham Shepard, pages 91, 319; to Ms Candida Lycett Green, page 92; to the Anthony Blunt Estate, page 100; to Mr Wim Swaan, page 107; to Mr Eric Bramall, page 109; to King's College Library, Cambridge, pages 110, 187, 189; to the Ashmolean Museum, Oxford, page 116; to Ms Ann Gould, page 136; to Christ Church, Oxford, pages 150, 259; to Mr John Hilton, page 158; to BBC Photograph and Archive, pages 193, 291, 300, 301, 311, 316, 340, 341, 431, 445; to Ms Eleanor Clark Warren, pages 197, 244; to Nancy Spender, pages 204, 205, 214; to Mrs Alice Kadel, page 238; to the *Belfast Telegraph*, page 258; to the National Library of Ireland, page 263; to Mr Nicholas Lee, page 264; to the Henry Moore Foundation, page 293; to Russell Sedgwick Ltd, page 306; to Godfrey Argent Ltd (photo by Walter Bird), page 326; to the National Portrait Gallery, London (photo by John Gay), page 347; to the Associated Press Ltd, page 362; to the Archaeological Survey of India, page 365; to Ms Corinna MacNeice, page 366; to Ms Beatrix Collingham, page 377; to Mr Patrick Leigh Fermor, page 379; to the Royal Commission on the Historical Monuments of England, page 389 (Crown copyright); to Mrs Dan Davin, page 392; to Studio Chadel, Paris (photo by

Sacha-Masour), page 408; to the Thomas Cook Travel Archive, page 413; to Mrs Sylvia Krige, pages 437, 439; to C.C.A. Personal Management, page 461; to Mr Richard Murphy, page 463; to the Faber and Faber Archive (photo by Mark Gerson), page 469; to B. L. MacGill (photo by George MacCann), page 479.

The author and publishers have made every effort to trace owners of copyright material. They apologize if any person or source has been overlooked in these acknowledgements, and they would be grateful to be informed of oversights.

CHAPTER I

The Pre-natal Mountain

And the pre-natal mountain is far away.
'Carrick revisited', *Collected Poems*, p. 225

Memory cannot go back that far, fades into myth, I find myself walking down a long straight passage hung with bead curtains. Through one curtain after another, like sheets of coloured rain, but I notice very little in the passage, only at the end there is a staircase. I go up it several flights, at the last floor but one there is a small window of cheap stained glass which throws a stain on the floor mingling with the pattern of the worn-out linoleum. The last flight of the stairs is uncarpeted and the top is all but dark. The top is a blind alley, a small lobby without any doors and the roof sloping down as in an attic. It smells very fusty. Close in under the roof, but I can hardly see it, is a trunk, an old-fashioned trunk with metal studs on it. On the lid of the trunk there are initials but I cannot see if they are mine. Anyway the trunk is locked.

The Strings are False, p. 36

Frederick Louis MacNeice would have liked the contents of his ancestral trunk to confirm his grandfather's belief that the family was descended from an Irish king, Conchubar MacNessa, the villain of the Deirdre saga. In later years, he was told that the name MacNeice derived more probably from Naoise, the hero of the same saga; after which, he said, 'I have, in defiance of natural history, claimed descent from both of them and in each case by Deirdre'. The sight of a poet, particularly an Irish poet, in search of a pedigree is not uncommon. One remembers George Moore's mischievous caricature of Yeats crooning over the fire 'that if he had his rights he would be Duke of Ormonde. Æ's answer was: I am afraid, Willie, you are overlooking your father.' The quest for origins was crucial to both poets, but MacNeice's wry self-mockery was a far cry from Yeats's habitual

solemnity on the subject. A more significant difference was the fact –
and MacNeice's delight in the fact – that among his ancestors were
numbered Roman Catholics as well as Anglo-Irish Protestants. 'Sing
the peasantry', Yeats instructed his successors in 'Under Ben Bulben',
but he never made the claim to kinship found in 'Auden and Mac-
Neice: Their Last Will and Testament':

> L[ouis]. And to my own in particular whose rooms
> Were whitewashed, small, soothed with the smoke of peat,
> Looking out on the Atlantic's gleams and glooms,
>
> Of whom some lie among brambles high remote
> Above the yellow falls of Ballysodare
> Whose hands were hard with handling cart and boat
>
> I leave the credit for that which may endure
> Within myself of peasant vitality and
> Of the peasant's sense of humour . . . .

'In the beginning was the Irish rain', begins one of MacNeice's
autobiographical fragments, but to a twentieth-century eye, peering
down the passage of time, the earliest figures to emerge from the 'sheets
of coloured rain' are eighteenth-century. The MacNeices of Stonehall,
a couple of miles from Ballysodare in County Sligo, 'were a feckless
lot', said the poet's father: hard-drinking, hard-riding Protestant
squireens, typical of those who gallop and tipple through the novels of
Maria Edgeworth and the *Personal Sketches and Recollections* of
Jonah Barrington. A land agent, Anthony MacNeice, made a runaway
marriage with Peggy Duke, daughter of a local Anglo-Irish Ascendancy
family. Perhaps as a consequence of this advantageous connection,
their eldest son Thomas is said to have owned a considerable amount
of land between Knocknarea and the sea. His brother Ferguson John, a
small farmer, married a Marjorie Lindsay, whose name suggests Scottish plantation ancestry. Their eldest son, William Lindsay MacNeice,
decided early in life to be a schoolmaster with the Irish Church Missions to Roman Catholics. The aim of such schools was to convert the
children of the frequently starving peasantry and, offering them food,
clothes, and a better education than the Roman Catholic hedge-
schools, they were fairly successful; although a number of their con-

verts subsequently reverted to the faith of their fathers. Graduating from the ICM Training College at Ballinasloe, County Galway, William MacNeice was sent to teach at the Mission school in Aughrus near Cleggan. There he met and married Alice Jane Howell, daughter of a Welsh coastguard stationed at Bunowen and his wife, a member of the Anglo-Irish family of Eccles who owned the Eccles Hotel at Glengarriff, County Cork. Alice had auburn hair on which she could sit and which she 'put up' for the first time at her wedding in 1855. She was sixteen years old.

In 1856, her husband was sent to run the Irish Church Mission School on the island of Omey, seven miles north of Clifden in County Galway. Twelve years before, an American evangelist, Miss Asenath Nicholson, crossing at low tide the strand linking Omey to the mainland, found

an island a mile in diameter, of one rude pile of stone, with a little patch now and then of green, without a road, the footpaths being so obscured by sand blown in from the beach, that guess-work was my only guide. Here were huts, some of stone, and some of mud; and here, too, were habitations dug in the sand, as rabbits burrow, and whole families live therein; an aperture to crawl in admits the inmates, serving as door, window, and chimney; on the ground straw is spread, which serves for table, bed, and chair. At each end of this island live the owners, called *lords*.

The miseries of that island must be seen to be believed.

She went on to describe the overcrowding and poverty and the peasants' hunger for knowledge. Two years after her visit, they were ravaged by a greater hunger when the potato crop failed. Many on the island took their place in the windswept graveyard overlooking the mainland, and the meals offered by the ICM school must have presented a strong argument for conversion.

The MacNeices flourished on Omey, Alice there giving birth to all but the eldest of her ten children. Two of them died and a third, John Frederick, born on 20 March 1866, was hastily baptized eight days later because he was thought to be failing. However, with what was to prove characteristic resilience, he survived. His eldest sister, Caroline, made him her special charge and taught him to swim in one of the island's white-sanded bays. He spent the first fifteen years of his life on

Omey and ever afterwards, his son was to write,

> Kept something in him solitary and wild,

> So loved the western sea and no tree's green
> Fulfilled him like these contours of Slievemore
> Menaun and Croaghaun and the bogs between.

In his father's school he learnt Latin and the beginnings of Greek, but not the Gaelic of his Roman Catholic schoolfellows.

On Sundays, when the weather was too bad for the Protestant islanders to go to church at Sellerna on the mainland, William Mac-Neice used to conduct services in the schoolhouse. The then Church of Ireland Bishop of Tuam was a friend and tried to persuade him to become ordained but, lacking a sense of vocation for this, William was content to remain a schoolmaster. He was a hot-tempered man and in 1879 bad relations with the local Roman Catholic clergy came to a head: specifically, a priestly head. The Revd William Rhatigan, a Clifden priest, was an ardent supporter of the Land League that was then demanding fair rents for Irish tenant farmers, fixity of tenure, and freedom of sale. He decided it was his right to teach the Catholic catechism in the ICM school. On 28 February, he was driven across to Omey in a cart and, walking into the schoolhouse, came face to face with MacNeice, who called him a blackguard and would have knocked him down if he had not backed out and driven off. As the story of their confrontation went the rounds of the Revd Mr Rhatigan's parish, it was 'improved'. One version had his arriving to assert his rights just as the Good Woman of the school was stirring the soup for lunch. She was said to have repelled him with her ladle, so that he fell, cutting his head on the doorstep. 'Blood' – even when imaginary – 'will have blood', and soon threats of vengeance were being uttered. MacNeice was worried that there might be repercussions, and two armed members of the Royal Irish Constabulary, sub-constables Sheehan and Dumphy, were assigned to the family for their protection. The policemen spent the night of Saturday 22 March in the MacNeices' house, and the following morning they accompanied the Omey Protestants as they set out for matins on the mainland. They crossed the island on a grassy track between outcrops of pink granite that petered out at the edge of the strand. Four hundred yards of ribbed white sand then brought them to the further shore, where another track led them uphill past the Roman Catholic church of Stella Maris at Claddaghduff. As they approached this, a crowd gathered and began to throw stones. MacNeice and sub-constable Sheehan were hit, and the Protestant party ran to take cover in the house of a farmer called Lynch. The sub-constables, their rifles half-cocked, tried to keep the mob from following the MacNeices inside, but were disarmed and 'cruelly beaten'. In the course of this fracas, one of the rifles was fired – accidentally, it would seem, and without causing injury (although a Catholic version had a woman killed; a woman who, in the Protestant version, died many years later). The mob smashed a window, through which someone climbed who then opened the back door for the rest. William MacNeice was knocked down and repeatedly kicked, and his daughter Charlotte was cut on the face by a stone. Further injury was prevented by a Roman Catholic priest, the Revd Mr Flannery, who luckily happened to be passing and persuaded the mob to disperse.

The following night, friends of the MacNeices brought a coach to the mainland side of Omey strand, and William, Alice, and their eight children were driven the sixty miles to Galway and put onto the Dublin train. The sister of one of the men who organized their escape lived into her nineties and recounted the earlier version of this story to William's granddaughter Elizabeth. 'My brother always told me', she said, 'that Fred [John Frederick] was very brave. Some of the others' – and she shrugged expressively – 'but Fred was very brave.' This may have been the first demonstration of his courage. It was not to be the last.

For much of his adult life John Frederick MacNeice allowed his name to be printed Frederick John or F. J., but he seldom signed it that way. His brothers and sisters, nephews and nieces called him Fred or Uncle Fred. His second wife wanted a name of her own for him and she and her relations always called him Derrick. When he became a bishop, he decided to use John F. as his signature, and I will follow his daughter who in her memoir calls him John.

The flight from Omey left some of his brothers and sisters with a fear and bitterness that led them to reject Connemara, but for John it was the prelude to a long life largely devoted to spreading the Christian gospel of love and reconciliation between all classes and creeds in Ireland.

The outcast family moved first to Athlone, and shortly afterwards William MacNeice was appointed to the ICM training college in Dublin. They settled in a pleasant house in Clonsilla that became a meeting place for the young men and women brought up from the country for training by the ICM. John finished his schooling at a Dublin day-school where, at the age of seventeen, he won a medal for oratory, encouraging his father's hope that he might become a barrister. John, however, felt himself drawn to the calling that the Bishop of Tuam had proposed to William. Before he could be ordained he had to have a degree and, since his father could not then afford university fees, John went to work as a schoolmaster at an ICM Boys' Orphanage near Clifden and, for a time, at Dr Benson's school in the Dublin suburb of Rathmines. By the time he was twenty-five he had saved enough and, in January 1892, entered through the gates of Trinity College, Dublin. It was probably at his father's house, sometime in the early 1890s, that he met a young woman whose family had been connected with the Irish Church Missions almost as long as his own.

Elizabeth Margaret – always known as Lily – Clesham had been born on 18 October 1866, only seven months after John MacNeice, and brought up on her father's farm in the townland of Killymangan outside Clifden, seven miles from Omey. Unlike the MacNeices of Stonehall, the Cleshams – originally Clishams – were not natives of Connemara. In the late eighteenth century one John D'Arcy, a young man with landlordly aspirations, had acquired a large tract of bogland and imported (probably from the Hebrides) a family of stonemasons, the Cleshams, to build him a suitable seat at Clifden. With local labour doing the heavy work, an outer wall was raised, pierced by a mock-medieval gateway flanked by battlemented towers. From this, half a mile of serpentine drive led down to a massive castle (with crusader dripstones and fake loopholes) overlooking Clifden Bay. Once his castle had been erected, D'Arcy commissioned the Cleshams to build a town at Clifden. Famine interrupted this venture, D'Arcy died, and his family went bankrupt. His son Hyacinth, however, became Rector of Clifden and joining forces with another Protestant clergyman, the Revd Alexander Dallas, founded the Irish Church Missions.

Martin Clesham, born a Roman Catholic in 1831, was converted to the Church of Ireland around 1865, the year in which he married Christina Rosetta Bush, whom the D'Arcys had brought over from London to be a nurse in their Clifden orphanage; but when Lily was two her mother died during an outbreak of scarlet fever at the orphanage. The girl grew up with a maturity beyond her years, caring for her father who had been badly lamed in a sectarian brawl, and running his household. At eighteen she left home for the ICM Training College in Dublin, after which she taught for a time in one of their Dublin schools. When she and John MacNeice met at Clonsilla, it is easy to see why they were attracted to each other. There is an intensity in the gaze, an easy assurance in the stance, of the young man in the sepia photograph (by Lauder Bros. of 32 Westmoreland Street, Dublin). Hand on hip he looks every inch the orator. Lily Clesham's blue eyes liked what

Lily Clesham and John MacNeice

they saw, and by the end of 1892 she and John were engaged. Absence may have made their hearts grow fonder, because that same year she was transferred to the ICM school back at Ballyconneely near Clifden. Her father, now old and infirm, came to live with her.

John MacNeice graduated from Trinity in 1895 and was promptly ordained for the parish of Cappoquin in County Waterford. His salary of £120 a year would not support a wife, not even when supplemented by the purse of sovereigns his parishioners gave him in 1899 when he was appointed to Trinity Church, Belfast. Thanking them for this, he wrote:

Few curates have ever been treated by Rector [Archdeacon Burkitt] and people as I have been by you; it was your own goodness and not any merit on my part which made you think me what you wished a clergyman to be – Never had curate a kinder rector; never had man a better friend. I can never forget him, I can never forget you either. I have you in my heart . . . .

Another man – the curate's son-to-be, for example – leaving the green fields and gentle speech of Waterford for the harsher ways of Belfast, might have been tempted to see the transition as an Expulsion from the Garden, but not the Revd John. Though brought up in the West, he had learnt the realities of city life in Dublin and he loved a challenge. He was to find no shortage of challenges in Belfast.

Holy Trinity Church – in curt Ulster parlance commonly shorn of its adjective – stood in Trinity Street, off the larger and longer Clifton Street which, in 1843, when the church was consecrated, was the bottom of the Antrim Road. Although at right angles to the handsome Clifton House, the bulk of its congregation were mill-workers drawn from the populous district of Millfield. The new curate liked his new rector, the Revd Richard Clarke, as much as his old, but after three years he was moved again: this time to St Clement's Church in Bally-macarett, a poorer working-class district east of the River Lagan. St Clement's, an iron church on the Beersbridge Road, had been erected in the late 1890s. Its first incumbent, the Revd W. Peoples, was an able and good man, but soon after its opening he fell foul of a certain section of his congregation. On Sundays, there were unruly scenes in and around the church, and it was decided to close it for a 'cooling off' period. A smaller iron church, St Donard's, about four minutes' walk away, was opened, but almost at once Mr Peoples resigned.

Early in 1901, John MacNeice was appointed curate, and the following year incumbent, of the reopened St Clement's. The church had a debt of £1,000 and no rectory. A change in salary, however (to £150 a year), made possible another change, and in June 1902 John and Lily were married in Christ Church, Clifden. After a honeymoon in the Lake District, they went to live at 211 Albertbridge Road, Ballymacarett. Lily was now thirty-five. For the past eleven years she had been living and working by the sea, with the Connemara mountains all around and no city nearer than Galway, sixty miles to the south. For her, the transition to the backstreets of Belfast – backstreets noted for their roughness and bigotry – did seem like the Expulsion from the Garden. She took a strong dislike to the North of Ireland, which was to remain with her for the rest of her life. This is not to say that she did not make many friends in Ulster, but one of her greatest consolations was the companionship of her father, who moved with her to Ballymacarett and with whom she never tired of talking of the lost world of the West.

Her husband was only to remain Rector of St Clement's for about a year, but during that time his parish succeeded in paying off its debt. That was not his only challenge, however, and some sense of the other problems he encountered is conveyed by his account of an experience at a social meeting in St Donard's Church:

One who was well known in the congregation for his ultra zeal for orthodoxy – as some conceived it – had a number of people round him, to whom he was speaking excitedly and somewhat as follows:-

'Yon man who took the service on Sunday morning was a Puseyite. It is easy to know a Puseyite. There are three special marks, and he had all three.' Having spoken of marks one and two, he added, 'and, in the third place, remember this: he was clean-shaven – that is one of the most certain marks of a Puseyite.'

At this stage I ventured to put in a word. I suggested that it might not be wise to be influenced too much by the third point. 'You all remember,' I said, 'Dr Kane, the Grand Master of the Belfast Orangemen: he was clean-shaven: surely he was not a Puseyite.' 'He was clean-shaven,' replied our instructor, 'and that was the chief fault that was in him. If he had lived a little longer a deputation would have waited on him concerning that very thing.'

John MacNeice encountered somewhat similar opposition when, finding that Holy Communion was celebrated only once a month at St Clement's, he instituted a weekly Eucharist at 8 a.m. on Sundays. He was bitterly execrated for this innovation: it was 'the thin end of the wedge', leading straight to Rome, but he had the courage of his convictions. This storm in a communion cup soon subsided, and the weekly Eucharist was soon an established feature of the St Clement's calendar.

In the spring of 1903 John was instituted as Rector of Trinity Church, replacing the Revd Richard Clarke, and a week later, on 24 April, Lily gave birth to their first child. She was christened Caroline Elizabeth in her father's new church, and a month later the family moved to a larger house in a more salubrious neighbourhood. Number 1 Brookhill Avenue was one of three two-storey detached houses, each

No. 1 Brookhill Avenue

with a good-sized garden behind and at both sides. A bay window to the right of the front door let in the light to a generous sitting-room. John and Lily were happy in their new home and in their new parish and doubly happy when, on 31 March 1905, a second child was born and William Lindsay joined Caroline Elizabeth in the nursery. Over the months that followed, however, their delight became tinged with unease at 'Willie's' slowness in learning to walk and talk. Doctors were consulted and in due course he was diagnosed as a mongol (or, as we would now say, Downs Syndrome) child. For years his parents could not bring themselves to accept this, hoping against hope for signs of improvement. Lily, in particular, tortured herself with a search for other explanations. What had she done or failed to do that might account for Willie's condition? Finally, she seems to have convinced both herself and John that their son's backwardness was the result of a childhood accident: a nurse had allowed his pram to run away down a grassy slope and he had been thrown out at the bottom. For the rest of her life Lily tormented herself with self-lacerating questions: 'Why did I employ that nurse? Why wasn't I there? If only ... if only ....'

Other shadows began to gather at 1 Brookhill Avenue. In 1906 old William Lindsay MacNeice died at his house in Clonsilla (where his wife had died two years before), and that September there was another death in the family. Just before Lily's fortieth birthday, John took her and her invalid father and the two children away for a holiday in a farmhouse near Carrowdore, County Down. For the first few days the old man was well, receiving his two-year-old granddaughter's tribute of seaweed and shells as he sat in his chair on the porch. Then, quite suddenly, he developed pneumonia, and the holiday ended with his death and burial in Carrowdore churchyard.

Lily felt the loss of her father very deeply. They had lived together so long and so harmoniously, talking often of Connemara, that his death seemed the severance of her lifeline to the West. She still had friends in the Clifden area, but she seldom saw them and her new friends in the North were only a partial compensation. She and her husband remained devoted to each other, but his time and attention were increasingly taken up by his work. He was tireless in the performance of his pastoral duties, much in demand on committees, and the school-boy orator had matured into a powerful preacher and lecturer. A fortnight after her father's death, Lily wrote to her sister-in-law:

Fred is better. He started off this morning at 9.30 for a clerical meeting and returned *this evening* at 7 and remained about half an hour and flew off once more. It is now 10 p.m. and he is still out!! That is the sort of life he leads – no wonder he is *thin*!

It is very lonely for me now. I had so much to do before that I feel the loss all the more.

His absence and the loss of her role as a daughter were soon to be replaced by a new presence in the house and new demands on her role as mother. On 12 September 1907, in an upstairs room at 1 Brookhill Avenue, a third child was born. He was christened Frederick Louis – Louis after his godfather, Louis Plunkett – in Trinity Church, and was always known as Fred or Freddie until, in his rebellious teens, he abandoned his patronymic.*

Lily was very ill after this birth and took some time to recover her usual health and spirits, but both were restored by the family's annual seaside holiday the following year. Ever since his boyhood swimming lessons on Omey, her husband had loved the sea and used to say that he could never see an island without wishing to reach it or a mountain without wishing to climb it. In 1908 they took a house at Kilkeel, County Down, and spent several happy weeks bathing, walking, and visiting friends. Their daughter was always to remember sitting in the little drawing-room while John read aloud to Lily Burns's 'John Anderson my jo, John'.

Some weeks after they returned to Belfast, on 8 November, the rector noted in his diary: 'Interviewed re Carrickfergus. Left myself in the hands of Bishop and nominators.' The circumstances behind those laconic sentences were as follows. For some twenty years the Revd George Chamberlain had been the much-loved Rector of St Nicholas' Church, Carrickfergus, a town ten miles from Belfast on the northern shore of Belfast Lough. He was suffering from Bright's disease and had finally become bedridden. No hopes were held out for his recovery, he resigned, and a successor had therefore to be sought. When a parish of the Church of Ireland becomes vacant, a committee of nominators –

---

* I have called him Louis (or MacNeice) throughout.

Lily and Louis

some parochial, some diocesan – meets to choose a new incumbent, whose name is then presented to the Bishop for approval. In the case of Carrickfergus, the nominators duly met but could not agree. One wanted the Revd Chamberlain's curate, the able and popular Mr Bradley, to succeed him. Others thought Mr Bradley too young and proposed another candidate. The nominators met again on more than one occasion, but there was still a deadlock and the matter was referred to the Bishop of Down and Connor and Dromore, John Baptist Crozier. The Bishop said that he would appoint neither Mr Bradley nor the other candidate, but would put forward several new names to the nominators. The name chosen was that of J. F. MacNeice, who on 10 November wrote in his diary: 'Nominated to Carrickfergus. Visiting sick when word came. Wrote to Bishop accepting.'

CHAPTER 2

The House by the Harbour

I was born in Belfast between the mountain and gantries
　To the hooting of lost sirens and the clang of trams:
Thence to Smoky Carrick in County Antrim
　Where the bottle-neck harbour collects the mud which jams

The little boats beneath the Norman castle,
　The pier shining with lumps of crystal salt;
The Scotch Quarter was a line of residential houses
　But the Irish Quarter was a slum for the blind and halt.

'Carrickfergus', CP, p. 69

The origin of the name Carrickfergus, like that of the name MacNeice, is lost in the no man's land between myth and history. The poet and his sister grew up believing it 'a name to be proud of – we knew that it meant the Rock of Fergus who had been some great man in the dim past, but I disliked its abbreviation Carrick which in the local voice sounded like a slap in the face'. Their father took a less romantic, more historical view:

It is held by some authorities of repute that Carrickfergus means 'Crag' or 'Craig-na-fairge', the rock in the water or the rock in the sea. It is well known that until comparatively recent times the great rock was surrounded by water. But inasmuch as there are traditions that connect the town's name with a great hero, a descendant and progenitor of Kings, and himself the first Ulster King of Scottish Dalriada, it is not surprising that these traditions are preferred to the less romantic and less interesting explanation. We put the death of Fergus [shipwrecked and drowned off the great rock] somewhere after 531 A.D.

It has been said that the history of Carrickfergus 'is the history of Ulster writ small'. Plundered by the Danes in AD 960, the little harbour town was the key to the Anglo-Norman hold on Ulster. John de Courcy, conqueror of the Province, began the construction of the great grey-green castle on its outcrop of dark basalt between 1180 and 1204. It was captured by King John in 1210; captured again in 1690 by Frederick, Duke of Schomberg, for his master, William of Orange, who in June 1690 landed in the harbour with his courtiers and a large body of troops. In February 1760, John Wesley was one of those who saw the castle fall again, to the forces of the French commander Thurot (born Farrell), whose triumph was short-lived, as he was killed in a sea-battle some days later.

When John MacNeice wrote to the Bishop accepting the nomination, he could have had no idea that Carrickfergus was again to be the scene of conflict, with himself unwittingly cast in the role of invader. At breakfast on 11 November, Elizabeth saw her father look up from his newspaper, exclaiming: 'Hullo! There's a row at Carrickfergus!' Indeed there was. His newspaper reported:

On Tuesday night an impromptu meeting of the parishioners of [St. Nicholas Church] was held in the Town Hall, Carrickfergus, to protest against the appointment of the Revd. Mr. MacNeice of Trinity Church, Belfast, as rector of the parish in the room of the Revd. George Chamberlain, resigned. The hall, notwithstanding the short notice of the meeting, was filled to overflowing. When the Revd. Mr. Chamberlain's resignation was announced there was a feeling that the Revd. W. H. Bradley M.A. the curate-in-charge, should be appointed to the office. A memorial, signed by all the Select Vestry with the exception of the two ex-officio members, who are churchwardens, and by almost the entire congregation, was forwarded to the parishioners, and the latter feel that their wishes should have had consideration. It was pointed out to the nominators that the parish was never in a more flourishing condition, and that it would be in the interest of the church that the Revd. Mr. Bradley should have the appointment . . . .

It was resolved that a public meeting be immediately called, and a petition signed and presented to the Revd Mr MacNeice, informing him of the parishioners' views.

The following day an anonymous letter, headed 'Parochial Nominators', appeared in the *Belfast Newsletter* referring to the report. The writers took exception to the statement that parochial nominators were 'elected that the voice of the parish might be heard through them' and went on to point out that, under the Constitution of the Church of Ireland, the nominator had to declare before acting: 'I nominate such person only as I believe in my conscience to be ... fitted.' The letter ends:

The parochial nominator is chosen by the parishioners as the most fitting person to nominate a clergyman for the vacant parish, and if he allows himself to be influenced by popular opinion he fails in his duty and shows himself to be unfit for the solemn responsibility entrusted to him.

A couple of days after the protest meeting, the local weekly paper, the *Carrickfergus Advertiser*, came out. The meeting was very fully reported and in addition there was a long letter from Mr J. Herron Lepper, who wrote:

I feel that the way in which the recent appointment of rector was made is an insult to the inhabitants of Carrickfergus ....

Now I come to the behaviour of our parochial nominators. This triumvirate of busybodies has succeeded in getting a gentleman appointed as rector whom next to nobody here will support, if he sees fit to accept the appointment in the face of our indignant remonstrances ....

Here is a parish of over two thousand practically unanimous in demanding what we have a right to demand, a clergyman to tend us whom we know and love ....

Rule by the Land League would be more tolerable, for it at least conforms to the will of the majority: rule by Rome would be more tolerable, for it at least does not pretend to listen to the popular voice, but these local despots assume both absolute power and infallibility while pretending to be guided by the will of the people. Such conduct is hideously like hypocrisy of the worst description ....

The law of the land permits us to choose the men who shall take care of our bodies, our properties, our children's education, all that is dear to us physically, and in what concerns the care of souls are we to submit like a pack of schoolboys, and accept an unknown pedagogue without a murmur? Surely we are of age, and know best ourselves the spiritual medicine needed in this parish!

A deputation of four men – one the author of this letter – was sent from Carrickfergus to urge John MacNeice to withdraw his acceptance of the nomination. By way of preparation, Lily polished the dining-room table as if for a party and went out to buy flowers. No record remains of what was said over the shining table, but the deputation left without any firm promise of withdrawal. Next, a meeting of the ladies of the parish was called and a formidable Ascendancy figurehead, Mrs George Kirk of Thornfield, came over from London to preside. In the course of a powerful speech, she said:

I think it is our bounden duty to put on record the opinion of we women members of the congregation of St. Nicholas with regard to this appointment of a stranger ... as I feel convinced that those in highest authority cannot realise as we do the strength of our feelings of disappointment and amazement that our unanimous wishes should go for nothing in a decision which will in all probability influence the spiritual welfare of the parish for many years to come.... There is absolutely no personal feeling whatever against the gentleman chosen by the nominators. The question is almost entirely one of principle....

The meeting passed a resolution protesting 'in the strongest possible manner against the appointment of a rector in direct defiance of the almost unanimously expressed wishes of the members of the congregation'.

At this point the MacNeices' good friend and Louis' godfather, Louis Plunkett (known to the family affectionately as L. A. P.), became so concerned with the likely effects of this campaign, particularly on Lily's health and happiness, that he too tried to persuade John to withdraw his acceptance. John agreed to do so if – but only if – the Bishop also agreed with this decision. They met and the Bishop urged strongly against withdrawal. He made it clear that after all that had happened there could be no possibility of his instituting Mr Bradley to the benefice, even should John MacNeice stand down. 'I must send either you or x', said the Bishop. 'If I send x he'll be dead in six months.' John said that this remark did not suggest a very favourable prospect for himself but the Bishop replied: 'Ah! you're different. They won't kill you.'

From the time of this meeting, so far as John was concerned the matter was settled. He had given his promise to the Bishop, and he now considered his appointment to Carrickfergus a call of the '*ecclesia Dei*' – the expression by which he usually referred to the Church in his charge. But L. A. P. still disapproved. He tried again to persuade his friend to withdraw and, when that failed, he asked Lily to ask her husband not to go. She did so and her husband said he would withdraw his acceptance if she wished it, but that if he did so he would feel that he must also resign from the ministry. Lily was too loyal a wife to ask for that. So plans went ahead, and the date for the Service of Institution to St Nicholas' Church, Carrickfergus, was fixed for Wednesday, 25 November 1908.

Only two days before the induction another meeting of protest was held in Carrickfergus. The hall was packed and the feeling was practically unanimous. Mrs Kirk, who had presided over the former ladies' meeting, made another speech. In the interval she had written to the Bishop asking for an interview and she read aloud his reply:

Dear Mrs. Kirk,
I am sorry I cannot have the pleasure of seeing you to-day. The matter about which you write is one on which, alas! I know a great deal too much, and it is one which concerns the laws of the Church of Ireland, and in connection with which Churchmen all over my diocese are asking is the Church of Ireland to be ruled in accordance with her own statutes or by popular clamour. I would not be fit for the office of Bishop if I failed to carry out the laws and ordinances of the Church, and in doing so I bitterly regret that the Church has not the loyal support of yourself and others whom I thought the Church could rely on for loyalty to her laws and submission to the cause of God.

Yours truly,
John Down and Connor

On the morning of 25 November, the new rector and his wife set off for the Service of Institution, accompanied by a number of other clergy and friends from Belfast. The opposition, meanwhile, was gathering its forces. The manager of a local linen mill disapproved of the appointment and gave his mill girls the day off to voice their protests. When the rector's party arrived at Carrickfergus railway station, it was to be greeted by a jeering crowd. The police were also there in force and formed a guard for the short walk from the station to the church. The head constable warned Lily that it would be safer for her not to walk beside her husband – rotten eggs were flying and more dangerous missiles were feared – but she disregarded his advice. As soon as the rector's party had passed through the churchyard's wrought-iron gates, the police locked them, thus excluding the greater part of the angry crowd. Some of those shut out mistook the tall and imposing Archdeacon of Connor for John MacNeice and he, incensed by their insults, stepped up to the gates and shaking his fist thundered: 'I'm not your rector and I'm glad I'm not!'

The service itself passed off without further incident. It had been planned to follow it with the customary tea-party for members of the parish in a local hall, but the head constable said he could not guarantee the visitors' safety, and a muted little party was held behind the locked doors of the Vestry. The police then escorted them back to the station, where the ladies were locked in the waiting-room until the Belfast train arrived. Their sanctuary had windows all round, up near the ceiling, and the distorted faces of the mill girls who had climbed up to scream and scrabble at the glass were to haunt Lily for the rest of her life. She and her husband reached Belfast safely that evening, and his diary records that next day he returned to Carrickfergus to visit the former rector and the Church Schools.

The parishioners of St Nicholas, meanwhile, decided on a policy of 'passive resistance'. They would contribute no money for the upkeep of the parish, and would in all possible ways boycott the new rector. During the previous week, some had given up their pews and removed their cushions and prayer books. Others decided that they would continue to attend the church, but would neither put money in the collection plate nor speak to the rector. The action of those who withheld their subscriptions did not affect his salary, but it did make it impossible for him to keep a curate and, hence, increased the work he had to do himself.

Mr Bradley took charge of the services in St Nicholas Church for the last time on Sunday, 30 November. There was a very large attendance and when the collection came around,

The plates were presented to the occupants of seat after seat without the slightest response, some of the congregation gazing at the plate which was held before them with an expression of puzzled interest, as though it were a rare and valuable object which they had never seen before and might not be permitted to look upon again.

This gesture was somewhat nullified by the action of an octogenarian, Miss Maria Johns, who with considerable ostentation put in a crackling five-pound note. Mr Bradley, it should be said, had tried unsuccessfully throughout the previous six weeks to persuade his supporters to abandon their campaign. On 7 January, he was nominated as rector to the smaller neighbouring parish of Lordematown, where he was to remain – on the best of terms with John MacNeice – for many years.

Later in January 1909 the family moved to Carrickfergus. With characteristic generosity, the new rector insisted that his bedridden predecessor and his family should remain in the rectory, while the MacNeices took possession of a smaller house, 5 Governor's Walk, facing the harbour. Its front door opened on the street, the farther side of which was flanked by the harbour wall, so that in rough weather spray would lash the windows. The rector liked its closeness to the sea as well as to the historic castle (a stone's throw to the left) and to his church. A three-storey house, it had been built in 1830 – taller than its neighbours – as a befitting residence for the Manager of Kelly's Coal Yard next door. From the ground floor, where a dining-room over-

Carrickfergus Castle and 'the house by the sea' today, seen from Governor's Walk. No. 5 is visible beyond 'A. Davidson, Sculptor'

looked the harbour, an elegant circular staircase led up to a spacious drawing-room, whose three tall windows commanded a wider view of the bustling harbour with its castle and Belfast Lough beyond. The staircase curved on up to family bedrooms on the second floor, attics and servants' rooms on the third.

Lily never liked the house. It had no garden, and even before the carpets were down there was an incident distressingly similar to the one that had so disturbed her on the day of her husband's Institution. The McCaughen family had called to pay their respects and, while they were talking in the dining-room, the windows darkened with menacing faces of children from the town. It would have been customary for other members of the parish to follow the McCaughen's example, and Lily laid in two large tins of assorted biscuits for the expected callers. None came and, after a week or so, she gave a shrug and said: 'Well, if no one else is coming to eat these we may as well have them ourselves.' The hostility lasted for about a year, but the new rector performed his duties (and those of the curate he could not afford) so well that opposition to him and his family melted away, and in due course he came to be as loved and respected as in his previous parishes. It is hard to avoid the conclusion, however, that events proved the justice of Louis Plunkett's fears for Lily. Despite the friendships of the later years at Carrickfergus, she was deeply scarred by the circumstances of the family's arrival and initial reception, and something of this damage must have been transmitted to her children.

Louis' first memories were of the house in Governor's Walk: the stained-glass window on the landing, the trunk in the attic, the harbour and beyond it the sails on the Lough. He could remember something also of his first sea-crossing – to visit an uncle in Wales – probably in 1909. His impressionist depiction of his early years owes much of the manner of its brushwork to Joyce's *Portrait of the Artist as a Young Man* and, as with many memories of childhood, certain details seem transposed:

There were five of us in the family – my father and my mother and my sister and my brother and I – but there were many more people in the house. The red soldiers, for instance, who by day were tiny, you could knock them over with a finger, but by night they were ten foot high, came marching straight for you, drumming, and not the least change on their faces. There were people too in the cracks of the ceiling, in the mottling of the marble mantelpieces, in the shadows of the oil-lamps and the folds of the serge curtains.

Had redcoats entered his play and his dreams by the time he was three? It seems more likely that these were memories of his early days and nights at the rectory: both houses had marble mantelpieces, oil-lamps, and serge curtains. But if, as seems probable, Louis' life at this period was relatively unclouded, his mother suffered a further setback just when it looked as if the tide of hostility might be ebbing. In 1910 she was diagnosed as having a uterine fibroid tumour. This was causing intermittent attacks of illness, but her spirits lifted early the following year when, following the death of the Revd George Chamberlain, the MacNeices could move at last into the larger, lighter rectory, far from the dirt and noise of the harbour, on the other side of town.

CHAPTER 3

The House in the Garden

In my childhood trees were green
And there was plenty to be seen.
'Autobiography', *CP*, p. 183

Carrickfergus Rectory in 1985 (drawn by T. McNally)

St Nicholas' Rectory was a Victorian villa, built for the previous incumbent in a pleasant pink brick with a roof of grey slate tiles. It stood on the North Road which climbed steadily upwards into a country of low hills and small farms. The milkman's cows passed twice a day and on market days a slow procession of orange carts creaked by the gate. The rector was further from his church and the centre of his

Louis and Elizabeth in 1910

parish, but Lily in particular delighted in a new-found sense of space indoors and out. The house had fifteen rooms: a sombre red dining-room with a harmonium, a faded yellow drawing-room with a piano, and a large kitchen with a range, yellow flagstones and shelf-lined walls. Lily was a good housekeeper and introduced into her new domain a rhythm very different from that of Governor's Walk. Elizabeth would remember how the 'house ticked with the seasons, and we kept up all the traditional ceremonies. We picked mayflowers on May Eve, we rolled eggs in the fields on Easter Monday, my mother taught us all the Hallowe'en games'. She played the harmonium and the piano. She persuaded her husband to allow Elizabeth to take dancing lessons, and she talked constantly to her children – as formerly to her father – of Connemara. The very name soon seemed to Louis

too rich for any ordinary place. It appeared to be a country of windswept open spaces and mountains blazing with whins and seas that were never quiet, with drowned palaces beneath them, and seals and eagles and turf smoke and cottagers who were always laughing and who gave you milk when you asked for a glass of water. And the people's voices were different there, soft and rich like my father's (who made one syllable of 'heron' or 'orange') . . . .

Lily tried hard, though unsuccessfully, to prevent her children from acquiring an Ulster accent and dialect. She took emotional likes and dislikes to the sound of words and would not allow them to use those she disliked. Her husband, on the other hand, had a scholar's interest in the derivation and deployment of words and liked them to be used with precision. In more playful moods, he could throw off respectable doggerel on any subject under the Irish rain, and would occasionally carry on a rhyming correspondence with his friends. Between them, in their different ways, they transmitted to their children a sense of the importance of language, its colours, contours of meaning, and cadence:

My father would seat me on his knee and imitate the train from our town to Belfast, chugging and whistling and stopping at all stations – Trooperslane, Greenisland, Jordanstown, Whiteabbey, Whitehouse, Greencastle, Belfast. And then the train back again – Greencastle, Whitehouse, Whiteabbey, Jordanstown, Greenisland, Trooperslane, Carrickfergus.

'Place names were pregnant things then', imbued with magical powers of exfoliation like Jack the Giant-killer's beans, even names nearer at hand than those of the stations on the local branch-line:

Going up the North Road . . . we first passed the Busky Burn, a dim little stream full of rusty tins but glorified by its name, then Love's Loney (a dialect improvement on the English Lovers' Lane) and so to Mile Bush where our choices were three: north up the Red Brae (there was nothing red about it but the name seemed to suit its steepness, the carthorses had to take it zigzag), or right along the Sullatober Road, a musical purplish name, or left along the 'Ballymena Road', equally musical though, as we found out later, it went nowhere near Ballymena. Also within walking distance were Bonnybefore, Woodburn, Trooper's Lane and Eden, the last conducive to a split mind, for I always thought of the Garden as I approached it . . . .

MacNeice introduced his impressionist depiction of his rectory childhood with the words: 'The second house was in a garden'. The sentence is revealing in that it seems to ascribe priority to the garden rather than the house, and it is clear from both his and his sister's writings of and about those years that their rich fantasy life was centred in the garden rather than the house. From having no garden at all in Governor's Walk, they now had an immense acre 'with a long prairie of lawn and virgin shrubberies', a tennis court, a vegetable garden, and apple trees good for climbing, all enclosed by a hawthorn hedge too high for a four-year-old to look over.

Apart from the immediate family and the members of the animal kingdom introduced by Lily – cats, dogs, and fierce red hens – there were two other inhabitants of this Unfallen World. Presiding over the kitchen was the cook Annie, a buxom girl still in her teens from a farm in County Tyrone. She was the first Roman Catholic Louis had known, 'and therefore my only proof that Catholics were human'. She was a fast and efficient worker, who did Irish crochet work in her spare time:

We would watch the shamrocks and roses growing from her crochet hooks while in a gay warm voice she would tell us about Fivemiletown where she came from and the banshees and fairies and cows of the Clogher valley. They had nice rhymes out there – Lisnaskea for drinking tea, Maguire's Bridge for whisky – and County Tyrone sounded like a land of content.

Presiding over the garden was Archie White, the gardener, 'in whose presence everything was merry'. The opposite of Annie, with whom however he was on good terms, he was elderly with snow-white hair; an Orangeman proud of playing a flute in the Twelfth of July procession (until rheumatism got the better of his legs); and an erratic worker. He seldom turned up before noon, but the children would watch for his coming because, like Annie, he was a natural story-teller, given to romancing, largely about himself and always in the third person: 'Archie's the great fella now, aye, Archie's the queer fella for work, ye wouldn't find his like, I'm telling ye, not in the whole of Ireland.' He preferred children, cats, and birds to adults and would entertain the rector's 'weans', as he called them, to snatches of verse remembered from his kindergarten: 'A bee met a wasp once runnin' by' or 'The cat sat by the barn-door spinnin''. Archie could neither read not write, but he and Annie, the Protestant and the Roman Catholic, made an important contribution to the children's developing awareness of the intertwined mythologies of their country.

They were daily reminded of the wider world beyond the rectory garden by the trains that ran along a raised embankment fifty yards or

Archie White

so to the south of the hawthorn hedge. There was the one 'with a clanky little engine and a long, long funnel, ricketing along its silly little lines . . . all its buffers jangling, every now and then letting out a snort', but more exciting was the swift transit, twice a day, of the non-stop boat-train for the Larne-Stranraer steamer. In the summer of 1911, Louis had his first real taste of that wider world ('Going to Wales was too far back'), when the family took a holiday in Portstewart, a small seaside resort on the north coast of County Antrim. His initial anguish at having forgotten his toy boat evaporated as the train pulled up at the station, but where was the sea? Portstewart Station is in open country, a mile and a half out of town (either as being more convenient for the Big House, or to discourage day-trippers). To alleviate the disappointment, the rector produced a paper bag of preserved ginger and, leading the expedition, said it would only be a little while now. It was a long walk for short legs, but Louis never forgot being greeted suddenly, as they reached the crest of the hill, by 'a strong salt breeze and a high smell of herring and there down below us was blueness, lumbering up against the wall of the fisherman's quay, ever so or never so blue, exploding in white and in gulls'. They stayed in poky lodgings overlooking the sea; Louis sharing a bed with his mother, who was fearful she might 'overlay' him. They climbed by cliff paths to the battlemented Dominican college and played on Magilligan Strand, one of the longest and smoothest in Ireland. But Louis' most abiding memories of that holiday were revelations of space: one, on a road between high walls of 'an endless stretch of a windblown something, something not I nor even my father and mother could ever, however we tried, walk to the end of'; the other,

of space and distance, but distance cut on a curve and outlined in white. The Atlantic was already for me the biggest thing this side of God but so far I had only appreciated its size head on, my back to the land and nothing but water in sight. Now I found it even more revealing suddenly to perceive the shore outlining and underlining the ocean till both disappeared simultaneously as one's eyes strained to stretch after them.

Returning from such immensities to the confines of the house in the garden, he found both perspectives and shadows lengthening. Outdoors, there was Archie whose forte was cutting hedges. He would set up a stepladder and, taking a long plank, would rest one end on a step, the other on a wooden box, and he and the small boy would stand up there as on a captain's bridge. Archie's clicking shears revealed what the hawthorn had hidden: the cemetery beyond the garden. Three tall obelisks of Aberdeen granite came into view first. Louis found them frightening, especially when Archie would say 'Thon's a bad ould fella' and, snatching up a stick, pretend to shoot the tallest and blackest of the obelisks (inscribed 'In memory of James Woodside and his wife Catherine Isabella Brown'). The ship's boy on the captain's bridge could see, beyond the cemetery, Belfast Lough in the distance, and at night,

> Our lights looked over the lough to the lights of Bangor
> Under the peacock aura of a drowning moon.

Indoors, there was Miss MacCready. As Lily's bouts of illness became more frequent, she engaged what was called a Mother's Help. The children soon discovered that Miss MacCready was all that their beloved Annie was not:

her face was sour and die-hard Puritanical, she had a rasping Northern accent. The daughter of a farmer in County Armagh, she knew all there was to be known about bringing up children; keep them conscious of sin, learn them their sums, keep all the windows shut tight and don't let them run for it is bad for their hearts.

It was the end of *laissez-faire*. Miss MacCready nearly pulled your ears off when she cleaned them and she always got the soap in your eyes. When she carried you off in disgrace your face would be scratched by the buckle of her thick leather belt. Though small she was strong as leather and we soon developed new reflexes when we saw the slaps coming. Believing in economy she made dresses for my sister out of the funeral scarves with which my father was presented at funerals.

Miss MacCready 'was much possessed by death'. She was always talking of dying and, in winter when the rectory trees had lost their leaves, would gather the children at the window to watch the funeral processions winding into the cemetery from the North Road. She was an authority on Hell:

hell-flames embroidered her words like Victorian texts. I realised now that I was always doing wrong. Wrong was showing-off, being disobedient, being rude, telling stories, doing weekday things – or thinking weekday thoughts – on Sundays. I had done so much wrong I knew I must end in Hell and, what was worse, I could imagine it. Sometimes when Miss MacCready had jerked me and thumped me into bed she would look at me grimly and say: 'Aye, you're here now but you don't know where you'll be when you wake up.'

Louis began to be frightened by the shadows between the oil-lamps, even the shadows of rabbits his mother's hands made on the nursery wall, and more frightened still by the dark.

His lengthening perspectives, and perhaps a sense of shadows at home, appear in a remarkable letter written to his sister, from Tuam, at Christmas 1911:

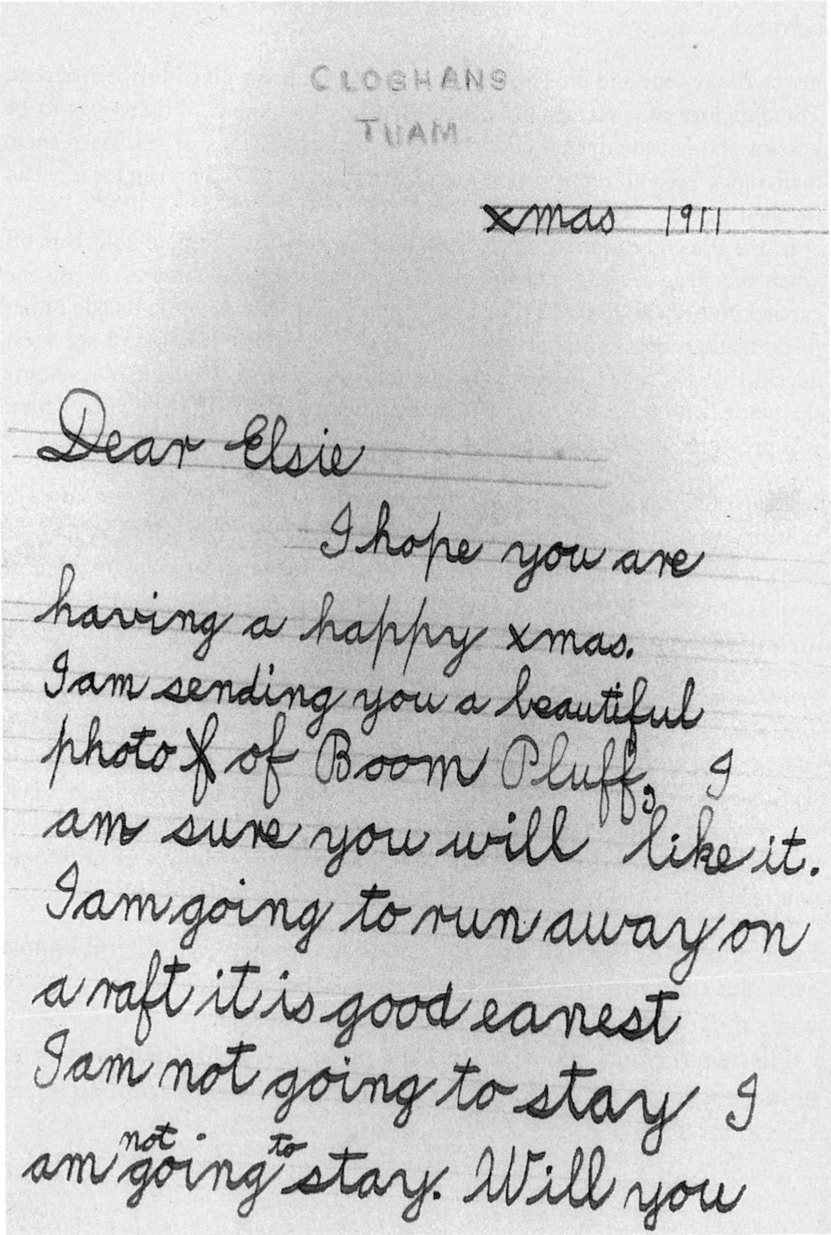

CLOGHANS
TUAM

~~xmas   1911~~

Dear Elsie
                    I hope you are
having a happy xmas.
I am sending you a beautiful
photo x of Boom Pluff. I
am sure you will like it.
I am going to run away on
a raft it is good eanest
I am not going to stay I
am ^not going ^to stay. Will you

accompany me if I call
for you. Write & tell me
if you will. I hope you will
as you will be very useful
on the raft. There will be a
watch-tower & a fort with
heaps of amunition in it, &
have the sleeping place
beside the stores.
Christopher Chippie & my-
self will be there. We will
have plenty of provisions
as we will have to go in-
to the interior of North
America. We will go where

3

the lions howl in the
night-time. We will keep a
fire burning all night, as you
wild beasts hate fire.
I will disguise myself in my
Indian suit and then
they will be friends with
us. I am giving you
notice so as you will be
able to make your costu-
-me. Must now close
with Pats love

The letter ends:

Private
Have you any more friends to run away [with], when you are writing

Selby,	Victor,	Dudley,	Susy,	Elsie
1	2	3	4	5

Christopher	Marjorie
6	

I am sending you a list of special friends. Mind you are ready for I will arrive in may ore june, this is a private letter, no one knows about this letter page good by

Even if one makes allowance for the influence of *Huckleberry Finn* or some similar adventure story, presumably read aloud in the nursery, this is an impressively imaginative and articulate piece of work for a four-year-old.

The second year at the rectory opened well. One day the children were taken up the hill to watch the newly launched *Titanic* heading for

The *Titanic* in Belfast Lough

the sea. In June, Lily took the children once again to Portstewart, but she was less cheerful than usual, taking little part in their games, sitting and staring for hours at the Atlantic rollers breaking on Magilligan Strand. The rector also had much on his mind. As a committed Home Ruler, he was distressed by the way in which the introduction of the third Home Rule bill had inflamed the militant opposition of the Ulster Unionists. Their leader and commander-in-chief was the formidable Sir Edward Carson, a Dublin-born lawyer who had come to prominence with his devastating cross-examination of Oscar Wilde in the Queensberry libel case of 1895. Although he stood for much that the Rector of Carrickfergus most disliked about the North of Ireland, John MacNeice wrote of him with characteristic accuracy and generosity:

He had great qualities of head and heart; he had courage, enthusiasm, quickness, eloquence. As a strategist he was more than a match for Mr. Asquith [the Liberal Prime Minister] and Mr. Redmond [leader of the Irish party in the House of Commons] combined. Under his direction the situation seemed to improve daily. He stressed the things which appealed inside and outside Ulster. He did not worry about the Pope. He reminded Ulstermen of their birthright. Were they to be driven out of the larger unity into which they had been born, and which meant a larger and freer life, and to be forced, against their will, to accept an inferior citizenship?

Demonstrations were held all over Ulster, and it soon became clear the Unionists were making preparations to resist Home Rule by force. At this junction an Ulster Covenant was proposed and enthusiastically welcomed. The actual contents of the document were not disclosed until almost the day on which it was to be signed, but its widely publicized message was clear: that through it would be secured Ulster's place in the British Empire.

On the day of its signing, 28 September 1912, the streets of Carrickfergus were decorated with bunting and Union Jacks. Orangemen and members of the Unionist Club marched in procession to services of dedication in the Joymount Presbyterian Church and the Parish Church of St Nicholas, where the lessons were read by Mr A. E. Dobbs, DL, who was to be the first to sign the Covenant, and in a courageous sermon John MacNeice explained why he would *not* sign it. There seemed, he said, to be four views taken of the Covenant:

First there is the view of those who take it to mean a policy of physical force, and who are persuaded that the circumstances justify such a policy. Secondly, there's the view of those who say it does not mean a policy of physical force, and who sign it in the belief that it does not. Thirdly, there's the attitude of those who look at it simply as a resolution against Home Rule, and a demand for an appeal to the nation. Those who view it in any of these three ways can, of course, sign it with a clear conscience. And lastly, there's the attitude of those who try to study the Covenant primarily from the Church's standpoint. Amongst these there are some who think that it means a call to arms, and who also think that as the Church of Christ is in this land to interpret the life of Christ and to exhibit the mind of Christ, she cannot sound that call. They do not censure or criticise those who take a different view – far from it. All they say is – 'Let each man be fully persuaded in his own mind.' But they do feel strongly that the Church as a Church, fighting for her own life, must fight under Christ's banner, and in Christ's way, and need not borrow the weapons of the kingdoms of the world .... Furthermore, they think that Ireland's greatest interest is peace, and they shrink from a policy which, as is avowed, in the last resort, means war, and worse still, civil war. They fear that even the avowal of such a policy may add to the dissensions that are already too characteristic of Irish life and intensify the bitterness that many of them hoped was fast dying away. This is the attitude of a minority, possibly a small minority. This is my own attitude .... I do not ask anyone to adopt my view. I may, of course, be mistaken in my interpretation of Christ's life and of the Church's duty, but I am entitled to hold the opinion I have expressed, and I make no apology for holding it ....

Mr Tommy Robinson, the butcher, probably spoke for most of the brethren assembled in St Nicholas that morning when, leaving the church, he said: 'That was a grand sermon the rector gave us. But he spoilt it all at the end by telling us he wasn't going to sign the Covenant.'

At six o'clock that evening a meeting was held in the Kilroot Orange Hall, which concluded with the signing, by men and women in numbers exceeding all expectations, of the following Declaration:

Ulster's
Solemn League and Covenant.

Being convinced in our consciences that Home Rule would be disastrous to the material well-being of Ulster as well as of the whole of Ireland, subversive of our civil and religious freedom, destructive of our citizenship and perilous to the unity of the Empire, we, whose names are under-written, men of Ulster, loyal subjects of His Gracious Majesty King George V., humbly relying on the God whom our fathers in days of stress and trial confidently trusted, do hereby pledge ourselves in solemn Covenant throughout this our time of threatened calamity to stand by one another in defending for ourselves and our children our cherished position of equal citizen-ship in the United Kingdom and in using all means which may be found necessary to defeat the present conspiracy to set up a Home Rule Parliament in Ireland. ¶ And in the event of such a Parliament being forced upon us we further solemnly and mutually pledge ourselves to refuse to recognise its authority. ¶ In sure confidence that God will defend the right we hereto subscribe our names. ¶ And further, we individually declare that we have not already signed this Covenant.

The above was signed by me at_____
"Ulster Day." Saturday, 28th September, 1912.

God Save the King.

Bonfires were lit that night on the hills around Carrickfergus, and many houses on the sea front were illuminated in honour of Carson and his associates. 'He will be remembered', John MacNeice told his daughter, 'as the man who broke the unity of Ireland.'

The tension of those days must have thrown another shadow across the rector's household; a tension manifested for the children in the servants' conflicting attitudes towards the Covenant: Archie and Miss MacCready would have welcomed it as strongly as Annie would have deplored it. The episode in general, and John MacNeice's stand in particular, can have done nothing for Lily's peace of mind. Around Christmas she was back in bed, but recovered and seemed much as usual. On 2 January, however, her husband's diary record: 'Lily ill again.' Some mornings later she went to Belfast to see a gynaecologist, who told her she needed an immediate hysterectomy. She returned in tears, that news having triggered off a depression from which she was never completely to emerge. It seemed that she believed, despite medical evidence to the contrary, that Louis' difficult birth had caused her uterine fibroid; a belief transmitted to her son, who grew up convinced at some psychological level that he was responsible for his mother's illness and death.

On 18 March the rector wrote in his diary: 'Prayers with Lily, Elsie, Freddie. Private Hospital stayed over 2 hours.' Surgically, the operation was a complete success. The children were taken to visit their mother in the Belfast nursing-home and told she would be home shortly. She came back, but her depression came with her. Much of the summer she was in tears. A nurse came to look after her, and most afternoons she was taken out for a drive in a phaeton. Elizabeth would always remember how her mother

and the nurse would sit on the main seat and one child was always taken to sit on the little seat facing them. I don't know what Louis felt on these drives. I enjoyed them, but at the same time the scenery became intermingled with my mother's sorrow. We used often to pass within sight of a little house far in the distance in the hills; I thought that it was like a face and the windows were eyes full of tears and it always looked like this to me in later life.

The rector's diary for 20 August records: 'Lily awfully bad.' And five days later he took the painful step of transferring her to a

nursing-home kept by a friend in Dublin. Neither Elizabeth nor Louis
ever forgot the morning of her departure. They were playing in the
garden, trying unsuccessfully to attach a rope to a stick, and asked her
to help. Elizabeth would recall how

Miss MacCready (who latterly had come to speak to our mother as if to a
child) came out and said quite sharply to her: 'What are you doing there?' 'I
don't know,' replied Mother, 'the children asked me to', and she went into the
house to get ready to leave. She gave last injunctions to Miss MacCready and
Annie. Our unpractical father was not to be asked questions about our clothes
or food or health, for he would not know the answers; they were to use their
own good judgment and were always to give us plenty of milk.

Louis remembered his mother 'walking up and down the bottom path
of the garden, the path under the hedge that was always in shadow,
talking to my sister and weeping'. Writing that sentence twenty-seven
years after the event, he has imaginatively ordered his memories to
conform to biblical paradigms – a dejected woman about to be ejected
from a garden, and another woman weeping beside a tomb in another
garden: Genesis 3 conflated with St John 20 and with the psalmist's
'walk through the valley of the shadow of death'.

    Some friends, who owned one of the rare motor cars in the neigh-
bourhood, then arrived to drive John and Lily to the Dublin train.
Their three children stood at the gate and waved. They never saw her
again.

CHAPTER 4

Black Dreams

When I was five the black dreams came;
Nothing after was quite the same.
'Autobiography', *CP*, p. 183

Everyone expected Lily to return. A month after she left she sent Louis a present for his sixth birthday, but an entry in her husband's diary that week speaks of receiving an 'appallingly doleful letter'. Elizabeth also began to get sad little letters, but they soon stopped and she was told she must write no more to her mother until she was better. With her departure, Miss MacCready took over the running of the rectory, a change of power no doubt responsible for Louis' first rebellion:

Thursday was Mrs. M'Quitty's Day and we always had stewed steak. Mrs. M'Quitty, the charwoman, was very stout and friendly, she had a son who was a fisherman and she had given us our cat but she had to have stewed steak. I could not bear stewed steak, I found it too tough to swallow, had to keep the pieces in my cheek till after dinner, then spit them out in the shrubbery. So one spring Thursday, as we were spending the morning with Annie raking up new-cut grass, I planned that, when the gong went, I would hang behind and have no steak. So the gong went and I hung behind, crawled in under some laurel bushes at the side of the lawn. In a few minutes they came out and called for me but I did not answer. This was achievement, I felt, something entirely new, I had planned to do something outrageous and outrage was working. The steak too must be getting cold.

The response was gratifyingly dramatic: Miss MacCready, Mrs M'Quitty, and Annie all shouting – then screaming – round the garden. He heard the charwoman say: 'Sure he may be killed on the roads; the master has the polis out looking for him.' Louis was alarmed to think

Willie, Louis (reading) and Elizabeth in the Rectory garden

that the polis were after him, but not as alarmed as he was later to see the rectory rooster, looking 'like the Devil with great scarlet wattles and crest', leading a coven of hens straight for his hideout. He scrambled out, to be caught by Miss MacCready and told he 'was bound for Hell'. His response to the rooster may have been prompted by her regular insistence that a cock crowing in the night was a warning of death. She was very superstitious and took great note of such portents. The nursery furniture was infested with death-watch beetle, or some similar insect, and when on a quiet afternoon the ticking would begin, Miss MacCready would never fail to lift her hand and say: 'Hark! the death watch!' (Louis probably thought she was referring to a sinister form of wrist-watch.) The rector, not surprisingly, strongly disapproved of superstition and would have been appalled to know it was rife under his own roof. The children were careful not to tell him, partly because both he and Miss MacCready would have been angry, and partly because superstition, for all its terrors, had an element of glamour that they would have been sorry to lose. The rector and the Mother's Help hardly ever came face to face. Elizabeth acted as a messenger between them and used to amuse herself by reporting what one said to the other. She was present at lunch when her father and a visiting clergyman were discussing corporal punishment. Afterwards, she was delighted to tell Miss MacCready: 'Daddy says he disapproves of corporal punishment for girls.' This brought the impenitent reply: 'You can tell him his own daughter gets the plenty of it.' The little go-between learnt when to keep her mouth shut. She would tell her father: 'Miss MacCready's father said he would as soon have the Kaiser as King George any day. The Kaiser is a good Protestant, Miss MacCready's father says.' And the rector would reply: 'Just the kind of ignorant, ill-informed statement, I would expect a man like Miss MacCready's father to make.' That, however, was not relayed to the nursery.

Gradually, over the weeks and months following Lily's departure, new routines, new rituals became established. Breakfast was as ample as ever: 'The same porridge on the side table – each one helping himself – the same breakfast service, the same triangular loaves of shaggy bread.' Later, Louis would have his lessons from Miss MacCready in the nursery, with the window always tight shut. When the rector lunched at home, Elizabeth ate with him and was delighted to avoid the midday meal in the nursery, which Miss MacCready prepared. In the afternoon, when it was not raining too hard, she would take the three children for a walk up the road to a point called Mile Bush and back again. The route was seldom varied because Miss MacCready 'disliked going through the town; you never knew what you might catch'. On their return there would be tea at the long narrow nursery table – strong tea laced with sugar – and sometimes, for a treat before bed, Miss MacCready would give them thick beef sandwiches lined with mustard, or a cold drink made from cream of tartar. In *The Strings are False*, Louis speculates whether this diet might not have exacerbated his dreams.

These got worse and worse. Where earlier I had had dreams of being chased by mowing-machines or falling into machinery or arguing with tigers who wanted to eat me I now was tormented by something much less definite, much more serious. There was a kind of a noise that I felt rather than heard, 'ah . . . ah . . . ah', a grey monotonous rhythm which drew me in towards a centre as if there were a spider at the centre drawing in his thread and everything else were unreal.

'Oh God I do not want to have any dreams. If I am going to go to sleep, do not let me have any dreams. And if I am going to have dreams, do not let me go to sleep, God, please I will do anything if only You keep me awake.' But I always went to sleep all the same. One night I woke up and yelled, my father came up from downstairs, there was light and his voice, he told me nothing would hurt me. I felt quite safe when he had gone but next morning Miss MacCready was very angry; my father had forgotten to go down again to the study and had left the lamp burning there all night. I was a very wicked boy and might have burnt the house down.

On the last Christmas Eve of his life, Louis said to his sister: 'You and I, Elizabeth, remember so much about our childhoods, yet we seem to remember such different things'. She viewed Miss MacCready in a kinder light, remembering how she kept up the seasonal traditions established by their mother; how she could unbend and even let her hair down:

whenever my father left home for a few days, a kind of restraint seemed to lift from the house and we even held a mild Saturnalia. For one thing, there was no longer any objection to noise. I don't remember that my father himself ever did lay down any embargo upon noise. But it had been impressed upon us by my mother when she left that we must not worry him, we must remember how often he suffered from bad and painful indigestion and how hard he worked; we must try to be quiet when he was at home. So that when he was away, the feeling of responsibility for his well-being lifted from us and perhaps it may have done so for Miss MacCready also. At all events, we were always rather gay at these times. Miss MacCready often asked such people as Mrs McCaughen to tea in the nursery and there was a general spirit of laissez-faire. In the evenings we stayed up later and would sit by the kitchen fire listening to Miss MacCready and Annie capping each other's stories of the countryside. I was kept up later still as company, for both women were slightly nervous as regards possible burglars, when my father was away. And a sort of ritual came into being. Miss MacCready, Annie and myself went last thing round the whole ground floor carrying a small hand-lamp and testing every shutter and every bolt. When on this journey we reached the piano, I always sat down and played *The Harp that Once* with both women standing solemnly behind me.

Elizabeth never denied or sought to excuse Miss MacCready's harshness towards her brother, and it is clear that he suffered much more than Elizabeth from the puritanical spinster's taboo against tenderness. She could neither offer nor receive demonstrations of affection. She believed that men were more naturally sinful than women. Had not Louis 'rebelled' as soon as she became responsible for him? She viewed him as a problem, whereas the ten-year-old Elizabeth was a companion as well as a charge. The eldest child had her social contacts established before her mother died, but while she could go to parties by herself, Louis tended to be invited only by those who were prepared to invite Miss MacCready and the mentally handicapped Willie as well – a double deterrent.

One of the saddest consequences of Lily's departure was a widening gap between the children and their father. He was desperately worried about his wife's failure to respond to treatment and no doubt they reminded him of her predicament and theirs. He wrote to a friend: 'When I see the children playing and laughing, I know that I should rejoice, and I do too but sometimes their laughter almost shocks me.' In later life, his daughter came to believe that he was probably undergoing a minor nervous breakdown at this time. He sought escape from his grief and worry in overwork, and the children saw him less and less. Coming in at night, frequently cold and wet and always tired, he would kiss them, try to say something cheerful, and then retire to his study. Louis in bed would hear him 'intoning away, communing with God. And because of his conspiracy with God . . . was afraid of him'. That voice on the verge of nightmare became associated in his mind with two other sounds that from the first he found alarming, the foghorns from the lough and the bells of St Nicholas.

There were also the terrors of Church. The church was cruciform, and the rectory pew, being the front pew of the nave, looked out on to the space where the chancel and the nave and the two transepts met. The transept on our left was on a higher level and was reached by a short flight of steps; the end wall of it was occupied by a huge Elizabethan monument to the Chichester family who had then been the power in the land. The father and mother, who were each very large, knelt each under an arch, opposite each other, praying; below them, much smaller, was a Chichester brother who had been beheaded by the rebels, and between them, like a roll of suet pudding, on a little marble cushion

43

was a little marble baby. None of these marble people worried me at all; what I disliked were the things that hung high up on the wall on either side of the monument's narrower top. A decayed coat of mail, a couple of old weapons, a helmet. I could not see the coat of mail when I was sitting, thanks to the solid front of the first pew in the transept, but, whenever I had to get up, there it would be, older and older and deader and deader, yet somehow not quite dead enough.

The Chichester Monument in St Nicholas Church

On Sundays, once Louis had learnt to read, he would be given a Bible open at the Book of Revelation when his father stood up to preach, but as he grew older and began to pay more attention to what was said and sung in church, he became increasingly alarmed by what he heard – especially about sin and the wages of sin.

Religion never left us alone, it was at home as much as in church, it fluttered in the pages of a tear-off calendar in the bathroom and it filled the kitchen with the smell of silver-polish when Annie, who might at the same time be making jokes about John Jameson, was cleaning the Communion plate.

With their mother's departure and their shortage of friends, Elizabeth and Louis became indispensible to each other. She was of the opinion – an opinion probably deriving from Miss MacCready – that anything *modern* was evil and anything *ancient* was good. She, her brother wrote later, 'took refuge in a cult of the Old and I took refuge in fantasy; she shared her antiquarianism with me and I shared my fantasies with her'. Prompted perhaps by her father's interest in Irish history, she invented a Great Queen (or Mrs) MacMiss, 'but Louis' imagination took over and a whole host of invisible people came to live in the trees and bushes and sheds'. Prominent in this mythology were the Good Queen MacMiss, the Bad Queen McMiss and another Queen, Ina Kee (who was younger than the Good Queen, gentle, and very beautiful), and Keddy Bock. The adult Louis called the last of these 'my oracle, my familiar and my general consolation', and it is clear that the other principal *dramatis personae* were shadow projections of their mother, Miss MacCready, Annie, and Elizabeth.

The original of the Good Queen, meanwhile, was in sorrowful exile, and on 25 December the rector wrote in his diary: 'Quiet Xmas, Poor Lily in hospital.' To John MacNeice's domestic anxieties were now added political anxieties, as he watched the formation and preparation of four armies: the Ulster Volunteers, Larkin's 'Citizen Army', the Irish Volunteers, and the Sinn Fein Volunteers. The British Government judged the situation in Ulster to be so explosive that it increasingly deployed units of its own army – the fifth in Ireland – to keep the peace. One beautiful spring morning, that of 21 March 1914, a hundred men of the Yorkshire Light Infantry arrived in Carrickfergus. John MacNeice described the scene:

The great Norman Castle, the symbol of England's rule in Ulster for over seven hundred years, threw its shadow into the clear water. Not far off lay one of His Majesty's ships in which the troops had come from Kingstown. Blue-jackets in small boats conveyed them to the pier. Numbers of people crowded together near the harbour.

Some of the women who looked on were almost in tears. Through that day the wildest rumours were in circulation, and were believed. It was stated that the leaders of the Ulster Volunteer force were to be seized that night, that the warrants for their arrest had come.

Later, the rector met a boy with two rifles ill-concealed under his coat on his way to act, if needed, as sentry outside the home of an Ulster Volunteer officer. No doubt John MacNeice had that encounter in mind when he climbed into his pulpit next morning to say:

What is the first duty of a Christian clergyman, and of a Christian congregation? Isn't it to put their strength into the things that make for peace? Surely there is no one so reckless as to wish for civil commotion, or strife, to say nothing of civil war? If this dear land of ours is to be stained with human blood, then I say that that will be a black crime, an awful tragedy, and that the consequences will be such as no man living can foresee. Our immediate duty, locally, is plain. It is to do all in our power to maintain order. As loyal subjects of the King we shall exhibit no antagonism to the soldiers of the King. On the contrary we shall show them that we welcome them most cordially to our neighbourhood. Let us see that no provocation is given by us. Let our words and actions, and whole bearing be worthy of our cause, and of our religious professions. And while we resolve not to give offence, let us also resolve not to take offence. After all, it is a stronger thing not to retaliate than to retaliate. Let us do the stronger thing, the more Christ-like thing.

The Yorkshires stayed in Carrickfergus, as peaceably as the rector could have wished, until the outbreak of war, when they marched away, many of them to graves in France. Among the columns of Irish Volunteers that followed them to the same destination were two brothers of the boy-sentry John MacNeice had met on the evening of 21 March. Louis must have watched the soldiers go and heard them singing. Annie and Miss MacCready were repapering the nursery. 'At the top of the new paper there was a little coloured border and as I watched this border advancing round the room under the ceiling I thought it's a long way to Tipperary.'

In late November 1914, all three children caught measles, their eyes were bandaged, and they were put in the same room. Louis would have welcomed this, because his bed had recently been moved into his father's room. The rector was himself sleeping badly, tossing and groaning through the night, and his son was desperate 'to be asleep before he arrived with the lamp and his own gigantic shadow'. On the morning of 18 December, John MacNeice came in and told the children that their mother had died. Louis was to remember that

Elizabeth began to cry but, being unable to cry, I dived down under the clothes and lay at the bottom of the bed where I hoped they would think I was crying. I felt very guilty at being so little moved but decided that when I grew up I would build my mother a monument. And everyone would know that I had built it.

Buried in that womb-like cave, he envisaged a monument, no doubt in marble, like that in his father's church to the Chichester mother, father, and children.

The very different monument that he would in due course raise was brought nearer by one of the many presents he was given that Christmas: *Aunt Louisa's Book of Nursery Rhymes.* Louis and Elizabeth had

of course learnt many of these from their mother years before and now, aged seven and eleven, might have been thought too old to enjoy such a book. Enjoy it they did, however, reading it over and over and chanting the rhymes aloud. Those comforting spells brought back the uncomplicated world of childhood they had shared with their mother. Nursery rhymes were to have an important influence on Louis' poetry, and *Aunt Louisa's Book* occupied an honoured place in his bookshelf, until finally he gave it to his daughter.

Just as Miss MacCready's superstitions and Archie's Ulster mythology were competing with Christian doctrine for the boy's imagination, so his ear was impressed with sacred as well as secular cadences: those of the Bible, his father's Book, and of the hymns first heard as his mother's hands moved over the dining-room harmonium or the drawing-room piano. He warmed to their 'melancholy poetry' as to that of such secular poems as Hopkins's 'Binsey Poplars' and the ballad of Sir Patrick Spens encountered in his first anthology. Nostalgic poetry particularly appealed to him because he 'was always looking back to some preceding, hardly remembered period as a kind of Golden Age'. Graduating from that anthology, he found a kindred spirit in Tennyson, whose velvet-bound selected poems was the first book by an individual poet to come into his hands. It was at seven, and probably in the aftermath of his mother's death, that he began writing poetry himself. His recipe was simple, as he explained:

use 'thou' instead of 'you' and make the ends of the lines rhyme with each other; no specific emotion or 'poetic' content required. Here is a poem about a live parrot which I had seen in a neighbour's house:

> O parrot, thou hast grey feathers
> Which thou peckest in all weathers.
> And thy curled beak
> Could make me squeak;
> Thy tail I admire
> As red as a fire
> And as red as a carrot,
> Thy tail I admire,
> Thou cross old parrot.

Many poets have had a less auspicious début. The boy has his eye on his subject, and has learnt from nursery rhymes how to bring his poem round to closure.

This was followed by an ode to a stuffed monkey, seen in an old lady's parlour, which began:

> O Monkey though thou art stuffed
> Thou hast very often roughed
> A night out in the wild forést . . . .

A letter to Elizabeth contains a revised version of 'a piece of poetry about "A great old Kangaroo"'. These subjects show the influence of a secular text elevated to the status of a sacred book and, indeed, as his later account makes clear, associated in his mind with the most sacred of all:

My favourite book was *Cassell's Natural History*, a large Mid-Victorian work in two volumes, heavy to lift, illustrated with engravings which are so much more romantic than photographs. This book had the charm of its period, being long-winded, discursive and moralistic, full of quotations from the poets and curious anecdotes. The first section, on the primates, had an alarming series of illustrations of brains and skeletons; many of the skeletons were climbing up trees. Many of the pictures were action pictures; there was one called 'the Lion, the Tiger, and the Jaguar', where these three animals were engaged in a threesome battle in the jungle, regardless of the fact that there is no jungle in the world which contains all three species. On the other hand there were some very sumptuous still lifes, such as an almost full-page engraving entitled 'Food of American Monkeys'. Every so often there was a coloured plate – a naked man playing with a squirrel (must have been Adam) . . . .

Another letter to Elizabeth contains a poem focused on a wild landscape with no sign of the animal kingdom, but showing an important technical development in its use of a refrain:

I have made another
piece of poetry. It is.

    The water sound
Gurgles and bubbles and are
believe believe
    In a wild country

The Cliffs are high
Against the sky
In a wild country

The Suns great ray
Makes hot the travellers way
In a wild country.
Do you like it.
With Love from Freddie.

The water sound
Gurgles and bubbles around
In a wild country
The Cliffs are high
Against the sky
In a wild country
The Suns great ray
Makes hot the traveller's way
In a wild country.

Cliff and water, fixity and flux: clear as a fingerprint in these lines of the child are the co-ordinates and configurations of the poems of the man. Louis' literary endeavours did not meet with unqualified encouragement. Miss MacCready indeed showed unqualified discouragement in throwing his diary on the fire because, she said, it was bad for his handwriting. She also disapproved of what she called 'book-reading' and forbade it except at certain times.

In March 1916, the rectory became an even darker place when Annie, who had been the children's 'bulwark for so long against puritan repression', left to get married. She was succeeded by Mrs Knox, an elderly woman with a witch's sharp nose and a line in sadistic horror stories. 'There was one about a little boy who filled a slice of bread with pins and covered the points of the pins with butter and jam and gave it to his sister and she died.' She engaged in screaming-matches with Miss MacCready and was soon dismissed. Willie, now eleven, was sent to an institution for the mentally handicapped in Scotland, and the exodus continued with the departure of Miss Mac-Cready. Elizabeth and Louis wept at her going, but cheered up when her successor proved to be a gentle and gullible Englishwoman, Miss Heward. It was now the children's turn to tell the gothic stories, as they introduced her to Ulster's violent mythology.

Violence was in the air:

a huge camp of soldiers
Grew from the ground in sight of our house with long
Dummies hanging from gibbets for bayonet practice
And the sentry's challenge echoing all day long;

> A Yorkshire terrier ran in and out by the gate-lodge
> Barred to civilians, yapping as if taking affront:
> Marching at ease and singing 'Who Killed Cock Robin?'
> The troops went out by the lodge and off to the Front.

The Western Front was not the only Front. There was violence nearer home, the more shocking for being unexpected. Easter had always been the rector's favourite festival, but on Easter Monday, 24 April 1916, there took place an Easter Rising very different from the one he had so recently celebrated. His newspaper next day reported a battle in the centre of Dublin. Between 700 and 800 volunteers of the Irish Republican Brotherhood and members of the Citizen Army had seized several of the principal buildings, and proclaimed an Irish Republic. The British responded to force with greater force, shelling their positions from a Royal Navy gunboat on the Liffey. John MacNeice was horrified by the week of fierce fighting that followed, in which 450 people were killed and 2,614 wounded, and by the no less brutal but more cold-blooded sequel. The leaders of the Rising were tried by court martial and, in early May, shot by firing squad in a prison yard.

Some months later, there was worse news from France. With the start of the Battle of the Somme in July 1916, the war entered a new and even uglier phase, and perhaps in response to the increasing attention accorded the rector's newspaper, his son that autumn started his own. He stitched together sheets of coarse paper and divided them into columns:

The columns were devoted to War News (Red Indian wars), verse, archaeological discoveries (illustrated), sensational accounts of improbable happenings and a domestic section of practical suggestions and reproofs directed at Miss Heward, Elizabeth, the cook, the dog, the cat and the hens . . . .

Concerned at the amount of time Louis was spending in writing his newspaper and his diary, and dissatisfied with a governess who set the children foolish essays rather than introducing them to Shakespeare, the rector now decided to take a hand in their education. He began to teach them Latin, succeeding with Louis better than he knew:

I began to introduce Latin words into my newspapers and one day, when I went to a tea-party with tigerskin rugs on the floor, I kept declining the noun '*dux*' in my head and that made everything taste better. '*Ducibus ducibus*' I said, and this private pattern in my mind fitted in somehow with the stripes on the tigers and knowledge was power and a wind blew down the vistas.

Other vistas opened in 1917. On 19 April John MacNeice remarried. His bride, Georgina Beatrice (known as 'Bea') Greer, came from the wealthiest family in the neighbourhood. Now in her forties, she had grown up dividing her time between Seapark, a big house on the shore of Belfast Lough, and a mansion overlooking Regent's Park in London. Her family had originally been Quakers but she, for a number of years, had been a member of the congregation of St Nicholas' Church, and there her long white gloves had attracted Louis' attention. Although he and Elizabeth had had many pleasant visits with their father to Seapark, and the rector had told them of his impending remarriage, Louis actually heard that the ceremony had taken place – in London – from Miss Heward, and was outraged. 'My father had no right to go turning things upside down. When my stepmother came home I would show her what I thought; her life would just not be worth living.'

With her arrival, things were indeed turned upside down. She would have no Roman Catholic servants, and brought with her a cook and a housemaid who had been employed by her mother. They took part in the formal family prayers she instituted for the now solidly Protestant household. The children had hitherto said their prayers at a parental knee. Late Dinner replaced High Tea, to Louis' initial displeasure. More to his liking was

a stack of books on Foreign missions. I picked my way through the maze of new furniture and devoured the adventures of the missionaries – in India, Burma, China, Uganda, Paraguay and Ungava. I decided to be a missionary too, preferably in a jungle with lots of wild animals; in the end I should be martyred and clergymen would use me in sermons for a noble example.

Miss Heward left and Elizabeth was packed off to an English boarding school, where her stepmother hoped she would lose her Northern Irish accent. Her brother missed her greatly but, to his surprise, found most other aspects of the new order marked improvements on the old. Contrary to his expectations, his stepmother 'brought so much comfort and benevolence with her' that he abandoned his plans of guerrilla action, other than the occasional deliberate naughtiness to salve his conscience 'for acting the role of dear amusing child, selling [his] savage birthright for a swansdown cushion'. One such piece of mischief proved unexpectedly instructive. He was caught by the new housemaid flooding the yard with a hose.

She said it was *her* yard (the yard where I had always played) and I had no right to come into it; she would skelp my father himself if he was to come fooling round her yard. This tirade of hers pained me like blasphemy; I had never heard anyone speak like that of my father, and it made it worse that I felt she could skelp him – or anyone else for that matter – if she wanted to; she was my conception of an ogress. Later I found that it was she who thought she was the victim of a tyranny – had spent her life, she told me, carrying coals; carrying coals from six in the morning; break the back on you, carrying coals.

We do not know how much later he found that out, but the incident seems to have prompted an early stirring – perhaps the earliest – of his social conscience.

That summer it was decided that Louis should follow Elizabeth to Sherborne, the boys' preparatory school being no great distance from the girls' school. Shortly after his tenth birthday, however, he fell ill, and it was not until the middle of November that he took his seat in the boat-train for the Larne-Stranraer steamer and watched the Carrickfergus cemetery and the house in the garden fall behind.

CHAPTER 5

Sherborne

I went to school in Dorset, the world of parents
    Contracted into a puppet world of sons
Far from the mill girls, the smell of porter, the salt-mines
    And the soldiers with their guns.
                     'Carrickfergus', *CP*, p. 70

Acreman House, home of 'The Prep' (as The Preparatory School, Sherborne, is still commonly called), is a three-storey stone mansion, built in 1855, that looks out over wide lawns to the yellow sandstone tower of the Abbey Church. Few of the attractions of Sherborne,

Acreman House

however, would have been visible on the winter evening when the MacNeices – father, stepmother, and son – came to the end of their journey. Their arrival was probably not unlike that of another family two months later.

Picture them if you will, getting out at a chilly railway station, amid hissing gusts of steam and the hoarse gargle of gas-lamps, and climbing into a melancholy horse-drawn cab that smells of old leather and musty straw, and follow them as it bears them clip-a-clop through dimly lit streets of brown stone houses that suddenly resound to the chime and boom of a great clock high up in the misty dusk. . . . The cab staggers up a long gritty drive between trees and deposits the little shivering family in front of a big door with a big brass bell, which, when pressed, produces a remote internal clang. Hardly has a white-capped maid opened the door, making a slight dip as she does so, than a pale light in the hall beyond wavers into a glare and there, suddenly, is a big man, his face beaming with smiles, and a big voice. . . . This clearly, is the Headmaster, Mr. Littleton Powys.

The second of eleven children of the Revd Charles and Mary Powys, Littleton was his father's favourite son, perhaps because he had the distinguished appearance and generous nature of his supposed fore-bears, the ancient Welsh princes of Powysland, but had not inherited from his masochistic grandmother (née Knight) the deadly *night*shade said to run in the veins of his more famous brothers, John Cowper, Theodore, and Llewelyn.

When the big door closed behind them that November evening, the MacNeices were shown into a study lit by gas lamps incomparably more brilliant than the oil lamps of the Carrickfergus rectory.

The headmaster stood in this miraculous light and his voice filled the room like a bell and his smile filled the room. He was ebullient with health, smelling of tweed, and high up under the ceiling from between the perfect teeth in his classic squirearchic face courteous phrases flowed out, rolled to the walls. Assurance that all was well. Oh yes, the headmaster said, we'll look after him. With great strides rocking the house he led my parents and me to my dormitory.

In the corridor, they heard a sound that Louis must have counted a good omen: a harsh Northern Irish voice. Mrs Powys explained: 'That is our Irish master teaching the boys. He comes from Portadown.'

('Well,' said Mrs MacNeice to her husband later that evening. 'We've come a long way to have Freddie taught by someone from Portadown.') In the dormitory, the circling lighthouse beam of the headmaster's smile produced reflected smiles from the two new boys already in bed in dormitory Number One, smiles that vanished as soon as the headmaster and the MacNeice parents withdrew. Louis was astonished by the sudden metamorphosis of his new companions:

The blond one, who had been so cherubic to my father, changed on the instant into a leering imp, his voice charged with malevolence, his nose twitching like a rabbit's. The dark one backed him up; both were delighted to have someone junior to themselves. 'Where's your little cocky?' they said.

Despite this reception and the rigours of his new environment, Louis wrote home cheerfully on 21 November to 'My dear Daddie and Madre'. He sent them sketched plans of the dining-room, his classroom and dormitory, together with news of a new interest – rugger – and an old one. As part of the Cult of the Old shared with Elizabeth, he had begun collecting fossils and now reported finding some in a local quarry, but was forbidden to bring them back to school. Looking back at his initiation into school life, he remembered

My first piece of Prep (preparation) was Rep (repetition). I learned by heart 'The Burial of Sir John Moore'. One by one the boys got up from their benches, stood before Mr. Powys, buried Sir John Moore. I felt very proud I could bury him as well as the others.

After watching so many burials from the rectory window, he might have been forgiven for considering himself something of an expert on this rite. His letters make no mention of his success, but in his first month he has to learn another elegy, Gray's 'Ode on the Death of a Favourite Cat', and Browning's 'Home-Thoughts, from Abroad'.

In the school stories that had shaped his optimistic expectations of Sherborne, 'the Irish boys or girls ... did what they liked and were always popular'. The blond boy in the dormitory cannot have read the same stories, for he took to bullying this particular Irish boy, who one night planned his revenge. Next morning Louis hunted him out in the changing-room and attacked him without preliminaries. He made him cry by pulling his hair, and left the battlefield triumphant. One of the

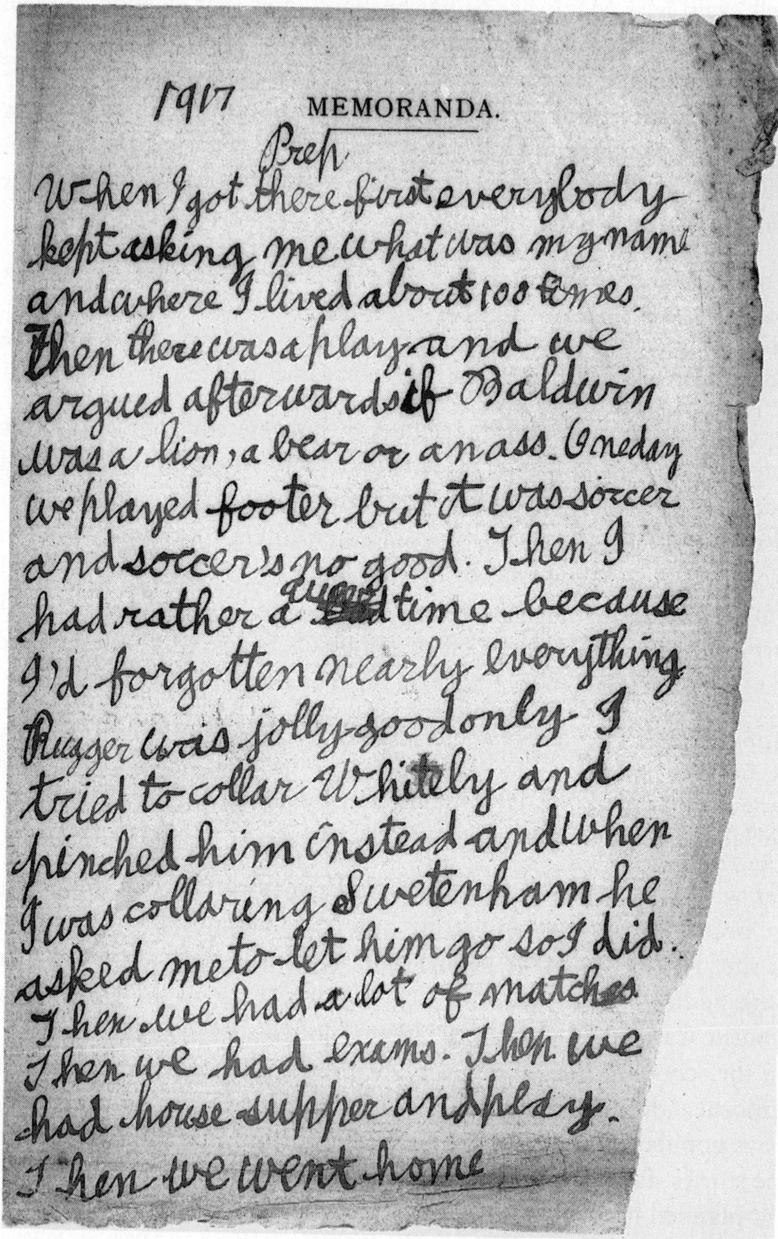

1917   MEMORANDA.

Prep

When I got there first everybody kept asking me what was my name and where I lived about 100 times. Then there was a play and we argued afterwards if Baldwin was a lion, a bear or an ass. One day we played footer but it was soccer and soccer's no good. Then I had rather a rummy time because I'd forgotten nearly everything Rugger was jolly good only I tried to collar Whitely and pinched him instead and when I was collaring Swetenham he asked me to let him go so I did. Then we had a lot of matches Then we had exams. Then we had house supper and play. Then we went home

Louis' own report on his first term

58

older boys, however, said 'Is that what they teach you in Ireland?' and the word went round that the wild Irish boy was spiteful. To counter-act this and advance his ambition of being popular, he took to giving away his twice-weekly allocation of sweets and to playing the comedian:

the boys laughed at the way I turned my feet out. Very well; if they found me funny I would be funny on purpose, so funny that my company would be precious. Always doing something unexpected. My family helped me by sending me from Ireland a new pair of boots much too big for me. They were very uncomfortable, kept filling with pebbles and grit, but a great asset. I turned my feet out all the more, and oh how the boys laughed. The headmaster took me aside, told me it was bad to be a buffoon, but I paid no attention. The laughter of the boys was intoxicating.

Soon he preferred school to home. 'Popularity was achievable by recipe; at school one was a person, at home one was just a child.' In *The Strings are False*, he records his surprised discovery that he was no athlete, but no sense of this emerges from his Sherborne letters, which from March 1918 are mostly addressed to 'My dear Madre'. Sport in general and 'footer' in particular is their major topic, with food a distant second.

Poetry could not be forgotten with Mr Powys around who, during the two winter terms, used to read to the assembled school every evening he was free from 6.30 to 7 o'clock, with a view to encouraging 'in an informal way a love of literature'. On May Day he read aloud Herrick's appeal to Corinna 'going a-Maying': 'Get up, get up for shame'. 'He read it with such gusto, booming like a belfry, you felt you must rush out at once, jump over hedges.' Later that month Louis wrote home:

Things in Summer Term different from other terms

(1) caterpillars
(2) butterflies
(3) cricket
(4) exchanging stockings on Monday
(5) collecting flowers
(6) going out after tea
(7) no gas

(8)   bats
(9)   balls
(10)   nets

This list shows the influence of Littleton Powys, whose 'religion was natural history and he strode through the country like a walking belfry. Ding! a something-or-other fritillary. Dong! a this or that orchis.' The use of *religion* and *belfry* suggest a subconscious identification with the Rector of Carrickfergus, and it would seem that Louis was beginning to see Powys as an idealized father-figure. He was an Enthusiast – for literature (Latin and Greek which, with Scripture, he taught, as well as English); for cricket and rugger; for collecting things. He encouraged Louis to collect fossils: 'the other boys seemed so far ahead with butterflies and birds' eggs'. The letters of Louis' first summer term bear out his recollection that he felt like the princess in the fairy story:

you open your mouth and out come golden guineas. In the stand in the passage, empty in winter, there was now an efflorescence of butterfly nets – the first thing I noticed the first day of term. Nets of emerald green and peacock blue, voluptuous as ladies' dresses, suggesting sunswept prairies; even to handle one indoors was to feel yourself lord of summer.

And then came bathing. One day all the boys appeared at Break with bathing-drawers on their heads. Striped in different colours according to their powers of swimming. When we came back from bathing we fastened these drawers on the wall of the yard, stretching them out on two nails. From our classroom window we could see this wall and, as these garments dried, the colours became carnival-gay; sometimes when fully dried the wind would belly inside them, the wall would dance, beyond Latin grammar and sums we knew there were wind and water and a chute down which those boys who had passed a test would come sailing out of the sky like Jacob's angels.

On 21 June he reports: 'I swam 2 strokes yesterday. The bath is SPLENDID! GLORIOUS!' Later that month, his headmaster wrote to the rector: 'In every way he is getting on most satisfactorily. He seems to get enjoyment out of everything, cricket included. I think that life will never be dull for him.'

Going home for the holidays – Euston, Crewe, Carlisle, Stranraer, Larne, Belfast – images of the Great War eclipsed those of Caesar's winter quarters and the burial of Sir John Moore after Corunna. Louis sat in corridors, 'wedged between kitbags and rifles, half-choked with the smell of sweat, brass-polish, beer', and heard the four-letter words he had seen on lavatory walls. At home, the kittens were called Mons and Flu. A sallow clergyman came to tea with his father and talked about the War. ' "You wait," he said, "till the French get into Berlin!" His face shone as he thought of the bayonets.' Soon after Louis returned to school for the autumn term, 'the incredible happened.' As he described it to his stepmother:

MONDAY
In the middle of 'news' Mrs Powys came in and said that the Big School had hoisted a flag & sung the National Anthem [.] MacCarthy I was sent out to discover what had happened. While he was away an aeroplane went with a flag on it. We had a kind of service in the Lower, most of it singing [.] Half hol . . . .

WEDNESDAY
Fireworks instead of Prep. *Glorious*!

Palgrave's *Golden Treasury* now had pride of place on his desk and, under its influence, the apprentice poet underwent (said his adult self)

a coarsening of taste and a growing preference for what Yeats calls those 'crude, violent rhythms as of a man running'. Like most boys of that age, I liked the flashier heroics – 'The Burial of Sir John Moore', 'Hohenlinden', 'The Battle of Naseby', 'The Execution of Montrose' . . . .

The great majority of poems in *The Golden Treasury* related to events or emotions of which I had no experience – for example, all the martial poems, which were therefore – for me at any rate – poetry of escape. On the other hand, Herrick's 'Whenas in silks my Julia goes' geared in with my ordinary life, for I had seen with admiration people going in silks or something like them. Out of the whole book I preferred, at about the age of 11, the earlier and later poems to those in the middle. I disliked most of the pieces from the seventeenth and the eighteenth centuries, and the Romantic Revival bored me with the exception of some poems by Scott and – more surprisingly – by Wordsworth. I liked 'The Grammarian's Funeral', Fitzgerald's 'Omar Khayyam', Swinburne's 'Forsaken Garden', 'To Althea from Prison', 'Go Fetch to me a Pint o' Wine', 'Fear no more the heat o' the sun', and 'The Dowie Houms o' Yarrow'. And I liked, because it reminded me of church, Drummond's poem on St. John the Baptist.

I liked the above poems for various reasons. Browning gave me fascinating rhymes, 'Omar Khayyam' gave me neat and easy images and an epicureanism which I already found sympathetic, Swinburne gave me sensuous rhythm and nostalgia (I thought of overrun gardens which I had seen in Ireland).

Returning to his own 'house in the garden' for Christmas, romantic literature continues to claim his attention. 'My dear friends', he confides to his diary, 'I apologize for being so frightfully lazy but the White Company occupies most of my time'. Back at school he galloped through *The Coral Island*, *The Pickwick Papers*, *The Rose and the Ring*, *Quentin Durward*, and *David Copperfield*. Mr Powys's evening readings included *A Tale of Two Cities* and a magnificent rendering of Dryden's 'Alexander's Feast'. That spring Louis sent his stepmother a poem of his own, one about 'an enterprising pioneer' in an aeroplane, and shortly after, reported hopefully: 'There may be a passing aeroplane or airship going from England to Ireland soon.' That prophecy had not been fulfilled by 23 April, however, when he went home by the familiar steamer in company with the Irish maths master, Mr Lindsay, who had always been an ally of his. That holiday he played ninety games of tennis with Elizabeth (whom he now called Eek), winning about half of them, and together they baited their stepmother about Evolution, on which Louis, with his interest in fauna, flora, and fossils, now considered himself something of an expert:

She was immune even to my father who mentioned Evolution in the pulpit. No, my stepmother said, passing it off as a joke but piqued nevertheless, she for one was not descended from a monkey. 'But now your appendix,' Elizabeth would say, 'you only have one because you once had a tail; the appendix is no use now.' 'You mustn't say things like that,' my stepmother rejoined, at last getting red in the face at our precocious importunate blasphemy, 'of course it must be some use; otherwise God wouldn't have put it there.'

The following summer term his letters and diary entries become less regular, as the demands of cricket ('Mr Powys says I may be in the team next year'), swimming ('I can swim once across [the pool] now'), and Greek take up more of his time. On 1 July he notes in his diary: 'I tell a story in the dormy now. Scene = Central Africa.' It was the headmaster's practice, shortly after 9 o'clock each night, to 'go from dormitory to dormitory, and sitting on the boys' beds hear the tales of various doings'. He was to remember Louis' ability as a story-teller to be second only to that of this brother, John Cowper Powys.

On 29 July, Louis and Elizabeth returned home together, and it was probably this summer that their father took them to the Carrickfergus salt-mines:

We went on an outside car, clopping of hoofs and scuttling of pebbles, the country a prism for the sun was shining on the patchwork, but Elizabeth and I were impatient till we got there; we had always wanted to go down under the earth to the caves of crystal and man-made thunder, to the black labyrinth of galleries under the carefree fields, under the tumbledown walls, the whins and the ragweed. We descended a pitch-black shaft in a great bucket, at the bottom was a cross of fire and there sure enough was the subterranean cathedral and men like gnomes in the clerestories, working with picks.

This desired descent into a cave like a subterranean cathedral calls to mind an earlier descent into the womb-like cave at the bottom of a bed in which a boy, hearing of the death of his mother, resolved to build her a monument like the marble one in his father's church. The conjunction suggests an expanding constellation of associations: underground, darkness, mother, statue, and fossils.

This may also have been the holiday when Willie came home for a

Willie in 1915

fortnight. His brother, who had looked forward to this, had built him a hut in the shrubbery:

He and I were to sit in there together, eating leaves of nasturtium and sorrel, making believe to be explorers. But when he arrived he was changed, had forgotten how to go even up or down stairs. When he left in a fortnight to return to his Institution I felt a great relief but a guilt more than balanced it. And the bloom, I felt, had gone off the Dorset hills. And the boys at Sherborne seemed suddenly terribly young; I had learned their language but they could not learn mine, could never breathe my darkness.

There is no sense of darkness, however, in Louis' cheerful letters from Sherborne that autumn. His news is of rugger matches, Mr Powys's reading of *King Solomon's Mines*, an eclipse of the moon, and an outbreak of chicken-pox, to which he does not succumb. He spent Christmas as usual at Carrickfergus and, returning to school in January, reported on a postcard: 'saw stars from train to Sherborne'. Looking back at that journey from 1940, he remembered finding himself

wonderfully alone in an empty carriage in a rocking train in the night between Waterloo and Sherborne. Stars on each side of me; I ran from side to side of the carriage checking the constellations as the train changed its direction. Bagfuls and bucketfuls of stars; I could open my mouth to the night and drink them.

His letters that spring show him increasingly fascinated by the mysteries of the stellar text inscribed on the night sky. On 25 January, he echoes a favourite poem, 'The Ballad of Sir Patrick Spens': 'Yesterday we saw the "old moon in the new moon's arms"'; then reports that 'Rickett has lent me an astronomical book' [*Starland* by Sir Robert Ball], and adds in a PS: 'We can see Pegasus and Andromeda from the dormy window when we go up to bed.'

A later letter describes the breathless routine of an ordinary day:

1st bell get up.
2nd bell rush down to gargling, after that to breakfast.
After breakfast rush into the changing rooms and get your boots on. Then either read, do work, play in the yard, write, tidy locker or desk, build huts, do stamps, draw etc.

Bell. Prayers. Work. Break in which you do anything for a few minutes. Some people have milk and biscuits.

Work. 12.30–1. = anything you like. One of the best times for writing letters. You are sometimes kept in now.

1st bell for dinner comes as a warning. Everyone crowds into the changing-room.

2nd bell. Dinner.

There is a short time after dinner and then either a game, work on the field, drawing or a 'slack'. If there is a game there is a short time after it that is spare.

Bell. Work. Tea.

After tea, if it is fine, you go out.

Bell. Reading by Mr Powys. He is now reading a book about Zulus.

Another bell. Prep for an hour.

Another bell. Supper (bread & water or milk)

Another bell. Prayers.

Then you rush up to bed.

LIGHTS OUT

Neither his letters home nor his parents' letters to him mention the worsening situation in Ireland: the policemen ambushed by Irish Volunteers, the recruitment of the Black and Tans (mainly British ex-soldiers) to help the Royal Irish Constabulary in their efforts to check the spread of guerrilla violence that by 1920 had escalated into civil war. Returning to Carrickfergus three times a year, however, he could not fail to be influenced by his father's distress at the bitter legacy of the Partition he so deplored, and to which can be traced the poet's own lifelong hatred of violence; but there is no evidence that he read newspapers at school or gave much thought in term-time to the Irish Troubles.

He seems to have had few troubles of his own. At the end of the Spring Term, his headmaster wrote to the rector of Carrickfergus:

Freddie has an intellect which is distinctly above the average and it would be worth while his having a shot for a Scholarship next year. If he does at all creditably as he should do this should secure him a place in most Public Schools. I can't at all promise a *scholarship*. . . . Freddie is doing well here in every way & is obviously happy. He is full of interest in Everything so his life is never dull.

You would have laughed to have seen his get up at our Fancy dress ball. He posed as a prehistoric man and was really Excellent & by general accord won the first prize. There was more originality about his costume than was the case with any of the others.

What was original about his costume was its simplicity: a loincloth of old sacking, a necklace, coronet and bracelets of fossils, shells and pieces of wood.

Shortly before the dance was due to begin he ran out into the yard and rolled in the mud – to add, as he put it, verisimilitude to his get-up; and throughout the dance, in which he steadfastly declined to take part, he sat glowering in a corner and growled when approached.

The Cult of the Old had paved the way for his success as an ambulant fossil.

With the coming of summer, his letters again dwindled as his spare time was taken up with fossil-collecting, cricket, swimming, and shooting on the miniature range. He pronounced it 'a glorious term'. His work was also going well, and Powys was cautiously optimistic about his chances in the Marlborough Scholarship it had been decided he should sit. On 29 November he travelled to Bath, where he was met by his aunt Eva, his stepmother's youngest sister, who lived there with her friend Gertrude Hind, a 'folk poetess' (as Louis somewhat unkindly called her). Next morning, he was taken round the Roman Baths and the Abbey before catching the train to Marlborough, where they spent the night at the Ailesbury Arms Hotel. On 1 December, Louis took his seat at one of a phalanx of desks in the Marlborough College gymnasium and nervously awaited the first of his scholarship papers. Later, he reported to his stepmother:

Latin Translation with dictionaries. Quite nice. "Greek" without dictionaries. Horrid. Latin prose + dicts. Quite nice. Afternoon. English. ½ hour for tea at shop, much frequented by school. Latin & Greek grammar. Not very nice. Thursday. Had to get up about 6.15 for geometry.

Christmas at Carrickfergus was cheered by the news that he had done himself – and Mr Powys – justice, winning a Classical Scholarship to Marlborough. On the night of 3 January the family crossed the Irish Sea. Woken before midnight by the lurching of his bunk, Louis drowsily recited Newbolt's poem, 'Drake's Drum', to himself. They reached

London in time for him to embark on an expedition, the importance of which can be gauged by the detailed entry in his diary:

British Museum

January 4th –

After 4 P.M. when part of Mus. was shut went through Egyptian galleries etc. up staircase to mummy rooms with Louisa [another alias for Elizabeth?]. Egyptian rooms – First R. – Bodies of prehistoric men baked hard by sun. Skeletons. Box & basket burials – 2nd R. Mummies & mummy cases 3rd room later ornamented mummies.

During 3 days saw nearly all the rooms including Roman Galleries – (sculptured heads of Julius Caesar, Nero, Titus, Marcus Aurelius, Antoninus Pius etc); Graeco-Roman Rooms. (copy of Diadamerous, copy of Discobolus, Hermes); Demeter of Cnidos, Ephesus Room; Elgin Room (Theseus & 3 Fates, bust of Pericles); Phrigaleian & Werec'd rooms; Mausoleum (statues of Mausoleus & wife) Egyptian galleries (head of Thothmes III, statue of Rameses II, many black granite statues of Sephet, the fire goddess, stone Sphinx [?] cast of Smet Smet, "*Rosetta Stone*" … stone sarcophagi, bits of colossal statues; Assyrian Transept. (colossal human heads of bulls & [?] lions); – Manuscript Saloon – (Codex Alexandrinus, Magna Charta, letters of Wolsey etc, autograph works of poets [elsewhere in his diary he listed these; Spenser, Bacon, Milton, Defoe, Swift, Addison, Pope, Gibbon, Cowper, Burns, Byron, Shelley, Keats, Wordsworth], seals of Eng. sovereigns, Capt. Scott's menu for midwinter day at S. Pole; King's Library – first attempts at printing etc. Ancient maps (including 1 of Ireland with Karrickfergus) Mummies, pictures from Book of Dead, mummified cats, calves, crocodiles etc. Toys, scarabs, models of funerary boats, pottery

Upstairs – Central Saloon – (antiquities of stone & bronze ages, flint, iron etc.); Gallery of Roman Britain: (Head of Hadrian); Oriental Saloon – (oriental arms (swords armour helmets etc / netsukés, model of Chinese house etc) Gallery of Indian Religions – (monuments of Brahman religion, Vishnu Siva, Ganesa (elephant god) Hanuman etc., model of car of Vishnu), Buddhist Room. (wooden statue of Bodhisatva, pottery statue of Jokan disciple); Ethnographical Gallery – (idols, Peruvian pottery, weapons, Solomon Island canoes, imitation Africans of diff. types, portrait statuettes, canopys etc.). Also many other interesting rooms –

Many of these objects, sinking into the depths of memory and there preserved as by the peaty waters of an Irish bog, would be exhumed years later for use in poems. Most significantly, Egyptian mummies now entered the dark constellation of cave, death, fossil, mother, and statue.

Leaving London, the family travelled down to Wickham in Hampshire, where they stayed at Wickham Lodge, home of Admiral Sir Robert Swinburne Lowry KCB and his wife Helena, 'Madre's' oldest sister; before moving on to Bath for a few days with Aunt Eva. On 19 January, Louis returned to Sherborne to find himself head of Number Eight dormitory and therefore elevated to a spring bed. His first letter home spoke of a new master whose influence on the prep-school poet was to prove second only to that of Littleton Powys. 'Mr Hemstead', he wrote, 'is here all right, leaping about class rooms and scribbling tremendous xs that cover the blackboards.'

Mr Hemstead was an Oxford graduate with 'advanced' ideas, who treated the boys 'in what he called "his lectures", as though they were men of his own age'. He was appointed to teach English, History and Geography, but

told us we need not bother with History and Geography; all that really mattered was Keats. He was tall and slim, with small features and a mouth that could sneer, he wore a grey check suit with a grey check shirt and a grey check tie and grey check socks, and he left little islands of scent behind him in classroom and garden. He filled his room with a bust of Dante and Keats's death-mask, and wrote Greek verses on the wall which we thought were his own composition. Cricket, he said, was a classical game, an art, but rugby football was barbarous.

Mr Hemstead was an aesthete and in some ways the antithesis of the tweedy Mr Powys, 'so full of health and Natural History', so ardent an advocate for the manly sports. Mr Hemstead disapproved of the manly poems (like 'The Burial of Sir John Moore') so well represented in Palgrave's *Golden Treasury*. His favourite anthology was Sir Arthur Quiller-Couch's *Oxford Book of English Verse*, and he told his disciples 'that it was vulgar to admire Kipling or Macaulay's lays. Poetry should contain true emotion, should be about beautiful things, and should offer an escape from the drabness of ordinary life'. In Mr Hemstead's view of the literary landscape, the eighteenth century was a desert but he was an exhilarating guide to the romantic 'valleys, groves, hills, and fields' on either side. He lent boys books from his own shelves and then filled a bookcase in the Upper classroom. Louis listed the titles, which included:

Coleridge, Shelley & Keats (poems)
'Channels of English Literature. Epic & Heroic Poetry' (W. MacNeile)
'Recollections of the Lakes' (Thomas de Quincey)
'The Pilgrim's Progress'
'Lyric Masterpieces of Living Authors'
'The Works of E.A. Poe' (Vol II – Tales)
'Selections from Wordsworth' (Adam Fox)
'Poems of Today'
'History of King Arthur' (Vols I, II, III)
'Dorset Poetry & Poets' (H. Berkeley Sage)
'Apologie for Poetrie' (Sir Philip Sidney)
'Poetical Works of Keats'
'R.L.S.' (Francis Watt)
'The Life of Robert Louis Stevenson' (Graham Balfour)
'Keats' (W. Michael Rossetti)
'Piers Plowman' (W. Langland)
'On University Education' (Cardinal Newman)
'Byron and his Poetry'
'Keats and his Poetry'
'Shelley and his Poetry'
'A Child's Garden of Verses' (R.L.S.)
'Shelley, Byron & The Author' (Trelawny)

Louis could now rest on his scholarship laurels and for the first time in his life had both the leisure and the impulse to read voraciously. He cantered through *The Faerie Queene* ('nine Cantos today'), and finishing that, looked for knights and maidens elsewhere.

Inspired by Mr Hemstead I had read Malory's *Morte d'Arthur* sitting in a windowseat and reading with such concentration that my hair stuck to the paint of the woodwork. The book was very long but by no means too long for me; I revelled in the reiteration of incident; to go from joust to joust and count how many knights Sir Tristram or Sir Pelleas unseated was as exciting as reading the County Cricket batting averages. My friends and I found a table in an old summerhouse and became the knights ourselves, drawing lots for the leading names. On Sundays we rode about the country on branches of trees, each with an ashplant for a sword, and tried to use the Malory diction.

Back in the Upper, however, there were clashes of a less romantic kind. One day Mr Hemstead asked a boy in class: ' "Have you ever heard of Mazzini?" and the boy said, "No and I don't want to." Mr Hemstead, who had been born in Italy, flared into a rage that dwarfed Mr Lindsay's. "Damn you," he said, "Little middle-class brats." ' A more dramatic Vesuvian eruption was to follow.

He had offered a prize for an English essay – to be done in our own time and the entries voluntary – on some subject like the Poetic Function of the Imagination. The eldest among us were thirteen and none of us understood the title but Mr Hemstead seemed very keen on it, was always giving us hints, and a few of us – many weeks after the competition had been announced – were about to begin an assault on the Imagination when Mr. Hemstead suddenly in class asked us which of us were entering. No one was brave enough to hold up his hand. Mr Hemstead went white and tense; this, he said, was the end. He had done all he could to no purpose. Very well, in future he would meet us on our level. Savagely he tore a quire of foolscap into quarters, threw them at our heads. 'Spell,' said Mr Hemstead, spitting the words like a machine-gun, 'spell. It is all you are good for. Spell erysipelas, symmetry, asyndeton.'

He declared there would be no more English Literature that term and demanded the return of all books borrowed from his shelves. A fortnight later, however, he relented to the extent of organizing a celebration to mark the centenary of Keats's death, at which he gave a lecture, a master from The Big School recited 'La Belle Dame sans Merci' and Louis the 'Ode to Autumn'. This was followed by a debate on the motion (surely not chosen by Mr Hemstead) that 'Keats did not deserve the appellation of poet'. It was probably a lingering resentment at the master's tantrums that led to the motion being passed by sixteen votes to two (Louis' being one of the two.) From this point, Mr Hemstead's influence on the schoolboy poet waned, but he had confirmed Louis' belief in the Greek Spirit, had taught him much about poetry and mythology, and had converted the wild Irish boy with outsize boots to the pleasures of dandyism.

Term and March ended together. Passing through London, Louis saw Oxford win the Boat Race before going on to Holyhead and the now familiar steamer. Back at Carrickfergus, he read Matthew Arnold and *The Arabian Nights* with his stepmother and spent some time at

Seapark, her childhood home. On 5 May he returned to Sherborne for his last term. The weather that summer was good and he abandoned literature for cricket, tennis, and swimming.

On the Twelfth of July Powys came into my dormitory and said, 'What is all this they do in your country today? Isn't it all mumbo-jumbo?' Remembering my father and Home Rule and the bony elbows of Miss MacCready and the black file of mill-girls and the wickedness of Carson and the dull dank days between sodden haycocks and foghorns, I said Yes it was. And I felt uplifted. To be speaking man to man to Powys and giving the lie to the Red Hand of Ulster was power, was freedom, meant I was nearly grown up. King William is dead and his white horse with him, and Miss MacCready will never put her knuckles in my ears again. But Powys went out of the dormitory and Mr Lindsay came in, his underlip jutting and his eyes enraged. 'What were you saying to Mr. Powys?' Oh this division of allegiance! That the Twelfth of July was mumbo-jumbo was true, and my father thought so too, but the moment Mr. Lindsay appeared I felt rather guilty and cheap. Because I had been showing off to Powys and because Mr. Lindsay being after all Irish I felt I had betrayed him.

A fortnight later – after a last prize-giving ('I got a Horace') and a sex-talk that he could not understand – Louis took his divided allegiances back to Ireland. At the end of August there was a family holiday at Rhosneigr on the coast of Wales, and one Sunday they attended a church service at which, hearing the Gloria sung in Welsh, Louis 'thought what fun – always moving on, Sherborne to Marlborough, Sandstone to flint, Glory be and Glory be and the world is there for the having'.

CHAPTER 6

Sandstone to Flint

> ... changing school, sandstone changed for chalk
> And ammonites for the flinty husks of sponges,
> Another lingo to talk
> And jerseys in other colours.
> 'Autumn Journal', *CP*, p. 120

Moving on from Sherborne to Marlborough, Louis soon found that flint was harder and greyer and sharper than sandstone. Not that the Ailesbury Arms was any less comfortable on the evening of 15 September 1921 than it had been when he stayed there as a scholarship candidate; nor was 'the little red-capped town', round which he wandered with his father before supper, any less attractive. Next morning, they looked at St Mary's Church before walking down the handsome High Street to the Church of St Peter and St Paul at the other end, and on into the great court of the College. Neither can have had much idea of what to expect. John MacNeice had no experience of public schools, and there is nothing to suggest that either father or son had read *Tom Brown's Schooldays*, let alone *The Loom of Youth* or Beverley Nichols's fictionalized account of his days at Marlborough, *Prelude*, published only the year before. Indeed, if the rector *had* read these books, it seems unlikely that his son would have followed in Nichols's footsteps through the wrought-iron gates, under the bulldog eye of Sheppard, the College Porter since 1902.

'A' House, seen from the court, has a certain spurious William-and-Mary charm but, inside, it seemed to Louis 'a prison, a great square building of ugly brick, with a huge well down the centre surrounded by railed-in landings; you could look up from the basement, see the prisoners listlessly parading on every floor'. Some of them were usually to be found undergoing a form of punishment-drill known as 'Basements'. In this variant of the tread-mill, little boys were sentenced by others – one term or more their seniors – to trudge a certain number of times up and down the stairs between ground floor and basement. Louis' first letter home spoke of 'a horrible muddle about my form' (caused by a master confusing Maurice with MacNeice), but sounded surprisingly buoyant considering other discomforts of which he made no mention. Meals were taken in a great bleak hall and for the first few he had little to eat:

as soon as you entered the hall you were expected to stick a fork in your patty, a spoon in your porridge plate and so on, otherwise anyone else could 'rush' them as well as his own. There was also Condescending, the word 'condescend' being perhaps a corruption of 'Can't you send'. No one in the junior house could condescend till he was in his third term, then he could pass the word down the table 'Condescend the sugar – or the milk – third-termer', and the milk or sugar had to be sent up to him unless a fourth-termer or a fifth-termer liked to intervene and condescend it for himself on the way. Thus a new boy was always like Tantalus, about to help himself from a bowl or jug which just as he was reaching for it would be harshly condescended away.

Ignorance of his prison's layout and its lingo caused a more acute discomfort. It took him two or three days to learn where the lavatories (or 'rears') were – a large shed, open at each end to the wind and rain, divided into doorless cells – and the password that gained access to them: 'Please, sir, may I cross court?'

Then there was fagging. A fortnight after his arrival Louis reports:

I have been beaten three times in dormitory for inefficiency in waterfagging and timefagging. Timefagging is the worst. Someone yells 'time'. You say '2 and three-quarter minutes past' (you have to be exact to an ⅛th) then there is a space of about 1 sec. You repeat your former statement. This time of course it isn't believed – it must be later than that now.

Neither in his diary nor his letters does he sound distressed by these hardships. He likes his form-master, Mr Canning; is delighted to find stuffed animals, mummy cases, and fossils in the Natural History Society Museum; and is grateful for the steady supply of food parcels he has been receiving from home. A week later he has two more good things to report: a long walk with a friend in Savernake forest (and the sight of a deer), and the discovery of 'an old book about Marlborough'. In this, James Waylen's *History Military and Municipal, of the Town of Marlborough*, the admirer of Malory's *Morte D'Arthur* was intrigued to learn 'that the origin of Marlborough is Merlinbury after Merlin'. He also learnt that the sixty-foot 'Castle Mound', whose crown of conifers looked down on the back of 'A' House, had been raised in the Bronze Age, and in the eleventh century formed part of a Norman motte-castle. After 300 years in Royal hands, it fell into disrepair and by the end of the sixteenth century there was only 'an heape of rammell and rubbish witnessing the ruines thereof, and some few reliques of the walls remain within the compasse of a dry ditch'. The ground beyond it then became the site of a great Tudor house, property of the Dukes of Somerset, and when their branch of the Seymour family died out, was converted to a coaching inn. As the Castle Inn, it flourished from 1751 until, with the extension of the Great Western Railway in the early 1840s, the iron horse drove the coach horse off the London Road.

The clatter of hooves in court and stable-yard was heard again, however, in August 1843 when the great house of the Seymours, now Marlborough College, opened its doors to 200 boys, many of them sons of Anglican clergymen. These were promised a first-class education for an annual fee of thirty guineas (twenty guineas less than that charged for the sons of laymen). Like other public schools at that time, Marlborough soon became a violent place, hostility between boys and masters culminating in the open rebellion of autumn 1851, when 'one side smashed windows and furniture, set fire to rooms and assaulted officials, while the other side flogged and expelled with desperate diligence'. The headmaster (then, as now, known as the Master) resigned and was succeeded by two of Thomas Arnold's Rugby housemasters in turn who, introducing the Arnoldian tradition, set the College on a more civilized course.

Waylen's *History* had been published in 1854 and its successor, by Bradley, Champneys and Baines, in 1893, so Louis had to depend on less objective accounts of more recent events. He probably would not have heard that when his own Master, Dr Cyril Norwood, first entered the College Hall in 1916, it was to the jeers of many who resented the appointment of a former grammar-school headmaster. The snobs nicknamed him 'Boots' because he had weak arches and could not wear shoes. Four years later, he was beginning to repeat at Marlborough the success that had earned him an honorary doctorate in Bristol, and in 1921 his distinction was recognized nationally by his appointment as chairman of the Secondary Schools Examination Council. Much still remained to be done at Marlborough, however. For his predecessor,

the prefectorial system had been a way of shrugging off his own responsibilities rather than developing those of the boys. A pernicious pecking order ran from the Senior Prefect, usually a prize athlete who was *ex officio* editor of the school magazine, down through Upper School Captains, minor 'bloods' and juniors to the persecuted fags.

Norwood may have looked (as Maurice Bowra said) 'like an Edwardian policeman', but in character and cast of mind he more resembled a High Victorian headmaster in the Arnoldian mould. He had taken a double-first in classical moderations and *Literae Humaniores* at Oxford, and was a man of great courage, energy, integrity and vision. By the end of his Mastership many much needed reforms would have been introduced, but in autumn 1921 life at Marlborough was generally tough and occasionally barbaric.

Louis' parents would not have known this from his letters. He seems to have adjusted to the rituals of 'rushing', 'condescending', and fagging as equably as to the 'sweats' or frequent cross-country runs:

The town and the school of Marlborough are set down in a hollow and on all sides the downs rise in curves, bevel and grey and serene as perching doves; on the skyline there are one or two clumps of trees like hippopotamuses. On days too wet for games we were sent running over these downs with a time limit out and back; if you were late either way you were caned but, once you got used to this strenuous effort, these runs were exhilarating.

Louis liked it, even when it hailed and, returning breathless to the communal bathroom, took a sensuous pleasure in sinking into his tub, 'wonderfully relaxed in an underworld of steam and dim pink bodies humming Gilbert and Sullivan'. The diary and letters of his first term devote much of their space to sport, but on 20 November he tells his stepmother:

On Friday we had to write a fragment of a play in blank verse for Mr. Canning. The Subject was any bit of History from the time of Alfred the Great to the time of Edward I. I did something about Harold Hardrada.

There is no record of how Mr Canning responded to what Louis' diary less modestly described as 'some magnificent lines (??????) upon "The Fall of Harold Hardrada"', but evidently the seeds of his lifelong interest in Norse history and mythology had already been sown.

A month later, their school terms over, Louis and Elizabeth met at Waterloo Station and crossed to Dublin where they caught the now familiar train to Belfast. For Christmas, he gave his co-founder of the Cult of the Old 'a book about prehistoric men', and himself plunged into *Every Boy's Book of Geology*. Returning to England on 19 January, he was met at the station by his aunt Eva who, knowing of his interest in animals, took him to London Zoo. His detailed account of what he saw there brims with an enthusiasm markedly absent from subsequent letters that term. He was not unhappy but bored and, comparing his days in 'A' House with those at Sherborne, would later remember:

There was not the same multiplicity of interests, the same variety of play; everyone was careerist, obsessed with getting on in form or in games, with getting into a senior house, with keeping his place in the weekly or fortnightly class-lists and so avoiding caning.

The Master's verdict at the end of the Lent Term – 'I am afraid this is a distinctly disappointing report' – did not confirm his earlier optimistic forecast: 'If he can cure these faults [untidiness and unpunctuality], he will do very well indeed.'

With the coming of summer, however, Louis began to enjoy himself more. On a friend's bicycle, he made the first of many happy visits to 'Leigh Hill', home of Mrs Wasey (the sister of a Carrickfergus parishioner), whose tennis parties were famous among Marlburians for their strawberries and cream. The weather was good and, in June, he was able to report: 'On Saturday I did my record score here – 32 retired. I also took six wickets.' He was also scoring better in class, and the term ended with him passing the School Certificate exam he had been expected to fail. He had another success on that summer's family holiday in Perthshire: 'I helped to save Elizabeth from drowning. My stepmother hurt my feelings by saying "We must thank God you can swim so well" but my egotism survived this injustice.'

The Scottish holiday was also memorable for two less dramatic but more important incidents, whose significance Louis did not understand at the time, but would later reveal with the ironic stage directions and subtle scene-splicing of *The Strings are False*:

In Perthshire we were shown over a ruined castle by a white-haired, rosy-cheeked curator, biblical in speech and heartily God-fearing. My father said he was a very fine type – you would find that all over Scotland – and took the occasion to deplore the defects of the Irish peasantry. The pious old man reeled off his dates with gusto till he came to a crumbled stone relief showing the rear view of a woman with her dress drawn up revealing her buttocks. His face lit up, he asked us if we knew what this was. None of us knew; my father looked a little displeased. Ah, said the old man, it was a good old custom; pity it had gone out; in the good old days if a woman misbehaved herself they would hold her down like this and anyone that came by was welcome to give her a pandy. I was secretly delighted; what fun it would be to have a grown-up woman held down for you to smack her on the bare behind.

Another day in Perthshire we met a company of film actors including a girl with yellow yellow hair and tight-fitting riding-breeches. She was very fragile and no taller than I was, and a little-boy lust took hold of me though I had not yet reached puberty. Wherever we walked afterwards, in the glens or by the lake, I imagined little fantasies – how I would come here and find this girl alone and how I would wrestle with her. Her walking about in breeches was a challenge; I would chase her through the pine trees and catch her, then I would show her. Show her what? I really didn't know but there was a big word Pandy in the sky and it would be much more exciting somehow than wrestling with boys, though that was enjoyable enough.

Returning to Marlborough in September, he found himself promoted to the Classical Fifth which met 'in a most splendid classroom, with gilt writing round the walls'. He may not have known what to show the girl with yellow yellow hair, but at least he could now boast his own full-size Liddell and Scott Greek Lexicon, and was clearly enjoying a rich diet of Classics and English literature:

We have just got 100 Best Latin Poems in the Class. Vth. They consist mostly of Horace. Today we are doing three about political matters. This afternoon we go to Mr. Turner for either Vergil or Eng. Lit. Last time we did the 3rd Eclogue, I think. The book we have for Eng. Lit. discusses everyone important in turn. We are doing Ben Jonson and Herrick at present.

In retrospect, he would remember particularly how he liked

the glitter of Horace – O fons Bandusiae splendidior vitro – and admired his tidiness, realizing that English with its articles and lack of inflexions could hardly ever equal Horace either in concentration or in subtlety of word-order.

He warmed to his form master, Mr Emery, who introduced his class to a recent discovery shedding light on a civilization older than those of Greece and Rome, one in which Louis was already interested. Mr Emery read out a long extract from *The Times*' account of the findings, in Egypt's Valley of the Kings, of the tomb of Tutankhamun. 'He has a sort of forlorn hope that some lost Greek documents may be found among the papyri.'

Louis' taste for history was further gratified by his move in the New Year into 'C' House, oldest and grandest of the Senior Houses, formerly the great mansion of the Seymours. A pillared portico led to a flagstoned hall, off which a massive staircase climbed to his dormitory, 'a long high room with lime-green panelling, egg-and-dart moulding round the cornice and a series of majestic windows which looked out on an elegant velvet lawn bounded by scalloped yew trees'. He now spent most of his working days in an even larger room, 'a great tract of

C. House in the 1930s

empty air, cold as the air outside but smelling of stables, enclosed by four thin walls and a distant roof'. This was Upper School, one half of which was covered with desks and benches. The other half was empty. There were two doors and two fires: Big Fire was reserved for less than twenty boys, the oligarchy, and Little Fire for the hundred or so others. To be elected to Big Fire was a great honour, but one to which only athletes and those without the brains to move beyond Upper School could aspire. This cavernous room was the scene of barbarous rites described with anthropological detail in *The Strings are False*:

I have never been anywhere like Samoa, but I fancy that the rites of Upper School should interest professional connoisseurs. Our last meal in the great dining-hall was at 6.30 p.m. and an hour's preparation of work began in Upper School at 7.15. Those of us who belonged to Little Fire were expected to be sitting at our desks by 7.0 at the latest. The next quarter of an hour was a babel while we watched the members of Big Fire at their antics. Big Fire, although the oligarchy, had no responsibility except to be exhibitionist. Above them there were four Captains, aged about sixteen and invariably athletic. During the rest of the day these Captains belonged to Big Fire but from 7.0 to 7.15 they were Big Fire's enemies. The Captains were not due to appear until 7.15 when they would come in with canes in their hands and preparation would begin. Anyone out of his seat when the Captains entered was caned.

'Upper School' in the 1930s

This applied to Big Fire too, but whereas Big Fire would not have brooked our leaving our seats during their sacred quarter of an hour they were expected by themselves and by us to be on the floor till the last half-second. So they would spend the time barricading the doors against the Captains or making them ingenious booby-traps or else running whooping out of the building by one door, around through a yard and in at the other. Round and round till the Captains caught them. Sometimes all of Big Fire would be caught out of their places at once, and after preparation we would have the treat of a mass caning, standing in a large semi-circle while the Captains took a run and laid into their bosom friends.

The Captains entered at 7.15 but that did not mean we could all start working. The Captains marched up and down the alley-ways slapping the desks with their canes and inspecting the lids to see if they were flush; if the lid of any desk were even a quarter of an inch raised its owner was booked to be caned. Meanwhile the junior boys had to go round the hall 'scavenging', gathering up in their hands the fruit-peel, match-ends, fluff, muck and paper which had been lavishly thrown on the floor during the day, and carrying these nasty little handfuls to an enormous wastepaper-basket. The Captains would keep an eye on the scavengers and flick at their ankles with their canes if they scavenged too slackly.

The wastepaper-basket had another purpose. Once in a while – not more often than once a term – Big Fire decided that someone was undesirable and could therefore provide a Roman holiday. They would seize him, tear off most of his clothes and cover him with house-paint, then put him in the basket and push him round and round the hall. Meanwhile Little Fire, dutifully sitting at their desks, would howl with delight – a perfect exhibition of mass sadism. The masters considered this a fine old tradition, and any boy who had been basketed was under a cloud for the future. Because the boys have an innate sense of justice, anyone they basket must be really undesirable. Government of the mob, by the mob, and for the mob.

Upper School was the not inappropriate setting for Louis' introduction to Homer, whom he found 'richer than Virgil or Spenser, more congenial than Milton'. He responded to a poetry that could retain its colour and dignity while dealing with those who, 'whatever their titles, their exceptional beauty and prowess, are much like ordinary people in their squabbles, greeds, and jealousies'.

Newcomers to his form that term included John Betjeman, with whom Louis was never to feel altogether at ease, and Graham Shepard, with whom, from the first, he did. Betjeman 'envied Louis his brains because he and his lifelong friend Graham Shepard ... used to sit in chairs at the top of the Classical Fifth while their voices were still unbroken and I aged sixteen was near the bottom'. Graham, son of Ernest Shepard the artist, came from a more conventional Home Counties background than Louis, but seemed 'a stray from some other place or era, a surprising blend of precocious worldly-wiseness and faunal innocence'. He had the slightly wrinkled appearance and ast-ringency of a pickled walnut. Both wanted to be writers and were spending an increasing amount of time in the Memorial Reading Room and the grander Adderley Library on the ground floor of 'C' House. The boys had in common a sense of fantasy and a sense of fun that, as spring turned to summer, they indulged on long bicycle rides into the Wiltshire countryside. One such expedition, in May, came to seem emblematic of the progress from innocence to experience:

As we skimmed down southwards over the chalk country the hedges were still fresh and lathered with mays, the laburnums were tumbling gold and the sun raking the downland. Upon wheels we were free, were We, and as we passed under the beeches the light fell through in confetti.

They found a canal and, as swimming in the country was forbidden and 'nakedness on a towpath seemed a beautiful bravado', stripped and stepped in. The idyll was interrupted by the voice of a ragged tramp:

he was accusing us huskily, incoherently. We felt on the instant like unfledged birds, both guilty and outraged. Easy for us, he was saying, it was easy enough for us; how would we like to do a hard day's work? Graham said that we had to work too. The tramp laughed and spat. Never done a day's work in your lives, he said. His swarthy male contempt felt like a bludgeon on our puny white bodies. 'Books' Graham said. 'Books!' the tramp said and shambled away swearing .... 'Poor old bloke!' said Graham but he had spoiled our afternoon and we knew he was the enemy.

Ugliness, poverty, and despair; Reality threatening the Dream; Life was the enemy at the gates of Literature.

Louis spent his summer holiday at Carrickfergus, much of it reading Robert Louis Stevenson, which may account for the relish with which he remembered a perilous return in an open boat from Rathlin Island to the north coast of County Antrim. September found him back at Marlborough and in the Lower Classical Sixth, where Mr A. R. Gidney would appear

each day on the stroke of the clock, taking a long, firm and yet self-conscious stride to his desk, jutting out his jaw and looking us up and down like an inspecting colonel. He always wore the same clothes – dark grey flannel trousers, a collar and a dull green tie which every so often he would push up into position with a quick movement that implied 'What must be must be.' A moralist and a logician, very precise in diction, he was never tired of asking: 'What exactly do you mean by that?'

To Louis he seemed a melancholy figure, but with his sarcastic tongue, he terrorized the young Betjeman, who would strike back years later with a savage article in *The Spectator* and a poem, 'Greek Orthodox', which begins:

> What did I see when first I went to Greece?
> Shades of the Sixth across the Peloponnese.
> Though clear the clean-cut Doric temple shone
> Still droned the voice of Mr. Gidney on;
> 'That ὅτι? Can we take its meaning here
> Wholly as interrogative?'

Louis reported better of Betjeman's voice, heard through the door of the Adderley Library as he took part in the Buchanan Reading Prize: 'It was very dramatic'. Perhaps too dramatic: he came second.

Other contemporaries, and already closer friends than Betjeman, were Fortie Vesey Ross and Anthony Blunt, both mathematicians and sons of Protestant clergymen: Ross 'small and dark with a high bulging forehead', Blunt 'very tall and very thin and drooping, with deadly sharp elbows and the ribs of a famished saint'. Ross was determined to follow in his Ulster father's footsteps down the straight and narrow path; Blunt was determined not to. He had been born a fortnight after Louis, in the vicarage of Holy Trinity Church, Bournemouth, but when he was four, his father, the Revd Stanley Blunt, was appointed chaplain at the embassy church in Paris, and the family exchanged their south-coast respectability for the cosmopolitan glamour of *Le Corps*

Diplomatique. Anthony was brought up to look at works of art by his parents and, more importantly, by his elder brother Wilfrid, who had been named after the Byronic black sheep of the family. Wilfrid Scawen Blunt, the Victorian adventurer, diplomat and poet, is better described as a black *ram*, since he specialized in tupping titled ladies and 'corrupting' the servants of the Queen in his tireless campaigns for Irish, Indian and Egyptian independence. His younger namesake had inherited something of that rebellious strain and determined to become a painter rather than a parson, let alone a parson like his father, a 'strict Ruskinian' who did not encourage his children to look at anything later than medieval architecture. 'The Chaplain's house', Wilfrid wrote, 'was not a good jumping-off point for Bohemia', but jump they did. One of Anthony's earliest memories was of visiting the Louvre before the Great War and, in the years since, his education in matters artistic had progressed by leaps and bounds, thanks to his brother's enthusiastic tutelage and his own precocious intelligence. In the autumn of 1923, there was an exhibition of paintings by Old Marlburians, on which Anthony commented with acid authority: 'half of them are coloured photographs and the other half black and white photographs'.

At this stage, Louis' attitude to his parents was closer to that of the dutiful Ross than the rebellious Blunt. Intellectually, he was some way behind Anthony, but at Christmas carried back with him to Carrickfergus a good report from Norwood: 'He is putting commendable vigour into all that he does, and is acquiring in consequence much more force of character.' This shows in his handwriting, which over the previous year had grown more confident and spacious. The vigour, praised in the Master's report, was manifested not only in the classroom. Returning to Marlborough in January, he bought a new pair of fives gloves and a month later tells his stepmother: 'This day week we won the House Grounds Cup (rugger) in which I was playing. House has never won it before.'

Interestingly, he makes no mention of a literary event anticipated in another boy's letter home:

There's a new college paper coming out for the first time next Saturday called the 'Heretick'. It is a very high-brow sort of thing I believe. Blunt's got a lot to

The rugger player (front right)

do with it. He says it is meant to form a focus for the literary talent in the school.

Envisaged as a counterblast to the official College magazine, the staid *Marlburian*, *The Heretick* was intended, Blunt said later,

to express our disapproval of the Establishment generally, of the more out-of-date and pedantic masters, of all forms of organized sport, of the Officers' Training Corps and of all the other features that we hated in school life, not so much the physical discomforts – they were almost taken for granted – but, you might say, the intellectual discomforts of the school.

The new magazine's title had been suggested by Christopher Hughes, the art master, and the editors were John Betjeman and John Bowle. Bowle drew the cover illustration, which showed a scowling athlete, armed with a hockey stick, seated on a mound in front of rugby posts, being taunted by two fauns in a tree and a third – playing a pipe – behind him. The picture was captioned 'UPON PHILISTIA WILL I TRIUMPH.'

The Heretick appeared on 29 March. Betjeman's contributions, says his biographer, 'were a "Prodigies Song", a satire on the classical scholars among the boys; a short story entitled "Death"; and an account of a "Dinner of Old Marlburian Centipede Farmers in Unyamwazi, S.A."' The short story, however, seems more likely to be from another hand. The setting is, initially, a cemetery in which a woman comes to the narrator's side. He says:

I could not see her face and I could not hear her footsteps on the gravel, but I heard her weep. 'They buried me,' she said, 'they buried me. But I did not love him then' and then she disappeared into the laurels.

If this is the ghost of Louis' mother, when the scene shifts to a dream conflation of Marlborough College Chapel and St Nicholas' Church, Carrickfergus, there enters a figure resembling his father:

He was dressed in long white robes as a priest but, somehow, he seemed more heavenly. A shudder came over me, my heart gave a leap as he fixed his eyes on me and came towards me; quite definitely he wanted me to follow him. All was quiet save for an occasional cough and the inane stammerings of the prefect. I

THE HERETICK

"Upon Philistia will I triumph"

arose and followed him, the bench creaked but no one looked at me. We walked down the aisle together and none of the sleepy boys even glanced at us.

When we were out in the rainy night he said to me 'We are going to my Garden' and in silence I walked by his side across the windy field towards the cemetery.

Priest and narrator (father and son?) enter a mortuary Chapel like that in the Carrickfergus cemetery, where the narrator is told to wait. He thinks 'I longed for the man, in a way I loved him', as he watches him among the graves help the woman to her feet. Then together 'they seemed to go up to heaven fainter and fainter in the mist'. The story ends with the narrator saying, as Louis must often have said to himself: 'Do not think of it any more; shout for your house on the touch line, turn your back to his Garden, you will soon have enough of polished granite, a white cross or a broken pillar.' If this is from Louis' hand – and it is difficult to believe that it is not, given the *dramatis personae*, the Chapel/Church and Mortuary chapel, cemetery and Garden, polished granite and pillar – it is not surprising that he did not show it to his father and stepmother.

The Heretick made a gratifying stir: there were threats of Philistine violence against the Aesthete editors (that came to nothing) and, in the last chapel service of term,

Dr. Norwood preached a sermon and quoted the magazine's motto. If, he said, it meant 'overcoming the Philistine in all of us', it was a good thing; if it was 'an expression of intellectual snobbery', it was not a good thing. He took a tolerant stance and reproved the extremists of both camps.

Since *The Heretick* had escaped the flames, its editors embarked on a second issue and, on 29 June, Louis told his stepmother:

On Thursday, I forgot to say, the 'Marlburian' and a second number of the 'Heretick' came out. As for the last named, boys in Newman's [House] of the ultra-athletic non-anything else creed, stole the proofs and altering passages in an absurd fashion, sent them down to the printer so causing some trouble.

The second issue contained a Betjeman poem, a Shepard satire, and a Blunt essay on 'Art and Morality' that opened with Oscar Wilde's famous statement: 'There is no such thing as a moral or an immoral book. Books are well written or badly written. That is all.' The spirit of

Wilde also presided over an anonymous story, 'The Loverless Knight', that has a familiar situation and a recognizable narrative voice:

It was a stormy October night and Melisande was quite alone in her chamber. Melisande always sat alone. Besides the ancient servitors – who seemed but human expressions of the castle – she saw nobody at all, not even her father. For her mother had died at her birth, and he, on hearing that the child was a girl, had refused to see it, and shut himself up from the world. With his wife his hopes were buried.

Melisande has grown to womanhood and Pre-Raphaelite beauty, but subscribes to a Cult of the Old and lives in the past:

In the old days before Melisande was born there had been much gaiety at the castle. Her father, the eighteen years' recluse, had been famous for the splendour of his entertainments, and still more for the beauty of the halls wherein they were held. The wondrous tapestries with which they were adorned were the work of a great artist, Guy the Outborn, who had long ago disappeared from the World, killed, people thought, by Melisande's father because of his love for her mother the Lady Jehane. But in reality he had escaped with his life, though never again was he able to practise his art.

Yet in the happy time he had wrought many marvellous works, and of all these by far the most beautiful were the tapestries he had made for the proud Jehane, whereby she might remember her lover, and think kindly of him sometimes, in the long winter nights.

He took for his subjects the stories of old time: Arthur and the Table Round, Tristram and Lancelot, Guinevere and two Iseults, Merlin whom Vivien bewitched, and Morgan le fay the dark queen of enchantments whose unnatural offspring, Modred, was to overthrow her brother at the last.

All these Melisande loved passionately and lived her life among them, but there was one tapestry which she had caused to be hung in her own chamber, because it was dearer to her than all the rest. The story it told had never been heard before or seen at all. It was called 'The Tale of Sir Bertram, the Loverless Knight.'

On winter evenings, and often far into the night, Melisande would sit alone and weave wonderful romances in which she always took part, and Sir Bertram was her lover.

It is hard to believe that this great artist, the foreigner ('Outborn') with the passion for Malory's knights and ladies, is not a romantic projection of the poet from Carrickfergus.

Guy the Outborn returns, is admitted to the Castle, and walks straight to Melisande's chamber where at last the servitors find him:

the old man lay dead on the floor with a happy smile on his white lips and contentment in his glazing eyes. But of Melisande they could see no trace. She seemed to have vanished utterly, until one of the men who was lifting the corpse stiffened suddenly as with fear, and pointed to the tapestry in front of him crying:

'Look! Look!'

And when they looked they saw there Melisande, yet more beautiful than in life, and beside her was Sir Bertram, the loverless knight no longer.

Despite the debt to Wilde's *Picture of Dorian Gray*, it is a powerful and moving story, but hardly one to meet with approval in the Carrickfergus rectory. One wonders also how John MacNeice reacted to the close of his son's letter of 6 July:

The sands of my epistolary faculty are running out fast so I will conclude by saying that I hope you are all at the acme of health.

Much love
Louis

For what seems to be the first time, Louis has dropped his father's name – Freddie – in favour of his godfather's and that of one of his favourite authors, Robert Louis Stevenson.

CHAPTER 7

Playing the Fool

> The order of the day is complete conformity and
>   An automatic complacence.
> Such was the order of the day; only at times
>   The Fool among the yes-men flashing his motley
> To prick their pseudo-reason with his rhymes. . . .
>   'Autumn Journal', *CP*, p. 120

The Summer Term of 1924 ended for Louis on a jubilant note. He and Fortie Ross had put their names down for a shared study (or 'bin' in Marlborough lingo) and, to their surprise and delight, heard that the application had been successful. More immediately, there was the anticipation of his first extended visit to the other Ireland of his imagination: the fabled West. But for the Troubles, the family would have taken holidays there before but the rector, for all his nationalism, had said: 'How can you mix with people who might be murderers without you knowing it?' Now, however, things being quiet in Donegal, he decided to take the risk and, in August and an overloaded car, the family set off for a rented cottage overlooking Sheep Haven Bay. This fulfilled Louis' romantic expectations.

Farragh is not a proper cottage at all. It has an upstairs, a slate roof and a drawing-room and a dining-room apart from the kitchen. A redeeming attribute is its lack of a bathroom. There is one round flat thing to wash in to be handed round among the inhabitants.

They saw no sign of the Troubles, but there was one moment of farcical drama when, on a drive through the mountains, a little man emerged from a ditch to throw a heavy sack through the window of their car. It was found to contain not a bomb but boots. Far from sharing his parents' alarm, Louis resented their talk of southern 'law-lessness', even after the 'bomber' had been identified as the local drunk. The rector, however, subsequently redeemed himself in his son's eyes. 'Not only did he seem to know half the population by name but he cheerfully greeted the other half, confidently waving his walking-stick, and the other half replied "Good day, Father." I was pleased that he did not repudiate the "Father"'.

After days walking through wet heather or sitting on a foam-flecked rock in Sheep Haven, Louis spent his evenings by the turf fire, reading and rereading Yeats's play, *The Land of Heart's Desire*, and his early lyrics. For the first time, he had fallen under the spell of a living writer, a spell that, for all his later reservations about Yeats, would never let him go. Returning to school in September, he thanks his stepmother 'for the parcels of heart's desire', and his first poem to appear in *The Marlburian* echoes Yeats's 'The Stolen Child' and 'The Ballad of the Foxhunter':

Death of a Prominent Businessman

'Who are you that are twisted, brown,
Come to knock at the window pane?
I have got to attend to my business cares,
My speculations, my stocks and shares,
So leave me alone again.'
'One of the wee folk out of the hills
I clammer and hammer your window pane;
For your stocks and shares may wither and rot
E'er God forgets the forget-me-not;
And I NEVER will leave you alone again.
Come you away to the black peat bog,
The driving sleet and the drifting rain,
Where the wee folk weave from the pith of the reed
And the world is rid of financial greed
And the gentry dance in a chain.'
The shriek of an owl and the flit of a bat
And a single drop of rain,
And the old man's body lay dead in his chair,
But his soul had gone to taste the air
Away on the hills again.

A second poem in the same issue, 'The Dissolution of Valhalla', borrows its 'blood-red wine' from 'The Ballad of Sir Patrick Spens', its setting from Yeats's 'The Wanderings of Oisin' and the Norse sagas.

The summer had been a success and Louis started the Autumn Term in high spirits. He and Ross furnished their study, put their frying-pan and kettle to work, and had Shepard to tea. It would seem that he

Graham Shepard

introduced Louis to the pleasures of debating. On 3 November, Graham seconded the motion that 'Manners Mayketh Manne' 'with trifling though flowery arguments based on Tarzan of the Apes'; and, on a number of occasions over the next year and a half, Louis also took the floor, usually in defence of unpopular propositions. Another friend was spreading his wings this time in another direction. Anthony Blunt, fired with enthusiasm for art and especially modern art, proposed the formation of an Arts society under the presidency of an enlightened and hospitable master, the Revd Clifford Canning. However, the Art Master, Christopher Hughes, objected on the grounds that the *Art* Master should be president of an *Arts* Society. Blunt – unlike Betjeman

– disapproved of Hughes because he was a Saturday-afternoon water-colourist who thought that Art ended with the Pre-Raphaelites, and because he was Commanding Officer of the Marlborough Officers' Training Corps. Anti-militarist Blunt may have been, but he showed the greater tactical sense by promptly reformulating his proposal. Instead of an Arts Society, the Anonymous Society was founded, and Canning was again invited to be president. Understandably, he replied: 'Sorry, Hughes has made such a stink about this that I can't take it on now.' Another master, George Turner, was approached and accepted the invitation. Blunt read the first paper, 'an astonishingly dull piece on Titian – highly respectable. And then John [Betjeman] read one on Victorian art; that was extremely amusing, the real Betj. gaiety, and of course highly intelligent.' In November, Louis listened to a paper on Egyptian art, and agreed to produce one himself on 'Northern Fairy Tales and Sagas'. He was also elected to the less lively Literary Society and heard a boy read a paper on Wordsworth. These new activities did not eclipse the old. He told his stepmother:

John Betjeman (centre, back row) at Marlborough

I am feeling fairly pleased with life at present – house match yesterday, and one tomorrow, a game for ourselves today and abundance of victuals. . . .

My table is crowded with old and dusty tomes anent Ireland, Teutonic Tales, Burnt Njal, Mythology of the Aryan Nations etc. They emanate a pleasant though musty atmosphere of erudition. They are propped up on one side by the big Liddell and Scott and on the other by the elephant, representing the West and East, or intellect and muscle, if you prefer it.

He spent Christmas at Carrickfergus, probably writing there the three poems printed in *The Marlburian* of 18 February and the 'Norse paper' read to the Anonymous Society, meeting in Canning's attractive house, at the end of that month. An informed and eloquent introduction to the world and afterworld of the Eddas, the paper opens with an authoritative flourish:

The Norse World was rough and cold and jolly; it smelt of stockfish. It was inhabited by leathery, fair-headed people with a sprinkling of bears and trolls and Jötuns. Its gods were respectable anthropomorphic deities, who liked blood and beer and song. Its men took after them; they were all warriors or Skalds, that is in the heroic age. The heroic age ended with Christianity and the subjection of Iceland to Norway. Thereafter the gods became demons and the sagas gave way to fairy tales, and Boots took the place of Odin or Thor or Grettir.

While he was speaking, Canning's lanky black dog strolled in like a boar-hound and lay before the fire.

Louis was now a member of societies to which Ross did not belong; in the Upper Sixth, as Ross was not; and entering a phase of rapid intellectual development. Ross appears less and less frequently in his letters and, though there is no word there of coolness between them, *The Strings are False* describes a widening breach. 'His mittens and his morality and, even more, his occasional sentimentality' exasperated Louis into malice. Being with him was too like being with his family, 'and what was forgiveable in them seemed intolerably priggish' in Ross. Increasingly, Louis sought the company of the impenitent apostate Blunt and began to borrow his books on painting. One day when Ross was out, he borrowed and put up in their study three of Blunt's coloured prints: 'a Duccio Madonna, a Greco Holy Family and some picture by Altdorfer. When [Ross] came back and saw them he was so angry he almost burst into tears. The Madonna especially struck him as blasphemous, disgusting; he said her face was green.' After that, relations between them rapidly deteriorated farther, and Louis was relieved when Ross announced that he was going to leave Marlborough a year early.

This would make it possible for him to share a study with Blunt, whose influence is discernible not only in Louis' interest in Old Masters. In May 1925, a contemporary wrote home that 'Blunt has also painted a picture and I find that MacNeice (the Irish genius) turns out about one a day, some of which according to Blunt, are quite wonderful.' It was almost certainly with the embryonic art-historian that Louis began taking bicycle rides to neighbouring sites of architectural interest. Whereas his prep-school letters to his father frequently mentioned Bible reading or a sermon he had heard, he now writes of arches and pillars and, in the church at Aldbourne, monuments 'very like the Chichester memorial at home on a smaller scale'. Blunt's influence can also be discerned in a careful letter Louis writes that July not to his father but to his rich and generous stepmother:

I have been thinking out a question which is really rather important, though superficially trival. I have just read a life of the painter Van Gogh, which makes it seem almost absurd, but when I return to cold calculation I remember that I am not a Van Gogh and that conventions must be complied with. The public schools are a mass of conventions, most of which are local and ephemeral. One that is, I am afraid, rather more lasting is that which concerns dress. In the term-time provided one shows a modicum of tidiness, it does not really matter very much, but it is in the holidays (foolishly enough) that the public schools desire that one shall seem moderately well-dressed. By 'well-dressed' it means that one should have one suit which fits properly, i.e. which is tailor-made. Well, this has never really affected me, as living in Ireland I have every holiday regularly, practically escaped from the public schools and only returned to their sphere on the first day of each term. But henceforward my escape will be less and less sure for these reasons. Next term I shall probably be a captain and captains are more bound by this law than anyone else while more subject to curious eyes; if one does not obey this law, this is if one does not appear on public occasions in a tailor-made suit, one is regarded by the less reasonable half of the community as a half-wit and by the more reasonable half as an object of pity, which is still worse – and in either case where is one's authority? Of course, one can escape this if one can only manage never to appear on public occasions. This I have so far done more or less successfully as my only 'public occasions' have been departing and arriving. Departing I have gone a day early and escaped with speed while everyone else is in school and arriving, I have arrived late at night and got into bed with such alacrity that I have escaped notice. But even this is very difficult and a great strain and this term it will be quite impossible as after Camp most of us, including myself, will return to Marlborough before going home. Not only this but supposing anyone ever asks me to stay with them, which in the case of Ross or Blunt or Shepard is quite possible, I shall of necessity refuse. But, worst of all, next term, I presume, I shall go up to Oxford for the best part of a week for a scholarship exam. For these exams one always goes in one's holiday suits and where am I then? For no one could pretend that my brown suit serviceable as it is, fits me very well. Besides the trousers are now almost too short for me. Nor would I dare to go through London going home, for London on such days (as I know from experience) is thronged with Marlburians. And if Mr. Guillebaud ever proposed to take me (as the senior classical boy in house, which I shall be next term) to a Greek play at Oxford or anything of the sort I should either refuse or go with misery. Lastly, if as I understand, we are going to spend next holidays in Scotland, especially in Edinburgh, it is more than probable we shall meet a Marlburian. Such a meeting, or indeed the expectation of one, will keep me in a constant state of suspense.

After this parade of court-room rhetoric, he comes to his 'practical proposal': that his stepmother should pay for a tailor-made suit in lieu of birthday and Christmas presents. Not surprisingly, she agreed.

His special pleading on behalf of conventions that 'must be complied with' should be set against an attack on the conventions of home and school: this, a 156-line poem called 'The City of God', was written that summer for a Marlborough competition (which it did not win). It is a satire about a hymn-writer, to whom his venetian blinds say:

> 'Try another job.
> There's nothing in your hymns. The City of God,
> If it exists at all, is not like yours –
> A place of sickly smiles. It is mere tradition
> That makes you talk of harps and golden thrones
> And jasper. Why! THE item of the lot –
> The milk and honey – your sophistication
> Eliminates but leaves that rubbish in.'

The assault is two-pronged, against both substance and form. Avoiding rhyming stanzas that might be associated with the objects of his attack, he wrote in what he believed to be free verse, but 'was really dissipated blank verse, but I enjoyed writing it, for I had plenty to say and I liked to see the phrases pick themselves, unhampered by a rigid form, and I liked varying my cadences'.

Another long poem of the same period is more conventional but, in the light of his later development, more interesting. Untitled, it is about '... that confectioner's assistant who, under the inspiration of Marco Polo and other antiquities, forfeited his post and consequently ... exposing himself in a state of poetic folly to the elements, his life.' The rhyming lines that follow the Coleridgean 'argument' alternate between two modes. First, the mock-heroic:

> The unwashed lad
> As stamp-collector has his own romance
> Who culls the crimson fruits of Trinidad.

Tiring of tight-waisted eighteenth-century brocade, the young poet slips into something more consciously baggy and modern:

> The pleasure-boats have paddled all the day, holiday;
> Pay your penny, go away, come again on Saturday,
> The boats will be repainted and their pennons will be gay,
> The yellow fruit umbrellas in remote Kinsay
> Will catch the yellow sun-rays . . . .

This harlequin motley carries the Sitwell label. Someone, perhaps Blunt, had told Louis that his poems resembled these of the Sitwells, which he claimed not to have read. Remedying that omission, he liked what he found. 'Their little jazz fantasies seemed to me extremely exciting. They were in tune with the "child-like" painting of Matisse and the sentimental harlequins of Picasso's blue period.'

By the time the family holiday came around, Louis was much more comfortable in motley than his stepmother's new suit. He was a sour companion on his parents' tour of Scotland in a chauffeur-driven Austin saloon. Under Blunt's influence, the dutiful son of the rectory was fast becoming a sceptical rebel, who wanted cornfields to look like landscapes by Van Gogh, and was irritated by indiscriminate praise of the scenery:

My stepmother and father were hurt by my lack of enthusiasm, not realising that this was a deliberate façade hiding a brand-new enthusiasm, the bacchanalian chorus of adolescence. I was reading a book on Greek philosophy in order to prepare for a scholarship examination at Oxford and was swept away by Heraclitus, by the thesis that everything is flux and fire is the primary principle.

John MacNeice had thought of sending his son to Glasgow, 'as being both more moral and more industrious than Oxford', but those recommendations seemed even less compelling to Louis after his summer holiday than they had before. He and Anthony had long since set their sights on Oxford and Cambridge and, when not preparing for their respective scholarship exams, now whitewashed their new study and chose pictures for its walls – reproductions of a Picasso still-life and Cézanne's Mont Sainte-Victoire – to which, in due course, were added paintings of their own. The room was twelve feet long and six wide, with the door at one end and a window at the other. There were two tables and a bookshelf topped with decorated plates and lustre jugs, one of which would usually be full of flowers. Here they 'anticipated the life of the University, spending hours and hours in Socratic argument, in gossip, malice and risqué wit'. They read eclectically and voraciously:

it was either stark and realistic or precious and remote and two-dimensional. We read Tolstoy and Dostoievski and Beckford's *Vathek*, Thomas Hardy and Crébillon *fils*, Blake and Lucretius and books about Blake and Lucretius, lives of Cézanne and Van Gogh, the three Sitwells, Lord Dunsany's fairy stories, Edward Lear and T. S. Eliot and Aldous Huxley. Anthony had a flair for bigotry; every day he blackballed another musician, he despised Tennyson, Shakespeare, the Italian High Renaissance and Praxiteles, was all in favour of the Primitives, of Uccello, of the Byzantine mosaics, of Byzantine and Negro sculpture.

John Hilton, a muscular mathematician, was a friend of them both and a frequent visitor of their study where, he said, 'one sometimes got the impression that the closing scene of the Mad Hatter's tea party was being performed, with Louis in the role of dormouse being stuffed into the teapot'. He summed up the difference between them:

Anthony was then an austere hedonist living for disciplined gratification of the senses, with an eye for social esteem and seeking anchorage in system and scholarly detail. While Louis was a ribald seer, an anarchic and mocking seeker after the deep springs of action and faith or at least hope or at least a mythology which would keep hope alive in a world always transient and mostly trivial, sordid or brutal; though often ludicrous, sometimes brave and occasionally tender.

Their tastes and temperaments were complementary, which must be why they remained such firm friends, despite being competitive animals in a competitive jungle. Both reached the finals of the Buchanan reading prize (Anthony winning second place); both were eloquent in the Debating Society (of which Anthony was president) and the Anonymous, to which Anthony read a paper on Cubism and Louis one on 'The mailed fist of common-sense and how to avoid it'. This was delivered first to the Literary Society, on 11 October, and was rapturously received by an unusually large audience. The secretary's account of this 'feast of brilliance' runs to abnormal length, as does Hilton's account of the latter performance in a letter home:

It really was simply astounding; an amazing and magnificent conglomeration of dreams, fables, parables, allegories, theories, quotations from Edward Lear and Edith Sitwell, the sort of thing that you want to howl with laughter at, but are afraid to for fear of missing a word. He spoke in a loud, clear, fast matter-of-fact voice going straight on without a pause from a long story about two ants who fell into a river and went floating down in company with two old sticks and a dead dog, until they met a fish to whom they said 'stuff and nonsense; it's contrary to common sense to swim upstream; we won't believe it' and went on and were drowned in a whirlpool, while the fish swam on upstream until he met St. Francis of Assisi preaching to the fishes and gained eternal happiness.

What begins as a *tour de farce* develops into a passionate evangelical sermon that deserves to be quoted in full, but three brief extracts must suffice:

By all means live in the world for it is sense to do so and one must live in sense. But don't live in commonsense for that is no better than being one of the pages in a Bradshaw. Sense, you see, is the foundation on which nonsense stands, but commonsense is the very capacious pigstye hidden down in the valley. . . .

Every age has at least one champion of sense, that is of nonsense. Even Queen Victoria traipsing her tartan linoleums had the chance of reading Mr.

Edward Lear; even in the hiatus after the death of Pope there was the voice of Blake crying in the wilderness. And so today we have the Sitwells. . . .

The Sitwells place things in new positions. By expressing something in terms of something quite different they succeed in describing what we had previously thought indescribable – the feeling that comes to us in dreams, or on a dead hot day when we are alone. This, it must be remembered, is a pure feeling, it is not a matter of reason; it must therefore be described not rationally but emotionally. Emotional treatment is less limited than rational treatment and therefore more difficult, just as vers libre is more difficult than blank verse and blank verse than the rhyming couplet.

John Hilton was not alone in seeing Louis as 'a genius', a magician, and no one has described his magic better:

His mind and sensorium formed a sounding board, an echo chamber, a court in constant session, a living touchstone, a presence, a force in being. As on a dark clear night, there was a sense of depth without bounds and communication without muffling, or 'noise' in the communication engineer's use of the word.

And at the heart of darkness a glow like Christmas. For the opposite pole of his attraction – which had me mesmerised, entranced and largely enslaved – was something like a non-stop variety show. The glow would bloom and broaden and show itself to have been the simmering lull of a volcanic spout of flying flares, explosive bombards, growlings, roarings, incandescent missiles, black-encrusted rosy lava, steam, smoke and ash; candle grease, barley sugar and coloured witchballs. There was a highly conscious showman in control of all this and, when the main fires had sunk beneath their vents and the air was only lightly traced with sparks and wisps and mutterings, however concentrated his meditation there was no curtain between him and the outside world whether as spectacle or audience; one's behaviour was still under scrutiny and one's attention somehow demanded.

This was the eighteen-year-old who, on 8 November, went up to Oxford to sit for one of the three 'Postmastership' scholarships (worth £80 a year) for which he was eligible at Merton College. He was well-disposed to the College, having heard that it was the oldest in the University and had a Tintoretto altarpiece, 'which is not a Tintoretto, if one looks at it long enough'. He was not disappointed and, on his first morning, walking in his new suit (with a packet of Gold Flake cigarettes 'brassily blazing' in his pocket) from the cobbles of Merton Street into Christ Church, he was astonished by the immensity of Tom Quad:

Next came the fan-vaulted staircase round the single column soaring, soaring, till we found ourselves in the enormous hall, cluttered with little tables which creaked under anxious elbows. Here, roasting by the fire which all the same I admired for its old-fashioned extravagance, I drew on my store of examination tricks and admitted to myself half guiltily, 'I should really rather like to come up here.'

The magician's tricks proved successful and in December Mr Sargeaunt was able to paste an addition on to his report: 'He deserves hearty congratulations on his scholarship.' Beneath this, Norwood wrote: 'A boy of great promise, and I hope he will fulfill it.'

This success further boosted Louis' confidence and, from his first letter home the following term, his handwriting is larger, more rounded and seemingly more rapid. Anthony, who had won a scholarship to Trinity College, Cambridge, has been made a prefect,

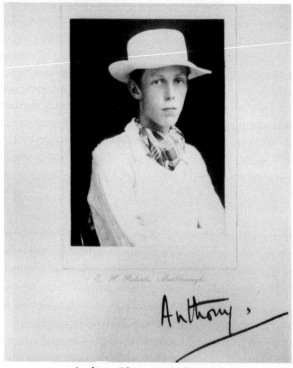

Anthony Blunt at Marlborough

'which is a great thing', and 'has brought back some really interesting new books – in particular two large ones on Negro Sculpture and Byzantine Art'. Tomorrow, he tells his parents, Mr Hughes is to read his paper on Art to the Anonymous Society. That meeting was to prove the most painful round in a long and ugly contest. Hughes had not forgiven Blunt for denying him the presidency of what, for all its alleged anonymity, was clearly an arts society; and, the previous November, he had rejected one of Wilfrid Blunt's pictures (of a mackerel) submitted for an exhibition by Old Marlburians, saying 'it was worthy of a pavement artist'. There had been fierce exchanges between the boy and the master at earlier Anonymous Society meetings, but none to equal those of this latest confrontation. Hughes's paper was a sharp attack on Blunt heresies and in the middle of it Anthony giggled. Hughes exploded in fury and tears: 'You've hurt me very much. I hope I'm now hurting you!' The giggle, however, showed he was not, and Blunt carried the day. Some weeks later, he completed his triumph by organizing an exhibition of large prints, borrowed from Zwemmers, in the school gymnasium. He was encouraged in this venture by Canning who, with his wife, came to tea in the aesthetes' study. Shortly afterwards, Louis was invited to tea by the admired Sargeaunt, who asked him 'if people in Ireland really spoke like the characters in the Playboy of the Western World' – perhaps an indication that he associated Louis with that role. If so, it was a compliment, because he thought the language of Synge's characters 'very fine and imaginative'.

Louis spent Easter at Carrickfergus and returned for a last term that was to seem an idyll. In May, he bicycled with Anthony and John Hilton to Avebury and back by East Kennet, where he climbed the church tower and rang the bell. There was a memorable reading of 'Vernal and Amorous Poetry' in the Cannings' garden beside the Kennet. Anthony read poems by Ronsard and du Bellay, and John would remember Louis declaiming

the *Pervigilium Veneris* with harsh resonance and a percussive menace in the refrain that was almost a threat.

He read verse with a vibrant, plangent, scrannel, sometimes harsh, almost raucous, sometimes warmly rolling voice, the tone even, emphasis usually subdued, vowel sounds given enormous value, consonants such as final r's rescued from English negligence – the word 'iron' becoming practically two syllables . . . . One hand would be held out sideways, palm down, moving slightly up and down in a rhythm unconnected with the verse as though to quieten an invisible dog.

The following month he contributed poems 'by a new poet', T. S. Eliot, to a reading organized by the Literary Society. A visiting American master, Mr Waring, introduced the poems and may well have introduced Louis to them. He was not an instant convert, finding them, initially, repellent: 'His subject-matter was ugly, I did not like his form, and I found him very obscure.' Soon, however, he began to respond to the 'patches of genuine nightmare relieving the drab realism', and then to see that the realism was not so drab after all. Discovering Eliot's principles, he warmed to his technique – 'the blend of conversation and incantation, the deliberate flatnesses, the quick cutting, the so-called free association'. A good deal of this Louis had already absorbed via the Sitwells, and although the Sitwellian influence is dominant in his own poems appearing regularly (and anonymously) in the *The Marlburian*, an Eliotelian note is almost certainly audible in at least one:

And the Spirit Returns . . .

The dark empoppied gypsy's daisy chain
Stretches across the barge-begrimed canal,
Past Sister Susey chatting to her pal
And the gnarled farmer prophesying rain,
Past the plump workhouse and the trite refrain
'Funds to be fostered by the liberal – '
(Oh, awfully liberal, who say, 'We shall
Give Abel a marble tomb by squeezing Cain!')
Past British workmen mopping British brows,
Past old French knights yellow in tapestry,
Past chinney endors of dark witchery,
Past winy seas of after-dinner drowse
To find a Queen upon the Sphinx's knee
Weaving a lotus wreath of Why's and How's.

Louis' contributions to *The Marlburian* this term were not confined to poems: there were three parts of a satirical prose serial, entitled 'Apollo on the Old Bath Road', and a modern fairy story, called 'Miss Ambergris & King Perhaps'. None of these was signed, but his name appears in reports of the Debating Society. Speaking against the motion 'That the Youth of to-day is degenerate',

Mr. MacNeice corrected a few errors of the previous speaker. By an adroit juggling of abstractions he proved him wrong. There followed a short attack on the enchanting delusion of the Good Old Days, and a simile about biscuits. We have developed our sense of humour, which is a great advance. A little story about Adam and an Ape, a quotation from Cornford and another from Catullus, completed this exciting oration.

In a debate on the motion 'That the General Strike was a Revolt justified by the Situation', 'MR MACNEICE recited a highly pertinent Limerick, mentioning a miner.' He was no doubt speaking against the motion since, in a letter home, he writes: 'If I had been at Oxford this term I should probably have rushed off to Hull to unlade fish. It would have been most amusing.' This underlines the truth of Blunt's retrospective summing-up:

we lived in this little self-contained world of art and literature, with no awareness of what was taking place in the outside world at all. Politics was simply a subject never discussed at all, and what happened to be going on at that time in Europe was no concern of ours. Inflation in Germany merely meant that one could get an incredibly cheap holiday! Fascism in Italy was something remote which we read about in the papers but we did not really take in. And even a thing like the general strike in 1926, my last term at school, was treated very largely as a sort of joke and one's elder brothers and one's parents went and did curious things; but it did not impinge as a real event on us at all.

Amusement was the great criterion. They bowled a hoop around the school, played catch with a huge painted nursery rubber ball, and generally set out 'to enrage the Boy in the Street'. One day they carried an easel and canvas down to the bathing place where Blunt wanted to do a composition of a corrugated iron shed. The master in charge, ignorant of the doctrine of Pure Form to which the aesthetes had been converted by the writings of Clive Bell, was scandalized. He told them 'it was strictly forbidden to take photos or paint pictures of the bathing place. When Blunt explained that he was only interested in the shed, the master grudgingly gave him permission to continue; provided, he said, you don't put in any *figures*.' The master's concern was no doubt intensified by the boys' reputation as decadent aesthetes, enemies of decency and convention, but Louis, at least, had no undue interest in *figures*. However, as many of his contemporaries were engaged in what he later called 'mild homosexual romances', he singled out 'a dark-haired boy of sixteen who had large grey feminine eyes and asked him illicitly to tea'. This romance advanced no further, and Blunt maintained that 'Louis was always, totally, irredeemably heterosexual'.

The golden sands of their Marlborough idyll were fast running out. They submitted some paintings for the school's Prize Day exhibition. 'Hughes was furious', Louis told his stepmother. 'He turned nearly all of them down after a violent argument with Canning and Mrs.' At this point, another voice entered the debate from an unexpected quarter. Prize Day was 28 June, and 700 stiff-collared boys and assorted members of their families were assembled in the newly completed Memorial Hall. George Turner (titular president of the Anonymous Society) had recently succeeded Norwood as Master of Marlborough, and he began his address by paying tribute to his predecessor, whose transformation of the school curriculum he credited with the record crops of Oxford and Cambridge scholarships: thirty in 1925, twenty-four in 1926. He singled out Anthony Blunt as Marlborough's star scholar of the year, adding: 'I cannot refrain from congratulating him also on his persistent efforts to interest an incurably sentimental society in modern aims in art and literature'. Louis observed that their philistine housemaster, Dr Guillebaud, was enraged at this, though he may have been mollified when the Master went on to say: 'Blunt and some others may go image breaking, but that is no bad thing so long as the hammer is swung fair and square at the image and not the heads of rival worshippers.'

The peace-maker was not to have the last word. The June issue of *The Marlburian* had carried an essay by Anthony. Entitled 'De Cubismo', it praised the achievements of modern art and attacked the 'evil tradition' of 'purely imitative' pictures, singling out Hughes's favourite Pre-Raphaelites as exemplifying a 'peculiarly English failing'. The French, he declared, had 'revolutionized the art of all European countries, except England'. To underline this point and undermine the influence of Hughes's Prize Day exhibition, Anthony organized a second exhibition of prints, one of which Louis bought. Hughes struck back in the term's last issue of *The Marlburian*. In reply to Blunt's 'De Cubismo' essay, he asserted that 'The critic and the artist are constantly at loggerheads, and this is partly because the critic does not understand the artist's point of view.' Brandishing his artist's licence, he harangued the young critic: 'Let the modernist . . . not think that he has a monopoly of the word Art; and let him get away from the amazing delusion that he represents the Old Masters.' Hughes may have had the last word, but Blunt probably had the last giggle.

There was a last meeting of the Anonymous Society, held in the Cannings' moonlit garden, to which several members came in a stolen punt; a meeting that ended with John Hilton's immersion in the Kennet. Louis' letter, giving his stepmother an account of this, ends '*Sic transit gloria mundi*', and he again resorted to the liturgical solemnity of Latin at the close of a last ritual:

At the end of term Anthony and I gave a tea-party in our study. When we had stuffed ourselves full we took the tea-set piece by piece, lovingly fondling the china, and threw it out of the window to smash on a blank wall opposite that was divided from our block by a narrow alley. Piece after piece fell in tiny fragments into space but we kept the best till last; the sugar bowl, still full of lumps, burst on the wall like a round of machine-gun fire and the large teapot sailed to its doom trailing tea from the spout. 'Ruins of Carthage,'* we said and washed our hands of Marlborough.

Louis left – for Officers' Training Camp near Tidworth – with his 'arms full of the flowers of five great years' – and, in his pocket, the *Poems* of T. S. Eliot.

---

* '*Delenda est Carthago.*' Plutarch, *Life of Cato.*

CHAPTER 8

Other Gods

Oxford crowded the mantelpiece with gods –
Scaliger, Heinsius, Dindorf, Bentley and Wilamowitz –
As we learned our genuflexions for Honour Mods.
'Autumn Journal', *CP*, p. 126

After the crashing chords of the Marlborough finale, Louis' Irish summer was a protracted anti-climax. He was reduced to repainting old croquet balls and playing golf with his father's curate. In the evenings he read Hardy's *Tess*, Lord Dunsany's recently published fairy-tale, *The Charwoman's Shadow*, and the poems of Christina Rossetti and Francis Thompson. There was a visit to the art galleries of Dublin described in one of a number of long and high-flown letters to Anthony, who was exploring the greater glories of Italy.

Eventually, however, October arrived and on Friday the 15th Louis passed through the gates of Merton, not now as a schoolboy supplicant but as a Postmaster (or scholar) of the College. He was shown to a set of rooms on the ground floor of the Founder's Quad: a living-room with his name over the door and narrow windows overlooking the lawn and lime trees of the Fellows' Garden that gave it a green underwater light; and a smaller bedroom overlooking the quad. He was delighted with these and with their *genius loci*, his seventy-year-old scout:

He was a tiny man designed by George Cruickshank, with a long ratlike moustache, a perky yet portentous manner, and a greasy bowler hat which he kept in the sink on the staircase. He was full of aphorisms, 'Brains runs in a family like wooden legs, sir'; of snobbery, 'The old Warden, now, he was a gentleman, I remember him riding his horse into the porter's lodge' or 'I could always tell when Lord Birkenhead had been drunk because then he would

The Front Gate of Merton College

hang his trousers over a certain picture'; and of a certain romanticism – he had seen the moon under an arch at Tintern Abbey.

He brought his 'young gentlemen' shaving water for their basins (though Louis would later claim to discover that China tea was preferable for this purpose), small coals for their fires, breakfast and luncheon on a tray. Dinner was taken by candlelight in the College's raftered hall, where scholars and exhibitioners sat apart from the 'commoners' at a separate long table with its own silver. Louis did not like the company, telling Anthony: 'all the other postmasters of this year are vile – so stupid – while those of earlier years are aesthetes with a slight gift for obscenity but pretty deplorable'. He soon found that most of his undergraduate contemporaries fell into one of three categories: the studious, the aesthetes (though these were pale shadows of their Wildean predecessors), and the hearties. Louis' problem – probably unperceived, certainly unadmitted – was that he had interests in common with some of each camp. His postmastership proved him studious, but he had not come up to Oxford to study: 'that was what grammar-school boys did'. He thought of himself as an aesthete and dressed as a dandy, but had neither the taste nor the money for the mindless excesses of the Bunthorn brigade. He had enjoyed rugger, cricket, and golf, and told Blunt he hoped 'to follow the Christ Church Beagles. Nice and brutal and invigorating'. There is no evidence that he did, perhaps because that would have seemed like defection to the hearties, natural enemies of the aesthetes.

Disappointed by his Merton contemporaries but eager for company, he allowed himself to be lured into a fourth camp even less to his liking than the others. A message intended for someone else in his passage was left in his room, inviting him to tea his second Sunday with an unknown Mr Moore. Arriving at a house in North Oxford, he found he had fallen among Plymouth Brethren:

The room was full of cake-stands and suspense and suddenly everyone stood up and Mr. Moore, our host, a genial, cunning old man, began praying in an over-familiar way which implied that we and God were all one jolly family. Then we ate. Mr Moore was puzzled by my presence but he took me into a corner and said I was welcome all the same and would I come again, they did this every Sunday; there was a young man from the Colonies, he said, a very fine athlete, who had told him just before he went down that there had been moments during his university career when he felt like going wrong but, whenever these temptations arose, he used to say to himself 'I'll just go up and have a cup of coffee with old Moore' and the situation was saved.

Veering to the other extreme, he was taken by a heavily powdered Old Marlburian to a party where the drink was not coffee but champagne, 'and all through the evening one pretty young man sat in the same armchair talking to no one except a stuffed spotted dog which he joggled up and down on its lead'. This couple, forebears of Sebastian Flyte and his teddy-bear Aloysius, remind one that Evelyn Waugh had left Oxford only two years before. The discovery, MacNeice wrote, 'that in Oxford homosexuality and "intelligence", heterosexuality and brawn, were almost inexorably paired . . . left me out in the cold and I took to drink'.

John Hilton, giving his parents an account of his friend's social success, told them that at the champagne party Louis had met 'the chief

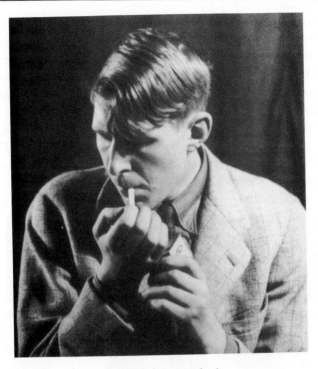

W. H. Auden at Oxford

Oxford poet'. This must have been Wystan Auden, who would later remember 'a tall languid undergraduate from Merton, rather foppishly dressed'. Though both had been born in 1907, Auden had gone up to Oxford the year before. Like many other aspiring poets, MacNeice in due course knocked at Auden's door in Christ Church's Peckwater Quad. He found him

busy getting on with the job. Sitting in a room all day with the blinds down, reading very fast and very widely – psychology, ethnology, *Arabia Deserta*. He did not seem to *look* at anything, admitted he hated flowers and was very free with quasi-scientific jargon . . . .

Despite their differences, Louis was always encouraged by their meetings. He recognized Wystan as someone else 'to whom ideas were friendly – they came and ate out of his hand', but at this stage the two were feeding – and feeding on – very different sorts of ideas. Louis did not fall under his spell as Day Lewis had already done and Spender would do the following year. Neither Auden nor MacNeice had, as yet, any interest in politics, unlike another Christ Church poet whom Louis met at this time. Clere Parsons, who had come up that term on a scholarship to read English, was tall and thin with a diabetic's pallor, a passion for poetry – particularly the poetry of E. E. Cummings – and what seemed to the self-centred aesthete MacNeice 'an invalid's fanaticism for politics' – particularly the politics of the Soviet Union. Parsons' reputation as an Oxford poet would soon rival Auden's. Louis respected both, but preferred the company of his old Marlburian contemporaries: John Hilton, whose ground-floor rooms in a Corpus annex were immediately opposite Merton, and Graham Shepard, then

'A tall languid undergraduate from Merton'

sharing a Lincoln attic with a cuckoo clock and blue beer glasses. MacNeice's most admired friend, however, was still Anthony Blunt, to whom he sent an account of a typical day:

morning to dreary lecture, an old vegetable cleric flapping a beard that had gone to seed, afternoon walked with Shepard along an endless suburban road – oh such arty houses with curtains to match the slates – tea in my rooms – sodden toast and crumpets, then [read] Charwoman's Shadow aloud to Shepard, . . . then a hearty dinner, then Hedda Gabler, then a Latin prose then this. Now I shall go to bed in my scarfs and a bath towel (clothing being insufficient)[.]

Later in October, Anthony paid a surprise visit to Oxford, descending on Merton like a meteor. Less surprising, and probably less welcome, was a visit at the end of November from Louis' father and stepmother. Since Anthony was now receiving the regular letters that had formerly gone to Carrickfergus, they no doubt wanted to see how Louis was settling in. Any fears that he might be succumbing to unwholesome influences were dispelled over tea in the Shamrock tea-rooms 'with Erse welcomes and Yeats's poems round the walls'.

Louis himself paid a visit, with Shepard, to Marlborough. It was not a success: 'the flowers of five great years' were starting to shed their petals. Particularly disillusioning was a talk with the once-admired Clifford Canning of which he sent a satirical account to Anthony, the arch-iconoclast. It was a time for pulling authority figures down from their pedestals, and none more gleefully than the Merton dons. There is no reason to suppose that he viewed them any more kindly in the Twenties than in the Forties when he pinned them to a cork board in *The Strings are False*:

Few of them were interested in teaching. They lived in a parlour up a winding stair and caught little facts like flies in webs of generalisation. For recreation they read detective stories. The cigar smoke of the Senior Common Rooms hid them from each other and from the world. Some of them had never been adult, their second childhood having come too early. Some of them had never been male, walked around in their gowns like blowsy widows or wizened spinsters. They had charm without warmth and knowledge without understanding.

His balanced cadences suggest a memory of Gibbon's indictment of 'the monks of Magdalen . . . who supinely enjoyed the gifts of the founder', and of one in particular, his tutor, who 'well remembered that he had a salary to receive and only forgot that he had a duty to perform'.

A fortnight after his arrival in Oxford, Louis had the satisfaction of seeing one of his poems, 'Seaside', printed in an undergraduate magazine, *The Cherwell* (albeit over the name Louis MacPeice). Two other poems and a prose piece followed later in the term. They would have caused the reverend MacNeice – now Archdeacon of Connor – some disquiet if he had seen them (as almost certainly he did not). All three show his son stalking bigger game than dons. 'In the Cathedral' is a dialogue between a Voluptuary and a Churchwarden, heavily weighted in favour of the former. More mysterious and more subtle is the prose piece, part parable, part sermon, in which pulpit rhetoric is deployed against those, among others, who speak from pulpits:

Fires of Hell

Brown sticks and coal, paper and that newspaper, wrapped in inertia. No prophet could find here a resurrection, no astrologer see stars here. Mr. Brown sat before the fire but the fire had not been lit. Mr. Brown had not been lit. Both fires were latent.

Mr. Brown was always looking for his spectacles. The young stood by and laughed. Mr. Brown was always looking for himself. He was a good butt as he jostled other Mr. Browns for young Brown to carp at, searching for a soul in Heaven's Woolworth's. On his mantelpiece were a clock and a Bradshaw, each other's complement and compliment. The canary was his only music.

One day he read *The Times* and next day he read *The Times* but one day he read *Cupid and Psyche*. The match cried in the wilderness and a knight of flame ran through the Sleeping Wood. The young Browns stopped laughing. For one day the flames leaped in self-expression, flapping pennons and jangling bells; then Mr. Brown turned back the quilt and the embers said goodnight. Gardens faded in the mind and office-stools returned.

These, he said, are but idle sentimentalities, the luxuries of effete and droning bees. They eat the honey of others and drink their honey-wine and thus intoxicated they paint the afternoon with idle melodies of drinking-catches. We must remove from the sound of their instruments that soporific and degrading strumming. Always we hear it when we have tea in the garden, so that we lie on our backs and close our eyes, floating back in that music as in a gondola to Utopian sands and the golden shore where Paniscus plays his pipe and the Graces sprinkle balm. To have tea in the garden is to hear the laughter of Cupid. Therefore, O my highly respectable audience, therefore all you sane and able-bodied persons, therefore all you athletes and aesthetes, you grocers and you drapers, you soldiers and you statesmen, you clerics, you philosophers, you chartered accountants, therefore you princes and rajahs and pedants, we shall NOT have tea in the garden.

Christian terminology – resurrection, soul in Heaven, voice in the wilderness – assists in the subversion of Christian values; and the Edenic associations of the rectory garden have now been enriched by sunlight on other lawns – Mrs Wasey's at Leigh Hill, Clifford Canning's beside the Kennet, those of the classical Arcadia and William Blake's Song of Experience:

> I went to the Garden of Love
> And saw what I never had seen:
> A Chapel was built in the midst,
> Where I used to play on the green.
>
> And the gates of this Chapel were shut,
> And "Thou shalt not" writ over the door . . . .

The aesthete author of 'Fires of Hell' was himself subjected to ordeal by terrestial fires when a gang of hearties, assuming (wrongly) that he was homosexual, raided his rooms, debagged him, and burnt some of his prettiest ties, including one depicting small parrots among jungle flowers. He was 'a little sad' about the ties, but not altogether displeased to be martyred in the cause of aesthetic principle. What his father would have called Self-respect had to be sacrificed: 'Self-respect was the Evil Genius of half the world's trouble-makers – of the sectarians and the militants, the nationalists and the imperialists, the captains of industry and the moral reformers.' Drink, therefore, became not merely a pleasure but a duty, undermining one's Evil Genius and, in an artist, promoting fantasy and the *dérèglement de tous les sens* advocated by Rimbaud.

At the end of term, Louis and John set out to walk the fifty miles to the Hilton home at Northwood but, reaching Aylesbury in the small hours of a misty morning, gave up and finished the journey by train. After a brief stay, Louis went on to the Blunts for a few days before crossing to Carrickfergus for Christmas. A month later, he returned to

England 'in a coal boat, 12 hours and a sea according to the Captain, would have made the devil sick'. Back in Oxford, he renewed his acquaintance with John Betjeman, visiting him in his candle-lit panel-led lodgings in St Aldates. There, on 24 January, he went to a party from which Betjeman's tutor, C. S. Lewis, returned to write in his diary:

I found myself pitchforked into a galaxy of super-undergraduates, including [John] Sparrow of the Nonesuch Press and an absolutely silent and astonishingly ugly person called McNiece [*sic*], of whom Betjeman said afterwards, 'He doesn't say much, but he's a great poet.'

Early in March, Louis organized a candle-lit reading of Shelley's 'The Cenci' in his living-room. Describing this occasion to his parents, Hilton wrote: 'Louis seems at last to have found a pleasant man at Merton who came and brought a skull which looked very well when I had provided it with radishes for eyeballs.' The pleasant man was probably Adrian Green-Armytage, 'a charming, slender, gentle person who went about for a time in a cloak'. He was to become Louis' closest friend in college. Also taking part in the play-reading were Graham Shepard and another new friend, Moore Crosthwaite, a handsome Old Rugbeian reading Classics – and *The New Statesman* – at Corpus. Moore's mother moved in Fabian circles and he was more politically conscious than the Old Marlburians. Already very knowledgeable about music and architecture, he was also 'a source of information on *savoir-faire* and *Salonfähigkeit*', and a discreet homosexual.

Like – and partly thanks to – his expanding circle of friends, Louis' literary horizons were also expanding. Shepard had introduced him to Joyce (on whom he wrote a paper which he read to Merton's Bodley Society); D. H. Lawrence was a recent discovery; and from Carrickfergus at Easter he wrote to Blunt: 'I am reading Aeschylus, Homer, Sophocles, Tchekov, Julian Huxley'. He still enjoyed the ancient authors, but not the way in which Latin and Greek language and literature were taught in the first half of Oxford's School of *literae humaniores*, the five-term course known as Honour Moderations (usually shortened to 'Honour Mods'). He grew to hate the precedence given to language over literature, the 'niggling over textual commentary', the memorization of emendations proposed by scholars such as Scaliger, Heinsius, Dindorf, Bentley, and Wilamowitz. Rejecting these false gods of his Mods tutors, 'the galloping Major' Edwards (formerly of the Indian Army) and R. G. C. Levens, MacNeice replaced them with a new set of Olympians: Nietzsche and D. H. Lawrence and Joyce. When he returned to Oxford in the last week of April, he spent less and less time in libraries, more on the river in a canoe he and Hilton had hired for the term. They had planned to hear the Magdalen choristers sing their hymn to Mithras from the top of the college's tower at sunrise on 'May morning', but Louis did not appear. John found him at ten, in his room and dressing-gown, and was treated to 'several torrential compositions' before he dressed and they set out, with stale rolls and oranges, to explore the Oxford canal. A riverside picnic with John, Graham and Moore Crosthwaite, the following week, was better provisioned: 'Curried prawns, brandy and ginger ale, cucumber, lettuces, grapefruit, and radishes, oranges, Florence cake and Burgundy, cheese biscuits and butter and other cakes.' There were other happy but unsuccessful expeditions in search of Bablock Hythe and Robert Graves's house in Islip. Under the influence of *The Waste Land* – a sacred text for undergraduates of the Twenties – they would also

paddle along the evil-smelling canal through the slums or up the Isis past the gas-drums. One May morning we were on this stretch of the Isis watching a dragonfly among the cow-parsley and shards on the bank when a goods train came over the railway bridge and we made a chant out of the names on the trucks – Hickleton, Hickleton, Hickleton, Lunt, Hickleton, Longbotham. This incantation of names at once became vastly symbolic – symbolic of an idle world of oily sunlit water and willows and willows' reflections and, mingled with the idleness, a sense of things worn out, scrap-iron and refuse, the shadow of the gas-drum, this England. Hickleton Hickleton Hickleton – the long train clanked and rumbled as if it had endless time to reach wherever it was going. The placid dotage of a great industrial country.

Remembering 1927 from 1940, MacNeice gives the scene a political dimension it would have had, if at all, only dimly for the poet entranced by the marriage of modern names and ancient meters.

MacNeice at twenty was romantic, as only those with no more than literary experience of romance can be, and 'always talking about the

Not Impossible She'. One day Moore Crosthwaite said to him: 'If you want to meet your Not Impossible She you must come to a lunch party I'm giving.' Moore, who was also reading Mods, had fallen under the spell of one of Oxford's most charismatic classicists, Professor 'Jacky' Beazley, who with his wife Marie kept open house for clever and charming undergraduates. Mrs Beazley was the guest of honour at

Mrs Beazley

Moore's lunch party in Corpus, invited with her daughter Mary to meet three of his more presentable friends. The Professor's wife was a celebrated Oxford 'character', who sailed through life like the well-endowed figurehead of a nineteenth-century clipper, trailing stories as a ship trails seaweed: she would not have a fire in her house or a dustbin outside it; waste paper was piled under the kitchen sink and removed once a week by a young woman she called 'the goose girl'. John Hilton, another of Moore's guests, noticed that Mrs Beazley had 'eyes like a witch that change shape all the time and a very long rather

Jewish nose'. He found her 'frightening, terribly quick and penetrating and almost oriental'. She spoke with the exotic accent of someone brought up in Smyrna, and her conversation was torrential and eccentric: 'Mr. Andrewes, we have had this discussion before. Why didn't you tell me?' Her laugh was a parrot's shriek. At Moore's lunch party she talked all the time – very whimsically, Louis thought – while her daughter sat in sulky silence 'like a Japanese doll, slight and dainty, her hair very black and skin very white'. Afterwards, Moore asked him if she would do for the Not Impossible She. 'No', he said, 'she would not.'

Perhaps with an eye to meeting a more possible She, Louis suggested to John that they should visit Paris in July. John was enthusiastic, but it was by no means certain that the Archdeacon would allow his susceptible son to make his first trip abroad to a city so renowned for its temptations. He 'thought the French a disgusting race because they used toothpicks'. Louis was staying with the Hiltons when good news came in the form of a telegram saying 'PRANCE TO FRANCE'. So prance they did – Louis swinging an Irish ashplant borrowed from Stephen Dedalus – off to the country of troubadours, symbolists, surrealists, impressionists and post-impressionists. On Anthony's recommendation, they took rooms in the Hôtel de Blois, Rue Vavin, a narrow street between the boulevards Raspail and Montparnasse, and set off to sample *la vie bohème*. French food and drink lived up to their expectations. They sat for hours at café tables behind mounting piles of saucers that had come bearing glasses of benedictine. Louis smoked interminable Gauloises, and with eyes narrowed against the stinging smoke they watched *le monde* go by. The *Quatorze Juillet* was approaching; the boulevards were pulsing with jazz bands, dancing couples and hooting traffic; and the night sky blazed with fireworks launched from bridges across the Seine. Louis, however, could not dance and neither he nor John had more than a few words of French. No girls with blue make-up accosted them – only, one night when the travellers had been locked out of their hotel and John was asleep on a bench, a greasy old man with a double chin and a broad black hat. Louis admired the hat, clearly the mark of a painter or a poet. '*Mais oui*,' said the old man, '*je suis poète*.' '*Moi aussi*', Louis replied, and delightedly accepted the offer of a bed for the night. 'This is the beginning', he thought. 'The next thing I know he will introduce me to Picasso.' But the next thing he knew, he was in an unromantic apartment at the top of a long staircase, being propositioned with obscene gestures. When these could no longer be ignored or misunderstood, he said: 'All right; you go back to your bed and I will join you; your bed appears to be bigger.' As the old man shambled off, Louis leaped into his own clothes, snatched up his ashplant, and thundered down the stairs. Elated at his adventure, he described it to John, who said – not unreasonably – 'You're a fool.'

They went to the Louvre, Notre Dame, the Moulin Rouge, and the Opéra, to which they were refused admission, as being improperly dressed. Louis, the dandy, disliked carrying things in his pockets, obliging John to act as both carrier and courier, a role he began to resent. At last, like Don Quixote and Sancho Panza, they set off for the country; taking a train to Fontainebleu and then, at nightfall, continuing by foot in the direction of Chartres. They slept for some time on the edge of a potato field; woke in a drizzle; and walked on with Louis discoursing about influences on Derain. At Chartres, they bought peasant straw hats to protect them from the vertical rays of sun, and sought shelter in the cathedral, which struck a responsive chord in the clergyman's rebellious son:

that stone should run away from the earth where it belonged, to lose itself not in heaven but in its own inner darkness, stirred something in my own unquarried depths, something which if not a 'death-wish' was at least a wish to escape – the same desire to escape which, outside on the west front, had elongated and emaciated the saints.

They returned to Paris by way of Versailles, where 'the formal gardens filled out a myth' for Louis, exciting his imagination as had the soaring stone of Chartres. They were shut in at closing time and had to climb out. Back then to more benedictines and piled saucers and the discharge of a commission from Moore Crosthwaite: the purchase of a 'modern painting' costing not more than £15. They found this a more restricting figure than they had expected but, after trudging through fifteen art galleries, settled on a small Gromaire (a painter of whom they had not previously heard). Carrying this canvas and their rucksacks, they missed their train home and slept a last night on a bench near the foot of the Eiffel Tower. They were woken by two gendarmes and an armed soldier convinced they were recapturing two young Spanish anarchists who had just escaped from a Parisian prison. Asked for his papers, Louis gave them a bookseller's bill, and it was some time before the anarchist-hunters grudgingly allowed them to prance home.

That September the MacNeices drove to Connemara. The Archdeacon had not been there for many years, and when the Atlantic came in sight, 'gnashing its teeth in the distance', he shouted 'The Sea!' in a voice that reminded his classicist son of Xenophon's troops crying '*Thalassa!*' They stopped to look for family gravestones in Ballysodare, where the Archdeacon asked a woman in a cottage doorway if there were any MacNeices now in the neighbourhood. 'Sure I married one myself', she said, and took them in to see his photograph. Their quest ended on the island of Omey. John MacNeice, trying to find the foundations of his family home among the rocks, was approached by a barefoot woman who said 'Which of them would ye be?' and reeled off a list of Christian names. He told her and she replied: 'Sure I knew ye must be one of them, the way ye knew the lie of the ground.' Louis had not been there before, but felt he knew it too:

It was a country I had always known, mournful and gay with mournful and gay inhabitants, moonstone air and bloody with fuchsias. The mountains had never woken up and the sea had never gone to sleep and the people had never got civilised. My father was remembering the stories the fishermen used to tell him about the houses and the towers were down there under the sea, and he was looking around for rookeries all the rooks had left, and his nostalgia would make him walk fast, swinging his stick, and then break off impatiently. 'Terribly backward,' he would say, 'terribly backward.'

When a few weeks later Louis returned to Oxford, it was to a set of more attractive panelled rooms on the first floor of the Founder's Quad. The host of a lunch party in the room below called his guests to silence to hear the feet of the poet (whom they presumed in the throes of composition) pacing to and fro. There was a candle-lit reading of *The Jew of Malta* in the new room; another of Louis' poems appeared in *The Cherwell* that term; but his tutors' warnings of impending disaster in the Mods exam were driving him back to libraries. He told Anthony he was thinking of 'going down' – leaving university – if he didn't get a second-class in Mods, which, he added, 'is quite probable'. Over Christmas, at Carrickfergus, he began a novel 'featuring' Blunt, whom he invited – with his brother Wilfrid – to deliver a sort of platonic dialogue to the Bodley Society towards the end of February. 'I suggest', he wrote, 'that you each compose a series of short lyrical, idyllic or satiric effusions on Life, Art etc. which you can then declaim in turn and my college will be frightfully pleased.' History does not record how pleased the college was.

In the weeks before his exam Louis 'hastily learned by heart some textual emendations by Wilamowitz, Scaliger and Co', which he duly regurgitated in the Examination Schools. Having done so, he went on a drunken spree for several days, starting with marsala at breakfast – in homage to Edward Lear. Returning to his father's teetotal rectory for Easter, he wrote to Anthony: 'Am still writing novel, even affecting a slight plot. Am giving you an embezzling mother and a fanatical father.' Affecting also a nonchalance he can scarcely have felt, he added: 'By the way I now believe in Providence; I got a 1st in Mods.'

CHAPTER 9

Paper Flowers

I hasten to explain
That having once been to the University of Oxford
   You can never really again
Believe anything that anyone says and that of course is an asset
   In a world like ours;
Why bother to water a garden
   That is planted with paper flowers?

                       'Autumn Journal', *CP*, p. 127

Louis's first letter to Anthony of the Summer Term replaced one affectation with another: 'To get a 1st is a mistake. I have never been so afflicted with ennui.' This he sought to overcome with social activity – a theatre trip to London, an expedition to Cambridge with other Old Marlburians for lunch with Anthony and friends – and a spicing of *anti*-social activity:

He spent last night climbing about on Merton roofs (though drunk) and capturing a large stone gargoil out of the sacred sacristi dropped it through the slate roof into the senior common room, where dinner was being served. They divining a special visitation from heaven fell upon their knees and Louis following through after the gargoyle was able to deliver a drunken metaphysical rant, which you will find recorded in all the forthcoming issues of respectable psychological and theological journals: he afterwards escaped by the buttery hatch.

The tone of this account suggests that the narrator, Shepard, was not himself present but was reporting the principal protagonist's version.

What would prove to be the most important event of Louis' term was his reintroduction by Moore to the Beazley family. They were living in a grand and elegant Queen Anne house, known as the Judge's Lodgings, in St Giles. It was 'scented like a potpourri and full of untouchable *objets d'art*'. Marie, the Professor's exotic wife, had been born the eldest child of Elise (née Gutman) and Bernard Blumenfeld (afterwards Bernard Bloomfield). A talented pianist, she studied under Leschetizky in Vienna and played admirably, 'though as might be expected some of her interpretations were highly unconventional'. As a young woman, she met David Ezra, member of a family that for nearly two centuries had been the leading Jewish dynasty in Calcutta. He fell violently in love with her, threatening to shoot himself unless she would marry him. Flattered by his passion and warming to his saturnine good looks, she allowed herself to be manoeuvred into a marriage that proved a failure. David's allowance from his father was inadequate for a man with a taste for ceramics and Persian rugs, a wife and, in 1908, a daughter. Christened Giovanna Marie Thérèse Babette, she spent her childhood at Ightham in Kent and, later, in a small house outside Maidstone. In 1916, her father joined the Army, rising to the rank of Captain before being killed near Amiens in August 1918. The following year Marie married J. D. Beazley, whom she had met at a party in All Souls in 1913 and come to love before David Ezra died. Beazley, probably the greatest classical scholar of his generation, pioneered the study and interpretation of Greek red- and black-figure vases. His appearance was as distinguished as his mind. Strikingly handsome in an ethereal way, this most intellectual of men was adored, cherished, dressed in scarlet shirts, and protected by his Marie, the least intellectual of dons' wives. Their beautiful house was a rich oasis in the otherwise arid desert of North Oxford, a place of refreshment for those who wished to drink from the pure wells of the Professor's learning, share the exotic fruits of his wife's conversation, or dance with his stepdaughter. Mary, as she was called to distinguish her from her mother, weighed less than seven stone, looked as fragile as porcelain, and measured her life by dance-cards kept in a lavendered box tied with ribbon. Said to be the best dancer in Oxford, she was in great demand, though 'she savoured too much of the hareem' for Harold Acton. When not dancing with one of her beaux, she was usually to be found 'lying on a sofa covered with Moorish embroideries as if she would never sit upright, much less stand, again.

She said standing made her feel faint.'

Louis, who did not dance, became a regular visitor at the house in St Giles, talking mainly with Marie whose kaleidoscopic reminiscences matched his own exuberant fantasies:

This was the first Jewish family I had known and I got in the habit of leaving two-thirds of myself outside when I entered their doors. This combination of Oriental indolence and elfin vivacity, of sophistication and primitive superstition, of sentimentality and worldly scepticism, I could only treat as a spectacle; I did not even try to take it seriously. I was as much amused by their serious discussions of horoscopes and the Evil Eye as I was by their deliberate jokes which had either the tang of the ghetto or a nuance of *La Vie Parisienne*.

Taking a leaf out of Moore's manual of etiquette, Louis invited Marie and her daughter to lunch in Merton, but made the mistake of including another woman in the party. Marie was *'utterly horrified'*. As her daughter later confided to their host, 'her mother had gone to countless lunch parties in Oxford, sometimes with a dozen men present, but never, never had any of their hosts dreamed of inviting another woman'.

Summer in Carrickfergus was even more of an anti-climax than usual. Detailed by his stepmother to accompany his father on a cruise along the coast of Norway, Louis first typed up his poems and sent them to Anthony with a letter saying:

Here they all are – title for the lot "Blind Fireworks"? Treat them well (they are in a set order) . . . .

(I am going to finish my novel in the Arctic Sea, it is growing in complexity & colour & characterization) most of my poems need reading several times over; also the prosody may be a little difficult – try reading them aloud[.]

This would seem to be the first mention of the title of his first book of poems; a title perhaps taken from a memory of the fireworks of *le Quatorze Juillet* 1927.

Predictably, Louis did not greatly enjoy the cruise. He had nothing in common with his fellow passengers – 200 middle-aged Americans and English spinsters – and talked to hardly any of them. Nor did he finish his novel, but read Nietzsche's *Also Sprach Zarathustra*, John Stuart Mill's *Logic* and *The Oxford Book of Medieval Latin Verse* instead. He had to dress for dinner every night, and at Spitzbergen there was a dance on shipboard to a gramophone whose playing of 'Dance, dance, dance, little lady' reminded him painfully of Mary. He got up early next morning and was somewhat consoled by the splendour of the view as Spitzbergen sank into the liner's wake: 'Diamond cut diamond; hard in the brilliant light the spikes of painful peaks .... a consummation of abstract art; it was not any more what I wanted.'

There had been some suggestion that he, John, and Moore might spend part of the summer archaeologizing with the Beazleys in Greece. When nothing came of this, he turned to other friends for distraction, writing to John:

You are to come here any time from 3rd Sept. on. Anthony is coming from the 1st.... My sister and I have been looking for mts for you to climb but of course Irish mts are very little. I am hopeful you will be a relief here. I am very lazy but full of good intentions e.g. to make an exhaustive study of 17th cent. English prose (e.g. Donne, Jeremy Taylor & Sir T. Browne [,] Milton etc.) & show how its cadences & imagery are a better union with God than any English prose before or since (except possibly Malory, in quite a different way, & of course mine); to write a Programme for the New Romantics; to write a tract on the Beauty of Guffaws; to write (this I really mean as my next book) a Baedeker's Guide to Purgatory; to write a Defence of Ostentation; to finish my novel & write a defensive preface; to write an explanatory preface to my poems which are to be called 'Blind Fireworks'; to do my last term's work, to do some work for next term's collections [a college examination]; to master the engine of the car; to learn the names of all garden flowers; to console you and Anthony because you'll need it in this rainy hell.

A principal topic of conversation at the Rectory was Elizabeth's approaching marriage to a young medical student, John Nicholson (whom Louis called Nonesuch and thought a bore), but this troubled the good-natured Hilton less than the bride's intemperate brother. Hilton enjoyed his stay. He had liked the Archdeacon and his wife when he first met them in the Shamrock tea-rooms and, on closer acquaintance, found them 'very delightful, especially Mrs MacNeice, who turns out to be a stepmother, but defies all the traditions of that tribe. In spite of being very deaf she is a great joke especially when fighting or arguing with Louis or prancing after him prancing.' The two friends climbed a hill (not a mountain), Knockagh, played golf and tennis, dined with an assortment of aunts (one, according to her nephew, lately engaged in gun-running), went over the Harland and Wolff shipyard, and John was treated to a reading of part of Louis' novel. By 12 September, Louis' twenty-first birthday, his guest had gone and he was depressed. The occasion was marked with a pair of gold cuff-links, but no other celebration, and he thought enviously of Auden in Berlin and the Beazleys on their working holiday in Greece. Oxford and October seemed intolerably distant.

Eventually they appeared, but almost at once Louis had to return to Carrickfergus for his sister's wedding on 18 October. It seems likely that he supplemented his father's teetotal hospitality with something more traditional, for that evening he and a bridesmaid rolled one of the wedding presents, 'a huge and hideous china jar', down the stairs to shatter at his stepmother's feet. He was glad to return to Oxford, but found himself lonely when he got there. Most of his friends were working, but he managed to lure Adrian, John, Moore and a couple of others to a high tea, 'the very highest ever had', in his room. It ended on a particularly high note with John, at the top of a chestnut tree, playing 'Here we go round the mulberry bush' on a tin whistle, while the rest of the company danced round the bole below.

A week later, most of the group set off in a hired car for lunch in Cambridge with Anthony and Leonard Woolf, publisher of the Hogarth Press, whom Anthony was hoping to interest in Louis' *Blind Fireworks*. The poet was at the wheel, but his mind may have been on his poems rather than the road for, swerving to avoid an oncoming Chrysler, he lost control of the car which, after several gyrations, came to rest on its side. He crawled out, muttering '*sic transit gloria mundi*'. Adrian suffered a broken collar bone, Moore a cut on the ankle, and while they were being treated by a doctor, Louis was found sitting by the roadside murmuring dreamily:

> Glory to God
> That we still are terrestial!
> Ichabod, ichabod,
> Our souls shall go to God
> Winging their way
> Through the regions celestial.
> Glory to God
> That we still are terrestial!

The car had to be abandoned and a slow bus delivered the survivors at Cambridge, but not before Blunt and Woolf had gone their separate ways.

With Mods behind him, and the final exams in ancient history and philosophy for 'Greats' (the second part of the course in *literae humaniores*) more than a year and a half ahead, MacNeice could give more time to poetry and poets. Auden had left Oxford with a third-class degree in English and a book of his poems printed by Stephen Spender, then an undergraduate at University College. He and Louis were – and were to remain – slightly wary of each other. MacNeice makes only one brief appearance in Spender's autobiography, *World Within World*, and MacNeice in *The Strings are False* writes ironically of his undergraduate contemporary: 'Spender was the nearest to the popular romantic conception of a poet – a towering angel not quite sure if he was fallen, thinking of himself as the poet always, moving in his own limelight.' Both had poems in *Oxford Poetry 1928*, an anthology edited by Clere Parsons. That term there were two more Old Marlburian recruits to the ranks of the poets – Bernard Spencer of Corpus and Edouard Roditi of Balliol – and both suffered the fate MacNeice had suffered before them. Spencer, son of a High Court Judge in Madras, wore a bow tie and sidewhiskers – one wing of which was forcibly removed by hearties who raided his room. He refused to shave off the other, 'continued to read *transition*, and to decorate his lampshade with "surrealist, mildly obscene figures in pencil"'. Roditi, like Spencer, both a poet and a painter, was the victim of three such raids in one night, the last of them led by 'the honourable Stanley, vowed enemy of all aestheticism'. MacNeice came to Roditi's defence with a triolet published in *The University News*:

After Mr. Roditi

> gOd is complaining
> > of the hOnourable Stanley.
> > it will not stop raining,
> > for god is complaining
> > that he rows without training
> > because he's so mANly
> gOd is complaining
> > of the honourable Stanley.

On a higher literary plane, Louis was revising the poems collected under the title *Blind Fireworks* and trying to find a publisher for them. After the failure of Anthony's attempt to introduce him to Leonard Woolf of the Hogarth Press, he approached Gollancz (where Moore's sister, Lexy, worked as a secretary), perhaps with no very high hope of success, since it seems likely that they had earlier rejected a collection of Auden's. Successful, however, he was, and probably before the end of the year heard they would publish *Blind Fireworks* the following spring.

Poetry was not Louis' only distraction that summer. The Beazleys had moved from St Giles to 100 Holywell Street, and he became an increasingly frequent visitor, but now he talked less to Marie than to Mary. They went for walks together and he was pleasantly surprised to find she had (she said) 'a passion for nature'. One day, encouraged by rum and a Mozart horn concerto, he found himself engaged to her. Neither saw the need at this stage of telling their parents, and Louis spent the last week of term almost entirely at 100 Holywell, where Mrs Beazley bafflingly remarked that he was 'just a stream to sit by and throw pebbles into'.

He returned to Carrickfergus in high spirits, for once, and wrote to Anthony: 'I filled the font in the church with holly so that 3 infants were pricked to death by my father short-sightedly plunging them into it.' In a more difficult letter he told Mary of his mongol brother, having been frightened to mention the fact before. Her response was alarming. He assured her that the condition was not hereditary and she replied that her family would have to have medical assurance of this. Since the Archdeacon and his wife knew nothing of the engagement and Louis was apprehensive about their reaction to the news, he could not enquire about a medical certificate, so the problem – for the moment – was shelved.

Back in Oxford for the start of term, he saw Mary every day for two or three weeks and found it wearing. Perhaps to help him forget the volcano smoking in Holywell, he deliberately mixed his drinks at a Merton lunch-party from which he reeled off, wildly drunk, into the insufficiently sobering rain. Unfortunately, he ran into a policeman who put him in a cell to cool off. By a pleasant coincidence, which Louis might not at the time have appreciated, the previous week he had read a paper called 'The Policeman' to the Pelican Club, a Corpus society, and on the morning of his arrest an Oxford paper had asked what the police were going to do about Mr MacNeice, since Mr MacNeice had read a paper about them?

The Merton authorities were not amused and some were for sending him down. His tutor, however, hoping he might get a First in Greats as in Mods (and Firsts were rare in Merton), told him to write a letter of apology to the Warden. A first draft of this argued at length that it was 'good for young men to get drunk because they need a spiritual catharsis', but Adrian convinced him that this could only earn him expulsion, and a final draft was more conventional. The Warden decided not to risk the loss of a potential First, but said he would write to the Archdeacon. Louis, preferring a showdown to being shown up, beat him to the draw, sending his father a telegram: EXPECT DONS LETTER DETAILING CHILDISH OUTBURSTS SO SORRY MERELY EMOTIONAL CRISIS FINDING MELODRAMATIC OUTLET AM NOW WELL OUT OF IT AND ENGAGED TO BE MARRIED GAUDEAMUS LOVE EVER WRITING = LOUIS [.]

His writing – to say he was engaged to a Jewess – dismayed the Archdeacon if anything more than the Warden's letter. Louis, confiding in his closest Oxford friend, told John (for the first time) that he was engaged; that Mary's grandfather would cut her out of his will if she married a Christian; and prophesied thunder and lightning from Carrickfergus. In the hope of averting the last of these, John sent the Rectory a telegram that included the sentence CAN VOUCH FOR LOUIS'S RATIONALITY and followed it up with a letter to Mrs Mac-Neice. This produced a reply from the Archdeacon confirming John's worst fears:

It was good of you to write. But how could you think I could approve Louis' choice? It is a terrible disappointment. It promises to both nothing but misery. I think it is shamefully wrong for Mrs. Beazley, that is if she had reason to anticipate an engagement.

Altogether I am very much crushed by the news. Could you not have saved Louis from his recent follies? Of course you could not: I must not be unreasonable.

This letter is for yourself. The thought of an engagement to a Jewess is dreadful.

If she is a religious Jewess it will be awful, & if she is an indifferent one it will be no better.

Louis' sister believed her father's reaction was not prompted by anti-Semitism so much as simple grief that his son's choice was not a good Christian, who would lead him back into the fold.

The Archdeacon's letter was followed by a telegram announcing the MacNeices' imminent arrival in Oxford and instructing Louis and John to meet them at the station. Telling his own parents of these developments, John wrote:

the stage is setting for a tip top storm. Picture the opposition of the Archdeacon, broad, magnificent, pontifical, Irish, backed by all the weight and majesty of the church and the darting, lightning, and witty Mrs. [Beazley]. She's got all the cards really, 'The idea of those country folk thinking their son such a great man in Oxford, that anyone should want him for their daughter.'

But before that we've got to meet these outraged parents. Think of trying to explain things to the deaf Mrs. MacNeice. The whole affair is too ludicrous for words. And not content with Mary and his drunkenness, Louis seems to have chosen the moment, perhaps unavoidably, for revealing that he cannot really call himself a Christian.

John liked Mary and thought her a good influence on Louis, 'getting him to go to bed in time, to smoke less and wear warmer clothes'; and when the MacNeices had arrived and summoned the unfortunate girl to appear before them in Merton, he told them so. Later, giving his parents an account of the next act of this comic opera, he wrote:

All the time Mrs. MacNeice was magnificent: her usual jocular birdlike self, prancing round the room, shaking her fist at Louis's pictures and covering them up with newspaper. The Archdeacon was thoughtful and silent except for a stupendous wink when Mrs. MacNeice was telling me how my telegram had arrived 'vouch for Louis's nationality' instead of 'rationality'.

The rest of us then went out, but going back to my room after a bit I found Louis and Mrs. M. there having left the unfortunate Mary face to face with the archdeacon. We went back and Mrs. M. took the place of the archd. as examiner. Then Mary went home and the rest of us (I having been absorbed into the family) took tea at the Shamrock.

Fortified by this breath of the old country the parents (?) sallied forth to battle. The opponents found themselves in perfect unison, agreeing that it was impertinent of Louis and, with a pleasing formality, that it should be called an understanding and not an engagement.

John's involvement in Louis' affairs was not only diplomatic; as a passable artist, he had been engaged to design a cover for a new literary magazine, *Sir Galahad*. This was published on 21 February with

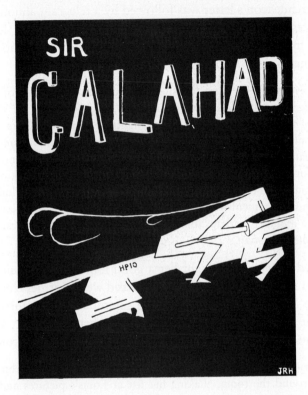

contributions by Harold Acton, Christopher Holme, Osbert Lancaster, Clere Parsons and his fiancée Sonia Hambourg, MacNeice, Roditi, Spencer, and Spender. Louis contributed a negligible prose piece and two more interesting poems, 'Epitaph for Louis' and (under the pseudonym John Bogus Rosifer) a villanelle entitled 'Paradise Lost', beginning

> Caught in Apollo's blended dream
> On the dim marge of Poesy
> My rose-red lips unlock to scream.

These mark an advance on most of Louis' poems to have found their way into print so far, but were written too late for inclusion in the little linen-backed book published on 18 March. This was dedicated 'To Giovanna' (the first of Mary's five names) and the poet's Foreword ended with an explanation of his book's title: 'I have called this collection *Blind Fireworks* because they go quickly through their antics against an important background, and fall and go out quickly.' He fails to say why their dark background is important, a characteristic evasion sensed by a reviewer of *Oxford Poetry 1929* who wrote:

Two of the most accomplished poets in this book, Mr. MacNeice and Mr. Calder-Marshall, ... are both, I think, afraid of giving themselves away. Hence their verse has the appearance of disguise – they have a double self, or at least they like trying to play the censor on the threshold of the unconscious.

The Foreword to *Blind Fireworks* warns its reader that 'several of these poems are founded on esoteric mythology'. Their references to Adonis, Pythagoras, and the Twilight of the Gods proclaim their modernist descent from Sir James Frazer and Jessie Weston by way of T. S. Eliot, but the dark background to the most impressive of MacNeice's *Blind Fireworks* is not a public but a private mythology – that, for example, behind the poet's

Reminiscences of Infancy

Trains came threading quietly through my dozing childhood
Gentle murmurs nosing through a summer quietude,
Drawing in and out, in and out, their smoky ribbons,
Parting now and then, and launching full-rigged galleons
And scrolls of smoke that hung in a shifting epitaph.
Then distantly the noise declined like a descending graph,
Sliding downhill gently to the bottom of the distance
(For now all things are there that all were here once);
And so we hardly noticed when that metal murmur came.
But it brought us assurance and comfort all the same,
And in the early night they soothed us to sleep,
And the chain of the rolling wheels bound us in deep
Till all was broken by that menace from the sea,
The steel-bosomed siren calling bitterly.

Written in 1926, this offers a map of the mythic terrain of the Mac-
Neice country that was to remain essentially unchanged for the rest of
his life. The trains that pass from the high ground to the west – from
garden to cemetery – on their way to the low ground by the sea, and
back again, have unmistakably feminine associations: 'threading
quietly . . . Drawing in and out, in and out, their smoky ribbons'. Their
gentle murmurs, 'Sliding downhill *gently* to the bottom of the distance'
would be echoed in a later poem:

> My mother wore a yellow dress;
> Gently, gently, gentleness.

The gentle murmurs of surrogate mother-comfort are succeeded by a
silent 'shifting epitaph' of smoke, as one after another the trains seem
to follow her underground, and the sleeping child forgets that 'now all
things are there that all were here once'.

Beyond the cemetery to the south-east was the rector's Church of St
Nicholas and beyond that the sea. The bells of the one and the
foghorns of the other – bells and sea are associated in several of the
book's poems – could be heard clearly from the Rectory, and Louis
came to associate both with his father. 'My mother was comfort and
my father was somewhat alarm,' he says in *The Strings are False*.
'When I was in bed I could hear his voice below in the study – and I
knew that he was alone – intoning away, communing with God. And
because of his conspiracy with God I was afraid of him.' The poem
makes the same transition from comfort to alarm, the voice he would
forever associate with his mother's replacement, 'The steel-bosomed
siren calling bitterly'.

MacNeice's own reading of this poem (twenty-three years after he
wrote it) is significantly different: significant in that the censor still
guards the threshold of the subconscious. Discussing 'Trains in the
Distance', as it came to be called, in his essay 'Experiences with
Images', he makes no mention of his mother, but speaks of 'certain
early contacts with both mental illness and mental deficiency (these
latter may explain the *petrification* images which appear pretty often in
my poems . . .)'. This explanation is at variance with the first such
image in the first poem of his first book – 'Death, the broken statue' –
and with the coffins, corpses, dirges, funerals, grave-clothes, obsequies,

tombs, and incessant references to marble in the poems that follow. These last may owe something to the marble tomb of the Chichester mother, father, and children in the Church of St Nicholas.

The poem that follows 'Reminiscences of Infancy' in *Blind Fireworks*, 'Child's Terror', shows the same mythic pattern. It begins in an Edenic garden:

> When I was small, each tree was voluble,
> Each shrubbery Dodona. I would sit
> In a prancing swing and soar through wonderful
> Confetti of green and blue.

The colours of Innocence are succeeded by those of Experience:

> Then autumn came, deciduous and bland,
> And drew its yellow lace across the window. . . .
> If I were the fuchsias I should weep in autumn
> Red tears to stain the years (white flowers in the dark),
> And when the snow came down I should call to nurse
> To come and brush away that marble tomb
> And give new water to the withering years.

As autumn has succeeded spring, night follows day, and the child – falling into a nightmare 'hole without a bottom' – cries out not to its mother, but to a nurse:

> Turn a light on my snowy counterpane,
> Tell me it is linen, it is not rock,
> Only tell me I am alive again
> And the sun will come again, the spring again,
> And the pampas grass will raise plume aloft again –
> And stop the clock, nurse, stop the clock.

Blind Fireworks is full of clocks, and this child's closing cry introduces the poles of fixity and flux that will generate the voltage of so many poems that will follow over the years.

Many other of the contents of this first book are not susceptible to such a biographical interpretation. More like fireworks, these go through their semantic antics and burn out quickly. As their most perceptive critic, Peter McDonald, has written: 'the self-consciousness of [*Blind Fireworks*'] use of mythological metaphor as deferral of reality entails a general retreat from reality'. The philosophy student of 1929, wandering through a walled garden 'planted with paper flowers', was in no great hurry to seek out reality, and the poet of 1929 held firmly to only two tenets: '(i) that what makes a poem a poem is its artificiality; (ii) that poetry is a pursuit for the few, that these few are the pick of humanity, and that when they speak they speak for themselves rather than for others'.

Louis spent the Easter vacation in Carrickfergus, writing to Mary – as she to him – every day. He also worked on his novel, which returned to Oxford with him as a completed typescript. John read it at the end of April and found himself

unable to give any useful criticism of it; trying, as always, to see him through it; except that it seems to demonstrate more of faith than of the morbid despair that his people fear they find in his work. It reproduces for me more vividly than I could have imagined possible the smells and cadences of Marlborough, but that is why I cannot criticize it.

Louis then sent that or another copy to William Heinemann. The publisher's most junior reader, Rupert Hart-Davis, must have responded encouragingly, since Louis wrote to thank him for 'smiling on my novel' and to say he was prepared to revise it 'to a certain extent but to make violent changes would be rather difficult'. His hopes came to nothing and the book was never published (indeed, no copy is known to have survived), although in 1930 John Betjeman feared that it had. He wrote to his Marlborough and Oxford contemporary, Patrick Balfour, who was then writing a gossip column for the *Daily Sketch*:

I have not read it yet, but I believe the new School book called 'Out of Step' by Derek Walker Smith (Gollancz) is really by Louis MacNeice – that fucking little Oxford Aesthete who lives near Belfast. If so it will be about Marlborough and about me – for I remember someone telling me that MacNeice had written a school story which contained a description of me. Please expose him so that he gets lynched – unless it is a Good Book – but I expect, if it is by this creature, it will be a sexless, complaining affair.

Fortunately, or unfortunately, Betjeman's fears proved groundless.

In 1929, MacNeice was playing a prominent role in Oxford literary circles. He was editor, with Stephen Spender, of *Oxford Poetry 1929*;

and, on 6 May, hosted a meeting of the University's Poetry Society, in his Merton room, at which Walter de la Mare read a paper on the craftsmanship of poetry. This was enthusiastically reviewed the following week in the second (and last) issue of *Sir Galahad*. Edited by MacNeice, it opened with a long editorial, entitled 'Our God Bogus', in which he repudiates the scepticism that 'showed itself in "Pure Form" (see Clive Bell who had no use for "Real Life") and in formlessness (which professed to be "real life" put down on paper)'. Like Plato proposing the banning of poets, he concludes:

Robert Louis Stevenson set himself to learn polite writing; this was bogus. For conventions are not rules of 'style', drawing-pins to fasten one's matter on the board. So we may ban the stylist (*qua* stylist). As we have banned the realist (*qua* realist). And the sceptic (*qua* sceptic). For all these are bogus. Whereas we are willing to admit ragamuffins like Mr. Cummings (for there is form in his disintegration) and poseurs like the Sitwells (for there is method in their madness) and pedants like Mr. Eliot (for there is life in his pedantry). But the transcendentalists (*qua* transcendentalists – who went out when the sceptics came in) we shall not readmit them. But assert without blushing the Hellenic platitude 'Remember that thou art neither a beast nor a god but a man' (which means a bit of each).

He admitted to subsequent pages of his magazine poems by his friends Hilton, Shepard, Spencer and Spender; prose pieces by Blunt ('Paris Exhibitions'), Green-Armytage, Hilton, and Sonia Hambourg, among others.

When not playing ring-master to Oxford's literary circus, he was usually to be found canoeing with Mary, dressed like a Dresden shepherdess, along the upper reaches of the Isis. On these expeditions he may have read to her from a second-hand copy of Sir Arthur Quiller-Couch's edition of *Early English Lyrics* that he gave her, tenderly inscribed:

To my Love
    Asking her not to
go away anywhere Ever because
I could not possibly bear it, but
to come and be my ~~own~~ own
Pusheen in a garret or possibly
Nonsuchery or at any rate
somewhere; for ever and ever to
be his Maire;
    from for ever and ever her
            Louis.

Relations with Mrs Beazley were predictably strained, but she did agree to accompany her daughter to another of Louis' lunch parties. This was hardly more successful than the first, since another of his guests was a sinister German baron, an ardent follower of Herr Hitler and the Nazi movement, about which Mrs Beazley (with her Jewish Viennese contacts) would have known more than her host.

After difficult negotiations with both sets of parents, it was agreed that Louis and Mary should spend much of the summer together – first with the MacNeices on the island of Achill, then with a Bloomfield uncle of Mary's at his villa in St Tropez. In August, they crossed to the west coast of Ireland and drove on, over causeway and bridge, to Achill. Haycocks and piled sheaves, hedges dripping with blood-red fuschsias gave way to an austere landscape of bog-grass and purple heather. There were turf-stacks beside the road and noble mountains in the distance. The MacNeices had rented a house on the northern coast and, from this, Louis and Mary made expeditions to Carrick Kildavnet Castle and the megalithic tombs on the purple flank of Slievemore. They swam in the green sea off Keem Strand and were walking along a road – he with his arm around her waist – when an old woman called out: 'That's a grand way for a girl to be – linked to a boy.' Mary liked Ireland, and Louis liked Provence 'with its garlic cooking and rowdy

The causeway over Achill Sound

cicadas and stars', but something was missing. As together they built domestic castles in the air, he wondered about his role as the Good Jewish Husband, and why he was no longer writing poetry.

When he returned to Oxford in October, it was to 26 St Giles, a house on the north side of the street shared with Adrian and Moore and 'two scrannel voiced landladies, half-sisters, who had just bought a vacuum cleaner and could not leave it alone'. The difficulty of getting down to work, after his summer's indolent idyll, was compounded by Mary who, having no work herself, would arrive on the doorstep every day at two o'clock. The next five hours would be spent in a recital of goings on at 100 Holywell, of Mary's worries and nightmares. After dinner, Adrian would fetch a jug of beer from The Lamb and Flag next door; Louis would at last pick up a book, but could only keep awake by reading it aloud to his friend. In the first of two long despatches to John (who, having 'gone down' in 1928, was now studying architecture in Germany), Louis says that he has practically been banned from 100 Holywell, because Mrs Beazley thinks him 'totally undesirable'. It seems likely that John's reply expressed surprise at the Beazleys' continuing opposition, prompting Louis to tell him something he had not divulged before:

The crux of the matter is that I have got an idiot brother (a 'mongol' i.e. non-hereditary.) Hence the greater part of my rows with Mrs. B. owing to my inefficiency in producing non-hereditary evidence.

I will now start at the beginning: my father was engaged to my mother for God knows how long & it seems to me that when they did marry they made rather a hash of all the more material side of it e.g. not taking proper precautions for child-birth etc. My birth was managed so rottenly that my mother had eventually to have a hysterectomy; after which she was ill off & on till she died for obscure reasons when I was just 7. Even the operation was done in a very crude manner which my sister tells me is now obsolete.

From the age of about 5 or 6 till 8 or 9 my sister & I (& my brother) lived all together at home without being in any way properly looked after; first we had a hopelessly uneducated woman from a farm in Co. Armagh who used to tell my sister how she would soon die because she (i.e. my sister) had so many colds, & what nasty things they would write on her grave-stone. Then we had a worthless zany or two; I think for several years I never had my teeth washed. As for my father he loomed about the house & hardly ever spoke to us. At one time I had to sleep in the same room with him & all night he used to moan & mutter & toss about.

My stepmother appeared when I was about 9. My brother was sent off to an Institute in Scotland & my sister & I were sent to school. As my stepmother's ideas were wholly quaker, mixed with a naive & charming innocence & a little snobbery, it was one dotty epoch on top of another. I always remained terrified of my father.

Once or twice while I was a little boy my brother was brought from Scotland to stay with us. Each time he seemed to be uglier & more monstrous & on one occasion I had to sleep in the same room for a fortnight; one morning he woke me up by beating me on the face with a shoe.

When I was at Marlborough I had already escaped from the 'fear of God' & the missionary atmosphere & general unwholesomeness. When I was 17, however, owing to a (sentimental &, I think, foolish) proposal of my sister, the family reinstated my brother at home. In case you don't know what Mongols are like, they are stunted & very ugly but very goodnatured; my brother, for instance, is talking & laughing all day long; he, of course, talks only very imperfectly.

The result of this was that while the rest of the family seemed even to enjoy it (as a Christian burden?) I became in a strange way hollow; I am only filling up again now. My only way out was to imagine it away, when I was not at home.

My family have always been making bloody mistakes; they sent (I am not quite sure of this but deduced it from writings in a margin) my sister to school at the age of 14 without telling her anything about adolescence etc.

Anyhow this is all irrelevant; the summer you stayed with me, my brother was away in England. I expected my family to let it out to you; I only objected to talking about it myself.

I seem to be writing this up more morbid than it was. I was really quite merry most of the time, & anyhow I devised an adequate scheme, or rather drift, of life. But then Mary came.

Here I crashed. We hove up to each other on Monday in the last week of the Christmas term & then we hove away again; I felt I was too hollow for anyone to marry. Besides I knew I ought to explain everything first.

On Tuesday, after being very sad and then merrily-&-sadly drunk the night before, I rushed off (after your lunch-party) to the Judge's Lodgings & we got engaged. Then (this is where I really was swinish) I didn't tell Mary anything about my brother. It all seemed a myth anyhow. Besides the world seemed sordid enough (e.g. Nonesuch) to spoil a myth before it spoiled itself.

We went to Cambridge the next week-end. Then I stayed with you, then with Anthony; while staying with Anthony I went (on the Sunday) up to Oxford & spent the afternoon with Mary & told her nothing; for, just as I thought of unloading it all, she said she had a horror of lunatics.

The next day (Sunday) [*sic*] I wrote her a long letter (from Anthony's house) all about it. Then began the complications which have been going on ever since.

This frank and touching 'Apologia pro Vita Mea' (as Louis called it) then proceeded to give a seven-page chronology of those 'complications': Mrs Beazley requesting assurances that mongolism was non-hereditary; these delayed, given verbatim, found insufficient; certificates requested, but still not forthcoming from the Archdeacon who, for all his promises, found it as hard to pursue the matter as his son.

Louis meanwhile was finding it hard to pursue philosophy. Hilton, reading *The Strings are False*, was surprised at the space given to his friend's philosophical thinking at Oxford, remembering his mounting impatience with grey abstractions; an impatience confirmed by such statements in Louis' later letters to him as 'Lots of lovely particulars; I suggest keeping generalisations out of it', and 'Philosophy should be kept strictly on the mantelpiece.' In *The Strings are False*, he called philosophy 'an exquisite engine of destruction', and the adjective suggests the satisfactions of fencing with intellectual swordsmen worthy of his steel. He evidently liked and respected his philosophy tutor, Geoffrey Mure, even when he told Professor Beazley that MacNeice would probably get 'a very poor 2nd' in Greats. Reporting this to John, he added: 'This is much more encouraging than anything they said about me before Mods. (Excuse conceit.)' Mure, a pupil of F. H. Bradley and 'one of Oxford's few remaining Neo-Hegelians', believed 'that neither logic nor ethics could be separated from metaphysics'. Louis was happy to be persuaded of this, since he

enjoyed metaphysics very much and hoped for a world-view. Whereas Mary only hoped for a house of her own. But it will be possible, I thought, to achieve a compromise; I can live with Mary in her house and still have a private wire to the cosmic outposts.

Mary being as determinedly anti-intellectual as her mother, and Graham, John, and Wystan having 'gone down', Louis was starved for intellectual conversation, but found it in one unexpected quarter:

I had met Father D'Arcy, the great Jesuit and authority on St. Thomas Aquinas, and he alone among Oxford dons seemed to me to have the glamour that medieval students looked for in their masters. Intellect incarnate in a beautiful head, wavy grey hair and delicate features; a hawk's eyes. I suspected his religion, of course, but it at least, I thought, has given him a *savoir-faire* which you do not find in these wishy-washy humanists; it was a treat to watch him carving a dish of game.

D'Arcy was said to be able to roll a cigarette with one hand while driving a car with the other and, more to the point, he it was who had written so perceptively of Louis' poems in *The Oxford Outlook* review of *Oxford Poetry 1929* observing that, 'as for Mr MacNeice, there are hardly any limits to his powers'.

Louis spent Christmas at Carrickfergus under clouds of parental disapproval and philosophy and, returning to Oxford in January, went into academic high gear as he had before Mods. Giving thought to life after Greats, he had told John 'I want to go to one of those universities like Leeds or Stellenbosch' (presumably because they were a long way from his parental orbit and Mary's), but in April he wrote to Anthony: 'I am just about to get a job of £1000 a year as the result of writing a flippant letter to the authority in question & enclosing an assassin-like photograph. Or rather, I should say he took it very well & has expressed a wish to see me.' The authority in question was either Oliver Thompson, Professor of Latin at Birmingham University, or, more likely, Professor E. R. Dodds, Professor of Greek. They had advertised for an Assistant Lecturer in Classics. The Merton authorities said that MacNeice 'was unquestionably gifted but unfortunately rather a difficult character and not always a steady worker – he spent too much time writing poetry'. The description attracted Dodds, an Ulsterman of high intelligence and granite-like integrity, himself 'a difficult character' (who had been expelled from school for 'insolence to the headmaster'), and a poet (of whom Yeats had said 'that he liked that young man's poems more than he liked that young man'). Louis' interview was a success. He and Dodds took to each other at once and, despite his tutor's heavily qualified recommendation, Louis was offered the job. Writing to thank Dodds for his hospitality, his telegram, and the confidence it showed in someone who was still an undergraduate, he touched on a personal problem:

As for digs, this raises a difficulty (or facility!) – in that I have some hopes of being married in the immediate future and, if possible, before I come to you in October. This has been for some time in the air and mainly depends on how much of a joint annual income my fiancée and I discover ourselves to have – apart from what I earn. I think it very probable that we shall find it feasible to get married.

I asked your wife whether the University objected to young lecturers being married, and she told me that they were at first a little taken aback by John Waterhouse producing a wife but that they were reassured when they found that it did not prevent him going about with the undergraduates. In my case (if I got married) I have an exceptional reason for confidence in guaranteeing no disastrous consequences – in that my future wife has been brought up in the family of an Oxford don and is, if anything, only too alive to the necessity both of industry in one's work proper and of phil-undergraduate activity ἐν παρέργῳ.* And I feel that, if married, I should prove in general more fit for my work.

Dodd's characteristically kindly response to this appeal gave MacNeice just the encouragement he needed as he came to his last academic hurdle, and more than compensated for a final counter-attack from 100 Holywell:

On the first day of Greats, my final examination, Mary was sent to see a prominent neurologist who allegedly told her I was mentally unsound; I had a psychosis and would sooner or later commit suicide. But why, she asked, would I commit suicide? Because I had a psychosis. But how did he know I had a psychosis? Because people who commit suicide always have psychoses. Unable to answer this logic Mary asked if it wouldn't be a good idea for him to see me. Quite unnecessary, he answered; he knew all about me that he wanted to. Besides, he had read one of my poems. The interview was a stalemate; the neurologist got his fee but Mary was depressed. I went on writing examination papers.

They were married on the morning of 21 June, the last day of the Summer Term, in Oxford Town Hall's Registry Office. Arriving there, late, in a taxi from which Mary emerged with a bouquet of roses, they were greeted by cheering crowds, mistaking her for the Princess Royal who was to make an official visit to Oxford that day. Graham accom-

* Greek for 'on the side'.

panied them to the Registry Office, but neither the Beazleys nor the MacNeices came to the wedding. Mary's best friend, Betty Cooke, would have been there had she not been recovering from an appendectomy in the Acland Nursing Home. Her sister Helen, however, had commissioned a Christ Church cook to make a little wedding cake, and this was eaten in the Nursing Home at the patient's bedside. That afternoon, Mr and Mrs MacNeice set off for the Lamb Hotel, Burford, and a honeymoon in the Cotswolds. They were very tired and looking forward to a long rest.

CHAPTER 10

Hazy City

I came to live in this hazy city
To work in a building caked with grime
Teaching the classics to Midland students . . . .
'Autumn Journal', *CP*, p. 115

None of the MacNeices' wedding presents can have been more welcome than the news that Louis had added a First in Greats to his First
in Mods. Writing to thank Dodds for his letter of congratulations, he
said he attributed this unexpected success 'entirely to Heaven and my
wife'; a curious explanation from an atheist whose wife had done more
to impede than to encourage his studies over the past two years. Dodds
– also an atheist, but one described by Father D'Arcy as 'the sort of
atheist a Jesuit enjoys talking to' – was surprised to receive a letter
from D'Arcy, saying that Providence had committed to his care a very
rare and exceptional person and that he must take this responsibility
seriously. Dodds drily commented on this charge: 'I doubt if I did for
Louis all that Providence and Father D'Arcy would have wished', but it
is difficult to believe that either would have found cause for complaint.
Over the years that followed, he and his wife Bet acquired the unsought
role of surrogate parents to the poet so emotionally and intellectually
remote from his own father and stepmother; and after MacNeice's
death, no father could have done more for his son's memory than
Dodds as his Literary Executor.

His first act on Louis' behalf, after appointing him, was to find him
somewhere to live. One of his more sociable acquaintances was the
Professor of Commerce, Philip Sargant Florence, an American educated at Rugby, Cambridge, and Columbia, who lived with his wife in
a red-brick, twenty-six-room Victorian mansion, called Highfield, in

Selly Park on the southern side of Birmingham. Mrs Florence, Lella, was also American. She had, wrote Louis,

a charming smile, violent red hair and vitality, had spent her life furthering causes; an evangelist in her teens, deputy of Henry Ford's peace ship, a protagonist of Birth Control in England. In her time off from political committees, peace campaigns and protest meetings, she would chop down trees with a long-handled axe or give evening parties to those who were elect and correct, to those who were Left and jolly.

Philip Sargant Florence had known Maynard Keynes at Cambridge; his sister Alix had married James Strachey, brother of Lytton; and these contacts had brought him briefly to the outer perimeter of the Bloomsbury Group. Lella, who was an activist rather than an intellectual, had a vision of Highfield as 'a better kind of Bloomsbury', a forum for debate, a salon for the enlightened shakers of society as well as for its makers. She, who had fallen in love with the house when she first saw it in 1929, had persuaded her husband to buy it, sweeping aside his objection that it was far too large for a family of four with the proposal that they should convert the extra space into flats. Helped by a local handyman, she made three of these in the house and turned a coachman's quarters and stables, across a cobbled courtyard, into a fourth. It was this flat that Dodds brought to the attention of his newly appointed lecturer.

At the end of their honeymoon, the MacNeices had gone, first, to stay at Graham's family home in Guildford; then, after a few nights with Mary's grandmother in London, they moved on to Oxford, where Louis took his degree and began preparing lectures for Birmingham. Hearing of the Highfield flat, they went up to see it; worried for a week or two over whether they could afford to pay a rent of £100 a year; and, early in September, decided they could. Louis had his salary, Mary an annual allowance of £300 a year from her grandfather and some small supplementary income from investments. They moved north on the 30th – taking with them Graham's gift of a marmalade kitten called Fuzby – and, after five days at the Hagley Grove Hotel (while their flat was being decorated), finally took possession of 'Highfield Cottage'. They found it transformed: bright as a gipsy caravan, with yellow window-frames, a blue front door, pink living-room and landing, yellow master bedroom, and rose-red dining-room. Over the coming months, Mary carried on where the Florences' painters (a couple called Frank and Joan Freeman) had left off, picking out every knob and lintel, every step of the stairs, in a different colour.

She got very annoyed if anyone used the phrase 'colour-scheme'. A colour-scheme for Mary was an affectation of aesthetes, a sheer fiction. She had met too many aesthetes in Oxford. To have colour-schemes was a sign of infertility. No, no, you paint your chest of drawers as the bird sings, and you paint your wardrobe also as the bird sings, and if it is a different bird so much the better.

She spoke in much the same way. Her letters ripple with bird-like chatter, as for example: 'To-day we invented a delightful game; which is racing between chestnuts along the road. There are heaps of them, & its really most exciting, & all our team have got names!' She was happy to have flown the parental nest and to be lining her own. The spoilt and lazy schoolgirl had become an energetic wife and – to her husband's particular satisfaction – an excellent cook.

He was less satisfied with other aspects of his new life. On 8 October he gave his first lecture. Preparing for this, he had skimmed through Tolstoy's *What is Art?* so that he could bring Plato more alive by linking him with Tolstoy. His choice of clothes had a certain relevance to this theme: 'he wore the Oxford undergraduate's uniform of sports jacket, and grey flannel trousers. But ... he did wonders with them, and never were the colours of jacket, shirt, tie and handkerchief more subtly matched and blended.' He was a poor lecturer, however; his public voice a monotonous drone, and by the end of the hour his audience looked as disenchanted as he felt. Birmingham was not a residential university. Its students came in by tram or train from their homes in the suburbs or nearby towns of the Black Country. Most male students in the Arts Faculty wore what had once been their best suits, 'sacred to Sunday', and many carried the briefcases, heavily pregnant with books, that earned them the contemptuous generic title of 'brown-baggers'. Many again were ill-fed and ill-prepared for university work. Their elegant new lecturer was well-fed but equally ill-prepared, in human terms, for what should have been *his* university work: kindling and sustaining their interest in the classics. Familiar only with the pastoral worlds of Carrickfergus, Marlborough, and Oxford, he was at twenty-three an intellectual snob, depressed by his introduction to the hazy city and its seemingly monochromatic inhabitants. For the moment, he withdrew – not by tram or train, but over the fields between Selly Park and the University – into the multi-coloured shell he shared with Mary.

> Life was comfortable, life was fine
> With two in a bed and patchwork cushions
> And checks and tassels on the washing-line,
> A gramophone, a cat, and the smell of jasmine.

Whoever was the first to get out of the new double-bed (from Heals) in the morning would put a record on the gramophone: Sophie Tucker, perhaps, or Elisabeth Schumann, or Segovia's guitar. At the other end of a day teaching 'Virgil, Livy, the usual round', Louis would walk home to supper, after which he and Mary might go to the cinema. Significantly, as he would later record in *The Strings are False* with the honesty characteristic of that book, these expeditions into the alien city were undertaken in a search not for urban reality – as experienced in the deepening Depression by less fortunate citizens of Britain's second largest city – but for romantic illusion:

The organist would come up through the floor, a purple spotlight on his brilliantined head, and play us the 'Londonderry Air' and bow and go back to the tomb. Then the stars would return close-up and the huge Cupid's bows of their mouths would swallow up everybody's troubles – there were no more offices or factories or shops, no more bosses or foremen, no more unemployment and no more employment, no more danger of disease or babies, nothing but bliss in a celluloid world where the roses are always red and the Danube is always blue.

Louis and Mary would hold hands on the twilit threshold of that celluloid world 'like a shopgirl and her boy-friend', but there the resemblance ended. They had no knowledge of bosses and foremen, no share in 'everybody's' troubles and dangers. Mary soon acquired a maid, however, and the lives of this Janet and her relations, together with the lives of the Florences' gardener, Robinson, and his son, Young Robinson, became major topics of conversation in Highfield Cottage.

But, for the MacNeices, they remained 'characters'; more solid than the figures on the cinema screen but, at least initially, inhabitants of a twilit zone between fact and fiction. For Mary, who nourished a fantasy of herself as a future Lady of the Manor (Mrs Beazley crossed with Lella Florence), these were prototypes of the 'domestics and under-gardeners and tenants all of whom would adore her and whom she would treat with the greatest kindness and educate in birth control and hygiene'.

Her first real friend in Birmingham was Bet Dodds, whom she could forgive for being an intellectual, because of her interest in domesticity and dogs. As a lecturer in the University's English Department, and the author of *The Romantic Theory of Poetry* (1926), Bet and Louis had even more in common. At the Dodds's small but comfortable late-Georgian house in Sir Harry's Road, Edgbaston, he would meet over the next few years many who would become close friends. There was a sadness at the centre of Bet's life: after two pregnancies had had to be terminated, due to the threat of eclampsia, she was forced to accept that she could not have the children she and her husband passionately wanted. Like others in the same predicament, she sought consolation in the breeding of dogs. Her success with Sealyham terriers prompted the MacNeices to buy an Old English sheepdog called Cherry, a pug called Prunella, and Betsy the borzoi (perhaps named in honour of Mrs Dodds): a trio Louis described as 'a haystack, a little Dutch cheese and a film-star to take out on strings'. The film-star was not so much a pet, one friend felt, as an aristocratic extension of her master. 'She's frightfully stupid', he would say, 'and very expensive to keep.' From reading two dog-papers a week, the MacNeices soon graduated to visiting shows and then to showing their own coiffed and pedicured animals. This hobby brought them – as the cinema had not – into contact with a wide range of people, from aristocrats to artisans. Thanks to Bet Dodds, the social education of the poet had begun. It was continued, on another front, by her husband.

The Professor (who was usually addressed as Dodds) had, like Louis, been to Oxford and, again like Louis, had nearly been sent down – not for drunkenness (the son of an alcoholic father, Dodds was the most temperate of men), but for failing to disguise his Irish Republican sympathies. His moral courage resembled that of Louis' father, and his

Mary and Betsy

new lecturer soon came to respect – though he could not emulate – his passionate commitment to teaching and the pastoral care of his students. He led his department by force of example, an example that would lead Louis to examine, question, and modify his own élitist system of values. Dodds was a brilliant scholar and, while he did not seek directly to influence Louis' teaching methods, he did urge him to do some research: 'Edit a Greek play perhaps.' The younger man was moved by his enthusiasm but, remembering his experience of the Oxford treadmill, did not fancy a scholarly martyrdom and decided that 'the halo of Wilamowitz' was not for him. Dodds then suggested literary history or criticism, as a result of which Louis began – but was never to finish – a book on Roman Humour. The problem was that he wanted to be a poet but, for reasons that would only later become clear

E. R. Dodds in 1937

to him, his muse had fallen silent. He therefore embarked on a second novel, working on it over the Christmas vacation. It was drafted by May, when he wrote to Anthony Blunt that it contained 'someone vaguely like you. . . . Only no one will think he's you because he's a) of medium stature and b) well-tailored.' He went on: 'If you think of a good nom de plume for me, do let me know. It seems reviewers blackball one if they know one's an academic. I want to keep my Christian name though.' At some point he settled – and probably not at Blunt's suggestion – on 'Louis Malone', a name with a good Irish pedigree ('Sweet Molly Malone') and just a hint of himself as the Romantic Solitary (Louis M[.]alone).

He sent a copy to Rupert Hart-Davis, who had written encouragingly about his previous novel. Hart-Davis found its successor 'readable'; offered to send it to Heinemann; and generously volunteered to read the proofs if it were accepted. His praise of a minor villain of the book, the Revd John Bilbatrox, produced an interesting response from the novelist:

By the way (as you say you like Bilbatrox) I hope to write a novel about North of Ireland clergyman (one of the few subjects I know something about) – mainly hypocrites but one, at least, hopelessly sincere.

Despite Hart-Davis's good offices, Heinemann did not accept the book. In January 1932, MacNeice tells Blunt he is revising it and, in March, writes triumphantly: 'my second novel, "Roundabout Way", which I had given to an agent, has just got itself accepted by Puttenham's* (all along with Marie Stopes)'. In October, he sent Blunt a parcel with a letter saying, less euphorically: 'Herewith my unhappy novel in its goddammed wrapper and full of other people's punctuation. I wrote it 2 years ago and am not now very interested in it, especially . . . seeing that it was a negative experiment, an attempt to write a novel according to popular standards "coherent".' This is probably an honest statement, but MacNeice's coolness may also owe something to embarrassment at the portrait of Blunt that his friend would find in the book. Hogley is unmistakable: a brilliant, cynical and witty young don, he dislikes women, has strong views on architecture, and is consistently described as the serpent in the garden: 'his head poised like a cobra' with a 'snaky smile'.

Roundabout Way is a light-hearted romantic novel (containing many references to romance and its cognates), in which Boy meets Girl, loses Girl, recovers Girl and, at the last, seems likely to live with her happily ever after. It is almost certainly a sequel to the earlier public-school novel, and chapters 8 and 9 describe a return to Hillbury/ Marlborough that may well be a recycling of material from the first book. *Roundabout Way* is unashamedly autobiographical. Devlin Urquhart, its orphan hero, has abandoned his course in philosophy at Oxford and been diagnosed, *in absentia*, by 'England's leading neuro-logist', Sir Randal Belcher, as suffering from '*Acute* psychosis . . . bound to end in suicide' – a diagnosis based on the subject's alleged wild behaviour and a paper glorifying intolerance 'and full of remarks about courtesans', delivered to an Oxford college society. Devlin runs off to disguise himself as a gardener, saying to the father of a friend (recognizable as John Hilton): 'SEX and LIFE are the two great things to avoid . . . that's why I'm going to be a gardener. I imagine you don't

* A misspelling of Putnams.

get either if you're a gardener.' His phoney Northumberland accent is recognized as such, and his cover blown, by Sir Randal's spirited and rebellious daughter Janet. She looks like Mary: has a roundish face, 'like a rather mischievous moon', white skin, dark hair, and 'a ballet dancer's figure'. She, too, 'dances like perfection' and wears chypre. More interesting are Devlin's resemblances to his creator: 'Thought of being taken to church when wan and little .... The smell of pew varnish, the marble skull opposite belonging to John Hogarth, the frightening intonations about *sin, hell, death*.' Devlin 'wished his mother was alive. Not his father though.' This reflection leads into a dream that seems a conflation of Louis' Scottish fantasy and his Marlborough dream – if such it was – of the maternal spectre in the cemetery:*

He dreamed he was straightway in the middle of a vast garden with tall threatening yew trees and an unending series of terraced lawns, of the smoothest possible grass, dotted with stone vases of flowers. Suddenly he was slipping into the house which had appeared from nowhere, and .... at last in a room where there was a table with a pot of tulips on it, he found a girl standing; and it flooded his mind at once that this was his own life's lady. Before anything could be said she vanished and he was running through the corridors crying. Coming out through the french window he saw her whitely slipping down the long darkening lawn; and he himself felt himself flying, skimming only a foot or so above the ground .... But that white flake in the distance inspired him till she disappeared round a great clump of yews. And he, flying round it in a rush of following wind, came to a dead stop. For there she was but she was stone. She was beautiful and white but only a stone statue.

The statue comes alive when the beautiful Janet enters the garden, sees through the under-gardener's disguise, and leads him away to learn that SEX and LIFE have their compensations after all. They are married, despite her father's disapproval (presumably in a registry office), and Devlin returns to Oxford, where he gets a First in philosophy, writes a thesis, and obtains a college Fellowship. The couple have a daughter, and the comedy ends with a modern variant of the traditional dance: a ride on a roundabout at Oxford's annual St Giles' Fair, which Mary and Louis had visited in September 1930.

* See pp. 77 and 85–6 above.

The reviews of *Roundabout Way* were brief, bland, and generally benevolent; very different from its author's own later, acerbic judgement: 'I was disloyal to myself, wrote a novel which purported to be an idyll of domestic felicity. Faking, I thought, doesn't matter so much in prose and one must at least keep one's hand in.' MacNeice had told Hilton, in April 1932, that 'I don't think I shall write many more short poems'. Poetry was too serious to be faked: 'To write poems expressing doubt or melancholy, an anarchist conception of freedom or nostalgia for the open spaces (and these were the things that I wanted to express), seemed disloyal to Mary.' Only two poems that Dodds would date 1931, and two from 1932, would find their way into his edition of the *Collected Poems*, but a new friendship would shortly help to prepare the ground for a new harvest of lyric poetry. Dodds, as Professor of Greek, had come to know the Honorary Secretary of the local branch of the Classical Association, Dr G. A. Auden, Professor of Public Health at the University. A man of great personal charm, he had studied classics and science at Cambridge; had since published papers on medical aspects of Greek Literature; and had passed on his enthusiasm for medicine in general, and psychology in particular, to his youngest son, the poet. Wystan and Louis had, of course, been acquaintances at Oxford. Louis had since given Auden's *Poems* (1928) a respectful review, and now, meeting again under the Doddses' hospitable roof, they became friends. In January 1933, he tells Blunt that 'Auden turned up and talked a good deal of communism'. Wystan's contact with German communists in Berlin and British communists and communist-sympathizers, such as Day Lewis and Spender, had all but converted him to St Marx's gospel that Clere Parsons had preached at Oxford. MacNeice, since arriving in Birmingham, had listened to many such sermons from Leftist writers staying with the Florences:

The word Proletariat hung in festoons from the ceiling. And yet I felt that they all were living in the study. The armchair reformist sits between two dangers – wishful thinking and self-indulgent gloom .... Naomi Mitchison after a fortnight or so in Russia gave a lecture at Birmingham University about the joy in the faces of the masses. It all seemed to me too pat.

Oxford, encouraging MacNeice's temperamental scepticism, had taught him never again to 'Believe anything that anyone says', unless and until he had the evidence of his own eyes. His view of communism he expressed in a wry poem of 1933, 'To a Communist':

> Your thoughts make shape like snow; in one night only
> The gawky earth grows breasts,
> Snow's unity engrosses
> Particular pettiness of stones and grasses.
> But before you proclaim the millennium, my dear,
> Consult the barometer –
> This poise is perfect but maintained
> For one day only.

The 'camp' phrase, 'my dear', suggests that Wystan was the communist addressed.*

The two poets had been approached, the previous autumn, by their Oxford contemporary, Geoffrey Grigson. They had known of – but not known – each other at university. Grigson had last seen MacNeice 'stalking in a cloak in the dusk of the purlieus of Merton College', not knowing they had more in common than he would then have supposed. Both were sons of clergymen and brought up by the sea and, though MacNeice was more brilliant and mercurial, each had a toughness and independence that the other would come to respect. Why Grigson had approached Auden and MacNeice was revealed in January 1933, when his magazine *New Verse* appeared with an editorial entitled 'Why'. He answered this question:

NEW VERSE ... has a clear function. When respectable poems (as it believes) are being written and forced to remain in typescript, it can add itself as a publishing agent to those few publishers who bring out (with conscience money) a few books of verse. It favours only its time, belonging to no literary or politico-literary cabal, cherishing bombs only for the everlasting 'critical' rearguard of nastiness, now represented so ably and variously by the *Best Poems of the Year*, the Book Society and all the gang of big shot reviewers.

Reminding his readers that *New Verse* can be bought for sixpence – the price of ten Players or a brief library borrowing of *Angel Pavement* or a

---

* A less likely addressee is Anthony Blunt, who many years later would recall that 'quite suddenly, in the autumn term of 1933, Marxism hit Cambridge'. He did not become a communist – and seems unlikely to have discussed communism with MacNeice – until sometime after 1933.

'bus fare from Piccadilly Circus to Golders Green', Grigson opened what was to prove the most influential poetry magazine of the 1930s with a poem of MacNeice's followed by one of Auden's. The former – which may have appealed to Grigson for autobiographical reasons, among others – shows a MacNeice very different from the Sitwellian poseur of *Blind Fireworks*:

Turn Again Worthington
(*or a thought for intending mystics*)

Upon this beach the falling wall of the sea
Explodes its drunken marble
Amid gulls' gaiety.

Which evercrumbling masonry, cancelling sum,
No one by any device can represent
In any medium.

Turn therefore inland, tripper, foot on the sea-holly,
Forget those waves' monstrous fatuity
And boarding 'bus be jolly.

Life and death, fixity and flux, are in contention: the sea's drunken *marble* and the gull's gaiety that might be thought to sanction the jollity enjoined upon the tripper as he boards his bus. This conclusion becomes more complicated when seen in relation to other of MacNeice's early poems: first,

'En Avant'
A Poem suggested by Marco Polo

Dead our Emperor rides in procession,
Forty horsemen after him.
Dead upon dead horses
With lances at rest and cakes in wallets.

Buses pass buses pass buses
Pass full of passengers.
Wooden upon seats of wood,
With pipe in mouth and coppers in pockets.

Foot in strirrups, clutch releasing,
Horse procession, bus procession,

> Mummy-head, wooden head
> Never ceasing, never ceasing,
> All dead, dead.

The image of bus as potential hearse recurs in MacNeice's 1933 celebration of his adoptive hazy city, 'Birmingham'. This, owing something to the death-in-life and life-in-death of the London of *The Waste Land*, sees 'On shining lines the trams like vast sarcophagi move'. They and the rest of the traffic are directed by a Pharaoh-like policeman, images deriving from MacNeice's boyhood visits to the Egyptian section of London's British Museum. This is confirmed by a poem of May 1933, 'Museums', whose opening rhymes have an associative as well as a musical connection:

> Museums offer us, running from among the buses,
> A centrally heated refuge, parquet floors and sarcophaguses . . . .

There the visitor can enter other people's 'marble lives' and martyrdoms before returning to the street,

> his mind an arena where sprawls
> Any number of consumptive Keatses and dying Gauls.

The buses, trams, taxis and trains that carry their passengers through MacNeice's poems are all variants of those trains of 'Reminiscences of Infancy' (1926) that, trailing smoky epitaphs, passed 'downhill gently to the bottom of the distance'. He was, like Eliot's Webster, 'much possessed by death', and nowhere is this – and its antithesis – more clearly set out than in 'The Glacier', written that July:

> we who have always been haunted by the fear of becoming stone
> Cannot bear to watch that catafalque creep down
> And therefore turn away to seemingly slower things
> And rejoice there to have found the speed of fins and wings . . . .

MacNeice is also much possessed by life, and these poems of the early Thirties rejoice in the rich detail of ordinary lives, ordinary music perceived as extraordinary:

> Down the road someone is practising scales,
> The notes like little fishes vanish with a wink of tails . . . .

> While the lawn-mower sings moving up and down
> Spirting its little fountain of vivid green . . . .

These poems have more to do with MacNeice's mother than his wife, but Mary would not have understood that – let alone have perceived it as 'disloyalty' – and when her in-laws gave them a Baby Austin, far from seeing it as proleptic of a hearse, the young couple revelled in the freedom it gave them to escape from the urban haze into pastoral Shropshire. They were, however, enjoying Birmingham more. At the start of the year, Mary had enthusiastically begun modernizing High-field Cottage with a view to having a child. They were at the centre of the Doddses' ever-expanding circle of friends. The Professor and his wife were passionate gardeners, and the MacNeices spent a happy day helping them construct a miniature rockery on either side of a rivulet that issued from the Doddses' lake in a waterfall which fed a lily pool and watercress bed. Another assistant gardener that day was John Waterhouse, a highly intelligent colleague of Bet's in the English Department, and already a good friend of Louis'. The snobbish young lecturer of 1930 was, moreover, beginning to find friends where he had least expected to find them – among his students. Dodds had intro-duced him to Walter Allen and Reggie Smith who, having been brought up in the same working-class street and gone to King Edward's Gram-mar School, had entered the university together in 1932. The ebullient Smith had founded the B.U. Socialist Society with three other male undergraduates and a young woman, at whose home he had met Wystan Auden, who was pursuing her handsome brother.

Louis and Mary were also delighted to welcome older friends to Highfield Cottage: John Hilton and his wife, Peggy, arrived in the middle of their honeymoon. John having qualified as an architect in the middle of the deepening Depression, had applied for a lectureship in the Birmingham University philosophy department. He was inter-viewed but unsuccessful. Moore Crosthwaite, turning up with his mother and sister, took the MacNeices out to dinner and, in February 1934, Graham Shepard arrived like John, with a new wife, Anne (who found Mary bossy and irritable, perhaps because she was pregnant). Another visitor, her childhood friend Helen Cooke, also found her more assertive than in the past. One morning, talking of poetry at

Peggy Stephens and John Hilton, after announcing their engagement in 1933

breakfast, she and Louis were interrupted by Mary yelling upstairs in bed. They went up to join her, whereupon Mary babbled like a fountain until Louis picked up – and with desperate deliberation dropped – a vase which, shattering on the floor, shocked her into silence.

In May, she went into a nursing home called The Dingle to have her baby, while her nervous husband went for a long walk down the towpath of a disused canal with George, the electrician who had helped modernize Highfield Cottage. Stopping for a drink, Louis left his ashplant, his Oxford talisman, in a pub. He had done this many times before and told himself he would go back to collect it. However, on 15 May, Daniel John MacNeice was born in The Dingle (weighing in at 6lb 14oz) and when, some weeks later, George told Louis that the pub in which he had left his ashplant was being demolished, he made no attempt to recover it. The father of a son, the author of two published books and others on the way, he was now his own man and had no need of that Joycean prop.

CHAPTER 11

Things Being Various

> World is crazier and more of it than we think,
> Incorrigibly plural. I peel and portion
> A tangerine and spit the pips and feel
> The drunkenness of things being various.
> 'Snow', CP, p. 30

1934 was a good year for MacNeice: he was feeling more settled at work and happy at home. 1933 had brought him an unprecedented catch of poems, and with the New Year they continued to come to his net: first, in January, his 'Valediction' to Ireland. This explores more fully the themes of 'Belfast' (September 1931), a poem in which the vision of the mature MacNeice is for the first time visible, and his voice audible. At its end,

> The sun goes down with a banging of Orange drums
> While the male kind murders each its woman
> To whose prayer for oblivion answers no Madonna.

'Valediction', bidding farewell to a country where 'arson and murder are legacies', looks back at Dublin, Belfast, and Killarney; the second of these the setting for MacNeice's 'Family Romance' (in Freud's famous phrase):

> This was my mother-city, these my paps.
> Country of callous lava cooled to stone....
> Cursèd be he that curses his mother. I cannot be
> Anyone else than what this land engendered me....

Loving and hating, he declares:

> I will exorcise my blood
> And not to have my baby-clothes my shroud
> I will acquire an attitude not yours
> And become one of your holiday visitors,
> And however often I may come
> Farewell my country, and in perpetuum . . . .

Where 'Belfast' had ended with subjectivity disguised as objectivity, 'Valediction', using some of the same terms, ends more powerfully because more personally:

> Good-bye your hens running in and out of the white house
> Your absent-minded goats along the road, your black cows
> Your greyhounds and your hunters beautifully bred
> Your drums and your dolled-up Virgins and your ignorant dead.

This poem has distressed and angered generations of Irish readers, leading some to reject MacNeice as an Irish poet. Examining the motivation behind such poems, Terence Brown suggests analogies with C. S. Lewis and Samuel Beckett, whose painful childhoods in isolated Protestant suburban houses were also exorcised in self-imposed exile. Death and distress darkened the boyhood of each of these writers, but sectarian violence was a more pressing reality in the Carrickfergus Rectory than in Lewis's New House or Beckett's Cooldrinagh. Mac-Neice's grandfathers both had personal experience of such violence; his parents' introduction to Carrickfergus may have seemed to him a factor in his mother's terminal depression; to say nothing of the horrors of the childhood described in his autumn 1929 letter to John Hilton.*

Dodds is a crucial figure in MacNeice's relationship with their mother-country and, in September, Louis joined him in Dublin where he was researching for a memoir of his friend Stephen MacKenna. It seems likely that MacNeice took the ferry to Belfast and saw his father and stepmother before heading south by train; a journey that prompted his poem 'Train to Dublin'. In this, he appears to emulate Dodds who once, crossing the Irish Sea in a ship full of uniformed Black and Tans, had failed to rise to the captain's toast: 'I give you the King':

---

* See pp. 138–40 above.

> All over the world people are toasting the King,
> Red lozenges of light as each one lifts his glass,
> But I will not give you any idol or idea, creed or king,
> I give you the incidental things which pass
> Outward through space exactly as each was.

Instead, MacNeice proposes a toast of his own to those *things* (increasingly, a key word in his poetry) that – like Thomas Hardy, 'a man who used to notice such things' – he was beginning to notice with delight:

> I give you the disproportion between labour spent
> And joy at random; the laughter of the Galway sea
> Juggling with spars and bones irresponsibly,
> I give you the toy Liffey and the vast gulls,
> I give you fuschia hedges and whitewashed walls.

After cataloguing the light and dark delights of the Irish landscape seen from his train, he turns to other things he was now learning to notice – those who people a landscape:

> And I give you the faces, not the permanent masks,
> But the faces balanced in the toppling wave –
> His glint of joy in cunning as the farmer asks
> Twenty per cent too much, or a girl's, forgetting to be suave,
> A tiro choosing stuffs, preferring mauve.

The poem ends with a coda of grateful celebration containing no hint of the bitterness and hurt of 'Valediction', written only eight months before:

> I would like to give you more but I cannot hold
> This stuff within my hands and the train goes on;
> I know that there are further syntheses to which,
> As you have perhaps, people at last attain
> And find that they are rich and breathing gold.

In Dublin, MacNeice felt 'born again', and with Dodds climbed up and ran down the Wicklow Mountains overlooking Dublin Bay. The Professor took his young colleague to tea with W. B. Yeats in Rathfarnham. The elegant lecturer was struck by the elegance of the Archpoet in his 'smooth light suit and a just sufficiently crooked bow tie'.

W. B. Yeats (by Howard Coster)

MacNeice was also struck by Yeats's hierophantic manner, though disappointed that his conversation was not about poetry but the phases of the moon and spiritualism. He spoke of the spirits then guiding his wife's automatic writing. Dodds, who was later president of the Society for Psychical Research, had the audacity to ask: 'Have you ever seen them?' Yeats was piqued by his presumption. 'No, he said grudgingly, he had never actually seen them . . . but – with a flash of triumph – he had often *smelt* them.'

It may have been Dodds who had persuaded MacNeice, in January 1932, to send his new poems to another great poet of his acquaintance, the publisher of Auden's *Poems* (1930), T. S. Eliot. Nothing was heard of these until April when MacNeice wrote again:

Dear Mr Eliot,

I met Father D'Arcy last week and he tells me that you have some poems which you received without any letter or explanation and which he thinks are mine. I think this is probable, as I sent you a large number of poems in January with a letter enclosed. The letter must have been lost owing to my use of a double envelope; I must therefore apologize.

As for the poems themselves I think that only a few of them stand on their own merits, but that as a collection and arranged in a certain order they would supplement each other and make an aggregate of some value. Whereas if I chose a dozen individuals, they would remain, perhaps, merely individuals. It seems to me (as far as I can see myself) that I am not sufficiently in a school for my poems to be readily significant; therefore they have to build up their own explanation. This is my apology for what may seem a haphazard mass of indifferent or casual verses.

My hope is that Faber and Faber's might publish a collection in book form.

Yours sincerely,
Louis MacNeice

Eliot replied that he found the poems 'very interesting work' but not quite justifying a volume. He softened the blow, however, by offering to publish some in his journal *The Criterion*, and inviting MacNeice to call and discuss the selection. 'The Creditor' and 'Trapeze' were published in the October issue, and in due course Eliot began sending him books to review.

In autumn 1933, MacNeice submitted a revised collection of poems. Eliot found this much improved, but still

not quite ripe for publication. I think that my feeling is largely a practical and tactical one. I think that a first volume ought, if possible, to be able to start off with one or two longish poems which will arrest the attention of the reader at once, and these, if possible, should be among the poet's most recent work. It seems to me that this book could be very much improved by re-arrangement, and by making it shorter; but I am not sure that it yet contains the poems that we want to start off with. I know that it is rather a tax upon your patience, but I have the feeling that if these suggestions strike you as having any value, the book may turn into something much more effective in six months' time.

MacNeice was happy to wait. By the time he received that letter he had written 'An Eclogue for Christmas', and in April 1934 told Eliot 'I have lately been writing some longer poems which, for want of a better name, I am calling "Eclogues".' The form had many advantages for him: meeting the request for longer poems, while giving scope to his developing interest in dramatic writing, and enabling him to extend the tradition of Virgil and Spenser into the twentieth century. In August, he sent Eliot a new typescript which, after a nail-biting delay, was accepted for publication the following spring. MacNeice's patience was amply rewarded by Eliot's praise:

I like the new poems very much, and the book seems to me to show a vast improvement over last year's. It seems to me that the new poems are quite the best that you have done, and if you go on in this way, you may have a few more to add or to substitute for a few of the earlier poems before the book goes to press. In any case I congratulate you on this collection.

The acceptance of his poems consoled MacNeice for a couple of literary disappointments. He had written a third novel, called *The F.[amily?] Vet*, which he described as 'a purgation of my grudges against my family'. It was turned down by Heinemann in March/April 1934 and, in June, he told Blunt he had withdrawn it. 'But not for good. I shall add some bits to it & then publish it when the right people are dead. My family, you see, have behaved so well lately that I feel it wld be a pity to get into a bldy mess with them.'

A first play also came to nothing. In February 1933, MacNeice told Blunt he was writing a play 'for the people in Dublin', probably the Gate Theatre. 'It is all about twins – Irish ones of course.' A year later, he writes: 'I am entirely changing my play; everyone is going to be electrocuted.' In June, he reports: 'My play is still unfinished – so protean – but I hope it will be done in London by a thing called, I think, the Groups Theatre. I am afraid it wouldn't be allowed in the I.F.S. [Irish Free State] as De Val[era]. wld take it personally.' This shows that *Station Bell* – as it would come to be called – had found the form in which it was submitted to the Group Theatre, which had been founded in 1932 by Rupert Doone and others determined to revitalize the English Theatre. In February 1934, this company had produced Auden's *The Dance of Death*. MacNeice would certainly have read the play – it was published in November 1933 – and may have seen the Group Theatre production (in which one of the principal singers was a young woman called Hedli Anderson). *The Dance of Death* may have influenced the final form of *Station Bell*, but just as Auden's European vision owes a good deal to Brecht, MacNeice's depiction of a fascist Ireland owes something to an Irish tradition exemplified by O'Casey and Yeats.

The inaction is set in a Dublin station buffet, where a fat woman proclaims herself Dictator of Ireland and sets up her headquarters. Her name, Julia Brown, may invite associations with Hitler's Brownshirts, but is clearly an alias also for Kathleen-ni-Houlihan, icon of Irish nationalism (later to be represented by a mannequin in the Dictator's triumphal procession). Escaping death at the hands of an incompetent communist bomber, Julia plans to blow up the boat-train carrying O'Halloran, a defector from her ranks, who has threatened to reveal in America that all the US armaments firms have crashed as a result of being undersold by her Irish Seaweed company. In Act III, she herself takes the train, but pulls the communication cord just short of Kilbishop Bridge, which then blows up with the bomb meant for the train, leaving Julia its prescient saviour. *Station Bell* is a satiric variation on the theme of 'Valediction'; the object of its attack, a country where the Catholic-turned-communist bomber declares 'I am the chosen instrument of God – I call him God for short'; where the Protestant Clergyman is 'genuinely a lunatic'; and the acclaimed Dictatress a scheming murderess. Station, train, and bell have the symbolic values – but none of the power – they carry in the poems, and the play was understandably rejected by the Group Theatre. MacNeice was not unduly discouraged, telling Doone that he planned to write another play that would be 'less of a compromise between two traditions' and more suitable for the Group.

His horizons – like his ambitions – were expanding: after the Dublin trip with Dodds, there were visits to London, long walks with Auden and John Waterhouse in the Black Country, and he was seeing more of them and his other friends in Birmingham. Mary's horizons, by contrast, had contracted. For a year following Dan's birth, she hardly left Highfield Cottage, but gave herself wholeheartedly to the nurturing of her son according to the methods advocated by the fashionable child psychologist Sir Truby King. That summer, it seemed possible that their Birmingham circle might be extended by the appointment of two friends to university positions. First, John Hilton applied for the post in the Philosophy Department for which he had applied the previous year. The previously successful candidate was moving on. This time Hilton was offered the job, but preferred to accept the simultaneous offer of the post of Director of Antiquities in Cyprus. Then Anthony Blunt (since 1932 a Fellow of Trinity College, Cambridge) applied for a new chair of Aesthetics at Birmingham. He was called for interview in October and Louis wrote to brief him: 'As to Grant Robertson [the Vice-Chancellor] remember that he is a snob; tell him about all the great men (both brains & titles) that you have known.' Blunt, himself a snob with connections in high places, was young and had relatively few publications to his credit. In November, MacNeice wrote to him again: 'The bloody old sots are, I fear, not going to have you. It's all because of your youth. . . . Dodds said that he did all he could & that Grant Robertson had liked you very much'. Dashed by this rejection, Blunt fell silent, prompting a postcard from MacNeice in the New Year: 'Do write & tell me if you're dead so that we can send flowers'.

After a busy year's teaching, marking of exam scripts, writing, and reviewing, he was ready for a holiday and rented a Cotswold farm-house for five weeks from the start of August. Situated in the village of Oddington – near Edward Thomas's Adlestrop – its attractions included a cow-byre plus cow. The MacNeices were accompanied by a large and formidable cook and a harrassed housekeeper. Mary played her Lady-of-the-Manor role and friends were invited to stay. First came Ernst Stahl, a gnome-like South African, lecturer in German at Bir-mingham University, and a fellow tenant of the Florences. Louis liked him because he was highly intelligent, a good listener and not too good at golf, which they played day after bright day on a nine-hole course overlooking the Vale of Evesham. After Stahl came John Waterhouse, with whom Louis and Betsy the borzoi once again went walking. She had to be lifted over stiles, prompting the village boys to shout: 'Here comes the sissy dog.' And after Waterhouse came Charles Katzman, invited at Mrs Beazley's request 'because he was poor'. Katzman was a Russian-American Jew, in his twenties, doing graduate work in Oxford, where – rumour had it – Mary's mother saw him looking at a boot in a Holywell Street gutter and said: 'Do you like old boots? So do I.' She also liked the look of *him*. Graham Shepard saw a resemblance to Clark Gable, 'but without such prominent ears, a big black fellow'.

He weighed two hundred pounds and had been an American College football star. Learning that he was looking for lodgings, Mrs Beazley offered him a room in 100 Holywell Street and when, sometime later, she and her husband were going away on holiday, she suggested that the MacNeices should invite him to Oddington. His visit was a success. Louis said he had 'the charm of a shaggy sheepdog who expects to be laughed at. Although his voice, too, was shaggy and he spoke very slowly he and Mary understood each other at once.' He and Louis had long talks about football. While he was there, Mary's schoolfriend, Helen Cooke, drove over to see them. At the end of her visit, she gave Katzman a lift back to Oxford and, since the Beazleys were still away, her parents had him to stay with them in Christ Church. When Mary heard this – and that he and Helen had gone for a walk in Osney – she was unaccountably angry and persuaded him to rejoin the MacNeice caravan when it returned to Birmingham in September.

That month, MacNeice's *Poems* was published. It was greeted by a letter that, unlike most letters he received, he kept – a clear indication of how much it meant to him:

My dear MacNeice,

I do like your poems – I'm astonished to find how much. Astonished, because like all modernist poems they have that outward air of being clever, and I do hate cleverness (usually failing to understand it). But most of these seem to me to have a live core which is the personality of their author, and a music and a dignity which grow naturally out of the core and aren't just a gummed-on decoration . . . .

Yours,
E. R. Dodds

Certainly, the book marks an astonishing advance on *Blind Fireworks*. The poet of the Gothic nursery has become the poet of the modern city, but an epigraph signals the link between them: διώκει παῖς ποτανὸν ὄρνιν. This phrase from *The Agamemnon* of Aeschylus (394) MacNeice translated – in the version that, with Dodds's encouragement, he had just begun – 'a boy / Who chases a winged bird'. It seems an image of the artist at work, the artist who asks or prays in 'An Eclogue for Christmas': 'Let all these so ephemeral things / Be somehow permanent like the swallow's tangent wings'. The good news with which this, the book's opening poem, ends – 'Christ is born' – bears no relation, however, to the bad news delivered by the Chorus of *The Agamemnon*. MacNeice's version muffles the original, which may be literally rendered: 'for a boy runs in chase of a flying bird after bringing an intolerable affliction upon his people; to his prayers no god will listen, but pulls down the unjust man that is conversant with such things'. It is hard to believe that MacNeice, in choosing this epigraph, was not hinting – if only to himself – at the burden of guilt (for his supposed part in the death of his mother) implied in his 1929 letter to John Hilton.*

His book follows the trajectory of his life to 1935: from the Ireland of 'Valediction' to the England of 'Birmingham' and back to 'Belfast'; then back again to England where at the book's end, he celebrates a birth balancing that of its opening Eclogue. His 'Ode' opens:

> To-night is so coarse with chocolate
> The wind blowing from Bournville
> That I hanker after the Atlantic. . . .

He has in mind 'the haystack- and roof-levelling wind, / Bred on the Atlantic,' that had inspired Yeats's 'Prayer for my Daughter'. MacNeice's prayer for his son,

> Let him have five good senses
> The feeling for symmetry
> And the sense of the magnet,

is linked, like Yeats's, to a prayer for Ireland: that both may survive 'the coming fury', the sound of the aeroplane that is for the younger poet 'our augury of war'. MacNeice has fewer certainties than Yeats to bequeath to his child:

> I cannot draw up any code
> There are too many qualifications
> Too many asterisk asides
> Too many crosses in the margin
> But as others, forgetting the others,

---

* See pp. 138–40 above.

Run after the nostrums
Of science art and religion
   So would I mystic and maudlin
Dream of the both real and ideal
   Breakers of ocean.
I must put away this drug.

Must become the migrating bird following felt routes
The comet's superficially casual orbit kept
Not self-abandoning to sky-blind chutes
To climb miles and kiss the miles of foam
For nothing is more proud than humbly to accept
And without soaring or swerving win by ignoring
The endlessly curving sea and so come to one's home.
And so come to one's peace while the yellow waves are roaring.

MacNeice's one certainty is that, for himself and his boy, the way forward must be the way of 'the winged bird' which, undeflected by

Father and Son

human codes and credos, relies on the evidence of its 'five good senses'. He had taken the same position, responding to 'An Enquiry' from Geoffrey Grigson in the pages of *New Verse*. To the question 'Do you take your stand with any political or politico-economic party or creed?' he replied: 'No. In weaker moments I wish I could.' And to the question 'As a poet what distinguishes you, do you think, from an ordinary man?' he answered: 'Dissatisfaction with accepted formulas. But most of the time one is not a poet and is perfectly satisfied.' The first review of his *Poems*, Stephen Spender's in *New Verse*, gave with one hand but took away with the other: 'The music is the most obviously "infectious" quality of these poems. It is too infectious'. Some other reviews were more positive but, by the time they were published, MacNeice had other matters on his mind.

He allowed himself to be press-ganged by his undergraduate friend, Reggie Smith, into playing centre-three-quarter for a rugger team of King Edward VI School Old Boys against the School's First XV. He was by half a dozen years the oldest Old Boy on the field, a drinker and a smoker, but Walter Allen remembers him playing 'with great dash' – if not the fluid elegance of Betsy, his borzoi. Katzman was still staying with the MacNeices and he, too, was invited to play rugger in Birmingham one Saturday. He wanted to accept, but had an appointment to see his Oxford tutor on the Friday, 11 October, so Louis said he would drive him down and back that day. Returning, he dozed at the wheel and, a mile from home, was hit broadside on by a larger car at a crossroads, where the other driver had right of way. MacNeice's car mounted the pavement and waltzed round two lampposts before coming to rest in the road ninety feet from the point of impact. Driver and passenger were both thrown out. Louis found himself sitting in the road, then found the car and wearily climbed into it. Only when the engine would not start did he notice 'that all the little gadgets on the dashboard were hanging out by the roots as if in some picture by Dali'. Katzman would not start either and was taken to hospital. Louis stumbled home, covered with mud and blood, to tell Mary what had happened. Together they went to the hospital, where Katzman was unconscious in a screened bed and a nurse asked the MacNeices if they were his nearest relatives. They said no, but asked to be telephoned if there was a crisis. Fortunately, there was not. Next morning, Katzman

woke up with a headache and concussion; Louis with what felt like –
but was not – a broken neck.

A few days later, Katzman was allowed out of hospital and returned
to Highfield Cottage to recuperate. Thanks to Mary's tender minis-
trations and his own powerful physique, he was soon able to go back
to Oxford. Louis meanwhile had sprained his ankle, running for a
tram, and was obliged to walk with two sticks. Other misfortunes
followed: he was prosecuted by the Police for dangerous driving, had
his licence endorsed, and received a demand for £80 from the driver of
the other car, a garage-proprietor. Then, on 18 November, a spark
from the sitting-room fire ignited first the floor and then the beams
beneath. Feeling a curious sense of catharsis, Louis carefully changed
his trousers, collected Mrs Florence's long-handled axe, and smashed
the cement base of the hearth to get at the burning beams. Mary then
threw water by the bucketful into the smoking hole, where it met the
fountaining jet of a hose held by a neighbour below. When the fire was
finally quenched, Louis felt only exhilaration, while Mary surveyed the
wreckage with a tragic face. Next morning she left him and Daniel for
Katzman and London.

CHAPTER 12

Moving

In short we must keep moving to keep pace
Or else drop into Limbo, the dead place.
'Letter to Graham and Anna', *CP*, p. 63

Their roles reversed, it was now Mary's turn to feel exhilarated. She called on the Shepards in their St John's Wood flat to tell them her news, and seemed more pleased with her acquisition of a new 'lump' coat than distressed or embarrassed at the loss of husband and son. Louis was devastated. Dorothy Baker, a student friend who saw him within days of Mary's departure, wondered whether he was not heading for a nervous breakdown. The shock of Mary's desertion may have reopened the old wound caused by his mother's desertion, as it seemed to her five-year-old son. The twenty-eight-year-old, however, was rescued by Lella Florence, who swept in to look after Dan and comfort and cook for the two of them. By 9 December, Louis was sufficiently recovered to write to Anthony Blunt, asking: 'Could you by any chance come & stay here next week-end?' He spoke of an undefined 'family crisis', but was not too self-absorbed to add: 'I want you to see the works of that local sculptor [Gordon Herickx], who is getting very hard up.' Mary's departure put Louis in touch – as never before – with the world and its woes. The morning paper and the evening news now kept him company. The day after he had written to Blunt, the world had word of another crisis involving a MacNeice.

The Archdeacon of Connor had been appointed Bishop of Cashel and Waterford in 1931 and, three years later, Bishop of Down and Connor and Dromore. He was no doubt pleased to discover that the earliest recorded Bishop of Connor was St MacNissi. He had been less pleased, on 27 October 1935, to have officiated at the funeral of Lord

Bishop John MacNeice in 1931

Carson, one of the architects of Ireland's Partition. As Louis had written to Blunt, his father, a passionate Home Ruler, 'had to sprinkle earth from the 6 Northern Counties on the coffin of . . . his lifelong bête noir out of a large gold chalice. That was hard on him.' What was to follow was harder still. Under the heading 'Bishop's Objection to Use of Union Jack', *The Times* of 10 December reported the outcome of a battle more savage than its measured sentences suggest:

Owing to the opposition of the Bishop of Down and Connor and Dromore (Dr. J. F. MacNeice) and other members of the Belfast Cathedral Board, the Union Jack is not to hang over the grave of Lord Carson in the Cathedral.

The Ulster Government suggested that the grave should be covered by a slab of granite from the Mourne Mountains, on which should be inscribed the one word 'Carson', that it should be surrounded by brass railings, and that, on the wall immediately above the grave, there should be a flagstaff with a Union

Jack, to be presented by a friend of the Cathedral. The Prime Minister told the Board that he considered that such simple embellishment of the grave would be in keeping with Lord Carson's nature.

When the suggestions came before the Board, however, the Bishop objected on the ground that the flag should not be brought into political associations. As unanimity could not be obtained on this point the Board decided that the flag and flagstaff should be omitted, but that the remainder of the scheme should be carried out.

When the Ulster Government proposed – 'suggested' is too tentative a verb – that the Union Jack should fly over the tomb of the man the Bishop held responsible for destroying the unity of Ireland, he wrote to the Deans of other British cathedrals asking if they had a Union Jack over any tomb other than that of a member of the Armed Forces. The answer was a uniform no. Armed with this, the Bishop refused to allow the precedent, standing his ground in face of thunderous criticism from parliament and press.

For all their differences of belief and temperament, the MacNeices had strong ties of family loyalty. Writing to Anthony, Louis said of his father: 'I will tell you more of that great man when I see you'; and Elizabeth drove up to Birmingham to help her brother look after his motherless son. She found Dan wearing a cream silk dress and red shoes, dancing to the record-player. Clearly Louis could not look after him unaided and, hearing of an unemployed middle-aged Scottish nurse, went up to Edinburgh to interview her. He must have thought her satisfactory because he agreed to employ her, but she does not appear in his autobiography's account of that Scottish expedition. This concentrates on another of his periodic assaults on his old Protestant enemy, Self-Respect. Mary, like his father and stepmother, strongly disapproved of Drink, so he celebrated his new-found independence by drinking flat champagne with a young poet who grew increasingly morbid as the evening progressed. 'I'm a dead man,' he kept saying, 'I'm dead today and you'll be dead tomorrow.' In a symbolic sense, his prophecy proved correct. The following evening, MacNeice was escorted from a drunken party to the Waverley Station by a young Scottish Nationalist carrying a glass of brandy like a candle before him. Having reached their destination, they drank perdition to the British Empire and smashed the glass on the platform. The train pulled out and soon 'the chain of the rolling wheels' had bound the poet in a sleep only broken at the approach of Birmingham. He 'had a throbbing head and a filthy mouth but felt somehow purified'.

Christmas was imminent and, hating the thought of spending it alone with Dan and his dour Scottish nurse, he joined Graham and Anne Shepard in a country inn overlooking the Severn near Tewkesbury. The day they arrived, 'the mist was so thick that the river had no further bank. A Lethe where everything ends and nothing begins.' On Boxing Day, they were invited to lunch by another Old Marlburian, John Betjeman, and his wife Penelope. Betjeman had not liked MacNeice much at school, and liked him less now (perhaps resenting his greater academic and literary success). Later, he wrote sourly in his diary:

MacN one hour late. P[enelope] very cold, like the lunch. I found MacN as gauche & literary & irritating as ever. I was obviously expected to mention his poetry but abstained from doing so. It seems to me to be Twilight Blunden. He brought a Borzoi with him. His wife has left him for a Jew – Reverted to type? Seemed unmoved by it. Mrs GHS[hepard] had a frightful dog which didn't like the indoor fireworks. A dismal party.

MacNeice returned to Birmingham, to 'intrigue, spiritual squalor and anxiety', mostly resulting from the machinations of his mother-in-law. Mrs Beazley first tried to effect a reconciliation but without success. Mary's pent-up resentment of her mother's tyrannical control of her life and loves erupts from a letter to Louis that catalogues seven damaging interventions 'in the name of "Mother-love"'. This is at once a hate-letter about her mother and a love-letter to 'Darling Louis'. Looking back, Mary realizes too late 'That the only person who has ever shown me what I feel is real love, in an all round sense – i.e. husband, mother, father, *everything* is <u>YOU</u>. <u>*That I SWEAR*</u>.' She evidently believed she and Louis had not used 'the only right contraceptive . . . . I was too squeemish, & you too thoughtful'. This probably means that he was considerate in his sexual demands. Katzman, by contrast, seems to have taken her by storm, with the result that she discovered in London she was pregnant. She told Louis, who 'felt very anxious, & offered to take [her] back', but she refused and went ahead with an abortion that she soon came to regret. Mrs Beazley, having done all in her power to prevent Mary's marriage, now embarked on a campaign to prevent her divorce from Louis and union with Katzman. She went to the American Embassy in London to acquaint the authorities with her daughter's 'moral turpitude' – one account of the story has her hinting at Mary's involvement with white-slave traffic – in an unsuccessful attempt to block her application for a US visa. Mrs Beazley then turned her guns on Mary's grandfather, telling him he must discontinue her allowance. Here, too, she met with defeat. The old man summoned his granddaughter, heard her story, and said that, 'though he failed to see why she was leaving such a good husband, he considered that her emotional life was no concern of his, and that he saw no reason why he should not continue to give her £300 a year.' Katzman left for America, to find a job, before Mary had obtained her visa, but not before Mrs Beazley had written letters to Oxford and Harvard trying to blast his career. There was a comic-opera scene on the boat, with Mrs Beazley and two muscular henchmen attempting to make the adulterer sign a document admitting his fault and renouncing Mary. She also made an effort to accost her daughter at Southampton Station. Mary simply turned her back on her. Returning to Oxford, Mrs Beazley commissioned an eminent rabbi to compose a lethal curse and asked one of her husband's most brilliant acolytes, Isaiah Berlin, to cross the Atlantic (all expenses paid) and deliver it to Katzman in person. Berlin told a friend of 'a séance lasting some 3–4 hours of uninterrupted Medea-talk. The combination of tigress, bore & femme fatale is really very odd: the effect is violent claustrophobia & a desire for solitude, with me as rare as rare.' Her would-be messenger did not ask whether he was to deliver it orally or in writing, but stayed away from 100 Holywell until the storm had blown over. That, however, was not before she had hired a private detective to 'shadow' her son-in-law in the hope of catching him *in flagrante delicto* with Daniel's nurse or a new maid, called Eva, whom she had insisted on appointing. How such a discovery would have advanced her cause, had the detective been successful (as he was not), is difficult to imagine.

The comedy in all this was lost on MacNeice. The mother-in-law he had hitherto regarded as an exotic eccentric revealed herself a monster, whom he would commemorate (though not name) in 'Auden and MacNeice: Their Last Will and Testament':

> And to the most mischievous woman now alive
> We leave a lorry-load of moral mud
> And may her Stone Age voodoo never thrive.

He had to contend not only with her calculated mischief but with such other humiliations as that unwittingly inflicted by a young friend and colleague in the English Department. Helen Gardner, hearing him and another man grumbling about the difficulty of moving through Twick-enham crowds at the Varsity rugger match (for which they had tickets) said: 'I always understood the secret was to take an attractive woman as a shield before whom the crowds would part. Why not take your wife, Louis?'

Before Mary's departure, there had been talk of him accompanying Anthony Blunt on a trip to Spain and, by 2 January 1936, that possibility had become a plan and he knew enough about Spanish politics to write: 'Perhaps there will be a revolution when we are in Spain.' Looking even further afield, MacNeice wrote to Eliot that he would like to give lectures in America that summer and asked him how to set about organizing these. Eliot gave him helpful advice that he would follow some years later:

I should advise you to try to get a temporary post in an American college or university, or an engagement to give some series of lectures. Such an experience would be amusing and not unprofitable in other ways than the financial emolument. Lecturing to Ladies' clubs I don't advise at all. It is only people like Hugh Walpole and Harold Nicolson who can make any money out of it.

Money was becoming a matter of concern for MacNeice. Having to pay wages to the new nurse as well as the old cook, he was heavily overdrawn. His father, however, came to the rescue with a cheque for £50 and Fabers made him a timely payment of royalties. He was finding Highfield Cottage oppressive: insomnia by night and squabbles by day between cook and nurse took their toll, and he began to go out more. Going out, he 'discovered Birmingham. Discovered that Birmingham had its own writers and artists who were free of the London trade-mark.' Friends like Reggie Smith and Walter Allen were less obsessed by politics than their contemporaries at Oxford and Cambridge who, in reaction against their bourgeois origins, were idealizing The Proletariat. The Birmingham novelists, like the

Birmingham surrealists, were free of social guilt and had a strong sense of self-identity. Perhaps it was because, as a writer and critic, he could see the faults in their writings, that Louis was even more impressed by the work of an artist in another medium. Gordon Herickx was a stonemason by day, a sculptor by night – in the summer months. In winter, exhausted from hacking frozen blocks in the stone-cutter's yard, he would listen to classical records on which he spent all his spare money. MacNeice, the writer who delighted in the athlete's co-ordination of mind and muscle, was fascinated by the sculptor at work:

It took him a summer to finish one piece of sculpture. He had made some very good portrait heads but was now chiefly interested in semi-abstract or symphonic pieces founded on some natural *motif*. The year before he had completed a 'cyclamen' and this year he was at work on a 'chestnut-bud'. To achieve these he had made a great many drawings of real cyclamens and chestnut-buds in every stage of their development, had then – without hurrying – allowed these to synthesise or crystalise into one dominant pattern, and had then taken a great slab of Hoptonwood stone (which cost much more than he could afford) and cut the arrested flame in it. Hoptonwood stone polishes beautifully and Herickx polished and finished every facet; his sculpture was meant to be seen from every angle, the cyclamen could even be rolled bottom upwards and still look in order, in key.

Herickx was no good at selling his work and, having a wife and children, he needed money. MacNeice understood his predicament only too well and was anxious to help. Back in December he had thought of Blunt as a possible patron and would later carry the cyclamen to Cambridge for him to see. First, however, he was himself to benefit from the bachelor Blunt's more prosperous circumstances.

Anthony bought both tickets for their Spanish holiday. They took ship from London docks in the last week of March. Also on board was another dapper Cambridge don, a lecturer in Spanish, shepherding three or four handsome undergraduates ('a favourite occupation of his', Blunt bitchily observed). They played piquet on board and talked about the Popular Front until the weather worsened and Anthony retired to be violently seasick. Arriving at Gibraltar, they went straight to Ronda, where they had dinner with the undergraduates and their shepherd who smugly prophesied – 'with a sly pride as if he were doing a card trick' – that Spain would soon have her spot of trouble. Next

Gordon Herickx, 'Chestnut Bud', 1935

day, Blunt and MacNeice went on to Granada, and then north through the mountains, to Madrid and the Prado, the object of their quest. Everywhere they went they saw the Hammer and Sickle scrawled on walls 'still plastered with posters from recent elections, ingenious cartoons showing the top-hatted banker in rout or political prisoners peering out from behind a grill in the gaping mouth of the capitalist'. The fascists and the rightist Falange party were protesting against the election, the previous month, of a Popular Front government of liberals, socialists and communists. In Madrid, Blunt and MacNeice saw their first political demonstrations, crowds braving cold and rain that the tourists were happy to escape in the warmth of the Prado galleries.

If Spain goes communist, Anthony said, France is bound to follow. And then Britain, and then there'll be jam for all. Which incidentally will mean new blood in the arts – in every parish a Diego Rivera. And easel-painting at last will admit it is dead and all the town-halls and factories will bloom with murals and bas-reliefs in concrete. For concrete is the new medium, concrete is vital.

MacNeice was aware – at least in retrospect – of the irony of Blunt proclaiming the coming of the New Kingdom while feasting his eyes on the productions of the Old. The influence of the art historian is every-where apparent in the poet's autobiographical account of their fortnight in Spain and section VI of his *Autumn Journal*. Blunt had taught MacNeice to 'read, mark, learn and inwardly digest' pictures when they were boys at Marlborough, and these writings show that he was an apt pupil. So, for example, coming upon

Greco's *Descent of the Holy Ghost* [he] was reminded of Yeats's poem *Byzantium* – 'flames begotten of flame'. And that is what Greco's pictures are. Their subject hardly matters; what matters is the incandescence of Greco himself, the Pentecost of his fingers, the counterpoint of aspiring brush-strokes. Those elongated saints of his are built for speed, their limbs lick upwards, the bellows is always blowing them.

MacNeice accepted Blunt's authority on matters of art history, but not his Marxist reading of history. Blunt said (in 1982) that his friend was 'politically incorrigible' and implied that the position he maintained in their Spanish conversations was essentially the same as in *The Strings are False*: 'the Marxist . . . forgets the end in the means, the evil of the means drowns the good of the end, power corrupts, the living gospel withers, Siberia fills with ghosts'. It is hard to imagine Blunt telling MacNeice of his involvement with the Soviet spy network, let alone trying to recruit him.

After a week in Madrid, with excursions to Avila, Segovia, Aranjuez, and Toledo, they went south again to Seville. On 12 April, Easter Sunday, they took to the streets in hope of 'a high-class carnival' but were disappointed to find, instead, a pathetic parade of bored young soldiers marching out-of-step. After lunch they went to their first – and last – bull-fight and found that no less anti-climactic. Returning then to Gibraltar, they stopped at Algeciras long enough to see a forest of clenched fists, a desecrated church, and the mayor 'being slightly stoned'. They spent much of their last night, at La Línea, listening to a drunk cursing in the street below;

> And next day took the boat
>   For home, forgetting Spain, not realising
> That Spain would soon denote
>   Our grief, our aspirations;
> Not knowing that our blunt
>   Ideals would find their whetstone, that our spirit
> Would find its frontier on the Spanish front,
>   Its body in a rag-tag army.

When, three years later, MacNeice wrote that coda to section VI of *Autumn Journal*, one would like to know whether he was conscious of the pun in 'blunt Ideals'.

Awaiting him in Birmingham was a lawyer's letter, which led him, on 25th April, to write a difficult letter of his own:

Dear Daddie & Madre,

I am afraid I must return for a moment to the subject which we usually avoid. I had meant to tell you that I was taking divorce proceedings against Mary but had postponed doing so in case an opportunity should arise for me to drop the whole business. The opportunity has not arisen and is now, I think, out of the question. Things on the other hand have moved much quicker than I expected and I was called up to London yesterday where the first part of the business went through successfully (if success is the right word.)

I do not know what your views on divorce are but I think you will see that in peculiar circumstances it is the necessary course, if only to give Mary a chance to reestablish herself. I naturally get the custody of Daniel and it is as well that this too should have been legally decided as Mary would otherwise be quite capable of making trouble over that at some point in the future. Technically it is still for some time open to her to attempt a reconciliation but I do not think that there is any likelihood of her doing this and this is, I think, just as well under the circumstances. I am sorry on your account that I have been forced to take this step. I do not think, however, that the affair will get the least publicity. It has occurred to me in that respect that it may save you some embarrassment if I don't come over to Belfast for a little time yet; my presence might make people inquisitive?

This is, I think, all I need say on the subject. I very much hope it doesn't upset you but, as I said, it seems to be an inevitable consequence of the situation. I talked about it with Elizabeth and she completely agreed. I shall be writing again soon. Daniel is very well. Term starts on Tuesday.

> love ever,
> Louis

Given the circumstances, it is hard to imagine a more considerate letter.

Some weeks later, MacNeice helped Herickx hoist the sculptor's cyclamen into his car and drove it down to Cambridge in the hope that Blunt's friend Victor Rothschild might buy it. Unfortunately, it did not harmonize with the Annunciation lilies in Blunt's 'coquettishly chaste' room, and the born-again Marxist was reluctant to promote the sale of a semi-abstract piece with no social message. After an evening with Blunt's friends, MacNeice concluded that 'Cambridge was still full of Peter Pans but all the Peter Pans were now talking Marx'. Next morning, he took his revenge on Dialectical Materialism and the homintern by getting drunk and insulting an exquisite evergreen don, whom Blunt had invited to lunch. Returning to Birmingham 'refreshingly jaded', he gave a lift to two of his host's most charismatic friends and was obliged to modify his opinion of the Peter Pans. As he wrote to Blunt,

I really must congratulate you on your university for producing this Cornford boy because obviously he is the one chap of the whole damn lot of you who is going to be a great man. There is still hope for the human race. As for Guy B[urgess] he is quite the nicest of your pals by a long way.

John Cornford was on his way to stand trial in Birmingham for causing an obstruction by distributing communist pamphlets in the city centre. Three months later, he would turn his back on Cambridge – where he had just gained a First in History and a research studentship – and head for Spain. He was killed in the battle for Madrid before the year was out, but not before he had written some of the most moving English poems of the Spanish Civil War. Burgess's career would follow a very different trajectory, leading to his defection – as a Russian spy – to the Soviet Union.

Before MacNeice and his passengers went their separate ways, Burgess said that all the young men in the streets of Birmingham looked queer. Reporting this to Blunt, MacNeice commented: 'I dare say they are, lucky creatures.' This and two later remarks of Blunt's – first, that 'Louis was beautiful' and, secondly, that he 'was always, totally and irredeemably heterosexual' – suggest the subsequent coolness between them may have been caused by embarrassment at an unwelcome advance.

MacNeice's irredeemable heterosexuality, however, was no bar to his friendship with Auden, which blossomed as that with Blunt faded. Together they attended an odd wedding on 20 May. In June the previous year, Auden had married Erika Mann, daughter of the novelist, so that she could obtain a British passport and leave Germany. He now arranged for her friend and fellow actress in the 'Peppermill' cabaret, Therese Giehse, to contract a similar marriage for a similar reason. Persuading his homosexual Birmingham friend John Simpson (who wrote novels under the name of John Hampson) to play the husband's part, Auden asked him 'What are buggers for?' Sharp at 9 o'clock on the day appointed, Auden and MacNeice arrived with the bride under the clock at Snow Hill Station. As marriage-broker and chief witness rolled into one morning suit, Wystan was Master of Ceremonies. Walter Allen was Best Man, Louis and Reggie Smith supplementary witnesses. The MC produced a five-pound note, with a flourish worthy of a conjurer's coloured handkerchief, and bought five tickets to Solihull, a posh suburb of Birmingham. In the train, with another flourish he produced the ring from his waistcoat pocket, gave it to Walter, and instructed him not to lose it. The bridegroom, who was very small, was waiting for his bride, who was very large, at Solihull station. Auden, masterful as ever, summoned a taxi for the Laurel and Hardyesque couple and their attendants, and ordered the driver to take them to Solihull Registry Office. This proved to be a hundred yards away. Upstairs, the formalities were duly observed, after which Auden shepherded his party back into the street and – saying 'We all need a drink' – led them to a mock-Tudor pub, where he ordered large brandies for everyone. All that was lacking was music, so the MC asked the barmaid if the pub had a piano. 'Yes, sir,' she said, 'but you can't play it.' Auden was indignant. 'Who's to stop me?' he asked, and was told: 'It's Mr so-and-so. He's dead. He's in there.' Following her pointing finger into the billiard room, they found a gleaming coffin on the green cloth. Auden led them back into the bar and ordered another round of brandies. Then, after finding them another taxi and another train, he presided over the wedding-breakfast at the Burlington Restaurant. Paying for this with a fistful of notes, he said: 'It's all on Thomas Mann.' Direction of the grand finale he delegated to MacNeice, who took the happy couple to the Futurist Cinema in John Bright Street for their honeymoon.

That registry office wedding would have reminded Louis of his own, and from it he returned to a flat that was now a torture-chamber of sharpened memories. It was time to move and, seeing an advertisement for a Lectureship in the Department of Latin at London University's Bedford College for Women, he applied on 27 May. His letter of application said:

I have published no classical work except occasional reviews but I am writing two books which should be completed within six months – (1) a verse translation of the 'Agamemnon' of Aeschylus, (2) a critical work on Humour in Latin Literature, which will be a book of about two hundred pages. If desired, I could send specimens of either of these in manuscript but am reluctant to do so as the 'Agamemnon' needs considerable polishing, while any one chapter of the other book will have to be revised again in relation to the whole when the book is finished. I have recently had the following non-classical work published:-

A collected book of poems, entitled 'Poems'
                    (Faber and Faber 1935)
An essay on Poetry in 'The Arts To-day'
                    (The Bodley Head 1935)
An essay on Sir Thomas Malory in 'The English Novelists'
                    (Chatto and Windus 1936)

On finishing my Latin Humour book I hope to make a Latin anthology, ranging from the earliest remains to the Fathers and consisting of passages picked not necessarily for their intrinsic merit but in order to illustrate, sometimes in an extreme form, certain tendencies of Roman culture.

He makes no mention of *Roundabout Way*. The most eloquent of three testimonials accompanying his application came from E. R. Dodds, who may already have given MacNeice another reason for leaving Birmingham: the news that Gilbert Murray was recommending him for the Regius Professorship of Greek at Oxford, the Chair Murray was himself shortly to vacate. MacNeice was short-listed for the Bedford post, but failed to get it; the news arriving within days of a letter offering Dodds the Oxford Chair. This intensified MacNeice's desire to leave Birmingham and, since his plans for a permanent move had come to nothing, he jumped at the chance of a working holiday, writing to Blunt: 'I hope to start for Iceland with Wystan Auden before the end of June (we are going to do a book about it for Cape full of verse epistles – Would you like an epistle?)' He was excited by the prospect, as was Auden, and for a similar reason: both as schoolboys had developed a passion for the Icelandic sagas. Wystan, in his 'Letter to Lord Byron', would boast:

> My name occurs in several of the sagas,
> Is common over Iceland still.

He set sail for Reykjavik early in June, but MacNeice was not with him, probably because neither his sister nor his stepmother could look after Dan and nurse until August. This proved providential, because early in July he received a letter from Bedford College inviting him to apply for a Lectureship in the Department of Greek. He did so and, on the 23rd, wrote to tell Blunt he had got the job and ask if he knew of a suitable vacant flat 'anywhere on the edge of Regent's Park (or Primrose Hill)'. Evidently he had by now overcome Rupert Doone's initial lack of enthusiasm for his translation of *The Agamemnon*, since, with a Group Theatre production in prospect, he went on to ask:

Do you know any good artist who for love (or possibly a small fee) would paint me a drop-curtain for the Agamemnon? I want a family-tree in the middle garlanded tastefully by pseudo-Greek motifs (Medusa's heads & such). Also I could do with chaps to paint scenery & minor gadgets such as shields & chariots.

Fabers, he said, were to publish his translation in the autumn and his own play, *The Rising Venus*, the following spring. Mary's departure had left him more time for writing and he had put it to good use. Ten days later, having deposited Dan and nurse with his sister Elizabeth in London, he returned in the small hours of the morning to his empty flat. Seeing 'little point in going to bed with no one in it', he put a stack of dance records on to the gramophone and sat down to write to Blunt again. A recent 'holocaust of letters & Mss' had seemed to him 'most satisfactory', but had involved a rereading that brought the past vividly to mind and left him feeling desolate and sentimental. He thought of Mary sadly, tenderly, and seemingly without bitterness:

M. was very narrow, I suppose, but she was very genuine. Narrow streams, as they say, run deep & have no mud & weeds . . . . Perhaps being married to M. was a sort of prolonged childhood – many toys, much comfort, painted furniture, running one's hand over materials, handtomouth idyll as all idylls are. But it went on too long & the habit is hard to break.

An epoch had ended: 'there is going to be a war which will wipe us all out', and in the meantime, on the domestic front, Fuzby the cat – like his mistress – had vanished.

On 4 August, wearing a new cloth cap bought out of £25 lent him by Auden's father, MacNeice set sail for Iceland, arriving there on the 9th. Auden was delighted to see him. He had spent most of his first month in Reykjavik, which he found rather dispiriting. He did not like the food – the sweet hot soups, tasting as if made with brilliantine and the endless dried fish: 'The tougher kind tastes like toe-nails, and the softer kind like the skin off the soles of one's feet.' Nor was there satisfactory liquor to wash it down: 'The beer is filthy, wine is prohibitive in price, and there is nothing left but whisky, which is not a good drink.' Auden most enjoyed the coffee, of which he later reckoned he 'must have drunk about 1,500 cups in three months.' On 13 July he had set off on a tour of western and northern Iceland. A week later, in Akureyri, he heard for the first time of the civil war in Spain. Reading the work of a poet who had died for freedom in an earlier war, he had a bright idea about the book that Fabers (not Cape) had commissioned him and MacNeice to write:

I brought a Byron with me to Iceland, and I suddenly thought I might write him a chatty letter in light verse about anything I could think of, Europe, literature, myself. He's the right person I think, because he was a townee, a European, and disliked Wordsworth and that kind of approach to nature, and I find that very sympathetic. This letter in itself will have very little to do with Iceland, but will be rather a description of an effect of travelling in distant places which is to make one reflect on one's past and one's culture from the outside. But it will form a central thread on which I shall hang other letters to different people more directly about Iceland. Who the people will be I haven't the slightest idea yet, but I must choose them, so that each letter deals with its subject in a different and significant way.

By the time MacNeice arrived, Auden had drafted the first part of his 'Letter to Lord Byron' and begun the second.

MacNeice spent his first week in Reykjavik, where Auden was making arrangements for an expedition they were to undertake with four boys from Bryanston and the master in charge of them, Bill Hoyland. The poets were on the quay to welcome the school party when their boat, the *Godafoss*, docked on 17 August. They had had a rough passage from Hull, but were allowed no time to recover. Auden took them briskly in hand. He supervised the leaving of luggage at the university hostel, the buying of oilskins, and saw them mounted on a string of horses meant for another party which – with a Viking disregard for social niceties – he had simply commandeered. Led by their guides, Stengrimur and Ari, they set off inland and by nightfall were at Gullfoss. There, the school party pitched their tents, and Auden was

Leaving Hraensnef

annoyed to discover that MacNeice (who was impractical even by the standards of poets) was expecting to share his and had no equipment of any kind other than an oilskin bought in Reykjavik. Auden's tent was small, conical, and lacking one section of its central pole. When he had put it up, inflated his blue and yellow pneumatic mattress – looking, as he did so, like something out of Brueghel – and adopted his favourite foetal position on it, there was little room for MacNeice. It began to rain and, in the small hours, the sodden tent collapsed. When the Bryanston boys woke, it was to see a patch of flattened canvas, but no poets. One of the boys, Michael Yates, thought: 'perhaps they had sneaked off to the nearby tin hut for coffee', but then the canvas undulated and two cross faces emerged.

The main object of the Bryanston expedition was to circumnavigate one of Iceland's central ice-fields, the Langjökull (or Long Glacier), and after breakfast the horses were saddled, panniers loaded, and the cavalcade set off. MacNeice, Hoyland, and three of the boys had never ridden a horse before and soon wanted never to ride one again. Gradually, however, they grew accustomed to the rhythm and Mac-Neice began to enjoy the spectacular sight of 'intense blue amethyst mountains castellating the glacier'. It took them eight days to circle the Langjökull, riding mostly in silence and single file. Often when they stopped, for their midday meal or in the evening, Auden would produce a camera with which he took a large number of eccentric pictures, some that would illustrate *Letters from Iceland* – the backside of a horse, half of MacNeice's head and shoulders at the mouth of their tent. Unshaven in his black oilskin, cloth cap worn back to front, he looks like an Irish tinker. Unfortunately, the photographer seems to have taken no snap of himself, but Michael Yates gives a vivid picture of another kind:

I can see him to this day in his full vile-weather regalia. According to his own account he wore flannel trousers over his pyjamas topped by riding breeches, two shirts, a golf jacket under his tweed jacket, and enormous brown gum-boots. When it rained he put on a long black oilskin and a bright yellow sou-wester with an old felt hat fastened on over it with a safety pin. When the weather was at its most vile he also put on yellow oilskin trousers reaching to the waist. The first time he tucked them into his gum-boots which immediately filled with water. Having pulled them out he looked, to quote Louis, as though

An Irish tinker

he had webbed feet – 'wisps of hair straggled over his forehead and when he walks he moves like something that is more at home in the water'. This extraordinary apparition seen from behind, jogging along on a pony scarcely as large as its rider, with his right hand hovering near his mouth as though smoking a cigarette, was a sight I was always to remember with affection.

The misery and irritation of the poets' first night under canvas was no augury of things to come. Auden found MacNeice 'the ideal travelling companion, funny, observant, tolerant and good-tempered', and many years later would say: 'I have very rarely in my life enjoyed myself so much as I did during those weeks when we were constantly together.' The meditative silence in which they rode was counterpointed by lively conversation when they were out of the saddle. MacNeice would capture something of the flavour of this in his 'Epilogue' to *Letters from Iceland*:

> And the don in me set forth
> How the landscape of the north
> Had educed the saga style
> Plodding forward mile by mile.
>
> And the don in you replied
> That the North begins inside,
> Our ascetic guts require
> Breathers from the Latin fire.

Their guides, sometimes navigating by compass, led them through fair weather and foul to the centre of Iceland in which, said MacNeice, 'there are only three kinds of scenery – Stones, More Stones, and All Stones. . . . The stones are the wrong size, the wrong shape, the wrong colour, and too many of them. They are not big enough to impress and not small enough to negotiate.' Negotiate them they did, however, without accident more serious than the distintegration of their one stove, and on 25 August were back in Reykjavik. There, the school party spent their last two nights in the university hostel, while the poets and Michael Yates were billeted in the local Lunatic Asylum. The doctor in charge was charming and hospitable, but caused consternation by trying to engage them in Latin conversation.

Hoyland and three of the boys sailed for England on 27 August leaving Auden, MacNeice, and Yates to make two last short expeditions. First, they took a boat up the coast to Borganes and a bus inland to a farm at Hraensnef where Auden had stayed earlier. He wanted his friends to share his experience of rural hospitality. This included use of the family harmonium, at which he thumped out the hymns and psalms he had been prevented from playing at John Simpson's wedding. An extensive repertoire of 'sacred songs' was not the least important bond between Auden and MacNeice. After a few days, forsaking country comforts, the travellers returned to Reykjavik where they again boarded a ship going north, but this time to the far north. It put in for a day at Patreksfjördur, and they made the mistake of walking sixteen miles over a lava-strewn headland to a whaling station. Rewarded there with a scene of carnage that was 'enough', said Auden, 'to make one a vegetarian for life', they glumly walked the sixteen miles back. Next morning they were in Isafjördur, just south of the Arctic Circle, drinking Spanish brandy from tooth-mugs in the Salvation Army Hostel, eating in the North Pole café. A crossing – rough enough to make MacNeice violently sick – brought them to Melgraseyri, where for three days they walked and rode on unaccustomed grass and Yates listened while 'Louis' endless dreams defeated Wystan's Freudian theories'. Returning then to Reykjavik, they boarded the *Dettifoss* which set sail for Hull on or around 10 September.

Back in his Birmingham flat, with only the gramophone to keep him company, MacNeice set about selling his thirty rose-trees and most of his furniture. Having cleared the decks somewhat, he could prepare for his farewell party. This took place on the last Saturday in September and began for Louis and some of his guests at a decorous dinner party *chez* Dodds. At 9 p.m. the blue front door of Highfield Cottage was opened to a torrent of guests, among them Professor and Mrs Auden, Wystan, the painters Nancy and William Coldstream, who were staying with the Audens, Stephen Spender, Rupert Doone and Robert Medley of the Group Theatre, Walter Allen, Gordon Herickx, Henry Reed, and Reggie Smith. At one point, the topic of conversation turned to the Group Theatre's forthcoming production of MacNeice's *Agamemnon* and Doone swung into a 'camp' performance of Cassandra: 'I see *fountains* of blood!' Dodds interrupted – 'You'll find *fountains* of blood rather difficult to stage' – to which Doone petulantly replied: 'Aeschylus is static, I'm dynamic, so fuck all!' In due course the Audens and Doddses left, taking with them the last semblance of professorial decorum, and the party began in earnest. In the small hours, someone threw a glass of brandy into the fire, and the resulting jet of flame scorched the seat of Henry Reed's trousers. Walter Allen remembered waking at first light, in a makeshift bed on the floor, to see the tall bald figure of Gordon Herickx standing at the window, surveying the grounds of Highfield and murmuring to himself: 'So this is how the poor live!' Somewhat later, MacNeice led the survivors off to breakfast on Guinness and eggs in Selly Oak village. Early in October, he packed his bags and set off for London.

CHAPTER 13

The Flower of Cities

> Later as a place to live in and love in
> I jockeyed her fogs and quoted Johnson:
> To be tired of this is to tire of life.
> Nevertheless let the petals fall
> Fast from the flower of cities all.
> 'Goodbye to London', *CP*, p. 545

MacNeice loved cities. Much as he might enjoy running over the Wiltshire downs or holidays on Achill, he was always happy to return to Belfast, Dublin, Oxford, Birmingham, and – most of all – London. City of Lights, the British Museum, the Zoo, the BBC, Faber and Faber, London was a place of romance and infinite riches, but riches revealed only to be snatched away from the boy on his way to school or the poet visiting his publisher. Taking the refrain of his love-song to London from the work of another provincial Celt, Dunbar's poem 'In Honour of the City of London', MacNeice used the flower image found in a more surprising context, a memory of his visit to Spain at Easter 1936: 'We saw the mob in flower at Algeciras'. The mob – so hated by Yeats – seemed natural, even beautiful, to MacNeice, who throughout his life would view cities as romantically as countless pastoral and Romantic poets view the country.

London, to the ear of the Sherborne schoolboy,

> was an ocean of drums and tumbrils
> And in my nostrils horsepiss and petrol.

But never before had he plunged into its crowds with the exhilaration he felt in October 1936. The Bedford College term was almost upon him and on 8 October he wrote to Mrs Dodds, who had herself just

Geoffrey Grigson

moved to Oxford: 'Yesterday I saw my girls. Twenty of them – one at a time. The last one brought me some tea but they were not exciting; neither lead-astray-ful nor did they look intelligent. Tended to fall over the chairs and things. They all say they need a lot of help.' He was staying with his sister in Highgate, with little spare time in which to search for something more permanent, but a sudden stroke of luck solved that problem. Geoffrey Grigson, editor of *New Verse*, was living in the attractive garden flat of 4 Keats Grove in the foothills of Hampstead, but with the collapse of the *Morning Post* (for which he had been a regular reviewer) he was forced to look for somewhere cheaper, and was happy to sublet 4a Keats Grove to a fellow poet. On 28 October, MacNeice wrote to Mrs Dodds: 'Grigson is moving out on 2nd. Distemper man starts on 3rd, Movers collect stuff on 5th & I get in with the grace of God on 6th.'

Next day, with many things more pressing than literary matters on his mind, MacNeice's *Agamemnon* was published. It was dedicated 'To My Father', and the translator must have been aware that his gesture of filial respect was complicated – if not subverted – by his Preface that asserted:

The family is physically, and therefore morally, a unit: the same blood runs in all, and through it descends an inherited responsibility which limits, without wholly destroying, the power of choice in each. The sins of the fathers are visited on the children, so the children are victims of circumstances. But the children, because they are of the same blood, are tempted to sin in their turn. If a man holds such a view he will tend simultaneously to vindicate the ways of God and kick against the pricks of chance.

MacNeice does not endorse Aeschylus's view, but his failure to repudiate it may have caused the Bishop some disquiet – particularly if he remembered the context of the Aeschylean epigraph to his son's *Poems* (1935). In a 'Note on my translation of the Agamemnon of Aeschylus' sent to Eliot in July, MacNeice had said:

This translation was primarily written for the stage. Of the many English translations already existent none of them seems to me to emerge as a live play. I hope that mine reads like a live play; in working to this end I have been prepared to sacrifice the parts to the whole. I have consciously sacrificed two things in the original: the liturgical flavour of the diction and the metrical complexity of the choruses. I have tried to make this translation vigorous, intelligible, and homogeneous. I have avoided on the whole poetic or archaic diction and any diction or rhythm too reminiscent of familiar English models. The dialogue is in an elastic blank verse; the choruses are unrhymed (occasionally they echo the cadences of the original). The translation is, I think, closer to the original than many; I first wrote a very literal version, line for line, sometimes word for word, and afterwards modified it with a view to form, intelligibility, and dramatic effect.

In the process of modification, an awareness of the play's relevance to his own life and times had been brought home to him. A draft prologue emphasized the importance of Helen's elopement as a cause of the action and noted that 'both Menelaus and Agamemnon are ruined by their wives'. On a more public level, events in Germany and Spain had persuaded MacNeice – like many others – that another European war was approaching, and a dark sense of history repeating itself shows, for example, in the Herald's speech:

If I were to tell of our labours, our hard lodging,
The sleeping on crowded decks, the scanty blankets,
Tossing and groaning, rations that never reached us –
And the land too gave matter for more disgust,
For our beds lay under the enemy's walls.
Continuous drizzle from the sky, dews from the marshes,
Rotting our clothes, filling our hair with lice.

In such passages, MacNeice fulfils the ambitions set out in the Note he sent to Eliot, breathing new life into the ancient lines of a translation which Dodds's successor as Regius Professor of Greek at Oxford, Sir Hugh Lloyd-Jones, considered 'the most successful version of any Greek tragedy that anyone in this country has yet produced'.

The play deserved a better production than the Group Theatre gave it on Sunday 1 November in the Westminster Theatre. Dodds, who had acted as midwife to the translation and was now acting as advisor to the production, found Rupert Doone 'determined at all costs to display his originality and he made a dreadful hash of the *Agamemnon*'. The *Time and Tide* theatre critic agreed, reserving his sharpest barbs for the costumes designed by Robert Medley in close consultation with MacNeice:

Aeschylus, it seems, would be dead unless modernized. So we had the curious spectacle of a chorus dressed in dinner-jackets and goggles . . . a watchman as a hooded monk. Clytemnestra with a headdress of a Chinese mandarin backed by a scroll, Agamemnon with a jester's cap, slaves in purple tarbushes and veils and close-fitting black tights, more slaves dressed like the Klu Klux Klan, Cassandra as an Arab from the shores of the Euphrates, with an Elizabethan ruff, and lastly Aegisthus in a Christmas cracker helmet and black evening cape. This might be thought enough; yet undoubtedly the *pièce de résistance* was the almost universal gloving of the cast.

Even more hurtful to the translator was a mournful remark of the silver-haired Yeats: 'We are assisting, my dear Dodds, at the death of tragedy'. He had the grace to add, however, that the translation deserved a better producer. *The Times'* critic was kinder, observing acutely that 'Mr Louis MacNeice has loosened the tormented magnificence of Aeschylean language, and has produced verse, often reminiscent of Mr Eliot's *Murder in the Cathedral*, of which the easy naturalism goes far to bridge the gulf of centuries'. He went on to praise the acting: 'Mr Robert Speaight and Miss Veronica Turleigh [Agamemnon and Clytemnestra], equally matched in a noble beauty of diction, lift the play to a great height of liturgical dignity'. This critic knew his Aeschylus and found it 'impossible to forgive' MacNeice for robbing Cassandra of 'the most wonderful exit in the whole range of tragedy' by giving her last lines to the leader of the Chorus. He approved, however, of a significant addition to the play: 'A choric ode from the *Choephoroe* is introduced by way of conclusion, and justifies its place both as a hint of the further horizons of the story and as bringing on once more a body of dancers who have several times delighted the eye and the imagination.' The newly appointed Lecturer in Greek at Bedford College defended himself against the criticism of his translation in a letter to *The Times* on 12 November:

In finding it impossible to forgive me for transferring Cassandra's last four lines to the leader of the chorus, [your critic] may suggest to the innocent reader that I am the first person to do this unforgivable thing. It is, on the contrary, a transference approved by many scholars and one which is theatrically defensible.

I was admittedly tempted to leave these lines to Cassandra, but I feel that it is more in the Greek tradition that the chorus should have them. Omitting the other arguments for the transference I would point out that, if Cassandra is given these lines, the chorus immediately after her exit break straight into their anapaests, which are entirely concerned with Agamemnon, and so make no comment, however indirect, upon the doom of Cassandra herself. I prefer not to make them so callous.

MacNeice's sense of a scene-change in his own drama was heightened by the arrival of a long envelope containing a certified copy of his divorce Decree Absolute. The loss of Mary increased the fellow feeling between MacNeice and his recently widowed landlord-to-be. They had long talks that winter, in which Grigson was treated to a full recital of the life-story usually reserved for the ears of sympathetic women. Grigson was intrigued by the contradictions of the sceptical romantic (so well-matched by the stinking elegance of his attendant borzoi), the melancholy and the wit, the confidences and the reticence. Much though he liked MacNeice, he never felt he knew him, but thought of him – very perceptively – as 'our Pasternak', seeing him, for all his

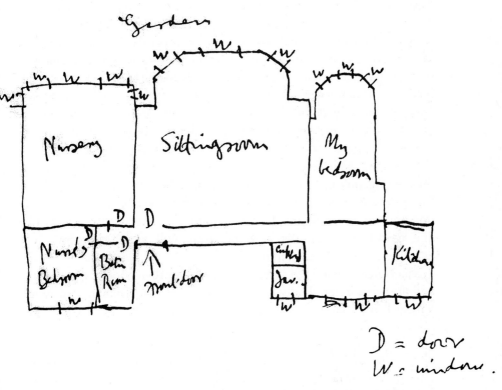

sorrows, 'always in terms of his delight in the Earth of the World'.

MacNeice was clearly delighted with Grigson's flat, into which he moved on 6 November. Number 4 Keats Grove had been built in 1812, three years before Wentworth Place, the house fifty yards down the road in which, from 1818 to 1820, Keats lived, loved, and wrote next door to Fanny Brawne and her widowed mother. The glory of each house was its garden: 4a was a 'garden flat'. Its front door opened into a corridor, which opened in turn into a handsome high-ceilinged sitting-room, whose French windows opened onto a wrought-iron staircase descending to the garden. The three principal rooms of the flat – nursery, sitting-room, and master bedroom – faced south and, even in November, were lit by the low sun striking through the branches of two large sycamores at the back of the garden. To the left and right of the sheltered lawn were shrubs and bushes, syringa and roses. If MacNeice hoped to share this little Eden with a descendant of Keats's nightingale, he was disappointed, but he was cheered to have the company of woodpigeons and owls.

One of the earliest and most welcome visitors to 4a Keats Grove was Wystan Auden, then living nearby, in an Upper Park Road maisonette, with the painters Nancy and William Coldstream. The two poets spent much of November and December together working on *Letters from Iceland*. The day before MacNeice moved in, Auden had written to Naomi Mitchison: 'Am up to the ears in a sort of travel book about Iceland. I've never enjoyed anything so much before, but I expect that's a bad sign.' MacNeice would later call the book 'a hodge-podge, thrown together in gaiety'. Both realized, rightly, that it had its faults. The gaiety that made it a pleasure to write makes it, in places, most notably Auden's brilliant 'Letter to Lord Byron', a pleasure to read, and in other places, the authors' 'Last Will and Testament', for example, somewhat self-indulgent.

MacNeice contributed three poems, half (or thereabouts) of a fourth and the prose letter, 'Hetty to Nancy'. His 'Letter to Graham and Anne Shepard' gives his reason for going to Iceland:

>   This complex word exacts
> Hard work of simplifying; to get its focus
> You have to stand outside the crowd and caucus.

Complementing that celebration of escape from the pains and pressures of the world, MacNeice's 'Eclogue from Iceland' offers a debate about the ethics of detachment and engagement between Ryan (MacNeice), Craven (Auden), and the ghost of Grettir Asmundson, 'last of the saga heroes'. Ryan identifies himself as an exile:

> I come from an island, Ireland, a nation
> Built upon violence and morose vendettas.
> My diehard countrymen, like drayhorses,
> Drag their ruin behind them.
> Shooting straight in the cause of crooked thinking
> Their greed is sugared with pretence of public spirit.
> From all which I am an exile.

MacNeice assigns to Craven his own experience of Spain the previous

Easter, in a passage that can be seen as almost a first draft of *Autumn Journal*, section VI:

> The bullfight – the banderillas like Christmas candles,
> And the scrawled hammer and sickle:
> It was all copy – impenetrable surface.
> I did not look for the sneer beneath the surface.
> Why should I trouble, an addict to oblivion,
> Running away from the gods of my own hearth
> With no intention of finding gods elsewhere?

Grettir the Strong advocates a more heroic course:

> Go back to where you came from and do not keep
> Crossing the road to escape them, do not avoid the ambush,
> Take sly detours, but ride the pass direct.

The Eclogue ends with the living convinced by the dead (it is implied) that engagement – 'Hatred of hatred, assertion of human values' – was now their only duty and their only chance. In this spirit, two months later, Auden would set off for Spain.

MacNeice's principal prose contribution to the book is the 'camp' letter, 'Hetty to Nancy', alias MacNeice to Blunt: 'Hetty' perhaps deriving from 'heterosexual', 'Nancy' from 'nancy-boy', homosexual. Michael Yates testifies to the accuracy of this diary/letter account of the journey round Langjökull in which Auden and MacNeice appear as two of a party of schoolgirls led by a mistress, Miss Greenhalge (Bill Hoyland). It has to be said that the gushing girl's school-story manner soon becomes tiresome, as do the in-jokes of 'Auden and MacNeice: Their Last Will and Testament'. This long poem in *terza rima* (appropriate for poets on the threshold of the Underworld) begins well, with generous bequests to the poet's families – as, for example:

> Lastly to Mary living in a remote
> Country I leave whatever she would remember
> Of hers and mine before she took that boat,
>
> Such memories not being necessarily lumber
> And may no chance, unless she wills, delete them
> And may her hours be gold and without number.

There are some good jokes in what follows:

> Item I leave my old friend Anthony Blunt
> A copy of Marx and £1000 a year
> And the picture of Love Locked Out by Holman Hunt.

But there are also far too many bad jokes, and most readers will arrive with a sense of relief at MacNeice's 'Epilogue for W. H. Auden'. Sitting late at night in 'lonely comfort', he reviews the companionable *dis*comfort of their weeks in Iceland, before saluting the 'lust for life' – in face of death – so engagingly demonstrated by Auden's contribution to their book, and ending his 'Epilogue':

> Still I drink your health before
> The gun-butt raps upon the door.

On 30 November Mary married Charles Katzman. She and Louis were still sending extraordinarily affectionate letters to each other. Addressing her as 'Darling Mary', he wrote: 'I do with all my heart wish you both everything you want & send you all my love as ever.' In a second letter the same day, he asked:

what *is* all this nonsense in your letters (a) suggesting that I don't like you as I did & (b) suggesting that you have ruined my life? What b -- ls! Or is it just fishing, sweetest? You know perfectly well (a) that I continue to like you as I did & (b) that you set my life on its feet a long time ago &, like Felix, it has been walking ever since. You've done your bit by me once & for good & I shall always be very, very grateful to you. For not only did you make me extremely happy, not only did I enjoy living with you very much indeed (though, as I now see quite clearly, it had to come to an end & it was lucky it ended with K. & not some other way) but you stopped me being a sap & that is no small service! So now, my dear, you must really quit worrying about me or thinking I am sad because I AIN'T.

Within weeks of their divorce, he had written a love-song – it was entitled 'Song' at its first appearance in print – for the girl who had been 'the best dancer in Oxford':

> The sunlight on the garden
> Hardens and grows cold,
> We cannot cage the minute

Within its nets of gold,
When all is told
We cannot beg for pardon.

Our freedom as free lances
Advances towards its end;
The earth compels, upon it
Sonnets and birds descend;
And soon, my friend,
We shall have no time for dances.

The sky was good for flying
Defying the church bells
And every evil iron
Siren and what it tells:
The earth compels,
We are dying, Egypt, dying

And not expecting pardon,
Hardened in heart anew,
But glad to have sat under
Thunder and rain with you,
And grateful too
For sunlight on the garden.

The garden of 4 Keats Grove is associated with other gardens, and with one most of all. Paradise has been lost, and again the 'sunlight on the garden' yields to the petrifying shadows of the cemetery, and gravity exerts its force. Almost a decade before, in the poem 'Child's Terror', the speaker lamented: 'I have lost my swing / That I thought would climb the sky'. Now, the recollection of that free flight is interrupted by a familiar sound. Maternal quietude is again succeeded by paternal din — church bells that explicitly identify father with God the Father, 'the voice of the Lord God . . . in the garden'. As in *The Waste Land*, 'then spoke the thunder', and MacNeice's association of thunder with divine imperatives is confirmed by the poem that immediately preceded 'The Sunlight on the Garden' in *The Earth Compels* (1938), their first publication in book-form. 'June Thunder' is attended by

Clouds like falling masonry and lightning's lavish

> Annunciation, the sword of the mad archangel
> Flashed from the scabbard.

Maternal sunlight is succeeded not only by paternal thunder, but also by paternal rain. As MacNeice's mother becomes associated with the fixity of stone, so his father becomes associated with fluidity in all its forms. The poem, propelled by its insistent rhymes, seems to move in a circle that, on closer inspection, proves to be a spiral; its end revealing a knowledge, a wisdom, not present at its beginning. Its vision extends from garden to grave and, in the space between, love teaches MacNeice to be as grateful for 'Thunder and rain with you' as for 'sunlight on the garden'.

The bells that rang out the old, rang in the new. Sometime in November or December 1936, walking back from Hampstead Heath with Betsy, MacNeice met Nancy Coldstream pushing her pram. They had known each other since, earlier in the year, Auden had introduced them in the Café Royal. She had thought he looked like a horse about to shy. They stopped and talked now in the street and, warmed by his 'black velvet voice', she remembered a sentence from Isaiah 44.16: 'Aha, I am warm, I have seen the fire.' They parted, each resolved to meet again. Before they did so, MacNeice met 'a girl called Leonora who was a musical actress, very tall, very blonde, all eye-veils, furs and egotism; dabbled in religion and poetry, mixed her conversation with French and German, and was painted by Royal Academicians'. This was almost certainly Leonora Corbett, whose conquests included A. A. Milne, in whose *Sarah Simple* she was to play the female lead in May 1937. She is said to have told a fellow actor, Griffith Jones: 'No-one can accuse me of having got here by my acting.' The affair with MacNeice ended, dramatically, with Leonora throwing a tea-table at him. As the flying tea-leaves scribbled their prophecy on the wall, the ex-lovers 'exploded into laughter' – perhaps, Louis thought, 'our one real moment of communion'.

Sometime before 7 January, when Auden left for Spain, he brought MacNeice back to supper at the Coldstreams' flat in Upper Park Road. At the end of the meal there was some debate – and eventually a competition – as to which of the men had the finest hair. The prize went to Bill Coldstream, but Nancy was fascinated by the length and lustre of the black locks that Louis unwound like a sikh's turban. After their guest had gone, that evening or another soon after, Wystan said to Bill with characteristic candour: 'Louis could be very convenient', keeping Nancy happy while he, Bill, got on with his painting. In their 'Last Will and Testament', the poets had left 'a call / To go a dangerous mission for a fellow creature / To Nancy Coldstream'. The nature of that call was not specified, but in February she agreed to go to Crufts Dog Show with MacNeice. Driving home, he lost his way and she was surprised at *his* surprise that she was not angry – as, he said, his wife and other women friends would have been. Another evening, when she and her husband had been invited to a party and Bill did not want to go, Wystan said: 'Why don't you take her, Louis?' He did; they drank too much; and she allowed him to take her back to his flat. He led her into his bedroom, locked the door, and, seizing her, bit her on the chin. She was furious, made him unlock the door and drive her home. Next time he was more gentle.

The delights and satisfactions of a new city, a new job, and a new love swept away the last vestiges of MacNeice's loneliness and depression. A new lust for life, a new creative energy took their place. Approached by the literary agent, Curtis Brown, with the news that Longmans were looking for someone to write them a book about the Hebrides, he took the bait. He wanted the money – both for itself and seeing it as 'a symbol of energy' – and having enjoyed the expedition to Iceland, proposed another collaborative venture. He would follow in the footsteps of Doctor Johnson to the Western Isles, accompanied by an artist, Nancy Coldstream; she to provide illustrations for his book (under her maiden name of Nancy Sharp). Longmans agreed, paying an advance of £75 that would cover the cost of the journey. Eliot was distressed to learn of his author's defection, but accepted his excuse that, since Longmans had proposed the book, he was not free to offer it to Fabers. With hindsight, MacNeice would come to see this as the first of a number of commissions for prose books for which he had no vocation, but which, he thought, 'I could do as well as the next man. It flattered me that publishers should ask me to do something unsuitable. The more unsuitable, the more it was a sign of power.'

Bill Coldstream raised no objection to his wife's part in the collaboration; her mother agreed to look after the children, Juliet and Miranda;

Nancy and Miranda Coldstream

and, on Saturday 3 April, the lovers caught the 10 a.m. train from Euston to Edinburgh. 'Auld Reekie' lived up to its nickname. The couple groped their way through the fog to a supper of haggis and whisky with Hector MacIver, an ardent Nationalist friend of Louis', before retiring to a mahogany catafalque in a sepulchral hotel. They spent most of Sunday in the National Gallery of Scotland, and next morning were up at 3 a.m. to catch the train to Mallaig on the west coast. From there they took a boat to Kyle of Lochalsh, at the northern end of the Sound of Sleat. Another boat carried them across the Minch to Stornoway on the Isle of Lewis, where they took a room in a hotel overlooking the harbour.

Next morning, Louis began gathering information for his book – from the editor of the *Stornoway Gazette*, from passengers in the afternoon bus to Ness, from a schoolmaster and his wife who lent them a wheelbarrow in which to carry their cases to a guest house. That night, their bed was so damp they slept in their greatcoats, but they woke to sunshine – almost the last they would see – and, after breakfast, began walking north. From time to time they would stop, Louis to write in his notebook or Nancy to draw on her sketching pad. Her trained eye – like Blunt's on the trip to Spain – showed him much that he would otherwise have missed, and she was rewarded with the words he found for things she could never have described. Over the days that followed, they settled into a companionable rhythm, walking, talking, their delight in each other's company compensating for boring food and damp beds. Louis fell ill in Miavaig, where for a day he groaned in bed, but was soon up and able to walk twenty-seven miles through the North Harris mountains to Tarbert. Next day, a boneshaking bus brought them to Rodel on the southern coast of South Harris, where they boarded a steamer to Lochmaddy in North Uist with a pair of Highland bulls. Two days later, they walked across seven miles of bog to Sollas airport and caught a small plane south to the Isle of Barra.

Black house, interior, showing central fire, by Nancy Sharp

There, they saw the sights: Nancy drawing Kisimul Castle, couchant on its rock in Castlebay, and Louis interviewing the uncrowned king of the island, Compton Mackenzie:

After various reminiscences of Ramsay Macdonald, H. G. Wells ('H. G.'), De Valera ('Dev'), F. E. Smith ('F. E.'), the Queen of England and the Archbishop of Canterbury, Mr. Mackenzie told me of his earlier years. He could read at twenty months, learnt Latin at four, Greek at eight, and at eleven was translating Shakespeare into Greek iambics. It was what was called being a prodigy; one finds similar cases in music. He had an extraordinarily good memory and could run the hundred yards in ten seconds. . . .

Mr. Mackenzie kept on talking. Every so often he would pop up from the sofa and stand on the white rug weighing himself on his feet and poising remarks as he poised the pipe in his hand.

Three days later, with the little *Loch Aline* due to leave for the mainland at midnight, MacNeice found he had only fourpence with which to get to Edinburgh, and was obliged to ask Mackenzie for help. He was given a lecture on the great grey seal and a letter to the ship's purser that persuaded him to cash a cheque for the penniless poet.

On their travels, Louis and Nancy had talked of marriage – he had said 'I'll give you a bull mastiff bitch puppy for a wedding present' – but the closer their train came to London, the larger the problems appeared. Nancy rang Bill from Euston and was troubled by how troubled he sounded, and her first evening home she rang Louis to say: 'It's not going to work.' He refused to accept that, and soon they slipped back into their old routine: Nancy running her household, painting when she had time, Louis caught up in the bustle of the Bedford summer term. His colleagues thought him 'polite but remote' and had the impression that he did not find 'either the classics in themselves or the teaching of them, particularly absorbing'. They were half-right: he did not enjoy teaching the ancient texts, but never ceased to enjoy reading them. As at Birmingham, his students found him more approachable out of class. He was happy to help the college's Reid Society organize readings and lectures by such of his friends as Auden and Spender, and would himself play a lively part in student discussions of poetry and politics. He was happier, however, with Nancy in his flat when Dan had been put to bed and the nurse was out. On nights when Nancy stayed, the nurse, who was becoming increasingly jealous, would protest by washing up into the small hours and banging saucepans in the kitchen sink (only a few feet away from the head of the lovers' bed).

He had told Mary of his two projected journeys round the Hebrides, and she wrote to him on 12 May – while her radio was reporting the Coronation of George VI:

I have been day-dreaming. And I thought how lovely it would be if I went to the Hebrides, put a shawl over my head, & took a herring in my hand: & then became your "native girl" – while you were there in the summer. My! Wouldn't that be fun!!! If you said 'yes' I would fly by the next boat.

Later in the letter, despair breaks through. She talks of suicide or leaving Katzman, adding: 'He knows that it is unlikely that I will stay with him *anyway*. And he is *sad*, but has promised that he would always help me. What do *you* say?' Louis could not give her the answers she wanted. She was miserable with Charles, missing Dan, and so desperate for news of him that, on 3 June, she wrote angrily threatening to ask her lawyer to force Louis to give her fuller and more frequent news of her son. Nothing, of course, came of this. Louis continued to write to her, but the demands of his new life took priority over the demands of the old.

In June his new play, *Out of the Picture*, was published. A painting called 'The Rising Venus' (as the play was originally called) – the first canvas to be completed by the painter, Portright – is no sooner delivered to his basement than it is seized by the bailiff. An artist's model, Moll O'Hara, says she will get it back for him. The scene then shifts to the Consulting Room of Dr Spielmann, a quack psychiatrist, who has to rely on his parrot, Bill, for diagnoses. (So MacNeice vents his spleen against the profession whose representative in Oxford had – without seeing him – diagnosed a psychosis that would result in suicide.) Dr Spielmann advises his patient, the beautiful film-star Clara de Groot, to cultivate an interest in Art. He takes her to an Auction Room where, in a sale that is a surreal parody of a church service (MacNeice satirizing the institution that darkened his childhood), she buys 'The Rising Venus'. Its velvet cover has yet to be removed and, before it is, Dr Spielmann conducts an experiment in mass hypnosis to impress his patient. He announces that the painter endowed his picture with magical power: everyone who looks at it falls in love with someone else in the room. 'The Rising Venus' is unveiled and the Auction Room is soon aswirl with waltzing couples. Act II opens in Clara's flat, with a Radio Voice announcing that war is about to be declared.

Dr Spielmann is called to Downing Street because 'The Prime Minister has gone mad'; and Clara, left alone with her newly acquired picture, dreams that she is visited by Spielmann's brother, Sholto, who has just resigned from the Government as Minister of Peace. She wakes to find Portright about to steal 'The Rising Venus' for which, it appears, she had been the unwitting model. He declares he loves her, that *his* picture is not worthy of her, and he takes her off to one of *her* pictures to see the real Clara de Groot. Later, returning to her flat for something she has forgotten, Portright meets and shoots the Minister of Peace whose policies precipitated the war, and is himself poisoned – as an act of mercy – by the devoted Moll. Enter then a *dea ex machina*; Venus steps forward 'out of the picture' and, in a long monologue to the audience, delivers a manifesto uniting the themes of the play – art, love, and death. The voice is unmistakably MacNeice's own:

> Man should not emulate the artist, Death.
> Let not man be contriving a frozen beauty;
> While he is here and now let him deal in here and now,
> Work and fight for meat and love,
> Gallant approximation, bravado of defeat.
> I am the principle of Unity and Division . . .
> I am the attempt to cover the abyss with grass
> And to spangle the grass with flowers
> And to put there cattle grazing the grass
> And young men picking the flowers,
> And to make believe through elaboration of pattern
> That life goes on for ever.

In a last scene, that enacts the end envisioned in the 'Epilogue for W. H. Auden', gun-butts rap on the door. Men 'in uniform with revolvers' come (too late) for Portright, and the play ends – as it began – with the voice of the Radio-Announcer.

The *TLS* reviewer of *Out of the Picture* rightly saw a debt to an Audenesque principle: 'Drama is not suited to the analysis of character, which is the province of the novel.' But he concluded that the play 'exhibits mental vigour, much amusement, and often brilliant writing, with dream-like rather than real characters.' The brilliance is mainly in the songs, arias (set to music by the young Ben Britten) that show a mastery of the short line counterpointing the longer, looser line of dialogue:

> Frost on the window,
> Skater's figures,
> Gunmen fingering
> Anxious triggers,
> Stocks and shares
> (The ribbon of the rich),
> The favourite down
> At the blind ditch.

Out of the Picture was to be produced by the Group Theatre in December, but in the meantime MacNeice was busy writing reviews for *The Criterion, The Listener, The Spectator*, as well as two books that would be delivered to their publishers before the end of the year: a new collection of poems and the Hebridean travel-book, *I Crossed the Minch*. In July, he made a second field-trip to the Hebrides, but this time on his own, Nancy being on holiday with her children in Bude. He took the Night Scot to Glasgow and, after a day in its Art Gallery, another night train to Oban, where he boarded an 'old friend, the *Lochearn*' on which he and Nancy had returned from Barra in April. He disembarked at Coll, an island to which Boswell and Johnson had been driven by a 'grandly horrible' storm. There he spent several days of determined walking before catching the *Lochearn* again, bound now for Coll's sister island of Tiree. After two days of rain, he was glad to move on to Barra, which reminded him of Achill where he had stayed with Mary in 1929. He had another woman in mind, however, the evening he left the island and, sitting in a deck-chair at the *Lochearn*'s stern, began a poem, 'Leaving Barra':

> The dazzle on the sea, my darling,
> Leads from the western channel,

> A carpet of brilliance taking
> My leave for ever of the island.

Carrying over the last word of the last line of each stanza to the end of the first line of the next, he himself weaves 'a carpet of brilliance' in which a figure finally appears:

> . . . you who to me among women
> Stand for so much that I wish for,
> I thank you, my dear, for the example
> Of living like a fugue and moving.
>
> For few are able to keep moving,
> They drag and flag in the traffic;
> While you are alive beyond question
> Like the dazzle on the sea, my darling.

Thinking of Nancy and pleased with his poem, he landed in high spirits at Lochboisdale on South Uist. Over the next few days he moved north, flying to Harris, before crossing over to Scalpay and back in a heavy rowing boat. He was given a lift to Tarbert, where he spent two nights and caught a bus going to Stornoway, but got out a mile beyond Loch Seaforth, leaving his kitbag (bought in Spain) to travel on ahead of him while he walked in a bracing wind. He took the wrong road, however, was caught in a deluge, and did not reach Stornoway until the following day. That afternoon, watching the annual sports in the nearby village of Barvas, he ran into his friend Hector MacIver, who invited him back to his house at Shawbost for the night. The following day in Stornoway harbour, MacNeice found a 'drifter', the *Fisher King*, that would take him out to see its ten-man crew shoot the nets. They caught little, but the wind in the Minch cleared the fumes of a night's heavy drinking with MacIver. There was another rousing night, at the Gaelic Concert (of the Lewis Pipe Band) and Grand Dance in Stornoway Town Hall, another trip to an island (Bernera), and Mac-Neice's working holiday was all but over. Unable to sleep in the smoke-room of the *Loch Ness*, bound for Oban, he came on deck at three in the morning and took a last look at the islands. 'The moon had an aura like a peacock's eye, Venus lay on a bank of cloud over Scotland, blue Vega was high over Skye.'

He was back in London for the publication of *Letters from Iceland* on 6 August. It was a considerable success. The Book Society had chosen it as their Book of the Month, and subscription sales of 8,000 copies necessitated an immediate reprint. Most reviewers were enthusiastic, though there were some that did not care for the 'Hetty to Nancy' section. *The Times*, however, singled out this 'delicious diary fragment' for special praise, and *The Oxford Times* thought these letters 'by far the liveliest things in the book'. MacNeice, reading a stack of reviews, was spurred by the adverse comments to write his co-author a letter, 'Hetty to Maisie', for inclusion in his new travel-book. Like much else in *I Crossed the Minch*, it is less good than the equivalent section of *Letters from Iceland*. This is probably because MacNeice thrived on company, and Auden's made the Icelandic lava-fields sparkle for him. Again, without the element of friendly rivalry, he tried less hard to entertain, and the Solitary Romantic sometimes found it difficult to keep his spirits up. Significantly, this was less a problem on the first journey, when his solitude was a fiction. Reading his account of their travels together, Nancy Coldstream was struck by the dark memories that did *not* appear: a sodden walk through a sinister gorge, their alarmed waking one night to a tolling bell, the Hebridean fortune-teller who told MacNeice he would not get the thing he wanted. Summing up, however in 'Hetty to Maisie', he complained that 'the natives didn't really take to me'; that he couldn't understand their Gaelic; that their 'religion is just too terrible' and their food little better. The best parts of the book are those furthest from the documentary mode: reminiscences of childhood, parodies of Pater, D. H. Lawrence, and Yeats, and – best of all – the poems. Three of these would appear in the new collection he was then assembling: 'Leaving Barra', 'On Those Islands (A poem for Hector MacIver)', a piece of verse journalism on a theme handled with more energy, more compression, in a poem that deserves to be quoted in full:

Bagpipe Music

It's no go the merrygoround, it's no go the rickshaw,
All we want is a limousine and a ticket for the peepshow.
Their knickers are made of crêpe-de-chine, their shoes are made of python,
Their halls are lined with tiger rugs and their walls with heads of bison.

.John MacDonald found a corpse, put it under the sofa,
Waited till it came to life and hit it with a poker,
Sold its eyes for souvenirs, sold its blood for whisky,
Kept its bones for dumb-bells to use when he was fifty.

It's no go the Yogi-Man, it's no go Blavatsky
All we want is a bank balance and a bit of skirt in a taxi.

Annie MacDougall went to milk, caught her foot in the heather,
Woke to hear a dance record playing of Old Vienna.
It's no go your maidenheads, it's no go your culture,
All we want is a Dunlop tyre and the devil mend the puncture.

The Laird o' Phelps spent Hogmanay declaring he was sober,
Counted his feet to prove the fact and found he had one foot over.
Mrs. Carmichael had her fifth, looked at the job with repulsion,
Said to the midwife 'Take it away; I'm through with over-production'.

It's no go the gossip column, it's no go the ceilidh,
All we want is a mother's help and a sugar-stick for the baby.

Willie Murray cut his thumb, couldn't count the damage,
Took the hide on an Ayrshire cow and used it for a bandage.
His brother caught three hundred cran when the seas were lavish,
Threw the bleeders back in the sea and went upon the parish.

It's no go the Herring Board, it's no go the Bible,
All we want is a packet of fags when our hands are idle.

It's no go the picture palace, it's no go the stadium,
It's no go the country cot with a pot of pink geraniums,
It's no go the Government grants, it's no go the elections,
Sit on your arse for fifty years and hang your hat on a pension.

It's no go my honey love, it's no go my poppet;
Work your hands from day to day, the winds will blow the profit.
The glass is falling hour by hour, the glass will fall for ever,
But if you break the bloody glass you won't hold up the weather.

The skirling rhythms of the Lewis Pipe Band are plucked from memory
to propel what MacNeice would later describe as 'a satirical elegy for
the Gaelic districts of Scotland and indeed for all traditional culture'.
He said 'the bad feminine rhymes are meant to suggest the wheeze of
the pipes'. Their air of hasty improvisation also suggests a new culture

that has no time for the civil harmonies of the old, the full rhymes of the traditional ballad. Time – the Decline of the West – is at one level what the poem is about, and nothing in it is more brilliantly controlled (while seeming to abandon control) than its timing: 'Bagpipe Music' quickens to a climax with the pumping repetition of 'It's no go . . .', then growls to a halt on a doom-laden note, the quintessential expression of Thirties' despair.*

The barometric glass might be falling, but others were still rising – Guinness glasses, black as a soutane, topped with a clerical collar – and the apocalyptic note was not the only note. The merrygoround kept turning, and the 'dance record playing of Old Vienna'. Louis was hard at work, but sometimes in the afternoon would leave his desk to play tennis with Nancy on courts near the BBC. She had once played for Cornwall and was good, as he in his spotless flannels, silk scarf tied loosely at the throat, was not. Afterwards, they might eat by candle-light in one of their favourite restaurants, Chez Victor or L'Etoile, whose formidable *patronne* Nancy once surprised by asking if she could paint her portrait. She was herself surprised with the reply: 'Many have wanted to ask that but none has dared. Yes, you may.' She also did two portraits of Louis: an oil and a charcoal sketch for the frontispiece of *I Crossed the Minch*. Nancy herself was attractively *gamine*, with blue eyes, arched eyebrows, and a mane of honey-coloured hair. Louis found her

an education – or rather illumination; so feminine . . . and so easily hurt that to be with her could be agony. She could be so gloomy as to black-out London and again she could be so gay that I would ask myself where I had been before I knew her and was I not colour-blind then. Of all the people I have known she could be most radiant.

She was less than radiant at the suggestion, from Louis or her husband, that they should set up a *ménage à trois*: she and her daughters, Louis and Dan, to live in the country; Bill to come down at weekends (no doubt with his laundry). It was becoming increasingly clear to her that Louis was better company as a lover than a husband. Bill thought of her as a decorative appendage, not as someone on whom to lavish time

---

* Compare this with MacNeice's poem of 1926, 'Glass Falling', *CP*, p. 4.

Louis by Nancy

or money, so she found it a marvellous change to be loved and cared for. 'That man', said Bill, 'must be spending £500 a year on you!' Louis showed more interest than her husband in her drawing and painting, and would sometimes show her new poems of his own.

As autumn drew on, he was involved in preparations and rehearsals for the Group Theatre production of *Out of the Picture*. Since their *Agamemnon* the previous November, the Group Theatre had been through stressful reorganization. There had been a move to find a more commercially rewarding alternative to their Sunday performances, and Eliot had tried to persuade Maynard Keynes to authorize a performance of *Out of the Picture* at the Arts Theatre, Cambridge. Keynes said no, agreeing with his wife, Lydia Lopokova, that the play was 'too . . . much an unhappy reaction against life'. The Group had no alternative but to continue with their Sunday performances, and *Out of the Picture* was staged at the Westminster Theatre on 5 and 12 December, in a form very different from that of the published text. The second part was radically revised and a long choral recitative added on the follies of a society drifting towards war. This, with Doone's choreography and Britten's music, was 'one of the most effective scenes ever created by the Group Theatre'. *Out of the Picture* was better received on the stage than on the page and, with the fall of the final curtain on 12 December, MacNeice had every reason to feel well satisfied with 1937, his 'year of wild sensations'.

CHAPTER 14

Summer is Ending

Close and slow, summer is ending in Hampshire . . .
'Autumn Journal', *CP*, p. 101

The skies might be darkening over Europe, but there was still sunlight on the garden of 4 Keats Grove. 1938 began auspiciously for Mac-Neice. On 7 January, he had good news of a collection of poems sent to Fabers some weeks before. Eliot wrote: 'I have read THE EARTH COMPELS last night, and am very much pleased with it.' He had a couple of minor editorial queries, but as soon as these were settled, he said, 'the poems can go straight to the printer'. The letter made no mention of an advance against royalties, which would not have surprised MacNeice, who understood the economics of poetry publishing, but money was more than ever a matter of concern to him. Life in London was more expensive than life in Birmingham. He was obliged to ask Dodds to lend him £20 and, shortly afterwards, Walter Allen saw him negotiate another loan.

Allen, now a freelance writer newly arrived in London, had been invited to speak to the Bedford College Literary Society about the contemporary novel. Having done so, he sat down expecting questions, but MacNeice, who was in the chair, at once brought the meeting to a close and led him from the room.

Outside, he asked: 'Have you got that thirty bob you owe me?' That I owed him thirty shillings was a fiction he clung to for several years. I hadn't, and he said philosophically: 'Oh well, we'll have to try the girls.' We went into a common room. 'Could anyone lend me ten shillings?' he asked, and immediately a dozen hands were rummaging in a dozen handbags.

The loan was no sooner raised than spent, at a Charlotte Street restaurant where the chairman gave the speaker (who was also a reviewer) a proof copy of *The Earth Compels*. Another day, the two friends met for lunch in the Café Royal and MacNeice, seeing a young man sitting at a table by himself, said: 'Look, there's Ben Britten. Let's join him.' MacNeice and Britten had been introduced by Auden in 1936, and the composer had since written music for the Group Theatre productions of *Agamemnon* and *Out of the Picture*. Now, at the Café Royal table, the talk was again of money. 'Was it easy, Louis wanted to know, to earn a living as a composer? Easier than for a poet? How much did Britten make a year?' The answer to the last question – '£15 a week', mainly from writing music for films – amazed the two authors, who were very impressed and very envious.

Wystan Auden and Ben Britten in New York, 1941

MacNeice had arrived in London knowing a number of literary and theatrical people, and his circle of acquaintance was widening all the time. In *The Strings are False*, he distinguishes between 'the old gang who were just literary and ... the new gang who were all Left'. As at Oxford, discovering that 'homosexuality and "intelligence", hetero-sexuality and brawn, were almost inexorably paired', MacNeice did not fit either stereotype and took to drink, so now in London he did not feel altogether comfortable in either gang – and continued to drink. This made him feel more comfortable in both. Next door in Keats Grove lived another Ulsterman and disillusioned Protestant Nationalist, Robert Lynd, described by Leonard Woolf 'as one of those impeccable journalists who every week for 30 or 40 years turn out an impeccable essay (called in the technical jargon of journalism a "middle") like an impeccable sausage, about anything or everything or nothing'. Lynd and his wife Sylvia, a brilliant and witty hostess, gave frequent literary dinner parties. At these, MacNeice met the old gang: 'J. B. Priestley, Oliver St J. Gogarty, Rose Macaulay .... They all of them had charm but, with the exception of Rose Macaulay, they talked as if the world were static.' MacNeice, like his contemporaries in the new gang, knew that history was on the move and in an alarming direction. He, too, wished it would change its course, but did not share the new gang's belief in the efficacy of committees: 'Committees to save democracy, to protect writers, to assist refugees, to pass, when every-thing failed, a measure of protest.' The new gang spoke and wrote about History (with a capital H) more than the old gang did. Earlier in the Thirties, the many Marxists and few Christians among them were generally agreed on one thing: that the History of the future would be better than that of the past. Much as MacNeice would have liked to believe this, he never could. His own experience of History – family History and Irish History – had left him with an underlying fatalism. He was sceptical of philosophical and political systems, sceptical of committees, sceptical of human motivation – not excluding his own. In the course of a 'Dialogue with my Guardian Angel' in *I Crossed the Minch*, he makes an admission that no other member of the new gang would have dared to make. 'With my heart and my guts', he says, 'I lament the passing of class. Of class, property and snobbery.' This is the voice of the dandy aesthete of 1930 rather (one might think) than that of the pub-haunting friend of 'Young Robinson', Walter Allen, or Gordon Herickx. Birmingham had brought MacNeice closer to the workers – in sympathy and understanding – than it would ever bring Auden, closer than London would bring Blunt, Day Lewis, or Spender. An Orwellian honesty, however, would always prevent him from concealing the inner self the others would deny, but time would increasingly reveal.

He saw through his friends of the new gang as he saw through himself, and his irony sometimes made them wary of him. 'Take the case of Stephen Spender', he says in *The Strings are False*, 'who was now living in a chic apartment with a colour scheme out of *Vogue*, a huge vulcanite writing-desk and over the fireplace an abstract picture by Wyndham Lewis'. One senses in MacNeice's detail both a sensuous delight in the objects he describes and a mischievous delight in the contrast they make with their owner's communist principles. He paints his portrait of Spender with the benefit of hindsight, but all the indications are that he viewed him as ironically in 1938, when the Group Theatre performed his *Trial of a Judge* at the Unity Theatre from 18–26 March. The play concerns a Judge who, having sentenced three fascist Blackshirts to death for murder and (reluctantly) three communists to death for carrying arms, is persuaded to rescind the sentence on the Blackshirts, but then recants the second judgement and is himself 'tried' and executed with the communists. The moral of this, as MacNeice identified, 'was that liberalism today was weak and wrong, communism was strong and right. But this moral was sabotaged by S's unconscious integrity; the Liberal Judge, his example of what-not-to-be, walked away with one's sympathy'. The communists and Fellow Travellers in the audience were troubled by this, and arranged a meeting – a trial of the author – following the last performance. It was, wrote MacNeice (using an adjective that might not have occurred to any other participant),

an exhilarating evening. There was a blonde girl, pretty and ice-cold, who got up and said that the play had been a great disappointment to herself and others in the Party; they had gone to the play expecting a message and the message had not been delivered; and *yet*, she said, there *was* a message to be given and they all knew what it was. She spoke precisely and quietly, never muffing a phrase (you could see her signing death-warrants). Certainly, S. answered, there was a message and they all knew what it was; an artist had something else to do than to tell people merely what they knew and give them just what they expected. The heckling went on. One after one the Comrades rose and shot their bolts. Marx, Marx and Marx. S. began to trail his coat; Marx, he said, was not necessarily what Marxists thought he was and anyhow you can't feed Marx to an artist as you feed grass to a cow. And another thing – the Comrades went on – this play gives expression to feelings of anxiety, fear and depression; which is wrong because ... S. said if they felt no anxiety themselves, well he felt sorry for them. Lastly, an old man got up, very sincere, very earnest, toilworn. There was one thing about the play, he said, which especially worried him; of course he knew S. could not have meant it, there must have been a mistake, but the writing seemed to imply an acceptance of Abstract Justice, a thing which we know is non-existent. S. deliberately towered into blasphemy. Abstract Justice, he said, of course he meant it; and what was more it existed.

After that S. gradually fell away from the Party; he had not been born for dogma.

MacNeice may mock Spender's inconsistencies, but no more than he mocks his own in *I Crossed the Minch*, and he clearly applauds the courage of the towering blasphemer. His portrait is fundamentally affectionate, though Spender might not have chosen it to hang above his fireplace.

For some months, MacNeice had been growing increasingly dissatisfied with his domestic arrangements: Keats Grove was further than he wished to be from Nancy's maisonette in Upper Park Road, and relations with the Scottish nurse were becoming strained. She resented Nancy's presence and Nancy was critical of the nurse, who persisted in treating Dan as a baby and kept him in his playpen until he was two and a half. MacNeice therefore nerved himself to find a new flat and a new nurse, although when he went flat-hunting with his sister and would say 'This could be the nurse's room', Elizabeth would object to the word 'nurse'. Her nephew now needed a nanny, but before she could be appointed, the Scottish nurse had to be disappointed. MacNeice hated this sort of confrontation, but on 10 April he was able to write triumphantly to Mrs Dodds: 'The crisis is over. She took it very well & nothing was broken. (I think I must have got a lot of tact.)' He was writing from the Bishop's House in Belfast, where he was depositing Dan before returning to search for a new flat and nurse or nanny. He told Mrs Dodds (to whom he now wrote more often than to her husband): 'I think I am going to live in an upper maisonette overlooking Primrose Hill (∴ very near the Zoo) with amazing views from the windows. Five rooms, lots of sun.' He was now looking, he said, for a father's help who '*Must* be placid, discreet & with lots of common sense, able to housekeep & cook, not snobbish, willing to go to Ireland etc. She will have good outings & be free of Dan from 9. till 4.0 five days a week.'

MacNeice himself had not been back to Northern Ireland since his self-imposed exile the previous April and, as so often, he approached his 'mother-city' gloomily. His 'conception of Belfast, built up since early childhood, demanded that it should always be grey, wet, repellent and its inhabitants dour, rude and callous'. This conception was shaken on the boat-train from London, when a Belfast man was friendly to the three-year-old Dan. They had a good crossing and disembarked in sunshine. The Bishop's House stood in Malone Road (which must have amused the Louis Malone who had written *Round-about Way*), with the Black Mountain at its back. For once, however, the mountain was not black but a luminous grey-blue, and the interior of the Bishop's ugly Victorian mansion was ablaze with azaleas. Unaccustomed light illuminated the portraits of earlier Bishops, the 'Grecian' black marble clocks, the furniture, books, and bric-à-brac of MacNeice's childhood. There, and driving between small fields on Saturday afternoon, and in Belfast Cathedral on Sunday, he felt strangely at home and strangely happy to be there. His father and stepmother were happy to have a grandson to fuss over – with five maids to help them, the extra work was hardly onerous – and, as the ferry drew away from the docks on Sunday evening, he looked back at a more benevolent Belfast. Some girls, standing at the ship's rail, were singing 'When Irish Eyes are Smiling' while his own eyes were delightedly recording what they saw:

As we went faster, crinkling the water a little, the reflections squirmed like tadpoles, the double reflections from the sheds regularly and quietly somersaulting. Two cranes facing each other conferred darkly. In the widening channel the lines of reflected lights behind us stretched in uncertain alleys like the lines of floating corks set out for swimmers. A black motor-boat cutting across them threw out shooting stars behind it. A buoy skated rapidly back-wards winking periodically red. Then the cranes and quays fell away and the channel opened into the lough – a single line of lights on each side – like a man stretching his arms and drawing a breath. Cassiopeia was tilted in her deck-chair over Antrim; Arcturus over Down.

He wrote busily for what remained of the Easter vacation. His Belfast letter to Mrs Dodds had asked her to tell the Professor he would start translating the *Hippolytus* – 'Have promised it to the Group Theatre for autumn' when he had finished his 'criticism book'. He had had those two projects in mind for some time. The translation he would never finish, unlike the 'criticism book', *Modern Poetry*, which had been commissioned by the Oxford University Press in February 1937. As originally conceived, this was to be a straightforward historical account of modern poetry from Housman and Yeats to 'the present day', but in September of that year, MacNeice wrote to his editor at OUP, John Mulgan:

I want to change the whole construction of it & make it much more personal. (There are so many books dealing with modern poetry in a series of chapters taking each poet or 'movement' in turn.) I want to call it 'Modern Poetry: An Essay in Autobiographical Criticism' and begin with several chapters analys-ing my own taste in poetry from when I began reading it up to the present moment, building on this certain conclusions as to the sort of poetry which is being written or can or ought to be written at the moment.

Mulgan agreed with this proposal, and MacNeice returned to the book with renewed enthusiasm.

His creative energy in the late Thirties was remarkable. On 28 April were published two of his four books to appear in 1938, *The Earth Compels* and *I Crossed the Minch*. Both are autobiographical and both, in a sense, travel books. As with the earlier *Poems*, *The Earth Compels* has an epigraph from a Greek tragedy MacNeice was then translating. This time, it is Euripides' *Hippolytus*:

δυσέρωτες δὴ φαινόμεθ' ὄντες
τοῦ δ ὅ τι τοῦτο στίλβει κατὰ γῆν

which may be roughly translated: 'We are manifestly all obsessively in love with this thing that glitters on the earth.' The book offers an impressionistic picture of a journey from brightness, 'The Sunlight on the Garden' (from which poem its title is taken), towards darkness; from Carrickfergus to Iceland and the Hebrides; from peace – by way of one World War – into the advancing shadows of another. The voice of the poems is the voice of someone in love with life that glitters on the earth, but someone who feels pursued like Coleridge's 'Ancient Mariner'. So, in 'Passage Steamer',

> Upon the decks they take beef tea
>   Who are so free, so free, so free,
> But down the ladder in the engine-room
>   (Doom, doom, doom, doom)
> The great cranks rise and fall, repeat,
> The great cranks plod with their Assyrian feet
>   To match the monotonous energy of the sea.
>
> Back from a journey I require
>   Some new desire, desire, desire
> But I find in the open sea and sun
>   None, none, none, none;
> The gulls that bank around the mast
> Insinuate that nothing we pass is past,
>   That all our beginnings were long since begun.
>
> And when I think of you, my dear,
>   Who were so near, so near, so near,
> The barren skies from wall to wall
>   Appal, appal, pall, pall,
> The spray no longer gilds the wave,
> The sea looks nothing more nor less than a grave
>   And the world and the day are grey and that is all.

From this steamer – on which a husband remembers his lost wife – we can look back to the 'Carrickfergus' steamer, and forward to the one 'Leaving Barra' with a lover on board who remembers someone 'alive beyond question / Like the dazzle on the sea'.

The Earth Compels is similarly alive, but its poems do not so much dazzle as glitter darkly. Several reviewers commented on a greater engagement with 'the world' than the earlier *Poems* had displayed.

Under the headline THE POETS GROW CLEARER, a leader-writer in the *TLS* said that MacNeice's new book shows him

continually aware of a grumbling and ominous world outside, in which he must do his duty. But his inclination is to write with delicate sensibility about his childhood, to make a curious pattern from the surface of everyday life, or to allow Iceland, which he has recently visited, to provide a romantic flight from reality.

Geoffrey Grigson, reviewing *The Earth Compels* in *New Verse*, put the emphasis on the world and the poet's perceiving self: 'the elegance in MacNeice's poetry is more one of sensuality now and less one of ingenuity, and the poems he is writing are the experiences of a lonely contemplative person, occupied with himself and with the world we share'. Grigson went on to claim: 'there is no other poet now in England who's such a good *writer* (Auden may be on a bigger scale altogether, but at present he does very often make a mannerism of his own inventions).' MacNeice would have been less pleased by Grigson's judgement of his other new book: 'I am not . . . writing much about *I Crossed the Minch*, because I do not think Mr MacNeice liked writing it, and so many of its weaknesses are irrelevant.' At the other end of the critical spectrum, the *Scrutiny* reviewer dismissed both books, together with *Letters from Iceland*, and regretted 'there are not many poets writing at the moment whom one wants to read'.

MacNeice may have been Scrutinized and found wanting, but his new books were widely – and generally well – reviewed; and he had other grounds for satisfaction. In May, he moved into 16a Primrose Hill Road, the maisonette overlooking Primrose Hill. It had five principal rooms: two in the roof – one for Dan and one for the nanny – and three on the floor below – a dining-room, a master bedroom, and an attractive sitting-room, described in a letter to a friend:

My desk is in the window & I have some awfully pretentious curtains – red & gold stripes. The walls are white & there is a thick carpet, warm grey. A lot of books on white shelves, an open fire, a large sofa, an armchair, a rockingchair, an ordinary chair & a card table.

Also in May he was 'recognized' – or confirmed – by a formal Resolution of the London University Senate 'as a Teacher of Classics at

Bedford College'. The consequent increase in salary helped with the wages of a new nanny, Miss Sophie Popper. A Hungarian Jewess, she was twenty-eight years old, small, cheerful, good at playing with Dan (who was recovered from the Bishop's House), and not one to clash saucepans in the sink when Nancy stayed late. MacNeice's life took on a new and happier rhythm. On sunny afternoons, Miss Popper and Dan would walk over Primrose Hill and down towards Regents Park to meet him as he returned from Bedford College on the south-west side of the Park.

There were many visits to the Zoo, because no sooner was the typescript of *Modern Poetry* despatched to the Oxford University Press than MacNeice began work in earnest on another commission. He had agreed to write a book for Michael Joseph on the subject of London Zoo. Designed for the armchair reader, this was to be more impressionistic than Julian Huxley's Official Guide to the Zoo. MacNeice had been fascinated by Zoos ever since his first visit as a schoolboy on holiday. He had come to think of the Zoo as 'a cross between a music hall and a museum', a place to be visited half because he liked looking at the animals and half because he liked looking at the people. It was also 'a nice sort of dream-world, and you can get into it for a shilling'. He had been thinking of his book for some time – had visited Edinburgh Zoo in July 1937, Bristol Zoo at the start of May – and had almost certainly begun writing it. On 1 June, he visited London Zoo again and, that evening, the lonely animal-watcher sat at the window of his Primrose Hill flat, looking out at a couple on Primrose Hill:

They lay facing each other, caressing, she with her hand on his hair, he with his hand in her bosom – for a long time lay there entranced and I could not see their faces. Then both sat up like puppets pulled by strings, their faces unflushed, perfectly matter-of-fact. He took out a cigarette, lit it, threw away the match like a man perfectly in control; she patted her hair, looked silently away into space. Spirals of blue smoke, ash tapped off into the grass, then Bang – both flopped down on the ground and resumed their loving. And all within earshot of the lions.

He worked on *Zoo*, writing little else, through June, July and the first half of August, taking the occasional break to watch tennis at Wimbledon or cricket at Lord's. There was a Bank Holiday weekend expedition with Ernst Stahl to see the Paris Zoo, and a flying visit with Nancy (who was illustrating *Zoo*) to Dieppe. They were eating lunch out of doors, at a table overlooking the harbour, when a group of hungry ragged children stopped to stare at them. Nancy said: 'We must go somewhere else.' 'Why?' replied Louis, not having noticed their audience. His lack of interest in children – hers included – she found troubling. Her daughters Juliet and Miranda being five and two, she painted at home. Every morning at 9.30, Bill Coldstream left the house for his studio and, at 9.45, their phone would ring. Answering it, Nancy would hear Louis' black velvet voice: 'What are you doing tonight?' If she said 'We're going to supper with X', he would reply 'Come and see me afterwards'. Sometimes, when their supper was some distance away and she knew they would be late, she would say 'I can't.' On those occasions, when the phone rang next morning, the black velvet voice would say reproachfully: 'I waited up for you half the night.' And the conversation would follow a depressingly predictable course: 'But I said I couldn't come.' 'I hoped you'd change your mind.' As the months passed, Louis' once-welcome attentions began to seem unreasonably possessive.

In August, however, that was only a small cloud on the horizon seen from 16a Primrose Hill Road. MacNeice was racing through the last chapters of *Zoo*. One day, when it was almost finished, Dan tripped over the telephone cord in the study, precipitating a white avalanche and his father's fury. Anger was in the air – and on the air from Germany and Spain – but it was easy to ignore it in High Tory Hampshire, where Louis, Dan and Miss Popper went on holiday after *Zoo* had been delivered to its publisher. They joined the Bishop and his wife at her sister Helena's comfortable house, Wickham Lodge in the village of Wickham, half way between Portsmouth and Southampton; and it was almost certainly there that MacNeice began drafting what many consider his masterpiece, *Autumn Journal*. At Birmingham, John Waterhouse had repeatedly urged his friend to write a long poem and when they met, shortly after MacNeice's Wickham holiday, he told Waterhouse he was following his advice and showed him part of the first entry in his *Journal*. A preliminary Note to the poem, written in March 1939, declared: '*I was writing it from August 1938 until the New Year and have not altered any passages relating to public events in the light of what happened after the time of writing.*' There is no reason to doubt the truth of this statement, and it would seem that Mac-Neice's sensitive antennae picked up in August 1938 distant echoes and vibrations of August 1914:

Close and slow, summer is ending in Hampshire,
  Ebbing away down ramps of shaven lawn where close-clipped yew
Insulates the lives of retired generals and admirals
  And the spyglasses hung in the hall and the prayer-books ready in the pew
And August going out to the tin trumpets of nasturtiums
  And the sunflowers' Salvation Army blare of brass
And the spinster sitting in a deck-chair picking up stitches
  Not raising her eyes to the noise of the 'planes that pass
Northward from Lee-on-Solent.

Hedges of funereal yew insulate those First World War generals and admirals from the fact that Herr Hitler's generals are only waiting for the harvest to be gathered, for trumpets other than those of silent nasturtiums and sunflowers to sound an end to peacetime preparations for war. The retired heroes in Hampshire do not reach for their spyglasses, nor do their sisters lift their eyes from their knitting, to wonder or worry about the planes from Lee-on-Solent.

MacNeice's 1935 essay, 'Poetry To-Day', had praised Auden, 'a journalist poet (I do not mean journalistic)', and had ended with 'a few predictions for the near future'. There would be less 'pure poetry', more 'psychological and political poetry', and more 'longer works (epics, epyllia, verse essays and autobiographies)' by poets. His predictions had been fulfilled, most notably by Auden, who wrote the text for what would prove one of the most successful documentary films of a decade fascinated by documentation: John Grierson's *Night Mail*. This travelogue was, of course, followed by others even more 'impure' – *Letters from Iceland* and *I Crossed the Minch* – that mingled auto-biography, factual documentation, and poetry. Only months before, MacNeice had sent the Oxford University Press the typescript of his *Modern Poetry*, at the centre of which were three autobiographical 'Case-Book' chapters ('Childhood', 'Public School', and 'Oxford'). The ground of his imagination was, therefore, prepared to receive the seed of his idea of a journal that would chronicle an autobiographical

journey from autumn into winter and perhaps beyond. It would have
everything that, in 1938, he asked of a poem: it would admit the
impurities of the world, the flux of experience, in a documentary form
that, for all its seeming spontaneity, would be directed into patterns on
a page – as images fixed on film – by the invisible imagination. We
cannot follow the making of *Autumn Journal* since no manuscripts
survive, but cannot doubt the maker's confidence and creative excitement as, after the poem's Old World overture, it gathers pace and picks
up a familiar rhythm:

> And I am in the train too now and summer is going
>   South as I go north
> Bound for the dead leaves falling, the burning bonfire,
>   The dying that brings forth
> The harder life, revealing the trees' girders,
>   The frost that kills the germ of *laissez-faire*;
> West Meon, Tisted, Farnham, Woking, Weybridge,
>   Then London's packed and stale and pregnant air.

The August air may have seemed stale to the returning holiday-
maker, though it is hard to believe that MacNeice was not happy to be
home from decorous Hampshire. He cannot have guessed, however,
what the pregnant air was shortly to bring forth, and to lull his reader
into his own excited anticipation, he salutes September as a month of
love: 'September has come, it is *hers*'. The lyrical aubade of *Autumn
Journal*'s fourth section gives way to the bitter fact that September will
not be Nancy's month so much as Hitler's. The August air had been
pregnant not with love but war.

Ever since March, when Hitler incorporated Austria into Germany,
it had been widely assumed that Czechoslovakia was next on his list.
On 4 September, Beneš, that country's President, agreed to all the
demands that the Czechoslovak Germans chose to make. They were
not satisfied with this and, on 13 September, attempted to revolt. The
attempt failed, but two days later Chamberlain flew to Munich and,
meeting Hitler at Berchtesgaden, offered the separation of the Sudeten
Germans from the rest of Czechoslovakia, on the basis of self-
determination. Beneš was forced to agree, on 21 September, by an
ultimatum from Britain and France that, unless he did so, they would

no longer support his country. Only the next day, Chamberlain, meeting Hitler at Godesberg, was confronted with new demands – nothing less than immediate occupation of the Sudetenland. When Britain, France, and Czechoslovakia rejected his Godesberg Memorandum, Hitler threatened war. Chamberlain returned to a London whose 'pregnant air' was quivering with banner headlines and wireless bulletins. On 26 September, the Foreign Office issued a warning: 'If German attack is made upon Czechoslovakia . . . France will be bound to come to her assistance, and Great Britain and Russia will certainly stand by France.' The fleet was mobilized and, on 29 September, Chamberlain again flew to Munich.

Earlier that week, a squad of Territorial soldiers had cut down the coronet of trees on the brow of Primrose Hill to make way for an anti-aircraft gun-emplacement. MacNeice was so depressed by this that he took a train to Birmingham and stayed a couple of nights with John Waterhouse. He showed him the start of *Autumn Journal*, and they spent the day listening gloomily to the wireless. The second evening they went to the Birmingham Hippodrome to be cheered up by George Formby – singing 'Cleaning Windows' and 'Chinese Laundry Blues' – and Florrie Forde, 'once a principal boy, now, with her voice gone still a music-hall sweetheart, sentimental as honeysuckle, vulgar as artificial violets, two hundred pounds of walking bonhomie and game to the last ounce of wobbling flesh'. MacNeice returned to London almost as Chamberlain arrived back from Munich, jubilantly waving the agreement he had signed with Hitler. That Friday evening, he told a cheering crowd: 'This is the second time that there has come back from Germany to Downing Street peace with honour. I believe it is peace for our time.' The following morning, MacNeice telephoned Walter Allen to say that, since there would be war by Monday and petrol, even if obtainable at all, would be rationed, he had just sold his car for £14. Would Allen join him for lunch at the Café Royal? The answer was obvious, and after a splendid meal, they took a taxi to a Tottenham Court Road cinema showing one of their favourite Westerns. It was raining when they came out, so they took another taxi to Oddenino's, where they had a few drinks before moving back to the Café Royal for dinner.

Monday 1 October brought no war to England, but that morning

'Peace for our time'

Hitler's troops marched into the Sudetenland. In England, the armed
services prepared for war while the universities prepared for term.
MacNeice pressed on with *Autumn Journal* and, looking ahead into a
darkening future, considered following Auden and Isherwood to
America. On 14 October he wrote to Eliot, asking if he could help him
arrange lectures at American universities over the Easter vacation. Eliot
promptly wrote to influential friends at Bowdoin and Bryn Mawr
Colleges, Columbia, Harvard, and Wellesley College; and it was
largely as a result of his good offices that MacNeice was able to set up
his lecture tour the following spring.

In October 1938, MacNeice heard from another of his admired
mentors, E. R. Dodds, who in his principled and practical fashion was
playing an active role in an important by-election for the City of
Oxford parliamentary seat. This was the British electorate's first
opportunity to express its opinion of the Munich Agreement. The
existing Labour candidate, Gordon Walker, was persuaded to stand
down 'as being too closely associated with Transport House orthodoxy
to have the necessary wide appeal' to pose a significant challenge to the

Government candidate, Quintin Hogg. Dodds was one of an informal delegation who persuaded A. D. Lindsay, the Master of Balliol College, to stand as a non-party candidate who would hope to attract anti-Munich voters, Liberal and Conservative as well as Labour. Campaigning vigorously for Lindsay, Dodds enlisted MacNeice's support in driving anti-Munich voters to the polls on Thursday 27 October. When the votes were counted, more had believed 'A vote for Hogg is a vote for peace' than that 'A vote for Hogg is a vote for Hitler'. Oxford had lived up to its reputation as the 'home of lost causes', and MacNeice drove disconsolately back to Primrose Hill. A fortnight later, he joined 300 professors, lecturers and students of London University in a march of protest against the ratification of the Anglo-Italian pact. A faded newspaper photograph shows him 'looking terribly respectable – mackintosh over his arm, and a flag on a long pole over his shoulder'. The *News Chronicle* reported him as saying: 'This is the first time that the staff of London University have done anything like this. It shows you how strongly some of us feel about it.'

In the middle of November, *Zoo* and *Modern Poetry* were published. Written to much the same recipe as *Letters from Iceland* and *I Crossed the Minch*, *Zoo* is less successful than its predecessors. An early chapter, 'The Zoo and London', shows MacNeice the philosopher-poet at his zestful best, but much of what follows is undistinguished journalism, and there are no poems. Kenneth Allott, reviewing the two books together in *New Verse*, put it well: 'Any single page has good things on it – an image, an anecdote or a turn of phrase, but I was weary before I put the book down simply because there was too much jewellery about, a profusion of images to mask, I thought, a flimsiness of thought.' Other reviewers were more generous – if less perceptive – and since *Zoo* was a Book Society Recommendation it sold well enough, though much less well than *Modern Poetry*, which over the years would prove one of MacNeice's most successful books. Subtitled 'A Personal Essay', it declares its purpose in the first sentence of its Preface: 'This book is a plea for *impure* poetry, that is, the poetry conditioned by the poet's life and the world around him.' An introductory chapter, 'A Change of Attitude', looks at the 'pure poetry' of the French symbolists and those who most notably extend that tradition,

Eliot and Yeats, before turning to the poets of his own generation with their very different political and cultural attitude to the world and their audience. The three autobiographical case-studies that follow give a personal context to MacNeice's theme and his subsequent discussion of the poets and poetry of the Thirties. Kenneth Allott was justified in calling *Modern Poetry* 'the least intimidating short cut to the under-standing of poetry (not just modern poetry) yet offered by an author to the ordinary man'; this, because the author saw himself and his con-temporaries as ordinary men: 'I would have a poet able-bodied, fond of talking, a reader of the newspapers, capable of pity and laughter, informed in economics, appreciative of women, involved in personal relationships, actively interested in politics, susceptible to physical impressions.' The extent to which this ordinary man shares the aspir-ations and apprehensions of those other ordinary men (and women), his readers, is nowhere more vividly illustrated than by the book's closing sentence: 'When the crisis comes, poetry may for the time be degraded or even silenced, but it will reappear, as one of the chief embodiments of human dignity, when people once more have time for play and criticism.' Just and generous as MacNeice's literary criticism is, it is – like Eliot's and Yeats's – a justification of his own principles. However, he shares with them a courtesy that enables him to acknow-ledge their influence and his continuing respect, while at the same time urging 'a change of attitude'.

MacNeice must have told Eliot of the long poem he was writing not long after he started it. By 14 October, the publisher is saying 'the sooner we can have the manuscript, the better it will be for giving the book an advantageous moment in the spring publications'. He asks in this letter for 'a statement about your new poem which would serve for the catalogue advertisement'. The statement that MacNeice sent on 22 November is what one would expect of 'a poet, able-bodied, fond of talking, a reader of the newspapers, ... involved in personal relation-ships, actively interested in politics':

Autumn Journal

A long poem of from 2,000 to 3,000 lines written from August to December 1938. Not strictly a journal but giving the tenor of my intellectual & emotional experiences during that period.

It is about nearly everything which from first-hand experience I consider significant.

It is written in sections averaging about 80 lines in length. This division gives it a *dramatic* quality, as different parts of myself (e.g. the anarchist, the defeatist, the sensual man, the philosopher, the would-be good citizen) can be given their say in turn.

It contains rapportage, metaphysics, ethics, lyrical emotion, autobiography, nightmare.

There is a constant interrelation of abstract & concrete. Generalisations are balanced by pictures.

Places presented include Hampshire, Spain, Birmingham, Ireland, & – especially – London.

It is written throughout in an elastic kind of quatrain. This form (a) gives the whole poem a formal unity but (b) saves it from monotony by allowing it a great range of appropriate variations.

The writing is direct; anyone could understand it.

I think this is my best work to date; it is both a panorama and a confession of faith.

By 5 December, MacNeice had written 1,700 lines of *Autumn Journal*. We have no way of knowing which sections they were, or when he saw how the personal theme would parallel the public one; the end of the love affair presaging the end of Peace. Certainly it was before 2 February 1939, when he sent Eliot the completed typescript; and it was probably before Christmas that he knew – even if he had not written – that

> The lady is gone who stood in the way so long,
> The hypnosis is over and no one
> Calls encore to the song.

Nancy had found their relationship increasingly claustrophobic, as MacNeice must have found it increasingly unsatisfactory. Then she met Michael Spender, Stephen's handsome, athletic, clever and charismatic elder brother. By Christmas she was in love with him, and out of love with Louis, though they would always remain affectionate friends. Perhaps not surprisingly, he did not like Michael Spender, but the lyrical tribute to Nancy in section IV of *Autumn Journal* and the leave-taking of section XIX ('I wish you luck and I thank you for the party') suggest that he was not utterly heart-broken at the party's end.

Ever since his visit to Spain at Easter 1936, MacNeice had closely followed the long slow agony of that country. His terse contribution to the Left Review pamphlet, *Authors Take Sides on the Spanish War*, in December 1937, probably reflected his distaste for the extravagant rhetoric some of his co-authors could be counted on to supply: 'I support the Valencia Government in Spain. Normally I would only support a cause because I hoped to get something out of it. Here the reason is stronger; if this cause is lost, nobody with civilized values may be able to get anything out of anything.' In December 1938, he was elected to the committee of the Association of Writers for Intellectual Liberty (an organization popularly known as FIL) and regularly attended its monthly meetings. The purpose of this body of university and professional people was 'to alert the public to the threat of fascism and war by means of lobbying, letters to the press, articles and meetings'. There were marches. On one of these, organized to demand arms for Spain, MacNeice and J. B. S. Haldane, the famous geneticist, carried the poles of a banner from Malet Street to Downing Street in a column chanting 'Arms for Spain!', 'They Shall Not Pass!' and, most popular, 'Chamberlain Must Go!' By December 1938, the Spanish Civil War was entering its last phase. The Republican offensive in the Battle of the Ebro River, launched in July, had failed. The International Brigades were withdrawn and, by 18 November, a Nationalist counter-offensive had crushed the Army of the Ebro. A month later, General Franco launched a new offensive in Catalonia, and soon Barcelona, the last bastion of the Republic, was under attack.

Early in December, MacNeice was invited to join a delegation of English writers due to visit Barcelona at the end of the month. He accepted, probably to get copy for a late section of *Autumn Journal* that would counterpoint the sixth section's memories of Spain in 1936. As the delegation's departure date approached, the other delegates dropped out (some, perhaps, discouraged by the bombing of Barcelona), and MacNeice decided to go on his own. Having deposited Dan and Miss Popper with his sister in Highgate, he had 'a fabulous dinner' at Prunier's with Ernst Stahl, after which they went on to spend Christmas in Paris. On 27 December, well insulated with food and drink against the cold, MacNeice caught a train to Perpignan. In his

Searching the wreckage in Barcelona

luggage he had a long piece of salami, a bottle of cognac, some biscuits, sugar lumps, and two tins of condensed milk. A diplomatic car drove him from Perpignan to the Spanish frontier, but there his papers were found not to be in order and, while the car went on without him, he took a bus back. The following day he had better luck: his new papers satisfied the frontier guards and a young Englishman gave him a lift to Barcelona, where he found a room at the Ritz. From that comfortable base, for the next nine days he walked or was driven (in a car from the Catalan Ministry of Propaganda) round the sights of the city: canteens, refugee colonies, the bombed cathedral, long lines of sleepers in the Metro. He had tea with Antonio Machado, since Lorca's execution the most famous poet in Spain; he watched a game of pelota and visited the desolate Zoo. On New Year's Eve there was an air-raid and, on his last day, he accompanied a convoy carrying food to Tarragona that was bombed on its way back. With a journalist's detachment he would come to despise, he made notes of this (as of everything else) to be reconstituted in the elegant prose of *The Strings are False*:

We lay down in the stony ditch and before our eyes a chain of bombs, six or eight, fell parallel with the road, so rapidly that I had no time to be frightened, merely thought what a wonderful show. First a big red flower and then another; then where the flowers had been, a powdery blue effulgence spreading upwards and outwards with scalloped edges, joining up with the next.

When he came to leave Barcelona on 9 January, the airport officials were puzzled by his notebook. 'What is this?' they said. '*Poesia*', MacNeice replied. The book was passed round. Then an American seaman, an ex-member of the International Brigade, appeared. 'What is that?' he asked. 'Just a few verses I wrote', answered MacNeice, feeling foolish. The American jerked his thumb at him. '*Propagandista!*' he said, and with that satisfactory explanation the notebook was handed back and the poet allowed to proceed. He broke his journey in Toulouse, and was shocked by the contrast (though he had not seemed unduly troubled by the contrast between the Barcelona Ritz and its refugee colonies). In the unravaged streets of Toulouse, 'people looked plump and complacent, smoking cigarettes and cigars; when you smoked you aroused no envy and the stubs lay ungathered in the ashtrays'. A late chapter of *The Strings are False* recaptures the onset of a desolate self-awareness. MacNeice found the French 'alien' in their smug prosperity: 'there was no danger or hunger to unite us . . . . they were self-centred for what else was there to be? It was all only too understandable but I still found myself hating them.' His pronouns ('us' and 'them') give him away, as he ruefully acknowledges: 'And I began to hate the English too who had passed by on the other side. Passed by under an umbrella. And then, very logically, I found myself hating myself.' This sense of personal shame underlies the Barcelona section of *Autumn Journal*, which must have been completed within weeks of MacNeice's return to England, since he sent the finished poem to Eliot on 2 February. He confesses:

> I have loved defeat and sloth,
> > The tawdry halo of the idle martyr;
> I have thrown away the roots of will and conscience,

and he resolves 'Now I must look for both', following the example of the people of Barcelona,

> The bearers of the living will,
> > The stubborn heirs of freedom

> Whose matter-of-fact faith and courage shame
>   Our niggling equivocations –
> We who play for safety,
>   A safety only in name.

MacNeice, the *propagandista*, ends this section with a direct address to his readers:

> Listen: a whirr, a challenge, an aubade –
>   It is the cock crowing in Barcelona.

The optimism has a hollow ring to it because the poet knew it was hollow: Barcelona fell to Franco's forces on 26 January, less than a week after an optimistic article by MacNeice, 'To-day in Barcelona', had appeared in *The Spectator*. The cock was crowing, not to welcome the dawn, but to echo the reproach of Simon Peter.

The post-Munich depression that deepened for the British Left with the fall of Barcelona was mitigated for MacNeice by several factors: first, the completion of *Autumn Journal*, his 'best work to date' and, secondly, Eliot's response to it. On 7 February he wrote,

I have read AUTUMN JOURNAL, and I think it is very good indeed. At times I was much moved, and what is still more unusual in the case of a single long poem, I found that I read it through without my interest flagging at any point. That is due partly to the dexterity with which you vary the versification, and, I think, to the fact that the imagery is all imagery of things lived through, and not merely chosen for poetic suggestiveness.

Eliot's only criticism was a mild questioning of emphasis on a political issue, which he viewed in a different light:

It is quite natural and proper that the Oxford by-election should be brought in, as that has a definite symbolic value, I am sure, for many people as well as for myself, as one of the historic points during last autumn. But I cannot help regretting that you simplify the issue so much in suggesting that the supporters of Quintin Hogg were mostly a pack of scoundrels. I think it is poor tactics to attribute motives, and that one is likely to overreach oneself in so doing. As a matter of fact, I think that one could make out a pretty good case for Lindsay's having been merely the less bad of two alternatives. Whatever one thinks of Hogg, Lindsay remains Goose Lindsay, and the alternative he offered was obsolete.

MacNeice met this criticism with a prefatory Note admitting 'over-statements in this poem' to be expected in a journal.

Other points of light in the gloom between his return from Spain and his departure for America were a rugby match – Ireland defeating England 5–0 at Twickenham – and a love affair. The only record of the latter is a posthumously published autobiographical novel, *Mrs Donald*, by Mary Keene. In January 1939, she was Mary Hunt, seventeen years old, slim and blonde, 'the most beautiful English girl I ever saw', said the poet Ruthven Todd. Her beauty had one blemish: an amputated lower leg, replaced by a tin substitute (held on by suction).

Mary Hunt in 1940

This did not prevent her sitting, as a model, for Lucian Freud, Augustus John, and Matthew Smith. She probably met MacNeice in one of the Soho pubs. All that we know is that she fell hopelessly in love with him – hopeless, because of what she perceived as an immeasurable gulf between them. Violet, the heroine of her novel, is described going to meet him:

Leaving the street she raised her eyes to the high calm sky, pink and effulgent with evening, her eyes fixing upon a glowing cloud edged with light in which she seemed to see Louis smile, his head held confidently there. She turned grasping at something, the brilliant cloud still fixed on her sight – the smile of the enlightened, she told herself – the great ones – poets. Louis was a poet and a painter and the awful fact made her see herself as a hollow sham, the belching clouds of sulphurous brown pressing down upon her brain, obliterating all she knew.

With her common understanding she must enter his great world, be blindly caught up in it. Oh farewell – she cried out to herself with an anguished thrust forward. She must get ready to act, and she felt tension grip her. Driving herself forward she looked down at the white silk blouse she wore, and felt the flowing breeze lift her hair, and raising her face she felt herself sail towards Louis – an unearthly creature like himself.

On the bus she imagined him – dark and magnetic, smiling indulgently at her old stupidity. On meeting him she had mocked him saying, 'I thought all poets were pale and drawn,' and he had turned to her intimately with a look that foreboded this other world and which ever since had held her in thrall. Her head turned upward and she struggled from drowning in the memory.

The romantic 'Louis' figure seems to have some of the characteristics of Henry Yorke, who wrote novels as Henry Green and was also at one time Mary's lover. Green had a wife, known as Dig, who was probably the model for the wife, Di, to whom Louis introduces Violet in Mary's novel. Yorke's wife was apparently tolerant of his infidelities, and Di raises no objection when the fictional Louis takes the young woman into another room, where they make love:

Violet felt she belonged to Louis, that the past was over and the future had come. It needed only that she be the person he wished her to be, to act, or rather live the part he wished her to play, live up to the idea he had formed of her, be the pale suffering unearthly creature he had discovered – be a poet like himself, and figure in his dreams.

Later, he gives her a book of poems. 'Inside he had written from L. to V. and the date, but – no love, no love, death-knelled in her mind, the echo of her own denial.' In fact, Louis gave Mary a copy of his *Poems* (1935) inscribed 'With love / Louis'. Writing her novel, however, she draws on a later present of his *Plant and Phantom*, inscribed 'For Mary, / May 7th 1941, / L.M.'.

Her fictional lovers take leave of each other in a scene that rings painfully true:

Louis, preparing to leave, was saying his farewells. He looked at Violet from where he stood at the bar, chatting to friends. To take her, so brilliantly new, to the party they were off to seemed a head-on clash of past and future. She wasn't properly dressed and now, as she felt his scrutiny, hardly in a party mood. She had no claims, he reminded himself, remembering the mutually embarrassed glance in which countless times he had put up barriers like a stretch of private ground between them. A void seemed to open up and carry him downstairs.

Violet instinctively felt his attitude, and felt herself stiffening. He would go now, she thought, and leave her there. She longed to move the great weight in her bones but felt as though she were made of clay which would crack if she moved. It was like those evenings after a marvellous time which they knew instinctively could not be repeated, and they fled from what was lacking between them. She felt him sail away, even now, on the ship. She would not feel, she must not care, only accept – quietly pretend that this was normal. She would not go into it, she would avoid the issue, and the agony would surge away – dreamlike . . . .

'Leave me here,' she said. 'I am expecting someone.' She could bear it, but only alone. She could not get up now and stumble out with him.

'I will send a postcard,' said Louis quickly, off to the party as if to present life to live, the knowledge that he might have taken her visible in their eyes, the final moment ceasing to exist except in nightmare regions.

Bedford College's Easter Term ended on 21 March. MacNeice deposited Dan and Miss Popper with his sister and her husband in Highgate, and was soon on his way to Southamptom and the *Queen Mary*.

CHAPTER 15

Talk of War

Only in the dark green room beside the fire
With the curtains drawn against the winds and waves
There is a little box with a well-bred voice:
    What a place to talk of War.
                        'The Closing Album', *CP*, p. 165

Much as MacNeice loved well-lit cities and the hum of the hive, nothing so quickened his imagination as lonely journeys in the darkness and silence beyond: 'it is easy', he wrote in the Introduction to *Varieties of Parable*, 'to identify with St Brandon and the others in their adventures on the western sea. The longest of these stories, The Voyage of Maeldúin, was used by Tennyson as the basis for a poem . . . . Such a voyage, like any form of quest, has an immemorial place in legend.' In March 1939, he had himself embarked in search of a legend: 'America . . . for people in the British Isles is a legend', especially, he might have added, for Irishmen brought up within sight of the Atlantic. He was disappointed, however, by both the *Queen Mary* and the Atlantic. The ship seemed like a hotel: 'you were hardly conscious of the sea, enclosed within shell upon shell of satinwood walls and sunk in club-room chairs'. Since he could not stand, like St Brandon or Odysseus, at a plunging prow gazing, salt-lashed, into the eye of the storm, he spent his time at the Tourist Bar observing his fellow passengers. Most were refugees, 'mainly Jews from Central Europe who covered their basic sorrow with volubility, fuss; only for a moment or two when they stopped troubling the water could you see the wreckage on the floor of their mind.' The image of shipwreck comes naturally to the romantic quester, as does the sympathy of the decent democrat. MacNeice had suffered greatly at the hands of Marie Beazley, Mary Ezra, and Charles

241

Katzman but when, in *The Strings are False*, he came to write his account of this crossing, he focused on the Jewish refugees and the horror still pursuing them:

The school-marm who came from Chicago explained to me, as if teaching me the ABC, that once a Jew moves into a street everyone else has to move out of it. 'Why?' I said. Because, she said gently, pitying my innocence, because they are so filthy in their habits; you should see what they throw out of the windows. But I had known a lot of Jews, I said.... 'Oh yes,' she said, 'you have quite a different *class* of Jews in England.'

Not that she was intolerant, she said, now what Hitler did to the Jews, she couldn't agree with that. But there was no doubt ... The tall old man, who was getting drunk, interrupted her, took the conversation to his bosom. 'I'll tell you something,' he said, 'and it's God's truth. You may not know it but I know it and I'm glad of it. One day soon the lid's going to blow off this country and every damn Jew's going to get what's coming to him. And will I be glad to see it!'

On the last morning of the voyage, MacNeice was not on deck in time to see the Statue of Liberty welcome the latest draft of 'huddled masses', but he continued to be aware of them even in the exhilaration of reaching the all but Celestial City. Walking up Second Avenue that first morning, he was accosted by unshaven beggars and with his eye for contradictions, contrasts, realized that 'there were two cities in this city, two cosmopolises, poor and rich. Glass and marble and banks like cathedrals on one hand; endless grimy streets on the other, with their iron fire-escapes showing, with bone and iron showing.'

Mary and Charles came to New York to see him and reinforced his awareness of the failure underlying and counterpointing the city's legendary celebrations of success. Mary was as talkative, Charles as taciturn, as ever. She told him of their life in Elizabeth, a 'dreary industrial limbo' on the outskirts of the city; how they had run a recreation ground, and then a library, for thousands of disadvantaged children; and how they had given that up for the chicken farm which she had wanted, or thought she wanted. Charles 'had farmed too though he still was a ballet fan. Now they never came to New York.' MacNeice makes no comment, but the voices so clearly audible behind his, for all their strenuous gaiety, are heavy with heartbreak.

He gave a lecture on modern English poetry at Pennsylvania State University on 28 March; at Princeton, probably later that week; at Hamilton College on 7 April; at Harvard (where he also gave a poetry reading) on the 11th; and at Wellesley College on the 12th. He was due to speak at Bowdoin College on the 18th, but had to cancel that engagement. His lectures earned him £80, leaving him about £40 out of pocket when he had paid his expenses.

His account of this first visit to America makes no mention of Auden, which is surprising, since one would have supposed their reunion to have been one of the high points of his trip. At the start of April, Auden and Isherwood left the hotel where they had been living, and moved – with Isherwood's boyfriend – to a cheap apartment on East 81st Street in the Yorkville district of Manhattan. On Maundy Thursday, 6 April, MacNeice and his two friends gave a reading, organized by the League of American Writers, under the title 'Modern Trends in English Poetry and Prose'. The first member of the audience to arrive was a twenty-two-year-old American poet, John Malcolm Brinnin, who had spent the greater part of his savings on a plane-ticket so that he could hear

three mortals who, as far as I was concerned, might have been Luke, Matthew and Mark, in haloes.

Louis MacNeice came first. Calm and handsome in a Donegal tweed suit and suede shoes, he read without the slightest change of emphasis poems that were either playfully light and intricate or casually grim and touched with the forebodings of Neville Chamberlain's England. Then came Isherwood. No bigger than a boy and with a smile broad enough to light up the room, he gave us a series of chatty anecdotes about the trip he and Auden had recently made to Chiang Kai-Chek's China. At last, Auden himself – reading from *Poems* and *On This Island* . . . .

Brinnin was not the only star-struck young man in the audience. After the reading he went backstage to find Auden talking to a blond teenager.

The youngster seemed decently shy and pleasant enough, I had to admit and, quite as I expected, Auden was being 'more than kind' to someone barren of any apparent credentials beyond fan club curiosity. Auden was also smiling an intrigued sort of smile, I noticed, and seemed actually to be prolonging a conversation he could only have wished to bring to a polite conclusion. Then I heard him ask the boy for his address and telephone number.

The name he wrote on the fly-leaf of the book Auden held out to him was 'Chester Kallman', who was to be his companion for the remaining thirty-four years of his life.

A meeting only a little less important for MacNeice took place, probably a few days later and at a *Partisan Review* party. Eleanor Clark was a beautiful, twenty-five-year-old writer of short stories, who had been married briefly to Trotsky's Czech secretary, Jan Frankl, with whom she had gone to Mexico some years before. MacNeice fell in love with her at first sight, or very shortly afterwards. She was flattered and excited by his excitement and vitality and wit. She did not ask him back to her furnished room on 11th Street, but went with him to the

Eleanor Clark in the 1930s

Queen Mary he reluctantly boarded in the third week of April. As the ship pulled out, he stood at the rail, searching the faces on the pier in mounting panic for one he could not find. Then consoled himself by 'talking' to her in a twenty-four-page letter. This insists that

The chief things are (a) that I love you & (b) that you have got to love me & (c) that if (a) & (b) are established, ((a) is anyway) things will be lovely & there is nothing really – except in the short run to be sad about. My love, I will talk about some other things in letters besides you & me (in case that is boring you) but just as the moment it is so on my brain – or heart – that you are really almost virginal (this has nothing to do with how many times you have slept with people; nor of course is it an insult) & that therefore we were probably quite right not to sleep together just now because that makes it (a) much more delicate but (b) much fuller of possibilities; when we have a lot of time, it will all evolve very naturally and beautifully. All the same I feel very Western Wind about it.* And you MUST COME, darling. There shall I be, waiting in the benighted old World, & if you don't come, I shall just give up the affections & turn Parisian. One of the first things I shall do in London is clear up the situation with my married friend. Of course, I have been clearing it up for some time – negatively, by explaining that I am no longer in love with her – but I had better now, I think, make it quite positive that I am definitely orientated elsewhere . . . .

Five pages later, he turned from private matters to the most public, a topic on which their views were diametrically opposed:

I have been thinking about this War question. You say, quite rightly, darling, that it will be just a dirty war of power politics, so what am I doing in it? All you are interested in is 'The Revolution' & you say that, if one is going to take action, the only thing to do is to foment the revolution directly. But look! if a war with Germany starts, it will be no damn good having an immediate revolution at home or a mutiny at the front. Because that will *not* (as you suggested) encourage the workers *in Germany* to revolt. It is much more difficult to revolt if your country is winning a war &, on your plan, Germany would be winning. (In Russia the war on that front was being lost.) . . . It

---

* Western wind, when will thou blow,
    The small rain down can rain?
  Christ, If my love were in my arms
    And I in my bed again!

    Anon, 15th [?] century

seems to me that the only hope in this War (if it happens) is for the people of England to enter into it on certain terms with the government (i.e. that it shall be terminated as quickly as possible by negotiation & with no Versailles nonsense.)

The following day, Saturday 22 April, MacNeice turned from political analysis to poetry, writing a poem on what he called 'the Still Centre theme', of which he later made a copy to send with this first letter. An ordinary moment in an ordinary coffee shop is cut like a celluloid 'frame' from the cutting-room floor, and held to the light of revelation:

Meeting point

Time was away and somewhere else,
There were two glasses and two chairs
And two people with the one pulse
(Somebody stopped the moving stairs):
Time was away and somewhere else.

And they were neither up nor down;
The stream's music did not stop
Flowing through heather, limpid brown,
Although they sat in a coffee shop
And they were neither up nor down.

The bell was silent in the air
Holding its inverted poise –
Between the clang and clang a flower,
A brazen calyx of no noise:
The bell was silent in the air.

The camels crossed the miles of sand
That stretched around the cups and plates;
The desert was their own, they planned
To portion out the stars and dates:
The camels crossed the miles of sand.

Time was away and somewhere else.
The waiter did not come, the clock
Forgot them and the radio waltz
Came out like water from a rock:
Time was away and somewhere else.

Her fingers flicked away the ash
That bloomed again in tropic trees:
Not caring if the markets crash
When they had forests such as these,
Her fingers flicked away the ash.

God or whatever means the Good
Be praised that time can stop like this,
That what the heart has understood
Can verify in the body's peace
God or whatever means the Good.

Time was away and she was here
And life no longer what it was,
The bell was silent in the air
And all the room one glow because
Time was away and she was here.

In the small round world of the poem, as in that of Keats's Grecian Urn, time has no place, but the poet soon found himself subject again to the tyranny of bell, clock, and radio, the time-bound routine of the white liner heading for Cherbourg and, at last, Southampton.

The London University summer term began on 25 April, and the following weekend MacNeice went down to Oxford, where the Doddses gave him whisky and much-needed moral support. He was missing Eleanor and depressed by the mood of the 'bloody little country' to which he had reluctantly returned. Eleanor's views may have helped to persuade him accept a request he would have preferred to decline. Some Labour supporters on the Bedford College staff asked him 'to speak to the girls on the significance of May Day, rally them to cut their lectures, go marching in the streets'. He did so, telling them also that 'they need not think that by marching on May Day they were serving the world but they might as well march all the same'. Writing to Eleanor the day after, he did not confess to this lukewarm support for the revolutionary cause. On 18 May, four letters later, he tells her: 'Autumn Journal . . . came out today'.

In the interim, he had quarrelled with Nancy Coldstream (agreeing to sit for a portrait painter of whom she disapproved), and so sent her copy of the book by post. It arrived as she was about to go shopping and she thrust it unopened into her bag. Taking it out in the Tube, she began to read – for the first time and with tears cascading down her cheeks – his account of their last autumn. Less privileged readers, ever since, have been held and compelled by an irresistible voice to follow MacNeice from Hampshire to Primrose Hill, by way of Ancient Greece and modern Ireland, Sherborne and Marlborough, Oxford and Birmingham. The voice is a living rather than a literary voice, though the living voice of a literary man; the voice of 'a man speaking to men', to use a Wordsworthian formulation not followed in the great Wordsworthian poem that lies behind MacNeice's. *Autumn Journal* is *The Prelude* of the Thirties, but it is a dramatic rather than a philo-sophical poem, sometimes recording emotions as they occur, some-times recollecting them, but seldom in tranquillity. History is a river on which Wordsworth in *The Prelude* looks back to the rapids of the French Revolution, whereas MacNeice can hear the premonitory thun-der of the Falls ahead. Memory is a structuring principle of both poems, but in *Autumn Journal* it is a post-Freudian, Proustian memory that flies back and forward like a weaver's shuttle, leaving past and present, public life and private life interwoven on the loom.

Section V, for example, opens calmly enough:

> To-day was a beautiful day, the sky was a brilliant
>   Blue for the first time for weeks and weeks
> But posters flapping on the railings tell the fluttered
>   World that Hitler speaks, that Hitler speaks
> And we cannot take it in and we go to our daily
>   Jobs to the dull refrain of the caption 'War'
> Buzzing around us as from hidden insects
>   And we think 'This must be wrong, it has happened before,
> Just like this before, we must be dreaming . . . .'

While other voices try to prolong the dream, that of the narrator breaks in to puncture it:

> But did you see
> The latest? You mean whether Cobb has bust the record
>   Or do you mean the Australians have lost their last by ten
> Wickets or do you mean that the autumn fashions –
>   *No, we don't mean anything like that again.*

No, what we mean is Hodza, Henlein, Hitler,
　　The Maginot Line,
The heavy panic that cramps the lungs and presses
　　The collar down the spine.
And when we go out into Piccadilly Circus
　　They are selling and buying the late
Special editions snatched and read abruptly
　　Beneath the electric signs as crude as Fate. . . .
The cylinders are racing in the presses,
　　The mines are laid,
The ribbon plumbs the fallen fathoms of Wall Street,
　　And you and I are afraid.

As the brilliant day ends – *Autumn Journal* is a poem of endings – we sense the accelerating river behind the shorter lines. The illusion of a speaking voice is assisted by the alternation of line-ending 'masculine' stressed rhyme-words (Line/spine) with 'feminine' unrhymed words (record/fashions) ending with an unstressed syllable; and the insistent repetition of the colloquial conjunction 'and':

What will happen next. What will happen
　　We ask and waste the question on the air;
Nelson is stone and Johnnie Walker moves his
　　Legs like a cretin over Trafalgar Square.
And in the Corner House the carpet-sweepers
　　Advance between the tables after crumbs
Inexorably, like a tank battalion
　　In answer to the drums.

Neither Nelson nor Johnnie Walker will say whether the answer is War or Peace (which they respectively represent), but the probability is suggested with psychological subtlety by the carpet-sweepers imaged as tanks. Day and section end together with an interweaving of some of the opposites and contrary states – men and women, creatures and machines, past and present – on which the poem is structured:

And factory workers are on their way to factories
　　And charwomen to chores.
And I notice feathers sprouting from the rotted
　　Silk of my black

Double eiderdown which was a wedding
    Present eight years back.
And the linen which I lie on came from Ireland
    In the easy days
When all I thought of was affection and comfort,
    Petting and praise.
And now the woodpigeon starts again denying
    The values of the town
And a car having crossed the hill accelerates, changes
    Up, having just changed down.
And a train begins to chug and I wonder what the morning
    Paper will say,
And decide to go quickly to sleep for the morning already
    Is with us, the day is to-day.

This is followed, as if with a dream, by memories of Easter 1936 –
'And I remember Spain' – as , in section XVI, 'reading the memoirs of
Maud Gonne', *A Servant of the Queen* (1938), MacNeice is prompted
by the word 'Servant' to

        remember, when I was little, the fear
    Bandied among the servants
That Casement would land at the pier
    With a sword and a horde of rebels;
And how we used to expect, at a later date,
    When the wind blew from the west, the noise of shooting
Starting in the evening at eight
    In Belfast in the York Street district;
And the voodoo of the Orange bands
    Drawing an iron net through darkest Ulster,
Flailing the limbo lands –
    The linen mills, the long wet grass, the ragged hawthorn.
And one read black where the other read white, his hope
    The other man's damnation:
Up the Rebels, To Hell with the Pope,
    And God Save – as you prefer – the King or Ireland.
The land of scholars and saints:
    Scholars and saints my eye, the land of ambush,
Purblind manifestoes, never-ending complaints,
    The born martyr and the gallant ninny;

The grocer drunk with the drum,
 The land-owner shot in his bed, the angry voices
Piercing the broken fanlight in the slum,
 The shawled woman weeping at the garish altar.

His diatribe still subconsciously directed by Maud Gonne's description of herself as 'A Servant of the Queen' – that queen being not Victoria, whom her soldier father served, but Kathleen ni Houlihan, icon of Ireland – MacNeice continues:

 Kathaleen ni Houlihan! Why
  Must a country, like a ship or a car, be always female,
 Mother or sweetheart? A woman passing by,
  We did but see her passing.
 Passing like a patch of sun on the rainy hill
  And yet we love her for ever and hate our neighbour
 And each one in his will
  Binds his heirs to continuance of hatred.

One of the qualities that makes *Autumn Journal* so moving, as Eliot said, is its honesty. MacNeice agreed with Wilfred Owen that 'All a poet can do today is warn. That is why the true Poets must be truthful.' No poet of the Thirties is more truthful when the truth is unflattering and likely to be unpopular. So, in this his most searching examination of Ireland's Irishness and his own, he asks and answers a more difficult question:

 Why do we like being Irish? Partly because
  It gives us a hold on the sentimental English
 As members of a world that never was,
  Baptised with fairy water;
 And partly because Ireland is small enough
  To be still thought of with a family feeling,
 And because the waves are rough
  That split her from a more commercial culture;
 And because one feels that here at least one can
  Do local work which is not at the world's mercy
 And that on this tiny stage with luck a man
  Might see the end of one particular action.

The dream of what Yeats called 'perfection of the work' leads, by way of a thundering jeremiad, to a recognition that his love and hatred are inseparable for the country whose legacy has been to undermine his own poetic project:

> she gives her children neither sense nor money
> Who slouch around the world with a gesture and a brogue
> And a faggot of useless memories.

Bitter Night Thoughts are an important element in *Autumn Journal*, but MacNeice had called the poem 'a confession of faith', and the closing lullaby of section XXIV ends with a vision of a possible future, a belief not in God but in man:

> Sleep, the past, and wake, the future,
>   And walk out promptly through the open door;
> But you, my coward doubts, may go on sleeping,
>   You need not wake again – not any more.
> The New Year comes with bombs, it is too late
>   To dose the dead with honourable intentions:
> If you have honour to spare, employ it on the living;
>   The dead are dead as Nineteen-Thirty-Eight.
> Sleep to the noise of running water
>   To-morrow to be crossed, however deep;
> This is no river of the dead or Lethe,
>   To-night we sleep
> On the banks of Rubicon – the die is cast;
>   There will be time to audit
> The accounts later, there will be sunlight later
>   And the equation will come out at last.

The accounts would later show this poem, published at the Thirties' end, to have caught the spirit of its decade as *The Waste Land* had caught that of the Twenties. New impressions were called for in 1940, 1943, 1945, 1946, 1948, 1964, and since 1966 it has been one of the jewels in the crown of MacNeice's *Collected Poems*.

Despite the success of *Autumn Journal*, his mind was now on the future rather than the past, a future in which Eleanor Clark was the central figure. She confessed she was scared of entering into an intense relationship so soon after the collapse of her marriage, and he replied:

I knew perfectly well in New York that you were not – in that sense of the word – 'wholehearted' (evidence: (a) several things you said, (b) several things you didn't say, (c) a curious physical impression that you had some kind of Hindenburg line pretty well intact which you were very reluctant to stop defending.)

This was perfectly natural, he said; there was no reason to suppose she would find herself in another mess; she should just 'come over' and let him show her the West of Ireland. A week later, he wrote to tell Dodds 'a minor tragedy has happened. Eleanor can't come to England this summer. Chief reason money but also work.' The best solution seemed for him to get a temporary academic job in America, but the Principal of Bedford College was only prepared to grant him leave if he found 'a really good substitute'. In the hope that this might be arranged, he made a formal application for leave of absence without salary for the academic year 1939–40, and on 20 June was able to write to Eleanor: 'I have blackmailed my old ladies into giving me a year's leave of absence. All against their principles but I suggested that otherwise I would quit.' Later in this letter, he mentions a new project: 'In August I shall be staying a bit in Ireland in a house by the sea with my family; will try & get healthy there & write this awful book about Yeats. After that no more books to order; I am sick of it.'

MacNeice had told Grigson some years before that he had given up rereading Yeats for fear of being influenced, but the Arch-poet's death in January 1939 seems to have removed that threat. On 1 March, MacNeice read a paper on 'Yeats' to a meeting of the Association of Writers for Intellectual Liberty, and that spring was commissioned by Oxford University Press to write a critical study of Yeats's work. He must have hoped this would make him some money but, more importantly, probably felt a need to 'have it out with Yeats' and define some of his own attitudes and priorities in relation to those of his fellow countryman. In a review of Yeats's posthumously published *Last Poems and Plays*, entitled 'Yeats's Epitaph', he adopts a tone similar to that of Auden's great elegy, 'In Memory of W. B. Yeats', first published (in the same magazine, the *New Republic*) on 8 March. Auden, addressing the great shade, had said 'You were silly like us'. MacNeice used the same word, saying that Yeats's more naïve enemies regard him as knave or fool all through – at best as a 'silly old thing'; his more naïve admirers regard him as God-intoxicated and therefore impeccable. It is high time for us to abandon this sloppy method of assessment; if poetry is important it deserves more from us than irresponsible gibes on the one hand or zany gush on the other.

Yeats, he went on, had two passions – Ireland and Art – both prominent in his last poems but, having for so long celebrated a static feudal Ireland, he had been brought round by the Irish Troubles to

an admiration, even an envy, for the dynamic revolutionary. His thought, in assimilating this element, became to some extent dialectical; he began to conceive of life as a developing whole, a whole which depends upon the conflict of the parts. He even began to write in praise of war, a false inference from a premiss which is essentially valid . . . .

MacNeice is correct in identifying the pernicious false inference drawn from an essentially valid premiss, but wrong in thinking Yeats's dialectical thought a late development. He had believed, with Blake, that 'Without Contraries is no Progression' since the early 1890s. The compassionate MacNeice recoiled from the 'inhumanity' that could sanction the murderous violence he so abhorred, but saluted Yeats's late recognition that even the highest, purest art is rooted in impurity:

> I must lie down where all the ladders start,
> In the foul rag-and-bone shop of the heart.

As soon as the Bedford College term was over, he began reading intensively for his Yeats book in the British Museum, where, ironically, his bag would be searched in case it contained an IRA bomb. Walter Allen, Reggie Smith, and Ernst Stahl were also working in the Reading Room and happy to join him for coffee, or a beer, or a cigarette sitting on the steps outside. Something of what he was thinking in the colonnade found its way into a poem, 'The British Museum Reading Room':

> Out on the steps in the sun the pigeons are courting,
> Puffing their ruffs and sweeping their tails or taking
>   A sun-bath at their ease
> And under the totem poles – the ancient terror –
> Between the enormous fluted Ionic columns

> There seeps from heavily jowled or hawk-like foreign faces
>   The guttural sorrow of the refugees.

He drafted this poem on the back of an envelope and showed it to Nancy Spender, who did not much like it. 'You think poetry should be about great things, don't you?' he challenged her. She did not, but said 'Yes'. Other poems were stirring in his head. On 27 June (the day his Bedford College colleagues appointed his substitute), he wrote to Eleanor that he had gone to the ballet 'with someone who never watches anything except Les Sylphides – escape, escape, escape'. Less than a week later, he told her: 'I am writing a new kind of poem; there are going to be 50 of them – very bleak, very simple, very objective, all in the 3rd peson.' One of the first – and best – of these was the poignant portrait of a marriage, 'Les Sylphides', whose completion he announced with some satisfaction a fortnight later. Another account of the painful transition from innocence to experience, also written in July, was 'Christina':

> It all began so easy
> with bricks upon the floor
> Building motley houses
> And knocking down your houses
> And always building more.
>
> The doll was called Christina,
> Her under-wear was lace,
> She smiled while you dressed her
> And when you then undressed her
> She kept a smiling face.
>
> Until the day she tumbled
> And broke herself in two
> And her legs and arms were hollow
> And her yellow head was hollow
> Behind her eyes of blue.
>
> . . .
>
> He went to bed with a lady
> Somewhere seen before,

> He heard the name Christina
> And suddenly saw Christina
> Dead on the nursery floor.

Truth, as so often, is stranger than fiction. What at first sight appears a surrealist fantasy is almost certainly a splicing of two memories: the first, of Elizabeth's doll; the second, of Mary Hunt 'who took her foot off before she went to bed'.

The June letter to Eleanor reported a brief visit to Belfast to take part in a radio discussion with an Irish poet of an earlier generation, F. R. Higgins. The BBC had asked them to talk about modern poetry, but Higgins made it clear from the outset that he only wanted to talk about modern *Irish* poetry and 'the rhythm of the race', a rhythm he declared broken or no longer functioning organically in the work of young English poets. MacNeice argued that the racial rhythm was not the only, or the most valid, one:

am I to take it that you think that today racial rhythm is more important for the poet than the international or extra-national rhythms we have mentioned?

Higgins: Yes, I would say racial rhythms are better for the poet who exists within the rhythm than the international rhythms that are only dimly perceived or felt by those who try to interpret them.

MacNeice: On those premises there is more likelihood of good poetry appearing among the Storm Troopers of Germany than in the cosmopolitan communities of Paris or New York.

Outpointed in that round, Higgins came back fiercely, attacking MacNeice as a defector:

I am afraid, Mr. MacNeice you as an Irishman, cannot escape from your blood, nor from our blood-music that brings the racial character to mind. Irish poetry remains a creation happily, fundamentally rooted in rural civilisation, yet aware and in touch with the elementals of the future. We have seen the drift of English poetry during the past few centuries – the retreat from the field to the park, from the pavement to the macadamed street, from the human zoological garden to the cinder heap where English verse pathetically droops today. You do not wish to repudiate us for that?

MacNeice, however, had the last word:

I have the feeling that you have sidetracked me into an Ireland *versus* England match. I am so little used to thinking of poetry in terms of race-consciousness that no doubt this was very good for me. However, I am still unconverted. I think that one may have such a thing as one's racial blood-music, but that, like one's unconscious, it may be left to take care of itself. You have been eulogising present-day Irish poets and damning present-day English ones whom you think of as drooping young men on a cinder heap. The last time I saw these young men, they were not very drooping and I do not think that their poetry droops either. However, whether their poetry droops or not, poets of the Auden-Spender school (which is now producing the most vital poetry in England) *are* attempting something legitimate. Compared with you, I take a rather common-sense view of poetry. I think that the poet is a sensitive instrument designed to record anything which interests his mind or affects his emotions. If a gasometer, for instance, affects his emotions, or if the Marxian dialectic, let us say, interests his mind, then let them come into his poetry. He will be fulfilling his function as a poet if he records these things with integrity and with as much music as he can compass or as is appropriate to the subject.

The debate continued long after the microphones had been switched off. It lasted through the night and ended in a characteristically Irish fashion. After Higgins had denounced MacNeice for twenty-four hours for having de-Irished himself, he asked him if he would like to belong to the Irish Academy of Letters. 'I said yes,' he told Eleanor, but added: 'they'll probably think better of it. The Irish Academy of Letters meets once a year in Dublin's only decent restaurant and gets so drunk they have to send the waiters away.' Later that day, 12 July, he watched a very different annual celebration – the Orange procession commemorating the Protestant victory at the Battle of the Boyne.

With the marchers' drums still reverberating in his head, MacNeice returned from the commemoration of one war to anticipations of another. 'Everyone told me that if I was going to America, I had better go quickly: war would break out within a month.' But he could not go to America, having as yet no job in prospect, and anyway there was something he wanted to do first. He had been planning to take Ernst Stahl on a tour of the West of Ireland, and the fatalist in him said: 'War or no war, you have got to go back to the West. If only for a week. Because you may never again.' In the middle of August, he was best man at Reggie Smith's registry-office marriage to Olivia Manning and, after taking them and their four guests to dinner

Orange Procession

at Chez Victor, he and Stahl set off for Ireland.

From Dublin, where by way of initiation Stahl was taken to the top of the Nelson Column, they went north to Cushendun Bay in Co. Antrim. Bishop MacNeice had rented a handsome country house there for the summer, and invited his children and their friends. It was called Rockfort, and Louis arrived to find his father and stepmother, his sister and her husband, Dan and Miss Popper, and Miss Popper's refugee father already installed. Every morning Louis and Ernst drove to Ballycastle to play golf, stopping to buy a newspaper on the way. On 24 August, this told them that Ribbentrop and Molotov had signed a Nazi-Soviet non-aggression pact. Hitler's next move was clear; the only question, when would he make it. 'Ought we to go back?' Ernst said. 'Certainly not', Louis replied, and they went on to play golf as usual. If they were to see the West, however, it was now or never, and a day or so later they set off in Elizabeth's ancient, growling Lea-Francis. They reached Galway on the last day of August. On Friday 1 September, they were leaning over a bridge, watching salmon 'facing upstream, oscillating slightly but keeping their places', when Ernst said: 'It is nearly time for the news'. He walked back to the hotel, leaving Louis to watch the salmon that would soon be 'gently swaying' in his poem 'Galway'. When eventually he, too, returned to the hotel, Ernst said: 'It's started. They invaded Poland last night.'

Ernst was now anxious to get back to England as quickly as possible, so Louis drove him to Dublin and saw him on to a night ferry. Not having the heart to return to Cushendun, he spent the Saturday drinking in a bar with Irish literary friends who, far from sharing his sense of catastrophe, only wanted to discuss variant versions of Dublin street songs. On Sunday morning, he was woken in his hotel with the news that England had declared war on Germany. That afternoon he went to a hurling match – 'Cork in crimson against Kerry in orange and black' – and tried to forget the greater conflict in the excitement of the lesser, but failed, and next day drove back to Cushendun.

Apart from one postcard in August, Louis had not written to Eleanor – who had herself been ill and writing little – since the middle of July, but now wrote to tell her:

Ernst Stahl in the 1940s

I am very worried about my father who seems in a decline. . . . comes down out of bed to listen to the radio & sits brooding on a map of Poland. The Times Lit. Supplement – damn them black – were crass enough to wire me for a war poem. (I didn't answer.) I have a whole batch of real poems however which I shall send you when typed.

These included a sequence entitled 'The Coming of War' (later to be called 'The Closing Album'), lovingly detailed views of town and country seen with Stahl: 'Dublin', 'Sligo and Mayo', 'Galway' and, perhaps most memorably, 'Cushendun':

> Fuchsia and ragweed and the distant hills
> Made as it were out of clouds and sea:
> All night the bay is plashing and the moon
>   Marks the break of the waves.
>
> Limestone and basalt and a whitewashed house
> With passages of great stone flags
> And a walled garden with plums on the wall
>   And a bird piping in the night.
>
> Forgetfulness: brass lamps and copper jugs
> And home-made bread and the smell of turf or flax
> And the air a glove and the water lathering easy
>   And convolvulus in the hedge.
>
> Only in the dark green room beside the fire
> With the curtains drawn against the winds and waves
> There is a little box with a well-bred voice:
>   What a place to talk of War.

The reader's eye is led – as by a zooming camera lens – down from the distant hills to the bay and, then, the whitewashed house protected by its walled garden. Entering the house, we are given a glimpse of the kitchen on our way to the sitting-room where, finally, the eye is brought to rest on a little box. It speaks, and what it says we learn from the mild voice of the narrator. At the poem's end, we are left looking at a world in which everything has been altered by the shocking revelation of the last word.

Louis was writing poems and letters to Eleanor about the progress of his plans for getting to America, but nothing else. On 14 September he told her 'that for some time now I have ceased from my academic vocation'. He would do no more work on his translation of Euripides' *Hippolytus* or the book on Latin Humour (to be called *The Roman Smile*). The critical study of Yeats had also come to a halt, but then something happened that must have made that book seem more relevant than the others. He met Walter Starkie, Professor of Spanish at Dublin University, who suggested that he apply for the Chair of English at Trinity College, Dublin, about to be vacated by Wilbraham Trench. Trench had been preferred to Yeats at the previous election. MacNeice liked the idea and duly applied, with strong support from Dodds and Eliot. He was then in correspondence with his publisher about another prose book,

to be called something like Plaudits & Aspersions or Blessings and Curses. Autobiographical but not in the usual way. A series of quick shots – with some more drawn-out ones – of the significant events of my life, not so much things I have done as things I have met; the padding left out & a pattern appearing through variations on several recurring themes; some of it – the more personal parts – in disguise, possibly fantasy. Roughly in chronological order, it would cover: – the North of Ireland, child's nightmares, Ulster mentality, Ulster religion, sadist mother's help, zany gardener, Orangemen: the last War, preparatory school in Dorset, a Dorset Powys, a 1919 Oxford aesthete: public school (Marlborough), games etc., sex fantasies, a dream about the Crucifixion, public school Picasso fans: Oxford, Auden & Spender etc., dons, drink: Jewry & marriage – treated obliquely: Birmingham, pigeon-fanciers, the Birmingham surrealists, provincial universities – maybe classical digressions: divorce treated obliquely: London from 1936, various odd travels, the Left: Barcelona New Year 1939 (a whole chapter): New York: finally Ireland again ending with news while in Galway of Germany invading Poland.

Eliot offered – and MacNeice accepted – a contract (with £100 advance) for this prose reworking and elaboration of the material of *Autumn Journal*.

The result of the Trinity College election would not be known for some months and, until it was, MacNeice could not finalize his American plans. He was finding his father's house gloomier than ever. They 'had family prayers in the morning but the god of the house was the radio. "And that is the end of the news." But it never was.' He found welcome distraction in the company of a new friend, George Mac-

Cann. A (then) surrealist painter, two years younger than MacNeice, he was one of those who justify Oscar Wilde's description of the Irish as 'the greatest race of talkers since the Greeks'. They were introduced in Mullens bookshop and took to each other at once. When MacCann said he had to go, MacNeice asked him where he was going? 'Down to the country', he replied. 'Can I come with you?' asked MacNeice, and they drove off together to 'Vinecash' in Co. Armagh, where George and his wife Mercy lived. This was a single-storey whitewashed cottage, surrounded by apple trees. It had a primitive kitchen; a dining-room with an open hearth, a long black table and two benches; three bedrooms; and a lavatory on the far side of a cobbled yard. After supper that first night, MacNeice read aloud from A. L. Lloyd's translation of Lorca's *Lament for the Death of a Bullfighter and Other Poems*, and showed a reluctance (the MacCanns would discover to be habitual) to go to bed. His hosts solved the problem by moving a spare bed into their room. By the end of that visit, the first of many, painter and poet had discovered they shared a love of art, poetry (including Greek poetry), rugby football, stout and Irish whiskey.

This new friendship did something to lighten the darkness of Mac-Neice's Belfast, but he was finding the city increasingly oppressive. Soldiers and patriotic posters in streets that were 'blacked out' at night (in case of air-raids) were continued reminders of war. Dublin was another world – 'a dance of lights in the Liffey, bacon and eggs and Guinness, laughter in the slums and salons, gossip sufficient to the day'. While awaiting decisions from Trinity and various American universities he had approached, MacNeice spent a good deal of time in Dublin's happier world. He talked of Yeats and painting with the poet's more gentle and genial artist brother Jack. He talked of Irish politics with Ernie O'Malley, who, at forty-one, was already a legendary figure in Ireland. As a medical student in 1916, he had found a rifle and spent the week of the Easter Rising as an amateur sniper. Some months later he joined the Irish Volunteers, became an IRA Captain, was captured and escaped to be wounded and captured again in the bitter civil war which followed the establishment of the Irish Free State in 1922. MacNeice hated the violence he represented, but could not help admiring the man of action, raconteur, and author of a brilliant memoir, *On Another Man's Wound* (1936). He spent much

Ernie O'Malley

(but not all) his time in pubs, and told Dodds he was in danger of sliding into his 'rashest entanglement yet'. Eileen Phillips was a Dubliner, no intellectual, but beautiful and capable, and their friendship – though platonic – flowered to a point at which he considered asking her to marry him. That he was able to speak of her in his still ardent letters to Eleanor suggests that such a marriage was never more than a conceivable consequence of his being unable to return to America. This possibility receded with the welcome offer of a job at Cornell University: a 'Special Lectureship in Poetry', from 12 February to 31 May, for a stipend of $2,000.

By the time he received this, he had slid into what was unquestionably his 'rashest entanglement yet'. One of his London friends, secretary of FIL and a leading light in the New Gang, was Margaret Gardiner. She 'knew everybody': had met D. H. Lawrence, climbed in

Margaret Gardiner (photographed by Nicholas Lee)

Snowdonia with I. A. Richards, and known Auden in Berlin. It was Auden who introduced her to MacNeice, when he was staying at 4a Keats Grove and working on *Letters from Iceland*. She lived nearby in Regency Hampstead, in a house full of fine paintings and sculpture by such of her friends as Ben Nicholson and Barbara Hepworth, and she studied Auden's friend with an artist's eye:

The MacNeices originally came from Connemara and it was in Connemara that I had seen rough-hewn versions of Louis – tall, proud, bony men with long faces, dark-haired and dark-eyed. That was the mould in which Louis was cast, differentiated by the full sensitivity of his mouth, his moody, grey, dark-lashed eyes and a camel-look of disdain. . . .

I was immensely impressed by Louis' dark good looks and what seemed to me an air of mystery. I was also, I suppose, rather piqued by the fact that he appeared to take no interest in me at all.

She soon found her first impression of his *hauteur* to have been mistaken: 'Louis was a friendly man, interested in people and without a trace of conceit'. They became friends, seeing each other at the monthly meetings of the Writers' FIL Committee and at parties. They saw *Stagecoach* together, and one cold afternoon she sat through a rugby match with him. Now, in late October 1939 , he invited her to join him in Belfast for a long weekend. They went to a party at George MacCann's house, drank too much, and next morning found themselves in bed together. It soon became clear that this episode meant more to her than to him. Returning to England, she confided to Dodds, who wrote sternly to MacNeice. He replied:

Dear E.R.D.,
Thank you very much for your letter. Of course I don't mind being talked to like that, in this case however I rather disagree with what you say. I am *not* in the habit of using my friends like prostitutes but I do feel guilty over M.G. as she is the only person I have ever had anything to do with without feeling in the slightest degree romantic about her. I don't know what account she gave you of the business but I expect you have gathered that it happened as a pure accident. I don't argue that such accidents are defensible & I don't pretend to have calculated at the time what its effects might be. If however I had done any calculation, I shouldn't have imagined that she would suffer over it. . . . she knew about my American fixation & other things. I don't know a bit what I *can* do for her. If & when I come to England, I shall of course see her but I don't see that that can do much good. You see, I like her very much but I haven't even the beginnings of any romantic feeling for her. & if she is, as you say, empty-handed, so are most people I know, including myself.

This letter suggests the depth and strength of the friendship between the two men; Dodds's rock-like integrity; and the honesty they have in common. MacNeice goes on to speak of his feelings for Eileen Phillipps, his stronger feelings for Eleanor Clark, and ends:

I am tired to death of polygamy. I should like to live somewhere monogamously & work eight hours a day. I do feel (though you probably won't believe me) very remorseful over M.G. but what can I do? If I try meeting her half way, it would only make things worse.

A month later, he told Dodds that Margaret had come to Dublin for the weekend and had said 'her visit did her good (I hope to God that is so). She was very nice & I really do feel extremely guilty over her. She says she will return to normal in time.'

MacNeice may not have been working eight hours a day, but he was working none the less – intermittently on Yeats and, with greater satisfaction, on a one-act play for (he hoped) the Abbey. *Blacklegs* is an O'Caseyan tragi-comedy, set on scaffolding round a church steeple. Three strike-breakers, a Professor and two labourers (Jim and Jack), talk with two women at adjacent windows of a nearby block of flats. Mrs Byrne (the name suggests a Roman Catholic) reviles and threatens them:

if there's one person will go to hell quicker than another isn't it a dirty Judas of a blackleg betrays the cause of the poor? (*She takes up a rug and shakes it out of the window.*) Much good it is me trying to air my room and two ruffians the like of you contaminating the sky every time I open the window. But it's not long you'll be fooling around on that steeple. A little bird told me something this morning. Did you ever hear tell of a gentleman called Rodd McGinn? Rodd McGinn was never a man to be patient. It's near a week now you blacklegs been on this job. A week you been at it and only two of you in hospital. But a little bird came to me this morning. 'Peep, peep, Mrs. Byrne', he says, 'Rodd McGinn is after winding his clock'. . . .

At the other window, Miss Wilson (the name suggests a Protestant) is, by contrast, friendly. Discovering that Jack's wife is in labour, she rings the hospital for news. Discovering also that he is the brother of Rodd McGinn (who has already put one strike-breaker in hospital), she warns him that 'Mrs Byrne is in with Eddie Ryan & you know how thick Eddie Ryan is with your brother'.

Mrs Byrne, having earlier called the Professor 'a dirty Judas', now plays that role herself and passes the word that brings Rodd McGinn up on the hoist. Revolver in hand, he interrogates the blacklegs, and lets Jim and the Professor go. Jack then explains that only by strike-breaking can he earn money he must have for his wife and imminent child. Unmoved, Rodd kills him – a death almost immediately counter-pointed by Miss Wilson's news of the birth of Jack's son, his mur-derer's nephew.

In his poem 'Dublin', MacNeice had written 'she will not / Have me alive or dead', and so it proved. The Abbey accepted *Blacklegs*, but wanted 'adjustments' and would never perform it, and on 6 December he heard that Trinity would not have him. On that day, H. O. White was elected to succeed Trench. This narrowed MacNeice's options and he immediately set about getting a visa for America and booking a passage. He had originally planned to take Dan and Miss Popper with him, but subsequently decided to leave them in Ireland under the benevolent eye of his father and stepmother. Miss Popper's father (now part of the Bishop's household) and his gallant attempts to keep everyone's spirits up with puns in a language he could barely speak (repeated into Mrs MacNeice's ear-trumpet) added a surrealist dimension to mealtime conversation. By Christmas, Louis' spirits refused to be lifted. He was preoccupied with travel arrangements and eager to be off. In the second week of January, he said his goodbyes and crossed to Liverpool where, on the 14th, he wrote two letters to Dodds in the Cunard White Star Line passengers' waiting room. The first asked him to look out for Eileen Phillips and Nancy Coldstream (whom Bill had now deserted). The second appointed Dodds his executor and made provision for what should happen to Dan in the event of his death. Having done his parental duty, he picked up his bags and boarded the RMS *Samaria*.

CHAPTER 16

The Pity of it All

Sleep and, asleep, forget
The watchers on the wall
Awake all night who know
The pity of it all.
'Cradle Song for Eleanor', *CP*, p. 190

The MacNeice who embarked on the *Samaria* was in a mood very different from that of the man who had disembarked from the *Queen Mary* nine months before. In the words of Auden's poem, 'September 1, 1939', he was now

> Uncertain and afraid
> As the clever hopes expire
> Of a low dishonest decade.

He was uncertain about his feelings for Eleanor and hers for him; uncertain about the direction and value of his book on Yeats; afraid of the approaching war, uncertain of what his role in it should be, and, more immediately, uncertain and afraid of what awaited the *Samaria* in the open sea. On the day that war was declared, a U-boat had sunk the Glasgow liner *Athenia* with the loss of 112 lives. By the end of September, nineteen more British ships had followed her to the bottom; and to the threat of the U-boat there was now added the threat of a new type of German magnetic mine. These had been laid in the mouth of the Mersey, and the *Samaria*'s departure was delayed for two days while the mine-sweepers went about their dangerous work. It was the 'phoney war' in miniature. As on the *Queen Mary*, many of the passengers were Jewish refugees from Central Europe, and two days with little to do but remember the horrors behind and imagine horrors

268

ahead were bad for nerves and tempers.

MacNeice was sharing a cabin with a young farmer from Winnipeg, and the two of them shared a table for meals with a German Jew who had done time in a concentration camp, his Swiss wife, and a middle-aged Catalan couple who had left Barcelona the day before the fascists entered. Morale on the ship improved when she got under way and every day brought her passengers closer to the New World. MacNeice walked the deck with the Spaniard who, having heard his views on politics, said with a smile of apology: 'I hope you don't mind, I think you are perhaps a little red.' He preferred playing ping-pong with a man whom everyone called 'Butcher', which was his occupation rather than his name:

He had a solid, loud body, a blunt red face, coarse hair, thick lips, enormous hands, the charm of brute self-confidence. His English was very bad – never tried to learn anything from books, he proudly explained – but he could say 'Blimey' in perfect cockney. He had been in London a year, working in a big butcher's shop in Whitechapel from 4.15 in the morning till 6.00 in the evening for £2.10s. a week; had had a room in Aldgate for ten shillings, spent a pound a week on food, had enough left over to watch football matches and take a girl to the pictures.

MacNeice found it a relief to turn from discussion of the ever-changing international political situation to homelier topics – football matches, girls, and pictures.

It had been spring when first he landed in New York. Now it was midwinter, but a beautiful face – missed on the quay in April – was there in January, with the promise of a brighter spring, and he 'went down the gangway to meet a nine months' longing'. Louis and Eleanor found themselves still in love – though they were still not lovers – and for ten intoxicating days she showed him the delights and splendours of New York. At the end of the first week of February, he wrote to Dodds:

I start Cornell next week, it sounds cushy. Have been in New York till now. As soon as I saw E. everything fell back into place; I must have been merely aberrant the last six months or so. Don't ask me what's going to happen next because I don't know. I think maybe it's about time I had a bout of ir-rationality. I feel I've been fitting myself into patterns for so long & (though you may be sceptical about 'romance'?) it is so exciting to find oneself timelessly happy; also I am going to write (at least I hope so) quite new kinds of poems. After which, no doubt, the deluge but I can't think about that now. I have *never* felt like this about anyone, it pervades everything. If I had imagined ideal people for years, I couldn't have come near it.

A train from Grand Central Station took him 'upstate', climbing through valleys flanked by wooded hillsides, to the little town of Ithaca. A taxi ride up Buffalo Street, the steepest gradient he had climbed that day, brought him to Telluride House on the south-west edge of the Cornell University campus. Rising four-square and wide-gabled from its hillside, this reflects the sober prosperity of its founder, Mr Lucien L. Nunn, who built and endowed it from his first fortune in the Telluride gold-mine in Colorado. Opened in 1910, forty-two years after the inauguration of the University, the house was to be the laboratory for an innovatory and very successful educational experiment. Every year, the Telluride Association would select, by examination, 'a group of young men of exceptional promise and give them release from all material concern, a background of culture, the responsibility for managing their own household, and the stimulation of dwelling with resident faculty members and eminent visitors'. Its founder had envisaged Telluride House as a foundry for the making of élite engineers, with the cultural 'finish' that he himself lacked. By the time that MacNeice shook the snow off his shoes and entered Telluride's cavernous hall as an 'eminent visitor', the proportion of engineers had shrunk to about half of the twenty or so resident undergraduates. This community differed from that of an Oxford college in that its intellectual life was much more intense, and more intense, too, than that of the rest of Cornell. Tellurideans tended to be robust – many worked as manual labourers in their vacations – without being Hearties, and intelligent without being Aesthetes. They were Good Americans, isolationist, suspicious of Europe in general and England in particular. They regarded the war as an imperialist war. Few if any had been to Europe, so their interaction with their European fellow residents was educationally important. In addition to the Anglo-Irish poet, there was Viktor Lange, a professor of German, and Maurice Barret, a dashing Frenchman, who was doing research and giving one course in French.

These three were guests of the Telluride Association, so for the first time in his life MacNeice was able to save money, benefiting from the favourable exchange rate when he sent the greater part of his salary back to his 'inhuman bank in King's Norton'. To earn this, he was required to teach poetry three mornings a week (Tuesdays, Thursdays and Saturdays) throughout the fifteen-week spring semester. The Cornell campus stands on the brow of a steep hill overlooking Lake Cayuga, one of the New York Finger Lakes, fed by streams – frozen in winter – that cascade through great gorges. The university buildings are themselves overlooked by a tall brick campanile, from which, morning and evening, there comes an improbable variety of chimes – hymn and nursery-rhyme tunes, folk-songs and college anthems. Woken by these, MacNeice would breakfast on philosophy and politics before climbing to an office in the English Department building that he shared with a young instructor called Jack Adams. He aimed to arrive with the mail, would always ask the time (he did not wear a watch), then read his letters and leave. He was happier talking to students than to colleagues – in part, no doubt, because he thought '99% of the world's literary criticism' was 'lousy' – and he and Adams soon developed a mutual dislike. The American resented MacNeice's Anglo-Irish airs and disapproved of the heretical gospel he preached. Believing poetry to be unteachable, he told his classes to suspect everything he said. He had too many students – about sixty in each course – who were too young; but their saving grace was their lack of self-consciousness.

'Have you ever written poetry?'
'Oh yes, I wrote a lot of poetry when I was about 16.'
'Why did you do that?'
'Because I was in love with a young lady and I wanted to please my mother.'
'You showed your poems to your mother?'
'Yes, I showed them all to my mother. I wanted her to tell me I would be a great poet.'

To his surprise, MacNeice enjoyed his teaching at Cornell and his students seem to have enjoyed him. *Autumn Journal* had been published in America on 24 January, and his rising reputation was earning him invitations to lecture or read his poems at other campuses. He spoke at Vassar on 21 February; at Buffalo on the 23rd; in Montreal on the 26th; at Skidmore College on 11 March; at Northwestern University on 4 April; and at Syracuse on the 16th. Cornell then offered to extend his appointment and, though nothing had been finalized, he cabled Bedford College with his resignation on the 27th. Eleanor had accompanied him to Vassar, a visit they both enjoyed, but for the next six months they met mostly in New York. His long, handwritten letters show him as much in love as ever; hers, shorter and typewritten, are affectionate but cool, the letters of a caring friend who desires no closer relationship – a situation MacNeice found difficult, but believed would change. As he told her:

it is my own (no doubt, rationally, indefensible) belief that eventually you & I are bound to gamble on each other – & that, if we don't, it will be an enormous mistake. It is a pity if you don't see it this way but, when one is as full of pros and cons as you are, I guess, darling, it may take one some time to see the obvious?

He told Mrs Dodds that his 'situation with E. remains v. good but v. peculiar . . . . She is still fretting about her work, has an almost Flaubertian conscience about it'. He was not dissatisfied with his own work – 'a new kind of poetry (very slight so far, but will gain body)' and the critical study of Yeats (now all but finished) – and was optimistic about the prose book outlined to Eliot on 14 September 1939.

In April, the news from Ireland took a worrying turn: Miss Popper wrote from the Belfast Union Fever Hospital to say that Dan had scarlet fever, and she, erysipelas. Both made a good recovery, however, and on 10 May she wrote with the news that she was getting married on the 15th of the month, but would return to Dan on the 23rd and stay with him until the end of June. Dan's father responded by asking his sister to send the boy to America, and to consult Dodds for guidance on how to get him a passport. Dodds urged MacNeice to leave Dan where he was, advice he was reluctant to accept, knowing that if he did, he would himself have to return – sooner rather than later – to look after him. The wisdom of Dodds's advice became clearer every day as the German armies approached the Channel and the seas became increasingly dangerous. In April, Hitler had invaded Denmark and Norway; on 10 May, Belgium and Holland; and, on the 19th, the battered British Expeditionary Force began its retreat towards Dunkirk. The following day, Eleanor wrote Louis a letter, which prompted a long reply that deserves to be quoted in full for what it reveals of his state of mind:

May 21st

Darling,

Your letter wasn't quite what I expected & I am really angry with you, instead of being merely upset as I thought I should be. I am now going to say a lot of things to you but, as they say, you asked for it. I thought you might accuse me of 'inhumanity' (which I shall explain about in a moment) but what in hell do you mean by telling me I have 'an awful lack of curiosity about the world'? I was curious about the world & suffering from my curiosity about it before you were born. And if you think you can judge my curiosity about the world by the fact that I don't look at newspapers when you're around, you show an appalling lack of feminine imagination. Apart from which, newspapers aren't the world anyway though one might think they were to judge from the conversation one hears at Eunice's [Eleanor's sister]. Secondly as for 4 months before coming over I had read 2 or 3 newspapers practically from cover to cover daily & had also spent half the day listening to the radio – all of which led nowhere – I felt being in America, a reaction against it. And if you think the only way 'the world' impinges on me is through my nerves, you are – I am sorry to say, darling – a fool. When for the last week I have been feeling steam-rollers go over me all the time, that wasn't just nerves; it was imagining (with my brain & also – if I may be hackneyed for want of a better word – with my heart) what this war is going to do to England & Ireland as I know them & to particular people whom I know there – & this doesn't just mean my bosom friends or ex-mistresses but it means people like my family's chauffeur (who joined the territorials) & the little electrician in Birmingham whom I probably told you about & it means people also whom I've never seen but whom I *know* much better than you obviously think I can know even the people I meet (more about 'knowing' people in a minute.) As for 'curiosity', darling, this seems rather a cheap Tu Quoque but you have in your time taken me aback by showing no interest in people I was telling you about – e.g. the German refugee butcher on the Samaria whom (in a non-sexual way) I practically fell in love with. As for looking at books 'off my field' I am no Wystan or Aldous Huxley & I don't value information for information's sake but you obviously have no knowledge of the sort of books I do look at & why; & once again you seem to forget the distracting effect sex has on one (in situations like mine at the moment) if you are judging my book-interests by what I do in your presence. Also, darling, our respective ways of looking at the world are perhaps appropriate to our branches of writing (poetry – to crib a book I have just been reading – being more concerned with internal reality – the pole of instinct – & the novel with external reality – the pole of environment) but you do seem to me every so often to distort the world by projecting ideological prejudices on to it – & one shouldn't do this even to damn an ideologist. e.g. it is all very well for you to say – if you are convinced of it – that Stalinism is horrible but, unless American Stalinists are very different from English ones, you are uttering a damned lie when you say – as you have said – that all Stalinists are horrible. (& I am not thinking of fellow-travellers or dilettantes like Stephen but in particular of a 100% Stalinist I knew who would, I suspect, still be a Stalinist if he were alive.) In the same way, darling – although I quite agree that you can have very good intuitions about people – you also do much too much facile labelling e.g. last year you had no use for Erika Mann [Thomas Mann's daughter and Auden's wife] & this year you think she's swell. & talking of labelling, it is high time you & Eunice dropped this little pixie myth about me (which means, I suppose, much the same as what you call 'automatically sheltered' in your letter) because, though no doubt superficially apt & amusing, it is completely false & if you are such the hell of an intuitive, you ought to be able to see beneath people's skin. If you want a formula for me (which will also explain our discrepancy much more nearly) it is that I am a peasant who has gate-crashed culture. & when I say that I am a peasant this isn't a figure of speech or an inverted snob romanticism, it is just a statement of fact, though very few people can see it except some people who have come from your 'lower classes' themselves &, having also gate-crashed culture, realise my curious position. Not that it is a bad position at all (it's why I'm able to write poetry that is not stale) but it does lead to the paradox – that one can talk better to the people one has gate-crashed on than to the people one feels more identity with. & you, darling, obviously judge my 'knowledge' of people or my 'curiosity' about them by my capacity for surface gestures towards them – which is very naive of you. Actually, darling, you are much more 'upper-class' in your attitude to people than I am just at the time when you are taking an intelligent interest & being sympathetic etc. e.g. if you & I were talking to a slum-dweller you would certainly make a much better job of the talking & the slum-dweller would think you were sympathetic & I was aloof. Because he couldn't recognise me, darling, not in a thousand years. For you he remains an external person & you feel *about* him; you may do much *more* 'feeling' than I do but I don't feel about him, I feel him plain & simple; I have an *internal* identity with him. This is what makes me very sceptical about all idealistic, or reformist, or humanitarian or call-it-what-you-will movements which come from 'above' – cult of the proletariat or getting to grips with 'facts'. For the upper-class mentality these remain 'facts' i.e. objective & they collect them & systematise them & try to do something about them & all the time, whether they know it or not, they are feeling superior. Even you, darling, when you say things like 'It's amazing the way those people live' are being superior. It doesn't seem to me amazing the way poor people live, though as the case may be, it may seem admirable or regrettable. There is nothing exotic in it for me, it's a stratum which is still (instinctively) intelligible to me, my relations are still living in mud-floored cottages in the West of Ireland.

Now a little autobiography on the subject of 'inhumanity'. You are not the first person who has thought me inhuman though the other people didn't think my inhumanity as established & final a state as you seem to. Again I think you are only looking at the skin – or perhaps, this time, a crust. You, darling, think I am 'automatically sheltered.' Well, *if* I am automatically sheltered, I'm sorry for the people who are not sheltered. This again you can't boil down to nerves &, if I go back to my childhood for examples, I don't do so out of self-pity or because I want you to think of me as a pathetic little boy – which is the last thing I want. The point is that by the age of 12 far from being automatically sheltered, I was extremely vulnerable to contacts with 'the world' & other people & I was vulnerable just because I was comparatively clear-sighted about them, because I could imagine myself into them whereas they couldn't imagine themselves into me. If in one's childhood one has had to act as interpreter for an idiot brother whom none of the adults could understand, if one has been kept awake half the night every night by a father moaning about his life, if one has got so that one winces in advance on behalf of one's family's reactions in any possible situation, the important effect is not the (admittedly heavy) effect on one's nerves but the terrifying, precocious development of insight. I am not exaggerating this, darling. By the time I was 12 I could sit in a classroom of little boys at my school & foresee pretty accurately what reactions *each* of them would have to anything anyone said or did; even when the foresight wasn't accurate the point was that I was imagining myself inside each of those boys, a thing which I guess they weren't doing in turn. Well, later I closed down on that, darling, because of the strain & because, in order to make myself, I couldn't keep on feeling on behalf of other people. And so I got this detachment or aloofness or whatever it should be called but if you think I am aloofness to the core & can't see behind what was only a protective crust, you are, darling, more short-sighted than I should have expected. One other point: you seem to think I have a purely aesthetic approach to the world. This is crazy of you. I suppose you think the reason I haven't got a lovely comprehensive world-view is that I amn't interested in world-views. When I was married I *did* try to do without a world-view but it was a failure & I have known for years that I must develop one & I am trying to develop one but I am damned if I am going to swallow Marx or Trotsky or anyone else lock stock & barrel unless it squares with my experience or, perhaps I should say, my feelings of internal reality. Also when you say my attitude leads to tiredness & the death-wish etc., I don't see that if I am either tired or have death-wishes at the moment, that is necessarily due to my attitude (at moments it is *you* who seem to me defeatist, especially in regard to work) but may quite understandably be due to circumstances which are not of my making at all. In the time between my two visits to America there was after all the outbreak of war, while on the private plane (though this, I suppose, was of my own making) I had (a) an absurd amount of work on hand, b) some very exhausting personal experiences, & – talking of being interested in people – with regard to people as individuals, when you have had 3 people within as many months pour out upon you all their inmost & most horrifying secrets & when you think it on the cards that any or all of them may commit suicide, you may tend temporarily to feel surfeited with individuals & turn for a change to the bathroom tiles or, as you say, to 'thinking about airplanes & rivers'; with regard to people in the mass, if you had lived in England last year, you might feel *temporarily* escapist in that respect too. Anyhow, darling, if you really can only see me from the angle you took in your letter, I think it's about time we wash up – if the world situation isn't going to wash us up anyway.

Seeing you've been 'honest with yourself' I might as well – this isn't just spite though there may be spite in it (I don't pretend not be spiteful) – be honest with yourself too. I think you think, darling, that I think you're some sort of angel but I don't & never have. I am completely in love with you but I am not, as they say, blindly infatuated. I am not blind to you either physically or any other way. e.g. I think you are astonishingly beautiful but this doesn't mean that I think you are perfect or that I forget I have seen people say with more beautiful legs. In the same way I don't think that as a character you are anything like perfect, you just happen to appeal to me very much (by the way, your complementation talk was off the mark; I didn't mean to ask you to complement me, at least not in the crude sense of atoning for my deficiencies.) So you may as well know what I think are your imperfections & then the air may be cleared a bit. Apart from your being upper-class (which is perhaps the most serious) I think, darling, that you are – in *some* respects (for God's sake don't think I mean absolutely) – immature, soft, 'inhuman' (though not in the same way as me) &, sexually inhibited, & to some extent self-deceiving. I first realised your immaturity (& perhaps also the others except the sex one) when we were walking with your mother up Fifth Avenue last year & you came all over pathetic little girl passing the hat-shops. & your softness manifests itself dialectically in a certain intellectual arrogance & in a contempt which spreads over people instead of being concentrated on institutions, also in a perfectionist attitude to work (Flaubert surely was softer than Shakespeare.) Also I think your revolutionalism is partly self-deceiving, a sort of couvade but that is too long to go into now. As to your sexual inhibitedness I don't say this on the strength of you & me because for all I know I am not at all your type but it comes out in a lot that you do & say & I think it is a great pity because, even if the novelist is more concerned with environment than instinct, I can't see how he can present the world at all adequately if he hasn't got *inside* knowledge of what is about the most important of the instincts. If he hasn't got that, his *internal* reality remains in a sense in the nursery.

Well, that's that, darling, for the present. I shan't be coming down this weekend though I shall probably go somewhere else & then to N.Y.C. next week. You see, I don't really accept your imputations except in a very modified form. I used to have a masochistic instinct to agree with things people said against me but I have given up pretending to agree when I don't, just for the fun of playing the lost soul. I am not a lost soul (though, if your view of me were correct, I should consider myself one), neither am I a little spring lamb gambolling for ever through meadows of inconsequence. That you should think of me as either makes me feel like taking the next boat for hell though even that I wouldn't do – not for that reason – because it would involve a defeat & I am prepared for you-&-me to come to nothing but I am not going to let myself come to nothing because of you.

Love,
L.

Eleanor responded to this broadside with a short conciliatory note. For some months, their letters make no mention of their criticisms of each other, but give the impression that an equator has been crossed and they are sailing into cooler waters.

Ironically, a combination of circumstances now led him to give her a present conceived in more passionate days. In September 1939, he had asked Eliot's permission to publish a limited edition of his new poems with the Cuala Press in Dublin, run by Yeats's sisters, 'Lily' and 'Lollie'. Eliot had no objection, and MacNeice duly sent the Weird Sisters (as Joyce called them) a thirty-four-page collection entitled *The Last Ditch*, dedicated to Eleanor Clark and introduced with a quatrain:

> Without heroics, without belief,
> I send you, as I am not rich,
> Nothing but odds and ends a thief
> Bundled up in the last ditch.

The author of these rather pretentious lines has taken his tone from Yeats, but it is not clear in what other sense he is a thief. The body of the book contains twenty-five poems, including three subsequently dropped from 'The Coming of War' sequence. It ends with 'Three Poems Apart (for X)' – X being Nancy Coldstream who, collecting her belongings from 16a Primrose Hill Road, found proofs of *The Last Ditch* on MacNeice's desk and wrote to him with justified asperity: 'may I ask quite simply & without tact, *why* was the poem which indeed had no possible connection with E, when written, nor (if what you say is true) any accurate detailed significance up until the time you sailed . . . included?' The printing of *The Last Ditch* was delayed by the death of Lollie Yeats, but the book was finally published in June. MacNeice sent Eleanor a copy for her birthday and, in an accompanying letter, apologized 'for the cynically-sentimental little versicle attached to your dedication – written on the spur of a very black moment'.

He was writing from 29 Fifth Avenue, New York, a smart apartment owned by her sister, Eunice Jessup, and her husband Jack, an editor with *Time* magazine. They had generously put their spare room at his disposal when he left Cornell in late May, and he was to stay with them until late July, revising his new book, *The Poetry of W. B. Yeats*. Eunice was pregnant and grateful for his good company when her husband was at work. One night she smelt smoke, traced it to the spare room, and found him asleep with his pillow on fire from a fallen cigarette. Shaken awake he said: 'Yeats says the smell of burning feathers is one of the seven mystic smells.'

In early July, the American Immigration authorities granted him a twelve-month extension of his visa, but later that month the British Government ordered him to return to the UK. Nelson-like, he turned a blind eye to that signal, having planned a more congenial journey with Eleanor. She was to be interviewed for a job by William S. Paley, President of CBS, at his holiday house on Mount Desert, and it was agreed that Louis would drive her there in his little blue Ford. At the end of the first day, they took a room in a hotel north of Boston and slept in the same bed – though still not as lovers. A second day's driving brought them to the New Hampshire fishing village of Newcastle, where they rented a sea-front room above the store of a lobsterman, Mr Luther Amerzeen. There, around midnight on 16/17 July, in a large double bed, Louis began groaning. He had a stomach-ache that grew steadily worse until, near dawn, Eleanor drove him to Portsmouth hospital, where he underwent an emergency operation for severe peritonitis. As soon as he was out of danger, Eleanor drove on to Mount Desert for her interview, was offered the job, accepted it, and returned to Newcastle. In the interim, the patient had contracted a streptococcal infection and, for a time, seemed likely to die. He survived this second crisis and was soon allowed to see visitors – Eunice Jessup, who told his surgeon not to charge him 'because he's a famous English poet', and Wystan Auden, who claimed their Oxford friend, Father D'Arcy, had said: 'Tell me if he's dying and I'll come and get him!'

Eleanor's mother had invited him to convalesce in her Roxbury Connecticut house and had arranged for him to be collected by an anglophile neighbour, a First World War air-ace called Batch Pond, who flew his own plane. Weather conditions, however, were unsuitable for landing when MacNeice was discharged from hospital at the end of August, but he was rescued by a kindly Professor of English whom he had met at Harvard in April 1939. F. O. Matthiessen and his partner, Russell Cheney, spent their vacations in a little wood-frame house on the coast at Kittery opposite Newcastle. Their guest was installed 'in a duck's egg attic' with a sumptuous double bed and, on 3 September, he wrote to Eleanor:

for a week I have been stuffing food & drinking Alsatian wines & pouring out poems in an unprecedented spate. I have written ELEVEN since coming here; what do you think is wrong with me? Five ballades (which, in spite of all the reasons to the contrary, seem to be alive & Matthiessen thinks so too), & a poem about the War called Jehu, & one about Picture Galleries, & an 80 line philosophical called Plurality (difficulty of content balanced by an easy, almost slick, metre & rhyme-scheme), & a naive-seeming kind of little ballad with refrain called 'Autobiography', & a short flat piece called 'Provence' but really a comment on human beings, & a hurry of short lines about smells.

The five ballads would appear in his *Selected Poems 1925–1940* but not – with 'Jehu', 'Picture Galleries', 'Plurality', 'Autobiography', and 'Provence' – in *Plant and Phantom*.

Cheney and Matthiessen were to leave for Mexico on 3 September, and MacNeice was planning to take the train into New York with them when Mrs Clark rang to say that Batch Pond would come for him that afternoon if the fog lifted. It did, and the gallant aviator, descending like a *deus ex machina* in his little black Monocoupe, carried him off to his hilltop airstrip. Mrs Clark welcomed him to Southover Farm like a Prodigal Son, and for a fortnight he entered the world of Eleanor's childhood, the world of his 'Evening in Connecticut':

> Equipoise: becalmed
> Trees, a dome of kindness;
> Only the scissory noise of the grasshoppers;
> Only the shadows longer and longer.
>
> The lawn a raft
> In a sea of singing insects,
> Sea without waves or mines or premonitions:
> Life on a china cup.

The Clarks' garden is coloured by memories of his own that had resurfaced, only days before, in his poem 'Autobiography':

> In my childhood trees were green
> And there was plenty to be seen.
>
> *Come back early or never come.*
>
> My father made the walls resound,
> He wore his collar the wrong way round.
>
> *Come back early or never come.*
>
> My mother wore a yellow dress;
> Gently, gently, gentleness.
>
> *Come back early or never come.*
>
> When I was five the black dreams came;
> Nothing after was quite the same.
>
> *Come back early or never come.*

The dark was talking to the dead;
The lamp was dark beside my bed.

Come back early or never come.

When I woke they did not care;
Nobody, nobody was there.

Come back early or never come.

When my silent terror cried,
Nobody, nobody replied.

Come back early or never come.

I got up; the chilly sun
Saw me walk away alone.

Come back early or never come.

The Fall there signalled by the changing colours – green, yellow, black
– alerts him to the signs of another Fall in Eleanor's childhood garden,
and to violence at its borders, as 'Evening in Connecticut' ends:

But turning. The trees turn
Soon to brocaded autumn.
Fall. The fall of dynasties; the emergence
Of sleeping kings from caves –

Beard over the breastplate,
Eyes not yet in focus, red
Hair on the back of the hands, unreal
Heraldic axe in the hands.

Unreal but still can strike.
And in defence we cannot call on the evening
Or the seeming-friendly woods –
Nature is not to be trusted,

Nature whose falls of snow,
Falling softer than catkins,
Bury the lost and over their grave a distant
Smile spreads in the sun.

Not to be trusted, no,
Deaf at the best; she is only

281

> And always herself, Nature is only herself,
> Only the shadows longer and longer.

The sun that presides over the close of both poems is 'chilly' and remote and, given MacNeice's childhood immersion in the language of his father's Bible, there may be a subconscious associative link with the Son of God. There are clearer links between these poems and another, written some weeks later, that again seems to conflate Eleanor's childhood with his own. This is a Lullaby, though he cannot call it that, since Yeats and Auden had already 'booked' that title. Instead, and less satisfactorily, he calls his poem

Cradle Song.

71

Sleep, my darling, sleep;
  The pity of it all
Is all we compass if
  We watch disaster fall.
Put off your twenty-odd
  Encumbered years and creep
Into the only heaven,
  The robbers' cave of sleep.

The wild grass will whisper,
  Lights of passing cars
Will streak across your dreams
  And fumble at the stars;
Life will tap the window
  Only too soon again,
Life will have her answer——
  Do not ask her when.

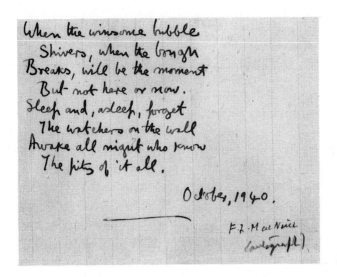

When the winsome bubble
Shivers, when the bough
Breaks, will be the moment
But not here or now.
Sleep and, asleep, forget
The watchers on the wall
Awake all night who know
The pity of it all.

                    October, 1940.

                         F. L. MacNeice
                         (autograph)

MacNeice's dialogue with his father is now more audible: the *only* heaven is 'The robber's cave of sleep' – that cave from which the sleeping kings emerge; the cave into which the five-year-old had tried to dive when his father told him of his mother's death. The nursery-rhyme simplicity of 'Autobiography' is succeeded by the distinct echo of 'Rock a bye Baby'. There are other, more distant, echoes. The poet who, some months earlier, had told his love that 'you & I are bound to gamble on each other', and that it was 'a pity' if she didn't see it this way, now knows what 'The watchers on the wall' know – watchers related to the watchman on Agamemnon's wall who, centuries earlier, knew 'The pity of it all'.

MacNeice's days in Eleanor's family home sharpened his sense of 'The pity of it all', and late at night on 10 October he wrote her a desperate letter:

When I think about leaving you, it half destroys me. Especially as you seem so pessimistic about it yourself. It would be much easier if I felt you had any confidence in a future for you & me . . . . But having to go so soon makes me feel as if I'm missing my last chance of contact with you. I don't mean sex-life; the dream character of this period makes that seem for the moment almost irrelevant – I want to sleep with you *very much* but I don't know if we should achieve a harmony in the circumstances; am always willing to try of course but still that's not the point at the moment . . . . I want you to *talk* to me.

He goes on to speak of his sense of needing to return to Europe which, he feels, she misunderstands: 'I think some of your criticisms of my poetry are true. I don't imagine for a moment that going to England is going to have any direct effect on that. But one's got to see to one's life first (whoso tries to save his art – by insulating it – shall lose it.)'

It seems unlikely that he and Eleanor ever talked in the way he wanted. In the middle of October, he went down for the weekend to the Katzmans' chicken farm near the town of Egg Harbour. Despite the intoxicating beauty of the Fall, 'the maple trees gone drunk with colour', it was a dispiriting visit. The house was chaotic, the farm did not pay, an expedition to Atlantic City ended with Mary and Charles bickering about each other's weight. That evening, she told Louis how she hated people, and Charles told him of his disappointment and frustrations. Their guest sat up late, listening to the rats behind the skirting-boards, 'wondering if it made any sense, with Charles who had once been a star American footballer and Mary who had been the best dancer in Oxford'.

The following week, he paid a more cheerful visit to Cornell – to collect his belongings – and no doubt thought of Charles again, watching the Cornell football team play the University of Syracuse. The erstwhile rugger-player disapproved of many features of the American game, but was lyrical about its 'one great elegance' – the forward pass: 'to see a man feint and then throw a long impertinent pass out of the palm of his hand into a space where no one is but suddenly someone appears and ball and man are wedded at the run, is exhilarating, almost a sacrament'. The impurist in him also enjoyed the razzmatazz framing the Big Game – the cheerleaders with megaphones, the rival brass bands marching and countermarching in the intermission, the ice cream and hot dog sellers shouting their wares.

He took the train back to New York on or around 20 October and found a bed, as Auden's guest, on the top floor of 7 Middagh Street in Brooklyn Heights. George Davis, fiction editor of *Harper's Bazaar*, had acquired this tall brownstone building near Brooklyn Bridge as a hive for himself and a swarm of artistic friends. In addition to Auden, who was soon playing the part of queen bee, these at various times included Carson McCullers, Benjamin Britten and Peter Pears, Paul and Jane Bowles, Golo Mann, and the striptease artist, Gypsy Rose Lee. Excellent meals were prepared and served by a huge, black, homosexual cook-cum-butler. 'When George Davis, giving an interview about the house to *The New Yorker*, said "It's a boarding house", the reporter understandably thought he had said "bawdy house".'

On 17 November, MacNeice wrote to tell Dodds that he would be 'sailing about the end of this month (no boat before)', and to give him instructions about printing his work and making provision for Dan, should he not survive: 'sorry to be such a bore but they say the North Atlantic is getting hotter & hotter.' Two days later, he wrote his last letter to Eleanor from American soil. He told her of a lunch with her sister, who had said that he and Eleanor were 'no go', and of his own feeling

that perhaps, darling, we ought to call it a day. You see, darling, you don't appear to need the sort of intimate relationship which I need so badly. I have tried to softpedal the sex business but the more I softpedal it, the more it obsesses me. I am not suggesting that you are immune to these things but various remarks of yours – e.g. about feeling ashamed with me, feeling more natural with other people – seem to imply that you will find yourself in those ways with other people & not with me. Well, if that is so, darling, I can't go back to Europe, especially with so much death about, & try to keep up a troubadourish relationship with you, all the driving-force of which comes from one side (my side.) I am not after all a cross between a Christian monk & an (intellectual) hearth-dog. The only way I can stop sex interfering with my work, general attitude, etc., is to have a sex-life. & I certainly shall have one when I go back. I don't suppose that will affect my (deeper) feelings to you at all but it will at least keep me from going crazy with frustration. I am sorry, darling, but I can't help it; I can't live on your plane.

Eleanor probably accepted the truth of this. They spent their last days together as affectionate friends and, in the last week of November, she saw him sadly climb the gangplank he had descended so happily ten months before. The *Samaria* slid away from the quay, and they waved goodbye across the widening gulf between them.

MacNeice, who from the first had been exhilarated by America, watched Brooklyn Bridge, the Manhattan skyscrapers, and the Statue of Liberty dwindle and disappear. His sense of loss was less sharp than he had feared, as the practicalities of the voyage competed for his attention. The first three people he spoke to were Irish, and he was delighted that two recognized him as a fellow-countryman. One was his cabin-mate – a drunken old man 'with a bogtrotter's face' and the racial gift of the gab. Interrupting MacNeice at his writing, he peered over his shoulder and said: 'Ye're a decent young man, . . . ye're deep as Hell's gates but grammar is grammar. Where is your full stops? Where is your apostrophe s's? I'm an old dumb Irishman bedamn but I know my apostrophe s's.' The decent young man was at work on the auto-biography that would eventually – and posthumously – be published as *The Strings are False*. A letter to Eleanor tells her he is anxious to get 'this prose thing' done, 'because it will finish up the old period & I shan't be troubled again by the things that are going into it. No more past.' He had drafted the childhood chapters iv to ix at Cornell in February or March, a draft that now seemed to him 'shockingly badly written' and in need of heavy cutting. On the voyage, he drafted chapters i–iii that describe the voyage and his two visits to America; starting his narrative with the end towards which subsequent chapters would move, until the circle was complete.

The *Samaria* put in at Halifax, Nova Scotia, on 29 November, and took on board 200 Canadian airmen and a number of British seamen, survivors of an armed merchant cruiser, HMS *Jervis Bay*, sunk on 5 November. For the last few nights of the voyage, the passengers were told to sleep in their clothes, because of the U-boat threat. When MacNeice took his shoes off, his cabin-mate protested: 'What will the people say if you go down into the life-boat in your dirty feet?' Fortunately, they never discovered. On 8 December, the *Samaria* reached the mouth of the Mersey and, on the 9th, they disembarked.

Disgruntled at having to pay £4 customs duty for 'Wystan's wolf-collar coat', MacNeice caught a Birmingham train and fell into conver-sation with two soldiers who had been at Dunkirk, one of whom said to the other: 'Cheer up, lad, you'll be in the Roll of Honour some day.' The war had reached Birmingham in the form of heavy bombing, and MacNeice spent two nights there, seeing the damage and visiting friends (including Auden's parents), before going on to Oxford. He stayed in the Doddses' High Street house, and went to see a doctor who told him that, despite feeling well, he was 'not technically fit & should probably be rejected by any medical board'. His operation had necess-itated a large incision from which his stomach muscles would take some time to recover. There is some evidence that, around this time, he volunteered for service in the Royal Navy, but was rejected on grounds of bad eyesight. Writing to tell his father and stepmother that he was safely back, he said he was thinking 'of trying to crash in on the BBC' and, in the meantime, wanted to finish a book. This was probably the new collection of poems – to be called *Plant and Phantom*, '(a phrase from Nietzsche describing Man)' – that he had described to Eliot in a letter of 24 September.

With no salary and little in the way of savings, MacNeice's first priority was earning a living. Some months before this, Faber and Faber had forwarded to him a letter from T. Rowland Hughes of the BBC Features and Drama Section, who wrote:

I have been discussing with Mr. Val Gielgud and Mr. Laurence Gilliam the possibility of persuading you to write for radio. I wonder if some aspect of Nazism and its influence or its victims would appeal to you as the theme of a radio programme. What I have in mind, of course, is something in the style of MacLeish's 'Fall of the City' and 'Air Raid'. We in this country have not yet been able to secure a first class poet for such radio programmes and I feel convinced that your lines would speak well.

He proposed a meeting but, perhaps because on his return MacNeice could not lay his hand on that letter or remember who had written it, he wrote instead to the Director General of the BBC, F. W. Ogilvie, who as President and Vice-Chancellor of Queen's University, Belfast (from 1934 to 1938), had become friendly with his father. While waiting for an answer, he went up to London in search of freelance work and stayed with Rupert Doone at 34 Wharton Street. He gave Eliot the typescript of *Plant and Phantom*; arranged to review films for *The Spectator* ('money for jam'); and called on Cyril Connolly at the office of his magazine *Horizon*, launched the previous year. In its issue of 12 December, Connolly had written: 'From America no travellers return, no American letters get written, and to ask for them is like dropping pebbles down a well. This is regrettable, for *Horizon* has suspended judgement on the expatriates.' It was a more charitable position than most on this contentious issue, and Connolly invited MacNeice to put the case for the defence in the February *Horizon*. This essay, 'Traveller's Return', far from claiming any credit for his own return, gave his motives as 'vulgar curiosity' and the thought 'that if I stayed another year out of England I should have to stay out for good, having missed so much history, lost touch'. He went on to argue, generously and persuasively:

For the expatriate there is no Categorical Imperative bidding him return – or stay. Auden, for example, working eight hours a day in New York, is getting somewhere; it might well be 'wrong' for him to return. For another artist who felt he was getting nowhere it might be 'right' to return. . . . The expatriates do not need anybody else to act as their *ersatz* conscience: they have consciences of their own and the last word must be said by their own instinct as artists.

Having given British readers an expatriate point of view, MacNeice set about giving American readers a British view of the war. In the first of five 'London Letters' to the leftist periodical *Common Sense* (edited by Alfred M. Bingham and Selden Rodman, former husband of Eleanor's sister Eunice), he described the effect of the war on Birmingham, Oxford and London. He was writing two days after one of its heaviest air-raids – timed to coincide with the tidal low-point in the

St Paul's, the Blitz, 1940

Dr Johnson Takes It

Thames – in which more than 10,000 fire bombs had fallen on the City of London, circling St Paul's with flame. The Bishop's son focuses his readers' attention on a lesser church, St Clement Danes in the Strand, but not to show the damage to 'sanctuary and choir', as Eliot would shortly do in 'Little Gidding'. Instead he shows them something undamaged, outside in the churchyard:

a statue of Dr Johnson still stands among the debris, unconcerned and pawky, with an open book in his left hand, looking up Fleet Street.

Last night they dropped a great number of incendiary bombs, stage-lighting London; you could have read a book in the streets a mile away.

The choice of image is significant, as is the transition from the great lexicographer – more concerned with the words on his page than with the destruction all round him – to that of his no less insouciant successor.

MacNeice probably had Eleanor and her Trotskyite ex-husband in mind when he turned to another subject: 'You will want to know about the Intellectual Front (I use this Stalinesque phrase deliberately). Well, there is no Front.' Most British intellectuals, he tells them, align themselves with the Labour Party, 'which is really more committed to winning the war than the Conservatives'. Recalling the remark of an American friend, that Britain today seems 'downhill and hopeless', he ends with a flourish:

Having just returned to this country I wish to say honestly and as someone who has never been patriotic and who loathes propaganda, that Britain at the end of 1940 seems a good deal less downhill than I have ever known it before. In fact not downhill at all.

Early in the New Year, MacNeice's letter to the Director General of the BBC resulted in his being called to interview at Broadcasting House. On 9 January, he was seen by E. A. (Archie) Harding, another Oxford intellectual with strong left-wing sympathies, and they took to each other at once. Harding, Chief Instructor of the BBC's Staff Training School, had the rich voice of a former radio-announcer and a passionate belief in the power of radio to entertain, instruct, and persuade. He would himself seem to have persuaded MacNeice to reconsider his views on patriotism and propaganda. By the end of the interview, the poet had agreed to try his freelance hand at writing scripts that would contribute to national morale.

CHAPTER 17

The Truth about Love

> Will it come like a change in the weather,
>   Will its greeting be courteous or bluff,
> Will it alter my life altogether?
>   O tell me the truth about love.
>   W. H. Auden, 'Some say that Love's a little boy'

He had written for the BBC once before – a short talk, 'In Defence of Vulgarity', broadcast in December 1937, and a year later had said in a letter to *The Listener*: 'Poets should certainly write plays, and probably

William Empson and Louis MacNeice

certain other forms of verse, expressly for broadcasting.' So far, he had not himself done this, though the radio had appeared as a powerful presence in *Out of the Picture*, *Autumn Journal*, and the poem 'Cushendun'. A number of other writers recruited by the BBC – William Empson and George Orwell among them – attended a six-week crash course in 1941 on how to be a propagandist. There is no evidence that MacNeice also graduated from 'The Liars' School' (as they called it) but, whether he did or not, he had a natural talent for the work – not for propagating lies (as Goebbels' henchmen were doing), but for memorably reinforcing aspects of the truth. Empson was devising programmes for transmission to China, and one of Harding's reasons for encouraging MacNeice was his experience of America (a country the British Government hoped to enlist as an ally). His first programme, 'Word from America', was an anthology of 'poems and songs of the American people'. This was followed by the more ambitious 'Cook's Tour of the London Subways', a fifteen-minute playlet, in which a Young Man encounters a Mrs Van Winkle Brown – who has not been to London since 1930 – and takes her on a tour of Underground stations converted to air-raid shelters. There, she and thousands of American listeners are introduced to the voices of a London down but not out, not downcast, not defeatist. Writing to Mrs Dodds, MacNeice boasted of demanding 'all sorts of sound effects' for this script, clear evidence that he had taken to the air. He told her that he was shortly going to Ireland.

He crossed to Belfast in the middle of February, spent some time with his father, and went on to see Dan, who was now six, at Cootehill in County Cavan. A bomb had fallen in the Bishop's garden, and it had been decided that Dan should go, for safety, across the border into the neutral Republic, either to Elizabeth Bowen at Bowen's Court or to Mrs MacNeice's cousin, Diana Clements, at Cootehill. Given the fact that the boy was part-Jewish and there were strong pro-Axis sympathies in the Bowen's Court area, Cootehill seemed preferable. He took a tearful farewell from the faithful Miss Popper and was packed off to join his step-cousins, Catharine and Marcus Clements, at Ashfield Lodge. His father found him much changed: very tall and impressively athletic. His grandfather had taught him to read, and father and son were happy to discover each other – effectively for the first time – on

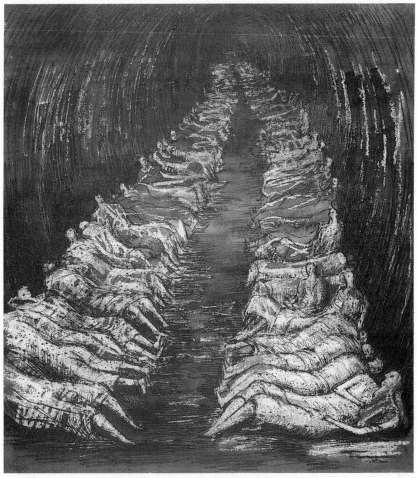

Henry Moore, 'Tube Shelter Perspective'

long walks in Colonel Clements' 400-acre estate.

Returning to England in early March, MacNeice spent a week in Oxford where – perhaps under Dodds's influence – he wrote a BBC script about the Athenian general Xenophon, hero of a fighting retreat (like that of the British Expeditionary Force to Dunkirk) from Kurdistan to the Black Sea. Ernst Stahl, now married and teaching in Oxford, allowed his friend to commandeer his dining-room table for the drafting of 'The March of the 10,000'. Much as MacNeice enjoyed the company of the Doddses and the Stahls, it was a relief to return to the comforts of Wharton Street, where he and Doone were cared for by Lady Constance Foljambe, who had kept house for Doone (and Robert Medley, now a camouflage officer) since 1933. Connie, he wrote to Eleanor,

looks like a hard-bitten char, was once, I believe, married to a clergyman from whom she ran away – but all that is legend & she cooks very nicely. She & I & the ex-ballet dancer [Doone] play Rummy nearly every evening with a great deal of bad language & recrimination. This helps to drown out the guns when they happen.

Clearly, too, he preferred the perilous excitement of London and its sense of shared community. Trying to explain himself to Eleanor, he wrote:

It's *not* patriotism, darling, & it's *not* sentimentality but I have the feeling that it's important that, while things are in such a mess here & just because they are in such a mess, people – especially people like me who have plenty to lose – should be *in* the mess continuing to be more or less human . . . .

Awaiting him in London were reviews of *The Poetry of W. B. Yeats*, which had been published towards the end of February. Apart from a predictable dismissal by *Scrutiny* ('not a bad but a superficial book'), they were generally favourable. The *TLS* gave the book a respectful middle-page article, and Kenneth Muir ended his *New Statesman* piece: 'the book is crammed with the most acute observation, and is one of the most brilliant critical works which have appeared for some time'. No review, however, would have pleased the author as much as the tribute from Richard Ellmann that was published after his death:

MacNeice's book on Yeats is still as good an introduction to that poet as we have, with the added interest that it is also an introduction to MacNeice. It discloses a critical mind always discontented with its own formulations, full of self-questionings and questionings of others, scrupling to admire, reluctant to be won. Yet mistrust of Yeats is overcome by wary approval, in a rising tone of endorsement. Then at the end MacNeice declares a kind of independence, as if this mode of thinking, feeling, and writing was 'no go', like the merrygoround and the rickshaw, and must be put aside as belonging to the past rather than the future.

Ellmann astutely links this conclusion to another – MacNeice's statement in the Foreword to his *Poems 1925–1940* (published in America on 17 February 1941): 'When a man collects his poems, people think he is dead. I am collecting mine not because I am dead, but because my past life is.' This book contained all but two of the poems of *Plant and Phantom*, published in England in mid-April. Dedicated 'To Eleanor Clark', it opens with 'Prognosis', which announces that

> The tea-leaf in the teacup
> Is herald of a stranger

and asks:

> Will his name be Love
> And all his talk be crazy?
> Or will his name be Death
> And his message easy?

The alternatives are familiar – the flux of life, the fixity of death – and, as in MacNeice's earlier poetry, the one is celebrated under the advancing shadow of the other. *Plant and Phantom* may not have the dramatic momentum of *Autumn Journal* but, as the *TLS* reviewer wrote of the new book: 'There is thrust and sparkle in almost all he writes, even when it is too fortuitous.'

'The Trolls' may be the only poem MacNeice wrote in the hectic spring of 1941. He was too busy writing prose: notably his 'London Letters' for Selden Rodman's *Common Sense* and scripts for a BBC series, aimed at America, about bombed buildings representative of the Anglo-American heritage. The title – if not the idea – of the series, 'The Stones Cry Out',* may have been MacNeice's. The conjunction of stone and voice would be a natural expression of his principal imaginative polarities, and he wrote the first of these fifteen-minute programmes: 'Dr. Johnson Takes It.' A dramatized visit to the damaged house in London's Gough Square, where Johnson wrote his dictionary, the sketch uses the figure of the heroic lexicographer – like MacNeice's earlier 'London Letter' – as an emblem of British tenacity and, by implication, a celebration of the language uniting the British and American peoples. A similar association of lives, language, books and

---

* 'but', the announcer added, 'the people stand firm!'

buildings appears in one of his articles, 'The Morning after the Blitz', an account of 'the Biggest Raid Ever' on the night of 16–17 April. This had lasted eight hours, and 450 planes had dropped 100,000 tons of bombs. Honest as ever, MacNeice admits:

All these shattered shops and blazing stores, this cataract of broken glass, this holocaust of hall-marked and dog's-eared property – there was a voice inside me which (ignoring all the suffering and wastage involved) kept saying, as I watched a building burning or demolished: 'Let her go up!' or 'Let her come down. Let them all go. Write them all off. Stone walls do not a city make. Tear all the blotted old pages out of the book; there are more books in the mind than ever have got upon paper.'

Old pages written by older hands than Dr Johnson's are celebrated in the second of MacNeice's scripts for 'The Stones Cry Out' – 'Westminster Abbey'. He takes his text from Ecclesiasticus, 44:

PREACHER: Let us now praise famous men and our fathers that begat us . . . .
1ST SPEAKER: Who lie under the nave and the transepts and the chapels behind the sanctuary.
PREACHER: Such as did bear rule in their kingdoms –
1ST SPEAKER: Edward the Confessor, Henry the Third, Edward the First, Edward the Third, Richard the Second, Henry the Fifth, Henry the Sixth and Henry the Seventh:
2ND SPEAKER: Edward the Sixth and Mary Tudor, Queen Elizabeth and Mary Queen of Scots.
PREACHER: . . . men renowned for their power, giving counsel by their understanding –
1ST SPEAKER: William Pitt, Earl of Chatham, Pitt the Younger and Charles James Fox –
PREACHER: Leaders of the people by their counsels –
2ND SPEAKER: William Ewart Gladstone and Benjamin Disraeli –
PREACHER: And by their knowledge of learning meet for the people, wise and eloquent in their instructions –
1ST SPEAKER: William Wilberforce and Richard Cobden, Sir Isaac Newton and Charles Darwin –
2ND SPEAKER: And the early Abbots and doctors of divinity –
PREACHER: Such as found out musical tunes –
1ST SPEAKER: Handel and Henry Purcell –
PREACHER: And recited verses in writing –

2ND SPEAKER: Chaucer, Spenser, Dryden, Tennyson, Browning, Kipling, Hardy.

London's social life was complicated by the Blitz, but not eclipsed by it. MacNeice was in a restaurant at the start of 'the Biggest Raid Ever' and, on 9 April, he was a guest at Stephen Spender's wedding party in a Chelsea studio. There, Margaret Gardiner found him, drunk and being harangued by Nancy Coldstream:

'How could you, Louis, how *could* you? With that woman? How could you?'

'Listen,' said Louis, 'Listen – '

'How could you?' Nancy insisted. She was beginning to cry. Louis put his arms around her.

At that moment, Stephen Spender appeared. He looked at them bewildered, since Nancy was engaged to his brother, then said: 'I thought you were going to marry Michael.'

The erstwhile lovers took no notice and Gardiner and Spender tactfully withdrew. Later that evening – after an air-raid – as the wedding party was crossing the square to a restaurant, Nancy noticed that two of the guests were missing.

'Where's Louis?' she asked. 'Where's Michael?' 'Somewhere around,' said Margaret Gardiner. 'Probably they've gone ahead.'

'Where are they?' she asked again. 'I must find them, I'm sure they're fighting.'

They were eventually found, at a table for two, talking amicably about polar exploration. MacNeice almost always managed to remain on good terms not only with his former lovers but with their subsequent partners.

The BBC, evidently pleased with his initial scripts, now offered him a staff position, subject to satisfactory references and 'positive vetting' by MI5. There was to be a three-month trial, at the end of which – all being well – his appointment (on a salary of £620 a year) would be confirmed. On 26 May, he wrote to warn Eliot that he would be asked for a reference and, on the 30th, announced to Eleanor:

I have just – with a certain amount of misgiving – signed on to the B.B.C. I guess this may prove rather cramping – though not so cramping as anything I might have been conscripted into – but at the same time, in spite of all the vulgarisation involved, the predominance of *quantitative* values, & the unhealth which goes with a machine that is largely propaganda (N.B. don't quote anything I say on this subject in public), it *has* its excitements & (what was less to be expected) its value.

The BBC was much younger than MacNeice. Although by the end of the Thirties, nine out of ten homes in Britain had a wireless set, at the start of the Twenties there had been none. The first regular broadcasting service in the country was organized by the Experimental Section of the Designs Department of the Marconi Company in February 1922. Some months later, it was agreed that a consortium of wireless manufacturers, the British Broadcasting Company, should be established as a monopoly under the technical supervision of the Post Office, with the Postmaster General ultimately responsible to Parliament for satisfactory standards of broadcasting. In October 1922, the BBC advertised for a General Manager and John Reith was appointed, a choice that determined the character and course of the ship (to borrow Reith's image) entrusted to his charge; one which a 'devoted, adventurous crew launched into uncharted and treacherous seas, where never sail was carried before'. So successful were they that the Crawford Committee, reporting in May 1926, recommended that the Company be reorganized as a public service and renamed the British Broadcasting Corporation. This it became on 1 January 1927, with Sir John Reith as its first Director General.

By 1932, when the BBC moved from Savoy Hill to its Art Deco building in Portland Place, the former Production Department had been divided into three: Review, Variety, and Drama. In 1936, the Drama Department was itself divided into three: Drama, Features, and Children's Hour. Two years later, Children's Hour became independent and the remaining Department was renamed Features and Drama, with Val Gielgud its Director, Laurence Gilliam Assistant Director of Features, and Moray McLaren Assistant Director of Drama. At the start of the war, this department had been moved first to Evesham, then to Manchester, and in May 1941 it returned to London with offices and studios in the buildings of Bedford College, whose staff and students had in turn moved to Cambridge.

Institutions tend to reflect the strength or weakness of the man or woman at the top. Reith, the BBC's Founding Father, had been an inspired appointment, and many of those whom he appointed were men of vision and creative vitality; none more so than the one to whom MacNeice reported – in the building he knew so well – on 26 May. Laurence Gilliam was a large man, not tall and austere like Reith, but broad in every sense of the word. A successful writer and producer of programmes, he was a notable champion of other writers and producers, actors and musicians, to whom he was 'Lorenzo the Magnificent'.

He was against those figures in the system who frustrated good ideas; administrators in general but network planners in particular. Inverted Micawbers, he called them, waiting for something to turn down. He was a comfortable, slow-moving, generous man with broad features and wiry grey hair. There was a curious African quality about him; if he had blacked-up he would, but for his blue eyes, have looked very much the tribal chief, a Basuto for preference, over-weight and proud of it. He laughed a lot. He liked good food and good wine. He was a good mimic. He could do real Digger talk, Cape Dutch and various north-country accents to perfection.

Gilliam was a natural leader who, as Douglas Cleverdon discovered, 'would always back a project that had a chance of success rather than reject one that might fail'. He, more than anyone else, was responsible for the development of features as a radio form.

The first major assignment he gave his new recruit showed his skill in matching scriptwriter to subject. The Ministry of Information wished there to be public acknowledgement of Britain's gratitude to America for fifty destroyers transferred from the US Navy to the British, and offered the BBC a couple of berths on one of these vessels patrolling the North Atlantic. Knowing that MacNeice had experience of that ocean, Gilliam gave him the job, assigning him as his producer and mentor a man who would become one of his closest friends. Francis Dillon – always known as 'Jack' – was then forty-one, a veteran both of 'Features' and the First World War. He, too, had experience of the sea in wartime, having landed at Archangel with Ironside's expeditionary force, and again at Constantinople with the occupying army. 'He was a man of infinite and strident wit, whose croaky voice had been raised to its unusual pitch by a dose of mustard gas in Flanders.'

Laurence Gilliam

Like Gilliam, Dillon was a good trencherman and a great drinker. He and MacNeice had nine days at sea in HMS *Chelsea*, their destroyer rolling all the time. Louis told Eleanor 'it was illuminating, though quite unsensational. The naval officers, mainly very young, were charming, though wonderfully uninformed about the world'.

The ship docked at Liverpool after breakfast on 29 June. The Captain then invited his BBC guests to his cabin for a drink, and his officers pressed them to stay for lunch before going ashore. They parted, it seemed, on the best of terms, but a month later a senior administrative officer of the BBC received a confidential letter from the Admiralty:

My Dear Nicolls,

We recently arranged facilities in H.M.S. CHELSEA, an ex-American destroyer, for Messrs. Louis MacNeice and Francis Dillon to prepare a programme intended for broadcasting to America in the Overseas Transmission.

'Jack' Dillon

I am extremely sorry to have to inform you that as the result of a report received from the Commanding Officer of H.M.S. CHELSEA on the conduct and deportment of these two gentlemen, we shall not be prepared to grant them further facilities to go to sea in H.M. Ships.

Yours sincerely,
F. R. Baxter.

Nicolls rang to ask for further information and, after speaking to Baxter, made the following note:

On the telephone he supplemented this by saying that Dillon and MacNeice arrived at 6.0 p.m. on board [presumably he meant 'on deck'] and had a drink or two in the ordinary way in the course of the evening. At 1.0 a.m. a terrific noise was going on in the Ward Room and the officer on duty went in and told them to shut up and go to bed. At 4.0 a.m. Dillon and MacNeice were alleged still to be in the Ward Room, very tight, and some action was taken against them. At 5.0 a.m. one of them is alleged to have tottered up on the bridge and been turned off by the Commanding Officer. At 7.15 a.m. they were found asleep in arm chairs in the Ward Room with empty glasses and bottles all round them, the Ward Room being described by one of the officers as looking like a pub on the morning after Bank Holiday.

The two scriptwriters were sternly interviewed, and MacNeice wrote a report that presented the events of their last night at sea in a somewhat different light:

On the last evening (June 28/9th), the ship being due to dock about breakfast time, we got the impression that there was rather a holiday spirit in the air; as this was our last opportunity of showing our friendliness, we were very ready to sit up and have drinks with anyone who felt like it. We began by swopping stories and later there was some singing; this was what was referred to in the report as the 'terrific noise', and we quietened down on request. After the singing had stopped, it is still possible that – owing to the small size and acoustic qualities of the ward-room – the conversation and laughter between Dillon, myself and some of the officers may have been more penetrating than we realised. A younger officer did come through the ward-room and say something like 'Don't make so much noise, chaps, there are people trying to sleep!' I wish to point out, however, that *if* anyone had told us to shut up completely or to go to bed, we should of course have complied; we had no wish to abuse the hospitality of the ship. (Incidentally, there was always someone sleeping off the ward-room at any time of the day or night.)

Some time after the singing stopped, we settled down to playing cards and so continued for a long time, having periodical drinks (all of which were entered in the mess sheet) but making very little noise; I myself was feeling pretty sleepy, not from drink but from a series of uncomfortable nights, and did not feel in the least like raising hell. When the game broke up, I went up on the bridge to have a look out for five minutes before going to bed and also to borrow a cigarette from a junior officer who was then on watch (I may add that for a landsman who was 'very tight' – the phrase used in the report – it would have been pretty difficult to get up the two ladders to the bridge when the ship was in motion). After this Dillon and I went to sleep in the ward-room. I had been accustomed to sleep there every night, sleeping in my clothes, while Dillon had the use of the Doctor's cabin. On this occasion the Doctor used his own cabin and Dillon took his place in the ward-room.

This was relayed to the naval authorities who, after further inquiries, told the BBC:

The Captain of H.M.S. Chelsea made no report on his own initiative and was not going to do so. Unfortunately he told his wife of the incident, and she, when passing through London, retailed it to naval friends, saying in effect that she did not think that H.M.S. Chelsea would want any more B.B.C. visitors for some time. This story reached Captain Baxter and he thought it necessary, and justifiably, I think, to trace the story to its source and either kill it or have it investigated. He therefore asked the Flag Officer at Liverpool for a report and the Captain of H.M.S. Chelsea was instructed to submit one.

Yet more reports – one from MacNeice – were called for, but gradually this storm in a gin glass subsided, and on 11 September he was again summoned for interview. A senior administrative officer lectured him on 'representing the B.B.C.' and afterwards wrote a final report, which ended: 'He is penitent, and I think, considerably shaken by the incident. He accepted this reprimand, and I told him that the confirmation of his appointment would no longer be held up.'

The radio programme that precipitated this furore, 'Freedom's Ferry – Life on an ex-American Destroyer', was rather more dramatic than the patrol on which it was based, involving the rescue of survivors from a torpedoed British Merchant ship. For this, MacNeice drew on remembered conversations with survivors of the *Jervis Bay*, as he would later draw on memories of this voyage for his poem, 'Convoy':

> Together, keeping in line, slow as if hypnotised
> Across the blackboard sea in sombre echelon
> The food-ships draw their wakes. No Euclid could have devised
> Neater means to a more essential end –
> Unless the chalk breaks off, the convoy is surprised.
>
> The cranks go up and down, the smoke-trails tendril out,
> The precious cargoes creak, the signals clack,
> All is under control and nobody need shout,
> We are steady as we go, and on our flanks,
> The little whippet warships romp and scurry about.
>
> This is a bit like us: the individual sets
> A course of all his soul's more basic needs
> Of love and pride-of-life, but sometimes he forgets
> How much their voyage home depends upon pragmatic
> And ruthless attitudes – destroyers and corvettes.

'Convoy' draws also on a submerged memory of a greater poem about a greater ship sunk in those waters – Hardy's 'The Convergence of the Twain (Lines on the Loss of the 'Titanic')'. Almost thirty years before, MacNeice at his mother's side had watched the *Titanic* on her trials in Belfast Lough, and now in the last stanza of his 'Convoy' there surfaces the ghost of Hardy's vessel:

> In a solitude of the sea
> Deep from human vanity,
> And the Pride of Life that planned her, stilly couches she.

'Freedom's Ferry' was well produced – Dillon's use of sound effects was particularly skilful – and so that MacNeice could himself learn about production, Gilliam sent him on a fortnight's course at the end of July. He told Eleanor he found it 'Just like being at school – sitting on hard benches – but technically fascinating though in places difficult for me with my unmechanical mind.' He proved an apt pupil and, producing one of William Empson's scripts later in 1941, impressed him both by his professional management of technical matters and his handling of the actors. Instead of calling for the run-through that Empson was expecting, MacNeice told them to go and have a drink. They did the programme with great verve and spontaneity.

Doone's Wharton Street house had so far survived the bombing, but houses in a parallel street nearby had not and it was decided to move to MacNeice's sister's house in Highgate. She was now working in Plymouth, where Louis had visited her in April when gathering material for a script in 'The Stones Cry Out' series. He was happy to move to Byron Cottage in North Road, Highgate, not only because it was safer than central London, but also because it was the house in which Housman wrote *A Shropshire Lad* and was 'surrounded by historic pubs all of which claim to have been patronized by Coleridge'.

Back in June, when Dillon and MacNeice were patrolling the Atlantic, the captain of their destroyer heard on his radio that the Germans had invaded Russia. The BBC was soon at work endeavouring to change British and American perceptions of their enemy-turned-ally, and MacNeice was asked to write a feature on Chekhov. This he was happy to do. Though he had never been intoxicated – like Blunt, Parsons, or Spender – by the idea of communist Russia, he had long been interested in its writers. The script he now produced, 'Dr Chekhov', was an impressionist radio portrait of a man who 'did everything gently'. This was not perhaps the quality in their new ally that the Foreign Office most wished to celebrate and, in the summer of 1941, they suggested a large-scale feature that would highlight Russian heroism. Dallas Bower, an experienced film-maker, was chosen to produce this. He chose the subject – Alexander Nevsky's defeat of his country's German invaders in 1242, the subject of Eisenstein's epic film – and chose, as his scriptwriter, the film critic of *The Spectator*. Bower had a copy of the film, used before the war to instruct television trainees in the art of camera, and this he now showed to MacNeice and Dillon. (Ironically, the film had been withdrawn from circulation in the Soviet Union following the signing of the Nazi-Soviet non-aggression pact in 1939.) MacNeice wrote a rousing script and went with Bower to the Soviet Embassy to record an introductory statement by the Ambassador, M. Maisky. A strong cast, headed by Robert Donat, and supported by the BBC Symphony Orchestra, the BBC Chorus and Theatre Chorus, conducted by Sir Adrian Boult, was assembled in Bedford School Hall, and poised to begin a 'live' recording on 8 December, when proceedings were suddenly halted. The air-waves were cleared for an important news bulletin: the Japanese had attacked Pearl Harbor. The shock of this intensified the drama of 'Alexander Nevsky' for performers and listeners alike.

MacNeice and Bower would sometimes meet in the Players' Theatre, a music hall that at the start of the Blitz had moved to a basement in Albemarle Street. A frequent performer there was a beautiful singer with a mane of red hair gathered into a chignon, called Hedli Anderson. MacNeice had seen her play the part of the Cabaret Singer in the Group Theatre's 1934 production of Auden's *The Dance of Death*; and she had seen him, three years later, at a rehearsal of *Out of the Picture* in the same theatre. He was bending over Betsy the borzoi, and she had noticed that they both had long elegant faces. In December 1941, she saw him again, sitting dejectedly in the corner of a party he had gate-crashed, and crossed the room to talk to him. Some days later, she invited Rupert Doone to Christmas dinner in her flat at 6 Maiden Lane, just off the Strand, and told him to bring Connie and Louis. Perhaps sensing a threat to the equilibrium of his Byron Cottage

Hedli Anderson

establishment, Rupert told Louis he was invited *after* dinner, and explained to Hedli that his friend had another engagement. He duly arrived after dinner and, sinking into a deep armchair, threw his legs over one of its arms and lit a cigar. He was more silent then the other guests – being both more sober and slightly offended at not being asked to the meal. Doone invited Hedli to tea at Byron Cottage the following day, and there she discovered that Louis had eaten Christmas dinner on his own in a Lyons Corner House. This discovery had the very effect that Doone had been anxious to avoid: she invited Louis to a compensatory supper, he invited her to lunch, and soon they were meeting regularly. One evening, returning to her flat, she found him sitting in the deep armchair and there seemed no reason for him to go home.

On 19 January, he wrote a letter to Eleanor trying to explain why she had not heard from him for so long. There were two reasons:

1) a sudden revulsion from America on my part & 2) a girl I had as good as decided to set up with. Since when Reason One has vanished (curious that you should come nearer to me via Japan) & Reason Two I have disposed of myself – rather brutally, I'm afraid. (I thought I'd decided on this Two thing & was all set up to go on with it but found myself being emotionally dishonest & traced that back to you.) Rather a repetition of that Irish episode in the Fall of '39 but this went much further & for quite some time, darling, I really did think that you-&-me was finished. It looks as if it takes a lot of killing.

If he was telling the truth – and he was an unusually honest man – the *coup de grâce* was nearer than he knew. Indeed, it seems likely that his change of heart about this girl he does not identify had less to do with Eleanor than with a girl he does not mention: a singer with a mane of red hair gathered into a chignon.

Hedli Anderson had been born Antoinette Millicent Hedley Anderson in 1907, the same year as Frederick Louis MacNeice. She, too, inherited Irish blood from both parents. Leaving an English boarding school at eleven, she lived in Switzerland for some years before returning to England to begin her musical training. She studied with Victor Beigel, a coach well known to Elisabeth Schumann and Lotte Lehman but, she came to see, 'quite, quite wrong for any little person who came to him to start singing'. Nevertheless, she followed him to Bayreuth and then to Hamburg, where she took lessons at the *conservatoire* and learnt some painful political lessons. Her landlady's son – unable to choose whether to be a communist or a Nazi – committed suicide; and her landlady's daughter – to keep her job – was forced to sleep with her fascist boss. In 1935, the girl with red hair moved to Berlin to study as an opera singer, but soon realized that both her voice and her personality were better suited to the smaller stage of sophisticated cabaret. She also realized that the increasing dangers of Berlin outweighed its diminishing delight and, returning to London in early 1934, headed for the Group Theatre and a role that might have been written for her – that of the Cabaret Singer in Auden's *The Dance of Death*. Eight months later, the Group Theatre's *Midnight Cabaret* featured 'Hedli Anderson in old and new songs of satire'. She created several roles in the first Auden-Isherwood collaboration *The Dog Beneath the Skin*, but it was their second, *The Ascent of F6*, in which she appeared as 'The Singer', that made her name. Britten, whose music – and Auden, whose lyrics – she had sung so well, then collaborated on a series of cabaret songs especially for her. Six were recorded in 1938–9 for the Columbia label, but the 'masters' were subsequently destroyed and only four songs have survived: 'Calypso', 'Johnny', 'Funeral Blues', and what came to be her theme-song, the one popularly known by its refrain, 'Tell me the truth about love'.

In the winter of 1941–2, she was singing Victorian music-hall songs – 'Jane, Jane of Maiden Lane', 'Driving in the Park', and 'Never Lost me Last Train Yet' – in the smoky underworld of the Players' Theatre. There she befriended a twenty-year-old Irish actress with something of her own verve and animal vitality. Julia – always known as Judy – Lang had heroine-worshipped Hedli ever since seeing her, while 'making up', fill the slight gap in her front teeth with melted candle-wax on a matchstick. Judy had been sleeping under the theatre's grand piano, but Hedli pronounced the basement damp, the other sleepers unsuitable company, and whisked her away to her spare room in 6 Maiden Lane. The patter of shrapnel on the skylight, however, kept her awake, and after a week she decided she preferred the perils of the Players' basement. From time to time she would return to Maiden Lane for a shower. One day she could not turn the water off and flooded the studio. She shouted to Hedli, who came at once and herself shouted: 'Louis, come and look what this *absurd* child has done!' He did. Judy was stark naked.

In spite of the shower and the patter of shrapnel on the guest-room skylight, she thought the flat a place of enchantment, and could conceive of no greater glamour than lying on Hedli's real fur rug (with Louis stroking her leg), while Ben Britten played the piano and Hedli sang her cabaret songs. She thought Louis 'a most lovely creature, loved his sardonic look, loved the fallen angel look of him, the long Irish head, the long Irish upper lip, and the delight with which that sardonic and rather tragic face broke into laughter.'

He had been working hard on new scripts: two of his features – in addition to 'Alexander Nevsky' – were broadcast in December, and two more were scheduled for March. Like many people living in the centre of London, he and Hedli were feeling the effects of broken nights and, in March, they escaped to Cornwall for ten days together. They rented a cottage on a cliff overlooking Polperro Bay. The daffodils were out and, with the sound of the sea reminding him of Carrickfergus, he told her the story of his life. Returning to London, they could see no reason why he should not move into 6 Maiden Lane, but Doone could. 'Louis can't live with you', he told Hedli. 'We need his ration-book.'

Death was no stranger to Londoners in 1942, but on 14 April he struck where he was least expected. Bishop MacNeice died that evening. 'It seemed a good way', his son told Dodds. 'He had just announced that he was going to retire this year & he wouldn't have liked being retired at all.' Louis went over to Ireland for the funeral and a memorial service, during which the Roman Catholic Bishop of Belfast – in a telling gesture of fraternal respect – said prayers for him in St Anne's Cathedral porch. Louis must have been moved by this and many other tributes to his father. As a child, he had been alarmed by him; as a boy, he had found him exasperating; and as a man, he had found him and his house depressing. He had long known, however, that his father was a 'great man' and, over the years to come, poems would plot the progress of his grieving and reconciliation with

> One who believed and practised and whose life
> Presumed the Resurrection. What that means
> He may have felt he knew; this much is certain –
> The meaning filled his actions, made him courteous
> And lyrical and strong and kind and truthful,
> A generous puritan.

After the funeral, Louis crossed the border to see Dan at Ashfield Lodge, where blazing daffodils may have reminded him of Polperro. Returning to London, he asked Hedli to marry him, and she agreed. Some of his friends wondered if he would have taken this step while his father was alive. This, however, is to underestimate the Bishop's generous humanity. He had welcomed Mary into his family and come to terms with her desertion of his son and their divorce. It is hard to believe that he would not have warmed to Hedli's warmth and welcomed a relationship that would give his son and grandson a replacement for the wife and mother they had lost. In due course, Dan received a letter from his father telling him he was about to marry a lady 'whom I know you'll love very much'; and, at the end of June, Hedli's parents received a telegram: AM MARRYING LOUIS MAC-NEICE TOMORROW. They were obliged to reply: WHO IS LOUIS MACNEICE?

At 9.30 on the morning of 1 July, Rupert Doone (who was reconciled by now to the loss of the ration-book) appeared at 6 Maiden Lane, with half a bottle of champagne. MacNeice came to the door.

'Have you got the ring?' Doone asked.

'No.'

'Then, you'd better go down to the Strand and get one.' The bridegroom went off, and returned with a platinum band. As a result of this unscheduled digression, the wedding party reached Caxton Hall Registry Office half an hour late. The Registrar told the groom: 'You have to pay 25 shillings for having been married before.' The groom did not have 25 shillings, so a hat was passed round to raise this sum. After the wedding, they were having lunch in an Italian restaurant when Hedli remembered she had a singing lesson booked for that afternoon, and rang to cancel it. 'Don't be silly,' said her teacher, Maggie Teyte. 'You can get married any day. Of course you must have your lesson.' So off she went, with her bridegroom in tow. That evening, Lorenzo the Magnificent gave them a magnificent dinner, and the wedding day ended with a Zulu dance through the streets of Soho.

The following day, Nancy Spender received a letter:

Darling,

Hedli and I are getting married this afternoon, otherwise I can't take her to Ireland, but it won't change anything between you and me.

All my love,
Louis

In due course, Eleanor Clark also received a letter:

Darling,

This is to tell you that I have got married — but not to anyone I had mentioned to you before.

This makes sense to me. I hope you understand?

What I said before about you & me perhaps is what really applies: we met on the top of a mountain & should leave it at that.

But I would like you to go on writing to me. Without post-mortems.

Be happy, darling,

love ever,

Louis

Another letter told Mercy MacCann of his marriage to Hedli and their plan to come to Ireland on about 20 July. Their honeymoon was probably delayed while Louis finished two feature programmes that were to be broadcast that month. As soon as he was free, they crossed to Belfast and stayed with Mrs MacNeice at 'Oakfield', a little white house overlooking Carrickfergus, into which she had recently moved with her mentally handicapped stepson, Willie, and a female companion who looked after him. Moving on to Portadown, they then spent some happy days with the MacCanns at Vinecash. Hedli had recently been singing Arnold Schoenberg's setting of Alberty Giraud's *Pierrot Lunaire* poems. Louis disliked the words of this song-cycle and, saying he would write Hedli something better, drafted 'The Revenant'

Louis MacNeice in 1942

on the Vinecash dining-room table. A cycle of twelve songs divided by eleven 'interludes' (of which he would publish only the last song), it is an interesting failure. The voice is that of a girl waiting for a lover who has gone to a war from which he returns as a ghost, but some of her memories are the poet's own:

> Seven years   I have been alone
> Fearing the future,   hoarding the past.
> The past is past,   yet let me take you
> Back to the bright garden of girlhood.
> I am alone   in Here and Now;
> There and Then   we were together.
> I will take you back   to There and Then;
> Come with me now   through seven years
> To the far-off days   before I met him
> When I was a girl   unlearned in love.
> Come with me now   to the gay garden
> When time was still   and I was young
> Hoping for life   hoping for love.

Seven years before, Mary had walked out of 'Highfield Cottage', and six years before that she and Louis had travelled across Ireland – from Carrickfergus to Achill – as he and Hedli were now doing.

From Vinecash they went to Cootehill, where Hedli made an electrifying impression on Dan, a seven-year-old used to Anglo-Irish ladies; then they took a train (with a turf-burning engine) to Westport and, shouldering rucksacks, walked on to Achill. They took a room in a small hotel where the German Ambassador to Ireland was then staying. He was presumed to be in radio-contact with Nazi Germany, and Ernie O'Malley, the old IRA hero, had offered to give MacNeice a letter of introduction to him – an offer gruffly rejected.

The last stage of the honeymoon was a visit – with Dan – to Dublin, where he and Hedli were introduced to Jack Yeats by the Cultural Attaché at the British Embassy, John Betjeman. Then Dan returned sadly to Cootehill, and his father and stepmother boarded the ferry on their way back to the blacked-out flat in Maiden Lane.

CHAPTER 18

A Birth and a Death

angels are frigid and shepherds are dumb,
There is no holy water when the enemy come . . . .
'Nuts in May', *CP*, p. 204

MacNeice's love for America – eclipsed by 'a sudden revulsion' in autumn 1941 – re-emerged with her entry into the war and shines through his radio scripts of summer and winter 1942: 'Britain to America', 'Halfway House' ('a programme presenting the American Expeditionary Force in Northern Ireland'), 'Salute to the US Army', and his major undertaking of the year, 'Christopher Columbus'. Ironically, the last of these, MacNeice's second collaboration with Dallas Bower, was triggered by the events that delayed the recording of their first collaborative venture on 8 December 1941. The attack on Pearl Harbor had brought America into the war, and no sooner had the BBC honoured one new ally with 'Alexander Nevsky' than it decided to honour another with a major programme marking the 450th anniversary of Columbus's discovery of America. This was entrusted to Bower, who again chose MacNeice as scriptwriter. As their earlier collaboration had been based on Eisenstein's film, this was to be based on Samuel Eliot Morison's magisterial biography, *Admiral of the Ocean Sea* (one of the titles Columbus had demanded from Ferdinand and Isabella of Spain). MacNeice at once began reading and rendering down Morison's fat book to reveal its skeletal narrative. This they discussed over a precious bottle of Drambuie during a January weekend at Bower's home in Essex, after which William Walton was asked if he would write a musical score to accompany MacNeice's text. He agreed, provided they could wait while he discharged certain other commitments. This suited MacNeice, whose play was conceived on an ambitious scale, and the programme – originally scheduled for March – was set back to 12 October, the actual anniversary of Columbus's arrival in the New World. MacNeice's original conception was 'essentially a one man, one idea programme' and, in an Appendix to the printed text, he wrote:

Construction and 'over-all' unity being in a radio play of primary importance, a heroic subject, such as the discovery of America, required an epic rather than a psychological treatment. The later career of Columbus, though vastly interesting from a biographical angle, would by transferring interest from the *muthos* to the character (i.e. to the character not only as distinct from but as opposed to the *muthos*), have broken the programme in two, confused the listener and given him possibly a feeling of anti-climax. This programme, moreover, was intended to celebrate the 450th anniversary of the discovery of America; in writing an anniversary programme for the Battle of Waterloo I would not include that picture from 1833 of Wellington in Apsley House – the duchess lying dead inside while the mob is breaking the windows. Similarly, with *Alexander Nevsky*, neither Eisenstein's film nor radio adaptation of it was bothered by the fact that Nevsky spent his later years appeasing the Tartars.

MacNeice's Columbus is a Marlovian overreacher, though the playwright was at pains to avoid the monotony of Marlovian blank verse, preferring a more flexible and Shakespearean interaction of prose and poetry. So, in Act Two, the prosaic talk of sailors is counterpointed by their Admiral's soliloquy:

'Where shall wisdom be found and where is the abode of understanding?
God makes the weight for his winds and he weigheth the waters by measure.'
They knew that I was to come.
Isaiah and Esdras and Job and John the Divine –
They knew that I was to come.
And the Roman poet, Seneca, knew it too –
. . . venient annis
Saecula seris quibus oceanus
Vincula rerum laxet . . .
'The time will come in a late
Century when the sea
Will loose the knots of fate

And the earth will be opened up
And the rolled map unfurled
And a new sailor sail
To uncover a new world.'
'The time will come . . .' The time has come already.
There are strange things happening.

Rhyme here contributes unobtrusively to the musical texture of the verse. Elsewhere, MacNeice would use it more formally, as in the beautiful song of the Cordoban Beatriz, who will bear Columbus's child:

> When will he return?
> Only to depart.
> Of his restless heart;
> Bondsman of the Voice,
> Rival of the Sun,
> Viceroy of the sunset
> Till his task be done.
>
> Though he is my love
> He is not for me;
> What he loves is over
> Loveless miles of sea
> Haunted by the West
> Eating out his heart –
> When will be return?
> Only to depart.

Christopher Columbus has forty-nine speaking parts and, on 12 October, a splendid cast – headed by Laurence Olivier in the title-role and Margaret Rawlings as Beatriz – was assembled in the Corn Exchange in Bedford. They were supported by the BBC Chorus and Symphony Orchestra, again conducted by Sir Adrian Boult, and the resulting programme was a resounding success. In the words of Asa Briggs, it 'created a sensation in artistic circles on both sides of the Atlantic'.

MacNeice had written the part of Queen Isabella's friend, Marquesa, for Hedli, and she did full justice to Walton's setting of her husband's songs. Their delight in their new life and shared success was

Louis, Hedli, and Robert Speaight rehearsing *Christopher Columbus*

compounded that autumn by the discovery that Hedli was pregnant. On Christmas Day, she prepared a celebratory lunch in her tiny kitchen. To give herself elbow-room, she despatched the men of the party – Louis, Anthony Blunt, John Hilton, and Ernst Stahl – to the local pub, The Peacock in Maiden Lane. When everything was ready, she appeared in their midst, brandishing a ladle, eyes blazing like a priestess, crying: 'The goose, the goose!'

Her flat was attractive and convenient – especially for Louis when the Features Department moved from Bedford College to Rothwell House in New Cavendish Street – but it was not large enough for a family and, in January 1943, the MacNeices moved to a rented house, 10 Wellington Place, NW8. This had the advantage for Louis that it overlooked Lord's cricket ground, but the disadvantage for Hedli that it had, initially, no stove. Their first night was shaken with gun-fire and, around five o'clcok in the morning, the revving of airforce lorries in a depot nearby. Setting off for work, the MacNeices found a barrier at the top of Cavendish Avenue guarded by a policeman who asked:

'Where have you come from?'

'10 Wellington Place.'

'But we evacuated this street last night', he said. 'There's an unexploded land-mine over the wall in Lord's.'

The baby was not due until July, but there was an addition to the household in January, when Dan arrived from Ireland wearing a three-piece suit of herring-bone tweed, with a fob-watch on a chain and a bulldog-headed walking stick (all provided by his generous step-grandmother). He hardly had time to adjust to Wellington Place before he was despatched to Springfield Grange prep school in Great Missenden, Buckinghamshire. It was a season of comings and goings. MacNeice's BBC secretary, Audrey Brayshaw, left to become a Land Girl and on 16 April her successor, Ruth Jones, wrote in her diary: 'Louis MacNeice made his first appearance – Very Sinn Fein looking, pleasant voice, but far away most of the time. Very quiet.' A week later she reports: 'He's to go to War Correspondents' Training Place on Thursday for a month.' He was to be assigned to a tank regiment in Kent for training, prior to secondment to the BBC's team of roving war correspondents. Hedli – now monumental in the seventh month of pregnancy – told Mercy MacCann: 'he will be away a great deal, in fact most of the time. For him I am pleased for myself I am very very sorry.' On 29 April, husband and wife – he in uniform, swagger-stick in hand – took a last turn round the lake in St James' Park and said a stiff-upper-lipped goodbye. Dramatically, this was the high point of MacNeice's 'military' career, which soon degenerated into farce. On manoeuvres in Kent, the commander of his tank told him to take over and he drove it into a wood. Then, one wet night, he was sheltering under the tank when it began to sink on top of him. He was pulled clear, but soon, perceived to be technologically incompetent and generally accident-prone, he was back – to everyone's relief – at the BBC.

His working day typically began sometime after 10 o'clock, when he would drift in like a thundercloud to the office he shared with Ruth Jones. He would look at the post, say 'coffee?' and raise an eyebrow. She would nod, and together they would go down to a seedy café near Rothwell House. She had never known anyone with less small talk, but he liked being brought up to date with office news, and soon the cloud would show a silver lining and the sun might emerge. He did all his writing at home – usually at night, with the help of a packet of cigarettes – and, back in the office, would push his manuscript over the desk to Ruth Jones, who would type it and push the typescript back to him. He never learnt to type himself, and she was surprised to learn that his long flipper-like hands could drive a car. Had she known of his success with women, she would also have been surprised by his formality. For a year he called her 'Miss Jones' and remained 'Mr Mac-Neice' to her.

She came to see his formality as the outward and visible sign of an inner integrity. She was impressed by 'his absolute truthfulness, and scrupulous attention to the repayment of even the smallest debts' – these always recorded in the little notebook he carried with him. Unlike some of his colleagues, he would never inflate his BBC expenses. This honesty had its disadvantages: he was slow to detect dishonesty in others – like the confidence-trickster who turned up at his house with a load of logs that he claimed the lady of the house had ordered, promising cash on delivery. MacNeice was surprised by the sum but paid it – to Hedli's fury when she returned.

On Monday 5 July, Ruth Jones recorded in her diary: 'Louis' baby born. Birds sang and the sun shone. He was terribly happy. A girl, 8lbs 1 oz, called Brigid Corinna. Wires to everyone.' The name was a good Anglo-Irish compromise, its Anglo half deriving from a Boeotian Greek poet of the second century BC, by way of a happy memory of Littleton Powys declaiming Herrick's poem, 'Corinna's Going A-Maying', as a summer Reveille in a Sherborne dormitory:

> Get up! get up for shame! the blooming morn
> Upon her wings presents the god unshorn.
> See how Aurora throws her fair
> Fresh-quilted colours through the air:
> Get up, sweet slug-a-bed, and see
> The dew bespangling herb and tree.

In the excitement of this birth MacNeice seems hardly to have noticed the appearance that July of a penchild bearing his name. *Meet the U.S. Army* – a twenty-four-page pamphlet, published by the Stationery Office at fourpence – had been commissioned by the Ministry of

Information 'for teachers to use as a basis for lessons in school'. It was a good choice of author, and he shows his hand in challenging Hollywood stereotypes, and in his evident appreciation of America and Americans, their customs and their slang ('richer and more colourful than our own'), and in their football's 'forward pass'.

For all his jubilant wires sent at Corinna's birth, one of her father's first and firmest friends would never hear the good news. On 20 September a corvette, HMS *Polyanthus*, was escorting a convoy from Londonderry to Newfoundland when she was sunk by an acoustic torpedo. All hands were lost, including Lieutenant Graham Shepard.

Lieutenant Graham Shepard

Ten years later, MacNeice would remember in *Autumn Sequel* how

> one day (I was living in Saint John's Wood
> In one small cell of London's half empty comb)

> His sister called and came upstairs and stood
> Quietly and said quietly 'We have lost
> Gavin'; a cobra spread an enormous hood

> Over the window and a sudden frost
> Froze all the honey left in the looted hive . . . .*

MacNeice responded to this death more immediately than to his father's. We are in some sense prepared for the death of an elderly parent, but the death of our first friend and contemporary forces us to confront our own death. In late September or early October, he wrote a radio script dramatically different from his recent propaganda pieces. 'The Story of My Death' sketches the life and death of a young Italian called Lauro de Bosis. A poet and the son of a poet, he writes a prize-winning play about Icarus, learns to fly a plane, then on 2 October 1931 writes 'The Story of My Death', and the following day scatters anti-fascist leaflets over the dome of St Peter's on a flight that ends when 'he falls into the sea'. MacNeice has him quote from *Adonais*, Shelley's great elegy for another English poet who died young, a poem he would himself shortly echo in an elegy of his own. *Adonais* ends with a prophetic foreshadowing of its speaker's death at sea:

> The breath whose might I have invoked in song
> Descends on me; my spirit's bark is driven,
> Far from the shore, far from the trembling throng
> Whose sails were never to the tempest given;
> The massy earth and sphered skies are riven!
> I am borne darkly, fearfully, afar;
> Whilst burning through the inmost veil of Heaven,
> The soul of Adonais, like a star,
> Beacons from the abode where the Eternal are.

Keats's star 'beacons' and Shelley's death at sea is remembered in the

* CP, p. 336. Gavin is a pseudonym for Graham in this poem.

opening movement of MacNeice's elegy, 'The Casualty':

> 'Damn!' you would say if I were to write the best
> Tribute I could to you, 'All clichés', and you would grin
> Dwindling to where that faded star allures
> Where no time presses and no days begin –
> Turning back shrugging to the misty West
> Remembered out of Homer but now yours.
>
> Than whom I do not expect ever again
> To find a more accordant friend, with whom
> I could be silent knowledgeably; you never
> Faked or flattered or time-served. If ten
> Winds were to shout you down or twenty oceans boom
> Above the last of you, they will not sever
>
> That thread of so articulate silence. How
> You died remains conjecture; instantaneous
> Is the most likely – that the shutter fell
> Congealing the kaleidoscope at Now
> And making all your past contemporaneous
> Under that final chord of the mid-Atlantic swell.

'The Casualty', subtitled '(in memoriam G.H.S.)', is also indebted to Yeats's elegy for an Irish airman killed – like Lauro de Bosis – over Italy: 'In Memory of Major Robert Gregory'. The problem of both poets – indeed the problem of all pastoral elegists – is how to present someone 'dead ere his prime' as a credible cause of Nature's lamentation, or the world's. Theocritus, Milton, Shelley, and Yeats, lamenting an absent shepherd, are able to magnify his virtues by their rhetorical strategies. MacNeice, however, by addressing *his* Shepard directly – 'You never/Faked or flattered' – makes such strategies impossible. Where Yeats can inflate Robert Gregory's importance by suggesting he would have been suitable company for the writers Lionel Johnson and John Synge and a notable horseman, George Pollexfen, MacNeice may not 'touch up' his 'snapshots' of Shepard:

> Here you are gabbling Baudelaire or Donne,
> Here you are mimicking that cuckoo clock,
> Here you are serving a double fault for set,
> Here you are diving naked from a Dalmatian rock,

Here you are barracking the sinking sun,
Here you are taking Proust aboard your doomed corvette.

Yes, all you gave were inklings; even so
Invaluable – such as I remember
Out of your mouth or only in your eyes
On walks in blowsy August, Brueghel-like December,
Or when the gas was hissing and a glow
Of copper jugs gave back your lyrical surprise.

For above all that was your gift – to be
Surprised and therefore sympathetic, warm
Towards things as well as people, you could see
The integrity of differences – O did you
Make one last integration, find a Form
Grow out of formlessness when the Atlantic hid you?

MacNeice knew and liked Shepard better than Milton knew and liked Edward King (the subject of his 'Lycidas') or Yeats knew and liked Robert Gregory* but, ironically, it is his honesty – and his respect for Shepard's honesty – that undermine his poem and prevent it from taking its place with Milton's and Yeats's masterpiece of rhetorical inflation. It may have been dissatisfaction with 'The Casualty' that led MacNeice, six months later, to return to the subject of Shepard's death. As with 'The Story of My Death', it takes the form of a radio drama, an impressionist portrait. Its title – 'He Had a Date' – picks up a word from the poem: 'you cannot from this date / Talk big or little'. The radio drama, however, tells a story very different from that of the poem. An opening statement, spoken by MacNeice himself, announces:

He Had a Date was conceived as a private news-reel of episodes from one man's life. The hero – who is not in the ordinary sense a hero (some might

---

* Yeats gives himself away when, in his hyperbolic celebration of Gregory ('Soldier, scholar, horseman, he, / As 'twere all life's epitome'), he echoes Dryden's satiric attack on another 'Jack of all trades', George Villiers, 2nd Duke of Buckingham:

> A man so various that he seemed to be
> Not one, but all mankind's epitome:
> Stiff in opinions, always in the wrong;
> Was everything by starts and nothing long . . . .

> 'Absalom and Achitophel', l. 545–8

dismiss him as a fool, a failure, or even a cad) – is a fictitious character but typical of his period. He belongs to a generation which was not sure of its bearings and to a class of which *he* was not sure himself . . . .

He was born in 1907 and died in 1942. He had – you see – a Date.

'Tom Varney' was born in the same year as MacNeice and Shepard. His life is presented in the form of 'a private news-reel', seen in his dying moments on a ship struck by a torpedo. He relives his nightmares as a child; at school, is teased for wearing boots ('only cads wear boots. People like grocers' sons'); wins a scholarship to Oxford and gains a First in Classical Mods. Thus far, the trajectory of his career follows MacNeice's rather than Shepard's, but from this point it diverges from theirs, before following Shepard's to its close. Varney abandons Greats; takes and abandons a job as a journalist; marries and abandons his wife Mary; joins the International Brigade in Spain; returns to England and joins the Navy. He is at sea, remembering that he has broken a date with Mary, when he sees the torpedo that occasions and cuts short his private news-reel.

MacNeice's dreamlike conflation of his life with Shepard's to depict a representative of their generation made a strikingly successful programme – Cleverdon called it 'a brilliant example of sceneless composition' – but, paradoxically, it is a portrait of failure. Tom Varney's last speech – from his watery grave – ends with a significant echo of Wilfred Owen's 'Let us sleep now':

'I am asleep at last. The Japanese flower opened in water. It did not open fully, the bearing was . . . not quite right. Was I a misfit? Maybe. I hurt my mother, my father, I hurt Jane and Mary. And I leave nothing behind me – child, work, or deed to remember. But I tried, you know, I tried. Believe it or not, I did have ideals of a sort. But I could not quite get the bearing. Now let me sleep: I'm tired.'

Shepard's death was a tragic waste of his potential, and in June 1944, it may have seemed to MacNeice that he himself had sold his birthright for a mess of propaganda. He had also a more specific cause for gloom.

The tides of war had now turned in North Africa, Eastern Europe, Italy and the Pacific, and preparations for the opening of a European Second Front were well advanced. Gilliam planned programmes 'to catch and repeat the greatest moment of tension in our time almost as it was being lived'. He wanted MacNeice to write a feature for D-Day. This he did, in a manner more realistic and less romantic than that of his more overtly propaganda pieces. A narrator tunes in to the thoughts of men waiting to go into action and of the women they left behind them, interweaving voices and sound-effects into a single stream of consciousness. Ruth Jones collected the script on 21 May. Her diary notes that it was recorded on the 30th but, on 2 June, she writes: 'After a lot of hoo-ha and talk by the policy boys they decided not to use the D-Day programme. Haley said it was very good but "too editorial". Louis very depressed and quiet and said he wouldn't do any more war programmes'. William Haley had been appointed Director General two months before and, with the benefit of hindsight, it is hard to quarrel with his verdict. When, four days later, the invasion of Europe began, Ruth Jones's diary recorded that Louis 'felt D-Day programme would have been exactly right in tone for the day'. It is hard to believe, however, that listeners' needs were not better served by John Snagge's radio reportage than they would have been by Mac-Neice's imaginative script. Its rejection darkened his next, 'He Had a Date'.

The day this was broadcast, 28 June, a flying bomb blew in some of the windows of 10 Wellington Place. The Allies may have been winning the war, but the German V-1s, unleashed for the first time on 14 June, brought back memories of the Blitz and were, if anything, worse for civilian morale than the more predictable raids of 1941–2. In July, Louis took Hedli and the children up to Scotland, where it was arranged they should stay until London was safer. While they were away, their house had a visitor.

A young woman in her twenties was travelling from her home in Edinburgh to her job in a department of the Foreign Office located outside London. Sitting next to her in the train was another young woman, who said she was a mother's help 'in a professor's family in St John's Wood'. Their train arrived in London too late for the civil servant to make her connection, and the mother's help suggested she spend the night with her, since her employers were away and 'wouldn't mind'. Many years later, she described what followed:

It was a warm summer evening, still light enough to see the small, tangled garden in front of the house. We entered a large room almost entirely filled by a long work-table of plain wood, just such a table as I myself always write on now. In another corner of the room was a Morrison shelter: this was a large bed with a steel canopy – in fact, an indoor bomb shelter. The place was generally unconventional. I thought, at first, unnecessarily so. It looked like eccentricity for its own sake. While my friend was preparing the rooms upstairs, I wandered through the house. One room had nothing but a mattress-bed on the floor. There was a handsome writing-desk and a marvellous library of books. It was a decidedly literary collection. I began looking through the titles.

I found two of the books, and then more, inscribed by famous novelists. Another was dedicated to a famous poet, and so was yet another.

I called upstairs to my friend, who was now having a bath. 'Is this the house of the famous poet?'

'Yes,' she called out, 'he writes poetry.'

The famous poet was Louis MacNeice, whose work I loved and admired tremendously. I had just been reading his poem 'The Trolls', written after an air raid . . . .

I ran outside to look at the house from the point of view of my new knowledge, to see the neglected garden and enter the front door and look at the strange rooms again. I touched the furniture. I tried the pencils which were lying on the desk, with an inward, inexplicable satisfaction. I had never met a real poet.

I have always known that this occasion vitally strengthened my resolve to become a writer. In the short story I wrote eight years later ['The House of the Famous Poet'], I reproduced some of the actual scenes of that event. The story tells of an imaginative meeting with a soldier, and a brush with death. It has taken me over 40 years to realise that the quality of the experience was intensified by fear of those flying bombs and the knowledge that destruction might fall at any moment, even on the house of the famous poet.

The writer was Muriel Spark.

MacNeice was back in London on 4 September and, true to his resolve, made no more war programmes – supported in this, as in everything else, by Laurence Gilliam. The text of *Christopher Columbus* had been published in March, prefaced by a long introduction that began with an apologia for 'a popular art-form which still is an art-form', and went on to consider requirements of the medium,

Muriel Spark

requirements of the audience, radio-drama and poetry, construction in radio drama, radio craftsmanship, the importance of 'story', radio production, the voices, the 'effects', and the music. Having failed – like many poets before him – to reach a wider audience from the stage, MacNeice's success in his new element set him exploring it with enthusiasm, intelligence and versatility. The months that saw the publication of his epic treatment of Columbus's quest heard his 'direct and very simple dramatisation of a Russian folk story'. 'The Nosebag' offered a brilliant demonstration of his theories in practice.

The story is central and swiftly unfolded. A good-hearted Soldier is rewarded for his generosity to three Beggars with a magic pack of cards and a magic nosebag. These enable him to outwit a troop of Devils that has taken over a country palace of the Tsar. The Soldier captures them in his nosebag and has them belaboured by Blacksmiths on an anvil until the Devil Captain swears to serve him whenever he is summoned. Only then are he and his troop released. The nosebag now provides the Soldier with food and drink, wife and son, but his felicity is threatened when the boy falls victim to the plague. The Devil

Captain is summoned and enables the Soldier to outwit Death. She, too, is captured in the nosebag. Decades later, the kingdom is over-populated and many, like the Soldier, are ready for Death. He releases her on condition that she takes him first, but she breaks her word and the story ends with a powerfully prophetic exchange:

LANDLORD: ... *I'm* going to give you a toast. You've had twenty-five years of service? Well; you're going to have more. Campaigns like you never dreamed of. You had a magic nosebag, I see you've lost it. Well, that don't matter, you've got something better. You've got a —
SOLDIER: I've got a terrible thirst. Give me your toast.
LANDLORD: You've got a fighting heart and a fighting arm. Well, now you're going to fight with 'em. That's what you're going to do, all through the centuries, you are. Tartars, Swedes, French, Teutons —
SOLDIER: That will all come when it comes. Give me your toast.
LANDLORD: All right, soldier. Here's to Mother Russia.
SOLDIER: Here's ... to Mother ... Russia!

The effect of this, on an audience that only a month before had heard of General Koniev's victory on the Ukrainian Front, may have been greater than that of MacNeice's overtly propagandist programmes, 'Salute to the USSR' and 'The Spirit of Russia'. Relaxed where those were rhetorical, 'The Nosebag' is written with economy and wit (returning to release his captive, the Soldier shouts: 'Death, are you alive?'); and, in MacNeice's production, voices, 'effects', and Russian music did full justice to his script. 'The part of the Soldier was magnificently embodied by Roy Emerton', and Peter Ustinov was a suitably fruity Tsar.

In July, the fortieth anniversary of Chekhov's death gave MacNeice the opportunity to refine one of his earliest features, and the first to have a Russian theme. 'Dr Chekhov' had been a feature-biography. Beginning on the morning of his last day, it ended with his death. Phases of his earlier life were presented through flashbacks, but because MacNeice had no experience of studio production, some of the transitions between past and present would have been unproducible but for the skill of the producer, Stephen Potter, who, as the script-writer gratefully acknowledged, 'saved the situation'. The revised version, 'Sunbeams in His Hat', which MacNeice himself produced, followed the central stream of consciousness with a dexterity learnt in writing 'The Story of My Death' and 'He Had a Date'. Influenced perhaps by the same 'death by water' that had prompted those earlier feature-biographies, he identified the Doctor's revised stream of consciousness more specifically with water. Chekhov's journey to Sahalin, the convict settlement, becomes more clearly a quest into the Heart of Darkness:

> (*A steamer is heard hooting in the distance. The next speech, delivered quietly and rhythmically, is really a soliloquy.*)
>
> TCHEHOV: (*dreamily*) Down the Volga and up the Kama. Days of rain and days of snow. First there was mud and then there was snow and then there was dust. First there was killing cold and then there was killing heat . . . . Innumerable muddy rivers . . . . Endless plains where the wind sings in the stunted birch trees. Further and further from civilisation. Miles and miles of snow and desert – Russian snow and Russian desert. Russia? Poverty . . . distance . . . disease. Tomsk and Irkutsk . . . further and further.
>
> (*Siberian music creeps in.*)
>
> TCHEHOV: Further and further on the road to Sahalin. Further and further on the road to Hell.

These rivers go underground to rise again in the recurrent dream of a river, recognizable as the Styx or Lethe, added to the revised versions:

> TCHEHOV: I told you, Olga, I told you. I've dreamt about it for years. It's like those rivers in Siberia. Great grey slippery stones on the bank; cold autumnal water; mist . . . mist over everything. It's all incredibly dismal and damp and I know that I have to cross it. Then I hear hooters in the mist.

'Dr Chekhov' had ended with his wife saying: 'Anton, doctor, did everything gently.' To this is now added a stage-direction and a speech:

> (*Silence and then the hooter of the steamer. Tchehov's voice is heard, speaking slowly in a great space.*)
>
> TCHEHOV: Which is the steamer for Odessa? . . .
> Where do we book our passage? Your passage and mine.
> For a future which *should* be happy.

The image of the steamer merges with that of Charon's ferry moving through the mist on the river of death.

Despite all the creative energy that had gone into scriptwriting and producing, MacNeice had managed to complete another book of poems. Ruth Jones had typed this and sent it off on 31 March and, in December, *Springboard* was published in an edition of 7,000 copies. This was by far the largest printing of any book of his poems to date – a reflection of the success of *Autumn Journal* (then on its third impression) and of the public's hunger for poetry, a regular wartime phenomenon. *Springboard*, it must be said, did not justify the high hopes of its readers. MacNeice probably sensed this. His dedicatory poem is an apologia:

To Hedli

Because the velvet image,
Because the lilting measure,
No more convey my meaning
I am compelled to use
Such words as disabuse
My minder of casual pleasure
And turn it towards a centre –
A zone which others too
And you
May choose to enter.

The poem does not say who or what compels this change, but we sense it is not 'the earth compels'. Nor is the 'zone' identified towards which his mind is turned, but the dominant use of that word in the 1940s was in the compound 'war-zone'. Not surprisingly, war is a dominant presence in the book – as it was in *Autumn Journal* and *Plant and Phantom*, but in a different way. Both earlier books had velvet images and lilting measures, and they seemed a natural expression of the eye perceiving, the voice recording, the public world intruding on the private. The poems of *Springboard* are much more public than private, more concerned with a reality external to the speaker. MacNeice's prefatory Note is as much an apologia as his dedication:

Many of my titles in this book have the definite article, e.g. 'The Satirist', 'The Conscript'. The reader must not think that I am offering him a set of Theophrastean characters. I am not generalising; 'The Conscript' does not stand for all conscripts but for an imagined individual; any such individual seems to me to have an absolute quality which the definite article recognizes.

One such title, 'The Casualty', belongs to a different sort of poem – not (I have already suggested) a successful one, but one in which the poet's private grief for his friend generates a warmth noticeably absent from the poems of more detached observation. What, one must ask, was the cause of this new detachment, this concentration on an external reality rather than an internal or a fusion of the two? Wartime pressure of external events can only be part of the answer: another part must be the pressure of a job that required – from a subjective poet – an objective response to those external events. It is simplistic to say (as many outside the Corporation have said) that 'the BBC was bad for MacNeice', or to say (as many inside the Corporation have said) that it was good for him. The final balance-sheet, with its credits and debits, is complicated, but it is clear that at this stage of his career the script-writer's work for the BBC upset the natural balance of the poet's perceptions.

One of the character sketches in *Springboard* seems to acknowledge this. It is hard to believe that he did not put something of himself into 'The Satirist':

> He is not creative at all, his mind is dry
> And bears no blossoms even in the season,
> He is an onlooker, a heartless type,
> Whose hobby is giving everyone else the lie.
>
> Who is that man with eyes like a lonely dog?
> Lonely is right. He knows that he has missed
> What others miss unconsciously. Assigned
> To a condemned ship he still must keep the log
> And so fulfil the premises of his mind
> Where large ideals have bred a satirist.

'The Satirist', however, does not have the last word. That is assigned to someone with a mind still capable of bearing blossom, a past master of 'the velvet image' and 'the lilting measure'. The voice of 'Postscript' is that of the Pasternakian MacNeice, both onlooker and inlooker:

When we were children words were coloured
(Harlot and murder were dark purple)
And language was a prism, the light
    A conjured inlay on the grass,
Whose rays to-day are concentrated
    And language grown a burning-glass.

When we were children Spring was easy,
Dousing our heads in suds of hawthorn
And scrambling the laburnum tree –
    A breakfast for the gluttonous eye;
Whose winds and sweets have now forsaken
    Lungs that are black, tongues that are dry.

Now we are older and our talents
Accredited to time and meaning,
To handsel joy requires a new
    Shuffle of cards behind the brain
Where meaning shall remarry colour
    And flowers be timeless once again.

It was oddly appropriate that a poet so obsessed with the passage of time, the ticking of the death-watch beetle in the wainscot, should have found a job dominated by the stop-watch. For the second year in succession, MacNeice was given the honour of writing the department's final feature. Ruth Jones's diary entry for Sunday 31 December 1944 gives a good sense of the BBC at work:

'The Year in Review' [Robert] Donat as narrator. Very good – lovely voice and good tempered .... Rita Vale with us, looking wonderful with Val [Gielgud, Head of the Features and Drama Department] trailing her all the time. Louis unable to conceal his surprise at Val's appearance in listening room. Laurence [Gilliam] and Michael Standing appeared in afternoon . . . and were a nuisance but finally disappeared without having insisted on any disasterous alterations. I very nervous because rather accurate timing needed, to be out on an exact second. David Godfrey P[roduction]. E[ngineer]. fortunately. Laddie [Ladbroke, senior engineer] around with an awful cold – swallowing double whiskies with great equanimity. Got Donat some tea very late as he had to go on rehearsing with Stephen [Potter], and waitress obstinately refused to give him anything but the best teapot which had to be polished .... Final run through O.K. Val appeared again, rather lit. When faced with an actuality housewife, who was speaking for the housewives of Britain, and looked it, he said stagily: 'Thank God I only deal with actors and actresses!'

In the New Year MacNeice was busier than ever. The previous August, he had agreed to write the screenplay for a film to be produced by Dallas Bower for Two Cities Films, a subsidiary of the Rank Organisation. A contract was signed in a Tottenham Court Road pub, The Rising Sun, with Cecil Day Lewis as witness. A November diary entry of Ruth Jones's – 'Dallas Bower prodding Louis about his beastly film' – suggests an exasperation probably as much his as hers. Six weeks later, he is 'being pestered by Dallas Bower for Pax Futura'. MacNeice's reluctance to turn to this is no doubt partly to be explained by all the BBC work he had on hand and his increasing weariness: at the end of 1944 he had written sixty-four scripts and produced most of them. Even so, he would probably have been less reluctant to turn to 'Pax Futura' if Bower's 'shooting script' (or narrative outline) had been more promising. Early in 1945, at over-long last, he began to write but without conviction. Subtitled 'A Film Fantasy of the Future of Aviation', the story is set in 1995. A huge 'Cunarder' of the air, the *Henri Grâce à Dieu*, is threatened by a villain called Xanthias, whose Bible is Nietzsche's *Thus Spoke Zarathustra*. He is outwitted by the Cunarder's captain, Flavius, described as 'The Cincinnatus of the modern world', and finally killed by him in a Buchanesque scene on the Wiltshire Downs. MacNeice's script is as dull as Bower's plot, and the only surprising thing about 'Pax Futura' is that either of its authors ever thought it had a future.

By the end of February, the Allied armies were closing on Berlin and, with the end of war in sight, Gilliam set MacNeice to work on a celebratory programme. 'London Victorious', a tribute to the capital's courage, spirit, and resilience, followed the formula of the earlier 'Salute to ...' features. It was pre-recorded on 3 April – 'Rather a dreary business', Ruth Jones confided to her diary. Two days later she wrote: 'Louis and family left for Northern Ireland.' They spent Easter with his stepmother at 'Oakfield' outside Carrickfergus and, on 28 April, Louis returned to London with Dan, who was due back at the Downs School in Herefordshire on 1 May.

By the end of April Hitler and Mussolini were dead and, on the afternoon of 8 May, Churchill announced victory in the House of Commons and the church bells rang. That night, MacNeice and Margaret Gardiner – now comfortable in each other's company again – wandered through the streets of the newly floodlit West End, dropping into pub after pub. In Whitehall, they saw a beaming Churchill at an open window making the V sign, and they paused to watch the dancing in Trafalgar Square. Next day, Ruth Jones noted in her diary: 'Everyone all day telling me where they had seen Louis ... and exactly how drunk he had been'. 'London Victorious' was broadcast on 18 May, and the following day he left to rejoin Hedli and Corinna (now nicknamed Bimba) in Carrickfergus.

VE Day in Piccadilly Circus

CHAPTER 19

To the Dark Tower

'Child Rowland to the dark tower came'
Shakespeare, *King Lear*, III. iv. 182

Climactic action was followed by anti-climactic reaction. Arthur Koestler prophesied: 'The interregnum of the next decades will be a time of distress and of gnashing of teeth. We shall live in the hollow of the historical wave.' MacNeice would learn the truth of that – but not yet, and not in Ireland. He was happy to be home and temporarily forgot his exhaustion in a burst of creative energy. To Gilliam he wrote: 'my old idea of a programme on "The Dark Tower" has suddenly blossomed out and I should like to get on with writing it within the next few weeks'. Gilliam responded encouragingly, as always, and in a departmental memo noted that MacNeice would be

at the disposal of Northern Ireland Programme Director with a view to preparing Features programmes on Ulster subjects either by himself or writers that he can discover and encourage . . . Mr MacNeice will also be working on various agreed projects for the Home Service, including "The Dark Tower" and "The Careerist".

In June, he told Gilliam: 'I am writing the Tower but it comes slowly – partly because virtue has gone out of me and partly because the subject is so austere that I can't do it in long sessions.' What had begun as a holiday was becoming a productive sabbatical. He asked Gilliam if it would be possible to have three months 'free from obligations to the institution', and his leave was extended until 10 July.

There were other reasons for his request: Hedli had been feeling unwell and had been told by a Belfast doctor she had an enlarged heart and must take life more quietly. It was easier for her to do this in

Ireland than in England. A happier reason for extending their stay was that Louis was writing poems again and loath to risk cutting off the flow of sap now rising from his roots. In 'Carrick Revisited', he returns to the place of his childhood, a place visited in his earlier 'Carrickfergus'. The new poem looks behind and beneath the simple autobiographical narrative of the old:

> Memories I had shelved peer at me from the shelf.

> Fog-horn, mill-horn, corncrake and church bell
> Half-heard through boarded time as a child in bed
> Glimpses a brangle of talk from the floor below
> But cannot catch the words. Our past we know
> But not its meaning – whether it meant well.

He knows – and we know – one at least of the voices heard in the 'brangle of talk': a voice long associated in his mind with 'church bell' and 'the sea' of the next stanza, the voice of his father. In 'Carrick Revisited', the poet finds himself in 'a topographical frame' between his father's sea and his mother's 'pre-natal mountain'. Other poems of this summer explore his ancestral – and now symbolic – topography with a depth of focus missing from so many *Springboard* poems. In 'Last before America', he sees 'long low islets snouting towards the west / Like *cubs that have lost their mother*' (my italics); and 'Under the Mountain' (part of a range that includes Yeats's 'Under Ben Bulben'), he perceives that

> when you get down
> The breakers are cold scum and the wrack
> Sizzles with stinking life.

The mountain of that poem is probably Slievemore (2,204 ft) on the northern flank of Achill Island. Mrs Barrett, the island's retired post-mistress, had found the MacNeices a cottage – 'Sandy Bank' in the village of Keel, on the west coast of Achill – where they spent the best part of that summer. Ernie O'Malley lived nearby at Burrishoole and, for some weeks when he and his family were away, the MacNeices took over their high house overlooking the Atlantic. Asking that his leave be extended beyond 10 July, Louis had offered to forgo a month's salary and suggested to Laurence Gilliam that he tell 'them' MacNeice was

(1) Irish – and have not been in my own country for three years and not for so long then – and (2) an (for want of a better word) artist – which means that I can do some hackwork all of the time, and all hackwork some of the time but not all hackwork all of the time.

'They' were persuaded, and MacNeice was told he need not return to the BBC until 1 September. For him and his family, it was one of the best of times. Convivial friends like the playwright Denis Johnston came to stay. Hedli was better, Dan and Bimba played on Keel strand. On 31 July, Louis wrote to Dodds: 'all of us are now blooming, full of eggs & ozone. During the last 2 months I have written eleven poems (after a year-long lull).' One of these was an elegy for his father, whom he remembered walking at the same sea's edge in the summer of 1929 and now follows down 'The Strand':

> White Tintoretto clouds beneath my naked feet,
> This mirror of wet sand imputes a lasting mood
> To island truancies; my steps repeat
>
> Someone's who now has left such strands for good
> Carrying his boots and paddling like a child,
> A square black figure whom the horizon understood –
>
> My father. Who for all his responsibly compiled
> Account books of a devout, precise routine
> Kept something in him solitary and wild,
>
> So loved the western sea and no tree's green
> Fulfilled him like these contours of Slievemore
> Menaun and Croaghaun and the bogs between.
>
> Sixty-odd years behind him and twelve before,
> Eyeing the flange of steel in the turning belt of brine
> It was sixteen years ago he walked this shore
>
> And the mirror caught his shape which catches mine
> But then as now the floor-mop of the foam
> Blotted the bright reflections – and no sign
>
> Remains of face or feet when visitors have gone home.

'The Strand' succeeds by implication where 'The Casualty' failed by explication. We are made to sense the speaker's love and admiration for his father, although the only love mentioned is the father's for the sea and Achill's three highest peaks.

Not surprisingly, 'The Dark Tower' embodies the deeper themes of the poems written that summer on the same table. In an Introductory Note to the published text, MacNeice wrote that his 'parable play' had been suggested to him

by Browning's poem 'Childe Roland to the Dark Tower came', a work which does not admit of a completely rational analysis and still less adds up to any clear moral or message. This poem has the solidity of a dream; the writer of such a poem, though he may be aware of the 'meanings' implicit in his dream, must not take the dream to pieces, must present his characters concretely, must allow the story to persist as a story and not dwindle into a diagram.

MacNeice's story is relatively simple. The hero, Roland, is brought up by his mother to follow in the family tradition, undertaking a quest that has claimed the lives of his forefathers and five older brothers. He watches a sixth, Gavin, trained by a Sergeant-Trumpeter to play 'the Challenge Call' before he, too, is despatched by his mother on the quest. In due course, a bell tolls for him and his name is added to the roll of honour. Roland, in turn, is trained by the Sergeant-Trumpeter and a Tutor, who tells him never to fall in love. He does – with Sylvie – but is sent off to talk to Blind Peter in a castle ringed by 'smothering yew-trees'. Peter tells him more about the Dragon he must seek and challenge, and more about his father:

> You're like your father – one of the dedicated
> Whose life is a quest, whose death is a victory.

His training completed, Roland takes leave of Sylvie and receives his marching orders from Tutor, Sergeant-Trumpeter, and Mother who gives him a last message:

Here is a ring with a blood-red stone. So long as
This stone retains its colour, it means that I
Retain my purpose in sending you on the Quest.
I put it now on your finger.

The Quester sets out and encounters and escapes a number of tempters: a soak and barmaid in a tavern, the seductive Neaera on a luxury liner, and Sylvie, whom he would have married had not the voices of Blind Peter, Gavin, and his Father persuaded him to leave her at the altar. The tempters' voices pursue him into the Desert, and are driving him mad, when suddenly the blood drains from the stone in his ring and he hears his mother say:

> On my deathbed I have changed my mind;
> I am bearing now a child of stone.
> *He* can go on the Quest. But you, Roland – come back!

Ecstatic at his reprieve, Roland throws the ring away, but hears it strike a stone that proves to be a gravestone inscribed:

> 'To Those Who Did Not Go Back –
> Whose Bones being Nowhere, their signature is for
>   All Men –
> Who went to their Death of their Own Free Will
> Bequeathing Free Will to Others.'

Uncertain whether to go forward or follow his footsteps back ('Are these my footsteps? But how small they look!'), he hears the pounding rhythm of his heart and sees the mountains closing round him. On their peaks stand Blind Peter, his brothers, the Sergeant-Trumpeter, his Tutor, and his Father. With their exhortations in his ears, and the Dark Tower rising from the ground in front of him, the Quester replies:

> I, Roland, the black sheep, the unbeliever –
> Who never did anything of his own free will–
> Will now do this to bequeath free will to others.

He then challenges the Dragon to 'Come out and do your worst' and sounds the trumpet call.

How are we to interpret MacNeice's dream of the Dark Tower? 'Roland, the black sheep, the unbeliever' – who learns Latin and ethics from a Tutor – is obvious enough. A note to the printed text tells us that 'The Mother in bearing so many children only to send them to their death, can be thought of as thereby bearing a series of deaths. So her logical last child is stone – her own death. This motif has an echo in the stone in the ring.' The Mother, associated with death, is as readily identifiable as the dedicated Father, 'whose death is a victory'. The

Bishop, who believed with St Paul that 'Death is swallowed up in victory', is the unmistakable representative of life temporal and eternal. Roland tells Sylvie:

> I will remember
> The mayflies jigging above us in the delight
> Of the dying instant –

much as Mary Ezra, the sylvan shepherdess of 1929, will remember Louis' love-poem 'Mayfly'. Roland's nearest and dearest brother, Gavin, is clearly an early version of the Gavin/Graham Shepard of *Autumn Sequel*; and the 'smothering yew-trees' encircling Blind Peter's castle are no less clearly those, close to the Marlborough castle mound, that had already featured in Devlin's dream in *Roundabout Way* (p. 152 above). When he reaches the Desert – known to Malory and Eliot as the Waste Land – Roland elects to follow his father's vanished footsteps *forward* across the sand (as in 'The Strand') rather than his own footsteps *back* to Mother. The Quester's allegiance is clear, even if the nature of his adversary and his trial are shrouded in the mists of futurity.

On 8 August, MacNeice wrote to Ruth Jones, who had been 'house-sitting' 10 Wellington Place:

Here at long last is the draft script of the Dark Tower. There's no great hurry for the typing – if you're working for Laurence; I'd rather not have anyone do it who's going to get my writing all wrong.

I'd like a good number of carbons; please send me one & keep the top copy in office; send one carbon to Tony (that is, if Laurence agrees to him composing). Tell him that, as before, I want the music done with the greatest economy – no long chunks on its own. And it's v. important that the Challenge Call (trumpet or other solo instrument) should be the sort of thing that makes one's hair stand up. The Music in the Tavern Scene should of course be banal, while the Forest music should be sinister – shivering twigs & murmuring shadows.

When Gilliam had read *his* carbon copy, he directed Ruth to send the composer's copy not to Antony Hopkins but to Benjamin Britten.

It had been one of MacNeice's most productive summers, and productive not only in terms of his own writing. He had encouraged a number of new scriptwriters, and had taken the typescript of Sam

Hanna Bell's 'Ill Fares the Land' to Achill, returning it with congratulations and detailed comments. 'Here follow', he wrote, 'some page by page notes (disregard them if they irritate!).' The name of another writer – one of several he was to introduce to the BBC – appears in Ruth Jones's diary entry for 3 September: 'Louis back in office looking very well and unofficial. Hedli brought me a little scarf. Reggie Smith came. Large man from Palestine radio ex-Birmingham, seeking job in Corporation – very like Laurence in wit and size.' Ten days later, her diary records the first appearance of another writer introduced by MacNeice: 'W. R. Rodgers came over to stay with Louis for a few days and see Laurence. A nice creature. Almost going to stay a week and suddenly remembered he had "a marriage".'

'Bertie' Rodgers was the minister of the oldest Presbyterian church in Ireland, Loughgall in Armagh; a minister as unlike the Revd J. F. MacNeice of Carrickfergus as it was possible to be. It was said that

the pulpit in Loughgall was so high that, on those Sundays when Saturday had been the night before, Bertie – as even that staid parish knew its pastor – could

Reggie Smith

Bertie Rodgers

stoop in a pause of his preaching, some cautiously contrived caesura, and retch gently, invisible to his devout and Sunday-sombre flock.

Rodgers was a poet, author of *Awake and Other Poems* (1941), and those who knew him in the years of his ministry – 1934 to 1946 –

recalled life then in Bertie's house as a sort of poem, one of his own poems. There was always sun or moonlight on apple blossom, endless talk of life and death in the small big house full of books and the small hours that never grew smaller, and a gay drift of laughing girls flitting innocently carnal through the orchard. And somewhere at the heart of it all would be Bertie, smoking his eschatological pipe, nodding a compassionate head to the saint and sinner in others and himself, anticipating indiscretion, confession, disclosure, revelation, with the omniscience of his calm 'I know, I know'.

Loughgall was only a few miles west of Portadown, and MacNeice had first met its engaging poet-minister at dinner with the MacCanns during his first visit to Vinecash in autumn 1939. They had met there many times subsequently – most recently in summer 1945, when

Rodgers had brought over to supper MacNeice's Merton contemporary, Harold Brooks.

The convivial minister was now in London to make plans for the production of his first script, 'City Set on a Hill', a programme about Armagh. MacNeice was to produce this in a BBC Belfast studio, and on 8 November he left for Ireland. Ruth Jones, who was to assist him – and see her brother, Phil, on his return from a Japanese POW camp – followed three days later. Her diary records details of the ensuing rehearsals and gives a good account of the grand finale:

Thursday 15 Nov. Rehearsal from 2 onwards. Rather hectic. Transmission 9.30–10.30. Ghastly crisis at the beginning when needle stuck in groove of first record. After that all went well. Rodgers there and a lot of people in listening room. Invited us to party at Loughgall. George Marshall asked Louis, [the composer, William] Alwyn and Rodgers for drinks after the show. Then we all went out in car to Loughgall. Louis with bottle of neat whisky, which kept us warm. Lovely Georgian house, lamps and huge turf fire and dogs barking when we arrived. More whisky and roast chicken and tea. Phil began to look very green, Alwyn to mellow and Louis even more mellow. Phil then went to bed. Rodgers and wife sang bawdy songs – i.e. the Ball at Kirriemuir. Story about his father and the tinker. His father: 'I'm no goat's foot.' Re the tinker: 'Isn't he the queer hare?' Alwyn playing flute and drumming on the log box. Louis and Rodgers dancing. I feeling dead sleepy at the end, went to bed.

Friday 16 Nov. Woke up earlyish. Sounds of fowl and animals. Hot water in the bathroom a comfort. Phil dressed. Presently we found Rodgers, who drew us into the bathroom to talk about trains, as the pump was making such a noise. We sat on the edge of the bath and Rodgers said 'I'm a bit throughother this morning.' I felt dreadful. We wakened Alwyn and had lot of tea. Rodgers' small daughter came in with very penetrating voice and broad accent. Later we wakened Louis with a cup of tea – he apparently had gone to bed at 8, first in the hay, and then had demanded food and finally slept in the sitting room. He appeared not looking too bad. Marie [Rodgers] appeared from the hay looking dreadful. We drove to George MacCann's cottage where we had sherry, and then to the train, leaving Louis with George. Arrived at the [Belfast] office. Everyone speaking well of programme.

In July, MacNeice had written to Dodds: 'I wish one could either *live* in Ireland or *feel oneself* in England.' This helps to explain the difference between 'The Dark Tower', written in rural Ireland, and Mac-

Neice's next play, written for the stage, that autumn in England. 'Eureka' is hard to categorize: too 'realistic' to be 'black comedy' in the normal sense, it is perhaps best described as 'grey comedy'. Set in London of the 1950s, it follows the rise and fall of Harvey Forgang, an idealistic freelance scientist, who discovers a happiness-inducing serum. This he tests – successfully but illegally – on patients in the Workhouse. His experiment is detected by representatives of the fascist government, who give him the choice of prison or working for them. He opts for the latter course, still hoping to put his discovery to humanitarian use; is elevated to the peerage as Lord Lostitt; but, in less than a year, injections of his serum are reducing thousands of dissidents and workers to smiling zombies. Finally, in Act Three , charged with presenting on television the government's Euthanasia Bill, Lord Lostitt finds his lost integrity and tells the people the truth about their murderous leaders. He escapes from the TV studio, but is cornered and killed at home – not, however, before the formula for his serum has been destroyed.

'Eureka' is an urbane urban play, a cerebral exercise, written in a free blank verse with none of the wild energy, the imaginative pressure behind 'The Dark Tower'. Attached to one typescript is a list of six 'proposed changes', dated 11 December 1945, but they were never incorporated and the play was eventually abandoned. The knowledge that it was a failure and a sense that the family could live – and he could write – better in rural surroundings may have prompted the MacNeices' decision to look for a house in the country. They then heard from Dallas Bower that his eighteen-year-old daughter, Pamela, was soon to leave Tilty Hill House in the Essex village of Tilty – where she had been a paying guest – because the tenant, a well-known painter called John Armstrong, was moving to Cornwall. She took the MacNeices over the house, parts of which dated from the fifteenth and sixteenth centuries. They liked its floorboards of hand-hewn oak, its outlook over fields and wood, and they agreed to rent it from its stockbroker owner for £100 a year. Before they could think of moving, however, Louis had to attend to some unfinished business.

For the third time in succession, Gilliam had given him the honour of devising the last feature programme of the year; and no sooner had his 'Threshold of the New' been broadcast than he began preparing for the production of 'The Dark Tower'. Two early decisions played a decisive part in the success of his 'parable play': the choice of Cyril Cusack as Roland, and the choice of Britten as composer. MacNeice would later dedicate the printed text to Britten, whose music he thought 'the best I have heard in a radio play'. Without it, he added, '*The Dark Tower* lacks a dimension'. It was first broadcast on 21 January, and responses were mixed. Hedli heard it at home in the company of Louis' Birmingham friend, now a BBC colleague, Dorothy Baker, who was then living with them, and their next-door neighbours, Goronwy Rees and his wife. Louis came in afterwards, on top of the world, only to be told by Rees that the play had been 'bloody awful'. Both had been drinking and the ensuing argument ended with a fight in which Louis was knocked down the stairs.

The Listener's reviewer asked 'what of "The Dark Tower"?' And replied:

An uncouth modern edifice, Baedeker might say. . . . We were conscious of a real poet's sensibility, of a wide power of matching new-minted phrase and stale jargon to make a language which should touch heart and mind and ear freshly. Yet the parable was very difficult to visualise: indeed, I think it was the poet's deliberate intention that it should be so. But the mind's eye, seeing nothing, was restless, and imagination refused to warm to the long-drawn dedicated venture. And yet, comparatively, how distinguished and original the idea and the idiom, with its acute musical commentary by Britten, melodrama in the true sense.

MacNeice's fellow poets, however, were more enthusiastic, no doubt perceiving that the play was a psychomachia rather than a melodrama. Day Lewis called it 'magnificient'; Bertie Rodgers said it was the 'most memorable broadcast I have yet heard'; and Henry Reed wrote:

Dear Louis,
    Forgive a fan-letter . . . . I found I was listening with an intentness I had never before been forced to give to anything except music on the wireless . . . . I am sure yours is the way radio must go if it is to be worth listening to; I have always thought your claims for its potentialities to be excessive; I now begin, reluctantly, to think you may be right, and am very glad.

In a postscript he added: 'it is difficult to rise and cheer in a letter'. MacNeice told MacCann it was his 'favourite programme to date. The public either loved it or loathed it (I have a heap of letters – ecstatic or virulent).' He went on to speak of the impending move to Tilty, and it was the prospect of their departure from London that prompted the MacNeices to discharge an ancient debt. T. S. Eliot had recently accepted *The Dark Tower and Other Radio Scripts* for publication and, to thank him for more than a decade of encouragement and support, he was invited to dinner.

Neither the poet nor the singer had any taste for housework and, after three years of neglect, 10 Wellington Place was filthy. Mice were everywhere – even in Hedli's grand piano – so an enormous cleaning operation was mounted. Dorothy Baker dusted and swept, while Louis washed and polished the cutlery and glasses. Hedli (who was a splendid, if messy cook) began preparing bouillabaisse at nine o'clock in the morning, and by seven-thirty in the evening the house and hosts were in an unaccustomed state of readiness. Eliot duly arrived, but in the deepest gloom. Then came Martita Hunt, the actress, and Louis' drinking companion and sparring partner, Goronwy Rees. Eliot was clearly ill at ease with Hedli, and not even the ebullient Rees could kindle the conversation until the principal guest made a (probably quite innocent) remark in which Martita perceived a *double entendre* and said: 'Now, now, Mr Eliot, don't be naughty!' This saved the evening. The funereal poet cheered up and finally went off arm-in-arm with Martita to find a taxi to Chelsea where they both lived.

In late March, the MacNeices moved to Tilty. Louis would write his scripts there, but was increasingly involved in meetings and production work in London. There were important changes at the BBC. Features had become a separate department on 31 July 1945, switching its focus from war to peace with such series as Robert Barr's 'It's Your Money They're After' (warnings to ex-servicemen with gratuities) and 'How' (to move house or to face Christmas). The Director General, Sir William Haley, had announced that, after the war, listeners would be given a choice of three full programmes: the Home Service, the Light Programme, and the Third Programme. The last of these offered particular scope to writers like MacNeice. It was to be inaugurated on 29 September 1946, and at the first Features Department meeting to discuss specifically Third Programme plans he suggested a 'psycho-morality' and a 'satirical fantasy'. By the summer he had been commissioned to translate these suggestions into two scripts: 'The Careerist' (discussed with Gilliam the previous year) and 'Enemy of Cant'.

MacNeice's work for the BBC in 1946 shows him to be a master of many modes. In an allegorical or 'psycho-morality' mode, 'The Careerist' follows 'The Dark Tower', tracing the progress of its 'hero-cum-villain-cum-victim' from cradle to grave. Jim Human is driven by a lust for power from deceit at school to a career as a corrupt pro-Nazi publisher who, having betrayed and ruined others, finally kills himself. In a no less socially aware but exuberant satirical mode, MacNeice wrote a 'Salute to All Fools' for April Fool's Day. The March Hare decides to get married – to Truth – and going in search of her meets Journalists' Truth, Poetic Truth, Tory Truth, and others familiar with the lady such as the Gael, who greets Hare and his agent, Nonesuch:

GAEL: I can see ye're English – the pair of yez.

HARE: English? Of course we're English.

GAEL: Ah poor fellows. There was nothing good ever come out of England. Sure *I* wouldn't use anything that was English.

NONESUCH: Except the language.

GAEL: Ah I only use that when I'm talkin' to black foreigners. When I'm here by meself I talk to meself in the Gaelic.

HARE: And do you understand yourself?

GAEL: I do. At times I do. There's great truth in the Gaelic.

HARE: Truth!

GAEL: Great and beautiful truth.

HARE: Nonesuch, we're on the track! Truth, sir, you say – Truth is a beautiful woman?

GAEL: She is, indeed she is. I know her well.

HARE: But she only speaks Gaelic, you say?

GAEL: What else would she speak? Isn't her proper name not Truth at all?

HARE: No? What is her name then?

GAEL: Cathleen ni Houlihan.

HARE: Cathleen ni – Nonesuch, make a note of that. And I must learn Gaelic. Buy me a grammar, Nonesuch.

GAEL: Why are ye wantin' a grammar?

HARE: Because I must speak with this lady. You're sure that she knows no English?

GAEL: Know English, is it? May the Round Towers turn square! Would she soil her delicate ears and be twistin' her beautiful mouth and pollutin' her pure green blood with a heathen language like that?

The streams of fantasy and wit that so captivated MacNeice's Sherborne dormitory may subsequently have gone underground at times, but could still resurface. In 'Enemy of Cant', he paid tribute to Aristophanes, whom he introduced as 'an author of infinite fantasy, a lover of slapstick and beauty, a good hater and hard hitter, a live man, an Enemy of Cant'. He might have been writing an epitaph for himself or the friend and fellow poet to whom he gave the part of Aristophanes – Dylan Thomas.

In a more light-hearted mode of folk-tale fantasy, he repeated the success of 'The Nosebag' with 'The Heartless Giant'. This time it was a Norwegian story he adapted. Six of a King's seven sons, returning

Dylan Thomas

home with their brides, are turned to stone by a Giant, who has hidden his heart – as an egg – in a duck in a well in a church on an island in a lake. The seventh son, Boots (played by Cyril Cusack), sets out to rescue them. On his quest, he helps a Raven (played by Dylan Thomas), a Salmon, and a Wolf, who in turn help him to rescue his brothers and their brides and a bride for himself. The story closed, as it had opened, with a song from a character called 'Picture Book' (played by Hedli).

In a fourth, historical mode – the only one showing a connection with MacNeice's wartime work – he wrote 'Enter Caesar', a programme to mark the 2,000th anniversary of the Roman legions' arrival in Britain. Like many of his propaganda features, and indeed like 'The Heartless Giant', it is constructed on the model of an ancient picture in a modern frame. From a classroom in which a schoolmaster equates Caesar with Hitler, the listener is led (as in a day-dream) into political infighting in ancient Rome, before being returned to the classroom again. These very different scripts all have one thing in common: a connection with the scriptwriter's childhood or schooldays. His early years had provided MacNeice's memory-bank with imaginative capital that would last him all his life.

Returning, as so often in his poems, to memories of his father, he had written:

> in using the word tame my father was maybe right,
> These woods are not the Forest; each is moored
> To a village somewhere near. If not of to-day
> They are not like the wilds of Mayo, they are assured
> Of their place by men; reprieved from the neolithic night
> By gamekeepers or by Herrick's girls at play.

The Romantic in MacNeice would always prefer the wild to the tame. He and Hedli soon discovered that Tilty – with their two-year-old Bimba at play in the garden – was not Achill. They found the natives less congenial, and Hedli became increasingly lonely and neurotic. She fretted at the impact of motherhood on her musical career and missed her musical friends. She envied Louis his London life and resented him returning late, having drunk but not eaten, often with a 'jagger' (such as Dorothy Baker or Bertie Rodgers) to deflect her wrath. In the middle of May, when those friends were staying at Tilty Hill House, it was decided that the anniversary of VE Day called for celebration in the local pub, The Rising Sun. Since Bimba was too young to be left on her own, Louis proposed that Hedli should join the men for the first half of the evening, and Dorothy for the second. Hedli was furious, refused to go at all, and retired to bed. 'You come', said Louis to Dorothy, and off they went. The evening was enlivened by a gipsy couple who did an intricate dance with coloured scarves. By closing time, Bertie and Louis were very drunk and, as Dorothy steered them back down the lane, the poets tried to repeat the gipsy dance with scarves of Queen Anne's lace. When they reached home they found to their amazement that Hedli had forgiven them and prepared a delicious supper. Not all evenings ended so well, and in July, the two women had a violent quarrel. Dorothy told Hedli she was 'a thoroughly vulgar woman' and stormed out of the house. She did not return.

Later that month, the MacNeices took a fortnight's holiday in a villa, rented by Hedli's parents, at Brissago, near Locarno in Switzerland. At the end of August, Louis went over to Belfast to produce Rodgers' 'Professional Portrait of a Country Parson'. By then his portrait was out of date, for on 1 June the Revd W. R. Rodgers, Minister of Loughgall, had become Bertie Rodgers of the Features Department of the BBC, sharing an office with MacNeice and the long-suffering Ruth Jones. Increasingly, too, they shared the mahogany bar or buttoned plush of the George in Great Portland Street. It was there that Dylan Thomas first introduced MacNeice to Bob Pocock, who would himself join the BBC and who later sketched a portrait of MacNeice:

I remember him standing at the bend of the bar in 'The George' ... with a group of us who were friends or cronies, *with* but not strictly *of* the company. You got the impression that he was sighting you through his eyes ... always with a notebook ready to hand for entering bets or debts at the back. And then again, he'd pick on a chance remark of yours and he'd say, 'Let me pick your brains, my dear fellah', ask a few questions and something would go down in the notebook for future use. If he didn't like anybody, he'd say, 'Ach, *that* fellah', and the worst thing he could say of anybody was 'He isn't warm.' And then you'd get that bent black safety pin of the eyes and hidalgo curl of the lip . . . .

In her own way, Hedli was as sociable as her husband; an effervescent entertainer, a participant where he was an ironic commentator; a conversational 'sprinter' where his strength lay in the midday and midnight marathons. At length, her increasing sense of exclusion from his London life led to their renting an upstairs flat at 33 Cheyne Walk. She used it a good deal at the start of the winter, when Mary Katzman came to London (on family business connected with a relative's death) and would baby-sit Bimba there. Louis had been apprehensive that Mary would try to win Dan back, and had insisted that she could only see him two or three times. This she did – appearing in a lambskin coat and a dramatic hat – but then fell ill with jaundice and was confined to her hotel for the rest of her visit. Events would show, however, that Louis' fears were well-founded: not surprisingly, mother and son were delighted with each other.

Back in June, Hedli had written excitedly to Mercy MacCann of additions to her repertoire: settings – written specially for her – by William Alwyn of Louis' 'Slum Song' and 'The Streets of Laredo', and settings by Elizabeth Lutyens of Auden's 'As I Walked Out One Evening' and 'Refugee Blues'. In due course, it was arranged that she would give a song recital at the Wigmore Hall on 17 November. The programme was to be in two parts: Ballads, Traditional and Romantic, and – after an interval – Modern Songs and Ballads; these including three by her husband and two by Apollinaire. The evening was a great success as she reported to Mercy: 'At last imagination had the upper hand & technique just followed up. It was *wonderful* for me! & the audience were so good! Everyone seems awfully enthusiastic – the same praise from singers, Actresses & a dancer.'

The year ended well for her husband also. In December, Gilliam approved his proposal for the dramatization of two Icelandic sagas that had excited MacNeice at Marlborough; the first of them – the Njal saga – to be divided into two programmes. He spent most of January and the first half of February 1947 at home, condensing Dasent's translation of that saga into seventy-five-minute plays whose action unfolds with the murderous logic of a game of chess. Each opens with the words of a Watcher, reminiscent of the Watchman of *The Agamemnon* and his own

watchers on the wall
Awake all night who know
The pity of it all.

The fascination of these violent histories for a poet who hated violence
was, in part, their analogy with a history of which he was both
inheritor and helpless watcher. As his *alter ego*, Ryan, had long ago
told Grettir in 'Eclogue from Iceland':

I come from an island, Ireland, a nation
Built upon violence and morose vendettas.

'The Death of Gunnar' and 'The Burning of Njal' introduce their
listeners to the inexorable escalation of murder engineered by a
woman, whom MacNeice may have associated with Clytemnestra and
Kathleen-ni-Houlihan. Against the advice of his friend, the lawyer
Njal, Gunnar marries Halgertha, whose two previous husbands had
died violent deaths. She immediately embarks on a course of action
that will lead to the death of the third. Despite Njal's honourable and
peaceable attempts to break the chain of murder and retaliation,
Gunnar finally goes down fighting. In 'The Burning of Njal', Gunnar's
mother sends her grandson out to avenge his father, thereby continuing
the murderous chain reaction. Njal and all but one of his family die in
the burning of their house. Kari, his son-in-law, escapes to track down
Fiosi, leader of the coalition against Njal, not – as one might expect –
to kill him, but to effect a final reconciliation.

The plays were broadcast on consecutive nights, 11 and 12 March,
and were well received. MacNeice was now due for a holiday and, with
the summer holiday season in mind, he was commissioned to produce a
Portrait of Rome. At the start of April, Hedli and the children crossed
to Switzerland to join her parents in Brissago. Louis followed by way
of Norway and Denmark, where he arranged a series of combined
poetry readings and song recitals to be given by himself and Hedli that
autumn. Then, at the end of May, he set off for ten days' sightseeing in
Rome. The resulting portrait, broadcast on 22 June, he cunningly
justified with a self-referential exchange between two British tourists,
one of whom has come from listening to a BBC 'Portrait of Rome':

EVELYN: One moment I thought it was Catholic propaganda and the next they
    were using bad language. And such a hotch-potch! Little bits of history all
    thrown together anyhow –
MARGARET: But it *is* a bit like that, isn't it?
EVELYN: What?
MARGARET: Well, Rome . . . .

MacNeice's impressionistic portrait communicates an equal delight in
the past of Byron, Benvenuto Cellini, Gibbon, Keats, and Virgil, and
the present of

The knife-grinder pedalling a stationary bicycle, . . .
Workmen in newspaper hats, made out of some of the thirty-odd dailies . . . .

A General Introduction to *The Dark Tower and Other Radio Scripts*,
published in May, reiterated and refined the case for radio drama
advanced in the Introduction to *Christopher Columbus*, and was followed by a rousing article in the *BBC Year Book* for 1947. Under the
title 'Scripts Wanted!' MacNeice addresses those 'hundreds of writers
perched upon pillars pretending to be St Simeon Stylites and whining
that nobody pays them for it'. He urges them to descend – like 'two of
the best writers of our time, V. S. Pritchett and Dylan Thomas' – and,
as freelances, work for 'one of the least interfering patrons there have
ever been'. He puts his most compelling argument last: 'I have just
reckoned that, were I not on the staff of the BBC, a single recent
programme of mine would have brought me – from three guaranteed
performances – rather more money than I once used to make in a year
as a University lecturer.'

Refreshed by his Roman holiday, he went back to ancient Iceland.
Grettir the Strong had introduced himself, in 'Eclogue from Iceland',
as

> The last of the saga heroes
> Who had not the wisdom of Njal or the beauty of Gunnar
> I was the doomed tough, disaster kept me witty;
> Being born the surly jack, the ne'er-do-well, the loiterer
> Hard blows exalted me.

MacNeice's radio adaptation compresses his red-haired hero's violent
life and death into sixty minutes. The scriptwriter, like the poet, can

dispense with narrative transitions, and here, for example, the passage of time is clearly conveyed by fanfares and proclamations of the yearly Assembly. Scriptwriter and subject had one thing in common – fear of the dark (Grettir having been cursed by the ghost of Glam) – and this enables MacNeice to make his 'doomed tough' a strangely sympathetic figure.

'Grettir the Strong' was broadcast on 27 July, to almost certainly the largest audience ever to hear a version of that saga. By then, MacNeice was preparing for his next BBC assignment. With a tragic irony only later to be revealed, he was required to turn his imagination from the cold North to the warm South, from Iceland to India on the eve of Partition.

CHAPTER 20

The Horror

So cast up here this India jolts us
Awake to what engrossed our sleep;
This was the truth and now we see it,
This was the horror – it is deep . . . .
'Letter from India', *CP*, p. 269

What a horror! What a nightmare!
Goethe's Faust, p. 246

In March 1947, Lord Mountbatten of Burma had succeeded Lord Wavell of Cyrenaica as Viceroy of India; his brief – the briefest ever given to a holder of that office – to return the Jewel in the Imperial Crown to its rightful owners. There were two principal claimants: the Hindu-dominated Congress Party, under the Presidency of Jawaharlal Nehru, and the Muslim League, led by Mohammed Ali Jinnah. It took Mountbatten little more than a month to recognize he had no chance of reconciling the parties, and in the first week of June he persuaded the British Government that the Jewel must be divided. Sir Cyril Radcliffe, an English barrister (who had never till then set foot in India) was appointed diamond-cutter, and given two months in which to determine the boundaries of a Hindu India and a Muslim Pakistan.

Punjab and Bengal, with almost equal numbers of Muslims and Hindus, would be bisected. The princely States would be urged to join one Dominion or the other. Everything would be partitioned, the Indian Army, the National Debt, the railway system, down to the stock of stationery at the New Delhi secretariat, and the staff cars of GHQ.

Having to decide when his plans for partition would take effect,

354

Mountbatten chose 14 August, a date with complex symbolic associations. The second anniversary of Japan's surrender in the Second World War, it represented a triumph both for Great Britain and for the Allied supreme Commander in South-East Asia, Admiral Lord Louis Mountbatten; and it represented a defeat both for Japan and for her allies, the so-called Indian National Army. Who would be triumphant, who defeated, on 14 August 1947, was a more open question.

To report and commemorate the transfer of power to the peoples of India and Pakistan, the BBC sent a joint Features and News team to the subcontinent. This consisted of an ebullient Welsh news reporter, Wynford Vaughan Thomas, MacNeice, his friend and one-time mentor, Jack Dillon, and a supporting staff of sound engineers. Dillon had been to India before. MacNeice had not and, brought up to think of it as a field of missionary endeavour, he had never had any desire to go there. As an undergraduate, India probably meant to him what it meant to 'Edward', the central British character in the first of the feature programmes he would write on his return: 'A spot of Kipling and a spot of Tagore and a stray conversation in the Oxford Union. And I didn't much like the Indians I met – or the photos of Indian temples – or all this yogi-cum-swami stuff.' MacNeice modified his views after meeting a young Indian novelist, Mulk Raj Anand, in the summer of 1939:

Mulk was small and lithe and very handsome, wore shirts, ties and scarves of scarlet or coral, talked very fast and all the time, was a crusader for the Indian Left. A conversation I had with him about Yeats brought up the subject of spiritual India. It was all a mistake, Mulk said, India was *not* spiritual, no Indian had even thought so until fifty years ago. India was earthy, matter-of-fact; it was the Anglo-Indians who had loudpedalled her alleged mysticism. . . . I asked him about yoga. Oh yoga, he said, that's not mysticism. His father, who was a craftsman, did yoga for an hour every morning, it merely increased his efficiency.

Mulk appealed to the dandy, the Home Ruler, and the writer in MacNeice, but there were strong prejudices still to be overcome. His radio script suggests how:

EDWARD: . . . Was all for the Indian nationalist but apart from that – well, I was allergic to India. So when last year I'm suddenly asked to go there –

well, my first reaction was No! But somehow, inside me, there was a
sort of little voice –

STILL VOICE: You don't want to go – and that is why you must go. You
think your world is already too big and complex. It is – but you must
complicate it further. You have Europe in your blood and one kind of
East in your church – but there is another kind of East from which
you've been too long parted. You must go back beyond Rome, Athens,
Jerusalem. The earth is not the moon, one can cross to the dark side, can
see how the other half lives. And even a glimpse of their lives may throw
some light on your own half. Look East, Eddie –

> 'Look East, where whole new thousands are!
> In Vishnu-land what Avatar?'

Come on, come on, start packing. Inklings and guesses at the bottom –
and squeeze in an open mind. Hurry up, Eddie. Your plane leaves next
week.

MacNeice's plane left on 6 August and, after stops at Cairo, Hab-
baniya (outside Baghdad), and Karachi, he arrived in Delhi on the 9th.
He had been reading *A Passage to India*, but next day set that aside in
favour of an armful of newspapers, hoping they would bring him up to
date with political developments. They were full of letters urging that
cow slaughter be made illegal throughout the new India, but he was
relieved to find that the sports pages carried the latest English county
cricket scores. Similarly bewildering (and frequently hilarious) con-
junctions of ancient and modern would confront him at every turn.

His first official engagement was the last cocktail party given by a
Viceroy in the viceregal house (described by MacNeice as 'Lutyens
Odeon'); his second, an interview with Dalmia, a millionaire indus-
trialist, who was heading a crusade for the protection of cows. Meeting
this Hindu 'Henry Ford of India' in his luxurious mansion, the lapsed
Church of Ireland poet asked him:

'This campaign of yours for cow protection, is it primarily religious or economic?' Answer from D: 'My dear young man, you cannot separate things like
that. Everything is one. Religions . . . they are the same thing.' Upon which I
wondered where do we go from here. Where we went in fact was to Dalmia's
scheme for world government: a benevolent autocrat (himself?) elected by a
committee of all the peoples. And no more democracy, which has been
disproved in the West. A decent standard of living guaranteed for all but no

limits on private enterprise as it is only just & kind that a hardworking man should be able to accumulate luxuries for his children (D., I'm told, has 8 wives). 'But I am very courageous man, I follow my own ideas.' And then, returning to the cow, the cow is like your mother, only more so; she *goes on* giving you milk. And even when she's past that & v. old, she still pays her way with her dung – 'I have statistics to prove that.'

The following evening, MacNeice attended the midnight session of the Constituent Assembly. Sitting high up in the Press Gallery of Lutyens's enormous circular Parliament building, he heard Nehru and Radhakrishnan speak and, at midnight, the chimes marking the transition to Independence drowned by the blast of a great braying conch ('the worst of both worlds', he told Hedli). On Independence day, he and Dillon joined the immense crowd thronging the Rajpath to see the Mountbattens ride in the state coach magnificently flanked by mounted lancers. After the ceremony, the speeches and the gun-salute, as the coach carried the last of the Viceroys back to his house for the last time, Nehru sat on top of the hood, 'like a schoolboy', Mountbatten reported. That evening, MacNeice met the President of the new Dominion at a reception in the illuminated gardens of Government House. He said he supposed the President was tired after dealing with the milling crowds. Nehru replied that he was fond of crowds and whenever he saw one had an impulse to rush into it and merge with it. 'But sometimes', he added, 'I have to rush *at* it and beat it.' He invited MacNeice to lunch the following Sunday, saying he wanted a change from talking politics; but, not surprisingly, politics asserted their precedence over poetry, a conference had to be called, and the meeting was cancelled.

The letters reporting these and subsequent events to Hedli show him revelling in the rich variety of his Indian experience, but concerned also with what was happening to her and the children – as well he might be, since she was about to move house. Shortly before he left, they had decided to leave Tilty for a handsome town house in London's Canonbury Park. A young Italian maid, Teresa Moroni, had been hired to help Hedli, and Louis eased his bad conscience by telling his wife not to exhaust herself but 'shamelessly exploit all the chaps we know. Reggie for instance, tell him it's good for his figure to move a spot of furniture.' There is no evidence of him writing to exhort all the chaps himself.

His letter of 25 August complains of 'far too many social engagements' but, for the first time, shows him aware that the cost of Partition was to be heavy in human terms:

V. Thomas came back last week from a recce in Lahore & Amritsar. He says the amount of killing & burning & still more the atrocity stories are exaggerated but recounts that the road between Lahore & Amritsar is cluttered up with 2 great rivers of pedestrian refugees, Hindus & Sikhs from the West & Muslims from the East & all of them utterly exhausted. What's happened in fact is an exchange of populations – but unintended & achieved most brutally. He thinks the violence is really not committed by 'mobs' at all but by little gangs of experts who treat the whole thing as a cricket match: the scores must be kept even.

The results of Sir Cyril Radcliffe's Boundary Commission had been announced shortly after the birth of the two Dominions on 15 August, with the consequences that Thomas reported and MacNeice would soon see for himself.

He left Delhi on the 26th in a BBC van heading for Peshawar. They broke their journey at Lahore and 'ran into some horrors there'. Two images, in particular, would remain etched on his memory. First, a refugee camp for Muslims from the East Punjab. MacNeice had been moved by the plight of the European refugees on the *Samaria*, but was appalled by the sight of 30,000 of the dispossessed, a wide sea of misery swollen by streams of overloaded trucks and bullock carts. A few hours later, he and Vaughan Thomas and two newspaper correspondents found themselves in the village of Sheikhupura which, the day before, had been the scene of 'communal trouble'. The hospital held 80 badly injured Sikhs and Hindus. They were covered with flies and attended by one doctor, apparently without equipment; 1,500 more were crammed into a schoolhouse.

A v. large number of these had been wounded with swords or spears & their white clothes were covered with rusty-brown blood. Some with their hands cut off etc. & again the hordes of flies. But hardly any moaning – just abstracted, even smiling in a horrible unreal way.

Refugees queueing for cholera injections

These survivors of the massacre saw the Europeans – many who could walk clustered round them – as representing some sort of order amidst the chaos, and suddenly Vaughan Thomas saw

a totally different Louis, one I never imagined existed. Louis the man of action. He ordered those people into a nearby lorry, we got some sort of structure going of a way to get them out of the refugee area into something like safety and there he was ordering people about, they were obeying him – a Louis who was no longer the detached observer but one deeply and proudly involved in the human dilemma.

Neither in his letters nor in any published account of this incident did MacNeice mention his own part in it.

When the BBC contingent could do no more, they drove on to Peshawar where, in a search for petrol, they stopped at the District Commissioner's office. They found a handsome young man at a desk busily blue-pencilling a piece of paper. 'Excuse me, gentlemen,' he said, 'I shall be at your service in a moment, but just at present I am composing . . . a curfew.' He got them their petrol and, a day or so later, they and their van were piloted up the perilous narrows of the Khyber Pass by a Muslim professor, 'who looked rather like Groucho Marx and seemed to have his old pupils in all the key positions'. This and a later expedition provided MacNeice with memorable images of power to set beside those of powerless victims seen on the road north. The professor introduced them to two formidable brothers: Dr Khan Sahib, former Prime Minister of the North West Frontier Province, and Khan Abdul Ghaffar Khan, founder of the Pathan Red Shirt movement. The first treated his visitors to cakes; the second to a 'militant-cum-pseudo-socialist' harangue ending with the statement that, if the Pakistan Government would not accede to his demands for a separate 'Pathanistan', 'we will do what we ought to do' – launch a revolution ('v. Irish in their approach to things', thought MacNeice). Both the cakes and the harangue had to be digested under the muzzles of rifles and revolvers in the hands of bandolier-slung retainers. The visitors were then introduced to a dozen or so tribal chiefs, who had come 370 miles from Waziristan to ask the former Prime Minister for permission to march into the Punjab to assist their fellow Muslims. They seemed to MacNeice

a wonderful collection who might have come out of Homer. Their whole mentality is sheer Border Ballad. As we were leaving, a late-comer, a great ox of a man with a great black turned-up moustache & diehard angry eyes, stood himself plumb in front of V.T. & me & poured out a stream of rhythmical Pushto (which sounds an attractive language, not like old ragbag Hindustani). This flow of eloquence was punctuated by an eloquent throat-cutting gesture (all their hand movements are terrific). It turned out that he was giving the roll-call of the tribes who would go with him to Delhi & explaining what they would then do to Delhi & in fact to the whole of India. No more Sikhs – throat-cutting gesture! No more Hindus – throat-cutting gesture! And if the British interfere – throat-cutting gesture! And if the Russians interfere – throat cutting gesture! Q.E.D. On the Frontier the 20th Century doesn't go.

At the end of August, the BBC recording van again left Peshawar, this time heading east into the mountains and, on 2 September, its passengers had another Kiplingesque encounter. A hair-raising sequence of hairpin bends brought them to the hill station of Gulmarg, where they had lunch at Government House with Sir George Cunningham, Governor of the North West Frontier Province. Here, with log fires blazing indoors and dahlias blazing outside at the edge of exquisite lawns, MacNeice was introduced to images of a different, but complementary, power. There were no rifles here, only one (faulty) telephone; and no blood-curdling tirades, only a quiet old man with far-away blue eyes and his other guest, a young officer's wife, hysterically talkative about a country she could not understand.

The following morning, from his hotel window, MacNeice had a vision of another India: 'A long dark ridge of mountains below & a long dark ridge of clouds above & in the canal of liquid clear sky between a thing like a tiny floating lion with snow on its mane' – the peak of Nanga Parbat, a hundred miles to the north.

The BBC party drove on to Kashmir, and there, as later from central and south India, MacNeice's long letters home record other images of great beauty and meetings with Indians – many of them writers – whom he greatly liked, but such gleams of light flash out against a deepening gloom. He arrived in Lahore on 13 September, two days later flew to Delhi, where he was horrified by the refugee camp at Purana Kila, a beauty-spot he had admired in August; and on the 23rd he flew to Calcutta on his own. The rest of the BBC team remained in the Punjab. At the start of October, he took a night train to Benares ('the most fascinating town I've seen') and, on the 4th, reached Lucknow, where he stayed in Government House as the guest of the acting Governor, the charismatic Miss Sarojini Naidu, whom he had met at the Viceroy's reception in Delhi. They had taken to each other at once. She too was a poet, known as 'the Nightingale of India', whose work had been translated into English and many Indian languages. She was also a feminist, a political activist, the first woman President of the Indian National Congress, and an energetic and charming person. One of her first acts as acting Governor had been to open Government House – suitably illuminated – to the public, who came flocking with such comments as 'in the other Governor's days not even a mosquito could enter here'. She now assigned her ADC to show MacNeice the sights of Lucknow and get him a drink whenever he needed one. In return for her munificent hospitality, he gave a poetry reading to an audience that included aggressive young communists, some of the

Miss Sarojini Naidu

Oct
~~Sept~~. 6ᵗ (Letter 13)

GOVERNMENT HOUSE,
LUCKNOW.

Cat-Heart Dearest,

As you might guess from this notepaper I'm staying now in yet another remarkable place (watercolours & antlers — shades of the Old Order). On Saturday, before leaving Benares, saw the most magnificent sunrise, hanging over the Ganges & coming clean through the Frenchman's house so that all the arched openings looked brimfull of liquid fire. And everything v. quiet; just the swish of people on their haunches sweeping & stray bits of ²⁰ˡᵒ chanting; single individuals appearing on the roofs & joining their hands in silent prayer.

Mrs Naidu has confirmed my brief impression that she's a terrific personality. She's 69, short & burly, with a funny wide mouth & a face a bit like the Queen of All the Monkeys. Enormously warm — & witty. She's fed-up with being Acting Governor (the Governor Elect is in the U.S.A. & keeps postponing his return) & says she feels in a cage here; especially resents being escorted everywhere by police; says she had enough of police when she used to go to gaol. But the country folk, she says, hail her on the road & say: 'You're not our Governor, you're our Mother.' When she arrived here to enter on her duties (Aug. 15ᵗ) she flung Government House (duly 'illuminated') open to the people who came flocking in with delight commenting that 'in the other Governors' days not even a mosquito could enter here.' She seems to have known all the chaps like Yeats & Huxley & is v. keen to know about the writers in England today, so-called 'Barons of Oudh' ('supposed to be about the most reactionary people in India'), and – behind screens – some purdah women.

From Lucknow he sent Hedli a poem first mentioned in his letter of 16 September and drafted in Calcutta. On 3 October, he had asked her to warn Eliot that he might want to add a poem 'of about fifteen verses of six lines each' to the end of the collection he had delivered to Fabers before leaving England. When his 'Letter from India / for Hedli' appeared in that book, *Holes in the Sky*, it had gained a further three verses. The finished poem begins as travelogue:

> Our letters cross by nosing silver
> Place of a skull, skull of a star,
> Each answer coming late and little,
> The air-mail being no avatar,
> And whence I think I know you are
> I feel divided as for ever.

The remoteness of husband and wife at opposite ends of the world is skilfully reinforced by the remoteness of the rhymes 'silver'/'ever' at the opposite ends of the verse. He goes on to tell her of a country

> where men as fungi burgeon
> And each crushed puffball dies in dust

until the Western observer loses his sense of the individual's identity and importance, and the world 'seems a mere sabbath of bacilli' – the 'sabbath' of his rectory childhood now nothing but a metaphor for the 'bacilli' of the new Science that has replaced the old Religion. It seems to him that Europe has

> written off what looms behind
> The fragile fences of our mind,
> Have written off the flood, the jungle.
>
> So cast up here this India jolts us
> Awake to what engrossed our sleep;
> This was the truth and now we see it,
> This was the horror – it is deep;
> The lid is off, the things that creep
> Down there are we, we were there always.

And always also, doubtless, ruthless
Doubt made us grope for the same clue,
We too sat cross-legged, eyes on navel,
Deaf to the senses and we too
Saw the Beyond – but now the view
Is of the near, the too near only.

I have seen Sheikhupura High School
Fester with glaze-eyed refugees
And the bad coin of fear inverted
Under Purana Kila's trees
And like doomed oxen those and these
Cooped by their past in a blind circle . . . .

Massacre and refugee camp are literally and figuratively at the centre – the heart – of the poem, but from this point the physical is overwhelmed by the metaphysical and the poem loses its way. It recovers somewhat at the end, when philosophical lecture turns to love letter, but one is left feeling that the poet has attempted too much too soon after lifting the lid on Pandora's box.

Returning to Delhi on 8 October, MacNeice rejoined the other BBC

Mahabalipuram

men, but five days later was off again, with Dillon and Vaughan Thomas, to see the painted caves of Ajanta, the rock-cut temples of Ellora, and the great city of Hyderabad. Vaughan Thomas then returned to London to prepare and rehearse his commentary for the Royal wedding in November, leaving his friends to continue their southern progress. On 21 October they were staying in Madras and drove out to Mahabalipuram to see its great temple fronting the sea. That evening, Louis wrote to Hedli: 'I really do intend to have a shot at that long poem. The lingam by the way is also to be noticed on humble little graves in the countryside.' Soon the first line of 'Mahabalipuram' would be stirring in his head: 'All alone from his dark sanctum the lingam fronts, affronts the sea'.

They went on to Trichinopoly, Madurai, and Trivandrum on Cape Comorin, where they swam and were served with a splendid picnic. At last, turning their backs on the Indian Ocean, 'the dark grim chargers launched from Australia', they headed north and reached England – after a stop at Cairo and the Pyramids – in the second week of November.

Louis was pleased to be home. Hedli and the children were delighted with the presents he had brought them, and all were delighted with 52 Canonbury Park South. Almost his first task in his new study was to

Bimba

prepare a set of lectures to be given at Liverpool University. As soon as those were out of the way, he sat down to distil his experience of the past three months into three of a series of six one-hour feature programmes on India and Pakistan. Contrary to his expectations, he had been excited and moved by the subcontinent. The title he chose for his first script, 'India at First Sight', has a surely subconscious but significant associative link with 'love at first sight'. MacNeice's 'India' (by which he refers to the subcontinent as a whole) says of herself:

> Mother of many yet always virginal,
> With a crescent moon in one hand and
>   a spinning wheel in the other,
> I go on with a constant flow like the Ganges
> Yet unmoved as Nanga Parbat.

She embodies the opposing principles that had long dominated his imagination: water and rock, flux and stasis. She contains multitudes of the living and the dead, but her gods 'dance in the rock'; 'I worship stocks and stones', she says and later speaks of 'two sons who were poets. One was a Hindu, one was a Muslim , both became famous.' It would seem that at some deep imaginative level Mother India is associated – like Mother Ireland – with an Irish Mother who died in 1914 and was also survived by a famous poet.

MacNeice's 'India' is richly polyphonic. In her many voices, she speaks a flowing poetry denied to the visitor, Edward, and 'the Western familiars of his mind', the voices of his colonial education – Nanny, Missionary, Uncle Howard – or all of those voices but one. The visitor's inner 'Still Voice' sometimes catches the flowing cadence and the rich particularity of the Indian voices, as the poet rises to the level of his subject. His BBC brief – to stress all that the new dominions had in common and notably their need for reconciliation – accorded with his inclinations. He does not avert his eyes from horror. His Mother India says:

You will meet me lying on my back in the gutter with my legs apart and my white skirt rusty brown and the flies like a black nebula spiralling over the spear-wound. Yes, and you will meet me dead. Many times over dead.

His theme, however, is reconciliation, the ideals celebrated by India's poet-sons Tagore and Iqbal, and by Buddha, whose saying (in the mouth of the Christian missionary) ends the programme:

> Never in this world is hatred ended by hatred.
> Hatred is ended by love.

'India at First Sight', broadcast on 13 March 1948, was a notable success in a difficult genre, a fact MacNeice must have recognized since he published a substantial section of it the following year under the title 'The Crash Landing'. His subsequent scripts in the 'India and Pakistan' series are workmanlike but do not sing. 'Portrait of Delhi' follows the pattern of his earlier 'Portrait of Rome'. With its fifty-three characters (some 'doubled up') it sketches the history of the city from its foundation to January 1948; ending as Gandhi ends his fast eleven days before an assassin's bullet would end his life. 'The Road to Independence' – again with fifty-three characters (some 'doubled up') – follows the footsteps and hoof-prints of representatives of the millions who travelled that road between John Company's arrival in India and his descendants' transfer of power on 15 August 1947. These programmes were broadcast on 2 and 23 May, the month that saw the publication of MacNeice's *Holes in the Sky*.

A book that begins with the London Blitz ('The Streets of Laredo') and ends with the partition of the subcontinent ('Letter from India') may be forgiven an air of unease, a measure of nostalgic retrospection, but some of its more perceptive reviewers detected a deeper disquiet. Denis Botteril found evidence of the mid-life crisis that afflicts most poets who reach maturity. 'Possibly neglect and disappointment have soured the spring of inspiration; more often it is the sudden and conscious realization of stylistic repetition and a desire to enlarge the technical scope.' The latter hypothesis would account for MacNeice's use of the longer line and more supple syntax – features of his writing for radio – in poems like 'The National Gallery' and 'The Stygian Banks'. Botteril detected 'a nagging touch of despair undertoning the collection' and a certain loss of spontaneity. The *TLS* reviewer was more critical: 'he has lost the proper compression of poetry'. But concluded: 'He remains one of the more important of our younger poets, and the only one of them, perhaps, whose attitude to life is a broad and genial humanism.' Terence Tiller, a fellow poet and member of the BBC Features Department, went further: 'Dylan Thomas and Louis MacNeice, almost alone and in their different ways, have maintained a high minimum and a sharply rising maximum of excellence.'

Thomas and MacNeice were spending an increasing amount of time in each other's company. When, in July, Hedli went to see her parents in Switzerland, Louis wrote to her: 'Dylan T. stayed the night at 52 & yesterday we gave up to recreation: – Lords in the morning, wine-bar at lunch-time, Oval (where I'd never been) in the afternoon & London Casino in the evening.' Hedli returned for the family holiday, in August, on the island of Sark. They crossed in a converted German motor torpedo boat and a Force Ten gale, intending to spend a fortnight as guests of Mervyn Peake and his family in *Le Châlet*, a handsome stone house on the highest point of the island. After two or three days, however, the wives quarrelled. Then a telegram from the BBC called Louis back to work on a programme and, as there was only one boat to Guernsey a week, the MacNeices had to leave at once.

At about this time, Louis was caught up in another quarrel. Geoffrey Grigson had criticized Edith Sitwell for writing about motherhood when she was childless, and Roy Campbell had sprung to her defence with a scything attack on Grigson in a review of his anthology, *Poetry of the Present*:

For Mr. Grigson, poetically impotent, suffers all the rages and infatuations of a cuckold at his own keyhole ... both his rage and infatuation are aroused by watching other people romping, frolicking, and performing feats with the Muses that he can't perform himself. His rage is often completely self-contradictory – at its worst it verges on abject hypocrisy, as when he attacked Miss Sitwell for writing of childbirth though she is childless: yet he is always writing about the War; and his own War-record is about as virginal as Miss Sitwell's contribution to the birthrate.

Grigson responded with a letter to Campbell, saying he forgave him because 'you have written some fine poems. You know I would not even bounce a ping-pong ball off your venerable nut.' To this, Campbell replied: 'If I was young enough to fight for you I am young enough for you to fight.'

Matters came to a head when the two poets met in the street outside the BBC. Campbell told Grigson to take off his glasses, which he did, whereupon Campbell slapped his face. By the time Grigson had recovered from his surprise and put his glasses on again, Campbell had vanished. That evening, MacNeice found Campbell at the bar of the George and said: 'I heard you had a fight with Grigson.'

'No.'

'Well, what did you do?'

By way of answer, Campbell gave him a mock slap on the cheek. 'Surely', said MacNeice, 'it was more like this', and slapped Campbell resoundingly across the face. The South African's nose began to bleed and MacNeice went home that evening with a black eye. By then, however, honour had been satisfied, Campbell had bought him a drink, and a lasting friendship had been established.

Some weeks after his return from Sark, MacNeice crossed to Dublin for the literary event of the Irish year. In January 1939, Yeats had died in the south of France and been buried at Roquebrune. Now his body was being brought home, in the corvette *Macha*, to be reinterred in

W. B. Yeats comes home

Drumcliff churchyard outside Sligo on 17 September. The brothers Bob and Maurice Collis had offered MacNeice a lift in their car and arranged to leave Dublin at 7.30 that morning. He arrived an hour later with another poet, Maurice Craig, and an apocalyptic hangover. They set off at high speed, took aboard a third poet, Austin Clarke, at Longford, and as they entered Sligo town, overtook the funeral cortège, which had processed at a more decorous pace from Galway.

A halt was now made for lunch, while the guard stood to attention round the coffin with arms reversed. By this time Louis MacNeice was much better. His appearance was hardly yet as should have been the mien of the most eminent poet present, but he was able to converse, a trifle diffidently, on general topics such as, [Maurice Collis's] diary surprisingly records, Indian sculpture, a subject alien to the occasion.

At about 2.30, the cortège set off for Drumcliff in a drenching mist, and the coffin was duly lowered into its grave in the presence of the poet's brother, wife and children, Eamon de Valera, Sean MacBride

Louis MacNeice in Drumcliff churchyard

(son of Maud Gonne and John MacBride), Erskine Childers, the Earl of Longford, five clergymen, and half the poets of Ireland. Maurice Collis's account of the great day ends:

It remained for Louis MacNeice to say the final word. He declared that the wrong body had been buried.* They had dug up at Menton the body of a Frenchman with a club foot. A mistake, but did it really matter? But was it certain he knew what he was talking about? Why, it's common knowledge in Menton, he assured us. Well, then, what do you think should be done? we asked. Can't do anything now, he said. Everyone then went back to the hotel for tea.

Ruth Jones, MacNeice's friend and 'secretary par excellence', had left the BBC at the end of July to have a baby. Her departure compounded the problems of a difficult propaganda programme he had been assigned to mark the opening of the United Nations Assembly in Paris. Having tried to breathe life into the dry bones of UNICEF, ICAO, WHO, IRO, and UNESCO in 'No Other Road', he turned his hand to more congenial projects: 'Trimalchio's Feast', a sprightly study of late-Roman decadence, and 'The Queen of Air and Darkness', a parable-play prompted by a haunting poem of Housman's:

> Her strong enchantments failing,
>   Her tower of fear in wreck,
> Her limbecks dried of poisons
>   And the knife at her neck,
>
> The Queen of air and darkness
>   Begins to shrill and cry,
> 'O young man, O my slayer,
>   To-morrow you shall die.'
>
> 'O Queen of air and darkness,
>   I think 'tis truth you say,
> And I shall die to-morrow;
>   But you will die to-day.'

---

* A Welsh poet, the late John Ormond, as a newspaper reporter in 1948, interviewed the doctor who had signed Yeats's death certificate and the sexton of the Roquebrune cemetery, among others, and believed this distressing rumour to be true.

MacNeice's 'young man' is a failed artist called Adam who, under the spell of a supernatural blind and malevolent Queen, devotes his life to the pursuit of power in her service. He becomes a dictator and, finally overthrown, understands the evil he has done and destroys the Queen who has destroyed him.

As usual, MacNeice produced his script himself. Commissioning a score from the composer Elizabeth Lutyens, he asked for 'music like blue velvet, dripping', and followed his normal practice of giving his principal actors brief impressionistic sketches of their parts, as he conceived them. He told Catherine Lacey, who played the Queen, that 'She should be both sinister and glamorous', and wrote to Julia Lang, his friend since their Maiden Lane days: 'Your part is that of Margaret [Adam's wife] . . . . Among other things she must be capable of being hypnotized. And we don't of course want any "poetry voice".' Mac-Neice was good at getting the best out of his actors and technicians, and 'The Queen of Air and Darkness' was a powerful and sombre programme, if less moving than its predecessor in this mode, 'The Dark Tower', no doubt because it did not have the same autobiographical intensity.

Before it was broadcast, on 28 March 1949, MacNeice was at work on the most ambitious project for radio that he would ever undertake. Earlier in the year, his colleague Archie Harding had proposed the commissioning of a new translation of Goethe's *Faust* to mark the 200th anniversary of Goethe's birth on 28 August 1749. Auden, who had good German and admired Goethe, was approached and declined. Harding then asked MacNeice, whose German was not good, and after some hesitation he accepted, provided that his old friend Ernst Stahl – now Reader in German at Oxford – would collaborate with him. Stahl agreed, and together they set about scaling down Goethe's mammoth masterpiece to fit the dimensions of six programmes. Side by side at MacNeice's desk in his Canonbury Park study or his Rothwell House office (shared with Bertie Rodgers and a shy new secretary, Margaret Clark), they went through Stahl's literal translation line by line, deciding what sections should be cut. In each case the decision was MacNeice's and, though the scholar winced to see the Dedicatory Poem, the Prologue on the Stage, major portions of the two Walpurgis Night scenes and of Acts I, III and IV of Part 2 fall to the cutting-room floor, he admired the 'consummate skill' with which his friend first solved the structural problems and then set about translating German poetry into English poetry.

The work gathered speed from 1 April when, with only seven months to go before the first programme, the BBC allowed its poet a period of leave. To Stahl's surprise, his lack of German proved a positive advantage. Freed from the inhibitions of bilingual knowledge, he allowed himself to be guided only by Stahl and his own intuitions. He refused to look at Shelley's translation – saying 'Shelley was slipshod' and not much of a poet – or any other. Far from slipshod himself, he showed particular ingenuity in adapting Goethe's many and varied verse forms: blank verse, free verse, two-beat lines, hexameters, trimeters, tetrameters, choric odes, and alexandrines. As the collaboration moved into its final phase, MacNeice rented a beautiful old house at Ménerbes in the south of France. Its owners, Tony and Terèse Mayer, had filled it with magnificent furniture, and there for two sun-drenched, mistral-swept summer months the translators and their wives worked and walked, ate, drank, and talked, until the task was done.

In retrospect, Stahl would say of his friend's translation:

There can be little doubt that the outstanding contribution he made is the rendering of the many and varied lyrical passages in both parts of *Faust*. He was not so successful in capturing the tone of the unsophisticated songs and ballads of Part 1, except when they are sardonic and irreverent. His unsurpassed achievements are his re-creations of the complex and subtle measures of such lyric masterpieces as the angelic choruses of both parts; Gretchen's elegiac prayer in the '*Zwinger*' scene and her poignant visions in the dungeon; and the opening scene of Part 2.

Nowhere is that achievement more impressive than in the translation of the concluding lines of the whole work:

Alles Vergängliche	All that is past of us
Ist nur ein Gleichnis;	Was but reflected;
Das Unzulängliche,	All that was lost in us
Hier wird's Ereignis;	Here is corrected:
Das Unbeschreibliche	All indescribables
Hier ist's getan:	Here we descry:

| *Das Ewig-Weibliche* | Eternal Womanhead |
| *Zieht und hinan.* | Leads us on high. |

MacNeice took a very long time over this rendering of the *Chorus Mysticus*, elaborating and refining it during one of those extended phases of withdrawn and abstracted concentration when he conceived and shaped his best poetry. I experienced such fertile periods of his creativity over the years in unexpected places, as when he wrote a section of *Autumn Journal* in a Paris bar. He took especial pleasure in arriving at his bold rendering of Goethe's phrase '*das Ewig-Weibliche*' having eschewed the current 'Eternal Feminine'. The neologism 'Womanhead' is a stroke of genius. Analogous to 'Godhead' this coinage admits the interpretation that man's ultimate transformation is consummated not by Womanhood at large but by its divine manifestation embodied in the Virgin.

Archie Harding, whom MacNeice described as '"the onlie begetter" of the whole project', also produced it. Stephen Murray played Faust, Howard Marion Crawford was Mephistopheles, and Matyas Seiber composed the music for all six programmes. Part I – in which God authorizes Mephistopheles to tempt Faust, the pact is made, Gretchen is loved, seduced, and dies – was broadcast on 30 and 31 October; a more abridged Part II on 10, 13, 17, and 21 November. In this, Faust recovers from the shock of Gretchen's death only to fall in love again, with Helen. They are miraculously transported to Greece, where she gives birth to a child, Euphorion, who dies and descends with his mother to the Underworld. With no more desire for love or beauty, Faust himself goes to his death and, just as Mephistopheles is about to claim the soul he considers his, choirs of angels snatch it from the jaws of Hell and carry it heavenwards to join the soul of Gretchen, supplicant before the *Mater Gloriosa*.

MacNeice, warming to Mephistopheles more than to the self-pitying Faust, gave the devil some of his best lines, and may have thought himself repaid when, at the year's end, he was himself transported – in Faust's footsteps – to Greece.

CHAPTER 21

The Sanguine Visitor

Idyllic? Maybe. Still there is hardly
Such a thing as a just idyl. The sanguine visitor dreams . . . .
'The Island', *CP*, p. 306.

The British Institute in Athens, one of four such in Greece administered by the British Council, was looking for a new Director. Who could be more appropriate – given Byron's place in modern Greek mythology – than a well-known British poet with a classical education? The BBC was approached, and it was agreed that the Corporation would allow MacNeice one and a half years' leave to take up the appointment. Before he could give his mind to the new job, however, he had to tie up loose ends of the old. The Third Programme had commissioned a new production of 'The Dark Tower' and this had to be completed, ending the post-war phase of his career in broadcasting as it had begun. He then proposed that Dylan Thomas should have his job while he was away – a proposal that did not find favour with his superiors in the Corporation.

Hedli, meanwhile, was packing furiously; finding friends to look after Dan until he went back to school (now Bryanston) in mid-January; and finding tenants for 52 Canonbury Park South. When these took possession of the house, they were furious to find it dirty, and had to be placated by Louis' new secretary. The MacNeices and their maid, Teresa Moroni, had by then left England. Landing in Athens on the first day of the 1950s, with a copy of his newly published *Collected Poems 1925–1948* in his luggage, the new Director of the British Institute inhaled a lung-full of Greek air and found it to his liking.

He was less enthusiastic about the flat that had been rented for them in Sina Street, on the steep southern slope of Mount Lykabetos. Number 36 had a front door of wrought iron and glass, opening onto a hall that offered a choice of stairs or lift. A frosted-glass door on the fourth floor admitted one to a room 'like a doctor's consulting room'. Its worst feature was its brown paint: its best, the floor-to-ceiling windows with a distant view of Mount Hymettos. Another frosted-glass door led to the dining-room, off which other frosted-glass doors led to the other rooms.

Much more attractive was the Institute of which MacNeice took command on 2 January. This was housed in a neo-classical building on a corner of Kolonaki Square, a green oasis in the heart of the city (but only a short walk from Sina Street), where pigeons strut in the shade of low leafy trees and the sound of traffic is muted by a splashing fountain. From the start, he liked his staff and they liked him. He delegated as much of the administration as he could and, though his involvement in office routines was minimal, the Institute functioned smoothly under his direction. He set himself to organize a lively programme of cultural events. One of the first was a poetry reading made memorable for many in the audience by his own harsh, nasal

The Playboy in Athens: MacNeice is second from right

377

rendering of 'Bagpipe Music'. He led play-readings of Shakespeare's *Troilus and Cressida*, Webster's *White Devil*, Eliot's *Family Reunion*, and his own 'Dark Tower'. Encouraged by the success of these, he embarked on a full-scale production of Synge's *Playboy of the Western World*, taking particular pains with his actors' Irish accents. The play ran for four nights in early May, and the day after the last performance he took the cast out to lunch in a village *taverna*. Not having quite emerged from their roles, they sat under olive trees and 'tired the sun with talking', while laden plates and jugs of *retsina* went round and round.

There were other, more decorous parties at the Institute. At one of these, an American student of medieval archaeology found himself talking to a handsome red-haired lady. He was telling her about a detention-camp for political prisoners, called Makronisos.

For Greeks the place was famous and, in certain circles, it was wiser not to speak of it, but in early 1950, with the Civil War barely at an end, it was only a few foreign visitors and international sub-committees with supposedly objective or perhaps philanthropic intentions that went there and usually chose to remain silent on what they had seen.

'Louis, come over here, this is interesting,' and after a few more vicarious heroics by me addressed to the straight and graceful husband with the expressionless look of someone either quite bored or quite receptive, that (amid the yelping and bared teeth and feathered hats) was that.

Until the occasion broke up and, having learned the identity of the famous poet whom I hadn't heard of, I – relentless literary snob – took care to reach the marble exit at the same time he did.

Something had clicked, and they took me home to dinner . . . .

So began one of the most important friendships the MacNeices would make in Greece. Kevin Andrews was twenty-five. Born in Peking, educated in England and at Harvard, he had served as a reconnaissance-scout with the US Army in the Po Valley campaign. Skills learnt in the war stood him in good stead when, after it, a fellowship at the US School of Archaeology in Athens led him into the mountains of the Peloponnese on a search for Crusader castles. Those barren ranges were then the setting of a brutal civil war and, often in great danger, Andrews became friends with combatants on both sides. His experience of those years gave him the raw material of *The Flight of Ikaros* (1959), which Patrick Leigh Fermor has called 'the most brilliant and penetrating book on the bitter and tragic aspects of Greek rustic life to come out since the war'. This engaging, flute-playing scholar gipsy helped to educate MacNeice, the lapsed classicist, in the grim realities of modern Greek history.

Another such tutor was Leigh Fermor, who had himself been Deputy Director of the British Institute immediately after the war. They and their wives discovered they had London friends – and much else – in common at a party following a song-recital given by Hedli on 4 April. Leigh Fermor was another stylish Anglo-Irishman, more Byronic than MacNeice, and ebullient where he was reflective. The poet would never lose his admiration for men of action, and must have been impressed by the story (soon to be the subject of a bestseller, *Ill Met by Moonlight*) of Leigh Fermor's leading role in the abduction of General

Patrick Leigh Fermor

379

Kreipe during the German occupation of Crete. Most importantly, the two Anglo-Irishmen respected each other as writers and shared a passion for poetry in general and Greek poetry in particular. They spent a good deal of time together, reading aloud random passages and challenging each other to guess the author. On one occasion, Leigh Fermor spoke of a Cretan friend who had opened a garage in Athens, then caught 'flu, and suddenly died. Without hesitation, MacNeice quoted an epitaph by Simonides:

Κρὴς γενεὰν Βρότακος Γορτύνιος ἐνθάδε κεῖμαι,
οὐ κατὰ τοῦτ' ἐλθὼν ἀλλὰ κατ' ἐμπορίαν.

[Here I lie, Brotachos, from Gortyn in Crete.
Not for this did I come, but for trade.]

Leigh Fermor would later remember

many evenings at Louis' flat, all perfect, hospitably abetted by Hedli, and in which Bimba – a very young, active, red-haired mite at the time – was a lively and amusing presence. In spite of their reservations about some sides of the Athenian life, they enjoyed going to *tavernas* as much as I did, and the retsina and the minstrels with violin, accordeon, and lute wandering from table to table singing island or mountain songs in which one could join, or old ironical and romantic numbers from long-forgotten musical comedies. Kevin Andrews was as assiduous a guide as I was in such evenings. There were several late visits to still unspoiled *bouzoukia* haunts in Piraeus and New Phaleron where the songs were very different: urban, low-life and dockside with a special rather apache-like delivery, originating among Asia Minor refugees, accompanied by long-necked mandolins and short tortoise-shell-bowled *baglamas* accompanied by very intricate dances scanned against the beat: solitary, double, or triune, with hands linked on shoulders while the words recounted some hard-luck-story or feud or ill-starred love, or the consolations, when the world was too much, of puffing at a hookah with hashish, which indeed sometimes went on in the back-rooms or cellars. (I had a passion for such haunts, felt I was plumbing the mysteries of the east, merging an Ottoman world with Byzantium and intrepidly advancing into a maze of louche and delinquent life.) Another craze, which I made them share once or twice, was exactly the opposite: taverns frequented by Epirotes and Macedonians still fresh from their home-sierras where zither, clarinet, lute, violin, a double bass, and long-drawn-out and sometimes howled Klephtic ballads from Roumeli and Pindus rent the air, telling of battles with Janissaries and rocky skirmishes with the Arnauts of Ali Pasha.

The MacNeices did not much care for the more boisterous, gregarious, and pace-forcing aspects of Athenian life, but through the Leigh Fermors they came to know and like the Greek poet Seferis and Ghika the painter. MacNeice, however, did not take to George Katsimbalis, the flamboyant editor of *The Anglo-Hellenic Review* portrayed in Henry Miller's *Colossus of Maroussi*. Someone, seeing them in conversation, said Louis looked 'like a man caught in a sharp shower without an umbrella'.

His Oxford friend, Moore Crosthwaite, was Counsellor at the British Embassy and, through him, the MacNeices were soon on good terms with the Ambassador, Sir Clifford Norton, and his engaging wife. The Director of the British Institute 'reported' to the Representative of the British Council, Wilfrid Tatham, MC, a former Olympic half-miler, army officer, and housemaster at Eton. He and MacNeice had little in common apart from an interest in cricket, but what might otherwise have been a good working relationship was rapidly undermined by a feud between their wives. Rachel Tatham was tall, slender, golden-haired, and snobbish in the grand manner. MacNeice's reputation had preceded him and, for some time after his arrival, many Greek intellectuals and students believed that *he* was the Representative and showed their amazement on learning that Tatham was. Left to himself, Tatham would have laughed this off, but his wife was not amused. She decided it was Hedli's doing, and tried to put Hedli down. Hedli, however, was unputdownable, a brilliant mimic with – on occasions – a wittily wicked tongue, and their clashes were soon an obsessive topic of dinner-table conversation.

At Easter, Dan flew out and the MacNeices went with Kevin Andrews to stay for a week with Paddy Leigh Fermor, who was looking after Ghika's beautiful house on the island of Hydra. This has since been destroyed by fire, but its essence survives in its owner's paintings and Leigh Fermor's prose:

The Ghika house was built in the late 18th century by the painter's great-great-great-grandfather. It lies above and beyond the town at the end of a precipitous ascent by mule or on foot – for the island, thanks to its steepness, is as empty of wheels as pre-Columbian America. A saddle of rock to the east, covered with white houses which flow down and fill a ravine that sinks to the shore, conceals the main town. This valley divides the seaman's from the shepherd's realm for the roughly ledged hillsides to the west, bare except for occasional almond and olive trees, are sprinkled with black goats. Beyond, in either direction, ascends a wilderness of grey and wrinkled mountains. The sea, showing through rugged hills, stretches away to the Argive coast. Islands follow each other along leagues of water that expand westwards towards the twin angular ghosts, forty miles away, of the Laconian peninsula and the inland sierras of the Peloponnese. White-walled and massive, built as a defence against the attacks of pirates, the house climbs the flank of the central water-shed in four dazzling tiers. It is one of the oldest in the island. A tilted fortress-like wall encloses its nine strata of tree-shaded terrace. This ziggurat is honeycombed with rooms, and elaborate cedarwood ceilings enclose the larger ones like the lids of caskets.

The friends walked up the mountain and through the terraced olive groves. They ate and drank and talked late into the nights, and after a long period of poetic drought, the first of MacNeice's *Ten Burnt Offerings* began to quicken in his head. As they walked down the steep lanes to the port, Andrews heard him muttering 'indistinguishable words'.

On 6 June, MacNeice left Athens again, to lecture at the British Institute at Patras. From there, he crossed the Corinth canal to pay his respects to the great shade of Byron among the swamps of Misso-longhi. Writing to George MacCann of this pilgrimage, he said: 'All I can say is: naturally he died. There are some Victorian-Romantic (v.bad) canvasses in Missolonghi Town Hall featuring highly combus-tive battles with Ibrahim Pasha on a white horse rampant doing the King Billy act.' That flippant note would find its way into the opening of 'Cock o' the North', the third of his *Ten Burnt Offerings*:

> Bad Lord Byron went to the firing, helmet and dogs and all,
> He rode and he swam and he swam and he rode but now he rode
>   for a fall;

but by the end of the poem he has identified himself with the dying poet:

> Mither! Mither! *Crede Biron!*

> Was it my fault you bore me lame . . . .
>   Mither! Mither! Blaw the bellows!
> My foreign doctors kill to heal
>   And the last licht leads to darkness.

Through the mask of Byron, MacNeice calls to the mother who awaits him in the final darkness.

He returned to a difficult situation: the British Council, planning retrenchment, decided to house the Institute in its own (less attractive) building. The merger was scheduled for September and MacNeice, who was then to become the Representative's deputy, was faced with the prospect of an office next to Tatham's. First, however, he could look forward to a summer holiday. Dan again flew out from England and, on 4 August, the MacNeices and their Greek maid, Ariadne, set off for her native island of Ikaria. Near their rented house was a concentration-camp like the one described by Kevin Andrews at their first meeting. Its 'political prisoners' included women and children, many with TB, who could be heard coughing at night. These, strangely, find their way into only one indifferent line of 'The Island', sixth of MacNeice's *Burnt Offerings*. In the second half of their holiday, he led the family on a tour of the mainland sites, including Mycenae, Tiryns, and Missolonghi, where they spent a night in what by morning they had discovered to be a brothel.

They returned to Athens in early September and, later that month, the Institute merged with the British Council. On 4 December, Mac-Neice escaped from the increasingly thunderous air of the office to give a series of lectures and poetry readings on behalf of the Council in Istanbul. It would seem he was also escaping from thunder at home. A long and contrite letter to Hedli apologizes for his 'behaviour' (obviously when drunk) and seeks to reassure her on an important point:

You must never, never think again that I'm in any way indifferent to – let alone hostile to! – your singing. I couldn't, if I tried, dissociate you from singing – you'd be quite a different person & not the person I fell for! There are perhaps 2 things which may have misled you:– (i) I have on occasion been irritable when, on my entering the house, you've raised a whole question of planning a programme which I thought had been settled 6 times already (this is

thoroughly unreasonable of me but it goes with my hatred of synopses &
schedules & all that; what I like is the *stuff*); (ii) when you're about to give a
concert I get so tensed up that I'm useless to you (unless I try to drink myself
out of it in which case I'm even more useless!) &, while you're giving it, I
sometimes – not always – am so desperately anxious that you should be at
your best in every single number (!) that I tend to remark on the fluffs etc
before I remark on the excellences. (I'm afraid I did this in your B[ritish]
I[nstitute] Concert when you say I got it wrong at that!). But .... even a
dumbard could see how your voice has come on in the last year or two –
including the period in Athens. . . . Anyhow do believe me, darling, that your
singing is of the utmost importance to me. Or, to put it another way, I'd as
soon stop writing as have you stop singing.

This letter spoke of the possibility that she might fly out to join him in
Istanbul, and it is evident from the last of the 'Ten Burnt Offerings' that
she did.

Returning on 16 December, they organized a Christmas dinner for
their friends. As this was ending, towards midnight, a phone call
invited them all to a larger and grander party at the British Embassy.
There the company was Anglo-Greek and included Athenian actors,
dancers, and writers. Before long Hedli was singing. Then Paddy Leigh
Fermor led rounds of Cretan folksong, and the party ended with
everyone dancing a Greek *Kalamatianos*. Hedli had offered Paddy a
bed for what remained of the night but, when she went into her
drawing-room next morning, she found him and Louis 'seated in
armchairs – dinner-jacketed like two wax works, grasping glasses that
were still half filled, their other hands raised as though making telling
points in some close-knit colloquy which had ceased in mid-sentence –
and fast asleep'.

The MacNeices' entrée to Embassy circles rankled with Mrs
Tatham, and their friendship with two members of the expatriate
community fuelled her resentment further. One, Peter Duval-Smith,
was a young South African staff member of the British Council, brilliant but unreliable. When Mrs Tatham was receiving guests at the
Representative's New Year's Eve party, in came Duval-Smith eating an
orange. Shaking hands, he left her with a palmful of pith and pips. In
due course, he was summoned to a disciplinary 'court'. Arriving half an
hour late, he was found guilty of 'persistent unpunctuality' and told he

would forfeit one year's increment of salary. This prompted him to leave the Council, and in due course MacNeice found him a job at the BBC. Another expatriate of whom the Tathams disapproved was Arthur Sewell, Byron Professor of English Literature at Athens University. By the time the MacNeices realized the extent of the enmity between the austere Representative and the flamboyant professor, they and Sewell had become friends. He was shortly to retire from his Chair and Tatham had hopes that he would be succeeded by Stephen Spender, who was about to visit Athens as a guest of the British Council. He came, stayed with Moore Crosthwaite, and gave a lecture on 'The Art of Autobiography', but was dashed to learn that he was not to be the new Byron Professor. Sewell, who was then in London, and anxious not to be succeeded by Tatham's candidate, had told one of the electors: 'what we need is an academic administrator'. Tatham was furious and decided – wrongly – that MacNeice had had a hand in the matter. The Representative and his deputy had adjoining offices with a connecting door, but were now communicating chiefly by terse memoranda.

Another welcome visitor to 36 Sina Street that spring was Dodds, for whom Hedli gave a mischievously memorable dinner party. The other guests were the British Ambassador, Sir Clifford Norton, C. M. Woodhouse, architect of Britain's wartime policy in Greece, Yannis Peltekis, a brilliant leader of the wartime Resistance who felt himself betrayed by that policy, and the guerrilla's friend and ardent admirer, Kevin Andrews. It was an explosive combination, and Dodds and the MacNeices enjoyed the conversational crossfire a good deal more than the other distinguished British guests. Dodds and Andrews struck up a friendship cemented a week or so later when they explored Mount Athos together.

They returned in time for Dodds to join Hedli, Louis and Dan on an Easter expedition to Crete. One morning, they set off from Knossos with a guide and a laden mule to climb Mount Ida. It was a long slog. Above the timberline, they met shepherds wearing monkish cowls and accepted the hospitality of their smoky cave. Hedli and Louis, next morning, decided they were in no condition for another day's climbing. The guide tried to persuade them all to turn back, but Dodds berated him in Homeric Greek and insisted on continuing, with Dan, to the mountain's chapel-crowned summit. Hedli and Louis, meanwhile, made their slow way down. The party was reunited that evening in the mountain village of Anoyia, which had been a nerve-centre of Cretan resistance during the German occupation. The streets were thronged, for it was Easter Eve, and at midnight the church bells rang, everyone shouted '*Christos anéste!** and even the atheist Anglo-Irishmen joined in the feast of the paschal lamb.

Sometime that spring, the younger wrote:

> all my years are based on autumn,
> Blurred with blue smoke, charred by flame,
> Thrusting burnt offerings on a god
> Who cannot answer to his name.

The previous September, MacNeice had written to Eliot:

I have been working lately on a set of longish poems (averaging *c* 140–150 lines), each in four sections. I call them *Panegyrics* and I think they represent what one calls 'a new development'. I have already written eight (but 4 of these still need considerable tinkering) and am about to start on a ninth.

He called his *Ten Burnt Offerings* 'experiments in dialectical structure'. The ninth takes the form of a letter to Hedli about the death of their cat, Thompson – its absence lamented in the first section, its presence celebrated in the second:

> To begin with he was a beautiful object:
> Blue crisp fur with a white collar,
> Paws of white velvet, springs of steel,
> A Pharaoh's profile, a Krishna's grace,
> Tail like a questionmark at a masthead
> And eyes dug out of a mine, not the dark
> Clouded tarns of dog's, but cat's eyes –
> Light in a rock crystal, light distilled
> Before his time and ours, before cats were tame.

This is fluent and vivid, but a question asked in the fourth section is not fully answered:

---

* 'Christ is risen!'

Sentimentality? Yes, it is possible;
You and I, darling, are not above knowing
The tears of the semi-, less precious things,
A pathetic fallacy perhaps, as the man
Who gave his marble victory wings
Was the dupe – who knows – of sentimentality . . . .

MacNeice told Eliot that these poems 'come from a common matrix and so overlap or lead on to each other'. The overlap between 'The Death of a Cat' and its sequel, 'Flowers in the Interval', a love poem again in the form of a letter to Hedli, is unlikely to be detected by a reader ignorant of the fact that 'Cat' was the poet's pet name for his wife –

you my galactic
Marvel of ivoried warmth, with your warm hair curled
Over the cool of your forehead and your ambivalent
Tigercat eyes . . . .

These poems – like the preceding 'Burnt Offerings' – are graceful and technically accomplished if not technically ambitious. Voluminous drafts testify to the trouble MacNeice took with them, but they lack the intensity of his best work and leave one with the suspicion that they might have been written for a listener's ear rather than a reader's eye. Certainly, they were the first fruits of his time in Greece to be heard on the radio.

The BBC – all but forgotten for a year – was now beginning to loom larger in his thoughts. Gilliam came out to Athens in July, and probably accompanied him on a return visit to Crete, in early August, and to a drama festival at Delphi. On the last day of the month the MacNeices left Greece and, after some days in Venice, reached England in mid-September. The 'Ten Burnt Offerings' were broadcast in a series of programmes, each with an introduction by the poet, over the next two months. Meanwhile, he was at work on a 'Portrait of Athens', along the lines of his 'Portrait of Rome', and another, more ambitious, feature programme, 'In Search of Anoyia', which draws its theme and its motifs from deeper levels of its author's experience. The protagonist, John, is an amateur archaeologist who, in labyrinthine dreams, returns to Crete – the island of Minos's labyrinth – to confront the horrors of first the Turkish and then the German occupation of Anoyia. MacNeice conflates his own experience with Leigh Fermor's when church bells ring to announce that 'black cattle are coming!' These are the Germans (metaphorically crossed with the Minotaur), who proceed to march the women and children away and burn the village to the ground. 'Some chaps thought it was done in reprisal for Kreipe but we'd kidnapped the General in April', a Cretan guerrilla explains. Hatred is eventually succeeded by love; another dream, in which John finds himself at a Cretan wedding, which turns out to be his own. In this programme and a less successful sequel, 'The Centre of the World, a picture of Delphi past and present', MacNeice can be seen worrying at questions of religious belief – central also to *Ten Burnt Offerings* – and extra-sensory perception. These are manifestations of a lifelong debate with his father and, at another level, with his surrogate father, Dodds, an active member of the Society for Psychical Research whose magisterial book, *The Greeks and the Irrational*, had just been published.

The winter of 1951–2 was not a happy one for Dan. Depressed and in revolt against Bryanston, he began to court expulsion. He broke into the Portman family vault, looking for jewellery among the bones, and buried in the walls of the school pottery-kiln shells stolen from the local airforce base. Eventually he was exiled to a Franciscan friary for the end of the spring term. This confirmed his distaste for holiness and, choosing to transfer to a London 'crammer' rather than return under a probationary cloud, he duly passed his 'O' levels. But hardly had he escaped from one unsympathetic and authoritarian regime, than he was threatened with another even more alarming. With his eighteenth birthday imminent, he was obliged to sign up for two years' National Service. His father wrote to George MacCann (who, during the war, had served in the Inniskilling Fusiliers), asking if he could jot down a few basic facts about the Regiment to help Dan get into it. At this point a letter from his mother brought the possibility of at least a temporary escape. Charles Katzman had left her in 1950 and she wrote that, if Dan would like to spend his summer holiday on her chicken farm, she would pay his fare to America and back. He was enthusiastic and, with some foreboding, his father let him go.

Louis and Hedli had another matter on their minds that summer.

They had fallen in love with a house. Not only was 2 Clarence Terrace an example of Regency architecture at its most magnificent, but it overlooked Regent's Park, was five minutes' walk from the BBC, and had at different times been home to Dame Nellie Melba and the MacNeices' Anglo-Irish friend, Elizabeth Bowen. It had been the setting of her novel, *The Death of the Heart*:

2 Windsor Terrace was lanced through by dazzling spokes of sun, which moved unseen, hotly, over the waxed floors. Vacantly overlooking the bright lake, chestnuts in leaf, the house offered that ideal mould for living into which life so seldom pours itself.

Clarence Terrace was owned by the Crown Estate and, when Elizabeth Bowen gave it up, MacNeice asked his better-connected publisher to sound out the Estate's office on his behalf. This Eliot obligingly did.

2 Clarence Terrace

The rent was agreed, the lease signed, and on 25 July the MacNeices moved into what was from the first their favourite house.

Louis' delight in his domestic circumstances softened his disappointment at the reviews his *Ten Burnt Offerings* – published earlier in the month – was receiving. He told a friend: 'Personally I think that this book breaks new ground, these poems being more architectural – or perhaps I should say symphonic – than what I was doing before.' His bad press he ascribed to the fact that his friends, 'having become successful, have largely stopped writing book reviews which have consequently fallen into the hands of younger & as yet less successful writers (who also, I think, tend to be jealous of me in particular because I have the kind of job which they pretend to look down on but in fact would be delighted to have!)' He was still insisting that *Ten Burnt Offerings* was his best book when he came to introduce his 1959 selection of *Eighty-Five Poems*. The writing had been on the wall, however, since 1951 – and the writing was his own:

> Do I prefer to forget it? This middle stretch
> Of life is bad for poets; a sombre view
> Where neither works nor days look innocent
> And both seem now too many, now too few.

CHAPTER 22

The Middle Stretch

The writing may have been on the wall, but in the summer of 1952 MacNeice was too delighted with the wall to be depressed by the writing. He had always liked the non-commitment of rented property, and he and Hedli both revelled in the elegance of 2 Clarence Terrace. They saw it as an outward and visible sign of their individual and shared success, though 'he'll have to work so hard to keep it up', she wrote to Kevin Andrews. A natural hostess, she liked the idea of presiding over an intellectual salon – provided she did not have to do the cleaning and, luckily, when Teresa left, Restituta joined the household. Broad-hipped, short, but with high-piled hair making her seem taller than she was, Restituta was as ebullient as Hedli and she liked housework. For more than a decade she would run 2 Clarence Terrace as effectively as Matchett, the housekeeper of Elizabeth Bowen's *Death of the Heart*, ran 2 Windsor Terrace.

That summer, Elizabeth Bowen had visitors at Bowen's Court: the American poets Stanley Moss and John Malcolm Brinnin. She told them of the Irish poet who had taken over her London house, and Brinnin, who had spent his savings thirteen years before to hear Auden and MacNeice read in New York, later called at Clarence Terrace. MacNeice was in, but his mind was elsewhere. As they talked, Brinnin became aware of his host's obsessive interest in the hands of the clock as they approached 'opening time'. When they were near enough, MacNeice took him by way of several pubs to watch a Test match at Lord's and, when rain stopped play, they took shelter in a second round of pubs, until it was Brinnin who was obsessively watching the clock hands as they inched towards 'closing time'.

MacNeice was more comfortable in the company of old friends, seasoned drinkers like Dylan Thomas, Reggie Smith, Bob Pocock (who had joined the BBC while MacNeice was in Greece), and Bertie Rodgers. He and Rodgers now had another reason for drinking together. They had been recruited as editors of a book it would take them the rest of their lives not to complete: 'a collection of essays on Ireland, a book that would transcend the fission of its subject, and display the real order which kept the dance of electrons contained'. This, to be called *The Character of Ireland*, was the dream – and would later become the nightmare – of a New Zealander working for the Clarendon Press; 'an Irishman who was not of Ireland; an apostate, but from a faith that was not the faith of MacNeice's recent fathers – to use Bertie Rodgers's distinction – a Catholic agnostic, not a Protestant agnostic'. Dan Davin was also a poet, the author of a book of short stories and two novels, a battle-hardened veteran of the New Zealand Division's campaigns in Crete and North Africa. Like MacNeice he had a first-class degree in 'Greats' from Oxford, a strong head, and a sharp wit.

Dan Davin

They had been introduced by Jack Dillon in The Stag, late in 1948, and had met in Oxford, ostensibly to make plans for *The Character of Ireland*, the following June. The prospective editors had an afternoon appointment with Davin, which it seemed they had forgotten. With rueful hindsight, he would remember

The afternoon passed and there was no sign of them, a portent that was not for years yet to be brought home to me, any more than the significance of that day's later sequel. About nine o'clock Bertie rang. Would I join them in the George bar? I flushed them under the window, on the red upholstery, the two of them, and Dylan Thomas. They had come from the other George in London, had drunk but not eaten in the train, and had had a few more jars in Oxford before Bertie nerved himself to ring. They were all three very tight: Dylan boisterous, Bertie portentously grave, and Louis's usual vigilant taciturnity betrayed by the fixture of his smile.

The Welsh wizard was in spellbinding form, spinning parodic versions of the Crucifixion story in the manner of Hemingway, Auden, Malcolm Muggeridge, Day Lewis, Spender, Rodgers, and finally MacNeice: 'Christ became a phoenix burning on Heraclitean fire, and then a Tophet, a top hat of fire, out of which Dylan juggled the rabbits of the one and the many.' Come closing time, they adjourned to Davin's house where his wife, Winnie, plied them with chicken and wine. Next day, with BBC programmes requiring their attention, the prospective editors of a book that had not been discussed caught the train back to London.

The pattern of this visit would be repeated many times over the next decade; the pretext – more often than the text – of *The Character of Ireland* enabling MacNeice to visit his Oxford friends, the Doddses, Stahls, and Davins, not to mention Hall Bros, the High Street tailors of his elegant tweed suits. After a second meeting, in March 1952, contracts were exchanged and soon a list of contributors included Elizabeth Bowen on 'The Big House', Frank O'Connor on 'English Literature', Sam Hanna Bell on 'The Six Counties', and John Hewitt on 'The Visual Arts'. Progress with the commissioning of essays slowed that autumn, however, as the editors' relations came under strain and the easy rhythm of their shared office was disrupted. Gilliam's wife, Marianne Helweg, left him for Rodgers, raising the question of whether he could continue to work in Gilliam's department. Mac-Neice, who had brought the two men together, felt obscurely involved in what he saw as a betrayal of the boss to whom he was devoted, and told Rodgers he should resign from the BBC which, that December, he did. Never one to carry his guilts lightly, Rodgers had another to shoulder the following year when his former wife, Marie, committed suicide.

As the autumn advanced, MacNeice acquired a domestic worry of his own: Dan was showing no sign of returning to England and, indeed, every sign of wanting to remain in America. His father, there-fore, asked Kevin Andrews – then in New York and pining for Greece – to contact Dan and discover what his intentions were. Andrews, accordingly, wrote to him and was invited down to the New Jersey chicken farm. He did not like Mary, nor she him. After he and Dan had gone for a walk, on which he talked of the charms of Europe and the possibility of their meeting in Greece the following year, the boy suffered an upset stomach and was put into his mother's bed. The sickroom was declared out of bounds to Andrews. He stayed on for two or three days, eating fried eggs, until it became clear to him that the patient would not emerge while he was there. Only when his departure had been announced was he admitted to the sickroom for a supervised goodbye. Hearing of the failure of his mission, Dodds responded curtly: 'That was rather like asking you to visit a lioness for the purpose of removing her cub.' On 3 December, MacNeice wrote wryly to George MacCann: 'Dan . . . is still in the Bad Lands of New Jersey, being Svengali'd by his Mamma.'

It may have been with some thought of mounting a rescue operation that he then asked the BBC for two months leave without pay. This was granted, and he and Hedli set about planning an American tour with their reading-cum-recital double act. First, however, he organized a brief trip to Belfast on BBC business that conveniently coincided with a rugby international, Ireland v. France, at the Ravenhill Ground. There would be many more such expeditions over the years, and always George MacCann would meet him off the ferry at seven o'clock in the morning. Together they would go back to the flat in Botanic Avenue for a ritual breakfast of bacon, duck eggs, kidney, liver, sausage, and potato-bread, all washed down with Bushmills Whiskey.

So fortified, they would sally forth at opening time to prepare for the clash of the titans. On 24 January, their patriotism was rewarded with a famous victory: Ireland defeating France by 16 points to 3. For MacNeice, a particular cause for celebration was the dazzling try scored by one of his heroes, Jacky Kyle. He told George MacCann: 'I'd give anything to be able to play like Jacky Kyle.' MacCann reported this to Kyle, who replied: 'I'd give anything to be able to write poetry like Louis MacNeice.'

Back then to London and, on 26 February, the MacNeices boarded the liner *Liberté* bound for New York. Their tour had been co-ordinated by Elizabeth Reitall, the beautiful and dynamic secretary of John Malcolm Brinnin, Director of the Poetry Center in New York, and was due to begin there on the day they in fact sailed. The evening arrived but not the performers, only – next day – a lackadaisical telegram of regret. The programme, billed as 'a Recital of Song and Verse' (Louis reading, Hedli singing), was rescheduled for 5 March, the day after the *Liberté* docked. It was a considerable success. The Mac-Neices spent the best part of a fortnight in New York, staying with the poet Ruthven Todd and his wife (who had been neighbours of theirs in Tilty), and on 17 March, St Patrick's Day, MacNeice wrote to Dodds:

About Dan. He sailed for England in a Dutch boat last Saturday, 14th, but did not come to see us & didn't even ring us up while he was in N.Y.C. for the day or two before sailing (I'd given him the address and telephone number) ... I gather that *if* he's rejected by the Army he wants to return here at once to dig in For Ever on the poultry farm ....

Later on the 17th, the MacNeices left New York for five nights on a New England farm with other old friends, the Irish playwright Denis Johnston and his wife Betty. The 22nd found them at Harvard where, that afternoon, Louis gave a reading at The Poet's Theatre and, at a party afterwards, met the poets John Ciardi and E. E. Cummings. The MacNeices stayed at Harvard for several days and were royally enter-tained. They moved on to Minnesota, where Louis read his poems on 6 April; then to Chicago, where he read on the 8th. Hedli gave a solo recital in New York on the 13th; and they did their double act at the Phillips Gallery in Washington, DC, on the 19th, and at Connecticut College on the 24th. They had a farewell drink with Brinnin on the

The Poetry Center, John Malcolm Brinnin, director

·· presents

HEDLI ANDERSON and LOUIS MacNEICE

A Recital of Song and Verse

At the Piano
OTTO LUENING

Thursday Evening, March 5, 1953 at 8:40

I.

In a harbor grene .... R. Wever

The Revenant .... Louis MacNeice

Bagpipe Music .... Louis MacNeice
LOUIS MACNEICE

I once was a Maid (Robert Burns) .... Arr. Ferdinand Rauter

The Bonnie Earl of Moray (Trad. Scottish) .... Arr. Benjamin Britten

Hie Balou (Robert Burns) .... Benjamin Britten
HEDLI ANDERSON

I am of Ireland .... W. B. Yeats

Dublin .... Louis MacNeice

Devil, Maggot and Son .... Translated from the Irish by Frank O'Connor
LOUIS MACNEICE

Johnny, I hardly knew ye (18th Cent. Irish ballad) .... Arr. Herbert Hughes

She moved through the Fair (Trad. Irish) .... Arr. Herbert Hughes
HEDLI ANDERSON

Suite for Recorders .... Louis MacNeice
LOUIS MACNEICE

Who is it that this Dark Night (Sir Philip Sidney) . . . . . . Thomas Morley
On a time the amorous Sylvie (Anon.) . . . . . . John Attey
When first Amyntas (Anon.) . . . . . . Henry Purcell

HEDLI ANDERSON

The Careless Gallant . . . . . . Thomas Jordan
It was All Very Tidy . . . . . . Robert Graves
Prayer in Mid-Passage . . . . . . Louis MacNeice

LOUIS MACNEICE

Mad Bess (Anon.) . . . . . . Henry Purcell

HEDLI ANDERSON

INTERMISSION

The Sunlight on the Garden . . . . . . Louis MacNeice
A Toast . . . . . . Louis MacNeice

LOUIS MACNEICE

Common Sense and Genius (Thomas Moore) . . . . . . French Air
Oft in the Stilly Night (Thomas Moore) . . . . . . Irish Air

HEDLI ANDERSON

The Colour of his Hair . . . . . . A. E. Housman
Naming of Parts . . . . . . Henry Reed
Prognosis . . . . . . Louis MacNeice
Prayer before Birth . . . . . . Louis MacNeice

LOUIS MACNEICE

The Streets of Laredo (Louis MacNeice) . . . . . . William Alwyn
   (Variations on a Cowboy tune)
Refugee Blues (W. H. Auden) . . . . . . Elisabeth Lutyens
Johnny (W. H. Auden) . . . . . . Benjamin Britten

HEDLI ANDERSON

The Death of a Cat . . . . . . Louis MacNeice

LOUIS MACNEICE

Steinway Piano
Stage Managers
Al Collins and Paul Trautvetter

26th and, two days later, stood at the rail of the *Liberté* as she headed for the open sea.

Scanning the passenger list in their first-class cabin, MacNeice spotted the name John Berryman – travelling tourist-class with his wife Eileen – and invited them up for a drink. They had not met before. Berryman, however, had heard Hedli sing 'Tell me the Truth about Love', beautifully, at a New Year's Eve party at Clare College, Cambridge, in 1938; and had heard Louis read (badly, he thought, though he did not say so) in New York the following April. They all liked each other and spent every evening of the six-day crossing together, drinking and playing *vingt-et-un*. They parted company when the *Liberté* docked at Southampton on 4 May – the Berrymans were going on with her to Le Havre – but they made plans to meet in London that year.

It was not a happy homecoming for the MacNeices. Louis, in particular, was worried about Dan, who since his return had been staying with his parents' Oxford friend, Helen Cooke (now Gleadow), and her husband Rupert in their Chelsea flat. Far from moving back into Clarence Terrace, Dan kept out of his father's way, eventually taking refuge in country hotels, rather than face arguments about his future. As he had hoped, he was rejected for National Service (on the grounds of poor eyesight), and now wanted to return to America and live and work on his mother's farm. She, having lost a second husband but recovered the affections of her long-lost son, was desperate to have him. He could not, however, re-enter America without an immigrant visa but, being under twenty-one, he needed the consent of both parents before he could apply. His father withheld his consent and Dan took legal advice. Soon they were only communicating through solicitors. The one acting for Louis set out his client's reasons for withholding consent in a letter to Dodds, who had been proposed as an arbitrator between the parties. He asked Dodds if he could approve six paragraphs of a letter he proposed to send to Dan's solicitor:

13. The mother is a woman of abnormally strong emotional feeling. She had then recently written a number of hysterical and unbalanced letters to relatives and friends in England. She is of strongly possessive nature, egotistical and unscrupulous. A number of her letters contained untrue and indeed contradictory statements.

14. There was and is no evidence that the Egg farm is a commercial success.

Indeed the information in my client's possession is that for long periods it has not paid its way and that but for the private means of Mary it would have failed long since. In the best of years it has 'Broken even' financially. In your letter you mention gross takings, but not net. The house is filthy and neglected. The greater part of the land is uncultivated scrub.

15. The social life in and about the Egg farm is extremely limited. . . .

16. In these circumstances my client did not and does not consider that this is the environment in which his son should spend those years of his life when his character is at its most formative stage.

17. Nor does he consider that it is likely to lead to a happy result for Daniel. His mother, having deserted her first husband, and lost the affections of her second, has obviously transferred her abnormally strong emotional feelings to her son. She is, as I have said, of a possessive character. If her son, without other qualifications, should remain with her for a few years he will find himself completely dependent upon her emotionally and financially. Without a diploma or any other formal qualifications he would find it very difficult to find alternative employment in the United States, where such matters are more highly regarded than in this country. If without her consent he should wish to move away from her and marry someone of his own choice he would find it very difficult to do so. If, on the other hand, her affections should change in the future (as they have done in the past) he would find himself in an equally difficult position – without means and without qualifications for suitable employment.

18. It has occurred to me that perhaps you may not be prepared to accept from my client what I have written in paragraphs 13, 14 and 15. I would, in that event, suggest that you should refer to Professor and Mrs. Dodds . . . who have an intimate knowledge of both my client and Mary, who knew them both at the time of their marriage, who have been in correspondence with Mary from the time of her departure with Mr. Katzman onwards and who have visited the egg farm since the war. Professor Dodds is anxious only for the welfare of the boy whom he has known since his birth and if he can be of any assistance to you in helping you to find the correct solution for his problem he will be happy to do so.

It is not difficult to sympathize with father, mother, and son in this sad tug of war and love.

MacNeice's low spirits were not lifted by his return to work. The previous spring he had compiled and produced a radio-anthology, 'Mourning and Consolation', to mark the death of King George VI, and was now commissioned to prepare a programme marking the accession of Queen Elizabeth II. 'Time Hath Brought Me Hither', an interweaving of national past and present, was broadcast on 31 May, two days before the Coronation. It was followed by another of Mac-Neice's radio exercises for the left hand, an interweaving of personal past and present. 'Return to Atlantis', an exploration of his relationship with America, prompted his memory to other returns.

Back in April 1944, he had told Eliot that *Springboard* would probably be his last book of short poems for some considerable time. He was planning to write a long poem, of which he could only say

(1) that the main characters will be imagined contemporary individuals, but will exist on two planes, i.e. the symbolic as well as the naturalistic.
(2) That there will be some inter-shuttling of past and present (though in a much more modified way than in Ezra Pound's Cantos).
(3) That the total pattern will be very complex, and in fact rather comparable to the 'Faerie Queen' in its interlocking of episodes, sub-plots, and digressions which aren't really digressions.

The Faerie Queene had been one of MacNeice's favourite poems since he was first introduced to it at prep school. He refers to it often in his literary criticism, and had produced it, in twelve radio programmes, during the last quarter of 1952. These prepared the ground for his own, long-deferred, long poem.

August brought memories of August 1938, his flat on the other side of Regent's Park, and the exhilarating start of *Autumn Journal*; also the painful awareness that, in the past two and a half years, his poetic output had been one short poem. Depressed by this and by his deteriorating relationship with Dan, MacNeice 'suddenly and quite cold-bloodedly decided to write another long poem hinged to an autumn season'. Another sadness may also have contributed to that decision and to the shape of the poem. Gordon Herickx had died in July, and a desire to revisit him and other of his dead friends in the Underworld may have called to mind the start of one of the most famous of long poems:

> *Nel mezzo del cammin di nostra vita*
> *mi ritrovai per una selva oscura,*
> *che la diritta via era smarritta.*

Like Dante in *The Inferno*, MacNeice found himself in the middle of
the journey of his life in a dark wood where the straight way was lost.
Adopting Danter's *terza rima* stanza, he embarked on a new poetic
journey:

> August. Render to Caesar. Speak parrot: a gimmick for Poll.
> Castle your king in sand; as the dog days die,
> I hate the grey void that crams the guts of the doll
>
> And deplore each megrim and moan I scrawled on the sky
> In my hand of unformed smoke those fifteen years
> A-going, a-going, ago.

Hating the greyness of mechanical civilization (symbolized by the
parrot), and repudiating his own documentary *Autumn Journal*, he
turns to celebrate the lives of friends whose voices challenged the
mindless chatter of Poll:

> Gavin and Gwilym, and Aidan, Isabel, Calum, Aloys,
> Devlin, Hilary, Jenny, Blundell, McQuitty, Maguire,
> Stretton and Reilly and Price, Harrap and Owen and Boyce,
>
> Egdon and Evans and Costa and Wimbush and Gorman: a choir
> That never were all together; four of them now
> Have left their stalls.*

Where *Autumn Journal* had danced to the music of history, Mac-
Neice intended *Autumn Sequel* to move to a more formal measure. It
was to embody 'the wedding of myth and topicality', with less 'newspaper material' and 'a corresponding increase in the topical *human*
element'. An early synopsis gave as the subject of Canto II: 'Gavin
(dead) lust and death – Gwilym the poet and Poetry – the Fall and the
Devil'. The resulting sketches of Graham Shepard (Gavin) and Dylan
Thomas (Gwilym) have a fine exuberance and do for MacNeice's
friends something of what Yeats's celebrations of Lady Gregory and
John Synge did for his. The wedding of myth and topicality is nowhere
more successful than in Canto III, where MacNeice continues his
journey (as so often in *Autumn Journal* and elsewhere) by rail:

---

* See Appendix A on p. 487 for the names masked by pseudonyms in *Autumn Sequel*.

> my train goes west
> Crossing the stockbrokers at Gerrard's Cross
>
> And passing one more golf course, shaved and dressed
> With yellow flags but empty; on and on
> Until we stop beneath Mount Everest.

In a film-studio at Beaconsfield, he undertakes another commission, devising a commentary for Thomas Stobart's film, 'The Conquest of Everest':

> We stop – and start. All Beaconsfield is gone,
> Each slick red wall and roof, each dapper row
> Of pompons and each deft automaton
>
> Trimming the lawns, all are submerged below
> The icefall tumbling from the Western Cwm
> Above which deserts of unsounded snow
>
> Brood, above which again one ominous plume
> Flies from the crest of what was Peak Fifteen
> Which even now knows fifteen brands of doom,
>
> Twenty-nine thousand and two feet high, a clean
> Rebuttal of the verities of Bucks
> Where a projector clamps it on a screen
>
> And I write words about it; gaps and rucks
> Are smoothed away, the silences of ice
> And solitudes of height washed out in flux,
>
> A weir of whirling celluloid.

In an essay of 1941–2, MacNeice had written: 'we're bound for the Holy Mountain'. He had recently published his study of Yeats who, in 1934, had written an introduction to a translation of Shri Purowit Swami's *The Holy Mountain*. That book and his glimpse of Nanga Parbat in 1947 have merged with the mountain and water of his own mythological terrain. So, at the Canto's end, returning to Clarence Terrace, his own expulsion from the Carrickfergus garden is subconsciously remembered and re-enacted:

> A harsh voice cries All Out – all out of Regent's Park,

Of Everest, of Eden – casts a doubt
If we were ever in. The whole massif is dark,

The one tree silent, one day (to-day) ruled out, all out.'

There is no single myth sustaining *Autumn Sequel*, as the Grail legend underpins *The Waste Land*, so much as a number of mythic fragments. On 19 October, MacNeice took the train to Oxford and, after a business lunch with Davin discussing *The Character of Ireland*, walked back to Merton. He then caught a bus to the village of Old Marston, where he found Dodds 'among his books', and in due course accompanied him to dinner in Christ Church. They sat late, talking with Ernst Stahl, and next morning MacNeice returned to London. Later, transforming that simple visit into two glowing cantos (XII and XIII), his pencil tapped no subterranean reservoirs of myth. Other cantos called for other strategies. The eighteenth, in the early synopsis, was to have been about the British Museum, Egypt, Assyria, and Greece; and the twentieth, about the Pythia.

On 9 November, however, MacNeice heard – first from Bob Pocock and then on the 9 o'clock news – that Dylan Thomas had died in America. That evening, a number of Thomas's friends assembled at 2 Clarence Terrace for a kind of wake. Margaret Gardiner would later recall how, when the other guests had left and she was putting on her coat to leave, Louis touched her arm:

'Don't go yet, you,' he pleaded. 'Please stay a little longer. Please.'
Seeing the look of desperation in his eyes, 'Of course I will', I said.
'Good-night, then', called Hedli, going up the stairs.
Louis and I went into the room where he worked; he stirred the fire and put on coal and we sat close to it, warming our hands. This death had hit him hard and although I couldn't share his grief, I could at least help him to fend off sleep and that, I realized, was what he wanted. He didn't dare to sleep that night, for sleep was too dangerously akin to death. He had to stay awake. So we sat and talked until a grey light began to trickle through the curtains and the first sounds of the wakening town could be heard, single and distinct before they gradually increased and merged into a general hubbub. It was after six; the night was over and I went home.

Ever since he was five and 'the bad dreams came', his nights had been visited with fears that did not trouble his days. He disliked sleeping in a room by himself, and now – with death in the next room, as it were – dared not surrender to sleep at all.

Before long, Canto XVIII of *Autumn Sequel* had become a 'Lament for the Makers' and for one in particular:

> A bulbous Taliessin, a spruce and small
>
> Bow-tied Silenus roistering his way
> Through lands of fruit and fable, well aware
> That even Dionysus has his day
>
> And cannot take it with him. Debonair,
> He leant against the bar till his cigarette
> Became one stream of ash sustained in air
>
> Through which he puffed his talk.

He was buried in Laugharne on 24 November. MacNeice (wearing shoes bought, with Dylan, for Yeats's funeral) followed his friend's coffin, in bright sunlight, to the grave. Afterwards, at the wake, he tried to comfort the weeping widow, saying:

'Look, Caitlin, that's not really Dylan in the box there. That's just the body, the shell of what he was. The real Dylan is with us, with all of us always, in his spirit, his words, his poems. He's got away from that box and he's beyond it. He can never die – don't you see, Caitlin?'

'No Louis', she replied, 'if he's not in the box, he's not in the bed either.'

MacNeice would put it better in an obituary: 'What we remember is not a literary figure to be classified in the text-book but something quite unclassifiable, a wind that bloweth where it listeth, a wind with a chuckle in its voice and news from the end of the world.'

When Thomas's funeral displaced the priestess of Apollo as the subject of MacNeice's Canto XX, he returned 'To Wales once more, grasping a golden bough', but it does not admit him to the Underworld. He cannot accept the conclusions of pagan myth or (though he considers the possibility of 'an afterlife') Christian theology. As his autumn journey nears its end, however, the sceptical poet seems to grow sceptical of his scepticism. The last three cantos are set on 23, 24 and 25 December and, when they were broadcast on 1 August 1954,

MacNeice introduced them with the statement that

the whole poem in a sense has been approaching Christmas. But if I were asked whether this were a Christian poem, I should not know what to reply. All I know is that I have been saturated from my childhood in Christian symbolism and that some of these symbols seem to me still most valid. And I would like once more to repeat Walt Whitman's lines:

> Do I contradict myself?
> Very well then I contradict myself . . . .

Returning from Norwich, where he had been taking part in the BBC's 'round the world' Christmas programme, he reflects:

> So it goes on, the train goes on, the horn
> Of horror sounds no longer; I can smell
> A waft of frankincense, maybe this morn
>
> Is really Christmas, maybe (who can tell?)
> The Kings are on this train. All that I know
> Is that good will must mean both will and well
>
> And that, crowded or empty, fast or slow,
> This train is getting somewhere. I return
> To my own seat and wait and, also serving, go
>
> Irrevocably forward.

MacNeice's echo of the Christian Milton's sonnet on his blindness – 'They also serve who only stand and wait' – suggests he was close to believing the truth of the message his father had so often proclaimed on other Christmas mornings.

The Stahls were guests at Hedli's Christmas dinner, but their cheerful presence at the decorated table could not compensate for a painful absence. After months of wrangling, Dan had obtained a Queen's Counsel's opinion that enabled the American Embassy to issue a visa, despite his father's opposition, and he had booked a passage on the *Flandre*. Father and son had not met for many months and Dan was not anxious to see him now. He was persuaded, however, by family friends that, if he did not say goodbye in person, he would live to regret it. Accordingly, on 9 December they met for a couple of hours at Eric Mosbacher's house. Rather than skate on conversational thin ice, they talked of *The Conquest of Everest*; Louis asking if Dan had noticed a technical lapse in the film. Close to the summit, one of the climbers had shown a bare hand – that could not have survived, ungloved, at such an altitude – indicating footage that must have been shot elsewhere. At the last, coming someway down the mountain, Louis gave Dan a green and brown plaid scarf (which he would put away like a religious relic and wear for the first time, thirty years later, when he visited his father's grave) and, ungloved, they shook hands.

Perhaps because Louis' relations with his own parents had been distant in different ways, he was never as close to his own children as they would wish. (At his death, Bimba would say she had lost the father she never had.) He loved them, but was not a demonstrative man and had difficulty in displaying either the affection or the attention that they needed. However, he felt Dan's defection – as it seemed to him – deeply, and it may be that, reopening the wounds of Mary's defection and that – again as it seemed to him – of his mother, Dan's departure contributed to his father's later periods of depression.

Dan appeared – only to disappear 'across the Atlantic' – in Canto XXIII of *Autumn Sequel*. On 20 January 1954, MacNeice told Eliot that he had 'now finished a complete draft' of the poem and, four days later, he read Canto XVIII, his 'Lament for the Makers', at the Globe Theatre in a programme entitled 'Homage to Dylan Thomas'. This he organized, with other members of the Group Theatre, to raise money for the Dylan Thomas Memorial Fund, which had been set up 'to assist his widow in the support and education of his three young children'. MacNeice was one of the distinguished signatories of a widely published letter announcing the Fund and calling for subscriptions. Over the next few months, he wrote dozens of letters soliciting contributions and, on 14 February, took part in another fund-raising reading. This was held at the Royal Festival Hall. More than 3,000 people came to hear him and Day Lewis, Spender and Watkins. They made a profit of £633.

John and Eileen Berryman, on their way home the previous summer, had contacted the MacNeices and been invited to a party at Clarence Terrace. They found their host in boisterous good humour, but sensed trouble in the air between him and Hedli. This may have been no more than a domestic trough of low pressure, but a climatic change was on the way. It came from the south: from Rothwell House where, with the growth of the BBC, MacNeice and his fellow producers were spending an increasing amount of time on administration. There were more and more letters, memoranda, and reports to read and write, more and more meetings to attend, with a consequent decline in creativity. MacNeice wrote nineteen programmes in 1943, but only three in 1953. This and the simultaneous decline in his poetic output were causing him to 'lament/The maker [he] might have been'. The more dispirited and frustrated he became, the more he drank. Listing his and Hedli's 'likes' and 'dislikes' in a letter, he put 'standing in pubs' among *his* likes and among *her* dislikes. He was standing there longer and longer at lunch-time and after work, talking to friends and colleagues – producers, actors, and actresses.

One of the actresses whose company he enjoyed was Cécile Chevreau. They had met in 1944, when Gilliam had introduced them, telling MacNeice: 'You must use this girl. She's good'. She was, and he did – in 'The Golden Ass' (1944), a revised version of 'He Had a Date' (1949), 'One Eye Wild' (1952), 'Twelve Days of Christmas' (1953), and 'Prisoner's Progress' (1954). His first new programme in 1954 had been an adaptation of Goronwy Rees's novel, *Where No Wounds Were*, a study of a Nazi prisoner during the Second World War. His second programme owed something to the first. MacNeice called 'Prisoner's Progress' 'a fable of imprisonment and escape'. The 'Browns' are at war with the 'Greys' and, in segregated sections of a prison camp, 'Grey' men and 'Grey' women are plotting escape. Their tunnels meet and, in due course, one man, Waters (MacNeice's choice of name is as significant as his title's variation on *Pilgrim's Progress*), together with one woman, Alison, reach the mountain that lies between the camp and freedom. Waters, a peacetime mountaineer, helps his companion up the steep ascent. They shelter in a cave, then discover they are in love, and have all but reached the summit when they hear the sound of pursuing dogs. This is followed by a burst of automatic rifle-fire, and 'Prisoner's Progress' ends with the ghostly strains of its theme-song, 'Lavender's Blue', on the accordion of a fellow-prisoner killed earlier in the play.

Alison was acted by Cécile Chevreau. After a rehearsal, MacNeice took her for a drink at The Cock Tavern, near Broadcasting House,

Cécile Chevreau

and said: 'I've got to tell you something.'

'What?' she asked.

'You know, don't you?' he replied.

'Do I?' she said.

'I love you. You know that, don't you?'

She had been aware of a new warmth in his manner towards her, and was physically attracted to him. He stroked her breast in the taxi on their way home (she dropping him at Clarence Terrace before heading north to prepare supper for her husband). From that there developed a tender friendship. They would often drink together and, for two years on and off, would lunch in a Soho Greek Taverna. They did once go to bed together, in Clarence Terrace, when Hedli was away. It was not a great success, but their tenderness continued.

Hedli as yet knew nothing of this, and the MacNeices had a tranquil summer holiday in Ireland. They returned to the good news that 'Prisoner's Progress' had been awarded the prestigious Premio Italiano Prize (worth a million lire, or about £575) and to the happy prospect of another break from the BBC. Louis had been granted three months' unpaid leave to enable him to take up a Visiting Lectureship in poetry and drama, financed with a grant from the Rockefeller Foundation, at Sarah Lawrence College in Bronxville, New York.

Taking the eleven-year-old Bimba back to boarding school, they embarked on the *Queen Elizabeth*, which reached New York on 27 September. Louis gave an inaugural lecture, on 'The Poet Today', at Sarah Lawrence on 5 October and, shortly afterwards, set off with Hedli on a whistle-stop tour of midwestern universities. Husband and wife gave joint recitals of poems and songs at the University of Kansas on the 15th; at the University of Iowa on the 18th; at the University of Minnesota, Duluth Campus, on the 19th; at Concordia College, Minnesota, on the 20th; at the University of Minnesota on the 21st; in Wilmington, Ohio, on the 25th; and at Geneseo College, New York State, on 2 November.

Returning to Sarah Lawrence, MacNeice set about directing student actors in an 'experimental production' of Euripides' *Hippolytus*. He took particular pains to coach them in the correct pronunciation and

Louis and Hedli on the *Queen Elizabeth*

rhythm of the Greek, and the play was performed with some success on 8, 9, and 10 December. In between rehearsals, there was time for expeditions to New York. On one of these there was a lunch with Eleanor Clark and her husband, Robert Penn Warren, at which Eleanor, then pregnant with her second child, fell over in the restaurant and injured her back. A doctor was called, who refused to treat her until a satisfactory fee had been agreed. Sadly, but not surprisingly, in view of their acrimonious exchanges, there was no meeting with Mary and Dan.

The MacNeices' return journey on the *Queen Elizabeth*, and indeed their 1954 American tour as a whole, were less happy than those of the previous year. Husband and wife had grown to dislike sharing a stage together, and Hedli would later trace the disintegration of their marriage to the jealousies and resentments of this trip. Their homecoming was less than happy for another reason. Awaiting them were the first reviews of *Autumn Sequel*. *The Times* had warmly welcomed Cantos I and II, when broadcast earlier in the year, but had reservations about the completed poem:

the main difference between *Autumn Journal* and *Autumn Sequel* is a disturbing one: it is the difference between the universal and the particular, prospect and retrospect. *Autumn Sequel* is nostalgic, not prophetic: it looks back over its shoulder beyond the fire-blackened pit of the war: it is, almost, an ironic gloss on its predecessor.

MacNeice could hardly argue with this, and must have expected some adverse reaction to what his title-page challengingly described as 'A Rhetorical Poem in XXVI Cantos', but he cannot have expected it to be gunned down in the hitherto friendly pages of *The New Statesman*. Entitling his review 'Lament for a Maker', A. Alvarez there handcuffed MacNeice to Auden and opened fire on them both:

Mr. MacNeice used to be a poet of two voices. One was that of the serious, sensitive, individual minor poet, the classics don. He was the best of the Oxford group, except for Auden, and the most responsible: his subjects less questionable, his dignity and curiosity in the right place, his responses more frankly, though no less deeply sentimental, his tone restrained and assured. He lacked that intolerable cuteness of his colleagues. Above all, he alone of them seemed genuinely to care for the intelligence. Even Auden had little time for that, working instead by sleights of cleverness and oddity which succeeded because he was very clever, very quick and very disturbed. Yet if the information came past it came primarily to lend an air to a pose. Not so Mr. MacNeice. When most himself he was a reflective poet and – this was least fashionable – unpretentious. Things, situations, ideas interested him more than his own case-book. He was sensitive, not nervy. Hence the success of *Snow*, *August* and *Morning Sun* and the nostalgic, though rather vague concern of *Autumn Journal*. That was his own voice.

The other voice was that of the Oxford man, smart, irreverent, quick with his cultured references, one of the Auden gang. It did not ring so true.

Autumn Sequel, Alvarez went on, 'is in his modish vein', and he pointed to a number of weak links in the long chain of MacNeice's *terza rima*. It does, indeed, contain some strained rhymes and mixed metaphors but fewer than he implies and they hardly justify his dismissive conclusion:

The voice no longer comes fresh from the page. But then how could it, when making the best of a bad job is the theme of the poem? .... The Thirties entertained. It was not, finally, enough. *Autumn Sequel*, like *The Age of Anxiety*, shows that they have become weary and knowing and bored with it all. All we can do is, with them, lament the makers they might have been.

There is no record of MacNeice's reaction to this review, but he was too good a critic not to recognize the validity of some of its charges; and it may have had a salutary effect in helping to make him the maker he would become.

CHAPTER 23

Visitations and Revisitations

The Indian Ocean is still like Belfast Lough.
Letter to Hedli, 5 November 1955

MacNeice may not have enjoyed his 1954 trip to America, but it did not quench his taste for foreign travel. On the contrary, hardly was he back before he had proposed a programme that would involve a journey (without Hedli) that had haunted his imagination for more than thirty years. After visiting the British Museum as a thirteen-year-old schoolboy, he had noted in his diary: 'Mummies, pictures from the Book of the Dead, mummified cats, calves, crocodiles etc. Toys, scarabs, models of funerary boats'. In January 1955, his proposal for a programme about the Nile was accepted, and on 24 February he flew to Cairo, where for three days he was shown the sights, before flying on to the Northern Sudan. From Khartoum, he flew south again to Juba. There, a congenial expatriate Scot lent him a car and driver to take him the hundred miles to Nimule on the Sudanese/Uganda border. With a servant and an armed Game Scout 'riding shot-gun' in the back seat, he felt like 'the Sahib on safari'. They reached the Rest House that was their destination after dark, but they could see the Nile below them. As he would later describe the river in a letter to Hedli, 'it kept talking away (approaching the Fula Rapids) in competition with the pressure lamp & the crickets until all three were drowned out by wind, rain & lightning.' At dawn, they crossed the Nile in a narrow canoe and walked for several miles along its bank, seeing buffaloes, elephants, and hippos – '4 great knobby heads, pinkish, as if wearing goggles'. These 'goggled hippo' would resurface, like much else in his letter, in a poem called 'The Rest House'.

Returning to Khartoum on 7 March, he flew to Aswan on the 11th

The PS *Sudan*

and boarded the paddle-steamer *Sudan* that was about to make its first trip to Cairo since the War. His initial impressions of the boat and his fellow passengers were not encouraging. He foresaw a trip that would be 'a *penitenza*', like his 1928 voyage to Norway with his father, but he soon found some congenial company and began to enjoy their stately progress down the great river. Every day after breakfast or after lunch, they would go ashore 'to look at Antiquities'. He was duly impressed by the majestic temples at Luxor and Karnak and by the richly decorated shafts and burial chambers in the Valley of the Kings. Every evening, when it grew too dark for the helmsman to see the ever-shifting sand banks, one of the crew would swim ashore with a rope and the steamer would be moored for the night. He told Hedli:

The brown hills go pink at sunset & the sand flats go sort of lilac. The other evening we passed, at a place called Beni Hasan, some very steep high cliffs with half way up a horizontal row of tombs in them, just like a row of portholes.

Once again, a letter serves as a draft of a poem – 'Beni Hasan':

> It came to me on the Nile my passport lied
> Calling me dark who am grey. In the brown cliff

413

A row of tombs, of portholes, stared and stared as if
They were the long-dead eyes of beasts inside
Time's cage, black eyes on eyes that stared away
Lion-like focused on some different day
On which, on a long-term view, it was I, not they, had died.

MacNeice's sepulchral reveries were interrupted on the afternoon of 23 March, when a BBC colleague appeared in a motor-launch and rushed him back to Cairo to give a talk on Egyptian radio. At the end of that week he flew to Alexandria and, three days later, to Athens (there 'renewing Auld Acquaintance'), in preference to Zurich and/or Paris where Hedli had suggested she might meet him. Returning to London, by way of Rome, in the first week of April, he set about organizing fragments from his Egyptian notebooks into another of his impressionistic portraits – this time, of a river rather than a city. The resulting programme, 'The Fullness of the Nile', was not one of his best. Information and poetry are less well integrated than in his 'Portrait of Rome', for example, indicating that it was an 'exercise for the left hand', undertaken while the right was busy with poems. One of these, 'Beni Hasan', had its first airing in the programme.

On 28 May, MacNeice was off again – to Edinburgh, where one night in a pub Robin Richardson of the BBC asked a friend if he had a car. The answer being 'yes', Richardson said: 'I've Louis MacNeice with me, rather the worse for wear, and we've got to get to Pitlochry. Could you drive us?' The friend agreed and the jolting of the Morris 8 sobered the poet sufficiently for him to realize that the driver was just the sort of 'character' he liked. Stocky and red-bearded, Sam Wells was a painter, sculptor, bar-fighter, and raconteur of explosive energy and considerable charm. They booked into a Pitlochry hotel and, when the other drinkers had gone to bed, the poet and the painter shared a last bottle of whisky. MacNeice was depressed and told Wells he was finished as a poet. 'Lightning never strikes twice', he said. Wells answered that he could show him a tree in Scotland that had been struck several times.

Next day, driving back to Edinburgh, they stopped to buy another bottle of whisky and drank it in a field beside a river. MacNeice returned to the subject of his stalled poems, saying 'I just can't get started', and once again Wells told him he was being defeatist.

They parted in Edinburgh, but the following morning MacNeice rang from his hotel to say he had remembered he was due at a meeting of the Dylan Thomas Memorial Fund trustees and wondered if Wells would drive him to London. The good-natured painter agreed. He was promised a bed for the night but, when they reached Clarence Terrace, Hedli looked him up and down with disapproval and said to Louis: 'You know perfectly well he can't stay with us.' The guest room was apparently occupied. Understandably embarrassed, Louis arranged to meet him for lunch next day in The Stag. When he turned up, Wells – to his amazement – was effusively greeted by Hedli. She brought him a drink and said, 'You must stay with us tonight.' He confessed his bafflement to Reggie Smith, who explained how, when MacNeice had told his friends of being rescued by a red-headed Scot, a Good Samaritan with a Morris 8, he (Reggie) had said: 'Oh, you mean Sam Wells.' Realizing that she had turned a friend of Reggie's from her door, Hedli hurriedly made amends: she insisted Sam stay for a week at 2 Clarence Terrace, and they were soon firm friends.

Sometime in the spring or summer of 1955, she learnt that Louis was involved with Cécile. The MacNeices were at a party in Wapping given by Bertie Rodgers. While the men were talking rugger, Hedli, Margaret Gardiner, and Olivia Manning went off to a pub. There, Olivia suddenly asked Hedli 'Have you seen anything of Cécile lately?' 'Cécile?' said Hedli, blankly. 'Yes,' replied Olivia, 'Louis' girl.' Not surprisingly, Hedli was distressed and angry, but her subsequent recriminations were to prove the grit that produced a black pearl.

On 29 July, the MacNeices left London for a family holiday in Dorset, where they rented a house, which was to be the setting for a darkly mysterious poem called 'House on a Cliff':

> Indoor the tang of a tiny oil lamp. Outdoors
> The winking signal on the waste of sea.
> Indoors the sound of the wind. Outdoors the wind.
> Indoors the locked heart and the lost key.
>
> Outdoors the chill, the void, the siren. Indoors
> The strong man pained to find his red blood cools,
> While the blind clock grows louder, faster. Outdoors
> The silent moon, the garrulous tides she rules.

> Indoors ancestral curse-cum-blessing. Outdoors
> The empty bowl of heaven, the empty deep.
> Indoors a purposeful man who talks at cross
> Purposes, to himself, in a broken sleep.

Hedli would later say that this poem 'has to do with Cécile'. She would not elaborate. The secret she was guarding may have been the fact that, in Dorset, her husband found himself impotent (a Freudian interpretation of 'the lost key' may not be too fanciful), but it is more important to recognize the poem's relation to MacNeice's personal mythology. This 'House on a Cliff' can be traced back – by way of 'the brown cliff' of 'Beni Hasan' (its tombs overlooking the Nile), by way of 'The Rest House' and the house of 'Cushendun' (both overlooking water) – to Carrickfergus Rectory with the ticking of its death-watch beetle, its windows opening on the cemetery and the sea; the house of the poet's 'dozing childhood', where every night the trains had brought him 'assurance and comfort',

> Till all was broken by that menace from the sea,
> The steel-bosomed siren calling bitterly.

The MacNeices returned from Dorset on 1 September, and Louis was soon preparing himself for another BBC expedition. He had never been to Yorkshire and, the year before, had suggested to Andrew Stewart (recently promoted from Head of North Region to Controller of Home Service) that he be commissioned to tour the county with his favourite Yorkshireman, the actor John Sharp. The proposal was accepted and, writing to his successor, Stewart commented: 'the interest here, as you will agree, is not so much in Yorkshire but in what MacNeice's imagination makes of the theme'. As so often, his imagination found a classical precedent.

A Yorkshire Virgil met an Irish Dante at Darlington Station, off a train from Edinburgh (where he had been attending the Festival) on 10 September, and together they set off in Sharp's Morris Minor on a slow circuit of North Riding pubs. By nightfall, they had reached the remote Tan Hill Inn, the highest pub in Yorkshire, and were talking to shepherds. One, tapping MacNeice with his stick, said: 'Nah then, tha allus wants ter put a Teeswater tup on a Wesleydale yow ter gie thee a sturdy cross that's thrang i't fleece.' Drugged with pipe-smoke, Louis nodded; then nodded off, waking later to hear what he thought was Danish – 'yahn, tayhn, mether, mimph, hither, lither, anver, danver' – but proved to be an explanation of sheep-counting. They spent the night in The Red Lion at Longthwaite, and next day continued their slow progress round the country. They saw West Riding towns, the East Riding coast, abbeys and great houses, the caverns at Stump Cross and the Dripping Well at Knaresborough. MacNeice was fascinated by the objects this had encased in stone: particularly a dead cat that must have reminded him of mummified cats in the British Museum and statuettes from the tombs of the Pharaohs.

Sharp introduced him to Harry Ramsden, owner of the famous fish and chip emporium; to Kit Calvert, renowned Methodist lay-preacher and translator of the Bible into Yorkshire dialect; to cattle-drovers, cricketers, instrumentalists, and members of the Upper Nidderdale Agricultural Society. 'They loved him', said Sharp. As a grand finale, they spent their last day at the Pateley Bridge Show, watching sheep-dog trials and a cricket match; listening to the Hammond's Sauce Works Prize Brass Band; and drinking John Smith's Magnet Draught at the rate of three pints to the hour.

However, before MacNeice could distil the experience of those nine days into the three ninety-minute programmes he was planning, Gilliam called him back to London and a new assignment. He and another scriptwriter, Ritchie Calder, were to prepare an ambitious programme for Christmas Day and, because of MacNeice's successful 'features' on India and Pakistan, he was chosen to gather material in those countries and Ceylon.

The eve of his departure was evidently darkened with a domestic storm caused by the situation with Cécile. Arriving in Karachi on 21 October, Louis wrote to reassure Hedli that Cécile 'needn't impinge' on their marriage:

I suggest just 4 considerations (after which I'll drop it & return to Pakistan etc.!). (1) There's lots of evidence that a woman can be fond, or even v. fond, of a chap without wanting to break up his home life. (2) As regards your 'pattern which repeats itself', a pattern might *appear* to be repeating itself up to a point (after all someone who has charm will continue to use charm) without there being any intention of developing it to where it had gone before

– especially if its previous development had painful associations. (3) If C. were primarily romantic as well as practical, she might prefer the pattern *not* to develop as before, while on practical grounds she would certainly see the snags of such a development. (4) Even if C. were impingement-minded, what happens after all does depend on A [himself]! And A. says there's *no need to worry*.

Karachi had swollen by a million refugees since he had been there before, and he was glad to move on to Lahore, where he got a permit to consume liquor, which had to be drunk in the 'Permit Room' of his hotel. (In this way, the Government of Pakistan allowed for the base needs of non-Muslims.)

Armed with a Midget tape recorder, he toured the city in search of voices for the Christmas programme, and was particularly delighted by the song (in couplets) with which a street sweet-seller hawked his wares. There, he began a song of his own, called 'Return to Lahore', a draft of which he included in a letter to Hedli of 28 October. By then he was in Delhi and, the following day, flew on to Madras and Ceylon, where for a week he recorded busily. One evening, writing to Hedli, he told her: 'Outside this hotel the Indian Ocean is grey – just like Belfast Lough.' Four evenings later, he wrote again: 'The Indian Ocean is still like Belfast Lough'. For MacNeice, every ocean was the Atlantic, his father's ocean and his own.

Returning to London, he began to put the Christmas programme together. It was to be called 'The Star We Follow', and would begin and end with a sentence he had heard many times in the church of St Nicholas, Carrickfergus: 'And, lo, the star, which they saw in the east, went before them, till it came and stood over where the young child was.' The ancient theme, however, was to have a modern dimension and, on 29 November, MacNeice and programme's co-producers, John Bridges and Gilliam, went up to Cheshire to record the pioneer of a new science, radio astronomy. Professor Bernard Lovell set the Magi's star in a modern context. He said:

Since the dawn of human consciousness man has studied the sky and the stars. During the last few hundred years telescopes have revealed more and more of the majesty of the universe . . . . Ten years ago at the end of the war I came to Jodrell Bank. The lorry-driver left me alone with a trailer of surplus radar equipment stranded in the mud of this Cheshire field with the fuel pipes of the diesel generator blocked with ice. Now in that same field we are surrounded with some of the best equipped laboratories in the world and I'm speaking now from a room full of complicated apparatus connected to a great steel structure which I can see out of the window. It's one of the many radio telescopes which we've built here during the last ten years .... The noise you are going to hear now is made by radio waves that have travelled through space for two hundred million years.

The music of the spheres – and that of the composer, Matyas Seiber, commissioned for the programme – introduced a selection of the voices MacNeice and Calder had recorded round the world and arranged with a linking commentary read by the actor Michael Hordern. 'The Star We Follow' was broadcast on the afternoon of Christmas Day, and was itself followed by the National Anthem and the Queen's message to her Commonwealth.

MacNeice's first programme of the new year had been written before he left for the East the previous October and, like 'The Star We Follow', had a biblical theme. 'Also Among the Prophets' tells the story of Saul's anointing by the prophet Samuel and subsequent fall from grace. This, too, had an important musical dimension and Seiber was commissioned to compose a score giving prominence to the harp with which David, first, calms the jealous king and, at the last, accompanies his lament for Saul and Jonathan. When the play was broadcast, live, on 5 February, MacNeice cut Seiber's coda. He wrote to the composer to apologize and explain that, for dramatic reasons, he had felt obliged to omit the lengthy final chorus, but Seiber was not mollified. There followed a sharp exchange of letters in which MacNeice quoted Archie Harding on the subject of incidental music for radio drama: 'composers', he had said, 'are not there to write beautiful music, they are there to help us when we need them'.

In this programme and those that followed it, we can hear MacNeice rehearsing instruments of central importance in his symbolism: the bardic harp (to be invoked in the title of his autobiography, *The Strings are False*), bell, and siren. 'Bow Bells', broadcast on 17 June, offered 'a salute to the mother church of Cockneydom ... St Mary-le-Bow ... destroyed in the Great Fire of 1666 and burnt once more through enemy action in 1941 ... now about to be restored'. A week after this programme had revisited MacNeice's London of the Blitz, shaken with bells and sirens, he crossed the Channel to gather material for another, similar short feature. On 24 June, he was in Rouen watching its citizens celebrate two things at once: the fifth centenary of the Rehabilitation of Joan of Arc, and the reopening of the city's famous cathedral. Both had been burnt by the British: Joan of Arc in 1431, and the cathedral in 1944 (by RAF bombers aiming for the bridges over the Seine). Rouen's docks reminded MacNeice of Belfast. He called his evocation of the city's past and present 'Spires and Gantries', and ended it with a weak poem which itself ends:

> So, between glamour and big business,
> Picture postcards and brass tacks,
> This town exists upon the surface –
> Yet such a surface can wear thin.
>
> And show us gulfs of joy and horror
> And bring a name of life, remind
> Trader and tripper, bell and siren,
> That Joan heard voices from within.

No less audible to the poet are the voices of his father's former church bells and the sirens of the Belfast shipyards.

He had revisited Carrickfergus in imagination, and probably in person, two months before. His stepmother had died, in her eighty-second year, on 8 April; her coffin was placed in St Nicholas on the 12th, and she was buried the following day. MacNeice admired and loved her, and in an oblique elegy, 'Death of an Old Lady', would conflate her passing with that of the great ship he had glimpsed on the grey Loch forty-four years before:

> At five in the morning there were grey voices
> Calling three times through the dank fields;
> The ground fell away beyond the voices
> Forty long years to the wrinkled lough
> That had given a child one shining glimpse
> Of a boat so big it was named Titanic.
>
> Named or called? For a name is a call –
> Shipyard voices at five in the morning,
> As now for this old tired lady who sails
> Towards her own iceberg calm and slow;

We hardly hear the screws, we hardly
Can think her back her four score years.

They called and ceased. Later the night nurse
Handed over, the day went down
To the sea in a ship, it was grey April,
The daffodils in her garden waited
To make her a wreath, the iceberg waited;
At eight in the evening the ship went down.

It is hard to account for the *Titanic*'s hold on the poet's imagination, other than to suggest a subconscious association between its loss (against a cliff of 'petrified' water) and the loss of his mother (to a psychiatric institution) in the same year, 1912. What is clear is that his lyric impulse had returned, as Sam Wells had prophesied, and at the end of August he sent Eliot the typescript of a new book of poems entitled *Visitations*. Welcoming it, Eliot wrote: 'It is a small collection but a good one, and I am very happy with it.'

While it is clear that MacNeice's writing for radio at times siphoned off creative energy that might otherwise have gone into poems, it is also clear that what I have called the work of his left hand could contribute to that of his right, and that the same blood supply, the same imagination, nourished them both. Having bundled off his new poems, he set to work on a new radio script. Called '*Carpe Diem*', it is 'a tribute to the Roman poet Horace' (long one of MacNeice's favourites) in the form of a portrait of 'a modern Horatian'. He is older than his portraitist – old enough to have fought in the Great War – but the voice is at once unmistakable and prophetic. Tended by the last of his loves ('. . . *age iam meorum finis amorum* . . .'), he remembers the others: one with whom he danced to the jazz of 'Alexander's Ragtime Band'; another with whom he danced in Trafalgar Square the night the War ended. And he remembers his father: how his face changed when he opened his morning paper to read of the loss of the *Titanic*; how 'he'd supported Asquith over Home Rule but . . . strongly disapproved of the Dublin Easter Rising'. The modern Horatian quotes a poem, 'The Character of a Happy Life', by Sir Henry Wotton, 'which more or less fits [his] father':

How happy is he born and taught
That serveth not another's will!

421

Whose armour is his honest thought,
And simple truth his utmost skill.

Whose passions not his masters are,
Whose soul is still prepared for death;
Untied unto the world by care
Of public fame, or private breath.

His father may have been 'rather a museum piece' but, by contrast, his son sees himself as 'a failure – to use that nasty word, an escapist'. '*Carpe Diem*' was broadcast on 8 October, by which time MacNeice was preparing to escape from Rothwell House for a month in the sun.

He had been approached in August by Sean Graham, Director of the Gold Coast Film Unit, who told him – over lunch – that he had admired one of his feature programmes about India and Pakistan, and suggested that MacNeice write a film script. In March 1957, the Gold Coast was to become the sovereign state of Ghana, the first of Britain's African colonies to be granted independence, and Graham was planning a celebratory film. MacNeice liked the idea; discussed it with Gilliam; and was allowed to take unpaid leave, on the understanding that he would also write a script for the BBC.

On 13 October, he flew to Accra and four days later wrote to Hedli: 'I am enjoying this place; it's more interesting, much more colourful, & jollier than, say, the Sudan.' He went to a Yam Festival and watched 'a great cavalcade of chiefs carried in so-called palanquins which are a cross between a canoe and a coffin', each of them shaded by a brightly coloured umbrella. One very minor chief, he reported, was said to have notepaper headed: 'Prince of Princes, King of Kings, Ruler of Rulers & Vice-Captain of the Accra Football Club.'

On 22 October, an engaging young Australian, Bob Raymond, drove him westward along the coast. They visited forts and ports before heading inland down arrow-straight jungle roads to Kumasi, the ancient capital of Ashanti. After one of the most exhausting weeks of his life, he returned to Accra and, two days later, was on his way to the Northern Territories. His letters to Hedli are full of the vivid detail that would reappear in his film and radio scripts: 'a woman making a pot without a wheel. A perfect circle; she smooths it with a large pebble & with leaves dipped in water.' Back again in Accra on 2 November, he heard the 'appalling bloody news' of the Anglo-French attack on Egypt. With the hatred of violence born of his Irish experience, he thought it an act of unprincipled colonial aggression and told Hedli: 'Eden & Co. must be off their heads.' A last expedition took him eastward to Togoland for five days, and on the 16th he flew home.

Before setting to work on his film-script, he wrote a radio one that had been long in gestation. Ten years earlier, he had written of a crippled busker:

> *Ave Maria*! A sluice is suddenly opened
> Making Orphan Street a conduit for a fantastic voice;
> The Canadian sergeant turns to stone in his swagger,
> The painted girls, the lost demobbed, the pinstripped accountant listen
> As the swan-legged cripple straddled on flightless wings of crutches
> Hitting her top note holds our own lame hours in equipoise . . . .

The singer was Wyn Cutler who, accompanied on the banjo by her husband, Bill, was a familiar figure in the streets of London's West End. They and the MacNeices had been introduced by the actor Stephen Murray and, while he was in Accra, Louis had asked Hedli to find out the songs in Wyn Cutler's repertoire. He now used her as the lead-in to an 'entertainment' for the turn of the year. 'From Bard to Busker' was broadcast on 30 December and travelled the roads with minstrels, skalds, and story-tellers from ancient Greece to modern Ghana. His interest in the figure of the story-teller influenced his next programme, 'The Birth of Ghana', broadcast on 22 February 1957. This is structured round a debate between an old Drummer, who believes in God and talks in proverbs, and a young Modernist, who believes in Progress and talks in clichés. Antithesis leads to synthesis, a marriage of old and new, but attentive listeners would have been in no doubt where the scriptwriter's sympathies lay. This perspective was to prove a problem when he came to write the film-script. Graham was more interested in Ghana, present and future; MacNeice was more interested in the history and traditions of the Gold Coast. Their collaboration came under strain. Graham was obliged to 'doctor' the script, and MacNeice did not like the result, *Freedom for Ghana*, when it was released in March.

One of the reasons why these scripts were unsatisfactory was because they were written with the left hand while the right was at work on a play. *Traitors in Our Way* – the title is first mentioned in a letter of 21 February to George and Mercy MacCann – is about different ways of betrayal. It is set on a ship, where a honeymooning nuclear physicist, Tom Carstairs, and wife, Portia, recognize a fellow passenger as Roger (disguised and travelling under the false name of Haffer), a former colleague of his and a former lover of hers. Years before, Haffer had defected to the Soviet Union, betraying thereby his country, his friend, and his mistress. Carstairs now proposes to expose him to the ship's security officer, Norton, but is stopped by his wife who says she will leave him if he does. Eventually, in the third act, Carstairs tells Norton, who takes Haffer off to interrogate him. They return, however, with revolvers (Norton having been persuaded by Haffer to turn traitor also and hijack the vessel). Portia sides with her husband, but then the ship's siren sounds the approach of an iceberg (foreseen by Portia in a dream), and the play ends with the passengers singing like those on the deck of the doomed *Titanic*.

Traitors in Our Way was accepted for performance by the Group Theatre in Belfast. MacNeice went over to see the producer, Harold Goldblatt, and the set-designer, George MacCann (and, incidentally, an international rugger match in which England defeated Ireland 6–0) in the second week of February. He returned for the first night on Saturday 23 March. John Boyd was not the only member of the audience to think it a bad play, but the theatre was packed and the play received respectful notices in *The Times* and *TLS*. The reviewer in the latter, however, criticized 'an unsatisfactory third act' and, in a letter to the MacCanns, MacNeice mentions having 'done a lot of rewriting'.*

Life at 2 Clarence Terrace that spring was enlivened by the presence of a genial Irish-American. Bill Alfred was a playwright and a tutor at Harvard, where he had met the MacNeices in 1953. Four years later, on sabbatical leave in London, he had gone to Rome in the hope of selling one of his plays. The deal did not materialize, and returning to England, broke, he was met at Heathrow by a note from Hedli saying 'Come and live in our flat for nothing.' He did, and was soon treated

---

* He produced it – revised and retitled 'Another Part of the Sea' – as a TV play on 6 September 1960.

like a member of the family. A staunch Roman Catholic, he went to mass every morning and would often talk with Louis about 'the old faith'. MacNeice told him his maternal grandfather, Martin Clesham, had been born into a Roman Catholic family, but had 'turned'. He himself, he said, sometimes had thoughts of 'turning back' and seemed sufficiently serious about this for Alfred to make inquiries. It transpired that, were he to 'turn', his marriage to Hedli would be counted invalid. These conversations with Alfred confirm, however, the impression conveyed by the last poem of *Visitations*:

> Yet after all that or before it
> As he sat in the cave of his mind (and the cave was the world)
> Among old worked flints between insight and hindsight,
> Suddenly Something, or Someone, darkened the entrance
> But shed a new light on the cave and a still small voice in the silence
> In spite of ill winds and ill atoms blossomed in pure affirmation
> Of what lay behind and before it.

The 'visitations' of MacNeice's title are those of the Muse and, as here (in 'the still small voice' of I Kings 19:2), a presence that must be divine. A desire for such a presence may have prompted its visitations. MacNeice would have welcomed a faith that united in his own person, and his own poetry, the divided loyalties of Protestant and Roman Catholic Ireland.

The new book of poems was published on 10 May. It was the Summer Choice of the Poetry Book Society, and he wrote in its *Bulletin*:

This is the first book of short poems I have published since 1948. In between I have published *Ten Burnt Offerings* (ten long poems which were experiments in dialectical structure) and one very long poem, *Autumn Sequel*, the point of which was missed by most of the book-reviewers; it was 'occasional' but not casual, being an attempt to marry myth to 'actuality'. While writing these longer pieces I was incapable of writing short ones. When the lyrical impulse did return, this interval of abstention, it seems to me, had caused certain changes in my lyric-writing – I naturally hope for the better. It is hard to put labels on one's own work but I like to think that my latest short poems are on the whole more concentrated and better organized than my earlier ones, relying more on syntax and bony feature than on bloom or frill or the floating image. I should also like to think that sometimes they achieve a blend of 'classical' and 'romantic', marrying the element of wit to the sensuous-mystical element.

The reviews were again disappointing. The *TLS* concluded: 'these poems confirm Mr MacNeice's existing reputation without necess-itating any drastic revision either way. They suggest the possibility of future development even if they do not altogether embody it here.'

In early July, MacNeice paid his third visit of the year to Ireland – receiving an honorary D.Litt from Queen's University, Belfast – and, that autumn, paid a third visit to India and the Far East. Leaving London on 14 October, he reached Delhi at midnight on the 16th and, the following day, began a busy schedule of meetings and recording sessions. His letters to Hedli – nine in the month he was away – are as faithful and full as ever, but lack the sparkle of those written ten years before. Eating by himself in cavernous hotel dining rooms, he has no Dillon, no Vaughan Thomas to talk to, and – worst of all – no drink. 'Prohibition has killed this place', he writes glumly to Hedli. 'I'm now going to take a swig of cold water from the thermos provided by the management.' The only alcohol to be found is in the company of uncongenial expatriates: at a cocktail party in honour of John Masters, who was 'rather pleased with himself', or in the Dacca Club, 'which is a parody of a Graham Greene scene at its seediest. Jute wallahs, unhealthy bank clerks, steamship executives (I asked one who'd been here 28 years if he'd noticed any changes in the Pakistanis since Independence & he said he'd never met any *before* Independence)'. It was a relief to move on to Singapore and Kuala Lumpur: 'Nice blue mountains near by, a most refreshing change after all the fly-blown flatness.' He was in Malacca on 11 November; Ceylon on the 13th; and back in London on the 18th. 'I *have* worked hard on this trip', he told Hedli, but had less to show for it than on previous trips, and little of the material he recorded would find its way into Gilliam's Christmas Day programme, 'The Commonwealth Remembers'.

Recovering from the effects of Prohibition, MacNeice spent Christ-mas at home 'on whiskey & an iron lung of Guinness', and then, feeling himself again, took Hedli and Bimba down to the Isle of Wight. They had recently acquired a cottage there, in the grounds of 'Brook

Hill', a house owned by J. B. Priestley and his wife Jacquetta Hawkes. She and Hedli had met at a London party – neither knowing who the other was – and Hedli had said she was looking for a cottage on the island. Jacquetta replied that she had one, a half-ruined shack, going for £5. A cheque was written on the spot and, when Jacquetta saw the signature, she said she would frame it. The MacNeices soon made the shack at least as habitable as an Irish cabin and named it 'Prospect Cottage'. They and the Priestleys became good friends, and Louis was delighted to discover that the composer, Gerald Abraham, also had a cottage near by. He had devised a score for MacNeice's 'Salute to the USSR' in 1942, and had since been one of his principal advisers on musical matters. With the Abrahams and Priestleys and the many other friends who would visit Prospect Cottage, the MacNeices would forget the bustle and business of London; and here, beside another ocean, the poet would remember Belfast Lough.

CHAPTER 24

All Over Again

And there was light
Before him as through a window
That opens on to a garden.
The first garden. The last.
'The Wall', *CP*, p. 506

The New Year's honours list of 1958 brought MacNeice a CBE, but his gruffly ironical response to congratulations on this and his honorary doctorate confirmed what had long been clear to his friends: that he set little store by such marks of Establishment approval. His account of an exchange with the Queen at the Investiture was revealing: 'Herself asked me "What do you do?" and I said, "Well, I do radio. I also write," she said: "Have you been doing it long?"' Far from being self-satisfied, MacNeice in the 1950s was increasingly dissatisfied with his life and work. During the war, Gilliam and his staff had been stars in the BBC firmament, and the Features Department remained in the ascendant for the next decade. The following decade, however, saw the rise of the Drama Department and the decline of Features. There were several reasons for this. With the breakdown of Gilliam's marriage, he lost something of his earlier zest and energy. As Douglas Cleverdon, one of his most loyal lieutenants put it:

Gilliam retained his magnanimity, his breadth of vision, his faith in the radio medium; but that faith was not shared by all his colleagues. His own physique was beginning to feel the strain of the way of life that his generous nature imposed upon it, and he could no longer inspire the collective response that had characterized the early days of Features.

Not only was the Department losing ground – and audience – to

Drama, but radio as a whole was losing both to television. This Gilliam had foreseen. Asked by the BBC's Senior Controller to comment on the rival service in 1947, he noted its lack of news coverage and added: 'A bulletin, with a gradually increasing proportion of picture reports from our own local units, located in key news centres, would surely build up a regular television audience faster than any other single development.' His prophecy was fulfilled in 1953 when, with the televising of the Coronation, the new medium dramatically increased its audience.

By 1958, the Features Department was in the doldrums. MacNeice's most recent contributions to its performance had been two undistinguished exercises in nostalgia, 'An Oxford Anthology' and 'The Stones of Oxford', and his two 1958 programmes, 'All Fools at Home' and 'Health in Their Hands', were no nearer the standard of his best work. Like some of his BBC cronies, he was drinking more and staying later in The Stag or The George. All too often he would return home – sometimes with a friend – after Hedli's carefully cooked supper had been spoilt. Not all his friends were friends of hers. The last to leave one of their parties was Peter Duval-Smith, who had joined the BBC (on Louis' recommendation) after his acrimonious departure from the British Council in Athens. In the small hours of the morning, Hedli asked their guest to drink up. 'Louis must get to bed', she said. 'He has a rehearsal at 9 o'clock tomorrow morning.' 'I'm not going till I've finished this bottle of brandy,' Peter replied. 'Please take the bottle,' she said. He did, finishing it in the street, then hurling it through his hosts' sitting-room window.

Thinking perhaps that a change would do MacNeice good, Gilliam persuaded him to go on a six-month television course from April to October. He went with no great enthusiasm and never wavered in his allegiance to radio, though intellectually he responded to the new challenges, opportunities, and technology of the new medium. In August, he was happy to be entrusted with a TV production of his own and directed two short plays by Strindberg, *Pariah* and *The Stronger*. That month was also enlivened by a visit from Kevin Andrews. Now married to E. E. Cummings's daughter, he was in reluctant self-exile from the Greek island of Ikaros, which his wife did not like, and was in London to oversee the publication of his book *The Flight of Ikaros*. He stayed at Clarence Terrace and, with the heightened sensitivity of someone whose own marriage was in difficulties, detected disharmony between Hedli and Louis. Her high spirits and Louis' gloom did not complement each other. Talking with them on one occasion of the problems of marriage in general, Andrews said, *de profundis*: 'Doesn't one stay put in a marriage because one's afraid of loneliness?' Louis replied: 'That's a very searching question.'

When, in October, he returned to Rothwell House, MacNeice found himself sharing an office with a younger poet, Anthony Thwaite, who had joined the Features Department as a trainee earlier in the year. The cub would enter the cage, keenly, at 9.30; the literary lion, coughing and wheezing, at 11.30. 'He would shuffle his papers, scribble a few notes, and at about noon would gesture with his head towards the window: "Going to The Stag?"' They would move off to the watering-hole together and, an hour or so later, would join the herd of actors and actresses, producers and writers in its midday migration down Great Portland Street to The George. The cub kept a wary eye on the dyspeptic lion and more than once felt his claws. He would not forget how, one morning,

as we sat at our facing desks in Rothwell House, I'd noticed him scribbling away in pencil (he always used pencil), gazing out of the window, scribbling again. Later, in the Stag, I asked him whether he'd been writing a poem. He fixed me with his most disdainful, supercilious camel look and said, 'Have you nothing better to do than watch what I'm up to of a morning?' Another time, in the George, when I was fairly drunk and therefore insolent, I remarked: 'Louis, I've often wondered why you've got that long line down one side of your face and not down the other'. To which he replied: 'And *I've* often wondered why *you* have no lines on *your* face *at all*.'

Thwaite would also be surprised, however, by MacNeice's kindness – most notably in 1963, when Douglas Cleverdon arrived at The George with news of Sylvia Plath's suicide. Thwaite had known her and was shocked, but someone else in the group made a disparaging remark about 'women poets'. MacNeice rounded on him and told him to shut up. 'Can't you see the man's upset, and rightly too?'

There were no new radio scripts from MacNeice's pencil in the months following his return from the television course, perhaps because he was at work on a stage play prompted by that experience.

MacNeice in the late 1950s

One for the Grave is subtitled 'a modern morality play' and set in a television studio, 'where the floor represents the Earth and the production gallery Heaven'. It would seem to owe something of its form to the formula of the TV programme, 'This is Your Life', which had been running since 1955.

MacNeice's hero, Everyman, appears on set expecting a quiz programme only to be told he is about to die. First, however, he is confronted by his angry wife (Maggie), a mistress (Eleanor), a son, a daughter, and his first love (Mary), with whom he once again watches the mayflies that dance above the river in MacNeice's poem, 'Mayfly'. Regressing further, he rapturously meets his mother on her return from what she calls a 'rest cure'. She brings him a book of Hans Andersen's tales (one containing a picture of Death) and an empty box of chocolates. In the play's less autobiographical, more satirical second act, Everyman survives the attentions of Admom (personifying the consumer society), Analyst, Marxist, and Scientist; then, turning his back on them, addresses the audience:

'Moriturus te saluto.' That's what the doomed gladiators cried out in ancient Rome to the Emperor. 'I who am about to die salute you.' But in *this* arena I say it to you, to each of you. (*He looks searchingly in different directions over the audience.*) Moriturus te saluto, Moriturus te saluto. Moriturus te saluto. I did not choose to be put in this ring to fight, I did not ask to be born, but a babe in arms is in arms in more senses than one and since my birth I've been fighting. Conscript or volunteer – I just don't know which I am – and it may have been a losing battle but at least I've been in it, I've been in it. And *les jeux sont faits* and *rien ne va plus*. To be a human being is a cause for grief – and for pride. Everyman must vindicate himself.

To do this, he calls for a conductor's baton and declares: 'If I cannot conduct my life, at least I'll conduct my death.' An oblong wooden box, painted to look like marble, is wheeled on. Everyman crawls towards it and is helped to climb in by a Gravedigger, whose voice, he says, sounds like his father's – but kinder. That voice leads him through a form of confession and prayer; then, as if pronouncing absolution, says: 'Everyman, here and now, I salute you in the name of Life.' Everyman asks his name, and is told: 'I've just said it.' Life has the last word – one familiar to MacNeice's father – as the Chorus sings:

> Oh Everyman, oh Everyman,
> A new day dawns for Everyman.

The word is Afterlife.

This conclusion, it must be said, is at odds with the words of the callous Director in his production gallery/Heaven, and would seem to reflect the unresolved conflict of belief and scepticism revealed in MacNeice's conversations with Bill Alfred. The play's theology may be flawed, but it has much more vitality – especially in its songs and other music hall elements – than *Traitors in Our Way*. The playwright was never to see it staged, but it was performed, very successfully, at the Abbey Theatre, Dublin, in October 1966.

The claims of the BBC could not be indefinitely ignored, but in January 1959 the reluctant producer found a way to combine business and pleasure. It was agreed that he should write a feature on rugby that would require his presence at a forthcoming international match. Accordingly, he was at Cardiff Arms Park to see Wales beat England (5–0) on 17 January. The resulting programme, 'Scrums and Dreams', he called a mixture 'of fact, fiction, and fantasy'; the Dreams being those of two Walter Mittyean spectators – one Welsh, one English – who project themselves into the heroic action played out on the green arena below.

In 1958, Howard Newby had succeeded John Morris as Controller of the Third Programme. He was aware that the BBC had not been getting the best out of MacNeice in recent years, and aware, too, of his interest in animals, arranged a lunch at the Zoo with him and Gilliam to discuss future programmes. Newby's praise of the symbolism in 'The Heartless Giant' prompted him to adapt another Norwegian folk-tale for radio. Helga, heroine of 'East of the Sun and West of the Moon', finds her prince only to lose him, but with the help of the Four Winds tracks him to a castle, where she rescues him on the eve of his enforced marriage to the Lady Longnose. The programme had its charm but lacked the intensity of MacNeice's best work, no doubt because his imagination was engaged elsewhere.

On 21 July, four days before his folk-tale was broadcast, he wrote to tell Davin he had finished the verse 'Prologue' promised for 'The Character of Ireland', that rough beast still slouching towards Oxford and never to be born. Peter McDonald has well and wittily described it as 'a failure in collaboration or a collaboration in failure' and has related it to its editors' own search for identity: 'MacNeice's interest in the project was at its strongest in the early 1950s and early 1960s.' His 'Prologue' should be read in the light of his recovered sense of personal and poetic identity.* He now has the confidence and courage to question the very assumption on which 'The Character of Ireland' was postulated:

> 'The Character of Ireland'? Character?
> A stage convention? A historical trap?
> A geographical freak? Let us dump the rubbish
> Of race and talk to the point: what is a nation?

* The poem does not appear in *CP*, but may be found in Appendix B, pp.488–91.

The poem's torrential, thirty-line, opening sentence prepares the way for his answer. It offers a landscape packed with symbolic detail:

> with salmon
> Hovering side by side, keeping position,
> Headed upstream like lovers, with cairns and turf-stacks
> Keeping position like hermits, with broken cliffs
> Keeping position like broken heroes, with waves
> Breaking upon them like time, with sunlight breaking
> Sideways through the clouds like a word of God . . . .

Salmon and cairn (as that supposedly marking the grave of Queen Maeve on Knocknarea), wave and cliff: the MacNeice country is no longer the outskirts of Carrickfergus, but now the whole of Ireland, a landscape subconsciously defined by the parents he has buried in it. He sees the Irish as 'Inheritors of paradox and prism', cloud and sunlight 'like a word of [his father's] God', and at his Prologue's end returns to his own beginnings:

> So the eye
> Can miss the current in a stream, the ear
> Ignore even a waterfall, the mind,
> Intent on solid fact, forget that water,
> Which early thinkers thought the source of all things,
> Remains the symbol of our life; yet never,
> No more than peat can turn again to forest,
> No more than the die, once cast, can change its spots,
> No more than a child can disavow its birthplace,
> No more than one's first love can be forgotten,
> If pressed, could we deny this water flows.

Having delivered his poem, MacNeice set about preparing for another assignment overseas. He had been invited by Professor Howarth of the Department of English at the University of Cape Town to give a series of lectures. His stipend would be paid from the UCT Students' Visiting Lecturers Fund (to which each student contributed ten shillings a year) and, since the Features Department had recently been ordered to reduce its staff, Gilliam was happy to save the cost of a senior salary for two months and allow him to accept the invitation.

He arrived in Cape Town on 3 August and was installed in the

Vineyard Hotel, a handsome Cape Dutch building surrounded by oaks and commanding a magnificent view of Devil's Peak to the east of Table Mountain. He found his hosts 'waiting for their 10 lbs of flesh' and, the following day, took his first class – of 300 students. Shaken by this, he was further daunted by his introduction to the English Department at a sepulchral party. Among those present was an undergraduate poet, Paul Gregorowski, who had been assigned to the distinguished guest as driver, guide, and social secretary. MacNeice had no talent for small talk and did not help the first flickerings of conversation on this occasion by announcing that, 'In Iceland, when they want to give a party, they take a lot of dead fish and bury them under the ice. When they feel festive, they dig them up and eat them.' Gregorowski went home bitterly disillusioned and wrote a Byronic anti-MacNeice skit, for which his clergyman father (who had given him £5 towards the expenses of his assignment) rebuked him: 'At nineteen, you have no right . . . .'

Next morning, he glumly drove out to the Vineyard to fetch his fallen idol, who looked more and more loftily disapproving as the young man reeled off the list of social engagements planned for the week. Gregorowski then apologized that he would have to desert him on Wednesday and Saturday, as he was pledged to watch a couple of rugger matches. 'Thank God!' said MacNeice, thawing instantly. 'Can I come too?' From that moment they were friends.

The visitor was required to give four public lectures on successive Thursdays. The first, entitled 'Yes-men and No-men', advocated artistic independence, resistence to the pressures of sect or party. When, in question-time, some radical students challenged MacNeice's position, the chairman tried to steer the discussion into calmer waters, asking him what he would do if he were offered the post of Poet Laureate. 'I should refuse it', he snapped.

His second public performance, a reading of light verse, was more of a success. He and his audience were now beginning to warm to each other and, after 'Bagpipe Music', there were shouts of 'Encore!' and tumultuous applause. The enthusiastic response to his choice of light verse may have prompted a poem of his own in that genre, 'Old Masters Abroad'. This, with its nod to Auden's 'Musée des Beaux Arts' ('About suffering they were never wrong, / The Old Masters'), has an

435

engaging element of self-satire:

> At Bablockhythe the stripling Ganges
> Burns on her ghats the scholar gypsy,
> There's a deathly hush on the rocks of Aden,
> Nine bean rows rise in the Kalahari.
>
> The faces listen or not. The lecturers
> Mop their memories. All over the static
> Globe the needle sticks in the groove.
> It is overtime now for the Old Masters.

The social merry-go-round was beginning to gather speed. He was guest of honour at dinners and parties – one of the most memorable in a bungalow clinging to a cliff face and overlooking white sand and line after line of breakers, luminous in the moonlight. His host that night was Jack Cope, one of South Africa's leading novelists and short story writers. MacNeice showed little interest in the springbok haunch, the lemon and meringue pie (prepared by the poet Sydney Clouts and his wife Marg), but great interest in Cope's Cape wines and brandy. They talked until two in the morning, when his host led him up the hundred steps to the clifftop road. Pausing at the top to look back over the ocean to the setting moon, MacNeice muttered 'Indescribable!' A few days later, Cope went down for a swim in the icy sea below his bungalow and on the beach met MacNeice with a new friend, Sylvia Shear, who lived in a flat nearby. He had been caught by a wave and was wet to the knees of his green tweed trousers but, far from minding, was clearly delighted by the sea – and by Sylvia.

In a letter of 10 August, he told Hedli he had written three poems and sent her the first, 'Half Truth from Cape Town'. Five days later, he sent her the second, 'Solitary Travel', but subsequent letters make no mention of the third. This was the love poem, 'All Over Again', addressed to Sylvia Shear, for whom he wrote out a fair copy sub-titled '(for Sylvia)'. A single torrential sentence, it has the circular movement of 'Meeting Point' and several of the poems MacNeice had still to write:

> As if I had known you for years drink to me only if
> Those frontiers had never changed on the mad map of the years

Sylvia Shear

And all our tears were earned and this were the first cliff
From which we embraced the sea and these were the first words
We spread to lure the birds that nested in our day
As if it were always morning their dawnsong theirs and ours
And waking no one else me and you only now
Under the brow of a blue and imperturbable hill
Where still time stands and plays his bland and hemlock pipe
And the ripe moment tugs yet declines to fall and all
The years we had not met forget themselves in this
One kiss ingathered world and outward rippling bell
To the rim of the cup of the sky and leave it only there
Near into far blue into blue all over again
Notwithstanding unique all over all again
Of which to speak requires new fires of the tongue some trick
Of the light in the dark of the muted voice of the turning wild
World yet calm in her storm gay in her ancient rocks
To preserve today one kiss in this skybound timeless cup

> Nor now shall I ask for anything more of future or past
> This being last and first sound sight on eyes and ears
> And each long then and there suspended on this cliff
> Shining and slicing edge that reflects the sun as if
> This one Between were All and we in love for years

In one sense, nothing has changed 'on the mad map of the years': between 'the first cliff' and the first sea, the lovers stand in their timeless moment as, in 'Meeting Point',

> the clock
> Forgot them and the radio waltz
> Came out like water from a rock:
> Time was away and somewhere else.

The bell that was silent in the earlier poem here ripples (into silence?) but will sound again and, at some level, the speaker surely knows for whom it tolls.

On 20 August, MacNeice gave his third public lecture, speaking expansively and well on 'The Irish Playwrights'. For him, the event of the evening was meeting Irma Roth, a beautiful and intelligent Afrikaner teacher soon to rival Sylvia in his affections. A week later, he gave a poetry reading, entitled 'A Poetic Autobiography', that was followed by a party at an elegant private house. There was a dance band and delicious food, both of which MacNeice ignored, and, since Irma and Sylvia were both present and he could not favour one above the other, he got drunk. There was no such problem on 29 August, his last day in Cape Town, much of which he spent with Irma (who told Jack Cope that, at one stage, she had to bite him in self-defence). The day ended with a historic party at which a group of writers – Cope, Clouts, Uys Krige, Ken Parker, Philip Segal and others – encouraged by MacNeice, decided to launch a literary magazine.*

Many friends saw him off at Cape Town airport: all were sad – Irma, distraught – and when, arriving in Johannesburg, he was shown to a bleak billet in a converted army camp, he felt sad and lonely himself. The following evening he wrote a letter to Sylvia Shear and another to Judy Powell, the actress he had first met (as Judy Lang) in

---

* The first issue of *Contrast*, edited by Cope, was published in December 1960.

All Over Again

(for Sylvia)

As if I had known you for years drink to me only if
Those frontiers had never changed on the mad map of the years
And all our tears were earned & this was the first cliff
From which we embraced the sea & these were the first words
We spread to lure the birds that nested in our day
As if it were always morning their dawnsong theirs & ours
And wanting no one else me & you only now
Under the brow of a blue & imperishable hill
Where still Time stands & plays his blessed & hemlock pipe
And the ripe moment tugs yet declines to fall & all
The years we had not met forget themselves in this
One kiss ingathered world & outward rippling bell
To the rim of the cup of the sky & leave it only there
Near into far blue into blue all over again
Notwithstanding unique all over all again
Of which to speak requires new tongues of fire some trick
Of the light in the dark of the muted voice of the turning wild
World got calm in her storm gay in her ancient rocks
To preserve today one kiss in this greyhound timeless cup
Not now shall I ask for anything more of future or past
This being last & first sound sight on eyes & ears
And each long then & there suspended on this cliff
Shining & shining edge that reflects the sun as if
This one Between was All & we in love for years .

Louis MacNeice .

'All Over Again'

the Players Theatre twenty years before. They had kept in touch since and he was godfather to her son Matthew. When her husband had left her, earlier in 1959, MacNeice had driven down to Cheltenham to see them, bringing Matthew a copy of a children's book he had written, called *The Sixpence that Rolled Away*. Now, in his draughty hut of corrugated iron, he gave her an account of his time in Cape Town: 'In less than 4 weeks I gave 47 lectures, did one radio production (*One Eye Wild*) & 2 radio talks. Not to mention the social side!' His final verdict sounded a familiar note (though not one that Judy, or perhaps he, would recognize): 'The best things in Cape Town are the mountains & sea; I like the idea there's nothing much between one & the Antarctic.' Finally, with an echo of his recent love poem (that Judy, of course, had not read), he came, obliquely to the point of his letter:

It would be very nice to see you. I don't know, darling, if you've taken in my set-up (the internal one, I mean)? Sometimes I don't understand it myself. I always say Never Again but it always happens. I hope you don't dislike me for it. I'm very, very fond of you – as you know. Please write to me. Lots of love. Louis.

This immodest proposal needs to be read in conjunction with a letter written the following day to Hedli:

Your remarks about Alcohol & Sex were a little unkind I thought across all these many miles. You're such an old beam-&-moter (see your New Testament) that you seem quite unaware that *you* very often don't take up *my* signals. When your mind is on higher things (I wonder if Brecht by the way really *is* higher than Drink!). *Of course* a lot of drink (see Shakespeare!) doesn't help the sexual act but, if it weren't for drink (I've told you this before but it never sinks in), I'd probably have vanished long ago to Tahiti or somewhere. My main comment however is that I don't think I'm any longer interested in Sex for Sex's Sake (how horribly sibilant!) & can't really get interested – drink or no drink – unless one's tuned in on the *other* wavelengths. Which so often (drink or no drink) we aren't – probably because we're both such egocentrics. Please don't take any of this amiss; everyone (including me) knows that you're extraordinary attractive for your age – it will be nice to be in bed again with you anyway.

It might be 'nice to be in bed' with Hedli, but 'It would be very nice to see' Judy. The conclusion is inescapable.

MacNeice was rescued from the army hut by an old acquaintance, Michael Silver, whom he had known since 1945 and who now installed him in the guest-room of his large house in the fashionable district of Inanda. Silver and his wife Ethell made his fortnight in Johannesburg a good deal more comfortable and pleasant than he had expected, but his lectures at the University of Witwatersrand were less successful than those in Cape Town. He was drinking too much, and word reached Jack Cope of an evening when he had swayed on to a platform before a large audience, raised a hand and said: 'I am the last of the individualists, thank God!' He repeated this several times, but could not continue and had to be helped from the stage.

Leaving Johannesburg in mid-September, he broke his journey in Salisbury to give a poetry reading at the University College of Rhodesia and Nyasaland, before flying on to meet Hedli in Milan. All too soon, he was back at the BBC with two projects competing for his attention: a script about the battle of Clontarf, fought on Good Friday 1014 between Irish and Norse armies; and another, envisaged as a fable, about contemporary South Africa. He had proposed the first at his lunch with Newby in April and, since his proposal had been approved, he turned to it first. 'They Met on Good Friday' he called 'a Sceptical Historical Romance'. The narrative begins where 'Burnt Njal' ends. Halgertha and her Icelandic followers, finding themselves hated in Iceland because of the burning of Njal, respond to an appeal from the Norse garrison in Dublin for help in what both sides know will be the decisive battle. At Clontarf, the forces of the Irish King Brian Boru defeat the attacking Vikings, but the old king is killed in his hour of triumph, and the programme ends with an exchange between his Harper and his Poet:

HARPER: Why are you not reciting? This is our farewell to Brian.
POET: I am tired of words. I spoke my farewell on the battlefield. You are
    lucky, harper.
HARPER: Why lucky?
POET: Words must be true or false; what you say on those strings is neither.
HARPER: I must do it alone then? The Farewell.
POET: My words might flatter the dead – or they might malign him. Yes, my
    friend; this time you must do it alone.
    (*Harp finale*)

The words of the Irish poet help to explain the sceptical title of his successor's autobiography, *The Strings are False.**

MacNeice's original proposal for 'The Battle of Clontarf' asserted 'that the leaders on both sides were as much the victims of power politics as their counterparts in the 20th century'; and his proposal for a programme about South Africa was to represent the evil effects of contemporary power politics. On 5 October, he sent a memorandum to Newby, which began:

When doing a new production of *The Dark Tower* in Johannesburg the other day, I realised once again what an excellent vehicle this fable type of play is for dealing with contemporary issues which might be too hot or too delicate for a more direct treatment. I have now a very strong compulsion to write a new piece of this kind about exactly this sort of issue . . . .

The Pin is Out would be set in an imaginary country whose population is divided into three main groups – the Alphas, the Betas, and the Helots. As I think it safer to keep colour out of this, the distinctions between these groups would be political, social or economic. The Alphas, who rule the country are the political élite. The Betas, slightly fewer in number, have cornered most of the wealth; their interests in nearly every sphere are opposed to those of the Alphas and the rift between these two groups is continually widening. The Helots, who greatly outnumbered the other two groups put together, are . . . . well . . . . helots – hopelessly backward and deliberately kept backward.

In spite of the obvious implied morals in this set-up, this programme would *not* be just a dressed-up thesis. My imaginary liberal-minded citizens are predisposed to welcome any stranger as if he were an angel; almost any relationship between them and him will be from the start a sentimental one. So my main story-line will be one of personal relationships between real characters. Tragic of course.

With this proposal he sent a detailed synopsis. Newby replied:

Your synopsis gives the impression that the country and characters are being disguised not so much for artistic reasons as to avoid trouble with South Africa House. Is there any reason (apart from that) why the play should not be realistic? And, if not, is it correct to describe it as a fable?. . . .

---

* The evolution of this title can be followed from its Shakespearean source ('The strings, my lord, are false,' *Julius Caesar*, IV.iii.291) by way of 'They Met on Good Friday', 'The Administrator' (where Shakespeare's sentence is quoted; *The Mad Islands and The Administrator*, p. 78), and 'Let's Go Yellow' (where it is quoted again; BBC cyclostyled script, p. 8c).

My fear is that your play will, because of the inhibitions, seem academic and literary in the wrong way. Artistically it requires either a bold realistic treatment, or a much franker transposition into the world of fable – insects or animals as leading characters.

MacNeice saw the force of these objections, but was as anxious to give his story as stylized a realistic treatment as would escape political interference from outside the BBC, and it was agreed that he would write a draft.

First, however, he had to compile another programme he had proposed: one that would marry 'the two extremes of pure radio features written for actors and pure "actuality" pieces concocted from tape recordings'. For this, he recorded boys and girls in London and Oxford and integrated their voices into a script for studio actors. The resulting 'Mosaic of Youth' was broadcast on 30 December, three weeks after 'They Met on Good Friday'.

In the New Year, MacNeice finished his draft of 'The Pin is Out'. The story begins in one of the 'indistinguishable airports' of his poem 'Solitary Travel'. Roscoe Brown, a British journalist on his way to Zero Land, is instructed by a fellow passenger in the political realities of the area. An election is approaching in which the Inners are likely once again to defeat the Outers for control of a country, most of whose people are vote-less Zeros. (The names of these groups are a marked improvement on those of the original proposal.) Brown, whose name situates him between black and white, falls in love with a beautiful liberal, Greta Bechstein (daughter of an Inner millionaire). She introduces him, first, to some Inner thugs and, then, to her Zero revolutionary friend Kularu, who finally kills her in disturbances following an Inner victory at the polls.

MacNeice's script is vibrant with hatred of the apartheid system and, at one point, he makes Greta say: 'this country's beyond satire. If Dean Swift were alive, it would stump him.' She is wrong. The strongest parts of 'The Pin is Out' are its satirical moments; the weakest parts, its love story. Greta is too one-dimensional a figure to be tragic. Echoing MacNeice's letter to Judy Powell and his poem, 'All Over Again', she proposes a picnic 'On a high cliff over the ocean where there's nothing between you and the Pole.' One may assume he had Sylvia Shear in mind when he gave Roscoe – homeward bound and ignorant of Greta's death – the last word: 'I thank God I met her and love her and perhaps she loves me and perhaps she will come to me but at least and above all else thank God she exists, she exists!'

In March 1961, the Sharpeville massacre in South Africa rendered this script out of date. MacNeice suggested he revise it, and Gilliam strongly supported him, but the Director of Sound Broadcasting, Lindsay Wellington, finally ruled

it would be a mistake for the Corporation to broadcast 'The Pin is Out'. Whether we regard it as 'fantasy inspired by a well-known contemporary situation' or as 'satire which has general validity for the Union', its effect must be to attack a Commonwealth Government at a particularly difficult moment in Commonwealth relations.

If the distance between Cape Town and London lent any enchantment to Hedli and Louis MacNeice's view of each other, it evaporated rapidly. The old lion was soon back at the BBC watering-holes, drinking late and looking for another lioness. He did not have long to wait or far to look. In December 1959, the actress he had cast as Halgertha in 'They Met on Good Friday' noticed him noticing her in a new way. Mary Wimbush was thirty-five, handsome rather than beautiful, with the carriage of a lioness. She and Louis had first met, in The Stag, when she was twenty-one – and tongue-tied in the presence of the poet. Her husband then invited him to her birthday party in 1947, and he came with a signed copy of *Plant and Phantom*. She had been acting in the 1949 production of 'The Dark Tower' when her marriage was collapsing, and had played in a number of his subsequent programmes. Early in 1960, he found her in The George, by herself, and suggested they move on to The ML (The Marie Lloyd, a drinking club much frequented by the Rag Trade). There, while he was ordering drinks, another woman friend of his came in and joined them. Mary drained her glass quickly and left. Meeting her again next day, Louis asked: 'Where did you get to yesterday?' 'I thought you wanted to drink with X', she replied. 'I asked you for a drink', he said, 'because I wanted to drink with *you*.' Soon they were meeting by design and he would find excuses for not going home. Once, after a long lunch together, he announced that he wanted to go to Stratford, so they

Mary Wimbush

caught a train to Berkhamstead (where she lived with her parents and her son Charles) and, collecting her car, drove to Stratford. They arrived too late to see a play and spent the night with the actor, Jack MacGowran. Other nights were spent in Bob Pocock's flat in Mecklenburgh Square, nights sometimes punctuated by phone-calls from Hedli trying to track down her errant husband.

As the trees of Regent's Park broke into blossom, spring found its way into MacNeice's poems, and he 'underwent one of those rare bursts of creativity when the poet is first astonished and then rather alarmed by the way the mill goes on grinding'. He gave Mary a typescript of 'Apple Blossom'. It begins:

> The first blossom was the best blossom
> For the child who never had seen an orchard;
> For the youth whom whisky had led astray
> The morning after was the first day.

And it ends:

> For the last blossom is the first blossom
> And the first blossom is the best blossom
> And when from Eden we take our way
> The morning after is the first day.

Images of Eden recur in other poems – 'Idle Talk' and 'The Wall', for example – and memories of childhood resurface over and over again, as the poet goes back to his beginnings and rewrites the first chapter of his life. His mother reappears – not in a poem, though one senses her presence behind several, but in a radio programme. Early in 1960, MacNeice and Thwaite jointly proposed a series of translations from the *Odyssey*, each to be made by a poet; and, on 8 March, he sent Newby a detailed scheme for twelve half-hour readings. This was approved and, sometime in the summer, he himself translated passages from Book XI in which Odysseus, visiting Hades, has a brief but moving meeting with 'the spirit of [his] departed mother'.

MacNeice's father would appear, later, in a weird and wonderful poem called 'The Truisms':

> His father gave him a box of truisms
> Shaped like a coffin, then his father died;
> The truisms remained on the mantelpiece
> As wooden as the playbox they had been packed in
> Or that other his father skulked inside.
>
> Then he left home, left the truisms behind him
> Still on the mantelpiece, met love, met war,
> Sordor, disappointment, defeat, betrayal,
> Till through disbeliefs he arrived at a house
> He could not remember seeing before,
>
> And he walked straight in; it was where he had come from
> And something told him the way to behave.
> He raised his hand and blessed his home;
> The truisms flew and perched on his shoulders
> And a tall tree sprouted from his father's grave.

In this dream-like variant of a parable heard in his father's house, his father's church, MacNeice's prodigal son comes home to be greeted by his father, not in person but in spirit. Possessed by that spirit, he blesses his father's house and, as his father's sayings descend like homing pigeons to mutter at his ear, his father's coffin sprouts a triumphant tree. This scenario, of course, is not an allegorical or symbolic representation of biographical reality so much as an adulterous prodigal's dream of forgiveness and renewal.

There might be blossom and new growth in Regent's Park and in Louis' life and work, but 2 Clarence Terrace seemed in the grip of winter. Bimba was puzzled by her father's increasing absences, Restituta was perplexed, and Hedli distraught. She went to see a psychiatrist and, unable to bear the unaccustomed silence of the house, took to walking the streets at night in great agitation. In June, she had a concert engagement in Nottingham. She asked Louis not to come, thinking his presence would make her more nervous, but he did. In her dressing-room before the concert, she said to him: 'Love me!' He answered, 'I do.' She sang in a state of high tension, and afterwards – from her bath – forced herself to ask him about 'the formidable woman' with whom he was involved. A painful talk ended with him saying: 'Let's see what happens.'

In August, she went to see her mother in Switzerland and wrote to him generously but in evident distress:

I know nothing of this new relationship, that it enriches you you tell me that you are committed you also tell me – Cannot this all be accepted? Why not let these two great strongholds exist side by side? instead of coming into conflict. They should after all complement each other. You are so large and so generous & so Tolerant surely there is space. They don't compare, they are utterly different.

It was too late. On 10 September, Hedli could take no more and, about to set off for a weekend in Prospect Cottage, she said to him: 'I think, Louis, you ought to go.'

Mary Wimbush was then on holiday in Sark. When she returned, she went to a pub in the Gloucester Road where she and Louis had arranged to meet. He came in looking like a lost dog. 'What's the matter?' she asked. 'Hedli's told me to go', he said. 'I've a taxi waiting outside with a suitcase in it.' They got the driver to take them to a hotel and, some days later, moved to a basement flat in Lexham Gardens.

On 27 September, MacNeice wrote to Dodds:

447

I gather various people have been talking to you about my break up with
Hedli. This must probably sound shockingly selfish (or silly) to you but I don't
think when, after *years* of things going wrong, something appears irretriev-
able, it's really so selfish giving up trying to retrieve it. But I'd like to talk to
you about this. The *positive* side (for me) is very good indeed; I feel it's worth
having lived for.

Valuing Dodds's good opinion as he did, MacNeice probably visited
him within the next few weeks to explain his situation. He was in
Oxford on a more cheerful mission early in the New Year; one for
which, as poet, critic, and sports enthusiast, he was uniquely qualified.
The university was in the throes of an election to the Chair of Poetry,
Oxford's quinquennial equivalent of Siena's colourful but savage
horse-race, the *Palio*, and MacNeice was commissioned to 'cover' the
preliminaries for *The New Statesman*. There were four runners: Robert
Graves, poet and novelist, and three distinguished critics – Helen
Gardner, F. R. Leavis, and Enid Starkie. All were celebrated controver-
sialists. Gardner had forcefully defended D. H. Lawrence's *Lady Chatterley's Lover* in its recent trial for obscenity; Leavis, the acerbic editor
of *Scrutiny*, was the best-hated critic in Cambridge; and Starkie, an
effective campaign-manager in the two previous elections, was now
campaigning for herself.

MacNeice made his rounds of the colleges and pubs, studying 'form',
picking up tips and slogans: 'A vote for Leavis is a vote for Lawrence
. . . A vote for Starkie is a vote for Rimbaud . . . A vote for Gardner is a
vote for Chatterley . . . A vote for Graves is a vote for Graves.' Filing
his report, he focused on two aspects of the election appropriate to the
birthplace of *Alice in Wonderland*:

To vote for the Chair of Poetry, an institution described by the outgoing
Auden as 'comically absurd', you need not even know the English language.
Nor need you to occupy the Chair; nothing in the statutes would prevent the
election of a Chinese botanist who would give three lectures a year, in Chinese,
on Leninist botany. . . .

The undergraduates of course have no say in all this but then, as one don
expressed it, 'the undergraduates are an eternal nuisance' (he was referring to
their alleged current hankering for publicity). Still, it is the undergraduates
who will benefit or suffer from a Professor of Poetry; it was they who got most
pleasure and profit from the company of Auden as he held court in the Cadena

over his morning coffee and it is they who stand to be most stimulated by the Old Scrutineer or the White Goddess. That either Graves or Leavis is likely to commit absurd generalizations and injustices in his lectures does not really matter. What undergraduates need is provocation. Auden's whinnying irreverences and *enfant terrible* eccentricities must have done them more good than crate-loads of scholarship.

It was characteristic of MacNeice that he should delight in – and contribute to – the comedy, but not overlook the serious issues escaping the attention of many senior members of the University. In the event (and to the satisfaction of *The New Statesman* correspondent), Robert Graves was elected Professor of Poetry.

MacNeice's happiness in the spring of 1961 was not unclouded. Having now to contribute to the costs of two households, he was worried about money. He and Hedli had never been savers and, though both were generous by temperament, they could not agree on the level of maintenance he should pay her. On 16 February, she wrote him a sad and revealing letter:

Louis, After 6 months of deep & rather bitter reflection about myself, I don't think I am a bad or vicious – or fundamentally violent person, but I *have* very strong feelings I am romantically naive I think – & I *did* put you on a pedestal & I just couldn't bear it when you behaved other – I also was vain enough to think I was the fundamental part of you, whatever happened – but somehow somehow in order to live I had to be angry, violent & then preoccupied but now that I am out of the wood of the emotional trouble – I AM terribly worried about your financial difficulties, & somehow I think if you can be generous now I shall be able to help later.

She said she was planning to let the first floor of 2 Clarence Terrace, and ended her letter with an appeal and a characteristic show of spirit:

Have just telephoned you – you still have the hard unfriendly voice. O Louis it is not necessary to be unfriendly any more – you sound like the aggrieved 'party' – surely rather unfriendly when you have everything you want & I have what have I? Life is too short Louis – Stop being a horse! H[edli]

He did have much of what he wanted – including advance recognition of his new book of poems. *Solstices*, a Spring 1961 Recommendation of the Poetry Book Society, was published on 10 March. It carried, as dedication, the phrase from Horace he had quoted, prophetically, in 'Carpe Diem' almost five years before: '... *age iam meorum finis amorum* ...': 'Come now, last of my loves.'

CHAPTER 25

Funeral Games

the names we read seem more than names,
Potions or amulets, till we remember
The lines of print are always sidelines
And all our games funeral games.
'Sports Page', *CP*, p. 534

The winter of 1960–1 brought a cold wind to the corridors of the Features Department. It came in the wake of a team of management consultants, called in by Gilliam's superiors to assess the efficiency of his operation and recommend ways of improving it. In due course, the inquisitors confronted the poet: 'We see, Mr MacNeice, that during the past six months you have produced only one programme. Can you tell us what you were doing the rest of the time?' His reply became legendary: 'Thinking'. He had, in fact, done a good deal more: producing a programme of his own poetry, as well as one by someone else (Zofia Ilinska's 'Night at Lamorran'), and playing his part in the planning of many others.

The management consultants' investigation may have contributed to his decision to loosen his ties with the BBC. Having made a fresh start in his private life and in his poetry, he found the courage to make a fresh start in his professional life; negotiating a three-year programme contract whereby, from 1 July 1961, he would work for the Corporation twenty-six weeks a year, and go freelance for the rest. His last programme as a full-time member of the BBC staff, 'The Administrator', was broadcast on 10 March, the day that *Solstices* was published, and it articulates many of his concerns at this time. Jerry, a professor of physics, has been offered the Directorship of a prestigious Institute, a promotion that would bring him power and money but cause him to abandon creative research for full-time administration. This he is loath to do. As he admits to his wife, Martha (played by Mary Wimbush): 'I'm escapist. Like an artist.' She wants him to accept the appointment as much as he wants to decline it, and their argument reveals tensions in their marriage. Martha had been involved with a married man, Robert (a colleague of Jerry's), and was pregnant with his child when he was killed in a car-crash. Jerry, who had been driving the car, had married her before the child, Sally, was born. Much of this emerges in dream sequences as Jerry sleeps on his decision. MacNeice originally intended him to wake – and the play to end – with his decision still not taken, but he was persuaded by others in the Features Department that the listening public would hate this and so, as he wrote, 'against my grain and the probability of his character made him follow his wife's wishes' and accept the Directorship. When he came to prepare the play for publication, however, he had ceased to work full-time for the BBC and, giving Jerry the courage for his own convictions, made him opt for research rather than administration.

MacNeice's Introduction to *The Mad Islands and The Administrator* suggests a further reason for his partial withdrawal from the BBC:

These two plays were both written for what some think an obsolescent medium. Obsolescent or not, sound radio, in Britain at least, is not the *mass* medium it used to be, television having stolen most of its public though it cannot take over most of its territory. Sound radio can do things no other medium can and, if 'sound' dies, those things will not be done. So I offer these two plays in print not only as readable pieces (or I hope so) in their own right but also as specimens of a peculiar genus which may soon become a historical curiosity.

Making a fresh start at fifty-four, he wanted to write poems rather than historical curiosities. Later in this Introduction, he wrote that 'one of the attractions of radio is that you can move so fast, almost as fast as dreams do: this is why the medium is a good one for dealing with dreams and why, the other way round, a dream technique suits the medium'. The same might be said of poetry, and dreams had provided MacNeice's poems with both substance and structure for almost as long as he had been writing. Making a fresh start in *Solstices*, he had returned to memories of childhood and now, mining deeper levels, his poems come full circle and themselves reinforced the circular pattern. In a Proustian day-dream, 'Soap Suds' takes the place of *madeleine*:

This brand of soap has the same smell as once in the big
House he visited when he was eight: the walls of the bathroom open
To reveal a lawn where a great yellow ball rolls back through a hoop
To rest at the head of a mallet held in the hands of a child.

And these were the joys of that house: a tower with a telescope;
Two great faded globes, one of the earth, one of the stars;
A stuffed black dog in the hall; a walled garden with bees;
A rabbit warren; a rockery; a vine under glass; the sea.

To which he has now returned. The day of course is fine
And a grown-up voice cries Play! The mallet slowly swings,
Then crack, a great gong booms from the dog-dark hall and the ball
Skims forward through the hoop and then through the next and then

Through hoops where no hoops were and each dissolves in turn
And the grass has grown head-high and an angry voice cries Play!
But the ball is lost and the mallet slipped long since from the hands
Under the running tap that are not the hands of a child.

In the primal garden of Carrickfergus Rectory, the poet's mother had worn 'a yellow dress' that, in his passionate retrospect, seemed to offer the first intimation of Fall. So now the remembered garden of Seapark (home of Thomas Macgregor Greer, only brother of the second Mrs MacNeice) is dominated not by a yellow dress but a yellow ball. Again there is sunlight on the garden and, as train wheels had revolved once at the perimeter of the Rectory garden, the ball revolves – it and the globes and the gong (all linked by their common adjective, *great*) reinforcing the circular movement of the poem. Again 'an angry voice' is heard in the garden. The ball – like mother, like Paradise – is lost and, as the round soap bubble bursts, the speaker is left looking at 'hands/Under the running tap that are not the hands of a child.'

The sea to which he had returned in that poem is the subject of another, 'Round the Corner', written in the same burst of creativity:

Round the corner was always the sea. Our childhood
Tipping the sand from its shoes on return from holiday
Knew there was more where it came from, as there was more

> Seaweed to pop and horizon to blink at. Later
> Our calf loves yearned for union in solitude somewhere
> Round that corner where Xenophon crusted with parasangs
> Knew he was home, where Columbus feared he was not,
> And the Bible said there would be no more of it. Round
> That corner regardless there will be always a realm
> Undercutting its banks with repeated pittance of spray,
> The only anarchic democracy, where we are all vicarious
> Citizens; which we remember as we remember a person
> Whose wrists are springs to spring a trap or rock
> A cradle; whom we remember when the sand falls out on the carpet
> Or the exiled shell complains or a wind from round the corner
> Carries the smell of wrack or the taste of salt, or a wave
> Touched to steel by the moon twists a gimlet in memory.
> Round the corner is – sooner or later – the sea.

The angry voice heard in the garden of 'Soap Suds' is perhaps that of the person remembered in this, as he was remembered in *I Crossed the Minch*:

The first time I went to the West of Ireland I drove in a saloon car with my father, and as we came over a hill, still some miles from the coast, my father, who had not been back there for many years, leaped in his seat under the constricting roof, and cried like Xenophon's troops 'The Sea! The Sea!'

As 'Round the Corner' comes round to the sea, we recognize that the poet has come round to his father. Round the corner of his memory there may also be the sound of another moonlit and windswept sea, that of Arnold's 'Dover Beach':

> The Sea of Faith
> Was once, too, at the full, and round earth's shore
> Lay like the folds of a bright girdle furled.
> But now I hear
> Its melancholy, long, withdrawing roar,
> Retreating to the breath
> Of the night-wind, down the vast edges drear
> And naked shingles of the world.

The controlled delicacy of the many poems of MacNeice's last three years is the more remarkable when seen in connection with the increasing loss of control in his drinking. He had long been a two-fisted drinker – whisky in one hand, Guinness in the other – but, having now more time on his hand since leaving the BBC, he had more glasses in them. How many more, Jack Cope discovered on 26 April. In London on a British Council Travel Grant, he had bought a copy of *Solstices* and been struck by 'the quality of swift and devastating insight and an almost magical simplicity of technique'. They met by arrangement in the foyer of Broadcasting House, and MacNeice proposed a drink with friends, followed by a curry supper in an excellent place he knew. Hedli was in The George but he avoided her, telling Cope he was worried that she might make a scene over 'another young woman' in his life. Drinks followed in quickfire succession. BBC people rolled in and out with the tide. Plans were made and unmade. MacNeice signed Cope's copy of *Solstices* and told him they should look out for broadcasting opportunities '*to make some money*'. From The George, they went by taxi to another pub and another and another. Cope kept reminding MacNeice of the promised curry supper. 'Yes – any minute', he would unconvincingly reply. By the time they reached The Load of Hay on Haverstock Hill, Cope estimated he had drunk a dozen beers and MacNeice more than double that. It was close to closing time, and the Irishman (who was still steady on his feet, as the South African was not) ordered a row of drinks and a half-jack of whisky to tide him over the rest of the evening. He then went to the telephone 'to whistle up some girls', but only managed to contact Nancy Spender, who must have heard the alcohol in his voice and declined to join them. When time was called, he emptied the last glass and, with his bottle in his pocket, swayed out into the cold night. A short walk brought them to a door at which MacNeice knocked. It was opened by his doctor, Jerry Slattery, and his wife Johnny, who took Cope into the kitchen and cut some sandwiches, which he ate gratefully. MacNeice looked at them, winced, finished his bottle of whisky, and fell asleep. The Slatterys told Cope this was a fairly common occurrence. MacNeice was almost living on alcohol and would sometimes go without food for days on end.

Cope met him several times more during his stay in London, but took care to avoid another pub-crawl. At their last meeting, in The Salisbury, he was struck by how fresh and clear-eyed he looked. After several rounds of Guinness, MacNeice produced a sheet of paper and asked his circle of friends if they would like to hear his new poem. They nodded. He read it solemnly and passed it to Cope, who, reading it to himself, was amazed that 'he could still rise to a beautiful and moving poem'. Afterwards, he could not remember its title or subject. Sensing how the evening would end, he made his excuses 'and slowly backed away, seeing him smiling and laughing among the crowd of friends, admirers and onlookers'.

Another night's drinking, with Bob Pocock, ended in Holborn Police Station. Next morning, a Black Maria drove them to Clerkenwell Police Station, where MacNeice gave his occupation as 'Writer'. When they appeared in court, the magistrate said: 'You wouldn't have much to write about last night.' The writer's own verdict on the incident was: 'Serve us right for drinking double rums.'

Money worries were one cause of such excesses: not only was he contributing to the cost of two households on a reduced salary, but he believed he would have to pay 'back tax' on rental income from the 2 Clarence Terrace flat. This fear proved groundless, but before it was dispelled he had sold some of his manuscripts and signed books and many of his duplicated radio scripts, for what he called 'blood money', to a dealer, Dr Jake Schwarz (whose name appears five times in his 1961 diary). He also accepted a commission to write a book on astrology. The extent and form of Hedli's maintenance was to become an increasingly contentious issue. As he told Mercy MacCann: 'I find it highly unsatisfactory to go on paying out money at random until a definite & permanent arrangement has been agreed upon as to how much she is to receive per year (& to avoid mutual embarrassment this must be done through solicitors).' Hedli was reluctant to approach her solicitors and, in August 1961, Louis told her he would make no more *ad hoc* payments until a settlement had been formally agreed. The matter was finally resolved on 11 July 1963, when Hedli obtained an order before a Registrar in chambers requiring Louis to pay her £650 per annum, less tax, payable monthly. Arrears accrued due under this order were to be discharged on or before 31 August 1963, and Louis was to pay all costs.

There was no room in the Lexham Gardens basement for Mary's son Charles so, on 19 June 1961, they and Louis moved up in the world to a larger and more attractive flat on two floors of 10 Regent's Park Terrace. Hedli, meanwhile, had decided to give up 2 Clarence Terrace and move to Ireland, where she opened the Spinnaker Restaurant – with wall paintings by George MacCann – in Kinsale. The faithful Restituta went to work for Elizabeth Nicholson, who was looking after her handicapped brother, Willie;* and Bimba (now seventeen and soon to start at the Slade School of Fine Art) moved into Regent's Park Terrace. Probably none of these moves affected MacNeice as much as the ending, at the end of June, of his own full-time employment with the BBC. Gilliam and many of the staff of the Features Department were sad to see him move out of his cluttered office in Rothwell House, but there were others, more highly placed, who were glad to see him go: those who had rejected 'The Pin is Out' and ('for reasons of local politics') his proposal for a 'People Today' programme on Sam Thompson, whose play 'Over the Bridge' was then enjoying a *succès de scandale* in Belfast. Mac-Neice's relationship with the BBC followed the pattern of his earlier relationships with other institutions – Marlborough, Oxford and Birmingham Universities, the British Council. He enjoyed the camaraderie of house, college, department; he excelled at his work, but was never an 'Institution man'. His political alignment, unlike that of many of his literary contemporaries, remained consistently left of centre, and it is clear that he was increasingly seen as subversive by the hierarchy of the BBC.

He celebrated his new freedom with a holiday, returning to the island of Sark with Mary and her son Charles. Early in the autumn, she and Louis were involved in a car-crash – an experience transmuted into a poem, 'After the Crash' – from which he emerged with badly bruised ribs. Before he had fully recovered he had another bruising encounter, with Hedli whom he arranged to meet in a London pub. Having bought her a drink, he popped a prepared question: 'Will you give me a divorce? I'm not coming back.' She refused, as advised by their mutual friend, the American poet, Allen Tate, who had told her: '*My* wife wouldn't give me one for five years and I'm so grateful to her!' Louis remonstrated, but she would not be shifted, and they parted amiably enough, with him saying 'Look after yourself' and her replying 'Enjoy yourself.'

* He died in 1968, his sister in 1981.

That autumn, in fulfilment of his part-time BBC contract, he under-
took a new production of his 1952 radio play, 'One Eye Wild', and
wrote a new one called 'Let's Go Yellow' (Fleet Street slang for 'Let's
go muck-raking'). Douglas Carson has argued that this 'was a thinly-
disguised account of the BBC's reaction to his programmes on South
Africa and Sam Thompson'. 'Bloody young Master Haman late of
Rugby and Oxford' has joined the staff of a big daily newspaper as
young Master MacNeice had joined the BBC. Haman's refusal to
exploit the grief of a racing motorist's widow causes him to be transferred from the News pages to the Diary, and he is subsequently fired for
exposing as a drug-dealer the son of a titled manufacturer worth
thousands of pounds in advertising revenue to the paper. When, however, it appears that, despite the embarrassing story (which the Editor
would have gladly suppressed), the manufacturer will continue to
advertise in the paper, the Editor adds hypocrisy to corruption by
declaring:

it's sometimes suggested that the policy of newspapers is influenced unduly by
the advertisers but, whatever may be the case with other papers, I think we
have now proved beyond any shadow of doubt that in *our* paper our sense of
duty comes first.

The circular movement characteristic of many of MacNeice's later
poems appears also in this play, when Haman offers a BBC producer
his *exposé* of Fleet Street. Asked if he has a title for it, he replies: 'I've
got one stamped on my heart . . . . It's a phrase they use in some *circles*
[my italics] – occasionally. Let's Go Yellow!'
   The programme was broadcast on 19 December 1961 and received a
favourable review in *The Listener* of 28 December, which particularly
praised MacNeice's ear for voices. He responded with a letter in the
issue of 4 January:

Like anyone who works in 'steam radio' I am naturally very gratified by a
favourable notice but I feel I should point out that your drama critic, in giving
such a notice to my programme 'Let's Go Yellow', handed a bouquet to the
producer that was really due to his cast. While I have in fact noticed that
'drunks' voices always go up at the end of a song', on this occasion I had no
need to explain this fact of life to the actors. I wish it were more generally
realised that in any radio production casting is half the battle.

His skill in this and other areas of production was noted that January by a visitor to Broadcasting House. There in Studio 8, the Indian writer, Ved Mehta, found him rehearsing an abridged version of his *Faust* translation and, with his own matchless ear for voices, recorded what he heard:

Surrounded by engineers and a secretary, he was sitting in a booth in front of a row of switches and gazing intently through the glass wall that separated him from a roomful of actors and actresses. Nervous tension, scattered instruction sheets, sound-effects records, and an array of mechanical apparatus gave the room the atmosphere of the cockpit of an airplane at the moment of takeoff.

'Mephisto, can you drop your voice an octave or so?' MacNeice said over the intercom. 'It should be deep.'

'Like the blue sea, Louis?' came the voice of Mephistopheles, in bass tones. He got a ripple of unsure laughter from the cast.

'All right,' MacNeice said. 'Let's take the scene through again.'

All concerned, on both sides of the glass partition, pencils in hand, turned to their scripts. A signal light went on, and a second later the studio was transformed into a cosmic stage by the contrapuntal voices of Mephistopheles, low and resonant, and Faust, high-pitched and distraught:

> 'I like to see the Old One now and then,
> And try to keep relations on the level.
> It's really decent of so great a person
> To talk so humanely, even to the Devil.'

> 'Here stand I, ach, Philosophy
> Behind me, and Law and Medicine, too,
> And, to my cost, Theology –
> All these I have sweated through and through,
> And now you see me a poor fool
> As wise as when I started school!'

Except during occasional interruptions from MacNeice ('Mephisto, point up "decent".... Faust, point down "ach"'), the poetry continued to vibrate and resound in the studio, but when Faust's assistant made his entrance into the study, the drama came to a stop. 'The door should be medieval – heavy and stiff on its hinges,' the producer said to the engineer, 'but it sounds modern.' None of the recordings from the sound-effects library of the B.B.C. were right; it required the mixing of two records – the scraping of a bunch of keys on a table and the shuffling of a chair – to reproduce, many minutes later, the lumbering door. It was, however, the arrangement of the effects for Easter Sunday that caused the longest delay. Recordings of bells – from Indian cowbells to the bells of the Cologne Cathedral – were assembled and reassembled, until there was an epiphany of sound, a flood of joyous clanging. Half an hour later, with one sound succeeding another, Easter was born to the slow, uneven strokes of Angelus bells.

The previous September, MacNeice had put forward a proposal for a 'modern morality' on an Irish theme; 'Seeing that Third are not interested in my Arthurian project, "The Remorse of Sir Gawayne", *and* seeing that for the last decade or more I have been pestered to write "another *Dark Tower*", I have a suggestion to make for the first quarter of next year.' This was accepted and in the first half of March he wrote, rapidly, 'The Mad Islands', a script based on the ancient Irish legend of the Voyage of Maeldúin. He had found this in P. W. Joyce's *Old Celtic Romances* and Alwyn and Brinley Rees's *Celtic Heritage*. It may have appealed to him because, as with 'The Dark Tower', its hero is sent on a mission by his mother. MacNeice's Muldoon had believed her dead, but she is found alive and sends him to sea in pursuit of his father's murderer, the Lord of the Eskers. His mission takes him – like Odysseus and Oisin – to a number of islands. He hears sirens and bells, but discovers at the last that his father, far from being murdered, was in fact the murderer of his mother's husband. The failed quest failed to provide the basis for a successful programme, and MacNeice apologized to Denys Hawthorne – who had played Muldoon – for giving him a weak part.

'The Mad Islands' was broadcast on 4 April and, shortly afterwards, his six-month BBC stint completed, the freelance poet came into his freedom again. Since Bimba had moved into the Regent's Park Terrace flat, he and Mary had been using the living-room as bed-sitter and study. They needed a whole house and, being unable to afford one in central London, began to look outside. They made an offer for one in Berkhamstead (near Mary's parents) but it was taken off the market and, in May, she found three cottages for sale as a single property in the Hertfordshire village of Aldbury. Two apple trees were blossoming in the garden of 39–43 Stocks Road (named after the nearby village stocks) and, remembering *Solstices*' opening poem, Mary fell in love

Denys Hawthorne

with the house and told Louis he should look at it. He did, noting with approval the Baptist Chapel next door and a bucolic pub, The Greyhound, only fifty yards away beside the village pond. Mary was waiting for him at Euston Station on his return. She hesitated to ask him what he thought of Aldbury and, when he said nothing about it, she feared the worst. At last, unable to contain herself, she burst out: 'Well, what did you think of the house?' 'Oh,' he said, 'we've bought that.'

It was not, of course, settled so simply. He had made an offer for the cottages, 'subject to survey', and it had been accepted. In due course, the surveyors checked the damp courses and tapped the beams, and MacNeice bought his first and last house for £5,200 (£4,000 of which was an interest-free loan from Mary's father, to be repaid at £50 a month). He would not take possession for another six months. In the meantime, happy with the pastoral prospect, but not yet manacled to a mortgage, he took ship – like Muldoon – to a mad island in the West.

The object of his quest was a dark tower – the Martello tower of Joyce's *Ulysses*, which had been refurbished and was to be opened as a museum on 'Bloomsday', 16 June 1962, forty years after the novel had been published (on Joyce's fortieth birthday, 2 February 1922). Appropriately, this museum of Joyceana was to be opened by his heroic publisher, Sylvia Beach, proprietor of the Shakespeare and Company bookshop in Paris. MacNeice crossed to Belfast, where he stayed with the MacCanns for the Whitsun weekend, before taking the familiar train south. Giving them an account of the week that followed, he wrote: 'At a conservative estimate the drinking during my 7 days there averaged 12 hours a day'. Much of it was done in the company of one of his favourite drinking cronies and conversational sparring-partners, Dominic Behan, author of *Teems of Times and Happy Returns*. MacNeice was staying with Behan, who annoyed him one evening, when – while drinking a whole bottle of whisky – he insisted that he was ten times the better writer because *Life Magazine* paid him ten times what *The New Statesman* paid MacNeice.

After several days of liquid preliminaries, Joyce Week began improbably, even by Dublin's high standards of improbability, with a ladies' fashion show in Kay Petersen's Anna Livia Boutique. She had cannily timed her first showing for 'Bloomsday Eve'. MacNeice was lucky enough to get a seat for this, as did Sylvia Beach and Madame Eugène Jolas (wife of the co-founder of the magazine *transition* which had published Joyce's *Finnegans Wake*). Behan was not so lucky: he got near the door but did not come in. MacNeice, who was covering Joyce Week for *The New Statesman*, reported: 'thirty-nine models, all "with Joycean titles" and some, such as "Molly Bloom", intended as "direct interpretations of Joyce's characters" – there was never a dull garment.'

Bloomsday itself began for him and other literati at Davy Byrne's, Joyce's favourite bar and the setting of the 'Lestrygonians' episode in *Ulysses*. Two 'freshly refurbished black and yellow four-wheeler horse cabs' were in attendance outside, waiting to carry them in style from the city centre to Sandycove and the Martello tower. This time, MacNeice did not get a seat: instead, he and Behan clambered aboard a taxi with a crate of Guinness. They were spotted by a friend, leaning, one out of the left-hand window, one out of the right, each brandishing a bottle. Reaching the tower, MacNeice took a quick turn round the museum before stationing himself at the entrance to the marquee erected for the occasion, in easy reach of the passing drink-trays.

He was back in Ireland that August, touring the west coast with Bimba in a small rented car (that, to his annoyance, had been 'souped down'). The high point of this happy expedition was their visit to the poet Richard Murphy in the Old Forge in Cleggan, Connemara (a fine house of pink granite he had built himself). He took them sailing to the island of Inishbofin in his converted Galway hooker, the *Ave Maria*.

Richard Murphy's *Ave Maria*

From there the MacNeices travelled to Sligo where, on 22 August, Louis lectured to the Yeats International Summer School. His topic that evening was 'Is Yeats a good model?' Some of those who heard him cannot remember his answer to that question, but only that 'he was a bit under the weather', perhaps a charitable euphemism.

Returning to England, he went back to work on his astrology book and would entertain his friends with such nuggets of information as: 'It seems that in Germany now the really highbrow astrologers calculate horoscopes with the help of *eight* purely hypothetical trans-Plutonian planets.' On 19 November, he took possession of the Stocks Road cottages and, on 22 December, he and Mary moved to Aldbury.

Charles came with them. Bimba stayed on in the Regent's Park Terrace flat, and her father – when working late – would sometimes stay there overnight, until it was sold at the end of January. She then rented a room in London with the allowance he paid her.

Ever since he had moved in with Mary the previous September, poems had continued to grow like coral, word upon word, in his head and in a succession of little blue notebooks carried in his jacket pocket. One of the few that it is possible to date, even approximately, is 'Goodbye to London'. Written before the end of the year, it takes its refrain from that of a poem then ascribed to Dunbar, 'In Honour of the City of London': 'London thou art the flour of cities all'. MacNeice rings a sombre change on this earlier poem's peal of celebration:

> Having left the great mean city, I make
> Shift to pretend I am finally quit of her
> Though that cannot be so long as I work.
>   Nevertheless let the petals fall
>   Fast from the flower of cities all.

Robyn Marsack shrewdly observes that MacNeice's opening line 'sets the tone of his poem: "great" here indicates both size and quality; although "mean" is pejorative, it hints at the opposite sense, as in Paul's declaration that he was "a citizen of no mean city" (Acts 21:39)'. The next three stanzas attempt Proustian evocations of the city as perceived by the child, the teenager, and the young man quoting Johnson: 'when a man is tired of London, he is tired of life'. I say attempt, because these lack the effervescence of such earlier London poems as *Autumn Journal* and 'The British Museum Reading Room' and, in each stanza, the lively movement of an opening tercet is undercut by the tolling couplet. With the fourth stanza, the war enters the poem and all that follows is anti-climax, disappointment, and a dying fall:

> Then came the headshrinking war, the city
> Closed in too, the people were fewer
> But closer too, we were back in the womb.
>   Nevertheless let the petals fall
>   Fast from the flower of cities all.

From which reborn into anticlimax
We endured much litter and apathy hoping
The phoenix would rise, for so they had promised.
    Nevertheless let the petals fall
    Fast from the flower of cities all.

And nobody rose, only some meaningless
Buildings and the people once more were strangers
At home with no one, sibling or friend.
    Which is why now the petals fall
    Fast from the flower of cities all.

Reminded of Dr Johnson's dictum, we are left with a sense that the poet is tired both of London and of life.

Similarly, in many earlier poems of 1962, the speaker seems less concerned with conducting a new life than with conducting his death (as Everyman put it in *One for the Grave*). Charon, in the poem of that name, is a conductor of a different kind:

The conductor's hands were black with money:
Hold on to your ticket, he said, the inspector's
Mind is black with suspicion, and hold on to
That dissolving map. We moved through London,
We could see the pigeons through the glass but failed
To hear their rumours of wars, we could see
The lost dog barking but never knew
That his bark was as shrill as a cock crowing,
We just jogged on, at each request
Stop there was a crowd of aggressively vacant
Faces, we just jogged on, eternity
Gave itself airs in revolving lights
And then we came to the Thames and all
The bridges were down, the further shore
Was lost in fog, so we asked the conductor
What we should do. He said: Take the ferry
Faute de mieux. We flicked the flashlight
And there was the ferryman just as Virgil
And Dante had seen him. He looked at us coldly
And his eyes were dead and his hands on the oar
Were black with obols and varicose veins

Marbled his calves and he said to us coldly:
If you want to die you will have to pay for it.

This is a brilliant development of the central image of an undergraduate poem, 'En Avant', that MacNeice had probably forgotten.*
Where that had been static, 'Charon' moves, inexorably but jauntily,
down to the last river and the last full stop. Much of the power of the
poem derives from its blending of ancient and modern, myth and black
comedy, ingredients of another late poem, 'This is the Life', involving a
similar descent:

Down the rock chute into the tombs of the kings they grope these battling
     sandalled
Elderly ladies in slacks and a hurry, their red nails clutching at hieroglyphics,
Down to the deep peace of the shelter, everything found, cuisine and service,
All the small ochred menials and livestock discreetly in profile, every
     convenience
Laid on free so that they may survive in the manner to which they are
     accustomed,
Gracious in granite – this is the life – with their minds made up for ever and
     the black
Sarcophagus made up ready for the night, they can hide their heads under the
     graveclothes
And every day in the dark below the desert will be one of both independence
     and thanksgiving
So they never need worry again as to what may fall out of the sky
But whenever they want can have a Pharaoh's portion of turkey and pumpkin
     pie.

The American tourists (perhaps from the PS *Sudan*) are satirized, but
so sympathetically that one must ask whether the satirist may not
himself believe what they only jokingly *profess* to believe: that 'this is
the life', a life preferable to that above ground.

Another such descent would end the collection of poems now taking
shape under MacNeice's hand. Its 'Coda' again moves from ancient
past and present towards a possible future:

---

* See pp. 155–6 above.

Maybe we knew each other better
When the night was young and unrepeated
And the moon stood still over Jericho.

So much for the past; in the present
There are moments caught between heart-beats
When maybe we know each other better.

But what is that clinking in the darkness?
Maybe we shall know each other better
When the tunnels meet beneath the mountain.

The person addressed and the future envisaged must be those of the dedicatory poem to the new collection, 'To Mary', and Edna Longley is surely right in seeing in the last line a reference to the meeting, in 1962, of the two ends of the tunnel cut through Mont Blanc. The memory of that moment of public history may, however, be conflated with a subconscious memory of an event in MacNeice's *private* history: his childhood visit to the salt-mines outside Carrickfergus. He and his sister, he says in *The Strings are False*,

had always wanted to go down under the earth to the caves of crystal and man-made thunder, to the black labyrinth of galleries under the carefree fields, under the tumbledown walls, the whins and the ragweed. We descended a pitch-black shaft in a great bucket, at the bottom was a cross of fire and there sure enough was the subterranean cathedral and men like gnomes in the clerestories, working with picks.

More than forty years later, it may be those salt-miners' picks that he hears 'clinking in the darkness'. This would accord with all the other memories of childhood mined in such late poems as 'Soap Suds', 'Round the Corner', 'Château Jackson', 'Children's Games', 'Star Gazer', and in the unscripted 'Childhood Memories' that MacNeice recorded for John Boyd in July 1963.

With the move to Aldbury, he and Mary began to 'know each other better'. He bought her a gold ring with the signs of the Zodiac incised on it, and away from the stresses and temptations of London, his drinking fell to a couple of pints of Guinness at lunch-time and a couple more in the evening. Their weekends were generally festive, with teenagers running in and out, the TV and gramophone on, good

food cooking, and Mary presiding with an engaging blend of home-
liness and glamour. Through all this – and oblivious to it – Louis
would be writing, drinking black tea, and eating ginger biscuits. His
concentration was remarkable: Mary once put the same record on time
after time to see if he would notice. He did not.

Their life together, however, was no cloudless pastoral. Each was
working – she in the BBC, and he on the astrology book he considered
hack-work – and each was subject to periodic fits of depression. He
could rescue her from hers, but she could not dispel his occasional
'cosmic glooms'. These and, specifically, the shadow of approaching
death darken his later poems –

> The lines of print are always sidelines
> And all our games funeral games [–]

though the darkness, like that of Yeats's last poems, is often lit by wit
and a certain gaiety.

Late in 1962 or early in 1963, he assembled them into a book-length
sequence, but before he could send it to Fabers he had to give it a title.
Finding the choice difficult, he gave the typescript to Anthony Thwaite
and asked his advice. They met one afternoon in The ML (which was
open, as pubs were not, between 3 o'clock and 5.30). Thwaite urged
him to call the book *Funeral Games*, 'but Louis opined that this title
would kill the book stone dead. He inclined towards something to do
with Pyres – *Pyres and Journeys*, *Pyres and Staircases*, *Pyres and
Corners*, *Pyres and Margins*: he jotted these down on a bit of paper'.
The typescript he sent off to Fabers was called *Round The Corner*. The
printer's 'specimen page' carried that title, but the poet subsequently
changed it to *The Burning Perch* (a phrase from the poem 'Budgie').
This was the first of three books he would finish in 1963. MacNeice, by
this point, may have been a serious drinker, but he was still producing
more and better work than most of his seriously sober contemporaries.
'Louis is tough,' George MacCann used to say. 'He could work hard all
day and drink hard all night and rise the following day ready to absorb
more punishment.' He continued to work not only hard, but also fast
and well, reviewing, for example, as acutely as ever; and a list of his
reviews of books of Irish interest would give eloquent testimony of his
lifelong concern with his native land.

A pride of literary lions: Spender, MacNeice, Tom Driberg, Auden, Eliot, Hughes

At the start of 1963, he set astrology aside while he wrote a set of lectures on a subject close to his heart. These, the Clark Lectures, were delivered in Cambridge, under the title 'Varieties of Parable', on 28 February, 7 and 14 March, 25 April, 2 and 9 May. The first defined the area he proposed to explore: the forms of 'double-level' writing – parable, symbolism, allegory, fable, fantasy, and myth. Succeeding lectures focused on Spenser and Bunyan; the Romantics (Coleridge, Shelley, and Blake, with a coda on Christina Rossetti and Hans Andersen); the Victorians (Lewis Carroll, Charles Kingsley, and George Macdonald); contemporary poetry and drama (Eliot, Auden, Muir, Ibsen, Beckett, and Pinter) and contemporary prose narratives (Beckett, Kafka, and Golding). As with the critical pronouncements of other poets, playwrights, and novelists, MacNeice's Clark Lectures shed valuable light on his own priorities and procedures. Discussing the relationship between Housman's poem 'Her strong enchantments failing' and his own radio play 'The Queen of Air and Darkness', he described Housman as an 'underrated poet with whom any history of modern English poetry might very well start'. He had just accepted another commission from his long-suffering friend Dan Davin; one that appealed to him much more than the now terminally paralysed *Character of Ireland*. He had agreed to edit an *Oxford Book of Twentieth-Century Verse* and proposed, he told Thwaite, 'to begin with Hardy and Housman, and then the bulk of the book would give solid prominence to Yeats, Eliot, Lawrence, Muir, Graves, Owen, and Auden. He was not at all sure about Edith Sitwell'.

Again, a remark in the last of his Clark Lectures is relevant to what may have been his last completed poem. Speaking of Beckett, he said: 'the absence of God implies the need of God and therefore the presence of at least something spiritual in man'. The poem 'Thalassa'* goes further:

> Run out the boat, my broken comrades;
> Let the old seaweed crack, the surge
> Burgeon oblivious of the last
> Embarkation of feckless men,
> Let every adverse force converge –
> Here we must needs embark again.
>
> Run up the sail, my heartsick comrades;
> Let each horizon tilt and lurch –
> You know the worst: your wills are fickle,
> Your values blurred, your hearts impure
> And your past life a ruined church –
> But let your poison be your cure.
>
> Put out to sea, ignoble comrades,
> Whose record shall be noble yet;
> Butting through scraps of moving marble
> The narwhal dares us to be free;
> By a high star our course is set,
> Our end is Life. Put out to sea.

The speaker might be Ulysses: MacNeice had quoted Tennyson's poem of that title in the radio script he had written with Ritchie Calder, 'The Star We Follow' (25 December 1955). In Tennyson's dramatic monologue, Ulysses speaks of his son and, in MacNeice's, a son speaks with the accent, the diction, and the confidence of his father. As the Bishop

---

* The Greek word 'sea' shouted by Xenophon's troops. See pp. 119 and 454 above. This poem may owe something to MacNeice's experience of sailing in Richard Murphy's *Ave Maria*.

would have recognized (and most critics of his son's poetry have not), this is a religious poem.

Memories of his father and mother were never far below the surface of MacNeice's mind and, after the last of the Clark Lectures, he agreed to write and record a talk about his childhood for his friend John Boyd. On the day set for the recording, Boyd met him in Rothwell House and (as he tells the story in his memoirs) MacNeice seemed surprised to see him:

> I said reproachfully, 'Your script didn't arrive in Belfast.'
> 'Oh, I'm sorry about that,' he said. 'Couldn't we do it another time?'
> 'No, I want you to do it now.'
> 'But I haven't written it,' he retorted edgily.
> 'Well, you should have, Louis. I've studio 8B booked from two to two-thirty. It's now a quarter to two. Time to scribble a few notes on a scrap of paper and do it off the cuff.'

Eventually, after further attempts at prevarication, he jotted down:

> 1st House: 2nd House; Dramatis Personae: Church and Castle: Walks: Houses: Books: Titanic and War.

> That was all, and it was enough to evoke the years he spent as a child in Carrickfergus ....
> At the end of the recording he looked across the microphone at me and said, 'Well, will that do all right?'
> 'Yes. Exactly what I wanted.'
> 'What about a drink now?'
> 'I feel like one,' I said, and I did.

In late June, he was in Ireland, covering President Kennedy's visit to the Irish Republic for *The New Statesman* and, on his return to England, wrote what was to prove his last radio play, and one of his best. On 11 January, he had sent the Assistant Head of the Features Department the following synopsis for an hour-long programme:

A PERSON FROM PORLOCK

This idea was given to me – some time ago – by H[ead of]. F[eatures]. It would take the form of a dramatised (fictitious) biography and the theme would be the recurrent frustration of the human individual by interruptions of the kind represented by Coleridge's "Person from Porlock" (the original reference

471

could be made clear in the opening Announcement). While my hero would be far from being a Coleridge, I *would* make him a (potential) artist, since the shattering or curtailment of artistic vision is a particularly concentrated and clear-cut example of the kind of frustration that can ruin a man's life.

The following is a tentative Synopsis, subject as usual to various changes in setting, technical detail, etc.

Synopsis

I   Hero (born c. 1917) in early adolescence, fixated on his Mother who is romantically Left-Wing (slump on of course at the time) and is already moulding him in her image. But enter 'person from Porlock' (i.e. Mother's lover) who persuades her to abandon her family – and political ideas into bargain. Long-lasting trauma for hero.

II   Hero as art-student c. beginning of World War II. Scenes of argument between him and male drinking crony and girl art student. Display of canvas – 'The rest's all here in my head'; he is just beginning to get somewhere in painting. But the Person from Porlock this time is the Call-up.

III   After the War, which hero has spent largely in Burma, having love-hate relationship with Army. Now demobilised but nostalgic for life of action (and delegated responsibility); doesn't feel he can paint again but has got job for, say, some firm like Shell and is in love. Along comes high-up Shell-man or such Person from Porlock and offers him a good job overseas for, say, three years minimum. Takes job, loses beloved.

IV   Home again, having broken contract. Is consequently out of job but trying to paint again. Has started affair with erstwhile Girl Art Student (now married). But owing to expensive habits acquired overseas is terribly in debt. Last purchase a very extravagant mammoth super-easel. Vision just breaking through again – half-finished canvas on easel – when Person from Porlock (Bailiff) enters and starts removing furniture, ending with easel after argument as to whether this is essential tool of trade or just piece of furniture.

V   Hero now bankrupt. Vision gone but becomes commercial designer, at which successful. Continues affairs with Girl Art Student. Enter private divorce detective (Person from Porlock). Girl Art Student, outraged, abandons hero for good. Hero's financial problems look worse than ever.

VI   Hero has inherited house (possibly from wicked mother) which he does up with skill, hoping to sell it for enough to get himself discharged (i.e. sum which few would offer). Re-enter Beloved who rejects Hero's over-tures but lays on interview with tycoon who may buy house. When interview due, re-enter Drinking Crony (Person from Porlock). Late for interview. Hero borrows car, drives drunk, crashes, loses teeth and licence. No sale of house.

VII   Hero still bankrupt but recovering vision. Takes sketching and climbing holiday in Wales or some such place. Gets cut off in blizzard on rock-shelf. Hears series of voices (including those of Mother, Beloved, Bailiff and Drinking Crony). But 'everything begins to come clear'. Then a voice announcing the last Person from Porlock (death).

I quote this in full because so much was to be changed in the writing. The Hero is a familiar compound of MacNeice himself and George MacCann, painter and veteran of the Burma campaign. The abandoning mother and the Girl Art Student, the divorce detective, debt, drinking, and car-crash are all taken 'from the life', and the experience on the mountain from life at second hand (*The Conquest of Everest*).

The synopsis was approved, though with the suggestion (fiercely resisted by MacNeice) that the Coleridgean title should be changed: his counter-proposal of 'Persons from Porlock' was accepted. Auden called the finished play 'a magnificent example of ... psychological drama', and it became that when, in the writing, MacNeice moved his story to a deeper symbolic level by giving his hero – Hank – an obsessive interest not with mountains but with caves. Taken pot-holing by his friend Peter for the first time, he exclaims: 'Talk about back to the womb! Difference is the womb was soft.' Hank speculates that his rejection by his mother may be what made him take up painting. We are clearly meant to suppose that it also made him take up pot-holing, which he finds 'excitingly timeless'. His girlfriend, Sarah, makes connections between these passions when she tells him his best paintings 'come from the depths'. One of his pictures of an underground cave is mistaken for a fan-vaulted church, and, asked if painting is his hobby, he answers: 'Hobby! It's my bloody cross.' MacNeice is remembering the childhood visit to the salt-mines described in *The Strings are False*: 'at the bottom was a cross of fire and there sure enough was the subterranean cathedral'. In the aftermath of that visit, he had a dream:

the gnomes had caught me, imprisoned me under the ground until I should find a certain jewel. A hopeless task; I wandered under the vaults groping

473

through heaps of shattered quartzite rocks. Then met another prisoner, a girl; we decided to give up the hunt, to brave the gnomes and make our escape to daylight. No sooner decided than we found ourselves in a lift, an enormous lift fitted up as a teashop; a middle-aged man was eating bacon and eggs; no one took any notice of us. So there we were going up, sometimes the lift would stop, people come in and get out, but no one took any notice. It was frightening but almost hilarious. Then as we rose to the light I do not know what became of the girl but I woke up.

More than forty years later, it is a memory of that dream which resurfaces when Mervyn, one of Hank's pot-holing companions, speaks of

the biggest cave in the world, the Carlsbad Cavern in New Mexico. Do you know it has an intake of five hundred persons per hour? They whiz down by elevator eight hundred feet and what do they find when they get there? A quick feed restaurant . . . .

Again, when the water-level rises in the underground stream, the so-called Stygian Trap in which he will drown, another memory rises. Hank says: 'I noticed a funny bit of crystal in there in the wall of the tunnel – No, my God, it's submerged!' When his end of the rope attached to Mervyn (who has gone ahead into a further cave) is swept away, Hank is advised by a third member of the team to wait. However, rather than fail his friend as he has failed himself and others before, he dives into the swollen stream to attempt a rescue. The final and most powerful movement of the play follows that of MacNeice's earlier 'He Had a Date'. In another dreamlike sequence, a drowning man is brought to a deeper self-knowledge by voices from his past, and it is eerily appropriate that the poet's last, bleakest, self-projection should come full circle, returning not simply to a cave (explicitly associated with the womb) but to the paternal stream under the maternal rock.

Once he had finished writing the play MacNeice set about casting and producing it. The concern with accurate sound-effects, shown in his recent production of *Faust*, led him to send a recording engineer with a pot-holer guide to the Settle caves on the Yorkshire moors. No doubt because he was fascinated by caves and had happy memories of his visit to Yorkshire with John Sharp, he decided to go too. He set off on 7 August, and the following day wrote to Bimba (who was staying with her grandparents in Switzerland):

I'm just back from Yorkshire where I spent yesterday recording effects in a cave for my next programme. We got a nice underground stream, also a waterfall, also general drippings. There were lots of stalagmites & stalactites, some of the latter very delicate. By contrast we returned to Leeds for the evening where we visited an ancient music hall called the Palace of Varieties, now much invaded by strip: there was one lurid act where the girl was chased by a gorilla.

I'm prerecording this programme which is called *Persons from Porlock* (the central character by the way is a frustrated painter!) this Sunday: it goes out on August 30th. The final person from Porlock is Death (in a cave) & has a Somerset accent.

This letter makes no mention of the fact that, while the final recordings were made, he had returned to the moors for a stroll (and no doubt a smoke). It was a wet summer and he was caught in a heavy storm that soaked him to the skin. Not until he was back in Aldbury did he change out of his wet clothes. When Bob Pocock met him in The George on 11 August, 'he looked feverish and tired, and his cough, always troublesome at the best of times, now obviously caused him pain. But when we advised him to go back to the country, he only exclaimed "Ach!" and cut his hand away in that dismissive way of his.' The following day, Dorothy Baker looked in at his office and found him having difficulty breathing. 'Louis, you've got bronchitis', she said. 'No,' he replied, 'it's only a cold.'

'You must go to bed.'

'I can't. I'm going to Ireland to stay with Richard Murphy.'

He did, eventually, go back to Aldbury and, on 20 August wrote to Bimba apologizing for 'his striggly handwriting' and explaining: 'I'm writing in bed, which I've been confined to for several days with a mystery temperature. Haven't smoked since last Thursday!' He sounded cheerful enough, however, and told her he had been reading *The Country Girls* by Edna O'Brien and rereading 'most of Carson McCullers & *The Power & the Glory*'. Three days later, he wrote again: 'Am still not recovered & am getting v. fed up with it.' Once or twice, repeating an old (half-serious) refrain, he said to Mary: 'Louis wants to be under green grass.'* She bought green rafia paper for the present she was going to give him on his birthday in three weeks' time. By Tuesday 27 August he was having great difficulty with his breathing, and she rang his sister to voice her concern. Elizabeth drove down to Aldbury – it was her first visit to Stocks Road – and recognizing that his condition was serious, asked him if he would agree to go into hospital. When he said 'yes', Mary knew that he knew it was serious.

Elizabeth drove him up to St Leonard's Hospital, Shoreditch, where her husband was senior surgeon and, that evening, rang Mary to say he had viral pneumonia. Mary went up to see him on Thursday and Friday. He had been given antibiotics, which had so far had no effect (probably because his constitution had been undermined by alcohol and tobacco), but everyone was sufficiently optimistic for Elizabeth to ring Bob Pocock with the message that Louis would like to see visitors. Accordingly, on the Friday evening, he and Laurence Gilliam went to the hospital. Pocock later described their visit:

Louis was in a private ward, propped up with pillows, taking sharp, painful breaths, and holding an oxygen mask. His hair had grown long, accentuating its greyness, so that he looked suddenly very much older. His eyes were lack-lustrous, except when coughing shook him and he lay back; then they had a hunted look. Above all, it was the exhaustion that was most disturbing: the utter and, one felt, the ultimate weariness that the face showed.

Laurence did his best, big and urbanely witty, the Savile clubman, retailing shop and gossip. It was a creditable act. Did he want anything – cigarettes? Louis raised his oxygen mask. Books? – there was a stack on the bedside table. Drink? – Louis closed his eyes. We stayed for about twenty minutes, and during that time he barely spoke. Then, just as we were about to leave, he suddenly pointed to the window and asked, 'What is there outside?' The prospect could scarcely have been more depressing: the two wings of the hospital, drab Victorian buff and Edwardian red brick, enclosed a sooty lawn with a shabby plane tree as centre piece. Beyond were high barracks of council flats. Laurence described the scene in faithful detail. It had been a day of showers, and the sun was going down in stormy colours. I had been a poor foil for Laurence's flow of talk, but now I said, 'And the sky, Louis, is by Blake.' The same sky had shown one evening five years before from the balcony of a

---

* 'We had always wanted to go down under the earth . . . under the carefree fields, under the tumbledown walls, the whins and the ragweed' (SAF, p. 75).

riverside pub at Rotherhithe, and I had made the same remark, adding 'Blake could be a pretty amateur painter at times,' and Louis had replied, 'Yes, and sometimes a pretty amateur poet, as well.' He may have remembered, for at least he gave a faint smile.

That evening, 'Persons from Porlock' was broadcast and many of those close to MacNeice heard it with great foreboding.

Other friends visited him. John Sharp drove up from Sussex in pouring rain: 'Very good of you, John,' said the patient, 'but bloody silly in this weather.' Dan Davin looked in to tell him that the Oxford University Press wanted to reissue his book on Yeats – 'His smile glimmered, but only to please me.'

Mary told him she would put Sabre, their new Great Dane, into kennels; close the cottage; and move to London over the weekend. On Sunday, Elizabeth rang her in Aldbury to say: 'You must come up, but don't go straight to the hospital or he'll be alarmed by the change of plan.' That day the patient disconcerted his doctors, gathered round his bed, with the quizzical question: 'Am I supposed to be dying?' At 1 a.m. on Monday, Mary and Elizabeth were called to the hospital. Mary stayed with him that day and the following night, telling him stories and talking of going to Paris (she for the first time), drinking Pernod at a pavement café. On Tuesday morning the colour returned to his face, which she took as an encouraging sign but Elizabeth recognized as a mark of impending death. Then, very quietly, at 10.20 in the morning of 3 September – St MacNissi's Day – Louis MacNeice put out to sea.

Afterword

The Times of 4 September carried an anonymous obituary (written, at least in part, Hedli believed, by Jack Dillon) that offered a just assessment of the man and his work:

It might be said that Louis MacNeice was a poet's poet. He never sought the easy limelit road to a mass audience. On the other hand he avoided the wilfully 'difficult' and esoteric. He brought a delicate and fastidious craft to the expression of a robust but equally fastidious mind. None of his poems could ever have been mistaken for another man's; few of his fellow-poets could match him in either fecundity or ingenuity.

The fellow-poet whose good opinion MacNeice most valued, T. S. Eliot, paid his own tribute in *The Times* of 5 September. A tribute of another kind was paid by George MacCann, who crossed the Irish Sea to do his old friend one last service: capturing in a death mask the high furrowed forehead, laughter ripples fanned out from the outer corner of each closed eye, the aquiline nose, full lips slightly parted, and firm chin.

The funeral, organized by Elizabeth Nicholson, was held on Saturday 7 September in St John's Wood Church. The previous evening, Hedli had telephoned Mary Wimbush to suggest they sit together. Mary could not face this and excused herself saying she felt she should sit with her family. The service was due to start at 11 a.m., but at a quarter past the hour mourners were still arriving, there was no sign of Hedli or the coffin, and the organist had all but exhausted his repertoire. Then Hedli arrived, majestic in a voluminous mantilla, to take her place in the front pew. Mary, holding a bunch of red roses, had long been seated, disconsolate, at the back. Finally, the coffin arrived, having been held up by dense traffic heading for Lord's, where Sussex

George MacCann's death mask of MacNeice

were playing Worcestershire in the final of the Gillette county cricket competition – an irony the occupant of the coffin would have enjoyed.

And so, at last, his funeral began. A young cleric kinsman, who bore a striking resemblance to the black-haired MacNeice of the Thirties, read the lesson. The congregation sang Bunyan's hymn, 'Who would true valour see', and soon emerged, blinking, into bright sunshine. The service had seemed to Bob Pocock, in one important respect, more like a wedding than a funeral, 'for the family were on one side of the aisle, and Mary with her relations on the other. And so it was afterwards

479

when we went to drink, as Louis would have wished: there were the two separate camps.' Hedli held court in a wine-bar, Mary in a pub, and George MacCann played the part of whipper-in between the two. Meanwhile, the poet's body was on its way to the crematorium and, in due course, his ashes were laid to rest in Irish soil – the Carrowdore churchyard grave of his mother and maternal grandfather.

On 13 September, the day after what should have been his fifty-sixth birthday, *The Burning Perch* was published. It was the Autumn Choice of the Poetry Book Society, and in a note for the society's Bulletin he had written:

When I assembled the poems in *The Burning Perch* (I am not happy about the title but could not think of anything better), I was taken aback by the high proportion of sombre pieces, ranging from bleak observations to thumbnail nightmares. The proportion is far higher than in my last book, *Solstices*, but I am not sure why this should be so. Fear and resentment seem here to be serving me in the same way as Yeats in his old age claimed to be served by 'lust and rage', and yet I had been equally fearful and resentful of the world we live in when I was writing *Solstices*. All I can say is that I did not set out to write this kind of poem: they happened. I am reminded of Mr. Eliot's remark that the poet is concerned not only with beauty but with 'the boredom and the horror and the glory'. . . .

. . . I would venture the generalisation that most of these poems are two-way affairs or at least spiral ones: even in the most evil picture the good things, like the sea in one of these poems, are still there round the corner.*

Some of the book's reviewers recognized – as Auden did from seeing certain of his friend's last poems in newspapers – that they were 'among his very best', but none perceived its relation to his earlier books; how it brought his work full circle.

A memorial service was held on 17 October in the Church of All Souls, Langham Place, under the lee of Broadcasting House. After the opening sentences, the psalm (*De Profundis*), and the lesson (St Matthew 6:19–7:5), there was sung, to a setting by Alan Rawsthorne, MacNeice's own 'Canzonet':

---

* The Editor of *The Poetry Society Bulletin* followed this note with a note of his own:

This contribution by Louis MacNeice must have been one of the last things he wrote before his death on 3 September 1963. He sent it with a letter dated August 26th, apologising for delay and saying 'my doctor won't let me go to London yet, so everything is awkward.'

A thousand years and none the same
Since we to light and love-light came;

A thousand years and who knows how
Bright flower breaks from charnel bough.

Tomb and dark grow light and green
Till blind men see, heart be seen;

A thousand years of flower and flame,
A thousand years and none the same.

There followed prayers, another rendering of 'Who would true valour see', and then Auden delivered the address:

He stood in the All Souls pulpit, high in the air with the morning light from Nash's tall, neoclassical windows behind him as though at any moment he might extend vast wings and flap his creaking way over the heads of the congregation, his face lined like a kindly toad peering this way and that to confirm Louis was not there, that the incredible had happened, Louis was no longer to be seen or talked to. The words were accompanied by a road drill from a neighbouring street.

John Boyd thought Auden's praise 'precise and generous'; others, that it was a curiously muted performance. Certainly it lacked the warmth of a later poem, 'The Cave of Making', he addressed to MacNeice. Later still, Hedli, who had known him best, would write the best – most accurate, most eloquent – tribute of all. She called it 'The Story of the House that Louis Built':

It was a handsome house with thick walls. The windows on the west side looked towards Connemara, Mayo and the Sea. Those to the south scanned Dorset, The Downs and Marlborough – the windows to the north overlooked Iceland and those to the east, India.

The front door was wide and always open.

The Antechamber was full of people coming and going, administrators, doctors, dentists, critics, power men and smooth business agents, the everyday encounter who would say if asked that Louis was shy, arrogant, cold, polite, unapproachable, they didn't really know him, they would say. . . .

The second chamber had a strong door opening into a big Room with a Bar against which Louis would lean watching the door for the unexpected and exciting. Those that entered had always something to offer, journalists with travellers' tales of distant wars, poets, actors, those who talked 'shop' be it of radio, music or mountain climbing. Louis would talk but more often listen, sometimes he would draw a small note book from his breast pocket and write a word or two or else jot down a small sum of money lent for a drink, or again he would pull his handkerchief out and make a knot in the corner, a reminder for something to be done. These handkerchieves still with their knots would be reverently washed and ironed by his maid.* The next door was locked to all but a few. This room had shabby furniture, comfortable chairs and an open fire – books everywhere, for in this room, with these few friends Louis felt at ease, safe from the unexpected blow or the verbal knife in the back. There he worked, to these few people he gave all his affection and loyalty. Beyond this room there was a very small one, just space for two: himself and a Welsh poet Dylan Thomas or an Irish W. R. Rodgers. With them he would, manuscripts in hand, discuss the making of poetry, but only with them. Beyond was a passage leading to a chamber whose ceiling was a glass dome through which stars could be seen. There Louis would be alone with God, or as he called them the Great Presences, Greek or Roman, or again Dante, Donne, Spenser and the Elizabethans, and closer, to Yeats, Eliot and Auden.

Perhaps humbly through them, he would measure his own achievement.

Upstairs there were two rooms, the first, rather bare, received the casual lady encounter or the tentative relationship of short duration.

The second room contained paintings, flowers, a grand piano and was elegantly furnished – there, the five ladies of his life lingered, some more than others. The first, a young girl 'with whom I shared an idyll five years long'. Through her he finally escaped from the Anglican church, background of his father. The next four all had worlds of their very own, a painter, a writer, a singer to whom he was married for eighteen years and a talented actress.

Over the lintel of that door was written Love, Loyalty, Loneliness and Disillusion.

On September 3rd 1963, with the words 'Am I supposed to be dying?', he quietly closed the door of the house he had built.

In one sense the house was still unfinished. It was completed by his loyal friend and executor, E. R. Dodds, who saw through the press or edited *The Mad Islands and The Administrator* (1964), *Astrology* (1964), *The Strings are False: An Unfinished Autobiography* (1965), *Varieties of Parable* (1965), *Collected Poems of Louis MacNeice* (1966), *One for the Grave: A Modern Morality Play* (1968), *Persons*

---

* The faithful Restituta.

from Porlock and Other Plays for Radio (1969), and *The Revenant: A Song Cycle* (1975).

As is often the case with poets, MacNeice's reputation entered the doldrums with his death. For too long his name had been bracketed with those of Auden, Day Lewis, and Spender, and increasingly it came to be seen that he was not a part of the MacSpaunday pantomime horse. Where then did he belong? 'For the English reader he appears to be Irish,' wrote Tom Paulin, 'while for certain Irish readers he doesn't really belong to Ireland.'

Appropriately, MacNeice, the 'poet's poet', was 'placed' – and his reputation re-established – by the next generation of Northern Irish poets, who found him a more congenial and exemplary model than Yeats. Derek Mahon and Paul Muldoon celebrated him in poems ('In Carrowdore Churchyard' and '7 Middagh Street', respectively); Muldoon gave him pride of place in his *Faber Book of Contemporary Irish Poetry* (1986); Tom Paulin, Peter McDonald, and Seamus Heaney, in their critical writings, have given perceptive accounts of his work; and Michael Longley has edited a new *Selected Poems* (1988) to replace Auden's original and now outdated selection.

MacNeice has been fortunate in his champions and critics (by no means all of them Irish). They have introduced him to successive generations of readers as the celebrant of a world that is unmistakably their own:

> Now the till and the typewriter call the fingers,
>   The workman gathers his tools
> For the eight-hour day but after that the solace
>   Of films or football pools
> Or of the gossip or cuddle, the moments of self-glory
>   Or self-indulgence, blinkers on the eyes of doubt,
> The blue smoke rising and the brown lace sinking
>   In the empty glass of stout.

No other poet of the Thirties – and not many since – would have had the honesty to follow such an evocation of the wage slaves' world with the tempter's whisper:

> 'But you also
> Have the slave-owner's mind,

> Would like to sleep on a mattress of easy profits,
>   To snap your fingers or a whip and find
> Servants or houris ready to wince and flatter
>   And build with their degradation your self-esteem . . . .'

The poet has the Bishop's integrity. He does not pretend to be other than he is, and his sympathies – unlike the sympathies of some other Anglo-Irish poets – were more commonly with the slaves than with the slave-owners. The early loss of his mother to the grave, a Downs Syndrome brother to an institution and, later, a wife to another man gave him a fellow feeling for the deprived and suffering, an admiration for

> The routine courage of the worker,
> The gay endurance of women.

His last book of poems is as 'much possessed by death' as his first, but both are enlivened by wit and wild gaiety, and it is hard to think of a *Collected Poems* that bears witness to a keener delight in the world and 'The drunkenness of things being various'. Hard to think of a poet's eye that sees with such Martian clarity and exuberance (before Martians were) how, for example, 'a pigeon scores an outer/On a scholarly collar'. Hard to think of a poet with a more consistent and distinctive voice. It is not an idiosyncratic voice like that of Hardy or Hopkins. It is not a voice that moves down a register in mid-career like Yeats's, or up a register like Eliot's. It is a voice of a man talking to men and women and children; a man in love with language and the play of language. Like other people in love, he wrote too much ('my trouble all my life', he told Hedli, 'has been *over*-production'), but so did Wordsworth. Writers must be judged by their best work, and how many English-speaking poets of this century have written better long poems than *Autumn Journal* or better short poems than 'Snow', 'The Sunlight on the Garden', 'The Strand', 'House on a Cliff', or 'Charon'? Michael Longley has rightly praised in MacNeice the zest that Mac-Neice praised in Yeats. For all their differences, the greatest Irish poets of our century have this in common: 'a leaping vitality – the vitality of Cleopatra waiting for the asp'.

APPENDICES
SELECT BIBLIOGRAPHY
NOTES AND INDEX

The *dramatis personae* of *Autumn Sequel*

Aidan	:	O'Malley
Aloys	:	Stahl
Blundell	:	René Cutforth [?]*
Boyce	:	Dodds
Calum	:	MacIver
Costa	:	Ghika
Devlin	:	Dillon
Egdon	:	Auden
Esther	:	Mary Ezra
Evans	:	W. V. Thomas
Gavin	:	Shepard
Gorman	:	Rodgers
Gwilym	:	Dylan Thomas
Harrap	:	Harding
Herriot	:	Gilliam
Hilary	:	Blunt
Isabel	:	Eleanor Clark
Jenny	:	Nancy Spender
McQuitty	:	Tom Agnew†
Maguire	:	MacCann
Owen	:	Littleton Powys
Price	:	Goronwy Rees
Reilly	:	F. R. Higgins
Stretton	:	Hilton
Wimbush	:	Herickx

* A Features Department scriptwriter/producer, drinking companion and friend of FLM and AMHM.
† A Belfast-born Chartered Accountant, Agnew lived with his wife, Ellie, on the ketch-rigged hooker, *Mary Ann of Galway*, on the Thames outside London and in other parts of the British Isles. They, too, were drinking companions and friends of FLM and, to a lesser extent, AMHM.

Prologue

The Romans looked the other way, the roads
Remained boreens and never ran on time:
With cattle raids and treachery, with tangled
Woods like dark intrigues, long since cut down
Only to leave intrigues, with will o' the wisps
Like un-thought-out ideals, with ragged walls
Gapped like a faulty argument, with haycocks
Sodden-grey and resigned like slaves, with cormorants
Waiting to pounce like priests, with blue hills waiting
Like women to shed their loneliness, with whins
Blazing like chronic birthdays, with explosions
Of rooks like jokes in crowded bars, with cries
Of black-faced sheep like black-faced ghosts, with tramps
Like thorn-trees walking, tattered and gnarled, with salmon
Hovering side by side, keeping position,
Headed upstream like lovers, with cairns and turf-stacks
Keeping position like hermits, with broken cliffs
Keeping position like broken heroes, with waves
Breaking upon them like time, with sunlight breaking
Sideways through the clouds like a word of God,
With grey gone amethyst, dun gone purple, green
Gone greenest yet, with rock and muck no longer
Rock and muck but light, light immanent, light transcendent,
Light that takes in all colour, then suddenly fades;
With all this flaring and fading, soaring and sinking,
Roaring and dreaming, caterwauling and song,
Day and decay, night and delight, joy and alloy,
Pros and cons, glitter and filth, this island,
Hitched to the sun that sets in the Atlantic,
Lumbers into her misty west. In vain

The Norman castle and the Tudor bribe:
The natives remained native, took their bribe
And gave their word and broke it, while the brambles
Swamped the deserted bastion. Thus today
Some country house, up to its neck in weeds,
Looks old enough to stand its ground beside
The bone-grey bog oak in the bogs. The old
Disorder keeps its pattern while the new
Order has gone stagnant, barely moving
Except for bubbles of gas or foreign insects
Skidding across the surface: in the dance-halls,
Even those in the Gaeltacht, siren voices
Ogle our mute inglorious saints and heroes
To brave the seas and join the glossy future.
Have with you to Ben Bulben! To the tourist
This land may seem a dreamland, an escape.
But to her sons and even more her daughters
A dream from which they yearn to wake; the liner
Outhoots the owls of the past. The saffron kilt
May vie with the Orange sash but the black and white
Of the press of the rest of the world scales down their feuds
To storms in a broken teacup. What is the Border
Compared with the mushroom fears of the dizzy globe
In which no borders hold? Yet at this phase
With her children either leaving and losing Ireland
Or remaining there to lose themselves, we can still
Take stock before we are silenced. What can we offer
To still make sense or leave a grateful taste?
'The Character of Ireland'? Character?
A stage convention? A historical trap?
A geographical freak? Let us dump the rubbish
Of race and talk to the point: what is a nation?
Have with you to the Post Office! Was it a nation
They gave their lives for, was it rather a gesture
That as in a poem, a play, a flourish of brushwork,
Gives meaning to an accident, in passing
Confirms what was not there? So in their passing

Did sixteen men impose upon their fellows
An unsolicited poetry? Which, needless
To say, as soon as it could relapsed to prose –
A land of priests and grocers. Here we are then,
If only for a little, asking questions
And staying, for a little, for an answer
Which well may melt in our hands. Of course there are facts,
However expurgated, inflated, doctored,
But what do they add up to? Some QED
We had not wished to demonstrate? As if
One kept the diary of a love affair
Leaving out all the part that is writ in water,
That interflow of feeling. Even so
We who were born in this land of words and water
Know that to judge a love by facts alone –
And even should the affair be ended – means
To say it never happened. Which is false.
What happened must persist. As the past persists
For all the siren voices of the liners
And, for all the standing scum in committee room and office,
Water elsewhere keeps flowing. Between the lines
Of prose we can glimpse the ripple, as through the holes
In the official mask we can catch the eye,
Clouded or clear, of one who is always one.
Facts have their place of course but should learn to keep it. The feel
Of a body is more than body. That we met
Her, not her, is a chance; that we were born
Here, not there, is a chance but a chance we took
And would not have it otherwise. The water
Flows, the words bubble, the eyes flash,
The prism retains identity, that squalor,
Those bickerings, lies, disappointments, self-deceptions.
Still dare not prove that what was love was not;
Inheritors of paradox and prism
And stigmatised to the good by the Angry Dove,
As through our soft and rain-shot air the sun
Can alchemise our granite or boulder clay,

So we, marooned between two continents
And having missed half of their revolutions
And more than half their perquisites can still,
Sophisticated primitives, aspire
In spite of all their slogans and our own
To take this accident of time and place
And somehow, even now, to make it happy.
Have with you to Maynooth or the Walls of Derry,
The Rock of Cashel or the Shannon Dam,
The vanished Claddagh or the empty Blaskets,
The Bells of Shandon, the Bog of Allen, the Boyne,
Mount Jerome or Mountjoy Prison or Croke Park,
Have with you to Lough Derg or Sandy Row,
The fuchsias of Letterfrack, the pubs of Letterkenny,
The crosses of Clonmacnois, have with you where you will
To any less heard-of places, dull grey dirty towns
Or small drab fields of ragweed, though not mentioned
In the record, even these were part of the affair
Like those off-moments when two persons feel
Their love assured because it seems so casual,
So usual, down to earth, common-or-garden,
Off-moments that are really inner moments
When they can afford to forget to say 'I love you'
And yawn and think of other things, which yet
Revolve around this absence. So the eye
Can miss the current in a stream, the ear
Ignore even a waterfall, the mind,
Intent on solid fact, forget that water,
Which early thinkers thought the source of all things,
Remains the symbol of our life; yet never,
No more than peat can turn again to forest,
No more than the die, once cast, can change its spots,
No more than a child can disavow its birthplace,
No more than one's first love can be forgotten,
If pressed, could we deny this water flows.

[First published in *The Listener*, 16 September 1971, pp. 360–1]

Select Bibliography

MacNeice Manuscripts, Typescripts, and Radio Scripts

Letters:
The BBC Written Archives Centre, Caversham Park, Reading, contains letters between FLM and members of the BBC staff.

The Beinecke Rare Book and Manuscript Library, Yale University, contains letters between FLM and EC.

The Berg Collection, New York Public Library, contains letters between FLM and Rupert Doone.

The Bodleian Library, Oxford, contains letters between FLM and the following: AMHM, EN, ERD and his wife, GBM, GMTBM, JFM, JH; letters from AMHM to Mercy MacCann; from Miss Popper and Nancy Spender to FLM; from Littleton Powys to JFM.

The Butler Library, Columbia University, contains letters between FLM and Bennet Cerf.

The Faber and Faber archive contains letters between FLM and TSE.

The HRC at Austin, Texas, contains letters from FLM to Geoffrey Grigson and Mrs Stephenson.

The Library of King's College, Cambridge, contains FLM's letters to AB, and one from Graham Shepard to AB.

The National Library of Scotland contains letters from FLM to Hector MacIver.

The Oxford University Press archive contains letters from FLM (concerning *MP*).

The Princeton University Library contains FLM's letters to Allen Tate.

The archive of Royal Holloway and Bedford New College, London, contains letters from FLM (concerning his lectureship at Bedford).

The Library of Trinity College, Dublin, contains postcards from FLM to F. R. Higgins, and letters to Denis Johnston and H. O. White.

Letters in private hands are so described.

Poems and Plays:
Location of individual items is given in footnotes. See Robyn Marsack, *The Cave of Making: The Poetry of Louis MacNeice*, 1982, pp. 159–60, for a description of the five major library holdings.

Radio Scripts:
The most complete collection is that the BBC Written Archives Centre, Caversham Park, Reading, but there are fine collections in the Berg Collection, New York Public Library, and in the Humanities Research Center, University of Texas at Austin.

Books by MacNeice (arranged chronologically)

Blind Fireworks (London, 1929).
Roundabout Way (pseud. Louis Malone) (London, 1932).
Poems (London, 1935).
The Agamemnon of Aeschylus (London, 1936).
Out of the Picture (London, 1937).
Letters from Iceland, with W. H. Auden (London, 1937).
Poems (New York, 1937).
The Earth Compels (London, 1938).
I Crossed the Minch (London, 1938).
Modern Poetry: A Personal Essay (Oxford, 1938; 2nd edn. 1968).
Zoo (London, 1938).
Autumn Journal (London, 1939).
Selected Poems (London, 1940).
The Last Ditch (Dublin, 1940).
Collected Poems 1925–1940 (New York, 1941).
The Poetry of W. B. Yeats (London, 1941).
Plant and Phantom (London, 1941).
Meet the US Army (London, 1943).
Christopher Columbus (London, 1944).
Springboard (London, 1944).

The Dark Tower and Other Radio Scripts (London, 1947; *The Dark Tower* repr. 1964).

Holes in the Sky (London, 1948).

Collected Poems 1925–1948 (London, 1949).

Goethe's Faust (London, 1951).

Ten Burnt Offerings (London, 1952).

Autumn Sequel: A Rhetorical Poem in XXVI Cantos (London, 1954).

Visitations (London, 1957).

Eighty-Five Poems, selected by MacNeice (London, 1959).

Solstices (London, 1961).

The Burning Perch (London, 1963).

The Mad Islands and The Administrator (London, 1964).

Astrology (London, 1964).

Selected Poems, ed. W. H. Auden (London, 1964).

The Strings are False: An Unfinished Autobiography, ed. E. R. Dodds (London, 1965).

Varieties of Parable (Cambridge, 1965).

Collected Poems of Louis MacNeice, ed. E. R. Dodds (London, 1966; 2nd edn. 1979 [with correction of misprints]).

One for the Grave: A Modern Morality Play (London, 1968).

Persons from Porlock and Other Plays for Radio (London, 1969).

The Revenant: A Song Cycle (Dublin, 1975).

Selected Literary Criticism of Louis MacNeice, ed A. Heuser (Oxford, 1987).

Louis MacNeice: Selected Poems, ed. M. Longley (London, 1988).

Selected Prose of Louis MacNeice, ed. A. Heuser (Oxford, 1990).

Selected Plays of Louis MacNeice, ed. A. Heuser and P. McDonald (Oxford, 1993).

Publication details of most of these will be found in *A Bibliography of the Works of Louis MacNeice*, ed. C. M. Armitage and Neil Clark (1973; 2nd edn. 1974). As far as MacNeice's prose contributions to books and periodicals are concerned, the Bibliography supplied by Alan Heuser in his *Selected Prose of Louis MacNeice* is comprehensive and accurate and should be used in preference to Armitage and Clark.

Books and articles containing material on Louis MacNeice

Allen, Walter, *As I Walked Down New Grub Street* (London, 1981).

Bergonzi, Bernard, *Reading the Thirties: Texts and Contexts* (London, 1978).

Boyd, John, *The Middle of My Journey* (Belfast, 1990).

Bridson, D. G., *Prospero and Ariel* (London, 1971).

Brown, Terence, *Louis MacNeice: Sceptical Vision* (Dublin, 1975).

—— and Reid, Alec, eds, *Time Was Away: The World of Louis MacNeice* (Dublin, 1974).

Carpenter, Humphrey, *W. H. Auden: A Biography* (London, 1981).

Coulton, Barbara, *Louis MacNeice in the BBC* (London, 1980).

Cunningham, Valentine, *British Writers of the Thirties* (Oxford, 1988).

Davin, Dan, 'Louis MacNeice', in *Closing Times* (Oxford, 1975).

Dodds, E. R., *Missing Persons: An Autobiography* (Oxford, 1977).

Gardiner, Margaret, *A Scatter of Memories* (London, 1988).

Genet, Jacqueline, ed., *Studies on Louis MacNeice* (Caen, 1988) includes essays by Hedli MacNeice, Terence Brown, Peter McDonald, Edna Longley, Derek Mahon, and Adolphe Haberer.

Grigson, Geoffrey, 'Louis MacNeice', in *Recollections: Mainly of Writers and Artists* (London, 1984).

Haberer, Adolphe, *Louis MacNeice 1907–1963: l'Homme et la poésie* (Bordeaux, 1986).

Heaney, Seamus, 'The Frontiers of Writing', *Bullán* (Oxford, Spring 1994).

Hewison, Robert, *Under Seige: Literary Life in London 1939–1945* (London, 1977).

Hillier, Bevis, *Young Betjeman* (London, 1988).

Holme, Christopher, 'The Radio Drama of Louis MacNeice', in J. Drakakis, ed., *British Radio Drama* (Cambridge, 1981).

Hynes, Samuel, *The Auden Generation: Literature and Politics in England in the 1930s* (London, 1976).

Johnston, Dillon, *Irish Poetry after Joyce* (Dublin and Notre Dame, 1985).

Keene, Mary, *Mrs Donald* (London, 1983).

Kermode, Frank, *History and Value: The Clarendon Lectures and the Northcliffe Lectures 1987* (Oxford, 1988).

Longley, Edna, *Louis MacNeice: A Study* (London, 1988).

Longley, Michael, Introduction to *Louis MacNeice: Selected Poems* (London, 1988).

McDonald, Peter, *Louis MacNeice: The Poet in his Contexts* (Oxford, 1991).

McKinnon, William T., *Apollo's Blended Dream: A Study of the Poetry of Louis MacNeice* (London, 1971).

Marsack, Robyn, *The Cave of Making: The Poetry of Louis MacNeice* (Oxford, 1982).

Maxwell, D. E. S., *Poets of the Thirties* (London, 1969).

Mendelson, Edward, *Early Auden* (London, 1981).

Moore, D. B., *The Poetry of Louis MacNeice* (Leicester, 1972).

Newby, P. H., *Feelings Have Changed* (London, 1981).

Paulin, Tom, 'The Man from No Part: Louis MacNeice', and 'In the Salt Mines', in *Ireland and the English Crisis* (Newcastle upon Tyne, 1984).

Rodger, Ian *Radio Drama* (London, 1982).

Rutherford, George, ed., *Carrickfergus & District Historical Journal,* vol. 7 (Carrickfergus, 1993).

Sidnell, Michael J., *Dances of Death: The Group Theatre of London in the Thirties* (London, 1984).

Spender, Stephen, *The Thirties and After: Poetry, Politics, People 1933–1975* (London, 1978).

Stoddard, F. G., 'The Louis MacNeice Collection', *The Library Chronicle of The University of Texas,* VIII, 4, Spring 1968.

Symons, Julian, *The Thirties: A Dream Revolved* (London, 1960).

Tolley, A. T., *The Poetry of the Thirties* (London, 1975).

Whitehead, Kate, *The Third Programme: A Literary History* (Oxford, 1989).

Notes

The sources of information and quotation in the text are identified below by the number of the page on which they appear. Quotations are identified by the first words quoted. Where there is more than one such note in a line, subsequent key words introduce it.

1: The Pre-natal Mountain

The principal source for this chapter is a Xerox copy, almost certainly incomplete, of a manuscript memoir of the MacNeice family written by the poet's sister, Lady Nicholson, in the late 1960s (hereafter EN, 'Memoir'). The whereabouts of the original are not known; the copy is in private hands. Information not attributed to other sources may be assumed to be taken from this.

Page

1 'I have, in defiance'. *I Crossed the Minch* (hereafter *ICM*), p. 26.

 'that if he had'. *Vale*, Ebury Edition 1937, p. 114.

 'self-mockery'. See also Louis MacNeice (hereafter FLM) to Anthony Blunt (hereafter AB), 29 March 1927:

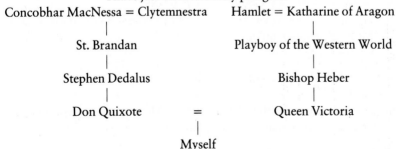

I have just discovered my pedigree.

Concobhar MacNessa = Clytemnestra   Hamlet = Katharine of Aragon

St. Brandan   Playboy of the Western World

Stephen Dedalus   Bishop Heber

Don Quixote   =   Queen Victoria

Myself

2 'And to my own'. W. H. Auden & FLM, *Letters from Iceland* (hereafter *LI)*, p. 237. When MacNeice's father read this poem, he remarked to his

497

daughter: 'There is only one mistake in it. The MacNeices were never peasants.' (William T. McKinnon, *Apollo's Blended Dream: A Study of the Poetry of Louis MacNeice*, hereafter *ABD*, pp. 6–7.)

2 'In the beginning'. 'Landscapes of Childhood and Youth', *The Strings are False* (hereafter *SAF*), p. 216.

3 'an island'. Asenath Nicholson, *The Bible in Ireland*, ed. Alfred Tresidder Sheppard, 1847, p. 245.

'ten children'. Caroline, Mathilda, Charlotte Ann, William Lindsay, Ferguson, Lindsay, Alice Jane, John Frederick, Ferguson John, Herbert.

4 'Kept something'. 'The Strand', *Collected Poems of Louis MacNeice* (hereafter *CP*). p. 226.

'On 28 February'. Testimony of the Revd Mr Rhatigan at the Clifden Sessions, 15 April, as reported in *The Galway Vindicator and Connaught Advertiser*, 16 April 1879.

'One version'. This version was recounted by EN to Richard Murphy, who relayed it to Jon Stallworthy (hereafter JS).

'MacNeice was worried'. This account of the event of 23 March is taken from evidence given at the Galway Assizes on 30 August, as reported in *The Galway Vindicator and Connaught Advertiser*, 2 August. Five men and a woman indicted for their part in 'a riotous assembly' and assault on sub-constable Sheehan were eventually acquitted.

6 'D'Arcy commissioned.' Desmond Bowen, *The Protestant Crusade in Ireland, 1800–1870*, 1978, p. 217.

8 'Holy Trinity Church'. Destroyed by German bombs in 1941, the church was relocated in the Ballysillan Road in 1956.

'St Clement's'. J. F. MacNeice (hereafter JFM), *The Church of Ireland in Belfast*, 1931, p. 53–4.

9 'One who was'. Ibid., p. 54.

12 'Louis Plunkett'. See 'Godfather', *CP*, p. 288.

'his diary'. The whereabouts of JFM's 1908 diary, quoted in EN, 'Memoir', are now unknown.

2: The House by the Harbour

The principal source for this chapter is EN, 'Memoir'. Information not attributed to other sources may be assumed to be taken from this.

14 'a name'. *SAF*, p. 218.

'It is held'. JFM, *Carrickfergus and its Contacts*, 1928, p. 12.

15 'On Tuesday night'. *Carrickfergus Advertiser*, 13 November 1908, p. 4.

16 'The parochial nominator'. *Belfast Newsletter*, 12 November 1908, p. 4.
    'I feel that'. *Carrickfergus Advertiser*, 13 November 1908, p. 4.
17 'I think it'. Ibid., 20 November 1908, p. 4.
19 'The plates'. Ibid., 4 December 1908, p. 4.
21 'Louis' first memories'. *SAF*, pp. 36–7.
    'uncle in Wales'. Ibid., p. 217.
    'There were five'. Ibid., p. 36.
22 'uterine fibroid tumour'. *ABD*, p. 7.

3: The House in the Garden

The principal sources for this chapter are FLM's two accounts in *SAF*, pp. 37–42 and 216–20. Information not attributed to other sources may be assumed to be taken from these.

23 'St Nicholas' Rectory'. The rectory was built in 1982 by Ezekiel Caters at a cost of £1,187 and 4d. See Jane Bell, 'A House with a Story to Tell', *Belfast Telegraph*, 6 March 1982, pp. 10–11.
    'the North Road'. EN, 'Trees Were Green', *Time Was Away* (hereafter *TWA*), ed. Terence Brown and Alec Reid, 1974, p. 12.
24 'The house ticked'. Ibid.
25 'she took emotional'. Ibid., pp. 14–15.
    'respectable doggerel'. Ibid., pp. 15–16.
26 'Archie White'. Cp. 'The Gardener', *CP*, p. 172.
    'the rector's "weans"'. EN, 'Memoir': 'I think Archie called us *weans* and *bairns*'.
27 'with a clanky'. Louis Malone [MacNeice], *Roundabout Way* (hereafter *RW*), 1932, p. 128.
28 'an endless stretch'. Cp. 'Mutations', *CP*, p. 195, and 'The Stygian Banks', IV, *CP*, p. 262.
    'Three tall obelisks'. FLM, 'Childhood Memoirs', *The Listener*, 12 December 1963, p. 990.
    'Our lights looked'. 'Carrickfergus', *CP*, p. 69.
    'Miss MacCready'. The 'Miss Craig' of *SAF*. I have silently substituted 'MacCready' for 'Craig' in all subsequent quotations from *SAF*.
30 'Dear Elsie'. Letter in private hands. Within the family at this stage, Elizabeth was known as Elsie.
33 'newly launched *Titanic*'. See 'Death of an Old Lady', *CP*, p. 463.
34 'Portstewart'. *TWA*, p. 15.
    'He had great'. JFM, *Carrickfergus and its Contacts*, p. 71.

35　'First there is'. *Carrickfergus Advertiser*, 4 October 1912.
　　'That was a grand'. *TWA*, p. 15.

37　'He will be'. Ibid., p. 16.
　　'she believed'. Ibid.
　　'and the nurse'. Ibid.

38　'Miss MacCready'. Ibid., p. 17.
　　'They never saw'. Ibid., p. 17. FLM does write of visiting his mother in hospital and rejecting her gift of a box of chocolates (*SAF*, pp. 42–3), but in a footnote to that account EN explains: 'the chocolate box episode took place on a visit paid to her by Louis after her operation six months earlier'.

4: Black Dreams

The principal source of this chapter is *SAF*, pp. 43–62. Information not attributed to other sources may be assumed to be taken from this.

39　'sad little letters'. *TWA*, p. 17.

40　'warning of death'. This and what follows in this paragraph derive from EN, 'Memoir'.

41　'The same porridge'. FLM, *Zoo*, 1938, p. 78.
　　'These got worse'. Cp. 'Intimations of Mortality', *CP*, pp. 28–9.

42　'You and I'. *TWA*, p. 11.
　　'whenever my father'. EN, 'Memoir'.

43　'When I see'. *TWA*, pp. 17–18.

45　'but Louis' imagination'. *TWA*, p. 18–19. See also *SAF*, pp. 51–2.

46　'The great Norman'. JFM, *Carrickfergus and its Contacts*, p. 77.
　　'What is the'. Ibid., p. 78.

47　'mother had died'. Lily died of tuberculosis in the Dublin mental hospital. She was buried beside her father in Carrowdore churchyard where FLM now also lies.

48　'Nursery rhymes'. See FLM, *Modern Poetry* (hereafter *MP*), p. 37.
　　'his daughter'. EN, 'Memoir'.
　　'the Bible'. *MP*, p. 35.
　　'was always looking'. Ibid., p. 38.
　　'use "thou"'. Ibid., pp. 39–40.

49　'O Monkey'. *Zoo*, p. 69.
　　'a piece of poetry'. Dated 'Monday morning' (probably spring 1915) and now in private hands.
　　'My favourite book'. *Zoo*, pp. 68–9.

51 'the water sound'. FLM to Elizabeth MacNeice, 23 October [1915].
'In March 1916'. *ABD*, p. 9.
'Miss Heward'. Miss Hewitt of *SAF*, pp. 56–60. I have silently substituted 'Heward' for 'Hewitt' in subsequent quotations from *SAF*.
'a huge camp'. 'Carrickfergus', *CP*, p. 69.

53 'Seapark'. The setting of 'Soap Suds', *CP*, p. 517.
'Roman Catholic servants'. Information given by EN to Dr Robyn Marsack.

54 'to Sherborne'. The children's rich stepmother paid their fees; FLM's being initially £82. 1s a year.

5: Sherborne

The principal published source for this chapter is *SAF* pp. 64–79 and 221–2. Information not attributed to other sources may be assumed to be taken from this.

56 'Picture them'. Oliver Holt, *Three Sherborne Memoirs*, privately printed, 1987, p. 5. For the headmaster's appearances in FLM's poetry, see 'The Kingdom', II, *CP*, p. 249, and 'Owen' in *Autumn Sequel*, Canto XXII, *CP*, pp. 419–21.
'father's favourite'. Richard Perceval Graves, *The Brothers Powys*, 1983, p. 6.
'masochistic grandmother'. Ibid., p. 1.
'Irish master'. Mr Lindsay, the 'Mr. Cameron' of *SAF*, pp. 65, 74, 78–9. I have silently substituted 'Lindsay' for 'Cameron' in all subsequent quotations from *SAF*.

57 '"Well" said Mrs MacNeice'. EN, manuscript notes on 'Characters connected to Sherborne Preparatory School', pp. 5–6 (Bodleian Library, hereafter Bod).
'My dear Daddie'. FLM customarily – and affectionately – addressed his stepmother with the Italian word for 'mother'.
'collecting fossils'. FLM to EN, Monday Morning (undated, but black-edged notepaper suggesting 1915. Letter in private hands.): 'have you found any fossils yet'.
'Ode on the Death'. FLM to JFM and Georgina Beatrice MacNeice (hereafter GBM), November [1917].
'Home-Thoughts'. FLM to JFM, 2 December [1917].

59 'in an informal way'. Littleton Powys, *The Joy of It*, 1937, p. 180.
'Things in Summer'. FLM to JFM, 19 May [1917].

60 '*belfry*'. See also p. 59 above.
'I swam'. FLM to GBM.
'In every way'. Littleton Powys to JFM, 30 June [1918].

61 'MONDAY'. FLM to GBM, November [1918].
'a coarsening'. *MP*, pp. 41–3.

62 'he galloped through'. Ibid., for 29 January, 9 February, and 14 March [1919].
'*A Tale of*'. Ibid., for 26 March [1919].
'Alexander's Feast'. FLM to GBM, 9 February [1919], and *MP*, p. 43.
'an enterprising pioneer'. FLM to GBM, Wednesday [late February or early March 1919].
'There may be'. FLM to GBM, 16 March [1919].
'Mr Lindsay'. See pp. 56–7 and 71.
'ninety games'. Diary for 24 April 1919.
'Mr Powys says'. FLM to GBM, undated.
'I can swim'. FLM to GBM, 22 June [1919].
'Greek'. FLM to GBM, 8 June [1919].
'go from dormitory'. Powys, *The Joy of It*, p. 162.
'He was to remember'. Ibid., p. 61.

64 '*King Solomon's Mines*'. FLM to GBM, 26 October [1919].
'an eclipse'. FLM to GBM, 9 November [1919].
'outbreak of chicken-pox'. FLM to GBM, 30 November [1919].
'wonderfully alone.' In *SAF*, p. 78, this journey is incorrectly dated January 1921. The experience was to produce the poem 'Star-gazer', *CP*, p. 544.
'We can see'. FLM to GBM, 25 January [1920].
'1st bell'. FLM to GBM, 29 February [1920].

65 'Freddie has'. Littleton Powys to JFM, 9 March [1920].

66 'Shortly before'. Holt, *Three Sherborne Memoirs*, pp. 12–13.
'a glorious term'. FLM to GBM, 23 May [1920].
'cautiously optimistic'. Littleton Powys to JFM, 20 November [1920].
'a folk poetess'. EN's notes on 'Characters connected with Sherborne Preparatory School', pp. 5–6 (Bod).
'Latin Translation'. FLM to GBM, 17 October [1920].

67 'use in poems'. See, for example, 'Birmingham', 'Mahabalipuram', and 'This is the Life', respectively *CP*, pp. 17, 273, and 538.

68 'Number Eight'. FLM to GBM, 23 January [1921].
'"Mr Hemstead", he wrote'. Ibid., Mr E. C. E. Hemstead is the 'Mr Charles' of *SAF*, pp. 76–8. I have silently substituted 'Hemstead' for 'Charles' in all subsequent quotations from *SAF*.

68 'in what he called'. Powys, *The Joy of It*, p. 168.
    'that it was vulgar'. *MP*, p. 45.
69 'Coleridge, Shelley'. FLM to GBM, [27 February 1921?].
    'nine Cantos today'. Diary, 10 February 1921.
70 'no more English'. Diary, 21 February 1921.
    'Ode to Autumn'. FLM to GBM, [March 1921].
    'Keats did not'. Ibid.
    'saw Oxford win'. Diary, 30 March 1921.
    'Back at Carrickfergus'. Diary, 2, 15, and 28 April 1921.
71 'I got a Horace'. See 'Memoranda to Horace', *CP*, pp. 539–43.

6: Sandstone to Flint

The principal published source for this chapter is *SAF*, pp. 80–92 and 223–6.
Information not attributed to other sources may be assumed to be taken from
this.

72 'the little red-capped'. Charles Hamilton Sorley, 'Rain', *The Collected
    Poems*, ed. Jean Moorcroft Wilson, 1985, p. 102.
    'he wandered'. Diary, 15 September 1921.
73 'Maurice with MacNeice'. FLM to GBM, 19 September [1921].
    'I have been'. FLM to GBM, 2 October [1921].
    'Mr Canning'. FLM to GBM, 25 September [1921].
    'Museum'. Diary, 22 September 1921.
    'food parcels'. FLM to GBM, 2 October [1921].
74 'an old book'. FLM to GBM, 9 October [1921].
    'that the origin'. P. 18. But see A. G. Bradley, A. C. Champneys and J. W.
    Baines, *A History of Marlborough College*, 1893, p. 11: 'As to the guess
    which connects [Marlborough] with Merlin, we may say with Camden
    that it is "ridiculous".'
    'one side smashed'. H. C. Brentnall and E. G. H. Kempson, eds, *Marl-
    borough College 1843–1943*, 1943, p. 3.
    'Boots'. See John Costello, *Mask of Treachery*, 1988, p. 72.
75 'distinction was recognized'. E. T. Williams and Helen M. Palmer, eds,
    Dictionary of National Biography, 1951–50, 1971, pp. 773–5.
    'The prefectorial system'. Bevis Hillier, *Young Betjeman*, 1988, p. 97.
    'like an Edwardian'. Reported by Professor J. E. Bowle to Bevis Hillier,
    ibid., p. 93.
    'On Friday'. FLM to GBM, 20 November [1921].
76 'some magnificent lines'. Diary, 18 November [1921].

76 'a book about'. Ibid., 24 December [1921].
'*Every Boy's Book*'. Ibid., 29 December [1921].
'His detailed account'. FLM to GBM, [20–1 January? 1921]. 'I cannot remember if the first zoo I visited was Dublin or London' (*Zoo*, p. 69). This seems to have been the first.
'If he can cure'. FLM's Marlborough reports are in Bod.
'Leigh Hill'. FLM to GBM, 21 May [1922].
'On Saturday'. FLM to GBM, 11 June [1922].

77 'in a most splendid'. FLM to GBM, 24 September [1922].
'We have just'. FLM to GBM, 1 November [1922].

78 'the glitter of Horace'. *MP*, p. 49.
'He has a sort'. FLM to GBM, 3 December [1922].

79 'I have never'. For a fuller account of 'basketing', see *ICM*, pp. 88–90.

80 'richer than Virgil'. *MP*, p. 48.
'whatever their titles'. Ibid.

81 'envied Louis'. John Betjeman, 'Louis MacNeice and Bernard Spencer', *London Magazine*, vol. 3, no. 4, December 1963, p. 63.
'pickled walnut'. John Hilton (hereafter JH), interview with JS.
'One such expedition'. See also 'The Cyclist', *CP*, pp. 229–30.
'Robert Louis Stevenson'. In a letter of 31 August 1923, FLM thanks his aunt Eva for her gift of several volumes by RLS: 'The whole tribe of Stevenson now occupies part of the shelf of honour'.

82 'Rathlin Island'. *SAF*, pp. 225–6.
'savage article'. John Betjeman, 'Dead from the Waist Down', *The Spectator*, 14 March 1958, pp. 320–21.
'Greek Orthodox'. John Betjeman, *A Nip in the Air*, 1974, p. 36.
'It was very dramatic'. FLM to GBM, 7 October [1923].
'Fortie Vesey Ross'. 'Reckitts' of *SAF*, pp. 93–6.

83 'strict Ruskinian'. AB, 'From Bloomsbury to Marxism', *Studio International*, vol. 186, November 1973, p. 164.
'was not a'. Wilfrid Blunt, *Married to a Single Life/An Autobiography 1901–1938*, 1983, p. 35.
'half of them'. Quoted by JH, Appendix B to *SAF*, p. 247.
'He is putting'. Bod.
'fives gloves'. FLM to GBM, 24 February [1924].
'This day week'. FLM to GBM, 12 February [1924].
'There's a new'. JH, Appendix B to *SAF*, p. 247.

84 'to express'. AB, 'From Bloomsbury to Marxism', p. 164.
'new magazine's title'. Hillier, *Young Betjeman*, pp. 101–2.

85 'were a "Prodigies Song"'. Ibid. Bevis Hillier, in correspondence, accepts

the case of my proposed re-attribution of the short story entitled 'Death'.

86 'Dr. Norwood'. Ibid.

'On Thursday'. FLM to GBM, 29 June [1924].

'There is no'. This essay so scandalized one parent that he threatened to remove his son from the school and, in the light of this and other protests, Norwood banned *The Heretick*. The games master violently objected to the opening article, which attacked the 'ludicrous pomposity' of the belief that 'the foundations of our mighty Empire are laid on the playing fields of our schools.' But it was Blunt's provocative piece on the Wildean theme of art and morality that caused an uproar. 'To call a work of art immoral is like calling an ink spot sympathetic,' he wrote, adding that: 'To say that a painting is immoral merely shews a lamentable incapacity for appreciation.' Blunt later claimed that his housemaster had provoked him to write the piece because he 'thought that the Matisse and Rouault which I had in my study were indecent.' This was confirmed by Hilton, who remembers that Blunt was 'at loggerheads with his housemaster over books picturing unclothed and amorous persons.' Costello, *Mask of Treachery*, p. 72.

88 'Much love Louis'. FLM to GBM, 6 July [1924].

7: Playing the Fool

The principal published source for this chapter is *SAF*, pp. 93–101 and 226–31. Information not attributed to other sources may be assumed to be taken from this.

89 'had been successful'. FLM to GBM, 13 July [1924].

'Farragh'. FLM to Ross, undated [August? 1924].

90 'for the parcels'. FLM to GBM, 29 September [1924].

'Death of a'. *The Marlburian*, LIX, no. 855, 23 October 1924, p. 134.

91 'The Dissolution'. Ibid., pp. 144–5.

'with trifling'. FLM to GBM, 4 November [1924].

92 'Sorry, Hughes'. Hillier, *Young Betjeman*, p. 100. Betjeman found Hughes, who took him on sketching expeditions into the Wiltshire countryside, a much more sympathetic figure than AB did.

'an astonishingly dull piece'. AB, in interview with Hillier. Ibid.

'Northern Fairy Tales'. FLM to GBM, 24 November [1924].

93 'I am feeling'. FLM to GBM, 2 December [1924].

'The Marlburian'. LX, no. 857, 18 February 1925, p. 31.

'The Norse World'. Manuscript Box B in the MacNeice Collection of the

Humanities Research Center, University of Texas at Austin (hereafter HRC).

93 'lanky black dog'. FLM to JFM and GBM, 3 March [1925].

94 'Blunt has also'. JH, *SAF*, Appendix B, p. 246.
'very like the'. FLM to JFM, 3 June [1925].
'I have been thinking'. FLM to GBM, 3 July [1925].

95 'practical proposal'. FLM to GBM, 8 July [1925].
'Try another job'. Manuscript Box C in the MacNeice Collection of the HRC.

96 'was really dissipated'. *MP*, p. 51.
'The pleasure-boats'. These lines from the 122-line manuscript draft (of Box C in the MacNeice Collection of the HRC) do not appear in the 72-line poem printed in *The Marlburian*, LXI, no. 871, 20 July 1926, p. 115.
'Their little jazz'. *MP*, pp. 51–2.

97 'one sometimes got'. *SAF*, Appendix B, p. 243.

98 'Anthony was then'. Ibid.
'paper on Cubism'. FLM to GBM, undated.
'It really was'. *SAF*, Appendix B, pp. 247–9.
'By all means'. Manuscript Box B in the MacNeice Collection of the HRC.

99 'His mind'. *SAF*. Appendix B, p. 240.
'which is not'. FLM to GBM, Friday [November 1925].

101 'has brought back'. FLM to JFM and GBM, undated [January 1926].
'it was worthy'. FLM to GBM, 6 November [1925].
'carried the day.' AB, interview with JS.
'if people in'. FLM to GBM, 14 November [1926].
'In May'. *SAF*, Appendix B, pp. 249–50.
'the *Pervigilium*'. Ibid., pp. 244–5.

102 'T. S. Eliot'. Minutes of the meeting on 13 June 1926.
'His subject-matter'. *MP*, pp. 56–9.
'And the Spirit'. *The Marlburian*, LXI, no. 866, 17 February 1926, p. 17.
'Apollo on the'. Ibid,. no. 869, 26 May 1926, p. 65; no. 870, 23 June 1926, pp. 90–1; and no. 871, 26 July, pp. 118–19.
'Miss Ambergris'. Ibid., LXI, no. 869, 26 May 1926, pp. 66–7.

103 'Mr. MacNeice'. Ibid., no. 870, 23 June 1926, p. 104.
'MR. MACNEICE'. Ibid., p. 81.
'If I had been.' FLM to GBM, undated [May 1926].
'we lived'. AB, 'From Bloomsbury to Marxism', *Studio International*, vol. 186, November 1973, p. 166.

104 'Louis was always'. AB, interview with JS.
'He turned'. FLM to GBM, undated [June 1926].
'Blunt and some others'. *The Marlburian*, LXI, no. 871, 26 July 1926, pp. 94–5.
'De Cubismo'. Ibid., LXI, no. 870, 23 June 1926. pp. 87–8.

105 'Louis bought'. FLM to GBM, 24 July [1926].
'Let the modernist'. *The Marlburian*, LXI, no. 871, 26 July 1926, pp. 112–13.
'Hilton's immersion'. Ibid. and *SAF*, Appendix B, p. 250.
'arms full'. Beverley Nichols, *Prelude*, 1920, p. 35.
'*Poems* of T. S. Eliot'. *MP*, p. 58.

8: Other Gods

The principal published source for this chapter is *SAF*, pp. 102–13, 232–8, and appendix B, by JH, 250–67. Information not attributed to other sources may be assumed to be taken from this.

106 'letters to Anthony'. AB's half of this correspondence has not survived.
107 'all the other postmasters'. FLM to AB, postmarked 23 October 1926.
108 'to follow'. Ibid.
'A message'. FLM to EN, postmarked 3 November 1926.
109 'a tall lanquid undergraduate'. W. H. Auden, 'Louis MacNeice', *Encounter*, November 1963, p. 48.
111 'morning to dreary'. FLM to AB, postmarked 23 October 1926.
'a satirical account'. FLM to AB, postmarked 6 December 1926.
112 'well remembered'. Edward Gibbon, *Memoirs of My Life*, 1796, ed. Georges A. Bonnard, 1966, pp. 52 and 56–7.
'Seaside'. *The Cherwell*, 30 October 1926, p. 81. The poem was reprinted, with minor alterations, as 'The Lugubrious, Salubrious Seaside' in *Blind Fireworks*, p. 66.
'Two other poems'. 'Harvest Thanksgiving', 13 November, p. 145; 'Fires of Hell', 4 December, p. 251; and 'In the Cathedral', 11 December, p. 303.
113 'a gang of hearties'. FLM to AB, postmarked 6 December 1926.
'on to the Blunts'. FLM to AB, postmarked 5 January 1927.
114 'I found myself'. Hillier, *Young Betjeman*, p. 136.
'Joyce'. FLM to AB, postmarked 7 February 1927. See also *MP*, p. 68.
'I am reading'. FLM to AB, postmarked 5 April 1927.
116 'Not Impossible She'. Richard Crashaw, 'Wishes to His Supposed

Mistress', line 2.

117   'Mr. Andrewes'. Professor A. Andrewes, interview with JS.

118   'more than £15'. JH gives this figure (*SAF*, p. 255) and his memory is probably more reliable than that of FLM, who says it was £30 (*SAF*, p. 235).

119   'The host'. A. S. T. Fisher to JS, 10 February 1985.

     'another of Louis' poems'. 'Reading by candle-light: Monday, October 17th, 1927', *The Cherwell*, 22 October, p. 24.

     'going down'. FLM to AB, postmarked 17 November 1927.

120   'he began a novel'. FLM to AB, postmarked [receipt] 2 January 1928.

     'I suggest'. FLM to AB, [January/February 1928].

     'Am still writing'. FLM to AB, postmarked 8 April 1928.

9: Paper Flowers

The principal published source for this chapter is *SAF*, pp. 113–29 and Appendix B by JH, pp. 255–84. Information not attributed to other sources may be assumed to be taken from this.

121   'To get a 1st'. FLM to AB, postmarked 4 May 1928.

     'He spent last night'. Shepard to AB, 18 May 1928 (King's College Library, Cambridge).

122   'though as might be'. Paul Bloomfield, unpublished typescript 'Additional Notes to Louis MacNeice's *The Strings are False*', p. 12. I am indebted to the late Mr Bloomfield, Mrs Beazley's brother, for much of the information about the family that follows.

     'she savoured'. Reported by Sir Isaiah Berlin, interview with JS.

123   'Here they all are'. FLM to AB, [July? 1928].

     'John Stuart Mill's *Logic*'. 'When I Was Twenty-One: 1928', *Selected Prose of Louis MacNeice*, ed. Alan Heuser (hereafter *SP*), 1990, p. 222.

124   'You are to come'. FLM to JH, [August? 1928].

125   'he was depressed'. 'When I Was Twenty-One: 1928'. *SP*, p. 222.

     'Glory to God'. Mr Denis O'Neill to Dame Helen Gardner, 21 August 1974.

126   'Auden had left Oxford'. Humphrey Carpenter, *W. H. Auden*, 1981, p. 82.

     'continued to read'. Bernard Spencer, *Collected Poems*, edited and with an Introduction by Roger Bowen, 1981, p. xvii.

     'The University News'. Vol. 1, no. 6, 24 November 1928, p. 192.

127   'rejected a collection'. Carpenter, op. cit., p. 113 *n.*

127 '*Blind Fireworks*'. FLM to AB, 29 December [1928?]: 'I shall be amused if Gollancz takes the novel'.
'I filled the font'. Ibid.

128 'It was good'. JFM to JH, 2 February 1929.

129 'Louis' sister believed'. EN in interview with Dr Robyn Marsack.

130 '*Sir Galahad*'. There is a rare copy in Bod.

131 'To Giovanna'. Mary MacNeice (hereafter GMTBM)'s own, tenderly inscribed, copy of *Blind Fireworks* was almost certainly stolen by Louis' friend and fellow poet, Ruthven Todd. See Geoffrey Grigson, *Recollections*, 1984, pp. 43–4.
'Two of the most'. M. C. D'Arcy, 'Oxford Poetry, 1929', *The Oxford Outlook*, X, no. 50, November 1929, p. 380.

132 'a later poem'. 'Autobiography', *CP*, p. 183.
'bells and sea'. For example, 'Sailor's Funeral', 'The Sunset Conceived as a Peal of Bells', and 'ΓΝΩΘΙ ΣΕΑΥΤΟΝ'.
'certain early contacts'. *SP*, 160.

133 'the self-consciousness'. Peter McDonald, *Louis MacNeice: The Poet in his Contexts*, 1991, p. 57.

134 'that what makes'. *MP*, pp. 73–4.
'smiling on my novel'. FLM to Hart-Davis, postmarked 18 [illegible] 1929, in private hands.
'I have not read'. Hillier, *Young Betjeman*, p. 112.

135 '*Sir Galahad*'. p. 30. There is a rare copy in Bod.
'Hellenic platitude'. A commonplace, found in such writers as Aristotle (*Politics* I. 2. 14, 1253^a 28) and St Augustine (*Homilies on the First Epistle of John* 8, 7–8). See Marcel Detienne, 'Entre Bêtes et dieux', *Nouvelle revue de psychanalyse*, 4 (1972), p. 230–46.
'*Early English Lyrics*'. Private collection.

136 'German baron'. *SP*, p. 226. FLM implies (*SAF*, p. 120) that he met the baron in 1928, but the fact that he wanted an introduction to Walter de la Mare indicates a 1929 meeting.

138 'totally undesirable'. FLM to JH, [autumn 1929?].
'The crux'. Ibid.

140 'This is much more'. Ibid.
'enjoyed metaphysics'. GMTBM is called Mariette throughout *The Strings are False*. I have silently emended this to Mary in this and subsequent quotations from that book.

141 'as for Mr. MacNeice'. *The Oxford Outlook*, X, no. 50, November 1929, p. 380.
'I want to go'. FLM to JH, [autumn 1929?].

141 'I am just about'. FLM to AB, postmarked 22 April 1930.
    'was unquestionably gifted'. E. R. Dodds (hereafter ERD), *Missing Persons*, 1977, p. 114.
    'insolence to the headmaster'. Ibid., p. 23.
    'that he liked'. Ibid., p. 59.
142 'As for digs'. FLM to ERD, 28 May [1930].
143 'wedding cake'. Helen Gleadow (née Cooke), interview with JS.

10: Hazy City

The principal published sources for this chapter are *SAF*, pp. 130–46, and ERD, *Missing Persons*, pp. 112–16. Information not attributed to other sources may be assumed to be taken from these.

144 'entirely to Heaven'. FLM to ERD, 29 July [1930].
    'Highfield'. For much of what follows about the Sargant Florences and their life at 'Highfield', I am indebted to an unpublished essay, 'Highfield: Birmingham's forgotten Bloomsbury', by Tracey E. Tobin.
145 'Graham's family home'. GMTBM to GBM, 9 July [1930].
    'Mary's grandmother'. GMTBM to GBM, 29 July [1930].
    'on to Oxford'. FLM to GBM, 6 August [1930].
    'decided they could'. FLM to GBM, 2 September [1930].
    '£300 a year'. Graham Shepard to JH, 14 February 1936.
    'Highfield Cottage'. FLM to GBM, 2 October [1930].
146 'Frank and Joan Freeman'. FLM to JH [summer or autumn 1930].
    'To-day we invented'. GMTBM to GBM, 21 September [1930].
    'he wore'. Walter Allen, *As I Walked Down New Grub Street*, 1981, p. 46.
    'sacred to Sunday'. Ibid., p. 32.
147 'Life was comfortable'. *Autumn Journal*, CP, p. 115.
    'new double-bed'. FLM and GMTBM to GBM, 24 September [1930].
148 'She's frightfully stupid'. Robert Medley, *Drawn from the Life: A Memoir*, 1983, p. 164.
149 'book on Roman Humour'. Chapters 1 and 2 of this are to be found in the MacNeice Collection of the HRC.
150 'someone vaguely'. FLM to AB, postmarked 11 May 1931.
151 'By the way'. FLM to Rupert Hart-Davis, 22 August 1931 (in private hands).
    'MacNeice tells Blunt'. FLM to AB, postmarked 21 January 1932.
    'my second novel'. FLM to AB, 6 March 1932.
    'Herewith my unhappy novel'. FLM to AB, dated by AB October 1932.

151 'his head poised'. *R W*, 1932, pp. 72 and 173.

'references to romance'. Ibid. See, for example, pp. 13, 14, 20, 47, 130, 136, 138 and 225.

'SEX and LIFE'. Ibid., p. 4.

152 'dances like perfection'. Ibid., pp. 254, 56, 109 and 112.

'Thought of being taken'. Ibid., p. 258.

'He dreamed'. Ibid., pp. 12–13.

'college Fellowship'. Ibid., pp. 259–63.

'St Giles' Fair'. FLM to JH, [autumn 1930].

153 'The reviews'. *TLS*, 10 November 1932, p. 840; *The Spectator*, 25 November 1932; and *Life and Letters*, December 1932, pp. 480–81.

'I don't think'. FLM to JH, 12 April [1932].

'a respectful review'. '*Poems*, by W. H. Auden', *SP*, pp. 1–3.

'Auden turned up'. FLM to AB, postmarked 19 January 1933.

'Day Lewis and Spender'. Carpenter, *W. H. Auden*, p. 148.

'Clere Parsons'. For a sympathetic memoir of Parsons, who died in 1931, see Grigson, *Recollections*, pp. 21–5.

154 'To a Communist'. *CP*, p. 22.

'quite suddenly'. AB, 'From Bloomsbury to Marxism', *Studio International*, November 1973, p. 167. See also Costello, *Mask of Treachery*, for Blunt's involvement with Marxism and Communism.

'stalking in a cloak'. Grigson, *Recollections*, p. 29.

'NEW VERSE'. *New Verse*, 1 January 1933, p. 2.

155 'Turn Again Worthington'. Retitled 'Upon this Beach', this appears with minor revisions in *CP*, p. 19.

'En Avant'. *The University News*, 10 November 1928, p. 124, and not subsequently collected.

156 'Museums'. *CP*, pp. 20–21.

'Reminiscences of Childhood'. Ibid., p. 3.

'The Glacier'. Ibid., p. 24.

'Down the road'. 'Sunday Morning', ibid., p. 23.

157 'While the lawn-mower'. 'August', ibid.

'miniature rockery'. FLM to JH [autumn 1933], and Dodds, *Missing Persons*, p. 112.

'The ebullient Smith'. Interview with JS.

'He was interviewed'. FLM to JH [autumn 1933], and JH's note on that letter.

'a new wife, Anne'. Interview with JS. See also FLM to AB, postmarked 3 February 1934.

158 'a vase'. Interview with JS.

158 '6lb 14oz'. FLM to GBM, 16 May [1934].

11: Things Being Various

The principal published source for this chapter is *SAF*, pp. 147–51. Information not attributed to other sources may be assumed to be taken from this.

159 'Valediction'. *CP*, pp. 52–4.
'Belfast'. Ibid., p. 17.

160 'Terence Brown'. Terence Brown, 'Louis MacNeice's Ireland', *Studies on Louis MacNeice*, ed. Jacqueline Genet and Wynne Hellegouarc'h, 1988, pp. 11–26.
'Train to Dublin'. *CP*, pp. 27–8.
'to emulate Dodds'. ERD, *Missing Persons*, p. 77.

162 'MacNeice wrote again'. 19 April 1932. This and other letters between MacNeice and Eliot are to be found in the archives of Faber and Faber.

163 'Very interesting work'. TSE to FLM, 18 May 1932.
'not quite ripe'. TSE to FLM, 17 January 1934.
'I have lately'. FLM to TSE, 2 April [1934].

164 'I like.' TSE to FLM, 5 October 1934.
'But not for good'. FLM to AB, postmarked 8 June 1934.
'It is all about twins'. FLM to AB, postmarked 6 February 1933.
'I am entirely'. FLM to AB, postmarked 3 March 1934.
'My play is still'. FLM to AB, postmarked 8 June 1934.

165 'The inaction'. There is an incomplete typescript of the play in the HRC, and a complete stage version in NYPL/BC. *Station Bell* was produced in 1937 by R. D. Smith for the Birmingham University Dramatic Society. See Allen, *As I Walked Down New Grub Street*, p. 95.
'less of a compromise'. FLM to Doone, 22 July [1934]. See Michael Sidnell, *Dances of Death: The Group Theatre of London*, 1984, pp. 207–10.
'visits to London'. FLM to AB, n.d. [1934], and ibid., postmarked 30 November 1934.
'John Waterhouse'. Interview with JS.

166 'Director of Antiquities'. JH's note to a series of letters from FLM in autumn 1934.
'As to Grant Robertson'. FLM to AB, postmarked 24 October 1934.
'The bloody old sots'. FLM to AB, postmarked 10 November 1934.
'Do write'. FLM to AB, postmarked 15 January 1935.

166 'and reviewing'. For books reviewed, see Armitage and Clark, *A Biblio-graphy of the Works of Louis MacNeice*, 1973, pp. 63–4.
'Do you like'. Professor A. Andrewes, interview with JS.
'Clark Gable'. Shepard to JH, 14 February 1936.

167 'Helen Cooke'. Helen Gleadow (née Cooke), interview with JS.
'My dear MacNeice'. ERD, *Missing Persons*, p. 117.

168 'for a boy'. Aeschylus, *Agamemnon*, ed. Edward Fraenkel, 1950, vol. I, p. 115.

170 'Dissatisfaction'. *New Verse*, 11, October 1934, pp. 2 and 7.
'The music'. *New Verse*, 17, October/November 1935, pp. 17–19.
'Some other reviews'. See, in particular, *Scrutiny*, December 1935, pp. 300–302, and *Poetry* (Chicago), May 1936, pp. 115–17.
'Walter Allen'. Allen, *As I Walked Down New Grub Street*, pp. 46–7, and Reggie Smith, interview with JS.

171 'sprained his ankle'. FLM to JH, 15 November [1936].
'demand for £80'. FLM to AB, postmarked 20 November 1935.
'on 18 November'. It seems probable that GMTBM left on 19 November and that FLM at once wrote an angry letter to her mother, who replied on the 20th: 'I forgive you your letter since I know who is driving you' (Bod). Apparently, Mrs Beazley had had some previous correspon-dence with her daughter, leading FLM to believe she had encouraged GMTBM to bolt.

12: Moving

The principal published sources for this chapter are *SAF*, pp. 152–64; Car-penter, *W. H. Auden*, pp. 197–202; and Michael Yates, 'Iceland 1936', in *W. H. Auden: A Tribute*, ed. Stephen Spender, 1974, pp. 59–68. Information not attributed to other sources may be assumed to be taken from one of these.

172 'a new "lump" coat'. Ann Shepard, interview with JS.
'Dorothy Baker'. Interview with JS.
'Lella Florence'. Ibid.

174 'The answer'. These letters are in Bod.
'I will tell'. FLM to AB, postmarked 20 November 1935.
'She found Dan'. Primrose Stevens, interview with JS.

175 'in his diary'. This is in the possession of the Library of the University of Victoria, British Columbia, Canada. I am indebted to Mr Bevis Hillier for bringing it to my attention.

175 'in the name'. GMTBM to FLM, undated but probably early 1936.
'the only right'. GMTBM to FLM, 19 March 1936.
'felt very anxious'. GMTBM to FLM, undated but probably early 1936.
176 'a campaign'. Paul Bloomfield, unpublished typescript 'Additional Notes to Louis MacNeice's *The Strings are False*', p. 7.
'though he failed'. Graham Shepard to JH, 14 February 1936.
'Mary simply turned'. Ibid.
'a séance'. Sir Isaiah Berlin to JH, undated.
'a private detective'. FLM to GMTBM, 10 November 1936 (2 letters in private hands), and Paul Bloomfield, unpublished typescript.
'Auden and MacNeice'. *LI*, p. 245.
177 'Helen Gardner'. Interview with JS.
'a trip to Spain'. FLM to AB, postmarked 10 November 1935.
'Perhaps there'. FLM to AB, postmarked 2 January 1936.
'I should advise'. TSE to FLM, 20 January 1936.
178 'Blunt bitchily observed'. Interview with JS. AB says FLM is mistaken in implying (*SAF*, p. 158) that they met this man first in Ronda.
180 'slightly stoned'. AB, interview with JS.
181 'And next day'. *CP*, p. 112.
182 'to Cambridge'. *SAF*, pp. 156–7, asserts that this Cambridge weekend was *before* the trip to Spain but FLM's letter to AB of 7 May [1936] shows that it was *after*.
'I really must'. FLM to AB, 7 May [1936].
'I dare say'. Ibid.
183 'remarks of Blunt's'. Interview with JS.
'an odd wedding'. My account of this is indebted to Allen, *As I Walked Down New Grub Street*, pp. 55–8, and Carpenter, *W. H. Auden*, pp. 196–7.
184 'letter of application'. This and other letters between FLM and Bedford College are to be found in the MacNeice file, Royal Holloway and Bedford New College archive.
'E. R. Dodds'. Other testimonials came from R. G. C. Levens and G. R. G. Mure, two of FLM's Oxford tutors. The Vice Chancellor of Birmingham University and TSE were also named as referees, but neither was asked for a reference.
'Gilbert Murray'. ERD, *Missing Persons*, p. 124.
185 'failed to get it'. FLM to AB, postmarked 15 June 1936.
'I hope to start'. FLM to AB, postmarked 24 May 1936.
'write to Blunt'. FLM to AB, dated by AB 'p.m.3.viii.1936'. This annotation should probably read: 'p.m.2 and/or a.m. 3.viii'.

186 'Auden's father'. Ibid.
'The beer'. *LI*, p. 215.
'must have drunk'. Ibid., p. 42.
'I brought'. Ibid., pp. 141–2.

189 'I have very rarely'. W. H. Auden, 'Louis MacNeice', *Encounter*, November 1963, p. 49.

190 'Epilogue'. *LI*, p. 259.
'there are only'. Ibid., p. 177.

191 'thirty rose-trees'. FLM to AB, 23 July [1936].
'Aeschylus is static'. R. D. Smith, interview with JS.
'So this is how'. Allen, *As I Walked Down New Grub Street*, p. 94.

13: The Flower of Cities

The principal published sources for this chapter are *SAF*, pp. 164–71, and *ICM*. My account of FLM's friendship with Nancy Spender is based on interviews with her. Information not attributed to other sources may be assumed to be taken from one of these.

192 'We saw the mob'. *Autumn Journal*, *CP*, p. 112.
'was an ocean'. 'Goodbye to London', *CP*, p. 544.

193 'Yesterday I saw'. Letters from FLM to ERD to Mrs ERD are in Bod.

194 'The family is'. FLM, trans. *The Agamemnon of Aeschylus*, 1936, pp. 7–8.
'This translation'. Faber archive.
'both Menelaus'. Draft 'prologue' in NYPL/BC. See Sidnell, *Dances of Death*, pp. 209–16, for the fullest account of the first staging and reception of MacNeice's *Agamemnon*.

195 'If I were to tell'. *Agamemnon*, pp. 31–2.
'the most successful'. ERD, *Missing Persons*, p. 116.
'determined at all'. Ibid., p. 132.
'Aeschylus, it seems'. *Time and Tide*, 7 November 1936, p. 1562.
'better producer'. ERD, op. cit., p. 132.
'Mr. Louis MacNeice'. *The Times*, 2 November 1936, p. 12. Sidnell makes a pertinent comment:

'Eliot saw the effect of his influence on the production and was influenced in his turn. In his new play, *The Family Reunion*, he was making use of *The Choephoroe* not as translator but as a modernizer whose work of adaptation would be so radical as to leave the "original" almost undetectable. As he confronted the problems of how to integrate the chorus and how to present the Eumenides, the example of *The Agamemnon* was useful, and not wholly negative. He decided to put the Eumenides in evening dress, like the Chorus in the *Agamemnon*. He afterwards considered this a mistake, but his Chorus, similarly clothed, was insinuated into the everyday world of the play with more success' (*Dances of Death*, p. 216).

196   'A choric ode'. This chorus does not appear in the printed text. It was reproduced in *The Group Theatre Paper*, no. 4, p. 13.

'divorce Decree'. This, dated 2 November 1936, gives the grounds of divorce as GMTBM's adultery with Charles Katzman (Bod).

'our Pasternak'. Grigson, *Recollections*, pp. 72–6.

198   'woodpigeons and owls'. FLM, *Zoo*, p. 67.

'Am up to the ears'. Quoted in Carpenter, *W. H. Auden*, p. 205.

'Letter to Graham'. *LI*, p. 33.

'I come from'. Ibid., p. 126.

199   'The bullfight'. Ibid., p. 127.

'Go back'. Ibid., p. 133.

'Auden and MacNeice'. Ibid., pp. 236–58.

200   'Epilogue for W. H. Auden'. Ibid., pp. 259–61.

'what *is* all'. FLM to GMTBM, 10 November 1936 (2 letters in private hands).

'Song'. *The Listener*, January 1937, p. 151.

'The sunlight on the garden'. *CP*, pp. 84–5.

202   'Leonora Corbett'. See Ann Thwaite, *A. A. Milne: His Life*, 1990, pp. 386–7.

'No-one can'. Ibid.

203   'a call/To go'. *LI*, p. 253.

'since Longmans'. FLM to TSE, 28 March [1937].

206   'either the classics'. Mrs F. Wilkinson, Senior Lecturer in Classics at Bedford College, as quoted in *ABD*, p. 27.

'student discussions'. Ibid.

208   'Man should not'. *Out of the Picture*, pp. 116–17.

209   'exhibits mental'. *TLS*, 24 July 1937, p. 540.

'Frost on'. *Out of the Picture*, p. 54.

211   'on 6 August'. Carpenter, *W. H. Auden*, pp. 225–6.

'*The Times*'. 6 August 1937.

'*The Oxford Times*'. 13 August 1937.

'Hetty to Maisie'. This he dates 1 August (*ICM*, p. 228), which must be an error since *LI* was not published until 6 August.

212   'a satirical elegy'. MS note for an Argo recording (HRC archive, FLM Works 20).

214 'stressful reorganization'. Sidnell, *Dances of Death*, chapter 8.

215 'too ... much'. Keynes to TSE, 7 May 1937, quoted in Sidnell, *Dances of Death*, p. 217.

'one of the most'. Ibid., p. 222.

14: Summer is Ending

The principal published sources for this chapter are *SAF*, pp. 165–98, *Zoo*, and 'To-Day in Barcelona', *SP*, pp. 67–70. Information not attributed to other sources may be assumed to be taken from one of these.

216 'I have read'. TSE to FLM, 6 January 1938.

'to lend him £20'. FLM to ERD, 14 February 1938.

'Outside, he asked'. Allen, *As I Walked Down New Grub Street*, pp. 109–10.

217 'MacNeice and Britten'. Britten's diary records that the three met for a meal – 'very rowdy and pleasant' – on 15 December 1936. Donald Mitchell and Philip Reed, eds, *Letters from a Life: Selected Letters and Diaries of Benjamin Britten*, 1991, p. 783.

'£15 a week'. Allen, *As I Walked Down New Grub Street*, p. 110.

218 'as one of those'. *Beginning Again*, 1964, p. 127.

'With my heart'. *ICM*, p. 127.

219 'benefit of hindsight'. ERD, who edited *SAF*, can only date this chapter post December 1940. See p. 12.

'*Trial of a Judge*'. See Sidnell, *Dances of Death*, chapter 11, for a full account of this.

220 'Nancy was critical'. Interview with JS.

'the word "nurse"'. FLM to Mrs ERD, 10 April [1938].

221 'conception of Belfast'. *Zoo*, p. 78. My account of this weekend is based on chapter V of this book, 'A Personal Digression'.

222 '*Modern Poetry*'. J. Mulgan to FLM, 8 February 1937 (OUP archives).

'I want to change'. FLM to J. Mulgan, 25 September [1937] (OUP archives).

223 'Passage Steamer'. *CP*, p. 72.

224 'continually aware'. *TLS*, 7 May 1938, p. 315. *The Earth Compels* is favourably reviewed on p. 314.

'the elegance'. *New Verse*, summer 1938, p. 17.

'there are not many'. Geoffrey Walton, *Scrutiny*, June 1938, pp. 93–5.

'My desk'. FLM to Eleanor Clark (hereafter EC), 18 May [1939].

'as a Teacher'. Letter from the secretary to the Academic Registrar,

University of London, to the Principal of Bedford College, 19 May 1938.

225 'good at playing'. Miss M. P. Stevens, interview with JS.
'On sunny afternoons'. Dan MacNeice (hereafter DM), interview with JS.

226 'a flying visit'. Nancy Spender, interview with JS. She cannot remember the precise dates of this visit.
'unreasonably possessive'. Ibid.
'Dan tripped over'. Interview with JS.
'Wickham Lodge'. EN to JH, 30 August 1977.
'he told Waterhouse'. Interview with JS.
'*I was writing*'. CP, p. 101.

227 'Close and slow'. Ibid.
'Poetry To-Day'. In Geoffrey Grigson, ed., *The Arts Today*, 1935.
'a journalist poet'. Ibid., p. 56.
'a few predictions'. Ibid., pp. 64–5.

228 'And I am in'. CP, p. 102.

229 'Walter Allen'. My account of this day is indebted to Allen, *As I Walked Down New Grub Street*, pp. 115–16.

230 'Eliot promptly wrote'. Copies of TSE's letters are in the Faber and Faber archive.
'as being too'. ERD *Missing Persons*, 1977, p. 131.

231 'looking terribly'. Mrs E. A. Serpell, quoted in *ABD*, p. 29 fn. 5. The source of the photograph is unknown.
'This is the first'. *News Chronicle*, 14 November 1938.
'Any single page'. *New Verse*, January 1939, pp. 20–21.

232 'the least intimidating'. Ibid.
'I would have a poet'. MP, p. 198.
'When the crisis'. Ibid., p. 205.

233 '1,700 lines'. FLM to TSE, 5 December 1938.

234 'I support'. SP, p. 42.
'to alert the public'. Margaret Gardiner, *A Scatter of Memories*, 1988, p. 128.
'On one of these.' Allen, *As I Walked Down New Grub Street*, p. 111.

237 'Listen: a whirr'. CP, p. 150.

238 'a rugby match'. See *The Times*, 13 February 1939, p. 6.
'*Mrs Donald*'. Published in 1983, this has a biographical epilogue written by Mary Keene's daughter, Alice Kadel, to whom I am indebted for further information about her mother.

239 'Leaving the street'. *Mrs Donald*, pp. 11–12.
'Violet felt she'. Ibid., p. 59.

240 'Inside he had'. Ibid., pp. 80–81.
'Louis, preparing'. Ibid., pp. 96–7.

15: Talk of War

The principal published source for this chapter is *SAF*, pp. 199–215. Information not attributed to other sources may be assumed to be taken from this.

241 'it is easy'. *Varieties of Parable*, 1965, pp. 11–12.
243 'Pennsylvania State'. *Faculty Bulletin*, 21 March 1939.
'Princeton'. FLM to JFM, [May–June 1939].
'Hamilton College'. *Hamilton Life*, 12 April 1939.
'Harvard'. *Harvard Crimson*, 11 April 1939.
'Wellesley College'. *Wellesley College News*, 20 April 1939.
'Bowdoin College'. *Bowdoin College Calendar*, no. 50, 17–24 April 1939.
'His lectures earned'. FLM to JFM, [May–June 1939].
'a cheap apartment'. Carpenter, *W. H. Auden*, p. 257.
'three mortals'. J. M. Brinnin, 'On First Meeting W. H. Auden', *Ploughshares*, vol. 2., no. 4, 1975, p. 32.
'The youngster'. Ibid., p. 34.
244 'Eleanor Clark'. Interview with JS.
245 'The chief things'. FLM to EC, Friday [21 April 1939].
246 'Meeting point'. *CP*, p. 167.
247 'the Doddses gave'. FLM to EC, 2 May [1939].
'he had quarrelled'. FLM to EC, 8 May [1939].
248 'she began to read'. Interview with JS.
'To-day was'. *CP*, p. 108.
'But did you see.' Ibid., pp. 108–9.
249 'What will happen'. Ibid.
'And factory workers'. Ibid., p. 110.
250 'remember, when'. Ibid., pp. 131–2.
251 'Kathaleen ni Houlihan'. Ibid.
'All a poet'. JS, ed., *The Poems of Wilfred Owen*, 1985, p. 192.
'Why do we like'. *CP*, pp. 132–3.
252 'she gives her'. Ibid., p. 134.
'Sleep, the past'. Ibid., p. 153.
253 'I knew perfectly'. FLM to EC, 25 May [1939].
'a minor tragedy'. FLM to ERD, 1 June [1939].
'a really good'. FLM to ERD, 2 June [1939].

253 'formal application'. FLM to Miss Monkhouse, 12 June 1939 (Bedford
College archive).
'I have blackmailed'. FLM to EC, 20 June [1939].
'On 1 March'. This meeting, in the Group Theatre Rooms, Great
Newport Street, WC2, was the second in a series on 'Realism in Litera-
ture', and was chaired by Cecil Day Lewis.
'Yeats's Epitaph'. *New Republic*, 102, vol. 26, no. 24, June 1940,
pp. 862–3.

254 'more naïve enemies'. *SLC*, p. 117.
'an admiration'. Ibid., p. 118.
'I must lie'. W. B. Yeats, 'The Circus Animals' Desertion', lines 39–40.
'Out on the steps'. *CP*, pp. 160–1.

255 'I am writing'. FLM to EC, 2 July [1939].
'Les Sylphides'. FLM to EC, 16 July [1939].
'Christina'. *CP*, pp. 174–5.

256 'who took her foot'. Reported by AMHM to JS.
'am I to take'. This and the two subsequent quotations are taken from
'Tendencies in Modern Poetry', *The Listener*, vol. 22, no. 550, 27 July
1939, pp. 185–6.

257 'they'll probably'. FLM to EC, 16 July [1939].

260 'I am very worried'. FLM to EC, 9 September [1939]. The poems were
sent with his letter of 18 September.
'Cushendun'. *CP*, p. 165.

261 'Walter Starkie'. FLM to ERD, 24 September [1939].
'Dodds and Eliot'. TSE's testimonial of 10 October 1939 is in the Faber
and Faber archive.
'to be called'. FLM to TSE, 14 September [1939].

262 'they were introduced'. Mercy MacCann, interview with JS.

263 'rashest entanglement'. FLM to ERD, 13 October [1939].
'considered asking'. FLM to ERD, 6 November [1939].
'Special Lectureship'. FLM to ERD, 22 November [1939].
'knew everybody'. Allen, *As I Walked Down New Grub Street*, p. 109.

264 'The MacNeices'. Gardiner, *A Scatter of Memories*, p. 117.

265 'Louis was a'. Ibid.
'Dear E.R.D.'. FLM to ERD, 6 November [1939].
'her visit did'. FLM to ERD, 5 December [1939].

266 'a one-act play'. FLM to ERD, 19 November [1939].
'if there's one'. This and subsequent quotations are from a carbon copy
of the typescript in Bod. There is an MS 'first draft' in NYPL/BC.
'Dublin'. *CP*, p. 163.

266 'accepted *Blacklegs*'. FLM's note on the NYPL/BC manuscript.
267 'adjustments'. FLM to ERD, 8 December [1939].
'Miss Popper's father'. FLM to ERD, 28 November [1939].

16: The Pity of it All

The principal published source for this chapter is *SAF*, pp. 17–35. Information not attributed to other sources may be assumed to be taken from this.

269 'I start Cornell'. FLM to ERD, 5 February [1940].
270 'a group of young'. Morris Bishop, *A History of Cornell*, 1962, p. 410.
'Viktor Lange . . . Maurice Barret'. *Telluride Newsletter*, vol. xxv, no. 6, post-Convention 1939, p. 7. For FLM at Telluride, see *Telluride Newsletter*, vol. xxvi, no. 3, March 1940, p. 2; no. 4, May 1940, p. 2; no. 5, June 1940, p. 4.
271 'inhuman bank'. FLM to Mrs ERD, 22 March [1940].
'Jack Adams'. Interview with JS.
'99% of the world's.' FLM to Mrs ERD, 22 March [1940].
272 'He spoke at'. Dates from FLM's letters to EC.
'Bedford College'. FLM did not confirm his resignation in writing until 8 September, when he concluded his letter: 'since the end of April I have had a rather worrying time and so seem to have let a lot of things lapse'.
'it is my own'. FLM to EC, 11 March [1940].
'situation with E.'. FLM to Mrs ERD, 22 March [1940].
'Miss Popper wrote'. Miss Popper to FLM, 6 April [1940].
'Dodds urged MacNeice'. ERD to FLM, 6 June 1940.
277 '"Lily" and "Lollie"'. FLM to TSE, 14 September [1939]. Yeats's sisters, 'Lily' and 'Lollie', had been christened Susan Mary and Elizabeth Corbet, respectively.
278 'may I ask'. Nancy Spender to FLM, 10 February 1940.
'for the cynically-sentimental'. FLM to EC, 3 July [1940].
'Yeats says the'. Interview with JS.
'twelve-month extension'. FLM to EC, 8 July [1940].
279 'not as lovers'. EC, interview with JS.
'on 16/17 July'. FLM to ERD, 18 August [1940].
280 'if the fog lifted'. FLM to EC, 3 September [1940].
'Evening in Connecticut'. *CP*, pp. 185–6.
'Autobiography'. Ibid., pp. 183–4.
282 'Cradle Song for Eleanor'. Ibid., p. 190.
283 'see it this way'. FLM to EC, 11 March [1940].

284 '20 October'. FLM to EC, 'late at night, Thursday morning' [10 October 1940].

285 'When George Davis'. Carpenter, *W. H. Auden*, p. 304.

'that perhaps, darling'. FLM to EC, 'Tuesday afternoon' [19 November 1940].

286 'No more past'. FLM to EC, 'Thursday' [28 November? 1940].

'childhood chapters'. *SAF*, pp. 11–12.

'shockingly badly'. FLM to EC, 6 December [1940].

'29 November'. FLM to EC, postmarked 29 November 1940.

'HMS *Jervis Bay*'. FLM, 'The Way We Live Now', *SP*, p. 80.

'What will the people'. Ibid., p. 81.

'Cheer up, lad'. FLM to EC, begun 6 December [1940], postmarked 11 December.

287 'not technically'. FLM to JFM & GBM, 'Sunday' [15 December 1940].

'bad eyesight'. 'I have no documentary evidence for this fact, but was assured of its veracity by various people who knew him well at the time, including Mrs. Ann Shepard. Cf. the obituary note in the *Guardian*, 4 September 1963: "Mr. Laurence Gilliam, Head of Features, Sound, remembered yesterday that MacNeice joined the B.B.C. after he had returned from the U.S. and volunteered for the Navy but had been turned down because of his eyesight".' McKinnon, *ABD*, p. 32.

'of trying to crash'. FLM to JFM & GBM, 'Sunday' [15 December 1940].

'a phrase from Nietszche'. This phrase appears as an epigraph to the book: *ein Zwiespalt und Zwitter von pflanze und von Gespenst.* Nietzsche, Preface to *Thus Spake Zarathustra*. The sentence from which these words are taken may be translated: '[But whosoever is the wisest among you, even he is only] a hermaphroditic disunion of plant and phantom.'

'I have been'. T. Rowland Hughes to FLM, 7 March 1940 (Bod).

'F. W. Ogilvie'. Barbara Coulton, *Louis MacNeice in the BBC* (hereafter *LMBBC*), p. 46.

'money for jam'. FLM to Mrs ERD, 10 February [1941].

'From America'. *Horizon*, 3, 12, p. 281.

288 'Traveller's Return'. Ibid., 3, 14, pp. 110–17; and *SP*, pp. 83–91.

'For the expatriate'. FLM had already defended Auden's decision to leave England for America in *Horizon* 1, 7, July 1940, pp. 462 and 464. See also *SP*, pp. 74–7.

289 'a statue of'. *SP*, pp. 102–3.

290 'Having just returned'. Ibid., p. 105.

290 '(Archie) Harding'. *LMBBC*, pp. 35, 40 and 42.

17: The Truth about Love

The principal sources for this chapter are *LMBBC*, pp. 35–59, and Douglas Cleverdon's unpublished monograph, 'The Art of Radio in Britain 1922–1966', that he was kind enough to lend me. Information not attributed to other sources may be assumed to be taken from one of these.

291 'In Defence of Vulgarity.' *SP*, pp. 43–8.
'Poets should certainly.' *The Listener*, 1 December 1938, pp. 1194–5.

292 'six-week crash course'. Sir William Empson, interview with JS.
'Word from America'. Broadcast 15 February 1941. Scripts written by FLM for the BBC are listed in the Bibliography to *LMBBC*, pp. 204–7, and are to be found in the BBC Written Archives Centre at Caversham Park, near Reading.
'Cook's Tour of'. Broadcast 25 March 1941. FLM describes spending 'most of a night . . . down in the biggest subway station' in his 'London Letter [2]: Anti-Defeatism of the Man in the Street', *SP*, pp. 106–11.
'all sorts of sound'. On 10 February [1941].
'Dan should go'. DM, interview with JS.
'His father found'. FLM to EC, March [1941].

293 'The March of the 10,000'. Broadcast 16 April 1941.

294 'comforts of Wharton Street'. Medley, *Drawn from the Life*, pp. 149–50.
'looks like a'. FLM to EC, 24 January [1941].
'It's *not* patriotism'. FLM to EC, 9 February [1941].
'not a bad but'. W. H. Mellers, *Scrutiny*, vol. ix. no. 4, March 1941, pp. 381–3.
'The *TLS* gave'. *TLS*, 29 March 1941, p. 150.
'the book is crammed'. *The New Statesman and Nation*, vol. xxi. no. 531, 26 April 1941, p. 440.
'MacNeice's book on'. Foreword to a Faber paper covered edition of *The Poetry of W. B. Yeats*, 1967, p. 11.

296 'Prognosis'. *CP*, pp. 157–8.
'There is thrust'. *TLS*, 19 April 1941, p. 194.
'Dr. Johnson Takes It'. Broadcast 5 May 1941.

296 'All these shattered'. *Picture Post*, vol. 2, no. 5, 3 May 1941, pp. 9–12, 14. Also *SP*, pp. 117–22.
'The Stones Cry Out'. Broadcast 27 May 1941.

297 'How could you'. Gardiner, *A Scatter of Memories*, p. 120.
'They were eventually'. Ibid., p. 121.
'positive vetting'. FLM to ERD, 29 April [1941].

298 'devoted, adventurous', J. C. W. Reith, *Into the Wind*, 1949, p. 100.

299 'He was against'. P. H. Newby, *Feelings Have Changed*, 1981, p. 29.
'He was a man'. D. G. Bridson, *Prospero and Ariel*, 1971, p. 32.

300 'it was illuminating'. FLM to EC, 19 July [1941].
'a confidential letter'. This and the subsequent reports concerning this
incident are to be found in FLM's personal file, BBC Written Archives
Centre, Caversham Park.

303 'Freedom's Ferry'. Broadcast 16 July 1941.
'Convoy'. *CP*, p. 200.

304 'In a solitude'. 'The Convergence of the Twain', *The Complete Poems of
Thomas Hardy*, ed. James Gibson, 1976, p. 306.
'Just like being'. FLM to EC, 6 August [1941].
'the run-through'. Sir William Empson, interview with JS.
'but houses in'. *SP*, p. 121.
'The Stones Cry Out'. Broadcast on 24 November 1941.
'surrounded by historic'. FLM to EC, 19 January [1942].

305 'Dr Chekhov'. Broadcast 6 September 1941.
'MacNeice and Bower'. Bower, interview with JS.
'she had seen'. AMHM, interview with JS.
'she saw him again'. DM, interview with JS.

306 'One evening'. AMHM, interview with JS.

307 'quite, quite wrong'. AMHM, quoted in the obituary by Donald
Mitchell and Philip Read, *The Independent*, Saturday 10 February
1990.

308 'Tell me the truth'. Mitchell and Reed, op. cit.
'making up'. Judy Lang, interview with JS.
'a most lovely'. Ibid.

309 'It seemed a good'. FLM to ERD, 25 April [1942].
'Roman Catholic Bishop'. Primrose Stevens, interview with JS.
'great man'. FLM to AB, postmarked 20 November 1935.
'One who believed'. 'The Kingdom', *CP*, p. 253.
'to see Dan'. FLM to ERD, 25 April [1942].

310 'whom I know'. Interview with JS.
'Darling, Hedli and I'. Quoted from memory by Nancy Spender, who
has lost the original.
'Darling, This is'. FLM to EC, 9 July [1942].

311 'Giraud's *Pierrot Lunaire*'. AMHM's Introduction to Louis MacNeice,

The Revenant / A Song-Cycle for Hedli Anderson, 1975.

312 'he would publish'. 'The Revenant', *CP*, pp. 199–200.

'Seven years'. 'The First Interlude' from *The Revenant / A Song-Cycle for Hedli Anderson*, p. 10.

'impression on Dan'. DM, interview with JS.

18: A Birth and a Death

The principal published source for this chapter is *LMBBC*, pp. 57–76. Information not attributed to other sources may be assumed to be taken from this.

313 'a sudden revulsion'. FLM to EC, 19 January [1942].

'his radio scripts'. These four programmes were broadcast, respectively, on 26 July, 25 September, 4 October, and 12 October.

'entrusted to Bower'. See Dallas Bower, 'MacNeice: Sound and Vision', in *TWA*, pp. 97–102.

314 'Construction and'. *Christopher Columbus*, 1944, p. 88.

'Where shall wisdom'. Alan Heuser and Peter McDonald, eds, *Selected Plays of Louis MacNeice* (hereafter *Plays*), pp. 48–9.

315 'When will he'. Ibid., p. 31.

'created a sensation'. Asa Briggs, *The History of Broadcasting in the United Kingdom*, vol. 3, 1970, p. 585.

316 'The goose, the goose!'. JH, interview with JS.

'the MacNeices found'. AMHM, interview with JS.

317 'he was despatched'. DM, interview with JS, and FLM to GMTBM, 12 April [1943], in private hands.

'he will be away'. AMHM to Mercy MacCann, 21st [April 1943].

'On manoeuvres in'. AMHM, interview with JS.

'His working day'. In what follows, I draw on an interview with Ruth Jones (now Winawer), her subsequent letter to me, and extracts from her diaries of 1943–8 (in private hands).

318 'Boeotian Greek poet'. See D. L. Page, *Corinna*, 1963.

320 'The Story of My Death'. Ruth Jones collected this script for typing from 10 Wellington Place on 5 October. It was broadcast on the 8th.

321 'The Casualty'. *CP*, pp. 245–8.

'dead ere his prime'. Milton, 'Lycidas', line 8.

322 'He Had a Date'. It was produced by FLM and broadcast on 28 June 1944.

323 'Let us sleep now'. 'Strange Meeting', line 44.

325 'It was a warm summer'. Muriel Spark, 'Footnote to A Poet's House',

The Independent Magazine, 5 November 1988, p. 59.

327 'LANDLORD. . . . *I'm* going'. *The Dark Tower and Other Radio Scripts*, 1947, pp. 132–3.

'propagandist programmes'. Broadcast on 12 April 1942 and 8 November 1943, respectively.

'The part of the'. *The Dark Tower and Other Radio Scripts*, pp. 101–2.

'saved the situation'. Ibid., p. 16.

328 'A *steamer is*'. Ibid., p. 79.

'TCHEHOV. I told'. Ibid., p. 95.

'(*Silence and then*'. Ibid., p. 98.

329 'To Hedli'. *CP*, p. 191.

'Many of my titles'. *Springboard*, p. 7.

330 'The Satirist'. *CP*, p. 210.

'Postscript'. Ibid., p. 214.

332 'Dallas Bower prodding'. 16 November 1944.

'being pestered by'. 28 December 1944.

'written sixty-four scripts'. *LMBBC*, lists 62 in its Bibliography, pp. 204–5. It omits 'Homage to Stalingrad', 27 September 1942, and 'They Shall Rise Again: 10 Nanking', 22 October 1944.

'The Cincinnatus of'. 'Pax Futura', typescript owned by Mr Dallas Bower, p. 12.

333 'In Whitehall, they'. Gardiner, *A Scatter of Memories*, p. 124.

19: To the Dark Tower

The principal published source for this chapter is *LMBBC*, pp. 77–97. Information not attributed to other sources may be assumed to be taken from this.

334 'The interregnum of'. *The Yogi and the Commissar*, 1945, p. 111. MacNeice read this book approvingly. FLM to ERD, 31 July [1945].

335 'Carrick Revisited'. *CP*, pp. 224–5. An HRC fair-copy is dated 'June 1945'.

'Carrickfergus'. *CP*, pp. 69–70.

'Last before America'. Ibid., pp. 226–7.

'Under the Mountain'. Ibid., p. 227.

336 'The Strand'. Ibid., p. 226.

337 'by Browning's poem'. *Plays*, p. 113.

'You're like your'. Ibid., p. 126.

'Here is a ring'. Ibid., p. 128.

338 'On my deathbed'. Ibid., p. 143.

338 'To Those Who'. Ibid., p. 144.
'Are these my footsteps?' Ibid., p. 145.
'I, Roland, the'. Ibid., p. 147.
'The Mother in'. Ibid., pp. 410–11.

339 'Death is swallowed'. I Corinthians 15:54.
'I will remember'. *Plays*, p. 123.
'Mayfly'. *CP*, pp. 13–14.

340 'Reggie Smith came'. Gilliam, initially, arranged a short-term contract for Smith to replace Ted Livesey at BBC Birmingham.
'the pulpit in'. Dan Davin, 'At the End of his Whether: W. R. Rodgers (1909–1969)', *Closing Times*, 1975, p. 29.

341 'recalled life then'. Ibid., p. 26.

342 'Harold Brooks'. Interview with JS.
'I wish one'. FLM to ERD, 31 July [1945].

343 'eventually abandoned'. On the title-page of the HRC typescript FLM has written 'draft of abandoned stage play – with notes'.
'They liked its'. AMHM to Mercy MacCann, June [1946].

344 'the best I have'. *The Dark Tower*, p. 22.
'Louis came in'. Dorothy Baker, interview with JS.
'An uncouth modern'. *The Listener*, vol. xxxv, no. 889, 24 January 1946, p. 124.

345 'T. S. Eliot had'. TSE to FLM, 25 October 1945.
'Neither the poet'. Dorothy Baker, interview with JS.

346 'The Careerist'. For a fuller account of this programme (broadcast 22 October 1946), see *LMBBC*, pp. 88–90.
'Salute to All Fools'. Ibid., pp. 85–6.
'GAEL. I can see'. *The Dark Tower*, p. 184.

347 'Enemy of Cant'. Broadcast 3 December 1946. See *LMBBC*, pp. 86–7.
'The Heartless Giant'. Broadcast 13 December 1946. See *LMBBC*, pp. 87–8.

348 'Enter Caesar'. Broadcast 20 September 1946.
'in using the word'. 'Woods', *CP*, pp. 230–31.

349 'Dorothy told Hedli'. Dorothy Baker, interview with JS.
'Louis went over'. He crossed on the 28th. The programme was broadcast on 1 September.
'I remember him'. 'Louis MacNeice, a radio portrait', broadcast 7 September 1966 (script in BBC Written Archives Centre, Caversham Park).

350 'Hedli had written'. Letter postmarked 6 June 1946.
'At last imagination'. Letter postmarked 22 November 1946.

351 'watchers on the wall'. 'Cradle Song for Eleanor', *CP*, p. 190.

351   'I come from'. Ibid., p. 41.
'where he arranged'. AMHM to Mercy MacCann, postmarked 22 April 1947. These arrangements had to be cancelled because of FLM's subsequent Indian assignment.
'sightseeing in Rome'. FLM to Ruth Jones, 26 May [1947] (in private hands), and *ABD*, p. 36.
'Portrait of Rome'. Script in the BBC Written Archives Centre, Caversham.
352   'Scripts Wanted!' *BBC Year Book 1947*, 1947, pp. 25–8.
'Eclogue from Iceland'. *CP*, p. 42.
'Grettir the Strong'. See *LMBBC*, pp. 92–4.

20: The Horror

The principal published source for this chapter is *LMBBC*, pp. 98–114. Information not attributed to other sources may be assumed to be taken from this.

354   'Punjab and Bengal'. James Morris, *Farewell the Trumpets: An Imperial Retreat*, 1978, p. 488.
355   'A spot of Kipling'. 'India at First Sight', broadcast 13 March 1948. The script of this shares no more than its title with the article in *SP*.
'Mulk was small'. *SAF*, p. 209.
'His radio script'. 'India at First Sight', broadcast 13 March 1948.
356   'Look East, where'. Robert Browning, 'Waring', part II. iii, lines 24–5.
'after stops at'. FLM to AMHM, 10 August [1947].
'last cocktail party'. On 11 August.
'interview with Dalmia'. On 13 August.
'This campaign of'. FLM to AMHM, 16 August [1947].
357   'Mountbatten reported'. Morris, *Farewell the Trumpets*, p. 491.
'shamelessly exploit all'. FLM to AMHM, 8 September [1947].
358   'The results of'. 'The awards of the Boundary Commission [for the partitions of Punjab and of Bengal] have, as was generally expected, been unpopular with both sides, but much more so with the Muslims than with the Hindus'. 'New Frontiers in India', *The Times*, 19 August 1947. Riots, reprisals, burnings, killings, followed: 'The Sikh Rising', ibid., 27 August. See also 'Final Boundaries of New Dominions', ibid., 18 August.
'ran into some horrors'. FLM to AMHM, 31 August [1947].
'A v. large'. Ibid.

359 'a totally different'. 'Louis MacNeice, a radio portrait'.
'Excuse me, gentleman'. *SP*, p. 168.

360 'militant-cum-pseudo-socialist'. FLM to AMHM, 5 September [1947].
'a wonderful collection'. Ibid.

361 'A long dark'. Ibid.
'the most fascinating'. FLM to AMHM, 3 October [1947].
'in the other'. FLM to AMHM, 6 October [1947].

364 'he sent Hedli'. FLM to AMHM, 8 October [1947].
'Letter from India'. *CP*, p. 268.

365 'Returning to Delhi'. FLM to AMHM, 9 October [1947].

366 'I really do'. FLM to AMHM, 21 October [1947].
'Mahabalipuram'. *CP*, p. 273.
'They went on'. FLM to AMHM, 27 October [1947].
'the dark grim'. 'Mahabalipuram', *CP*, p. 273.

368 'The Crash Landing'. *Botteghe Oscure*, 4, 1949, pp. 378–85. India opens this extract by saying: 'It is always a crash landing – when I come up to meet you. With the red earth on my sandals and the brass jug on my head . . . .'
'Possibly neglect'. *Life and Letters*, February 1949, pp. 111–13.
'he has lost'. *TLS*, 5 June 1948, p. 315.

369 'Dylan Thomas'. *Poetry London*, 16 September 1949, pp. 27–8. See also Tiller's review-article, 'Around Louis', *London Magazine*, October 1980, pp. 83–6.
'Dylan T. stayed'. FLM to AMHM, 21 July [1948].
'Then a telegram'. Maeve Gilmore, *A World Away: A Memoir of Mervyn Peake*, 1970, p. 72; and Sebastian Peake and AMHM, interviews with JS. AMHM spoke of the quarrel.
'For Mr. Grigson'. *Poetry Review*, August/September 1949, p. 290.
'If I was young'. David Wright, 'A Poet and His Dragons', *Sunday Telegraph Magazine*, 6 May 1979.
'Matters came to a head'. AMHM, interview with JS. See Victoria Glendinning, *Edith Sitwell: A Unicorn among Lions*, 1981, pp. 283–4; also Davin, *Closing Times*, p. 53, and Peter Alexander, *Roy Campbell / A Critical Biography*, 1982, pp. 211 and 215. Misled, I think, by Campbell's later annotation on a letter of June 1946 from Stephen Spender, Alexander proposes a 1946 date for the Campbell/MacNeice encounter, and a 1949 date for the Campbell/Grigson encounter.

371 'A halt was'. Maurice Collis, *The Journey Up*, 1970, p. 84.

372 'It remained for'. Ibid., p. 85.
'secretary par excellence'. FLM to Ruth Jones, 3 August [1948].

372 'No Other Road'. Broadcast 19 September 1948.
'Trimalchio's Feast'. Broadcast 22 December 1948. See *LMBBC*, pp. 105 and 108–9.
'The Queen of Air'. See *LMBBC*, pp. 109–11.

373 'Stahl agreed'. See E. L. Stahl, 'The "Faust" Translation: A Personal Account', in *Time Was Away*, ed. Terence Brown and Alec Reid, 1974, pp. 67–71, for the fullest account of this collaboration.

374 'He refused to look'. Stahl, quoted in 'Louis MacNeice: A radio portrait'.
'There can be'. Stahl, 'The "Faust" Translation: A Personal Account' in *Time Was Away*, pp. 69–70.

375 ' "the onlie begetter" '. FLM, *Goethe's Faust*, 1951, p. 10.

21: The Sanguine Visitor

The principal published source for this chapter is *LMBBC*, pp. 113–26. Information not attributed to other sources may be assumed to be taken from this.

376 'The Dark Tower'. It would be broadcast twice during FLM's absence in Greece: on 30 January 1950 and 16 May 1951.
'Dylan Thomas'. See Paul Ferris, ed., *Dylan Thomas: The Collected Letters*, 1985, p. 737.
'Louis' new secretary'. Margaret Clark, interview with JS.
'*Collected Poems*'. This had been grudgingly reviewed in the *TLS* of 28 October 1949, p. 696.

377 'like a doctor's'. 'The Death of a Cat', I, *CP*, p. 318.
'Institute functioned smoothly'. My account of FLM in the Institute in much indebted to letters from its former Librarian, Miss Beatrix Collingham.
'a poetry reading'. On 7 February. This and subsequent 1950 dates are taken from FLM's desk diary (Bod).

378 'in early May'. 3–6 May.
'For Greeks the'. Kevin Andrews, 'Time and the Will Lie Sidestepped: Athens, the Interval', in *Time Was Away*, ed. Terence Brown and Alec Reid, p. 103.

379 'the most brilliant'. 'Kevin Andrews' [obituary], *The Independent*, 7 September 1989.
'*Ill Met by Moonlight*'. By W. Stanley Moss, 1950.

380 '[Here I lie'. Patrick Leigh Fermor to JS.

380 'many evenings at'. Ibid.
381 'like a man'. Beatrix Collingham to JS.
'The Ghika house'. 'The Background of Ghika: Thoughts on a Greek Landscape', *Encounter*, 41, February 1957, pp. 61–2.
382 'indistinguishable words'. Andrews, *Time Was Away*, pp. 107–8.
'All I can say'. FLM to George MacCann, 22 June [1950].
'*Ten Burnt Offerings*'. *CP*, pp. 291–4.
383 'coughing at night'. DM, interview with JS.
'The Island'. *CP*, p. 307.
'be a brothel'. DM, interview with JS.
'You must never'. FLM to AMHM, 8 December [1950].
384 'evident from the last'. *CP*, p. 322: 'you are the air/Through which you flew to what was once Byzantium'.
'*Kalamatianos*'. Beatrix Collingham to JS.
'seated in armchairs'. Patrick Leigh Fermor to JS.
385 'found him a job'. John Press, interview with JS.
'The Art of Autobiography'. FLM to TSE, 7 May [1951].
'what we need'. Hal Lidderdale, interview with JS.
'terse memoranda'. Andrews, *Time Was Away*, p. 106.
'dinner party'. Andrews to JS.
'Dodds and Andrews'. ERD, *Missing Persons*, pp. 184–5.
386 'Easter Eve'. Ibid., p. 186, and DM, interview with JS.
'all my years'. 'Day of Renewal', *CP*, p. 313.
'I have been working'. FLM to TSE, 20 September [1950].
'experiments in'. *Poetry Book Society Bulletin*, May 1957.
'death of their cat'. *CP*, pp. 318–21. The cat is named in FLM to ERD, 15 May [1950].
387 'come from a common'. FLM to TSE, 20 September [1950].
'Flowers in the Interval'. *CP*, pp. 321–6.
'Voluminous drafts'. In HRC and NYPL/BC.
'Portrait of Athens'. Broadcast 18 November 1951. See *LMBBC*, pp. 116–18.
'In Search of Anoyia'. Broadcast 11 December 1951. See *LMBBC*, pp. 124–5.
388 'The Centre of the World'. Broadcast 28 January 1952. See *LMBBC*, p. 125.
'His father wrote'. FLM to MacCann, 17 April [1952].
'with some foreboding'. Gardiner, *A Scatter of Memories*, p. 125.
389 '2 Windsor Terrace'. Elizabeth Bowen, *The Death of the Heart*, 1938, p. 276.

389 'Eliot obligingly did'. TSE to FLM, 29 January 1952.
390 'MacNeices moved into'. FLM to GMTBM, 26 July [1952].
'Personally I think'. FLM to Mrs Stevenson, 21 March [1953] (HRC).
'Do I prefer'. 'Day of Renewal', *CP*, p. 309.

22: The Middle Stretch

The principal published source for this chapter is *LMBBC*, pp. 126–43. Information not attributed to other sources may be assumed to be taken from this.

391 'the non-commitment'. Corinna MacNeice (hereafter CM), interview with JS.
'he'll have to work'. Kevin Andrews to JS.
'John Malcolm Brinnin'. Interview with JS.
392 'a collection of essays'. Davin, *Closing Times*, p. 47.
'an Irishman who'. Ibid.
393 'The afternoon passed'. Ibid., pp. 48–9.
'Christ became a'. Ibid., p. 50.
'list of contributors'. See Peter McDonald, 'The Fate of "Identity": John Hewitt, W. R. Rodgers and Louis MacNeice', *The Irish Review*, 12, Spring/Summer 1952, pp. 72–86, for a fuller account of *The Character of Ireland* saga.
394 'and told Rodgers'. See John Boyd, *The Middle of My Journey*, 1990, pp. 92–4.
'That was rather'. Kevin Andrews to JS.
'a ritual breakfast'. Mercy MacCann, interview with JS.
395 'Ireland defeating France'. See 'An Irish Rugby Triumph', *The Times*, 26 January, p. 9.
'Kyle, who replied'. Mercy MacCann, interview with JS.
'Their tour had'. J. M. Brinnin, interview with JS.
'playwright Denis Johnston'. FLM to ERD, 17 March [1953].
'at Harvard'. J. M. Brinnin and W. Alfred, interviews with JS.
398 'invited them up'. Eileen Simpson, interview with JS.
'Berryman, however'. John Haffenden, *The Life of John Berryman*, 1982, p. 109.
'13. The mother'. P. R. Kimber to ERD, 15 September 1953 (Bod).
399 'Mourning and Consolation'. Broadcast 8 February 1952.
400 'Return to Atlantis'. Broadcast 5 July 1953.
'The Faerie Queene'. MP, pp. 46–7.

400   'He refers to it'. See the indexes to *SLC* and *Varieties of Parable*.

      'suddenly and quite'. Introductory note to the BBC recording of *Autumn Sequel*, Canto 1, broadcast 28 June 1954.

401   'August. Render to'. *CP*, p. 331.

      'Gavin and Gwilym'. Ibid., p. 332.

      'the wedding of'. Introductory note to the BBC recording of *Autumn Sequel*.

      'Yeats's celebrations'. See, for example, Yeats's poem 'The Municipal Gallery Revisited'.

402   'my train goes'. *CP*, p. 340.

      'We stop – and'. Ibid., pp. 340–41.

      'we're bound for'. *SP*, p. 140.

      'A harsh voice'. *CP*, p. 343.

403   'MacNeice heard'. Pocock, interview with JS.

      'Don't go yet'. Gardiner, *A Scatter of Memories*, pp. 129–30.

404   'a bulbous Taliessin'. *CP*, pp. 404.

      'wearing shoes bought'. Ibid., p. 411.

      'Look, Caitlin'. As reported by FLM to Jack Cope and by him to JS.

      'What we remember'. *Encounter*, vol. II, no. 1, January 1954, p. 12.

      'To Wales once'. *CP*, p. 410.

405   'Do I contradict'. These lines, printed as epigraph to *Autumn Sequel*, are taken from Whitman's 'Song of Myself'.

      'so it goes'. *CP*, pp. 438–9.

      'they met for'. DM, interview with JS.

406   'across the Atlantic'. *CP*, p. 425.

      'profit of £633'. Sean Day-Lewis, *C. Day Lewis: An English Literary Life*, 1980, p. 216.

      'They found their'. Eileen Simpson, interview with JS.

407   'lament/The maker'. *CP*, p. 349.

      'Listing his and'. FLM to Mrs Stevenson, 21 March [1953] (HRC).

      'You must use'. Cécile Chevreau, interview with JS.

      'an adaptation of'. Broadcast 16 March 1954. See *LMBBC*, p. 141.

      'Prisoner's Progress'. Broadcast 27 April 1954. See *LMBBC*, pp. 141–3.

      'After a rehearsal'. Cécile Chevreau, interview with JS.

408   'Prisoner's Progress'. Misreported in *The Times* of 24 September 1954, p. 8, as 'Mr. MacNeice's television work The Prisoner's Journey'. Mac-Neice had declined suggestions that he should submit his play for this prize, but Dorothy Baker had persuaded Gilliam to add it to the BBC's list of submissions. Dorothy Baker, interview with JS.

410   'there was a lunch'. Eleanor Clark, interview with JS.

410 'Hedli would later'. AMHM, interview with JS.
'Cantos I and II'. Broadcast 28 June 1954, and reviewed in *The Times*, 5 July 1954, p. 11.
'the main difference'. *The Times*, 20 November 1954, p. 8.
'*The New Statesman*'. 11 December 1954, p. 794.

23: Visitations and Revisitations

The principal published source for this chapter is *LMBBC*, pp. 149–65. Information not attributed to other sources may be assumed to be taken from this.

412 'Mummies, pictures from'. Diary, 4 January 1921 (Bod). See p. 67 above.
'Northern Sudan'. FLM to AMHM, 27 February, 3 and 8 March [1955].
'it kept talking'. FLM to AMHM, 8 March [1955].
'The Rest House'. *CP*, pp. 452–3.

413 'the PS *Sudan*'. FLM to AMHM, 23 March [1955].
'Every evening'. FLM to AMHM, 17 March [1955].
'The brown hills'. Ibid.
'Beni Hasan'. *CP*, p. 452.

414 'Hedli had suggested'. FLM to AMHM, 23 March [1955].
'The Fullness of the Nile'. Broadcast 3 July 1955.
'on 28 May'. FLM's BBC diary.
'They booked into'. Sam Wells interview with JS.

415 'wondered if Wells'. Ibid., and AMHM, interview with JS.
'Hedli, Margaret Gardiner'. Margaret Gardiner, interview with JS.
'House on a cliff'. *CP*, p. 462. AMHM, told JS that 'The house was in Dorset'. See Tom Paulin, *Ireland and the English Crisis*, 1984, pp. 78–9, for a perceptive discussion of this poem.

416 'has to do with Cécile'. Interview with JS. In 1970, AMHM spoke of FLM's impotence to DM and his wife.
'Till all was broken'. 'Trains in the Distance', *CP*, p. 3.
'on 1 September'. FLM's BBC diary.

417 'said Sharp'. Interview with JS.
'I suggest just'. FLM to AMHM, postmarked 22 Octobver 1955.

418 'was particularly delighted'. FLM to AMHM, 26 October [1955].
'Return to Lahore'. *CP*, pp. 453–4.
'Outside this hotel'. FLM to AMHM, 1 November [1955].

418 'The Indian Ocean'. FLM to AMHM, 5 November [1955].

420 'Spires and Gantries'. Broadcast 29 July 1956.
  'So, between glamour'. 'Visit to Rouen', *CP*, p. 454.
  'she was buried'. *Belfast Telegraph*, 9 April 1956. FLM's BBC diary has
  no entry between 11 and 14 April.
  'Death of an Old Lady'. *CP*, p. 463.

421 'It is a small'. TSE to FLM, 17 September 1956.
  '. . . *age iam meorum*'. Horace, Odes, IV, 11, lines 31–2.

422 'a great cavalcade'. FLM to AMHM, 21 October [1956].
  'Prince of Princes'. FLM to AMHM, 17 October [1956].
  'a woman making'. FLM to AMHM, 10 November [1956].

423 'Eden & Co.'. FLM to AMHM, 2 November [1956].
  '*Ave Marie!*' 'Street Scene', *CP*, p. 234.
  'had asked Hedli'. FLM to AMHM, 2 November [1956].

424 'letter of 21 February'. In private hands.
  'Boyd was not'. Boyd, *The Middle of My Journey*, p. 99.
  '*The Times* and *TLS*'. Of 26 March and 16 August 1957, respectively.
  'letter to the MacCanns'. Of 2 April [1957].

425 'MacNeice told him'. William Alfred, interview with JS.
  'Yet after all'. *CP*, p. 469.

426 'these poems confirm'. *TLS*, 7 June 1957, p. 350.
  'Prohibition has killed'. FLM to AMHM, 16 October [1957].
  'John Masters'. FLM to AMHM, 19 October [1957].
  'which is a parody'. FLM to AMHM, 28 October [1957].
  'Nice blue mountains'. FLM to AMHM, 5 November [1957].
  'I *have* worked'. FLM to AMHM, 9 November [1957].
  'on whiskey &'. FLM to George MacCann, 31 December [1957].

427 'would frame it'. Dr Gerald Abraham to JS, 10 October 1984, and
  LMBBC, p. 138.

24: All Over Again

The principal published source for this chapter is *LMBBC*, pp. 166–79.
Information not attributed to other sources may be assumed to be taken from
this.

428 'Herself asked me'. Kevin Andrews to JS, 31 December 1982.
  'decline of Features'. Douglas Cleverdon, 'The Art of Radio in Britain
  1922–1966' (unpublished typescript, p. 54).
  'Gilliam retained his'. Ibid.

429　'A bulletin, with'. Briggs, *The History of Broadcasting*, vol. 4, 1979, p. 218.

'two undistinguished exercises'. Broadcast on 22 and 24 September 1957.

'two 1958 programmes'. Broadcast on 1 and 7 April 1958.

'The last to leave'. John Press, interview with JS.

The Flight of Ikaros. Later reviewed by FLM in *The Observer* of 1 March 1959. See *SP*, pp. 217–19.

430　'Doesn't one stay'. Kevin Andrews to JS, 31 December 1982.

'a younger poet'. Anthony Thwaite, 'Memories of Rothwell House', *Poetry Review*, vol. 78, no. 2, Summer 1988, p. 11.

'as we sat'. Ibid., p. 12.

'Can't you see'. Ibid.

431　'*One for the Grave*'. Published in 1968.

'a modern morality'. *Plays*, p. 201.

'Mayfly'. *CP*, pp. 13–14.

432　'Moriturus te saluto'. *Plays*, pp. 246–7.

'it was performed'. See *Evening Press*, 4 October 1966, p. 4; *Irish Independent*, 4 October 1966, p. 6; *Irish Press*, 4 October 1966, p. 5; and *Irish Times*, 4 October 1966, p. 4.

433　'Scrums and Dreams'. Broadcast on 3 April 1959.

'East of the Sun'. Published in *Persons from Porlock and Other Plays for Radio*, 1969. See also *LMBBC*, pp. 170–71.

'MacNeice's interest in'. Peter McDonald, 'The Fate of "Identity": John Hewitt, W. R. Rodgers and Louis MacNeice', pp. 83–4.

434　'reduce its staff'. Cleverdon, 'The Art of Radio in Britain', p. 54.

435　'waiting for their'. FLM to AMHM, 5 August [1959].

'In Iceland, when'. Paul Gregorowski, interview with JS.

'I should refuse'. Jack Cope to JS, 19 August 1985. This letter is the principal source for my account of FLM in Cape Town. Information not attributed to other sources may be assumed to be taken from this.

'Old Masters Abroad'. *CP*, p. 501.

436　'MacNeice showed little'. Marjorie Clouts to JS.

'Half Truth from'. *CP*, p. 499.

'Solitary Travel'. Ibid., p. 500.

'All Over Again'. Ibid., p. 513.

'Meeting Point'. Ibid., pp. 167–8.

438　'The first issue'. See Jack Cope, 'The World of *Contrast*', *English in Africa*, 7, no. 9, September 1980, pp. 1–21.

'converted army camp'. FLM to AMHM, 1 September [1959].

440 'The Sixpence that'. First published in America as *The Penny that Rolled Away* (1954).

441 'Michael Silver'. Interview with JS.
'a poetry reading'. On 14 September.
'HARPER: Why are you'. *Plays*, pp. 300–301.

442 'that the leaders'. FLM to P. H. Newby, 17 April 1959 (Bod).
'When doing a'. Bod.
'Your synopsis'. P. H. Newby to FLM, 6 October 1959 (Bod).

443 'Solitary Travel'. *CP*, p. 500.

444 'MacNeice suggested he'. FLM to P. H. Newby, 21 June 1960 (Bod).
'Gilliam strongly supported'. L. Gilliam to the Assistant Director of Sound Broadcasting, 18 July 1960 (Bod).
'it would be'. Wellington to Gilliam, 2 August 1960 (Bod).
'Mary Wimbush was'. My account of Mary Wimbush and FLM largely derives from an interview with her.

445 'underwent one of'. 'Louis MacNeice Writes . . . [on *Solstices*]', *Poetry Book Society Bulletin*, no. 28, February 1961, *SLC*, p. 223.
'Apple Blossom'. *CP*, p. 473.

446 'in other poems'. Ibid., pp. 487–9 and 506.
'MacNeice and Thwaite'. See Thwaite, 'Memories of Rothwell House', p. 12.
'himself translated passages'. Broadcast 20 October 1960.
'The Truisms'. *CP*, p. 507.

447 'I know nothing'. AMHM to FLM, postmarked 15 August 1960.

448 'A vote for Leavis'. 'That Chair of Poetry', *SLC*, p. 225.
'*Alice in Wonderland*'. Ibid., p. 226.
'To vote for'. Ibid., p. 228.

450 '. . . *age iam meorum*'. Odes, IV 11, lines 31–2.

25: Funeral Games

The principal published source for this chapter is *LMBBC*, pp. 179–90. Information not attributed to other sources may be assumed to be taken from this.

451 'His reply became'. Thwaite, 'memories of Rothwell House', *Poetry Review*, vol. 78, no. 2, Summer 1988, p. 12.
'his own poetry'. 'Readings on Record', broadcast 18 September 1960.
'Night at Lamorran'. Broadcast 27 December 1960.

452 'I'm escapist'. FLM, *The Mad Islands and The Administrator*, 1964, p. 76.

452 'against my grain'. ibid., p. 8.
'These two plays'. iIbid., p. 7.

453 'Soap Suds'. *CP*, p. 517.
'a yellow dress'. 'Autobiography', ibid., p. 183.
'as train wheels'. See 'Trains in the Distance', ibid., p. 3.
'Round the Corner'. Ibid., p. 518.

454 'The first time'. *ICM*, p. 22.

455 'the quality of'. Jack Cope to JS, 19 August 1985. My account of Cope's meeting with FLM is taken from this letter.

456 'Serve us right'. Bob Pocock, interview with JS.
'pay "back tax" '. Mary Wimbush, interview with JS.
'book on astrology'. Published in 1964.
'I find it highly'. Letter of 12 March [1962].
'obtained an order'. This document and an affidavit by FLM, dated 22 March 1963, are in Bod.

457 'After the Crash'. *CP*, p. 524.
'Look after yourself'. AMHM, interview with JS.

458 'One Eye Wild'. Broadcast 14 November 1961.
'Douglas Carson'. In a lecture, entitled 'Ariel and Caliban/Louis Mac-Neice and the BBC', delivered at the John Hewitt Summer School, 2 August 1991.

459 'Surrounded by engineers'. Ved Mehta, *John Is Easy to Please*, 1971, pp. 51–3.

460 'Voyage of Maeldúin'. FLM to George and Mercy MacCann, 12 March [1962].
'The Mad Islands'. And published in *The Mad Islands and The Administrator* (1964).
'into his freedom'. FLM to George and Mercy MacCann, 29 March [1962].
'village of Aldbury'. FLM to George and Mercy MacCann, 16 May [1962].

461 'Well, what did'. Mary Wimbush, interview with JS.
'£50 a month'. FLM's affidavit, dated 22 March 1963, in respect of AMHM's application under Section 23 of the Matrimonial Causes Act, 1950, for periodical payments (Bod).

462 'stayed with the MacCanns'. FLM to George and Mercy MacCann, 25 June [1962].
'Teems of Times'. FLM reviewed this in *The New Statesman*, 24 November 1961, pp. 795–6.
'New Statesman paid'. Ibid.

462 'thirty-nine models'. FLM, 'Under the Sugar Loaf', *SP*, pp. 246–52.
'spotted by a friend'. Martha McCulloch, interview with JS.
'MacNeice took a quick'. Ibid.

463 'the *Ave Maria*'. See Murphy's book of poems, *Sailing to an Island*
(1963). FLM signed the ship's visitors' book on 19 August.
'he was a bit'. John Keohane, interview with JS.
'It seems that'. FLM to George and Mercy MacCann, 12 November
[1962].

464 'Goodbye to London'. *CP*, pp. 544–5.
'In Honour of the City'. James Kinsley does not include it in his Oxford
English Text edition of *The Poems of William Dunbar*, 1979.
'sets the tone'. Robyn Marsack, *The Cave of Making: The Poetry of Louis
MacNeice*, 1982, p. 139.
'when a man'. Boswell's *Life of Johnson*, 20 September 1777.

465 '*One for the Grave*'. p. 75.
'Charon'. *CP*, p. 530.

466 'This is the Life'. Ibid., p. 538.
'Coda'. *CP*, p. 546.

467 'To Mary'. Ibid., p. 515.
'Edna Longley'. *Louis MacNeice / A Study*, 1988, p. 169.
'*The Strings are False*'. P. 75.
'Childhood Memories'. Broadcast on 29 November 1963 and published
in *SP*, pp. 267–73.

468 'cosmic glooms'. Mary Wimbush, interview with JS.
'but Louis opined'. Thwaite, 'Memories of Rothwell House', p. 12.
'Budgie'. *CP*, p. 539.
'He could work'. Boyd, *The Middle of My Journey*, p. 218.
'list of his reviews'. See 'A Bibliography of Short Prose by Louis Mac-
Neice', *SP*, pp. 275–92.

469 'Varieties of Parable'. They were published with this title in 1965.
'underrated poet'. *Varieties of Parable*, p. 110.

470 'to begin with'. Thwaite, 'Memories of Rothwell House', p. 12.
'the absence of'. *Varieties of Parable*, p. 142.
'Thalassa'. *CP*, p. 546. 'It may have been sketched years before. Texas
holds a typed carbon-copy contents list for *Springboard*, with autograph
additions and deletions, which includes the title "Run Out the Boat",
dated January 1944. On another contents list for the volume, the title "Run
Out the Boat" is inserted between "Prayer Before Birth" and "Brother Fire",
then deleted, with "Thalassa" substituted. Unfortunately, there are no
corresponding manuscripts' (Marsack, *The Cave of Making*, p. 158).

471 '1st House'. Boyd, *The Middle of My Journey*, pp. 218–19. For a transcription of FLM's talk, 'Childhood Memories', see *SP*, pp. 267–73.
'*New Statesman*'. See FLM, 'Great Summer Sale', *The New Statesman*, vol. 66, no. 1686, 5 July 1963, pp. 10 and 12.
'A PERSON FROM'. This and correspondence with Newby relating to the proposed change of title are in Bod.

473 'a magnificent example'. FLM, *Persons from Porlock and Other Plays for Radio*, 1969, p. 7.
'Talk about back'. *Plays*, p. 358.
'excitingly timeless'. Ibid., p. 359.
'come from the'. Ibid., p. 379.
'fan-vaulted church'. Ibid., p. 380.
'Hobby! It's my'. Ibid., p. 382.
'At the bottom'. *SAF*, p. 75.

474 'the biggest cave'. *Plays*, p. 368.
'I noticed a'. Ibid., p. 386.

475 'on 7 August'. FLM to JH, 6 August [1963].
'he looked feverish'. Bob Pocock, 'Louis MacNeice'. Apparently a radio-portrait written in 1963–4, this lacks the normal BBC front-sheet giving rehearsal and transmission dates and times, and I can find no evidence that it was ever broadcast (Bod).
'Louis, you've got'. Dorothy Baker, interview with JS.

476 'Mary knew that'. Mary Wimbush, interview with JS.
'Louis was in'. Pocock, 'Louis MacNeice'. This and other accounts of FLM's last days suggest that Dr Slattery was incorrect in telling Nancy Spender that FLM's death 'was totally unnecessary. He got all the wrong treatment. They made him stop smoking [his 60 a day] and cut him off all human contact' (Nancy Spender, interview with JS).

Afterword

479 'for the family'. Pocock, 'Louis MacNeice'.

480 'Hedli held court'. Denys Hawthorne, interview with JS.
'reviewers recognized'. See, for example, Terence Tiller's unsigned review in the *TLS*, 22 September 1963, p. 746.
'among his very best'. 'Louis MacNeice', *Encounter*, November 1963, p. 48. This obituary was written before Auden had read *The Burning Perch*.
'Canzonet'. Published for the first time in the order of service.

481 'He stood in'. Newby, *Feelings Have Changed*, p. 145.

481 'precise and generous'. Boyd, *The Middle of My Journey*, p. 217.
'The Cave of Making'. W. H. Auden, *Collected Poems*, 1976, p. 521.
'The Story of'. *Studies on Louis MacNeice*, 1988, pp. 9–10.

483 'For the English'. Paulin, *Ireland and the English Crisis*, p. 75.
'Now the till'. *CP*, p. 105.
'But you also'. Ibid.

484 'The routine courage'. Ibid., p. 87.
'my trouble all'. FLM to AMHM, 5 November [1957].
'Michael Longley'. Introduction, *Louis MacNeice: Selected Poems*, 1988, p. xxiii.
'a leaping vitality'. FLM, *The Poetry of W. B. Yeats*, 1941, p. 232.

Index

Page references in **bold** type denote illustrations.

Betjeman, Penelope, 175
Bible, FLM influenced by language
of, 48, 282
Bingham, Alfred M., 288
Birkenhead, Lord, 106–7
Birmingham, 147, 165, 177–8, 182,
183, 192, 216, 219, 261, 286, 288
'Birmingham', 156, 168
Birmingham Hippodrome, 229
Birmingham University, 457; FLM
offered Assistant Lectureship in
Classics, 141; FLM at, 145–9,
206; as a non-residential
university, 146; Socialist Society,
157
Bishop's House, Belfast, 220–21,
225, 292
Black and Tans, 65, 160
Blacklegs, 266–7
Blake, William, 97, 99, 254, 469,
476–7; *Songs of Experience*, 113
Blind Fireworks, 123, 124, 125, 127,
131–4, 155, 167
Bloomsbury Group, 145
Bloomsday (16 June 1962),
462–3
Blumenfeld (later Bloomfield),
Bernard, 122
Blumenfeld (later Bloomfield), Elise,
122
Blunt, Anthony, 117, 124, 172, 219,
316, 487; at Marlborough, 82–4,
91–4, 97–8, 100–101, 100,
103–5, 180; and art, 83, 91–2, 93;
influences FLM, 93–4, 96;
compared with FLM, 98;
scholarship to Trinity College,
Cambridge, 100; in Italy, 106;
visits Oxford, FLM begins novel
'featuring', 120; FLM visits in
Cambridge, 121; car accident,
125, 126; and *Roundabout Way*,
150, 151; communism, 154n, 180,
182, 304; Fellow of Trinity, 166;
fails to obtain Birmingham post,

166; Spanish holiday with FLM,
177, 178–81, 205; and Soviet spy
network, 180; friendship with
FLM fades, 183
WRITINGS: 'Art and Morality', 86;
'De Cubismo', 104, 105; 'Paris
Exhibitions', 135
Blunt, Revd Stanley, 82
Blunt, Wilfrid, 83, 101, 120
Blunt, Wilfrid Scawen, 83
Blunt family, 113
Book Society, 154, 211
Boswell, James, 209
Botteril, Denis, 368
Boult, Sir Adrian, 305, 315
Bowdoin College, 230, 243
Bowen, Elizabeth, 292, 389, 391,
393; 'The Big House', 393; *The
Death of the Heart*, 389, 391
Bowen's Court, 292, 391
Bower, Dallas, 305, 313, 332, 343
Bower, Pamela, 343
Bowle, John, 84
Bowles, Jane, 285
Bowles, Paul, 285
Bowra, (Sir) Maurice, 75
Boyd, John, 424, 467, 471, 481
Bradley, F. H., 140
Bradley, Revd W. H., M.A., 13, 15,
17, 19–20
Brayshaw, Audrey, 317
Brecht, Bertolt, 165, 440
Bridges, John, 418
Briggs, (Lord) Asa, 315
Brinnin, John Malcolm, 243, 391,
395, 396
Brissago, near Locarno, 349
Bristol Zoo, 225
'Britain to America', 313
British Broadcasting Corporation
(previously British Broadcasting
Company; BBC), 192, 295, 387,
389, 443, 444, 455, 458; Higgins/
FLM discussion, 256–7; wants
FLM to write for radio, 287;

Wavell, Archibald, 1st Earl, 354
Waylen, James: *History Military and Municipal, of the Town of Marlborough*, 74
Webster, John: *The White Devil*, 378
Wellesley College, 230, 243
Wellington, Lindsay, 444
Wellington Place, London (10), 316–17, 324–5, 339, 345
Wells, H. G., 206
Wells, Sam, 414–15, 421
Wesley, John, 15
'Westminster Abbey', 296–7
Westminster Theatre, 195
Weston, Jessie, 131
White, Archie, 26, 27, 28, 37, 48
White, H. O., 267
Whitman, Walt, 405
WHO (World Health Organisation), 372
Wickham Lodge, Hampshire, 68, 226
Wigmore Hall, London, 350
Wilamowitz-Moellendorff, Ulrich von, 115, 120, 149
Wilde, Oscar, 34, 86–7, 107, 262; *The Picture of Dorian Gray*, 88
Wilhelm II, Kaiser, 41
William III, King (William of Orange), 15, 71
Wilmington, Ohio, 409
Wimbush, Charles, 445, 456–7, 464
Wimbush, Mary, **445**; first meets FLM, 444; acts in FLM works, 444, 452; meetings with FLM, 444–5; moves with FLM to Lexham Gardens, 447; move to Regent's Park Terrace, 456–7; purchase of house in Aldbury, 460–61, 463, 467; works at BBC, 468; and FLM's final illness, 476, 477; and FLM's funeral, 478, 479, 480
Wolfe, Charles: 'The Burial of Sir John Moore', 57, 61, 68
Woodhouse, C. M., 385
Woolf, Leonard, 125, 126, 127, 218
'Word from America', 292
Wordsworth, William, 61, 92, 186, 248, 484; *The Prelude*, 248
Wotton, Sir Henry: 'The Character of a Happy Life', 421–2

Xenophon, 119, 293, 454, 470n

Yates, Michael, 188–91, 199
'Yeats' (a paper), 253
Yeats, Jack, 262, 312
Yeats, 'Lily', 277
Yeats, 'Lollie', 277
Yeats, William Butler, 61, 111, **162**, 165, 192, 195, 211, 222, 232, 252, 261, 262, 355, 468, 470, 480, 482, 483, 484; quest for origins, 1–2; on Dodds, 141; FLM on, 161–2, 254; burial in Ireland, 370–72, 370, 371, 404; FLM publishes study of, 402
WRITINGS: 'Byzantium', 180; 'In Memory of Major Robert Gregory', 321; *Last Poems and Plays*, 253; 'Prayer for my Daughter', 168; 'The Ballad of the Foxhunter', 90; *The Land of Heart's Desire*, 90; 'The Stolen Child', 90; 'The Wanderings of Oisin', 91; 'Under Ben Bulben', 2, 335
Yeats International Summer School, Sligo (1962), 463
'Yeats's Epitaph' (review), 253–4
'Yes-men and No-men' (public lecture), 435
Yorke, Dig, 239
Yorke, Henry (Henry Green), 239
Yorkshire Light Infantry, 45, 46

Zoo, 225–6, 231
Zwemmers, 101